Critical Perspectives on Globalization

The Globalization of the World Economy

Series Editor: Mark Casson
Professor of Economics
University of Reading, UK

Wherever possible, the articles in these volumes have been reproduced as originally published using facsimile reproduction, inclusive of footnotes and pagination to facilitate ease of reference.

For a list of all Edward Elgar published titles visit our site on the World Wide Web at
www.e-elgar.com

Critical Perspectives on Globalization

Edited by

Marina Della Giusta

Lecturer
University of Reading Business School, UK

Uma S. Kambhampati

Senior Lecturer
University of Reading Business School, UK

and

Robert Hunter Wade

Professor of Political Economy
London School of Economics and Political Science, UK

THE GLOBALIZATION OF THE WORLD ECONOMY

An Elgar Reference Collection
Cheltenham, UK • Northampton, MA, USA

© Marina Della Giusta, Uma S. Kambhampati and Robert Hunter Wade 2006. For copyright of individual articles, please refer to the Acknowledgements.

MC

Published by
Edward Elgar Publishing Limited
Glensanda House
Montpellier Parade
Cheltenham
Glos GL50 1UA
UK

Edward Elgar Publishing, Inc.
136 West Street
Suite 202
Northampton
Massachusetts 01060
USA

A catalogue record for this book is available from the British Library

ISBN-13: 978 1 84542 176 2
ISBN-10: 1 84542 176 0

Printed and bound in Great Britain by MPG Books Ltd, Bodmin, Cornwall

Contents

B   The Sustainability Critique

C   Gender and Globalization

Acknowledgements

The editors and publishers wish to thank the authors and the following publishers who have kindly given permission for the use of copyright material.

Blackwell Publishing Ltd for articles: Adrian Wood (1998), 'Globalisation and the Rise in Labour Market Inequalities', *Economic Journal*, **108** (450), September, 1463–82; Peter Newell (2002), 'A World Environment Organisation: The Wrong Solution to the Wrong Problem', *World Economy*, **25** (5), 659–71; Desmond King and Amrita Narlikar (2003), 'The New Risk Regulators? International Organisations and Globalisation', *Political Quarterly*, **74** (3), 337–48.

Center for Global Development for article: Nancy Birdsall (2002), 'Asymmetric Globalization: Global Markets Require Good Global Politics', *Center for Global Development Working Paper*, **12**, October, 2–18.

Clark University for article: Richa Nagar, Victoria Lawson, Linda McDowell and Susan Hanson (2002), 'Locating Globalization: Feminist (Re)readings of the Subjects and Spaces of Globalization', *Economic Geography*, **78** (3), July, 257–84.

Columbia University Press for excerpts: Saskia Sassen (1996), 'The State and the New Geography of Power', in *Losing Control? Sovereignty in an Age of Globalization*, Chapter One, 1–30, notes, bibliography; Dani Rodrik (2005), 'Feasible Globalizations', in Michael M. Weinstein (ed.), *Globalization: What's New?*, Chapter 8, 196–213.

Earthscan Publications Ltd for excerpt: Simon Retallack (2001), 'The Environmental Cost of Economic Globalization', in Edward Goldsmith and Jerry Mander (eds), *The Case Against the Global Economy: And for a Turn Towards Localization*, Chapter 17, 189–202, references.

Earthscan Publications Ltd, Edward Goldsmith and Jerry Mander for excerpts: Jerry Mander (2001), 'Technologies of Globalization', in Edward Goldsmith and Jerry Mander (eds), *The Case Against the Global Economy: And for a Turn Towards Localization*, Chapter 3, 45–57, references; Richard Barnet and John Cavanagh (2001), 'Electronic Money and the Casino Economy', in Edward Goldsmith and Jerry Mander (eds), *The Case Against the Global Economy: And for a Turn Towards Localization*, Chapter 4, 58–69, references.

Elsevier for articles: Korkut Ertürk and William Darity, Jr. (2000), 'Secular Changes in the Gender Composition of Employment and Growth Dynamics in the North and the South', *World Development*, **28** (7), 1231–8; Branko Milanovic (2003), 'The Two Faces of Globalization: Against Globalization as We Know It', *World Development*, **31** (4), 667–83; Robert Hunter

Wade (2004), 'Is Globalization Reducing Poverty and Inequality?', *World Development*, **32** (4), 567–89.

Financial Markets Center (www.fmcenter.org) for article: Jane D'Arista (2000), 'Reforming International Financial Architecture', *Challenge*, **43** (3), May–June, 44–82.

Food First Books for excerpt: Vandana Shiva (2000), 'War against Nature and the People of the South', in Sarah Anderson (ed.), *Views from the South: The Effects of Globalization and the WTO on Third World Countries*, 91–125.

Oxford University Press for excerpt: Susan George (2003), 'Globalizing Rights?' in Matthew J. Gibney (ed.), *Globalizing Rights: The Oxford Amnesty Lectures 1999*, Chapter 1, 15–33, notes.

Dani Rodrik and *Harvard Magazine* for article: Dani Rodrik (2002), 'Globalization for Whom? Time to Change the Rules – and Focus on Poor Workers', *Harvard Magazine*, **104** (6), July–August, 1–5, reset.

Routledge for excerpt: John Tomlinson (1999), 'Globalised Culture: The Triumph of the West?', in Tracey Skelton and Tim Allen (eds), *Culture and Global Change*, Chapter 2, 22–9, references.

Sage Publications, Inc. for excerpt and article: Rhacel Salazar Parreñas (2001), 'The International Division of Reproductive Labor', in *Servants of Globalization: Women, Migration and Domestic Work*, Chapter 3, 61–79; Dong-Sook S. Gills (2002), 'Globalization of Production and Women in Asia', *Annals of the American Academy of Political and Social Science*, **581**, May, 106–20.

Taylor and Francis Ltd (www.tandf.co.uk/journals) for articles: Ruth Pearson (2000), 'Moving the Goalposts: Gender and Globalisation in the Twenty-first Century', *Gender and Development*, **8** (1), March, 10–19; Takis Fotopoulos (2002), 'The Global "War" of the Transnational Elite', *Democracy and Nature*, **8** (2), July, 201–40; Arshin Adib-Moghaddam (2002), 'Global Intifadah? September 11th and the Struggle within Islam', *Cambridge Review of International Affairs*, **15** (2), 203–16; Lael Brainard (2002), 'A Turning Point for Globalisation? The Implications for the Global Economy of America's Campaign against Terrorism', *Cambridge Review of International Affairs*, **15** (2), 233–44; Christopher W. Hughes (2002), 'Reflections on Globalisation, Security and 9/11', *Cambridge Review of International Affairs*, **15** (3), 421–33; Christine M. Koggel (2003), 'Globalization and Women's Paid Work: Expanding Freedom?', *Feminist Economics*, **9** (2–3), 163–83; David L. Heymann (2003), 'The Evolving Infectious Disease Threat: Implications for National and Global Security', *Journal of Human Development*, **4** (2), July, 192–207; Naila Kabeer (2004), 'Globalization, Labor Standards, and Women's Rights: Dilemmas of Collective (In)action in an Interdependent World', *Feminist Economics*, **10** (1), March, 3–35; Robert Hunter Wade (2004), 'On the Causes of Increasing World Poverty and Inequality, or Why the Matthew Effect Prevails', *New Political Economy*, **9** (2), June, 163–88.

Zed Books Ltd for excerpts: Samir Amin (1997), 'The Future of Global Polarization', in *Capitalism in the Age of Globalization: The Management of Contemporary Society*, Translated by Beatrice Wallerstein, Chapter 1, 1–11; Nicholas G. Faraclas (2001), 'Melanesia, the Banks, and the BINGOs: Real Alternatives are Everywhere (Except in the Consultants' Briefcases)', in Veronika Bennholdt-Thomsen, Nicholas G. Faraclas and Claudia von Werlhof (eds), *There is an Alternative: Subsistence and Worldwide Resistance to Corporate Globalization*, Chapter 5, 67–76; Veronika Bennholdt-Thomsen (2001), 'What Really Keeps Our Cities Alive, Money or Subsistence?', in Veronika Bennholdt-Thomsen, Nicholas G. Faraclas and Claudia von Werlhof (eds), *There is an Alternative: Subsistence and Worldwide Resistance to Corporate Globalization*, Chapter 16, 217–31; Ha-Joon Chang and Ilene Grabel (2004), Introduction and Part I, Chapters 1–4, in *Reclaiming Development: An Alternative Economic Policy Manual*, 1–37.

Every effort has been made to trace all the copyright holders but if any have been inadvertently overlooked the publishers will be pleased to make the necessary arrangement at the first opportunity.

In addition the publishers wish to thank the Marshall Library of Economics, University of Cambridge, UK, the Library at the University of Warwick, UK, and the Library of Indiana University at Bloomington, USA, for their assistance in obtaining these articles.

Introduction

Marina Della Giusta, Uma S. Kambhampati and Robert Hunter Wade

Some commentators see globalization as economic liberalization, falling transport costs, or the Internet revolution. Some see it more broadly as the ascendancy of capitalism or as a replacement term for imperialism or modernization. Globalization is also seen as a *process* of cultural standardization in which a global media reinforces sameness and homogeneity around predominantly American models. These are ideological interpretations, and to some extent, remain distinct within the literature from definitions that concentrate on globalization as a *process*. Definitions in the latter category highlight changes in the spatial and temporal contours of life, so that time–space distance is annihilated. Time–space distantiation, a term coined by Giddens (1990), refers to the degree to which the friction of space has been overcome to accommodate social interaction. Technological progress, for instance, has decreased the time taken to travel anywhere, while telecommunications have virtually annihilated it making social interaction almost instantaneous. In this context, Held et al. (1999) describe globalization as the 'widening, deepening and speeding up of worldwide interconnectedness in all aspects of contemporary social life, from the cultural, the financial, to the spiritual' (Held et al., 1999, p. 2). McGrew (2000, p. 347) highlights worldwide connectivity and the deepening enmeshment of societies in a web of flows of capital, labour, ideas, images, weapons, criminal activity and pollution. Robertson (1992), in turn, identifies world compression and the intensification of global consciousness[1] as the two main aspects of globalization. World compression implies that the way we live our lives has immediate implications for people on the other side of the globe, while global consciousness is highlighted when we speak in terms of world order, international recessions and global biodiversity.

Whatever the definition, proponents of globalization accent the benign effects. Economically, they expect it to increase growth, decrease inequality and poverty across people and countries. Politically, socially and culturally, they hope that it will decrease differences, reduce xenophobia and lead to a global consciousness where the nation state is no longer the main unit of identity for individuals. Opponents of globalization, who range from those who are ideologically opposed to globalization, to those who see it as a value-free process, accentuate other effects. They argue that the socioeconomic costs of globalization are too high and the benefits are inequitably distributed. Politically, they claim that globalization has simply acted as a vehicle for American hegemony, and to a handful of powerful transnational corporations influencing political processes and even reforming international institutions to benefit them. Culturally too, they see damping down differences as the Americanization of the periphery and the dilution of cultural identity for millions across the globe.

In the context of the 'widening, deepening and speeding up of worldwide interconnectedness' and the compression of time–space distantiation, critics argue that the costs are often unanticipated. These might include the costs of unlimited growth on the environment, the increasing risk of diseases travelling across the world, financial contagion, international terrorism, cultural homogenization etc. In addition, there are distributional costs in terms of the exclusion of the poor (both individuals and countries) from the benefits of higher growth. It is the 'centers' that gain and in this sense globalization is seen to be no different from earlier phases of growth. Critics within this group (see chapters by Wade, Wood, Rodrik) have many, sometimes contradictory fears including the fear of jobs going to the South and away from the North, the fear that countries of the South will lose out from globalization, and that there will be a global international elite that gains while the vast majority of unskilled or low skilled workers in both North and South lose out.

These critiques focus on a number of questions. How can one explain Africa's unchanged GDP per capita even after innumerable structural adjustment loans and IMF standbys? How can the recurrent Latin American crises in countries considered to be 'models' by the globalizers be explained? Why do countries like Georgia and the Kyrghyz Republic – star pupils of globalization over the past decade and a half – find themselves in a worse position today than ten years ago? (Milanovic, Chapter 3). Amin (Chapter 1) argues that globalization has had these contradictory effects for a number of reasons. First, the global system has not developed new forms of political and social organization going beyond the nation state. Second, it has not developed economic and social relations capable of reconciling industrialization in the periphery with the pursuit of global growth. Third, it has not developed a relationship with Africa (other than an exclusionary one).

In this volume, we have included a number of papers that consider these arguments in more detail. The papers we have chosen reveal concerns that revolve around a number of issues:

1. Fears that globalization is not really as beneficial as claimed, including increasing growth, decreasing inequality and poverty. Much of the debate here relates to how globalization and its effects are measured.
2. Fears that even where these benefits exist, the system is excluding individuals, countries and even entire regions (like Africa) from enjoying these benefits. Such exclusion may involve the poor, the unskilled and uneducated, or women.
3. Fear that such exclusion creates the motivation for terrorism as well as facilitates its execution.
4. Fears that globalization has significant costs on the environment and on indigenous cultures.
5. Fears that globalization facilitates the spread of disease.
6. Fears regarding the negative externality effects of the global financial system, such as financial crises.
7. Fears that all of the above costs are reinforced because the global system has not developed a sufficiently strong political and social infrastructure transcending the nation state, which could regulate the process of globalization.

Fear that globalization does not have the benefits being claimed for it

A number of articles in this volume are concerned with refuting the World Bank notion that 'the good globalizers grow fast' and the bad ones who are unwilling to globalize grow less fast. Proponents of this view argue that countries which have liberalized and globalized have grown faster (and decreased poverty faster) than those which have not. Thus, China (and to some extent India) are seen to have begun to grow faster after their respective reforms, as in a previous generation did the East Asian economies.

Critics of this view (Wade, Birdsall, Rodrik, Milanovic), however, feel that the figures cannot be so straightforwardly interpreted. They argue that the process of 'selecting' the good globalizers based on trade ratios is flawed. First, globalizers are selected on the basis of trade/GDP ratios over which they have little control if their exports (especially of natural resources) decrease. In fact, these countries are only seen as globalizers because the World Bank measures globalization in terms of *changes* in levels of protection rather than the levels per se. Thus, Wade makes the point that 'to call relatively closed economies "more globalized" or " globalizers" and to call countries with much higher ratios of trade/GDP and much freer trade regimes "less globalized" or even "non-globalizers" is an audacious use of language' (Chapter 5).

Second, the successful (in terms of growth and exports) countries like China are not really good examples of neo-liberal economic systems. Thus, says Rodrik (Chapter 8), China's economic policies have violated most of the rules of globalization and China has only grown because it was able to innovate its institutions to suit local conditions, including the household responsibility system and the township and village enterprises, special economic zones and partial liberalization in agriculture and industry. This is also seen to be true of India, which according to Rodrik, has managed to increase its growth rate despite having one of the world's most protectionist trade regimes. In this context, Wade also argues that there is no reason to assume that the causality is from trade to growth. It could equally be from growth to trade.

Wade, in Chapters 5 and 6 in this volume, asks a couple of related questions. First, is globalization decreasing poverty and inequality and second, what causes increasing poverty and inequality? In answer to the first question, he carefully considers the evidence as it is presented and the reasons why this evidence may be flawed. He shows that the poverty headcount is sensitive to the precise level of international poverty lines (because of the income distribution around the lines). Second, the headcount is sensitive to the reliability of household surveys of income and expenditure. Third, China's and India's surveys are especially problematic and given that these countries have a very large weight in the poverty figures, these errors are magnified. Fourth, the World Bank introduced a new methodology in the late 1990s, which makes figures in the 1980s and the 1990s non-comparable. Fifth, the Bank's international poverty lines do not take account of basic needs such as clean water and healthcare. Sixth, average consumption is shifting towards non-essential services whose prices relative to food and shelter are lower in poor than in rich countries, giving the misleading impression that the purchasing power of the poor over essential consumption goods is increasing.

Only one main measure of inequality, concludes Wade, supports the liberal argument that inequality has decreased. Other plausible measures suggest world income inequality has not fallen over the past quarter century. And, if we look at 'polarization' measures (for example, the ratio of the top 1 per cent of income recipients over the bottom 10 per cent) or the regional gap measures (for example, the average income of the North over the average of Africa, Latin America or the former Soviet Union), the trends are clearly adverse, with East Asia being the exception.

The historical fallacy of the neoliberal claim that today's wealthy countries achieved their success though free market policies lies at the heart of Chang and Grabel's analysis of the merits of neoliberal development policies (Chapter 4). Both Britain and the USA, today's most forceful advocates of free trade, engaged (and still engage) in protectionist and interventionist policies, as did most of today's industrialized economies, with governments intervening to socialize financial and economic risks on many occasions (most recently in the case of the Iraq reconstruction). It appears that the difference between developed and developing countries therefore lies more in the relative success of the intervention, rather than its presence. The present record of neoliberal policies of trade and financial liberalization in terms of growth performance indicates that these policies are failing to deliver economic benefits, whilst simultaneously imposing increased vulnerability and social costs. As for globalization itself, Chang and Grabel argue that this has historically been, and still is, the product of political decisions rather than a consequence of technological progress. More importantly, they argue that it is the neoliberal form of globalization that is to blame for the deterioration in living standards across developing countries, rather than globalization itself, which both history and contemporary evidence show to be compatible with different and more or less open policy regimes.

Exclusion of individuals, countries and even entire regions

As indicated above, one of the main concerns expressed by writers in this volume is that while many people and countries have gained from globalization, there are others who are excluded from its benefits. In Susan George's succinct dictum, globalization is 'a process that allows the world market economy to take the best and leave the rest' (Chapter 12). The continuous creation of so many 'losers' means that politics is becoming not just about hierarchy or pie-sharing (as in preindustrial and post Second World War periods respectively), but also about sheer survival. The ethical question then becomes who has the right to survive and who does not.

Considering the reasons for such exclusion, Wade argues in Chapters 5 and 6 that it is because the current pattern of globalization is such that the high value-added and increasing returns activities remain in the developed countries, while the middle levels of the manufacturing value-chain, which face decreasing returns, are moving to developing countries. Multinational corporations are continuing to concentrate on advanced economy markets for their sales and advanced economies are moving towards the financial sector wherein there is a shift in the corporate culture from 'earned differentials' to 'winner takes all'. This ascendancy of finance is causing further income differentials. In addition, very little R&D is done outside the Triad (North America, Europe and Japan) and while East Asia is gaining ground, this has only served to displace the other developing countries even further (both to the developed countries and to East Asia). Finally, US primacy has increased and so has its autonomy to set the key parameters of aggregate demand in accordance with its own domestic conditions.

Birdsall (Chapter 10) highlights three ways in which globalization makes unequal opportunities worse. First, those without the right training and equipment are excluded from the benefits of globalization while those with higher education get increasing returns. Second, negative externalities raise new costs for the vulnerable and compound the risks faced by the weak and disadvantaged. Such externalities include financial contagion, which implies that even countries with relatively sound domestic policies are affected by problems elsewhere; global warming, contagious diseases, international crime and terrorism. Third, economic power is important because the rich and powerful can influence global rules to benefit them. Generally, political disabilities helping them in their daily living, preparing meals, shopping, assisting with baths and providing bowel and bladder care. Working conditions are difficult as both the pay and job security are low. There is also no training, health benefits, vacation or sick leave. Workers in this sector are mostly women and mostly poor, although their ethnic background varies, as does their origin, education and experience of the job as a one generation or traditional occupation. Perhaps the most striking feature of the occupation is that in a society that values independence over interdependence, the work is regarded as best done the more the work looks effortless, the worker invisible, and the customer appears to be independent, so that caregivers are 'handing over authorship of their caring work' (Rivas, 2002, p. 77). The author concludes by observing how such transfer occurs throughout American society between executives and secretaries as it does between children and mothers, although the former takes a business-like air when the receiver of care is labelled consumer and claims an independence that justifies the inequality in pay and working conditions between care receivers and care givers.

Increasing risks

Global risk maybe seen as an externality of globalization and includes risks relating to health, the environment, financial collapse and socio-economic destabilization. The papers included in this volume consider each of these separately.

International terrorism

The attempts at cultural homogenization and the exclusion of millions from the benefits of globalization have been seen as contributing to the international terrorist threat. Thus, some have argued that the September 11th attacks were directed at globalization, while others speculate that globalization is a direct casualty of such attacks. Adib-Moghaddam (Chapter 31), for instance, claims that the forces underlying September 11th question the legitimacy of the political, economic and cultural supremacy of 'Western' values. The universalization of standards of social interaction has resulted in globalization being seen as Westernization or even simply as Americanization because the US is the power pushing for such convergence in ways that serve to reinforce its global dominance. Globalization has resulted in the economic exclusion of states and individuals leading to disparities in welfare and military tension. It has also led to economic rivalry amongst states for economic resources and to economic dislocation. The exposure to external economic shocks and political risks has led to a discontentment with dominant regimes and to a radicalization of Islam, which is the only outlet for the expression of such opposition in states where political parties are banned or subjugated to the state. Globalization is also seen to have facilitated terrorist activities because it has decreased the sovereign control of states and it is in states where such control is weakest, like Afghanistan and Somalia, that terrorism has prospered. Globalization, as economic liberalization and improvements in transport and information technology, has also enabled international criminal and terrorist organizations to behave like multinational corporations and to move with greater ease across deregulated economic and territorial space. Such activity is further facilitated by the existence of an increasing number of extra territorial targets that can be attacked without entering more secure national borders. Hughes (Chapter 29) concludes that unless there is an effort to harmonize globalization with the state building efforts of other regions, there will be no solution to trans-sovereign terrorism.

Adib-Moghaddam argues that the global outreach of transnational terrorism adds a new dimension to globalism wherein the driving agents of globalization are not simply the Gateses and Soroses but also criminal groupings travelling the globe using English and Arabic and sharing a sense of belonging to a common cause with a universal ethos. In this context, he claims that September 11th reflected a globalization of violence and altered the traditional view of the security of geographical barriers. This new dimension of globalization means that states like the US, which are geographically separated from the devastation in other parts of the world suddenly find themselves in a situation where the meaning of geographical barriers and of the security associated with them has become obsolete. This is reiterated by Fotopoulos in Chapter 28, who claims that counter-violence in all its forms has increased significantly since neo-liberal globalization. Economic globalization concentrates power in the hands of the economic elite and political globalization in the hands of the political elite. Fotopoulos claims that September 11th was 'clearly an extreme form of popular terrorism directly related to the systemic violence built into the New World Order'.

Increasingly global health risks

The compression of time-space distance and the growing interconnectedness of people and countries has resulted in risks and threats that are only now beginning to be considered. Globalization implies that the boundaries of the nation state are extremely porous politically, physically and culturally. As Heymann writes in Chapter 27, outbreaks of disease have a potential or spread that transcends the defenses of any single country. Increasing travel (air, sea and land) implies that infectious agents, incubating in symptomless travellers can move between cities and slip across borders. AIDS and other diseases have eroded past confidence that high standards of living and access to powerful medicines will insulate Western populations from infectious disease threats abroad. In a closely connected and interdependent world, the repercussions of adverse events abroad easily cross borders to intrude on state affairs in ways that cannot be averted through traditional military defenses. International Health Regulations are designed to maximize the security against the international spread of infectious diseases while ensuring minimum impact on trade and travel.

Increasing financial vulnerability

The financial requirements to enter into the global money game are extremely high and this has resulted in a decrease in the number of financial houses and an increase in their size. They have therefore become harder to control, making the world financial system vulnerable to technical breakdown, to the consequences of short-term speculation and to freelance decision-making. When one thing goes wrong, it affects all others in this interdependent world system. As is well known, the rise of global financial markets makes it increasingly difficult for national governments to formulate economic policy or to enforce it. In a globalized system, wired together by technology capable of moving funds instantaneously around the globe at the behest of speculators and immune to regulation or control, more frequent catastrophes are likely. In

Chapter 3, Milanovic argues that it is the role of the international financial institutions like the World Bank and the IMF to moderate global capitalism.

Insufficient political system

Given the exclusion of certain individuals and countries by the process of globalization, a number of writers highlight the importance of political power in dictating the inclusion of some and the exclusion of others from the benefits of globalization. While the state may have influenced the spread of such benefits in the past, the erosion of the power of the nation state in the new globalized world has left a vacuum that other political entities are unable to fill. In addition, since economic globalization extends the economy but not the sovereignty of the state beyond its borders, the latter can no longer guarantee property rights and contracts. Birdsall, for instance, in Chapter 10 identifies the main problem of globalization as the integration of the global economy without the development of a healthy global polity. These writers therefore argue that a new set of international regulatory regimes and institutions is required to govern international economic relations.

Sassen, considering 'sovereignty in the age of globalization' in Chapter 2, puts forward three components of the new geography of power under globalization. First, a particular form of territoriality is taking shape in the global economy within which financial markets are increasingly global, Anglo-American law is monopolizing international business and international institutions like the GATT/WTO are becoming increasingly important. Second, new legal regimes are emerging. Third, the virtualization of economic activity is leading to a control crisis because these activities cannot be governed or controlled by the state. For instance, offshoring creates a space economy that is not within the regulatory umbrella of a state. In spite of this, however, control remains in the centre because when firms are very globalized, their central functions become more important and complex and these central functions are largely concentrated in the developed countries.

A number of solutions to this political vacuum have been proposed. Sassen argues that we need to create viable systems of co-ordination and order among the powerful economic actors globally and also that we need to consider the equity and distributive implications of such global integration. In Chapter 8, Rodrik argues that while barriers to trade in goods, services and investment flows have all been decreased over time, barriers to trade in labour services (the one market where poor nations still have something to sell) still remain very high. He goes on to indicate the costs and benefits that a relaxation of these rules would yield both to the developing countries and to their developed country hosts. In turn, Susan George maintains that charity will not provide an answer to this problem, but rather solidarity based on 'reciprocity, political choice, human organization and hard work rather than following the lazy way, which is to allow markets to make all social choices for us' (Chapter 12). She argues that it can be reformed to ensure fair redistribution at the global level. Her proposals include the introduction of the Tobin Tax on all monetary and financial transactions, pro-rata taxes on transnational corporation sales, the elimination of fiscal paradises and the adoption of corporate responsibility. If not, competition and the obligation to increase shareholder value imply that capital must have total freedom to cross borders and taxation should be avoided as much as possible, leading to an erosion of feelings of fulfilment and inclusion, and an increase in hopelessness for the losers.

In Chapter 11, D'Arista shows how financial liberalization poses a substantial threat to the sovereignty of nations, and argues that the public sector will need to reconstitute its powers if this is to be remedied. She puts forward three possible proposals: the setting up of a public international investment fund for emerging markets; organizing a new allocation of special drawing rights (SDRs) to provide relief from short-term debt burdens for countries; and third, finding an alternative to the dollar based, privatized international monetary system. D'Arista argues in favour of an international transactions and payments system managed by a public international agency in which cross-border monetary exchanges can be made in each country's own currency.

Peter Newell, in Chapter 16, provides a critical assessment of the discussion on the appropriate international institutions for ensuring environmental sustainability. He argues that much of this discussion assumes that the failure to ensure environmental protection stems from the inadequacy of the present international institutions, rather than from other causes (such as the lack of will to implement environmental standards, particularly by powerful nations). He highlights the problems that a world environment organization would create, particularly for developing countries, with the reproduction of power asymmetries that have characterized the operations of the WTO, the World Bank, and the other international organizations. This organization is expected to preside over a global market for environmental goods, even though environmental problems are closely associated with problems of entitlements and definitions of property rights which, Newell argues, are not at all well defined and therefore cannot really be dealt with at the international level. Furthermore, in these discussions what counts is the willingness to pay in order to establish the worth of environmental goods, but this assumes that those who do not have financial resources are not valuing the resources, as they do not pay for them.

In Chapter 17 – 'Melanesia, the Banks and the BINGOs: Real Alternatives are Everywhere (Except in the Consultants' Briefcases)' – Nicholas Faraclas turns our attention to the well established socioeconomic models alternative to capitalism, which are being threatened by corporate globalization exported by the Banks (World Bank, International Monetary Fund, and bilateral aid agencies) and the BINGOs (big international non-governmental development organizations). He challenges us not to accept the inevitability with which corporate globalization presents itself but to look at such alternative models, both remembering our own past and looking around the world today for inspiration. He chooses the example of Melanesia to show both how an alternative system functions and the ways in which it is now being attacked through a process of 'recolonization through accountability' to the World Bank and IMF. He vividly illustrates the process set in motion in Papua New Guinea by a poverty alleviation programme, following it through the various stages: the drying up of funds for the local NGOs that opposed the programme, the 'mushrooming' of NGOs for credit extension (flavour of the month in Washington but not what was needed), and the effects of the selection of 'potentially successful enterpreneurs' (mostly young males). He then moves on to describe Melanesian society, a non patriarchal society without nuclear families, one that was not interested in the accumulation of wealth but had food security and one that was based on collective decision-making. Faraclas also cites ample studies from archaeology pointing to the fact that very similar societies existed in the West in the past as well: 'the society of domination that neo-liberal economists present to us as normal is therefore quite the opposite' (p. 364).

The passive acceptance of the present system as natural and inevitable is a key theme running throughout the critical literature, emphasizing the dangers of becoming more and more passive citizens as we become active consumers. Jerry Mander's 'Technologies of Globalization' in Chapter 15 shows how this has been particularly the case in the adoption of many of the information and communications technologies associated with the spread of globalization. He argues that technologies have political implications since they catalyze systemic changes, and tries to explain why society has remained so passive towards them, regarding them as unequivocally positive or neutral at best, and not developed approaches for evaluating the effects caused by technologies before they become pervasive. Explanations of such passivity are to be found in the wave after wave of optimistic statements about technology that scientists and industries have divulged since the industrial revolution that have contributed to the creation of what he calls a 'techno-utopian vision' that has made the general advancement of society synonymous with technological change.

Also responsible for such uncritical acceptance is the pervasive individualism of modern society, leading individuals to evaluate only the effects of technologies for themselves, ignoring systemic or holistic effects that can only be appreciated through an evaluation of the social, political and ecological dimensions. He then proceeds to illustrate the implications of different technologies. Computer technology becomes an instrument for the acceleration of centralized power: trans-national corporations are able to use global networks on a scale and speed that makes individuals cyber empowerment pathetic by comparison. The speed of interactions and the replacement of personal with computer interactions are also having profound transformative effects on culture. This can be seen both in the studies of the effect of their widespread use in education (loss of ecological sensitivity and understanding) as well as in those that point to a loss of the sense of belonging and caring for shared geographically located cultures that correspond to politically defined entities. He doesn't go as far as to say that this is also explaining the loss of political participation but this could be inferred from his discussion. Every technology has a specific purpose, for example 'television serves as the worldwide imagery of the new global corporate vision; computers are the nervous systems that facilitate the setup of new global organizations; trade agreements wipe out resistance...' (ibid.) and the overall effect is adverse to democracy and diversity.

Conclusion

The consequences of economic globalization, or rather the globalization of the current economic model, are covered from a variety of angles by this collection of papers, which illustrate the cultural as well as the socioeconomic implications of the process. This has been succinctly summarized by Birdsall in Chapter 10, who argues that

> The dominant view seems to be that 'that poverty is declining worldwide and inequality after a century is levelling off is not a sign that all is well in our globalized economy. Proponents of market-led globalization need to recognise that the global economy, even if it is not causing more poverty and inequality, is not addressing those global problems either, and is ridden with asymmetries that add up to unequal opportunities. Social activists need to insist on the reform not the dismantling of the limited institutions for managing globalization's downside.

Birdsall's agenda for a new global politics requires a global social contract (including transfers to the poor), an attempt to address global market failures and just global rules together with full and fair implementation.

The sustainability and gender literatures challenge us not to accept globalization uncritically, or to assume that it is only to be achieved in its current form. We are thus led to see the implications of economic globalizations for the human rights agenda, the implications of the adoption of information and communication technologies, the costs to the environment and to alternative more sustainable socioeconomic arrangements of the adoption of the 'one size fits all' global economic model, and the gendered patterns to the process of globalization itself. By bringing closer to the reader the implications not just of decisions taken in the distant spheres of corporate actors and international organizations, but of our own individual behaviour as well, they suggest the way forward for the realization of a sustainability perspective based on an ethics of caring (for others however distant, for the environment, and for oneself), and on the empowerment that derives from knowing that other more rewarding choices are always possible.

Note

1. Robertson (1992) saw three sources of cleavages in the cultural arena – religious, legal and industrial. The religious cleavage is between fundamentalist Islam and Christianity (a cleavage that many would say is highlighted by events in the 21st century). The legal-diplomatic cleavage is between democracies and absolutist states (the East–West divide). The industrial cleavage is between cultures that emphasise rationality, individuality and impersonal authority relative to those that do not (the North-South divide).

References

Cheru, F. (2000), 'Transforming our common future: The local dimensions of global reform', *Review of International Political Economy*, **7** (2), 353–68.

Giddens, A. (1990), *The Consequences of Modernity*, Cambridge: Polity Press.

Hawthorne, J. (2001), 'Freedom in Context', *Philosophical Studies*, **104**, 63–79.

Held, D., A. McGrew, D. Goldblatt and J. Perraton (1999), *Global Transformations: Politics, Economics and Culture*, Cambridge: Polity Press.

McGrew, A. (2000), *Empire: The United States in the Twentieth Century*, (2nd edn.), London: Hodder and Stoughton.

Rivas, L.M. (2002), 'Invisible Labors: caring for the independent person', in B. Ehrenreich and A. Hochschild (eds), *Global Woman: Nannies, maids, and sex workers in the new economy*, New York: Holt, pp. 70–85.

Robertson, R. (1992), *Globalization: Social Theory and Global Culture*, London: Sage.

Part I
Systemic Critiques of Globalization

A Critiques of the Neo-Liberal Ideology Underlying Globalization

[1]

The Future of Global Polarization

Unequal Development and the Historical Forms of Capitalism

History since antiquity has been characterized by the unequal development of regions. But it is only in the modern era that polarization has become the immanent byproduct of the integration of the entire planet into the capitalist system.

Modern (capitalist) polarization has appeared in successive forms during the evolution of the capitalist mode of production:

(1) **The mercantilist form** (1500–1800) before the industrial revolution which was fashioned by the hegemony of merchant capital in the dominant Atlantic centres, and by the creation of the peripheral zones (the Americas) whose function involved their total compliance with the logic of accumulation of merchant capital.

(2) **The so-called classical model** which grew out of the industrial revolution and henceforth defined the basic forms of capitalism. In contrast, the peripheries – progressively all of Asia (except for Japan) and Africa, which were added to Latin America – remained rural, non-industrialized, and as a result their participation in the world division of labour took place via agriculture and mineral production. This important characteristic of polarization was accompanied by a second equally important one: the crystallization of core industrial systems as national autocentred systems which parallelled the construction of the national bourgeois states. Taken together, these two characteristics account for the dominant lines of the ideology of national liberation which was the response to the challenge of polarization: (i) the goal of industrialization as a synonym for a liberating progress and as a means of 'catching up'; (ii) the goal

2   CAPITALISM IN THE AGE OF GLOBALIZATION

of constructing nation-states inspired by the models of those in the core. This is how modernization ideology was conceived. From the industrial revolution (after 1800) up to the end of the Second World War the world system was characterized by this classical form of polarization.

(3) **The postwar period** (1945–90) witnessed the progressive erosion of the above two characteristics. It was a period of industrialization of the peripheries, unequal and uneven to be sure. It was the dominant factor in Asia and Latin America, with the national liberation movement doing its best to accelerate the process within peripheral states which had recently regained their political autonomy. This period was simultaneously, however, one of the progressive dismantling of autocentric national production systems and their recomposition as constitutive elements of an integrated world production system. This double erosion was the new manifestation of the deepening of globalization.

(4) **The most recent period** (since 1990) in which the accumulation of these transformations has resulted in the collapse of the equilibria characteristic of the postwar world system.

This evolution is not leading simply to a new world order characterized by new forms of polarization, but to global disorder. The chaos which confronts us today comes from, a triple failure of the system: (i) it has not developed new forms of political and social organization going beyond the nation-state – a new requirement of the globalized system of production; (ii) it has not developed economic and political relationships capable of reconciling the rise of industrialization in the newly competitive peripheral zones of Asia and Latin America with the pursuit of global growth; (iii) it has not developed a relationship, other than an exclusionary one, with the African periphery which is not engaged in competitive industrialization at all. This chaos is visible in all regions of the world and in all facets of the political, social and ideological crisis. It is at the root of the difficulties in the present construction of Europe and that continent's inability to pursue market integration and establish parallel integrative political structures. It is also the cause of the convulsions in all the peripheries in Eastern Europe, in the old semi-industrialized Third World and in the new marginalized Fourth World. Far from sustaining the progression of globalization, the current chaos reveals its extreme vulnerability.

The predominance of this chaos should not keep us from thinking

THE FUTURE OF GLOBAL POLARIZATION 3

about alternative scenarios for a new 'world order' even if there are many different possible future 'world orders'. What I am trying to do here is to call attention to questions which have been glossed over by the triumphalism of inevitable globalization at the same time as its precariousness is revealed.

The reader will no doubt have discovered that this analysis of world capitalism is not centred on the question of hegemonies. I do not subscribe to the successive hegemonies school of historiography. The concept of hegemony is often sterile, and is unscientific because it has been so loosely defined. It does not seem to me that it should be the centre of the debate. I have, in contrast, developed the idea that hegemony is the exception to the rule. The rule is conflict among partners which puts an end to hegemony. The hegemony of the United States, seemingly unchallenged today, perhaps by default, is as fragile and precarious as the globalization of the structures through which it operates.

The Present World System and the Five Monopolies of the Centre

In my opinion, the debate should start with an in-depth discussion of the new features in the present world system which are produced by the erosion of the previous one. In my opinion there are two new elements:

(1) The erosion of the autocentred nation-state and the subsequent disappearance of the link between the arena of reproduction and accumulation together with the weakening of political and social control which up to now had been defined precisely by the frontiers of this autocentred nation-state;

(2) The erosion of the great divide: industrialized centre/non-industrialized peripheral regions, and the emergence of new dimensions of polarization.

A country's position in the global hierarchy is defined by its capacity to compete in the world market. Recognizing this truism does not in any way imply sharing the bourgeois economist's view that this position is achieved as the result of rational measures – the said rationality being assessed by the yardstick of the so-called 'objective laws of the market'. On the contrary, I think that this competitiveness is a complex product of many economic, political and social factors. In this unequal fight the centres use what I call their 'five monopolies'. These monopolies

4	CAPITALISM IN THE AGE OF GLOBALIZATION

constitute a challenge to social theory in its totality. They are:

(1) **Technological monopoly**. This requires huge expenditures that only a large and wealthy state can envisage. Without the support of the state, especially through military spending – something liberal discourse doesn't mention – most of these monopolies would not last.

(2) **Financial control of worldwide financial markets**. These monopolies have an unprecedented efficacy thanks to the liberalization of the rules governing their establishment. Not so long ago, the greater part of a nation's savings could circulate only within the largely national arena of its financial institutions. Today these savings are handled centrally by the institutions whose operations are worldwide. We are talking of finance capital: capital's most globalized component. Despite this, the logic of this globalization of finance could be called into question by a simple political decision to delink, even if delinking were limited to the domain of financial transfers. Moreover I think that the rules governing the free movement of finance capital have broken down. This system had been based in the past on the free floating of currencies on the market (according to the theory that money is a commodity like any other) with the dollar serving *de facto* as a universal currency. Regarding money as a commodity, however, is a theory that is unscientific and the pre-eminent position of the dollar is only *faute de mieux*. A national currency cannot fulfil the functions of an international currency unless there is a surplus of exports in the country whose currency purports to serve as an international currency, thus underwriting structural adjustment in the other countries. This was the case with Great Britain in the late-nineteenth century. This is not the case of the United States today which actually finances its deficit by the borrowing which the rest of the world is forced to accept. Nor indeed is this the case with the competitors of the United States: Japan's surplus (that of Germany disappeared after reunification in 1991) is not sufficient to meet the financial needs occasioned by the structural adjustment of the others. Under these conditions financial globalization, far from being a 'natural' process, is an extremely fragile one. In the short run, it leads only to permanent instability rather than to the stability necessary for the efficient operation of the processes of adjustment.

THE FUTURE OF GLOBAL POLARIZATION 5

(3) **Monopolistic access to the planet's natural resources.** The dangers of the reckless exploitation of these resources are now planet-wide. Capitalism, based on short-term rationality, cannot overcome these dangers posed by this reckless behaviour, and it therefore reinforces the monopolies of already developed countries. The much-vaunted environmental concern of these countries is simply not to let others be equally irresponsible.

(4) **Media and communication monopolies.** These not only lead to uniformity of culture but also open up new means of political manipulation. The expansion of the modern media market is already one of the major components in the erosion of democratic practices in the West itself.

(5) **Monopolies over weapons of mass destruction.** Held in check by the postwar bipolarity, this monopoly is again, as in 1945, the sole domain of the United States. While it may be true that nuclear proliferation risks getting out of control, it is still the only way of fighting this unacceptable US monopoly in the absence of democratic international control.

These five monopolies, taken as a whole, define the framework within which the law of globalized value operates. The law of value is the condensed expression of all these conditions, and not the expression of objective, 'pure' economic rationality. The conditioning of all of these processes annuls the impact of industrialization in the peripheries, devalues their productive work and overestimates the supposed value-added resulting from the activities of the new monopolies from which the centres profit. What results is a new hierarchy, more unequal than ever before, in the distribution of income on a world scale, subordinating the industries of the peripheries and reducing them to the role of subcontracting. This is the new foundation of polarization, presaging its future forms.

An Alternative Humanist Project of Globalization

In contrast to the dominant ideological discourse, I maintain that globalization via the market, is a reactionary utopia. We must counter it by developing an alternative humanistic project of globalization consistent with a socialist perspective.

Implied in the realization of such a project is the construction of a

6   CAPITALISM IN THE AGE OF GLOBALIZATION

global political system which is not in the service of a global market, but one which defines its parameters in the same way as the nation-state represented historically the social framework of the national market and not merely its passive field of deployment. A global political system would thus have major responsibilities in each of the following four areas:

(1) The organization of global disarmament at appropriate levels, thus liberating humanity from the menace of nuclear and other holocausts.

(2) The organization of access to the planet's resources in an equitable manner so that there would be less inequality. There would have to be a global decision-making process with a valuation (tariffication) of resources which would make obligatory waste reduction and the more equitable distribution of the value and income from these resources. This could also be the beginning of a globalized fiscal system.

(3) Negotiation of open, flexible economic relationships between the world's major regions which, currently, are unequally developed. This would reduce progressively the centres' technological and financial monopolies. This means, of course, the liquidation of the institutions presently running the global market (the so-called World Bank, the IMF, the World Trade Organization etc.) and the creation of other systems for managing the global economy.

(4) Starting negotiation for the correct management of the global/national dialectic in the areas of communication, culture and political policy. This implies the creation of political institutions which would represent social interests on a global scale – the beginning of a 'world parliament' going beyond the inter-state mechanisms of the United Nations system that exist now.

Obstacles to the Realization of this Project

It is more than evident that current trends are not going in the direction described above and that humanist objectives are not those being fought for today. I am not surprised. The erosion of the old system of globalization is not able to prepare its own succession and can only lead to chaos. Dominant forces are developing their activities in the framework of these constraints, trying to manoeuvre for short-term gain and thereby aggravating the chaos. Their attempt to legitimate their choices by the stale ideology of the 'self-regulating' market, or by affirming that 'there is no alternative', or by pure and simple cynicism, is not the solution but part of the problem. The people's spontaneous responses to the degradation they experience, however, are not necessarily any more helpful. In a time of disarray, illusory solutions such as fundamentalism or chauvinism can be highly politically mobilizing. It is up to the Left – that is in fact its historic mission – to formulate, in theory and in practice, a humanistic response to the challenge. In its absence and until it is formulated, regressive and outright criminal scenarios will be the most likely order of the day.

The difficulties confronting the EU's European project right now are a good illustration of the impasse created by globalization through market mechanisms. In the first flush of enthusiasm over the European project no one foresaw these difficulties. Yet they were perfectly predictable by people who never believed that the Common Market by itself could create a united Europe. They said that a project as ambitious as this could not be accomplished without a Left capable of making it socially and culturally progressive. In the absence of that, it would remain fragile, and even a minor political accident could prove fatal. It was necessary, therefore, for the various European Lefts to make sure that each step of the integration was accompanied by a double series of measures: on the one hand, ensuring that profits went to the workers, thereby reinforcing their social power and their unity; and on the other, beginning the construction of a political system which would supersede the nation-state and could be the only unit that could effectively manage an enlarged market. This did not happen. The European project, in the hands of the Right, was reduced to purely mercantilist proportions, and the Left sooner or later simply offered its support without imposing any conditions. The result is what we see before us: the economic downturn has put the European partners in an adversarial position. They can only imagine solutions to their problems (notably unemployment) that are at the expense of others, and they don't even have effective tools for achieving those. They are increasingly tempted to retreat behind national barriers. Even the sincere efforts to avoid such action on the part of French and German politicians on both the Right and the Left have resulted only in rhetoric rather than effective pan-European action.

The EU's Europe is experiencing problems at the same time as the wider Europe is giving a new meaning to the challenge facing it. This ought to be an opportunity for the Left to rethink the European project as a whole and to begin the construction of a confederal political and economic 'big' Europe that is anchored on the left by a reconstructed and united European labour force. But it has missed this opportunity and, on the contrary, has backed the forces of the Right which were in a hurry to profit from the collapse of the Soviet Empire by substituting a kind of unrestrained, wildcat capitalism. It is obvious that the present Latin Americanization of Eastern Europe can only weaken the chances of success of a left-leaning pan-European project. That in turn can only accentuate the disequilibrium within the Europe of the EU to the benefit of the only partner able to profit from this evolution: a reunited Germany.

The crisis of the European project is one of the major challenges confronting the construction of the new globalization. But these inward-looking manifestations, these inadequate and tragic responses to the challenge of the construction of a renewed global system, are not found exclusively in Europe. They are seen throughout the former Third World, especially in regions marginalized by the collapse of the old world order (sub-Saharan Africa and the Arab Islamic areas), and also in the new Third World of the East (as in the former USSR and former Yugoslavia), where we see self-destructive involutions rather than valid responses to the challenge.

Possible Future Scenarios and their Inadequacy

Given this background, there are a few realistic scenarios which can be proposed. I will examine several of them and show that they do not constitute adequate responses to the demands posed by the construction of an acceptable and stable world order. They therefore do not provide a way out from chaos.

The European question is at the centre of theorizing about the future of globalization. With the breakdown of the European project and the threat of its disintegration, forces faithful to the European idea could find it useful, and possible, to regroup around their second best position, that is, a German Europe. There is reason to believe that in this scenario the British ship would sail close to American shores, keeping its distance from 'continental Europe'. We have already started down this path and some have even legitimated this choice by giving priority to the notion of the 'neutral management of money' (a technocratic concept based on ignorance of the political meaning of monetary management), and conferring it (where else?) on the Bundesbank! I do not believe that this caricature of the original European project can be truly stable since several European countries will not accept the erosion of their positions which it implies.

To make matters worse, the preferential position of the United States is not challenged by this scenario of a German-led Europe. Nor is it clear that there is anything in this project that could challenge America in any of the areas of the five monopolies discussed above. A German-led Europe would remain within the American orbit.

There is another possible scenario – for lack of an alternative – a kind of second edition, American hegemony. There are many variations of this. The most likely one is a 'sharing of the burden' associated with neo-imperialist regionalization: hitching Latin America to the US wagon and Africa to the German–European one (with some crumbs for France), and with the Gulf oil region and a 'common market of the Middle East' remaining the domain of the United States. The American presence is already felt by its military occupation of the Gulf and less directly by its alliance with Israel. Finally, there might be a certain symmetry, with South and South-East Asia left open to Japanese expansion. But there is no equality implied in this division among the three centres: the United States would retain its privileged position. Here, too, I do not believe that neo-imperialist options of this kind would guarantee the stability of the system. They would be disputed periodically by revolts in Latin America, Asia and Africa.

We should therefore focus our attention on Asia, which has been largely outside the Euro-American conflict. It has often been observed that Asia – from Japan to Communist China, Korea, and to a lesser degree certain countries of South-East Asia (Singapore, Thailand and Malaysia) and even India – has not been affected by the present crisis, and that these countries have registered successes in terms of growth and efficiency (measured by their competitive position on the world market). Nevertheless, one cannot leap ahead and say that Asia will be the locus of the next hegemony. Asia may have more than half the world's population, but this is divided among distinct states. In place of a vague concept of global hegemony, one could substitute the notion of Asia becoming the principal region of capitalist accumulation. It remains to be described in detail how this may be occurring already: the articulation between the different Asian nations, and between them and the rest of the world. And there are variants of this model. The easiest to imagine – the domination of the region by Japanese imperialism – is, in my opinion, the least plausible. Admirers of Japan's recent success too often underestimate Japan's vulnerability. It is because of this weakness that Japan remains tied to the US. Nor is it probable that China, or even Korea, would accept being subordinated to Japan. Under these conditions the maintenance of an inter-Asian equilibrium would depend on forces external to the region, and here again only the United States is a candidate for this role, which would in turn prolong its primacy on the world scene.

Nonetheless it is highly probable that the positions of these Asian countries will be reinforced within the capitalist world system. How will the United States react to this? All alliance strategies will, in my opinion, revolve around this question. It goes almost without saying that the future development of China threatens all global equilibria. And that is why the United States will feel threatened by her development. In my opinion the United States and China will be *the* major antagonists in any future global conflict.

Renewing a Perspective of Global Socialism

Current developments suggest different possible scenarios, none of which questions the realities of North–South polarization. The commanding logic of the capitalist system perpetuates the centre/periphery polarization. Its modes of operation are ever renewed and will in the future be founded on the five monopolies around which I have constructed my argument.

One could say that there is nothing new in this view because polarization is almost part of the natural order of things. I do not agree with this contention precisely because this polarization has been challenged over the past five centuries. Peoples peripheralized by capitalist world expansion, and who seemed for a long time to accept their fate, have over the past 50 years ceased accepting it, and they will refuse to do so more and more in the future. The positive political aspect of the universalization which capitalism inaugurated – and which can't get beyond its present truncated version – is the worm in the fruit. The Russian and Chinese revolutions began the attempt to go beyond the system on the basis of the revolts of peripheral people, and this will be continued in new versions. The final explanation for the instability of the world-system being built is found here. Of course, the conflicts that will occupy international attention in the future will, as always, not all be of equal importance. I would intuitively give determining priority to those involving the peoples of Asia and the dominant system. This doesn't mean others won't participate in this generalized revolt against polarization, just as it does not mean that transformations, and even progress, won't emanate from the very centres of the system.

In short, a humanistic response to the challenge of globalization inaugurated by capitalist expansion may be idealistic but it is not utopian. On the contrary, it is the only realistic project possible. If only we begin to develop it, powerful social forces will rally to it from all regions of the world.

This is the way to renew the perspective of global socialism. In preparation, ideological and political forces must regroup in order to be capable of combating the five monopolies which reproduce capitalism. This struggle will create conditions for mutual adjustment. In it we have to reconsider fundamental questions on the ideological cultural front: (i) the dialectic between the universal and the particular; (ii) the relationship between political democracy and social progress; (iii) the dialectic of so-called economic efficiency (and the way it is expressed, 'the market') and values of equality and fraternity; and (iv) the definition of a global socialist objective in the light of all the above.

On the political front we have to develop world organizational forms which are more authentically democratic so as to be capable of reshaping economic relations on the basis of diminishing inequality. In this perspective it seems to me that high priority should be given to reorganizing the global system around large areas which would group together scattered parts of the peripheries. This would be the place for the constitution of Latin American, Arab, African, South-East Asian regions, alongside China and India (the only continental countries on our planet). I propose that this objective receive priority treatment in any new agenda of the Non-Aligned Movement. These regional groupings do not exclude others, such as Europe or the former USSR. The reason for this political call is simple: it is only by operating on this scale that one can effectively combat the five monopolies of our analysis. The construction, in turn, of a truly global economic and financial system becomes possible on this basis.

Of course the transformation of the world always begins by struggles at its base. Without changes in ideological, political and social systems at the national level, any discussion about challenging globalization and polarization remains a dead letter.

This chapter contains in condensed form conclusions from discussions developed in:
Empire of Chaos (Monthly Review, 1983)
Re-reading the Post War Period (Monthly Review, 1994)
L'ethnicité à l'assaut des nations (L'Harmattan, 1993)
Mondialisation et accumulation (L'Harmattan, 1993)

[2]

ONE

THE STATE AND THE NEW
GEOGRAPHY OF POWER

Economic globalization represents a major transformation in the territorial organization of economic activity and politico-economic power. How does it reconfigure the territorial exclusivity of sovereign states, and what does this do to both sovereignty and a system of rule based on sovereign states? Has economic globalization over the last ten or fifteen years contributed to a major institutional discontinuity in the history of the modern state, the modern interstate system, and, particularly, the system of rule?

The term *sovereignty* has a long history, beginning with Aristotle, running through Bodin and Hobbes and the American

{ 2 }

and French revolutions, and arriving today at yet another major transformation. From being the sovereignty of the ruler, it became the will of the people as contained in the nation-state, that is, popular sovereignty. It was for a long time centered in a concern with internal order, a notion that influenced international law and politics for many centuries. Sovereignty often was "an attribute of a powerful individual whose legitimacy over territory . . . rested on a purportedly direct or delegated divine or historic authority."[1] The international legal system did not necessarily register these changes as they were happening. But by the end of World War II the notion of sovereignty based on the will of the people had become established as one of the conditions of political legitimacy for a government.[2] Article 1 of the UN Charter established as one of the purposes of the UN the development of friendly relations among states "based on respect for the principles of equal rights and self-determination of peoples"; the Universal Declaration of Human Rights of 1948, Article 21 (3), provided that the will of the people shall be the basis of authority of government . . . through elections. . . ."[3] What is significant here is that this was now expressed in a fundamental international constitutive legal document. "In international law, the sovereign had finally been dethroned."[4]

The sovereignty of the modern state was constituted in mutually exclusive territories and the concentration of sovereignty in nations. There are other systems of rule, particularly those centered in supranational organizations and emergent

THE STATE AND THE NEW GEOGRAPHY OF POWER

private transnational legal regimes, and earlier forms of such supranational powers reigned on occasion over single states, as when the League of Nations gave itself the right of intervention for the purpose of protecting minority rights. Systems of rule need not be territorial, as in certain kinds of kinship-based systems; they may not be territorially fixed, as in nomadic societies; or, while territorially fixed, they need not be exclusive.[5] In the main, however, rule in the modern world flows from the absolute sovereignty of the state over its national territory.

Achieving exclusive territoriality was no easy task. It took centuries of struggle, wars, treaties made and treaties broken, to nationalize territories along mutually exclusive lines and secure the distinctive concentration of power and system of rule that is the sovereign state. Multiple systems of rule coexisted during the transition from the medieval system of rule to the modern state: there were centralizing monarchies in Western Europe, city-states in Italy, and city-leagues in Germany.[6] Even when nation-states with exclusive territoriality and sovereignty were beginning to emerge, other forms might have become effective alternatives—for example, the Italian city-states and the Hanseatic League in northern Europe—and the formation of and claims by central states were widely contested.[7] Even now, there continue to be other forms of concentration of power and other systems of rule, for instance, nonterritorial or nonexclusive systems such as the Catholic Church and the so-called Arab nation.

{ 4 }

There have long been problems with the exclusive territoriality of the modern state. Inevitably, one thinks of Garrett Mattingly's account of the right of embassy in medieval Europe. After succeeding brilliantly at creating mutually exclusive territories, states found there was no space left for the protected conduct of diplomacy; indeed, diplomats often felt—and indeed were—threatened, as well as pelted with vegetables. Moreover, for activities not covered by specific immunities, diplomats could be tried in the courts of the host state, just like any other subject.[8] There were various intermediate forms granting specific immunities. For example, the right of embassy could often be granted without reference to a specific sovereign, allowing subject cities to negotiate directly with one another. This form of the right of embassy became increasingly problematic when the right to embassy became a matter of sovereign recognition. As Mattingly notes, having achieved absolute sovereignty, the new states found they could only communicate with each other "by tolerating within themselves little islands of alien sovereignty."[9] The doctrine of extraterritoriality was thus the answer, and its consequences are still evident today, as when a diplomat parks anywhere in the city with impunity, de jure.[10] In the long history of securing and legitimating exclusive territoriality, particularly in this century, a variety of extraterritorial regimes have accumulated. And then there is, of course, Hugo Grotius's doctrine of mare liberum, which remains with us today.[11]

THE STATE AND THE NEW GEOGRAPHY OF POWER

It is not enough simply to posit, as is so often done, that economic globalization has brought with it declining significance for the national state. Today, the major dynamics at work in the global economy carry the capacity to undo the particular form of the intersection of sovereignty and territory embedded in the modern state and the modern state system. But does this mean that sovereignty or territoriality are less important features in the international system?

Addressing these questions requires an examination of the major aspects of economic globalization that contribute to what I think of as a new geography of power. One much-noted fact is that firms can now operate across borders with ease; indeed, for many, this is what globalization is about. But I wish to examine three other components in the new geography of power.

The first of these components concerns the actual territories where much globalization materializes in specific institutions and processes. What kind of territoriality does this represent? The second component concerns the ascendance of a new legal regime for governing cross-border economic transactions, a trend not sufficiently recognized in the social science literature. A rather peculiar passion for legality (and lawyers) drives the globalization of the corporate economy, and there has been a massive amount of legal innovation around the growth of globalization. The third component I wish to address is the growing number of economic activities taking place in electronic space. Electronic space overrides all existing territorial jurisdiction.

{ 6 }

Further, this growing virtualization of economic activity, particularly in the leading information industries such as finance and specialized corporate services, may be contributing to a crisis in control that transcends the capacities of both the state and the institutional apparatus of the economy. The speed made possible by the new technologies is creating orders of magnitude—in, for instance, the foreign currency markets—that escape the governing capacities of private and government overseers.

Adding these three components of the new geography of power to the global footlooseness of corporate capital reveals aspects of the relation between global economy and national state that the prevalent notion of a global-national duality does not adequately or usefully capture. This duality is conceived as a mutually exclusive set of terrains where the national economy or state loses what the global economy gains. Dualization has fed the proposition that the national state must decline in a globalized economy.

Territoriality in a Global Economy

To elaborate on these three components of the new geography of power, I will begin with the question of the spaces of the global economy. What is the strategic geography of globalization or, more conceptually, the particular form of territoriality that is taking shape in the global economy today?

My starting point is a set of practices and institutions: global financial markets; the ascendance of Anglo-American law

THE STATE AND THE NEW GEOGRAPHY OF POWER

firms in international business transactions; the Uruguay
Round of the GATT and the formation of the World Trade
Organization (WTO); the role of credit-rating agencies and
other such delightful entities in international capital markets;
the provisions in the GATT and NAFTA for the circulation of service workers as part of the international trade and investment
in services; and immigration, particularly the cross-border circulation of low-wage workers. In my earlier research I did not
think about these subjects in terms of governance and accountability; here, I seek to understand the spatial configuration and
legal/regulatory regimes that specify them.

An aspect of economic globalization that has received the
most attention from general and specialized commentators is
the geographic dispersal of firms' factories, offices, service
outlets, and markets. One of many versions of this is the global
assembly line in manufacturing, perhaps most famously drama-
tized by the infamous case of IBM's personal computer carrying
the label Made in the USA when more than 70 percent of its component parts were manufactured overseas, typically in low-
wage countries.[12] Yet another version is the export-processing
zone—a special tariff and taxation regime that allows firms,
mostly from high-wage countries, to export semiprocessed
components for further processing in low-wage countries and
then to reimport them back to the country of origin without
tariffs on the value added through processing. There are now
hundreds of such zones; the best-known instance is the

{ 8 }

Northern Industrialization Program in Mexico, the so-called *maquiladoras*. In Mexico, there are plants from many different countries, including Japanese plants making auto parts and electronic components shipped to Japanese plants in the United States. Another common example is the offshoring of clerical work. So-called clerical factories are growing rapidly in both numbers and types of locations: they can now be found in China even though workers do not necessarily know English. The clerical work that is offshored involves largely routine data entering and is, in many ways, an extension of the common practice in the highly developed countries of locating back offices in suburban areas or shipping clerical work to private households. There are several other variations of this trend toward worldwide geographic dispersal and internationalization. Indeed, national governments have reason to know this well: they are forever struggling to capture the elusive taxes of corporations operating in more than one country.

From the perspective of the national state, specifically the state in highly developed countries, offshoring creates a space economy that goes beyond the regulatory umbrella of the state. And in this regard, the significance of the state is in decline. Here we can point only to the different ways in which globalization brings about this partial denationalizing in developing and highly developed countries. In much of the developing world, it has assumed the form of free trade zones and export manufacturing zones where firms can locate production facili-

THE STATE AND THE NEW GEOGRAPHY OF POWER

ties without being subject to local taxes and various other regulations; such zones exist in many Latin American and Asian countries. In these cases, an actual piece of land becomes denationalized; with financial operations, the process assumes a more institutional and functional meaning.

Conceivably, the geographic dispersal of factories and offices could have gone along with a dispersal in control and profits, a democratizing, if you will, of the corporate structure. Instead, it takes place as part of highly integrated corporate structures with strong tendencies toward concentration in control and profit appropriation. Large corporations log many of these operations as "overseas sales," and it is well known that a very high share, about 40 percent, of international trade actually occurs intrafirm, and, according to some sources, the proportion is even higher than that.[13]

There are two major implications here for the question of territoriality and sovereignty in the context of a global economy. First, when there is geographic dispersal of factories, offices, and service outlets in an integrated corporate system, particularly one with centralized top-level control, there is also a growth in central functions. Put simply, the more globalized firms become, the more their central functions grow: in importance, in complexity, and in number of transactions.[14] The sometimes staggering figures involved in this worldwide dispersal demand extensive coordination and management at parent headquarters. For instance, in the early 1990s U.S. firms had

{ 10 }

more than 18,000 affiliates overseas; less known is the fact that German firms had even more, 19,000, up from 14,000 in the early 1980s or that well over 50 percent of the workforces of firms such as Ford Motors, GM, IBM, and Exxon are overseas.[15] A lot of this dispersal has been going on for a long time, and it does not proceed under a single organizational form: behind these general figures lie many types of establishments, hierarchies of control, and degrees of autonomy.[16]

The second implication in terms of territoriality and sovereignty in a global economy is that these central functions are disproportionately concentrated in the national territories of the highly developed countries. This means that an interpretation of the impact of globalization as creating a space economy that extends beyond the regulatory capacity of a single state is only half the story. It is important to clarify here that central functions involve not only top-level headquarters but also all the top-level financial, legal, accounting, managerial, executive, and planning functions necessary to run a corporate organization operating in more than one and now often several countries. These central functions partly take place at corporate headquarters, but many have become so specialized and complex that headquarters increasingly buy them from specialized firms rather than producing them in-house. This has led to the creation of what has been called the corporate services complex, that is, the network of financial, legal, accounting, advertising, and other corporate service firms that handle the diffi-

THE STATE AND THE NEW GEOGRAPHY OF POWER

culties of operating in more than one national legal system, national accounting system, advertising culture, etc., and do so under conditions of rapid innovations in all these fields.[17]

As a rule, firms in more routinized lines of activity, with predominantly regional or national markets, appear to be increasingly free to move or install their headquarters outside cities, while those in highly competitive and innovative lines of activity and/or with a strong world market orientation appear to benefit from being located at the heart of major international business centers, no matter how high the costs. Both types of firms need some kind of corporate services complex, and the more specialized complexes are most likely to be in cities rather than, say, suburban office parks. Thus the agglomerations of firms carrying out central functions for the management and coordination of global economic systems are disproportionately concentrated in the highly developed countries, particularly, though not exclusively, in the kinds of cities I call global cities, such as New York, Paris, and Amsterdam.[18]

Another instance today of this negotiation between a transnational process or dynamic and a national territory is that of the global financial markets. The orders of magnitude in these markets have risen sharply, as illustrated by the estimated 75 trillion U.S. dollars in turnover in the global capital market, a major component of the global economy. These transactions are partly dependent on telecommunications systems that make possible the instantaneous transmission of money and information

{ 12 }

around the globe. Much attention has gone to the new technologies' capacity for instantaneous transmission. But equally important is the extent to which the global financial markets are located in particular cities in the highly developed countries. The degrees of concentration are unexpectedly high. For instance, international bank lending by countries increased from 1.9 trillion dollars in 1980 to 6.2 trillion dollars in 1991; seven countries accounted for 65 percent of this total in both 1980 and 1991. What countries? Yes, the usual suspects: the United States, the U.K., Japan, Switzerland, France, Germany, and Luxembourg.[19]

Stock markets worldwide have become globally integrated. Besides deregulation in the 1980s in all the major European and North American markets, the late 1980s and early 1990s saw the addition of such markets as Buenos Aires, São Paulo, Bangkok, Taipei, etc. The integration of a growing number of stock markets has contributed to raise the capital that can be mobilized through them. Worldwide market value reached 13 trillion dollars in 1995. This globally integrated stock market, which makes possible the circulation of publicly listed shares around the globe in seconds, functions within a grid of very material, physical, strategic places: that is, cities belonging to national territories.

New Legal Regimes

The operation of worldwide networks of factories, offices, and service outlets and the deregulation and global integration of

THE STATE AND THE NEW GEOGRAPHY OF POWER

stock markets have involved a variety of major and minor legal innovations. Earlier, I discussed the struggle to nationalize territory and form mutually exclusive sovereign territories, in particular the question of the right of embassy, which evolved into a form of extraterritoriality through which to resolve the tension between exclusive territoriality and the need for transactions among states. The impact of economic globalization on national territory and state sovereignty could be yet another form of such extraterritoriality, only on a much larger scale. My discussion about territory in the global economy posits that much that we describe as global, including some of the most strategic functions necessary for globalization, is grounded in national territories. Is this a form of extraterritoriality that leaves the sovereignty of the state fundamentally unaltered? Or is it a development of a different sort, one that affects the sovereignty of the state and partially transforms the notions of both territoriality and sovereignty.

To address these questions, it is necessary to examine the particular forms of legal innovation that have been produced and within which much of globalization is encased and further to consider how they interact with the state or, more specifically, with the sovereignty of the state. These legal innovations and changes are often characterized as "deregulation" and taken as somewhat of a given (though not by legal scholars). In much social science, *deregulation* is another name for the declining significance of the state. But, it seems to me, these

{ 14 }

legal changes contain a more specific process, one that along with the reconfiguration of space may signal a more fundamental transformation in the matter of sovereignty, pointing to new contents and new locations for the particular systemic property that we call sovereignty. As with the discussion of territory in the global economy, my beginning point is a set of practices and minor legal forms, microhistories, that can, however, accumulate into major trends or regimes—and I am afraid are about to do so.

Firms operating transnationally need to ensure the functions traditionally exercised by the state in the national realm of the economy, such as guaranteeing property rights and contracts.[20] Yet insofar as economic globalization extends the economy—but not the sovereignty—of the nation-state beyond its boundaries, this guarantee would appear to be threatened.

In fact, globalization has been accompanied by the creation of new legal regimes and practices and the expansion and renovation of some older forms that bypass national legal systems. Globalization and governmental deregulation have not meant the absence of regulatory regimes and institutions for the governance of international economic relations. Among the most important in the private sector today are international commercial arbitration and the variety of institutions that fulfill the rating and advisory functions that have become essential for the operation of the global economy.

THE STATE AND THE NEW GEOGRAPHY OF POWER

Over the past twenty years, international commercial arbitration has been transformed and institutionalized as the leading contractual method for the resolution of transnational commercial disputes.[21] Again, a few figures tell a quick and dirty story. There has been an enormous growth in arbitration centers. Excluding those concerned with maritime and commodity disputes—an older tradition—there were 120 centers by 1991, with another 7 established by 1993; among the more recent are those of Bahrain, Singapore, Sydney, and Vietnam. There were about a thousand arbitrators by 1990, a number that had doubled by 1992.[22] In a major study on international commercial arbitration, Yves Dezalay and Bryant Garth find that it is a delocalized and decentralized market for the administration of international commercial disputes, connected by more or less powerful institutions and individuals who are both competitive and complementary.[23] It is in this regard a far from unitary system of justice, perhaps organized, as Dezalay and Garth put it, around one great lex mercatoria, which might have been envisioned by some of the pioneering idealists of law.[24]

Another private regulatory system is represented by the debt security or bond-rating agencies that have come to play an increasingly important role in the global economy. Two agencies dominate the market in ratings, with listings of 3 trillion U.S. dollars each: Moody's Investors Service, usually referred to as Moody's, and Standard and Poor's Ratings Group, usually referred to as Standard and Poor.[25] Ten years ago Moody's and

{ 16 }

Standard and Poor had no analysts outside the United States; by 1993 they each had about a hundred in Europe, Japan, and Australia. In his study of credit-rating processes, Sinclair found that they have leverage because of their distinct gate-keeping functions for investment funds sought by corporations and governments.[26] In this regard they can be seen as a significant force in the operation and expansion of the global economy.[27] And as with business law, the U.S. agencies have expanded their influence overseas; to some extent, their growing clout can be seen as both a function and a promoter of U.S. financial orthodoxy, particularly its short-term perspective.

AMERICANIZATION

Transnational institutions and regimes raise questions about the relation between state sovereignty and the governance of global economic processes. International commercial arbitration is basically a private justice system, and credit-rating agencies are private gate-keeping systems. With other institutions, they have emerged as important governance mechanisms whose authority is not centered in the state. The current relocation of authority has transformed the capacities of governments and can be thought of as an instance of Rosenau's "governance without government."[28] This is a subject I will explore in greater detail in the next chapter. It has also spurred the formation of transnational legal regimes, which have penetrated into national fields hitherto closed.[29] In their turn, national

THE STATE AND THE NEW GEOGRAPHY OF POWER

legal fields are becoming more internationalized in some of the major developed economies. Some of the old divisions between the national and the global are becoming weaker and, to some extent, have been neutralized. The new transnational regimes could, in principle, have assumed various forms and contents; but, in fact, they are assuming a specific form, one wherein the states of the highly developed countries play a strategic geopolitical role. The hegemony of neoliberal concepts of economic relations, with its strong emphasis on markets, deregulation, and free international trade, influenced policy in the USA and the U.K. in the 1980s and now increasingly does so in continental Europe as well. This has contributed to the formation of transnational legal regimes that are centered in Western economic concepts.[30]

Dezalay and Garth note that the "international" is itself constituted largely from a competition among national approaches. There is no global law. Martin Shapiro, too, notes that there is not much of a regime of international law, either through the establishment of a single global lawgiver and enforcer or through a nation-state consensus. He also posits that if there were, it would be an international rather than a global law; in fact, it is not even certain that the concept of law itself has become universal, that is, that human relations everywhere in the world will be governed by some, though perhaps not the same, law. The globalization of law refers to a very limited, specialized set of legal phenomena, and

{ 18 }

Shapiro argues that it will almost always refer to North America and Europe and only sometimes to Japan and some other Asian countries.[31]

The international thus emerges as a site for regulatory competition among essentially national approaches, whatever the issue: environmental protection, constitutionalism, human rights.[32] From this perspective "international" or "transnational" has become in the most recent period a form of Americanization, though the process has hardly been smooth. Contestation crops up everywhere, some of it highly visible and formalized, some of it not. In some countries, especially in Europe, there is resistance to what is perceived as the Americanization of the global capital market's standards for the regulation of financial systems and standards for reporting financial information. Sinclair notes that the internationalization of ratings by the two leading U.S. agencies could be seen as another step toward global financial integration or as fulfilling an American agenda. Resentment against U.S. agencies is clearly on the rise in Europe, as became evident when Credit Suisse was downgraded in 1991 and, in early 1992, the Swiss Bank Corporation met the same fate. Conflict is also evident in the difficulty with which foreign agencies gain SEC standing as Nationally Recognized Statistical Rating Organizations in the USA. The *Financial Times*—to mention one example—has reported on private discussions in London, Paris, and Frank-

THE STATE AND THE NEW GEOGRAPHY OF POWER

furt concerning the possibility of setting up a Europe-wide agency to compete with the major U.S.-based agencies.[33]

The most widely recognized instance of Americanization is seen, of course, in the profound influence U.S. popular culture exerts on global culture.[34] But, though less widely recognized and more difficult to specify, it has also become very clear in the legal forms ascendant in international business transactions.[35] Through the IMF and the International Bank for Reconstruction and Development (IBRD) as well as the GATT, the U.S. vision has spread to—some would say been imposed on—the developing world.[36]

The competition among national legal systems or approaches is particularly evident in business law, where the Anglo-American model of the business enterprise and competition is beginning to replace the Continental model of legal artisans and corporatist control over the profession.[37] More generally, U.S. dominance in the global economy over the last few decades has meant that the globalization of law through private corporate lawmaking has assumed the form of the Americanization of commercial law.[38] Certain U.S. legal practices are being diffused throughout the world—for instance, the legal device of franchising. Shapiro notes that this may not stem only from U.S. dominance but also from common law's receptivity to contract and other commercial law innovations. For example, it is widely believed in Europe that EC legal busi-

{ 20 }

ness goes to London because lawyers there are better at legal innovations to facilitate new and evolving transnational business relations. "For whatever reasons, it is now possible to argue that American business law has become a kind of global *jus commune* incorporated explicitly or implicitly into transnational contracts and beginning to be incorporated into the case law and even the statutes of many other nations."[39]

All the reasons for this Americanization are somewhat interrelated: the rationalization of arbitration know-how, the ascendance of large Anglo-American transnational legal services firms, and the emergence of a new specialty in conflict resolution.[40] The large Anglo-American law firms that dominate the international market of business law include arbitration as one of the array of services they offer. Specialists in conflict are practitioners formed from the two great groups that have dominated legal practice in the United States: corporate lawyers, known for their competence as negotiators in the creation of contracts, and trial lawyers, whose talent lies in jury trials. The growing importance in the 1980s of such transactions as mergers and acquisitions, as well as antitrust and other litigation, contributed to a new specialization: knowing how to combine judicial attacks and behind-the-scenes negotiations to reach the optimum outcome for the client. Dezalay and Garth note that under these conditions judicial recourse becomes a weapon in a struggle that will almost certainly end

THE STATE AND THE NEW GEOGRAPHY OF POWER

before trial. Notwithstanding its deep roots in the Continental tradition, especially the French and Swiss traditions, this system of private justice is becoming increasingly Americanized.

The Virtualization of Economic Activity

The third component in the new geography of power is the growing importance of electronic space. There is much to be said on this issue. Here, I can isolate one particular matter: the distinctive challenge that the virtualization of a growing number of economic activities presents not only to the existing state regulatory apparatus but also to private-sector institutions increasingly dependent on the new technologies. Taken to its extreme, this may signal a control crisis in the making, one for which we lack an analytical vocabulary.

The questions of control here have to do not with the extension of the economy beyond the territory of the state but with digitalization—that is, electronic markets—and orders of magnitude such as those that can be achieved in the financial markets, thanks to the transaction speeds made possible by the new technologies. The best example is probably the foreign currency market, which operates largely in electronic space and has achieved volumes—a trillion dollars a day—that leave the central banks incapable of exercising the influence on exchange rates they are expected to wield (though may, in fact, not always have had). The growing virtualization of economic

{ 22 }

activities raises questions of control that also go beyond the notions of non-state-centered systems of coordination prevalent in the literature on governance.

The State Reconfigured

In many ways, the state is involved in this emerging transnational governance system. But it is a state that has itself undergone transformation and participated in legitimating a new doctrine about its role in the economy. Central to this new doctrine is a growing consensus among states to further the growth and strength of the global economy. This combination of elements is illustrated by some of the aspects of the December 1994 crisis in Mexico.

Mexico's crisis was defined rather generally in international political and business circles, as well as in much of the press, as the result of the global financial markets' loss of confidence in the Mexican economy and the government's leadership of it. The U.S. government defined the crisis as a global economic security issue with direct impact on the U.S. economy and pushed hard to get the U.S. legislature and the governments of other highly developed countries to come to Mexico's aid. It opted for a financial "solution," an aid package that would allow the Mexican government to pay its obligations to foreign investors and thereby restore foreign (and national) investors' confidence in the Mexican economy. This financial response was but one of several potential choices. For instance, there

THE STATE AND THE NEW GEOGRAPHY OF POWER

could conceivably have been an emphasis on promoting manufacturing growth and protecting small businesses and home-
owners from the bankruptcies faced by many in Mexico. And
the U.S. government could also have exhorted the Mexican
government to give up on restoring confidence in the global
financial market and focus instead on the production of real
value added in the Mexican economy. To complicate matters
further, this crisis, which was largely presented as a global economic security issue, was handled not by the secretary of
state—as it would have been twenty years ago—but by the secretary of the treasury, Robert Rubin, someone who had been
the so-called dean of Wall Street. There are two rather important novel elements here: first, that Treasury should handle this
international crisis, and, second, that the secretary of that
agency was a former top partner at Goldman, Sachs & Co. on
Wall Street, one of the leading global financial firms. My aim
here is not to point to even the slightest potential for corruption
but rather to raise the question of what is desirable economically, and how we define problems and their best solutions.

The shift in responsibility from the State Department to
Treasury signals the extent to which the state itself has been
transformed by its participation in the implementation of globalization and by the pressures of globalization. Many governments now see their responsibilities as going beyond traditional
foreign policy and extending to world trade, the global environment, and global economic stability.[41] This participation of

{ 24 }

the state in the international arena is an extremely multifaceted and complex matter, and one in which some states participate much more than others. In some cases, it *can* be seen as benevolent—for example, in certain matters concerning the global environment—and in others less so—as when the governments of the highly developed countries, particularly the United States, push for worldwide market reform and privatization in developing countries.

I confine the analysis here to the economic arena, where the international role of the state has been read in rather diverse, though not necessarily mutually exclusive, ways. For instance, according to some, much of this new role of states in the global economy is dominated by the furthering of a broad neoliberal conception, to the point where it represents a constitutionalizing of this project.[42] Others emphasize that effective international participation by national governments can contribute to the strengthening of the rule of law at the global level.[43]

Yet others see the participation of the state in international systems as contributing to the loss of sovereignty. One can see this in recent debates over the World Trade Organization, fueled by concerns that it imposes restrictions on the political autonomy of the national state by placing the principle of free trade above all other considerations. For example, some fear that it will be used to enforce the GATT trade regulations to the point of overturning federal, state, and local laws. This is then seen as jeopardizing a nation's right to enact its own consumer,

THE STATE AND THE NEW GEOGRAPHY OF POWER

labor, and environmental laws. It is worth noting here that many in the United States who supported the GATT did not like the role of the WTO because they did not like the idea of binding the nation to an international dispute-resolution tribunal not fully controlled by the United States.

An important question running through these different interpretations is whether the new transnational regimes and institutions are creating systems that strengthen the claims of certain actors (corporations, the large multinational legal firms) and correspondingly weaken the positions of states and smaller players. John Ruggie has pointed out that "global markets and transnationalized corporate structures . . . are not in the business of replacing states," yet they can have the potential for producing fundamental changes in the system of states.[44]

What matters here is that global capital has made claims on national states, which have responded through the production of new forms of legality. The new geography of global economic processes, the strategic territories for economic globalization, have to be defined in terms of both the practices of corporate actors, including the requisite infrastructure, and the work of the state in producing or legitimating new legal regimes. Views that characterize the national state as simply losing significance fail to capture this very important fact and reduce what is happening to a function of the global-national duality: what one wins, the other loses. By contrast, I view deregulation not simply as a loss of control by the state but as a

{ 26 }

crucial mechanism for handling the juxtaposition of the inter-state consensus to pursue globalization and the fact that national legal systems remain as the major, or crucial, instanti-ation through which guarantees of contract and property rights are enforced.

There are two distinct issues here. One is the formation of new legal regimes that negotiate between national sovereignty and the transnational practices of corporate economic actors. The second is the particular content of these new regimes, one that strengthens the advantages of certain types of economic actors and weakens those of others. Concerning governance, these two aspects translate into two different agendas. One is centered on the effort to create viable systems of coordination and order among the powerful economic actors now operating globally (to ensure, one could say, that the big boys at the top don't kill each other). International commercial arbitration and credit-rating agencies can be seen as contributing to this type of order. The second is focused less on how to create order at the top than on equity and distributive questions in the context of a globally integrated economic system with immense inequalities in the profit-making capacities of firms and the earnings capac-ities of households.

This second, equity-oriented agenda is further constrained by some of the order-creating governance issues arising from a global economic system increasingly dominated by finance. For now, I want to raise two larger questions of principle and

THE STATE AND THE NEW GEOGRAPHY OF POWER

politics: What actors gain legitimacy to govern the global economy and take over rules and authorities previously controlled by the national state? Do the new systems for governance that are emerging and the confinement of the role of national states in the global economy to promoting deregulation, markets, and privatization indicate a decline of international public law?[45]

I see an important parallel here. Certain components of the state's authority to protect rights are being displaced onto so-called universal human rights codes, a subject I develop in chapter 3. While the national state was and remains in many ways the guarantor of the social, political, and civil rights of a nation's people, from the 1970s on we see a significant transformation in this area. Human rights codes have become a somewhat autonomous source of authority that can delegitimize a state's particular actions if it violates such codes. Thus both the global capital market and human rights codes can extract accountability from the state, but they do so with very different agendas. Both have gained a kind of legitimacy.

It is clear that defining the nation-state and the global economy as mutually exclusive operations is, in my analysis, highly problematic. The strategic spaces where many global processes take place are often national; the mechanisms through which the new legal forms necessary for globalization are implemented are often part of state institutions; the infrastructure

{ 28 }

that makes possible the hypermobility of financial capital at the global scale is situated in various national territories. The condition of the nation-state, in my view, cannot be reduced to one of declining significance. The shrinking capacity of the state to regulate many of its industries cannot be explained simply by the fact that firms now operate in a global rather than in a national economy. The state itself has been a key agent in the implementation of global processes, and it has emerged quite altered by this participation. The form and content of participation varies between highly developed and developing countries and within each of these groupings.

Sovereignty and territory, then, remain key features of the international system. But they have been reconstituted and partly displaced onto other institutional arenas outside the state and outside the framework of nationalized territory. I argue that sovereignty has been decentered and territory partly denationalized. From a longer historical perspective, this would represent a transformation in the articulation of sovereignty and territory as they have marked the formation of the modern state and interstate system. And it would entail a need to expand the analytic terrain within which the social sciences examine some of these processes, that is to say, the explicit or implicit tendency to use the nation-state as the container of social, political, and economic processes.

The denationalization of territory occurs through both corporate practices and the as yet fragmentary ascendant new legal

THE STATE AND THE NEW GEOGRAPHY OF POWER

regime. This process does not unfold within the geographic conception of territory shared by the generals who fought the wars for nationalizing territory in earlier centuries. It is instead a denationalizing of specific institutional arenas. (Manhattan is the equivalent of a free trade zone when it comes to finance, but it is not Manhattan the geographic entity, with all its layers of activity, functions, and regulations that is a free trade zone; it is a highly specialized functional or institutional realm that has become denationalized.)

Sovereignty remains a feature of the system, but it is now located in a multiplicity of institutional arenas: the new emergent transnational private legal regimes, new supranational organizations (such as the WTO and the institutions of the European Union), and the various international human rights codes. All these institutions constrain the autonomy of national states; states operating under the rule of law are caught in a web of obligations they cannot disregard easily (though they clearly can to some extent, as is illustrated by the United States' unpaid duties to the United Nations: if this were a personal credit card debt, you or I would be in jail).

What I see is the beginning of an unbundling of sovereignty as we have known it for many centuries—but not always. Scholars examining changes in mentalities or social epistemologies have remarked that significant, epochal change frequently could not be grasped by contemporaries: the vocabularies, categories, master images available to them were unable

{ 30 }

to capture fundamental change. Suffering from the same limitations, all we see is the collapse of sovereignty as we know it. But it seems to me that rather than sovereignty eroding as a consequence of globalization and supranational organizations, it is being transformed. There is plenty of it around, but the sites for its concentration have changed over the last two decades—and economic globalization has certainly been a key factor in all this. Over the last ten or fifteen years, that process has reconfigured the intersection of territoriality and sovereignty as it had been constituted over the last century, after struggles lasting many more. This reconfiguration is partial, selective, and above all strategic. Some of its repercussions for distributive justice and equity are profoundly disturbing. And even in the domain of immigration policy, where the state is still considered as absolutely sovereign, the new web of obligations and rights that states need to take into account under the rule of law in the making of policy has caused conditions to change. I discuss these issues in the following chapters.

NOTES

1. The State and the New Geography of Power

1. Reisman 1990, 867.

2. Franck 1992; Jacobson 1996.

3. Reisman 1990; McDougal and Reisman 1981.

4. Reisman 1990, 868.

5. See the classification of different types of relationships between a system of rule and territoriality in Ruggie 1993.

6. See Anderson 1974; Wallerstein 1974; Giddens 1985.

7. See Tilly 1990. On the Italian city-states and the Hanseatic League in northern Europe, see the analysis in Spruyt 1994.

8. See Mattingly's (1988) account of the right of embassy in medieval times as a specific, formal right with only partial immunities.

9. Mattingly 1988, 244. See also Kratochwil 1986.

10. In this case, the site for extraterritoriality is the individual holding diplomatic status.

11. Grotius's doctrine was a response to the Dutch East Indies Company's effort to monopolize access to the oceans; it resolved the vacuum left by the failure of Spain and Portugal to agree on a division of the maritime trade routes.

12. There is a vast literature on this subject. See, e.g., Bonacich et al. 1994; Morales 1994; Ward 1990.

13. See United Nations Centre for Transnational Corporations (UNCTAD) 1993, 1995. The center was an autonomous entity until 1994, when it became part of UNCTAD.

14. I elaborated these issues in Sassen 1991. This process of corporate integration should not be confused with vertical integration as conventionally defined. See also Gereffi and Korzeniewicz 1994 on commodity chains and Porter's (1990) value-added chains, two constructs that also illustrate the difference between corporate integration on a world scale and vertical integration as conventionally defined.

15. More detailed accounts of these figures and sources can be found in Sassen 1994a.

16. See, e.g., Harrison 1994.

17. See Sassen 1991, 1994a; Knox and Taylor 1995; Brotchie et al. 1995; *Le Débat*, 1994.

18. It is important to unbundle analytically the fact of strategic functions for the global economy or for global operation from the overall corporate economy of a country. Traditional economic complexes have valorization dynamics that tend to be far more articulated with the public economic functions of the state, the quintessential example being Fordist manufacturing. Global markets in finance and

advanced services, however, partly operate under a regulatory umbrella that is market centered. This raises questions of control, especially in view of the currently inadequate capacities to govern transactions in electronic space. Global control and command functions are partly handled within national corporate structures but also constitute a distinct corporate subsector, which can be conceived of as part of a network that connects global cities across the globe. In this sense, global cities are different from the old capitals of erstwhile empires, in that they are a function of cross-border networks rather than simply the most powerful city of an empire. There is, in my conceptualization, no such entity as a single global city akin to the single capital of an empire; the category "global city" only makes sense as a component of a global network of strategic sites. See Sassen 1991. For the purposes of certain kinds of inquiry, this distinction may not matter; for the purposes of understanding the global economy, it does.

19. These data come from the Bank for International Settlements, the so-called central bankers' bank.

20. See Mittelman 1996; Panitch 1996; Cox 1987.

21. There are, of course, other mechanisms for resolving business disputes. The larger system includes arbitration controlled by courts, arbitration that is parallel to courts, and various court and out-of-court mechanisms such as mediation. The following description of international commercial arbitration is taken from Dezalay and Garth 1995. For these authors, international commercial arbitration means something different today from what it did twenty years ago. Increasingly formal, it has come to resemble U.S.-style litigation as it has become more successful and institutionalized. Today, international business contracts for the sale of goods, joint ventures, construction projects, distributorships, and the like typically call for arbi-

{ 104 }

tration in the event of a dispute arising from the contractual arrangement. The main reason given for this choice is that arbitration allows each party to avoid being forced to submit to the courts of the other. Also important is the secrecy of the process. Such arbitration can be institutional, following the rules of institutions such as the International Chamber of Commerce in Paris, the American Arbitration Association, the London Court of International Commercial Arbitration, or many others, or it can be ad hoc, often following the rules of the UN Commission on International Trade Law (UNCITRAL). The arbitrators, usually three private individuals selected by the parties, act as private judges, holding hearings and issuing judgments. There are few grounds for appeal to courts, and the final decision of the arbitrators is more easily enforced among signatory countries than would be a court judgment (under the terms of a widely adopted 1958 New York Convention).

22. Dezalay and Garth 1995; Aksen, 1990. Despite this increase in size, there is a kind of international arbitration community, a club of sorts, with relatively few important institutions and limited numbers of individuals in each country who are the key players both as counsel and arbitrators. But the enormous growth of arbitration over the last decade has led to sharp competition in the business; indeed, it has become big legal business (Salacuse 1991). Dezalay and Garth found that multinational legal firms sharpen the competition further because they have the capacity to forum shop among institutions, sets of rules, laws, and arbitrators. The large English and U.S. law firms have used their power in the international business world to impose their conception of arbitration and more largely of the practice of law. This is well illustrated by the case of France. Although French firms rank among the top providers of information services and industrial engi-

neering services in Europe and have a strong though not outstanding position in financial and insurance services, they are at an increasing disadvantage in legal and accounting services. French law firms are at a particular disadvantage because of their legal system (the Napoleonic Code): Anglo-American law tends to govern international transactions. Foreign firms with offices in Paris dominate the servicing of the legal needs of firms in France, both French and foreign, that operate internationally (Carrez 1991) (see *Le Débat* 1994).

23. Summarized in Dezalay and Garth 1995; see also Dezalay 1992.

24. Dezalay and Garth 1995. The so-called lex mercatoria was conceived by many as a return to an international law of business independent of national laws (Carbonneau 1990). Anglo-American practitioners tend not to support this Continental, highly academic notion (see Carbonneau 1990), and insofar as they are "Americanizing" the field, they are moving it farther away from academic law and lex mercatoria.

25. There are several rating agencies in other countries, but they are oriented to the domestic markets. The possibility of a European-based rating agency has been discussed, particularly with the merger of a London-based agency (IBCA) with a French one (Euronotation).

26. As the demand for ratings grows, so does the authoritativeness of the notion behind them. Sinclair (1994) considers this to be ill founded given the judgments that are central to it. The processes intrinsic to ratings are tied to certain assumptions, which are in turn tied to dominant interests, notably narrow theories of market efficiency. They aim for undistorted price signals and little if any government intervention. Sinclair notes that transition costs such as unemployment are usually not factored into evaluations and considered to be outweighed by the new environment created (143).

{ 106 }

27. Their power has grown in good part because of disintermediation and the globalization of the capital market. Some functions fulfilled by banks (i.e., intermediation) have lost considerable weight in the running of capital markets. Thus, insofar as banks are subject to considerable government regulation and their successors are not, government regulation over the capital markets has declined. Ratings agencies, which are private entities, have taken over some of the functions of banks in organizing information for suppliers and borrowers of capital. An important question is whether the new agencies and the larger complex of entities represented by Wall Street have indeed formed a new intermediary sector (see Thrift 1987).

28. Rosenau and Czempiel 1992.

29. See Trubek et al. 1993.

30. This hegemony has not passed unnoticed and is engendering considerable debate. For instance, a familiar issue that is emerging as significant in view of the spread of Western legal concepts involves a critical examination of the philosophical premises of authorship and property that define the legal arena in the West (e.g., Coombe 1993.)

31. See Shapiro 1993. There have been a few particular common developments and many particular parallel developments in law across the world. Thus, as a concomitant of the globalization of markets and the organization of transnational corporations, there has been a move toward relatively uniform global contract and commercial law. This can be seen as a private lawmaking system wherein two or more parties create a set of rules to govern their future relations. Such a system of private lawmaking can exist transnationally even when there is no transnational court or sovereign to resolve disputes and secure enforcement. The case of international commercial arbitration discussed earlier illustrates this well. See also Shapiro 1979.

NOTES

32. Charny 1991; Trachtman 1993. Two other categories that may also partly overlap with internationalization are important to distinguish, at least analytically: multilateralism and what Ruggle (1993) has called multiperspectival institutions.

33. See Sinclair 1994.

34. For a discussion of the concept of cultural globalization, see King 1991 and Robertson 1991, especially Robertson's notion of the world as a single place, what he calls the "global human condition." I would say that globalization is also a process that produces differentiation, but of a character very different from that associated with such differentiating notions as national character, national culture, and national society. For example, the corporate world today has a global geography, but it isn't everywhere in the world: in fact, it has highly defined and structured spaces; it is also increasingly sharply differentiated from noncorporate segments in the economies of the particular locations (such as New York City) or countries where it operates.

35. Shapiro 1993 finds that law and the political structures that produce and sustain it are far more national and far less international than are trade and politics as such (63). He argues that the U.S. domestic legal regime may have to respond to global changes in markets and politics far more often than to global changes in law. For the most part, he claims, national regimes of law and lawyering will remain self-generating, though in response to globally perceived needs. In my reading, it is this last point that may well be emerging as a growing factor in shaping legal form and legal practice.

36. The best-known instance of this is probably the austerity policy imposed on many developing countries. Such policies also point up the participation of states in furthering the goals of globalization, because they have to be run through national govern-

{ 108 }

ments and reprocessed as national policies. It is clearer here than in other cases that the global is not simply the non-national, that global processes materialize in national territories and institutions. There is a distinction here to be made—and to be specified theoretically and empirically—between international law (whether public or private), which is always implemented through national governments, and these policies, which are part of the effort to foster globalization.

37. Dezalay 1992. See also Carrez 1991; and Sinclair 1994.

38. Shapiro 1993.

39. Shapiro 1993, 39; Wiegand 1991.

40. Dezalay 1992.

41. Aman 1995, 437.

42. See Panitch 1996; Cox 1987; Mittelman 1996.

43. Aman, 1995; Young 1989; Rosenau 1992.

44. Ruggie 1993, 143.

45. See Kennedy 1988; Negri 1995.

References

Dezalay, Yves, and Bryant Garth (1995), 'Merchants of Law as Moral Entrepreneurs: Constructing International Justice from the Competition for Transnational Business Disputes', *Law and Society Review*, **29** (1), 27–64.

Mattingly, Garrett (1988), *Renaissance Diplomacy*, New York: Dover.

Rosenau, J. N. (1992), 'Governance, Order, and Change in World Politics', in J. N. Rosenau and E. O. Czempiel (eds), *Governance Without Government: Order and Change in World Politics*, Cambridge: Cambridge University Press, pp. 1–29.

Ruggie, John Gerard (1993), 'Territoriality and Beyond: Problematizing Modernity in International Relations', *International Organization*, **47** (1 [winter]), 139–74.

Shapiro, Martin (1993), 'The Globalization of Law', *Indiana Journal of Global Legal Studies*, **I** (fall), 37–64.

Sinclair, Timothy J. (1994), 'Passing Judgement: Credit Rating Processes as Regulatory Mechanisms of Governance in the Emerging World Order', *Review of International Political Economy*, **I** (1 [spring]), 133–59.

[3]

Pergamon

www.elsevier.com/locate/worlddev

World Development Vol. 31, No. 4, pp. 667–683, 2003
© 2003 Elsevier Science Ltd. All rights reserved
Printed in Great Britain
0305-750X/03/$ - see front matter

doi:10.1016/S0305-750X(03)00002-0

The Two Faces of Globalization: Against Globalization as We Know It [☆]

BRANKO MILANOVIC [*]
World Bank, Washington, DC, USA

Summary. — The paper shows that the current view of globalization as an automatic and benign force is flawed: it focuses on only one, positive, face of globalization while entirely neglecting the malignant one. The two key historical episodes that are adduced by the supporters of the "globalization as it is" (the Halcyon days of the 1870–1913, and the record of the last two decades of development) are shown to be misinterpreted. The "Halcyon days" were never Halcyon for those who were "globalized" through colonization since colonial constraints prevented them from industrializing. The record of the last two decades (1978–98) is shown to be almost uniformly worse than that of the previous two (1960–78). © 2003 Elsevier Science Ltd. All rights reserved.

Key words — world, globalization, growth, development theory, convergence

1. THE MAINSTREAM VIEW

The mainstream view of globalization, at least among the people who "matter" in the countries that "matter"—the vast majority of economists, many political scientists, and political commentators—is that globalization is a benign force leading us ultimately to the era of converging world incomes (as poor countries such as China open up to the world and see their incomes rise), converging institutions as democracy becomes a universal norm, and cultural richness as people of different background interact more frequently. The most famous, or notorious, reflection of that Pollyannaish view of the world was the early announcement by Fukuyama (1989) of the "end of history." Although the ethnic warfare since then has not disproved Fukuyama's (or rather Hegel's) view, since none of the ethnic warriors had an alternative civilizational blueprint—a point which is implied in Hegel's hypothesis—the more recent debates about globalization as well as the role of Islam—a society *with* an alternative blueprint—do show that the end of history is not around the corner.

It is only a slight caricaturization of this naïve view to state that its proponents regard globalization as a *deus ex machina* for many of the problems, such as poverty, illiteracy or inequality that beset the developing world. The only thing that a country needs to do is to open up its borders, reduce tariff rates, attract foreign capital, and in a few generations if not less, the poor will become rich, the illiterate will learn how to read and write, and inequality will vanish as the poor countries catch up with the rich. This is the view conveyed implicitly and subliminally by many serious papers and publications as, for example, in the Dollar and Kraay (2000) often-repeated statement that "the poor and the rich gain one-for-one from openness," [1] or in Sala-i-Martin's (2002) derisive statements about inequality and globalization. While, of course, the authors are careful enough not to explicitly make such statements (e.g., Dollar & Kraay do acknowledge that gains "one-for-one" are expressed in percentage terms, so that a poor person whose income is one-hundredth of that of a rich person will also gain one-hundredth of the rich person's gain), [2]

[☆] The paper represents author's own views only; the views should not be attributed to the World Bank or its affiliated organization.

[*] I am thankful to Dennis Arens, Nancy Bidsall, David Dollar, Bill Easterly, James K. Galbraith, Carol Graham, Elizabeth King, Ravi Kanbur, Mansoob Murshed, Martin Ravallion, Dani Rodrik, and Michael Ward for very valuable comments on an earlier draft of the paper. Final revision accepted: 24 November 2002.

they do leave their statement sufficiently ambiguous, thus allowing more explicit and wrong Pollyannaish views of globalization to find currency in the mainstream popular magazines and newspapers. There the heavy guns of the globalization debate are not embarrassed by the finer points of relative *vs.* absolute gains, or with percentages or logarithms: they simply state that globalization is good for everyone. For example, *The Economist* (2000, p. 82) in a review of the Dollar and Kraay article writes: "Growth really does help the poor: in fact, it raises their incomes by about as much as it raises incomes of everybody else." This is deemed insufficient to carry the (misleading) message. In the next paragraph, they continue: "On average, incomes of the poor rise one-for-one with incomes overall."

Moreover, the past too is harnessed to support this dominant view of globalization. The period 1870–1913, the heyday of imperialism and colonialism, is made to appear as the period of universal growth, and catch-up of poor countries as, for example, in Lindert and Williamson (2001, p. 1) who somewhat incredibly write: "globalization probably mitigated the steep rise in income gaps between nations. The nations that gained the most from globalization are those poor ones that changed their policies to exploit it..."

Thus, globalization is regarded as a benign and automatic force that, once certain preconditions are set in place ("sound" macropolicies, protection of property rights *etc.*), will inexorably lead countries and individuals to a state of economic bliss. We show here that this view of globalization is based on one serious methodological error: a systematic ignorance of the double-sided nature of globalization, that is, systematic ignorance of its malignant side. We show, first, how this methodological error leads to the misreading of the 19th century economic history; second, we argue that the Pollyannaish view of globalization severely distorts the lessons of the most recent period, 1980–2000, and third, we show how a more accurate and realistic reading of globalization requires, in many respects, different policies from the ones suggested by the naïve (or self-interested?) globalization cheerleaders.

2. THE TWO FACES OF GLOBALIZATION

In contrast to the view of globalization as a purely benign force which we have briefly sketched above are two other views. One, the Left view, regards globalization as a malignant force that leads to child labor in the South and takes away middle-class jobs in the North. For the Left, to be anti-globalization is a very difficult task since the Left is, by definition, internationalist. But what the Left resents is that today's globalization is led by a triumphant, and often, unbridled capitalism. Unbridled capitalism does produce the effects of which the Left complains: destruction of environment, obliteration of indigenous cultures (e.g., how many Mayas still speak Mayan?), and exploitation of the weak.

The conservative, and often xenophobic, Right also agrees that globalization is a malignant force. That view is more prevalent in Europe, with its history of xenophobia, than in the United States.[3] In Europe, globalization engenders not only fear of losing jobs to the poor masses in the South, but of losing cultural homogeneity that many European countries have acquired through a long process of obliteration of local cultures (where are the French Bretons today?) and three centuries of capitalist development. Their homogeneity is threatened, moreover, by the people of different color, culture, and way of life. Silvio Berlusconi's recent quip about Islam, Fallaci's (2002) diatribes against Muslim immigrants, and Heider's, Le Pen's and Fortuyn's political support is all part and parcel of the fear engendered by a more globalized society.

Can these two views, the dominant one, and the critical too, be correct? Yes, they can because globalization being such a huge and multifaceted process presents different faces to different people. Depending on where we live, whether we are rich or poor, where we stand ideologically, we are bound to see the process differently. But this is nothing new. Globalization as it played out from the mid-19th century to 1914 was also a contradictory force, with both its benign and malignant features. Thus, we believe, today too, as in the past, globalization has two faces: the benign one, based on voluntary exchanges and free circulation of people, capital, goods and ideas; and the other face, based on coercion and brute force.

3. BY RAILROADS AND GUNSHIPS

These two faces have been very clearly in evidence during the previous period of globalization a century ago. On the one hand, there was a manifold increase in output and trade between Western European countries and their overseas offshoots (the United States, Canada, Australia, and New Zealand); there were millions of Italian, Polish, or Irish migrants who traversed the Atlantic in search of a better life (and found it), bringing moreover a wage and income convergence between Europe and the United States by putting a downward pressure on wages in the United States, and allowing European wages to go up (O'Rourke & Williamson, 1999). Telegraph cables and railroads were built to bring the world closer and to accelerate the transfer of goods. In Cuba, the main producer of sugar, railroads were built before any existed in Italy or Holland (Bairoch, 1997, vol. 2, p. 574). Foreign capital flowed from the capital-rich England and France to the lands capital-poor, yet rich in opportunities, such as Argentina and Russia. In Keynes' (1998, 1918, pp. 11–12) famous phrase, wistfully regretting the passing away of a world that was destroyed by the Great War, a Londoner

could secure... cheap and comfortable means of transport to any country or climate without passport or other formality, could dispatch his servant (sic!) to the neighboring office of a bank for such supply of the precious metals as might seem convenient, and could then proceed abroad to foreign quarters, without knowledge of their religion, language, or customs...

While to the Keynes' Londoners, globalization indeed presented that clean, friendly face, was the same true for the others? Not really. Globalization was brought to the many at the "point of a gun," and many were "globalized" literally kicking and screaming, from Commodore's Perry ultimatum which opened Japan, to British and French gunboat diplomacy in Tunisia, Egypt and Zanzibar, to the Opium wars and gunboats that patrolled Chinese *internal* waterways. Worst of all, for many millions who were sold in slavery, or who toiled 16 h a day on plantations from Malaya to Brazil that too was globalization. Globalization was not merely *accompanied* by the worst excesses of colonialism; colonialism was not an accident. On the contrary, globalization *was* colonialism because it is through being colonies that most of the non-European countries were brought to the global world. The Dutch East Indies company that, according to conservative estimates by Maddison (2001, p. 87) pillaged during 1868–1930 between 7.4% and 10.3% of Indonesia's national income per year, [4] and the genocide in Congo that might have killed up to

10 million people, are only the worst excesses (see Hochschild, 1998).

Economists who deal in models of individual rational behavior are not well equipped to treat conquests and plunder. Thus, they prefer to stick to the "nice" face of globalization, to describe how the global working of the "invisible hand" brought late 19th century technological marvels. It is, for example, remarkable that in an influential article on the 19th century globalization by two distinguished economists, Jeffrey Williamson from Harvard and Peter Lindert from University of California (2001) never once were the words "colonialism," "colony," "slavery," or "colonization" mentioned. This omission is all the more interesting because 1870–1913 (or 1820 which they also choose as the beginning year) was not only the epoch par excellence of colonialism, but of slavery too. Just *pro memoria*, in the British colonies, slavery was banned in 1833; in the French colonies, after the 1848 revolution; in the Dutch colonies, it continued until 1863; in the (Southern) United States, it was abolished in 1865, while in Brazil, it went on until 1878. It is thus, to say the least, very odd to ignore the existence of slavery when talking about globalization in the 19th century.

From this "clean-shaven" world of voluntary exchanges, the unpleasant facts of slavery and conquest are simply banished. So, when we reflect on what globalization then brought to those who were enslaved, and to those who could "send their servant to the neighboring office of a bank" in London, are we surprised that people today might also have similarly divided views about globalization?

4. INCOME DIVERGENCE DURING THE 19TH CENTURY

The dominant, economists' view, of the 19th century globalization is indeed based on what Williamson calls "the Atlantic economy," that is, the exchange of goods, migration, and capital flows between Western Europe, and Northern America (where Argentina and Uruguay too make a few cameo appearances). As already mentioned, economists are well-placed to deal with this benign face of globalization because their key methodological construct is a self-interested individual, and when there is no external coercion (slavery or gunboats), economists can best study how individuals, following their own interests, bring out economic changes that our textbooks tell us should happen.

The problem with this approach is twofold. First, it applies only to a limited part of the world. Colonialism, pillage, and slavery were no less part of globalization than the voluntary movement of Irish peasants to the United States, or the voluntary transfer of British funds to Argentina. So, if we want to discuss the North Atlantic economy alone, the Williamson–Lindert approach is fine: they can afford to ignore the rest of the world. But, if we want to use the parable of the North Atlantic economy to argue that this is what globalization *is*, then it is wrong because it is only one, and possibly a less important, facet of globalization.

Second, and more importantly, we have to look more carefully at the claim that globalization brings convergence of income among the participating countries with poor countries growing faster and presumably catching up with the rich. This is an important tenet in the mythology of benign globalization because it is supposed to show the benefits of globalization reaped by the poor countries. (Notice that the proper unit of analysis here is country. We are not concerned with whether globalization makes the world more equal or not, in which case we would need to calculate inequality across world citizens, as for example done by Bourguignon and Morrisson (2000). Here, we are simply concerned with the so-called theory of convergence—namely that the poor countries, when they open up, grow faster than the rich.) Indeed Lindert and Williamson (2001) make that conclusion by showing the wage convergence between the densely-populated Western European economies and the sparsely populated (and resource-rich) "New World." As people migrate from Western Europe to the United States or Argentina, wages and income per capita converge. Apodictically, Lindert and Williamson write (2001, p. 13): "Real wages and living standards converged among the currently-industrialized countries between 1850 and World War I." They do accept that even as migration and trade contributed to wage equalization among the participants, capital flows which favored the richer countries (that is, flowed toward the rich rather than toward the poorer countries) were an "anti-convergence force" (p. 17). Yet, on balance, their conclusion is that "prewar [World War I] globalization looks like a force equalizing average incomes between

participating countries" (p. 18). But let us see if that was really so.

We have three sources of data on incomes (GDP per capita) for the period stretching from the early 19th century to 1913. They are produced by Maddison (1995, 2001); Bairoch (1997) and Prados de la Escosura (2000). The countries we want to include—and they are mostly the only ones for which the data are available—are those that were all part of the broader Atlantic economy, the key participants in globalization. These are the rich WENAO (Western Europe, North America, and Oceania) countries. Their number varies between 18 and 20 in Bairoch's series, 13 (but only in 1850) and 21 in Prados de la Escosura's series, and 19 in Maddison's data. [5] Consequently, the country coverage is fairly standard and constant.

We look at whether there was convergence or not of mean incomes (GDPs per capita) by calculating Gini coefficient across GDPs per capita of these countries, with each country being given the same weight. [6] If there is convergence, the Gini coefficient should go down. Yet as Figure 1 shows, the story is not at all that simple.

According to Bairoch, during the peak period of globalization 1870–1913, incomes between the rich countries continued to diverge: the Gini coefficient of their GDPs per capita increased by five Gini points, or by almost a third, rising from 15.8 in 1870 to 20.9 in 1913. According to Maddison, inequality is about the same at the beginning and at the end of the period. Both Bairoch and Maddison use GDPs per capita expressed in PPP (purchasing power parity) terms anchored, respectively, in US 1960 prices and 1990 international prices (Geary–Kramis dollars). Prados de la Escosura uses current PPP exchange rates—which means that his GDPs per capita are not comparable across time—to derive the rankings of about the same set of countries over 1850–1938. Only his data show an income convergence among the rich countries starting in 1860 and ending on the eve of the WW I. [7]

Thus, the evidence of income convergence among the subset of rich globalization participants which we were led to expect was the norm during the previous globalization episode turns out on a closer inspection to be far from watertight. We see that depending on the author and on the PPP rates used, rich countries show either a divergence, or stability, or convergence of their incomes during 1870–1913. [8]

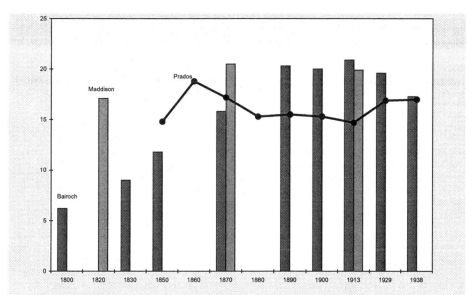

Figure 1. *The Gini coefficient of GDPs per capita of rich countries, 1800–1938. Source: calculated from Bairoch (1997, vol. 2, pp. 252–253), Maddison (1995, p. 194 & 2001, Appendix A), and Prados de la Escosura (2000, p. 24).*

Having criticized the dominant approach for showing only a selective picture of globalization, we need to extend it in two additional directions. First, we extend the picture over time by considering the same WENAO countries during the period prior to 1870, on a well-founded assumption that globalization had started by the turn of the 19th century. There we notice, according to Bairoch's data, a strong divergence during 1800–70—a divergence which makes sense when one reflects that at the turn of the 19th century income differences between European countries were minimal. The Gini, according to Bairoch, more than doubles from 6.2 in 1800 to 15.8 in 1870. Even Maddison's data show a significant increase in inequality, with the Gini rising from 17.1 in 1820 to 20.5 in 1870 (that is, by 20%). Thus, among the rich countries, once we extend our gaze past the peak period of globalization, there was a clear process of income divergence.

Second, we need to extend the analysis in space, by including other countries. Here we are, of course, on shakier grounds because none of the authors presents consistent series for both the rich (WENAO) countries and some of the most important future Third World countries. Yet, if we reflect that in 1760, Indian per capita

income was between 10% and 30% less to the British per capita income (Bairoch, 1997, vol. 2, p. 845), while in 1800, Chinese per capita income was equal or higher than the British,[9] it becomes clear that, on a *global scale*, there must have been divergence over 1800–1913, and that during the heyday of globalization in 1870–1913, divergence must have continued unabated.

Moreover, income *declines* among the non-European participants in the globalization process were an integral part of the process itself: Indian deindustrialization is directly linked to the British colonial commercial policy; large transfers out of Indonesia and most of Africa were part and parcel of globalization. Most important, a typical "colonial contract" or (more properly called) a "colonial *diktat*" (see Bairoch, 1997, vol. 2, pp. 665–669) precluded autochthonous industrial development of the conquered parts of the world. According to Bairoch, the "colonial contract" was the main cause of nontransmission of industrial revolution outside Europe since it implied that (a) colonies could import only products from the metropolis and tariff rates had to be low, normally 0%,[10] (b) colonial exports could be made only to the metropolis from which they could re-exported (c) production of manufactured goods that could compete with products of the metropolis was banned, and (d) transport between colony and metropolis was conducted only on metropolis' ships. Economic policy of the colonies (to the extent that there was any independent economic policy) was therefore entirely subjugated to the interests of the metropolis, the most important objective being to prevent industrial competition from the colony. [11]

While we lack, as already mentioned, generally accepted estimates of GDP per capita for the future Third World countries, we do have estimates of their levels of industrialization. Since these are closely linked with GDP per capita (and in the 19th century were even more so), [12] we can observe not only the relative decline of the Third World but its absolute impoverishment over the 19th century (see Table 1 reproduced from Bairoch, 1997, vol. 1, p. 404).

There we clearly see that other facet of globalization: there can be little doubt that globalization was responsible for the economic decline of the countries that at the turn of the 19th century were at about the same level of development as Western Europe, that is, India and China. For other conquered lands which were less advanced than Western Europe, 19th century globalization brought colonialism, which prevented their industrialization and thus development. Now, this is not to argue that the underdevelopment of the Third World was the *cause* of the First World's development as some hold (Frank, 1998). It suffices to take a much more moderate and well-argued position as Bairoch's and to see globalization and colonialism as a cause of Third World decline, but not as a cause of First World success—the latter one having been essentially endogenous to the West. [13]

In conclusions, we find first, that during the 19th century, globalization was accompanied by a growing divergence in income between the countries of the world, and second, that even among the leaders in this process, the rich

countries, there is no conclusive evidence that income differences did not widen. So, basically, it is divergence all around that was brought by the previous bout of globalization.

Let us now move to the interpretation of the more recent economic record made by the unconditional partisans of "real" globalization. [14]

5. MISINTERPRETING THE RECENT ECONOMIC RECORD

Consider Tables 2 and 3. Let us then suppose that we show them to a Martian visitor endowed with elementary arithmetic knowledge and tell him three things: first, that more growth (higher income) is better than lower growth (and lower income); second, that WENAO is the richest region and that we would ideally like to see differences between the rich and poor regions decrease; and third, that there are two periods of globalization. The first period (1960–78) comprises "import substitution" in Latin America and most of Asia, and Africa; Communism in Eastern Europe/FSU, China, Vietnam; and "welfare state" in the rich countries. The second period is the era "structural adjustment" in Latin America and Africa, "transition to market economy" in Eastern Europe/FSU, and "retrenchment of welfare state" in the rich world. Then we ask him to choose which period he thinks was better.

His decision should not be too difficult. He would first observe that whether he looks at the world mean unweighted GDP per capita only (so that each country counts the same) or at the population-weighted world GDP per capita, growth rate was between two and three times greater in the first period. Then, he will notice that whatever region he selects, and whatever concept of growth he uses, growth rate is always higher in the first period than in the second. That would provide him with some additional confidence that the first period was better.

Table 1. *Level of industrialization (manufacturing output per capita), 1800–1913 (UK 1900 = 100)*

	1800	1830	1860	1880	1900	1913
Total developed countries	8	11	16	24	35	55
Total Third World	6	6	4	3	2	2
Memo:						
United Kingdom	16	25	64	87	100	115
United States	9	14	21	38	69	126

Source: Bairoch (1997, vol. 1, p. 404).

Table 2. *Unweighted regional GDP per capita levels and growth rates, 1960–98*[a]

	GDP per capita (in 1995 international prices)			Growth rate of GDP per capita (%, p.a.)	
	Year 1960	Year 1978	Year 1998	1960–78	1978–98
Africa	1,514	2,147	2,432	2.0	0.6
Asia	1,971	5,944	7,050	6.3	0.9
Latin America	3,458	5,338	6,329	2.4	0.9
E. Europe/FSU	2,093	5,277	4,851	5.3	−0.4
WENAO	8,257	14,243	20,990	3.1	2.0
World	3,277	5,972	7,456	3.4	1.1

Source: Own calculations using the data from World Bank SIMA (Statistical Information Management and Analysis) database, countries' statistical yearbooks, Maddison (2001) and Penn World Tables.
[a] Each country is one observation.

Table 3. *Population-weighted regional GDP per capita levels and growth rates, 1960–98*[a]

	GDP per capita (in 1995 international prices)			Growth rate of GDP per capita (%, p.a.)	
	Year 1960	Year 1978	Year 1998	1960–1978	1978–1998
Africa	1,539	2,007	2,033	1.5	0.1
Asia	963	1,945	3,967	4.0	3.6
Latin America	3,297	5,460	6,353	2.8	0.8
E. Europe/FSU	2,206	5,361	4,290	5.1	−1.1
WENAO	9,792	16,438	22,594	2.9	1.6
World	3,058	4,940	6,498	2.7	1.4

Source: Own calculations using the data from World Bank SIMA (Statistical Information Management and Analysis) database, countries' statistical yearbooks, Maddison (2001) and Penn World Tables.
[a] Each country is one observation, but each observation is weighted by country's population.

He might then remember our instruction that we would also like regional incomes to converge. Yet there too, he will notice that according to unweighted GDP per capita, in the first period, two out of four poorer regions grew faster than WENAO, while in the second, all of them grew slower than WENAO. If he wanted to confirm that finding by looking at what happened to an average citizen of each region, he would notice again that in the first period, average per capita incomes in Eastern Europe/FSU and in Asia grew faster, and in Latin America about the same, as in WENAO. But in the second period, average incomes in Africa, Latin America and Eastern Europe/FSU were about stagnant or mildly declining (with per capita growth rates ranging from −1 to +0.8 p.a.), while WENAO grew by 1.6% p.a., and Asia, mostly thanks to China, by 3.6% p.a. Thus, he would conclude that, by the regional convergence criterion, the first period was better.

In addition, we might provide our Martian visitor with some further statistics. Consider Figure 2 which shows the average GDP per capita growth rates of all countries in the world (save the rich WENAO) during 1960–78 and 1978–98. Out of 124 countries, 95 grew faster in the first period. Notice not only that most of the dots are to the right of the 45-degree line, but also that there is a large number of the dots in the Southeastern quadrant. These are countries whose growth rates have switched from being positive—and often highly so—in the first period, to being negative in the second. [15]

Then, our Martian visitor would come back to us, and naïvely announce that he has definitely concluded that the first period was better since most countries grew faster then, and most of the poorer regions tended to catch up with the rich world. He would think that the test was rather easy and that he had done pretty well. [16]

Unfortunately, our Martian is not a good economist. Our mainstream economist would have to convince him that the *second* period—the period of structural adjustment and globalization—was actually better. It would be a hard sell, but it could be done. First, our economist would concede the fact that there was a divergence in countries' performance

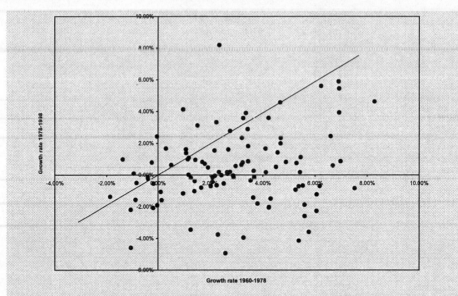

Figure 2. *Average real GDP per capita growth rates in 1960–78 and 1978–98 (124 non-WENAO countries). Source: World Bank SIMA (Statistical Information Management and Analysis) database, countries' statistical yearbooks, Maddison (2001) and Penn World Tables.*

since the end of the 1970s and that poor countries have tended to grow slower (or even to decline) than the rich countries. As shown in Figure 3, the Gini coefficient of the GDPs per capita of all countries in the world, after being roughly stable during 1960–78, has inexorably risen since 1978, from a Gini of about 46 to a Gini of 54 today—a huge increase of almost 20%.

The economist will claim however, that the divergence in incomes is due to some "bad" countries which, unwilling to globalize, have chosen the wrong policies. So, he would like to expunge the world of these "bad" countries and to show that there was indeed a convergence in incomes among countries that adopted "good" policies and globalized.

This approach, the "weeding" of the "bad" from the "good" countries was adopted by Dollar and Kraay (1999) and by the recent World Bank report on globalization (World Bank, 2002). These studies select countries that are globalizers using the ratio of exports and imports over GDP (that is, trade openness) and then show how highly open countries' GDP per capita has either tended to catch up with rich countries' GDP per capita, or how their growth rates have gradually accelerated from decade to

decade as openness ostensibly progressed. We shall show in detail, largely following Rodrik (2000), what is wrong with this selection criterion. But before we move to that, consider the prelude. Since the catch-up is defined in terms of mean *population*—weighted income of the "globalizers," and since China is among these, and since China has had such a remarkable growth record over the last two decades, the authors should not have even bothered to include other countries. All that is needed to obtain the desired conclusions is that China's growth accelerate (as shown in World Bank, 2002, Figure 1.12). [17]

Because China is a favorite example of the "openness is good for you" school, it is worth considering in somewhat greater detail. Now, one may find it rather strange that the key proof of beneficence of global capitalism is provided by one of the few remaining Communist countries. Of course, the partisans of "real" globalization argue that China is a Communist country in name only, and that what matters is its integration with world economy and *de facto* introduction of markets. Yet, the fact that a Communist country's record is wheeled out to defend capitalism is not merely a *boutade*. Almost one-third of China's

TWO FACES OF GLOBALIZATION

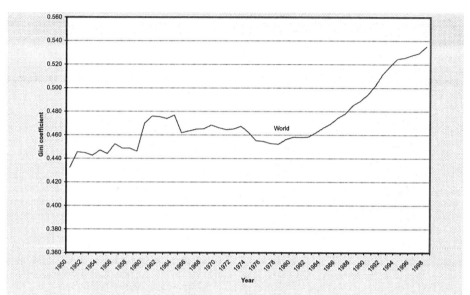

Figure 3. *Gini coefficient: Unweighted inter-national inequality, 1950–98. Source: Milanovic (2002). 144 countries included. All current countries (e.g., Russia, Bangladesh, Serbia, etc.) projected backward in order to avoid spurious Gini increase due to a greater number of observations/countries. Each country/year is one observation.*

industrial output is still produced by state-owned enterprises, and almost 20% of total GDP, a fraction higher than in any country in the world save for North Korea, Cuba, and a few former Soviet republics—a level of state involvement unlikely to be endorsed by mainstream economists. [18] Second, one of the preconditions for China's growth was arguably the set of policies that is also anathema to today's mainstream view: nationalization, widespread and free education at all levels, impediments to the free circulation of labor which kept lots of people from migrating into cities, land reform and abolishment of large landholdings—all hardly a favorite policy prescription for a developing country. Finally, little noticed is a paradox pointed out by Weitzman and Xu (1997) that, by far, the most dynamic sector of the Chinese economy is that of Township and Village Enterprises (TVEs) whose property rights are the very example of nontransparency: a TVE is legally owned by a "community," village or a township, is run by managers, or capitalists, and seeks private capital but pays no dividends. In effect, TVE is all that an efficient enterprise should *not* be. Yet it is this sector that shows the most significant progress. Thus, China, on these grounds alone, can

hardly be taken as an example of success of the current mainstream economic policy prescriptions.

The very process of "selecting" the good globalizers based on trade ratios is flawed, as argued by Rodrik (2000). He points to several technical and data-selection problems in the Dollar and Kraay analysis, of which two seem most important. First globalizers are selected based on a combination of an outcome indicator (trade over GDP) over which policymakers have no control and another which they do control (level of tariff rates). [19] There is an additional problem with this selection criterion. As Birdsall and Hamoudi (2002) show, most of "nonglobalizers" were *unwilling* nonglobalizers in the sense that their trade/GDP ratios had declined because their exports were heavily dependent on natural resources and primary commodities whose terms of trade declined in the 1980s. Consequently, countries' export revenues dropped, and they in turn had to curtail imports, reducing trade/GDP ratios on both accounts. In addition, they ran into balance of payments problems that required contractionary policies, and it is therefore not surprising that there was a positive correlation between openness and growth. Birdsall and

Hamoudi (2002, p. 5) write: "Dollar and Kraay have not isolated the benefits of 'participating in the global trading system', but rather the 'curse' of primary commodity dependence." Second in both India and China, which, as mentioned, are used as the prime examples of "good" globalizers, the main trade reforms took place after the onset of faster growth. The Chinese case is, as Rodrik (2000) writes, well known: high growth began in the early 1980s, while trade liberalization followed more than a decade later. Throughout the 1980s and until 1995, the average weighted tariff rate in China was about 40% (Figure 4)—a rate twice as high as the average for developing countries, and more than four times the average of industrialized countries. [20] It was only in 1996 that the average tariff decreased to 26%, and has since decreased further to a level of about 16%.

Rodrik (2000) shows that the same pattern holds for India: while growth accelerated in the early 1980s, trade reform did not start until 1991–93. There, too, growth and expansion of trade took place under the protection of an even higher tariff wall than in China: in the 1980s, the weighted tariffs averaged 80–90%, and gradually came down, to the still very high level of about 40% (Figure 4). Dollar and Kraay (1999) have clearly fallen prey to one of (what Bairoch & Kozul-Wright, 1996 call) the enduring myths of economic theory, namely that "liberalization [is] an important driving force behind rising trade." On the contrary, trade often increased the most during the mild protectionist phases, since the latter saw acceleration in growth, and it is growth that generally leads to trade—not *vice versa* (Bairoch, 1997, p. 310; Yotopolos, 1996).

How hazardous the *Globalization, growth and poverty* report's (World Bank, 2002) conclusions are can be observed from the two figures below which chart China's and India's per capita growth rates and their average weighted tariff rates over 1980–99. Notice that in the India graph, it is very difficult to see any correlation between the two: the growth rate oscillates around 4% p.a., no matter what happens to the tariff rate. The China graph is not much different, except that there, if anything, we notice a correlation between the slowdown in growth rate in the last five years and a reduction in tariff rates—a relationship that is exactly the opposite of the one the World Bank report claims to have found. We cannot put much store by this finding: it obviously covers a very short period, and the rate of

growth responds to a myriad of factors other than tariff rates. But the figures illustrate the perils of a monocausal approach to the evidence.

The authors of World Bank (2002) are aware that their preferred causality, low tariff rates ⇒ high export and import growth ⇒ high GDP growth cannot be proven. [21] They are aware also that both China and India grew behind very high protective walls. How then do they deal with these issues? With respect to the first point, they do so in a rather peculiar manner, as throughout the report there are scattered statements denying that causality can be inferred from or proven by their numbers. But these statements are often ignored, and there are a number of precisely such—causal—statements. [22] The second point is elegantly circumvented by showing the *change* in average tariff rates among the "globalizers" and "non-globalizers" (World Bank, 2002, p. 36). But since we saw that China and India had particularly high tariff rates, it is not surprising that they reduced them more than say, Barbados or Belize which started the 1980s with tariff rates of 15%.

Our conclusion regarding the most recent period of globalization is twofold.

—The last two decades, which witnessed expansion of globalization, are, in terms of overall growth and income convergence between poor and rich countries, vastly less successful than the preceding two decades.

—The attempt to explain divergence of incomes by "eliminating" the countries with "bad" policies and focusing solely on those with "good" policies is flawed because the successful countries, and China in particular, did not follow the orthodox economic advice. One can be pretty confident that if China had exactly the same policies, but a miserable record of economic growth, those who hail it now would flaunt it as an example of how harmful to growth are state ownership, undefined property rights in TVEs, and high tariff barriers.

6. THE TWO NARRATIVES AND THE NEED FOR "READJUSTMENT OF ADJUSTMENT"

We can illustrate the difference between the dominant focus on the benign aspect of globalization alone from a more even-handed presentation of globalization's two sides: the

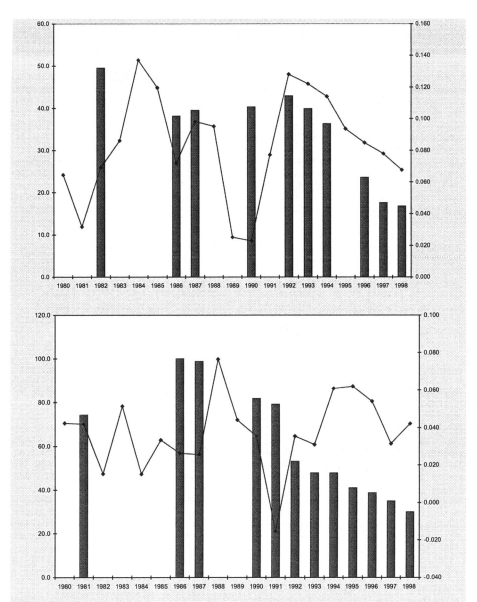

Figure 4. *China's (above) and India's (below) real annual GDP per capita growth rate, and average weighted tariffs. Source: Growth rates from World Bank SIMA database; traiff rates from Francis Ng (World Bank). Traiff rates are bars (levels shown on the left axis), growth rates (in fractiles) are lines (levels shown on the right axis).*

benign and the malignant. Consider the following two historical narratives of the same set of events.

The dominant narrative goes approximately as follows. Toward the end of the 18th century, there was Industrial Revolution that spread from Europe slowly and unevenly, to the rest of the world. At the end of the Napoleonic wars, the world entered a period of almost uninterrupted peace lasting 100 years. During that period global capitalism appeared: it spread to the rest of the globe, connecting Europe with the Americas, Asia, Africa. The leading countries of the period grew the fastest, their incomes converged as trade blossomed, people freely migrated to better places, and capital flowed wherever it wanted. Then, suddenly, the calamity of WW I struck, the world was inflamed, Communism and Fascism emerged, nationalism and protectionism became rampant, trade declined, countries' incomes diverged, until another, worse, calamity of the WW II struck. For a period after the war, global capitalism could not get a free rein because large parts of the globe fell under the Communist sway. It is only in the 1980s, as China liberalized and the Soviet empire broke up and abandoned Communism, that globalization, with its attendant growth for most, if not all, could resurge. "Happy days are here again," but we must not forget that the ogres of nationalism and protectionism lurk behind the corner. So give freedom to capital, let profit be your guide, and growth is guaranteed to all.

This is, with some poetic embellishment, the most common view of events of the last two centuries, perhaps (one might surmise) because the people who subscribe to that narrative have tended to experience only the benign side of globalization. The objective of that narrative is not to stimulate discussion, but to stifle it, similarly to the dominant narratives used in the Communist countries where too the main purpose of the accepted view of history was to generate the acquiescence to the dogma. The point is well made by Said (2002):

> In this day, and almost universally, phrases such as "the free market," "privatization," 'less government' and others like them have become the orthodoxy of globalization, its counterfeit universals. They are staples of the dominant discourse, designed to create consent and tacit approval... The main goal of this dominant discourse is to fashion the merciless logic of corporate profit-making and political power into a normal state of affairs.

It is relatively easy to explode this rosy story of the world, told by the first narrative. One needs only to ask three simple questions: (a) where are conquest, colonialism, and slavery in this narrative? (b) how does the narrative explain the outbreak of WW I? and (c) why did capitalism

suddenly become more tamed and civilized ("social market economy") after the end of WW II? To answer these questions, consider the following narrative of the same events.

After the technological and social revolutions occurred in Europe, its Northwestern part became the most advanced region of the world. It set out, at first timidly and often out of adventurism, then more seriously to conquer the rest of the world. As Europe conquered other countries, the winners established rules that were economically advantageous to themselves, developed further the already-existing slave trade, and by flooding markets of their colonies (devoid of independent commercial and economic policy) with their own manufactures, contributed to colonies' deindustrialization. All the while, gross coercion, wars, and even genocides went on in the colonies—perhaps not much noticed in Europe. So, the days of universal peace were quite far from being truly so.

European powers bent on conquest were, at the same time, in a struggle with each other. Their imperialism begot the Great War—the very war whose impossibility, because of intricate economic ties between leading countries, was proclaimed in the famous Angell book published just years prior to the carnage. After a truce of 20 years, the Second WW erupted—a straight continuation of WW I. Fascism was defeated but Communism came out stronger and spread to cover one-third of world's population. Under Communist threat from the outside, and under pressure of growing social-democratic and Communist movements at home, the capitalist regimes, already enfeebled by the Great Depression, conceded to dramatic and far-reaching social reforms. The nature of wild capitalism of the 19th century changed dramatically with the introduction of unemployment benefits and pensions, paid vacations, 40-h working week, guaranteed and free education, health care for all, trade unions, and protection of workers' rights. In the Third World countries that became liberated, dreams of industrialization and catching-up could be realistically entertained as countries grew quickly and import-substitution became the dominant approach to development. But then under the shock of rising petroleum prices, high interest rates, and large debts, Third World growth sputtered. In the West, the ideological pendulum swung against the welfare state. The social-democratic movement weakened, the collapse of Communism eliminated the external threat, and made global capitalism again, as in the 1870s, entirely free to pursue unhindered its objectives of profit maximization—without much regard for social consequences.

To question the profit objective is not to denigrate its importance, much less to argue that it should not be an important, perhaps the most important, criterion. But it should not be the sole criterion. It needs to be tempered by other considerations, akin to the way that national capitalisms after WW II were "civilized" by the role of the state and strong social-democratic parties. The erection of "financial viability" as the only acceptable norm will not lead to imperialist wars as it did in 1914, but will exacerbate the negative effects of global capitalism which we already see, and which have grown in importance during the last decade or so—precisely the period during which the earlier constraints on the free play of capital were weakened or abandoned. [23] Let me mention a few of these effects: very high and/or increasing spatial and interpersonal inequality, blatant theft of public resources masquerading under the name of privatization and cheered on by most economists and international organizations, growth of slums, deteriorating labor conditions, return of the long-forgotten diseases such as tuberculosis, declines in education enrollment rates, dramatically increased mortality in most of the former Soviet republics and Africa, deforestation, growth of worldwide networks of mafias and drug cartels, even modern-day slavery through development of piracy and abduction of women and children for prostitution. [24] Capitalism left to itself will always produce these effects. If people want to sell themselves, why should not they? If parents do not want to send children to school, why not allow them the choice? If university education is no longer free, perhaps a child from a poor family can borrow to pay for it? If people do not have money to pay for a cure or a drug, what else can be done to ensure cost recovery? [25]

While overt colonialism is a thing of the past, the rules are far from being even-handed as between the poor and the rich countries. They are slanted in favor of those who wield power. Khor (2001) gives some examples from the multilateral trading system: the well-known example of intellectual property rights, [26] differential treatment of subsidies (subsidies for R&D are exempt from counteraction while the subsidies used by developing countries, for industrial upgrading, are not), standards that are being set without effective participation by the less-developed countries (LDCs), and the high costs of raising and pursuing a trade dispute. We can compare the last point to the problem that Jewish survivors in Eastern Europe faced in trying to get the money impounded by the Swiss banks: how is a grand-mother surviving on $100 a month, and not speaking English or French, going to sue a Swiss bank?

Because we are now dealing with global capitalism, the role of "moderator" can no longer belong to the nation-state, but to international (global) actors. It is where the international financial institutions (IFI), such as the World Bank, enter. Continued misinterpretation of the disastrous results brought to most of Africa, Latin America, and Eastern Europe by about two decades of unabashedly free market policies will not prompt a review of these policies, and will, on the contrary, allow their continuation with probably equally bad results. [27] It is therefore incumbent on us to examine the actual results, and not the ideology of what these policies *should* have brought had they worked as originally intended. We must thus address some uncomfortable issues. Let me mention but three.

(i) How to explain that after sustained involvement and many structural adjustment loans, and as many IMF's Stand-bys, African GDP per capita has not budged from its level of 20 years ago? Moreover, in 24 African countries, GDP per capita is less than in 1975, and in 12 countries even below its 1960's level. [28]

(ii) How to explain the recurrence of Latin crises, in countries such as Argentina, that months prior to the outbreak of the crisis are being praised as model reformers. [29]

(iii) How to explain that the best "pupils" among the transition countries (Moldova, Georgia, Kyrghyz Republic, Armenia) after setting out in 1991 with no debt at all, and following all the prescriptions of the IFIs, find themselves 10 years later with their GDPs halved and in need of debt-forgiveness?

Something is clearly wrong. [30] Maintaining that globalization as we know it is the way to go and that, if the Washington consensus policies have not borne fruit so far, they will surely do so in the future, is to replace empiricism with ideology. Unfortunately, it has been done before, but the consequences were not very good.

NOTES

1. In effect, the very first sentence of the abstract reads: "Income of the poor rises one-for-one with overall growth."

2. In another of their papers, Dollar and Kraay (2002) do make a point that for (a) countries cursed by "poor geography" (e.g., Mali or Chad) or (b) those with inefficient or exploitative institutions, trade liberalization alone cannot be expected to bear much fruit.

3. As Anderson (2002) rightly points out, to the European antonym: internationalism *vs.* nationalism, the United States, somewhat uniquely, presented a different one: internationalism *vs.* isolationism. Hence specifically European xenophobia rooted in ethnicity and "blood and soil" was never much of an ideology in the United States.

4. Even in terms of the Dutch income at the time, the amounts were staggering: the transfers amounted to between 5.5% and 8.9% of Dutch GDP over the period of 60 years. This dwarfs the Marshall plan whose net transfers were about 4% of recipients' countries GDP over the period of about five years (Bairoch, 1997, vol. 3, p. 120). Of course, it makes puny today's official aid contributed by the rich countries which is about 0.3% of their GDPs.

5. The countries are: Austria–Hungary, Belgium, Denmark, Finland, France, Germany, Greece, Ireland, Italy, Netherlands, Norway, Portugal, Spain, Sweden, Switzerland, United Kingdom in Western Europe; United States and Canada in North America, and Australia and New Zealand in Oceania. Note that Finland, Ireland and Norway were not independent countries for most of the period; Greece, up until 1830, while Germany and Italy are presumably included in their post-Unification shapes.

6. This is a variant of the so-called σ convergence, but a preferred one, we hold, because Gini is a better and more common measure of inequality than standard deviation.

7. One explanation of the fact that inequality measured by using current exchange rates (Prados) declines, while inequality measured using PPP-constant exchange rates increases (or stays the same) is that price structures between the countries have become more similar (see Dowrick & Akmal, 2001, p. 16).

8. By the way, even the alleged divergence (Lindert & Williamson, 2001, pp. 18–20) during the interwar "globalization backlash" is not evident: according to Bairoch, incomes *converged* during that period, according to Prados de la Esconsura, they diverged.

9. Braudel (1984, p. 534), using Bairoch's calculations, gives Chinese GDP per capita as $282 (at US 1960 prices). According to Bairoch (1997, vol. 2, pp. 252–253), British GDP per capita in 1800 was $240. Maddison (2001, p. 90) estimates British GDP per capita in 1820 at $2,121 (in 1990 international dollars), China's GDP per capita at $600, and India's at $533. If we then set United Kingdom = 1 in both Bairoch and Maddison, China is 1.17 in Bairoch and 0.29 in Maddison; India is 0.7–0.9 in Bairoch, and 0.25 in Maddison. Although the differences between the two authors are often large for other countries as well (e.g., Maddison gives Australia's GDP per capita in 1850 at $3,070; recalculated in the same prices, Bairoch's estimate for the same year is $1,680), differences in the estimates of the Chinese and Indian GDP per capita are even larger.

10. Their maximum was often set at 5%, but at times when such a maximum was imposed for fiscal reasons (as in India in 1894), British industrial interests demanded that a similar local tax be imposed on Indian products so "as not to discriminate British exports" (Bairoch, 1997, vol. 2, p. 860). After the first Opium war, Britain imposed to China a maximum tariff range between 5% and 9%. In a historical curiosum, note that similar tariff preferences were imposed by Venice, and later by Genoa, on the declining Eastern Roman Empire from 12th century onward (see Runciman, 1932).

11. Parts of the "colonial contract" (e.g., ban on production of competing manufactured products) applied to the European offshoots as well. This was, in effect, one of the main motivations behind the drive for American independence. North American producers were not allowed to process pig iron, and had to sell it to Great Britain only where of course it would be processed and reexported (Bairoch, 1997, vol. 2, p. 667, & vol. 1, p. 462).

12. The correlation between level of industrialization and GDP per capita in both 1900 and 1913 is about 0.7 (calculated from Bairoch, 1997).

13. Furthermore, if we extend the origin of globalization back in time, say dating it from the European

conquest of the Americas, then the same conclusion is only reinforced. The Spanish conquest produced a dramatic decline in population and average incomes in the South and Central America (note that prior to the conquest, Central America's urbanization rates were probably greater than Europe's, Bairoch, 1997, vol. 2, p. 546), while growth of slave trade did the same for Africa.

As Bairoch (1989, p. 238) writes: "...I hasten to insist on the fact that if colonization did not play an important role in explaining 'why we [the West] became rich,' it played a crucial role in explaining 'why they [the Third World] remained poor' and even why, at a certain stage of history, 'they became poorer.'"

14. For those who have not had the chance to follow Communist jargon, the "real" is a pun on the "real socialism," the appellation invented by the Soviets in the 1970s, and similarly meant to convey the feeling that their Communism, like today's globalization, was the only right one—because "real."

15. All the current countries are projected backward using their past republican/provincial growth rates. This therefore represents probably the most detailed country growth database (see Milanovic, 2002). The main building blocks for the database were World Bank SIMA, countries' statistical yearbooks, Penn World Tables, and Maddison (2001). All GDPs per capita are expressed in 1995 international dollars.

16. The first, to my knowledge, to have noticed and discussed, with a great wealth of detail and econometrics, the discrepancy between the "improved" policies in LDCs during the last two decades, and more than disappointing results (worse than in the previous two decades) is Easterly (2001a,b).

17. This is incidently the wrong way to formulate the convergence question. Convergence is always defined in terms of *countries*. If we were interested in whether the world were becoming a more equal place, the proper way would be to study distribution of income among all *citizens* of the world. The criterion used in World Bank (2002) is neither, and is moreover the only one capable of producing the desired results.

18. These numbers refer to 1998 and include only the value added of industrial and construction sector State-owned enterprises (SOEs). They do not include mixed-ownership sector or TVEs. Calculated from the *Statistical Yearbook of China* (1999), pp. 55, 432, 473.

19. As Rodrik (2000, p. 1) writes: "Saying that 'participation in world trade is good for a country' is as meaningful as saying that 'upgrading of technological capabilities is good for growth' (and equally helpful to policy makers)."

20. Based on World Bank calculations by Francis Ng (downloadable from <www.worldbank.org/research/trade>).

21. The choice of this particular causality is all the more intriguing since there is no reason whatsoever why high exports (themselves a components of GDP) or imports should be bad for growth. I do not know if anyone has ever made such a claim. At issue is precisely the low tariffs $\Rightarrow$ high growth causality, which would be very hard to prove.

22. I do not know how to interpret otherwise statements such as: "As they reformed and integrated with the world market, the 'more globalized' countries started to grow rapidly, accelerating steadily from 2.9% in the 1970s to 5% throughout the 1990" (World Bank, 2002, p. 36), or the statement approvingly taken from Lindert and Williamson (2001), "We infer that this is because freer trade stimulates growth in Third world economies today, regardless of its effects before 1940" (World Bank, 2002, p. 37). Or as Dollar and Kraay (2001) write: "We provide evidence that, contrary to popular beliefs, increased trade has strongly encouraged growth and poverty reduction and has contributed to narrowing the gaps between rich and poor worldwide."

23. Gunter Grass (2002) puts it as follows: "In the fifties, sixties, and even in the seventies, a relatively successful attempt to civilize capitalism was made across Europe. If one assumes that socialism and capitalism are both indegenous, wayward children of the Enlightment, they can be regarded as having imposed certain checks on each other. Even capitalism was obliged to accept certain responsibilities. In Germany this was called the social market economy... The consensus broke down in the early eighties. And since the collapse of the Communist hierarchies, capitalism—recast as neoliberalism—has felt it could run riot, as if out of control. There is no longer a counterweight to it. Today even the few remaining responsible capitalists are raising a warning finger... and see neoliberalism repeating the mistakes of communism—issuing articles of faith that deny that there is any alternative to the free market and claiming infallibility."

24. Kanbur (2001) writes of the spread of "obnoxious goods."

25. The day after I distributed the first version of this paper, a newspaper article in the *Washington Post* tried to answer the question why, more than a decade after the end of Communism in the Soviet Union, and two decades after the rejection of Maoist legacy in China, a Maoist movement in Nepal (a multi-party democracy) is making progress and can claim support among most of Nepal's peasantry. The explanation (Odenheimer, 2002) is worth quoting *in extenso*

"The World Bank and the International Monetary Fund often made economic conditions worse for poor Nepalese. Heeding advice from the Bank and the IMF, the Nepali government cut state subsidies, including those that helped farmers buy fertilizer and seeds. The country's education and health systems were privatized to the point that most Nepalese, even if they work 14-h days, cannot afford to send their children to school or take them to the doctor when they are sick. Meanwhile, the World Bank supported huge hydroelectric and other massive infrastructure projects that brought windfalls to international companies and corrupt Nepali officials, while utility costs for the average Nepali continued to rise. In the face of this poverty and corruption, the Maoists have been playing the role of Robin Hood. Tenant farmers told me that they had been freed from the grip of their landlords after a few well-placed Maoist threats. Maoists have swooped down on agriculture banks and recaptured the land deeds that had been put up for collateral by poor farmers who had taken development loans that they couldn't repay. The Maoists set up people's courts where disputes were tried without fees or bribes. Women used the people's courts to successfully prosecute cases of wife beating and rape. Agents who enticed village girls to India and then sold them as prostitutes in Bombay—which happens to about 5,000 young Nepalese women a year—were caught and punished. Previously they often escaped by giving a cut of their profits to officials."

26. That poor countries have no money and expertise to enforce even the rules that may favor them is well known. I have recently noticed that there is such a thing as French feta cheese. But I remember how Armenian cognac, known to all under such a name, had to change its appelation because "cognac" is a registered trademark.

27. For a review of these policies see Easterly (2001a,b).

28. Meanwhile, from a much higher level, US GDP per capita has increased by a third since 1975, and has doubled since 1960.

29. Including in the World Bank report on globalization, issued a month before the Argentine crisis, where Argentina proudly belongs to the group of "well-known" reformers (World Bank, 2002, p. 35). It has been demoted from that august group though in Dollar and Kraay (2002) published in February 2002. By then the crisis was all too obvious. Note that that in 1999 and 2000, The Heritage Index of Economic Freedom, an ultra right-wing think-tank, scored Argentina's economic policies about the same as Chile's, that poster-child of the neoconservatives. Even in 2001, Argentina was scored only marginally worse (2.25 *vs.* Chile's 2), yet much better than 3.25 given to Brazil.

30. The typical excuse that the policies were right but were badly implemented is wrong and is a very lame excuse indeed. It reminds me of the constant litany under Communism, that the Communist ideas were very good, but were either poorly implemented, or people were too wicked for such beautiful ideas. (I saw through that when I was less than 20. I am surprised that many smart people do not see through similar excuses today; but then it is true that, at 20, I did not have a stake in *not* seeing the truth.) A policy that does not take into account the actual situation and people as they are is inadequate. Furthermore, it is not true, even on IFI's reckoning, that the governments always failed to fully implement the programs. Even when they did implement them, the results—as in the transition countries—were often relentlessly bad.

REFERENCES

Anderson, P. (2002). Internationalism: a breviary. *New Left Review*, March–April, downloaded from Available: <http://www.newleftreview.net/index.shtml>.

Bairoch, P. (1989). The paradoxes of economic history: economic laws and history. *European Economic Review, 33*, 225–249.

Bairoch, P. (1997). *Victoires and deboires* (3 vols.). Paris: Gallimard.

Bairoch, P., & Kozul-Wright, R. (1996). Globalization myths: some historical reflections on integration, industrialization and growth in the world economy. United Nations Conference on trade and development, Discussion paper no. 113.

Birdsall, N., & Hamoudi, A. (2002). Commodity dependence, trade and growth: When 'Openness' is not Enough. Center for Global Development Working Paper No. 7; Available: <http://www.cgdev.org/rp/publications.html>.

Bourguignon, F., & Morrisson, C. (2000). The size distribution of income among world citizens, 1820–1990. *American Economic Review.*

Braudel, F. (1984). *The perspective of the world: Civilization and capitalism, 15th–18th century.* New York: Harpers & Row.

Dollar, D., & Kraay, A. (1999). Trade, growth and poverty. Policy research working paper no. 2199, World Bank, Washington DC.

Dollar, D., & Kraay, A. (2000). Growth in *good* for the poor. Policy research working paper no. 2587. *Journal of Economic Growth, 7*(3), 195–225.

Dollar, D., & Kraay, A. (2001). Trade, growth and poverty. Finance and Development, 38, (3). Downloaded from http://www.imf.org/external/pubs/ft/fandd/2001/09/dollar.htm.

Dollar, D., & Kraay, A. (2002). Spreading the wealth. *Foreign Affairs* (January/February).

Dowrick, S., & Akmal, M. (2001). Contradictory trends in global income inequality: a tale of two biases. Version March 29, 2001. Downloaded from <http://ecocomm.anu.edu.au/economics/staff/dowrick/worldinequ.pdf>.

Easterly, B. (2001a). The lost decades: developing countries' stagnation in spite of policy reforms, 1980–1998. Mimeo. Downloaded from <http://www.worldbank.org/research/growth/pdfiles/lost%20decades_joeg.pdf>.

Easterly, B. (2001b). *The elusive quest for economic growth: Economists' adventures and misadventures in the tropics.* Cambridge and London: MIT Press.

Fallaci, O. (2002). La rabbia e l'orgoglio. *Corriere della Sera*, September 29.

Frank, A. G. (1998). *Re-orient.* Berkeley: University of California Press.

Fukuyama, F. (1989) The end of history. *National Interest,* Summer.

Grass, G. (2002). The 'progressive' restoration: a discussion with Pierre Bourdieu. *New Left Review,* March–April. Downloaded from <http://www.newleftreview.net/index.shtml>.

Hochschild, A. (1998). *King Leopold's ghost.* Boston: Houghton Mifflin Co.

Kanbur, R. (2001). On obnoxious markets. Downloaded from <http://www.people.cornell.edu/pages/sk145/papers.htm>.

Keynes, J. M. (1998). *Economic consequences of the peace.* New York: Penguin Books.

Khor, M. (2001). The multilateral trading system: a development perspective. Mimeo, *World Network,* December.

Lindert, P., & Williamson, J. (2001). Does globalization make the world more unequal. National Bureau of Economic Research, Working paper 8228. Cambridge MA: NBER.

Maddison, A. (1995). *Monitoring the world economy 1820–1992.* Paris: OECD, Development Centre Studies.

Maddison, A. (2001). *World economy: a millennial perspective.* Paris: OECD Development Centre Studies.

Milanovic, B. (2002). Worlds apart: the twentieth century's promise that failed. Manuscript, downloadable from <http://www.worldbank.org/research/inequality/>.

Odenheimer, M. (2002). Where Stalin has admirers, and Maoists fight on. *Washington Post,* April 7.

Rodrik, D. (2000). Comments on 'Trade, growth and poverty' by D. Dollar and A. Kraay. Mimeo, October. Downloadable from <http://ksghome.harvard.edu/~.drodrik.academic.ksg/>.

O'Rourke, K., & Williamson, J. (1999). *Globalisation and history: The evolution of a nineteenth-century Atlantic economy.* Cambridge, MA: MIT Press.

Prados de la Escosura, L. (2000). International comparison of real product 1820–1990. *Explorations in Economic History, 37,* 1–41.

Runciman, S. (1932). *Byzantine civilisation.* London: Edmond Arnold.

Said, E. W. (2002). The public role of writers and intellectuals. The 15th Jan Patocka Memorial Lecture, October 24, delivered at IWM Institute, Vienna.

Sala-i-Martin, X. (2002). The disturbing 'rise' in global income inequality. Mimeo, March.

The Economist (2000). Growth is good. May 27, 82.

Weitzman, M., & Xu, C. (1997). Chinese Township–village enterprises as vaguely defined cooperatives. In: J. Roemer (Ed.), *Property relations, incentives and welfare.* Proceedings of a Conference held in Barcelona, Spain, by the International Economic Association, June 1994, London: MacMillan Press.

World Bank (2002). *Globalization, growth and poverty: building an inclusive world economy.* Policy Research Report. Washington, DC: World Bank.

Yotopolos, P. (1996). *Exchange rate parity for trade and development.* Cambridge: Cambridge University Press.

[4]

Introduction

Reclaiming Development

'There is no alternative.' This is the famous pronouncement by former British Prime Minister Margaret Thatcher when she was faced with widespread opposition to her programme of radical neoliberal reform during the 1980s. Thatcher's dictum captures the triumphalism, hubris and closed-mindedness with which the neoliberal orthodoxy has dominated discussions of economic policy around the world during the last quarter of a century.

This book begins with the premiss that the 'no alternative' dictum is fundamentally and dangerously incorrect. As we demonstrate in great detail throughout the book, feasible alternatives to neoliberal policies exist that can promote rapid economic development that is equitable, stable and sustainable. Some of these are proposals for strategies not yet adopted, to be sure. But many others have already proven their worth in practice across the globe. We offer them here in order to shatter the idea that there is no alternative, and to contribute to the vigorous campaign now underway across the globe to 'reclaim development'.

The timing of this book is propitious for three reasons. First, there is now abundant and increasing evidence that the economic policies associated with the neoliberal agenda have failed to achieve their chief goals, and have introduced serious problems, especially in the developing world. Second, there is a great deal of historical and current evidence that there are multiple routes to

2 Reclaiming Development

development. We argue that successful development is the result of diverse types of economic policies, the majority of which run counter to the policies advocated by neoliberal economists today. Third, at the present juncture the unbridled confidence of neoliberal economists seems to be faltering. In fact, a good deal has been published of late by neoliberal economists who tell us that they have grown disenchanted with certain aspects of the neoliberal policies embodied in what is commonly known as the 'Washington Consensus'. This apparent 'rethinking' of the development agenda has led some commentators to identify an emergent 'post-Washington Consensus' or 'post-neoliberal' policy agenda. Prominent examples include the book by Pedro-Paul Kuczynski and John Williamson titled *After the Washington Consensus* (2003) and a much-discussed study of financial globalization by a team of International Monetary Fund (IMF) economists (Prasad et al., 2003).

There are reasons to be encouraged by efforts to rethink development policy by key architects of the original Washington Consensus policies.[1] However, the spin on this new work inaccurately claims that the architects of the Washington Consensus have now 'seen the light', and have genuinely moved to a new way of thinking that transcends their previous policy prescriptions. This, in fact, is not at all the case. Instead, this new way of thinking merely seeks to save the core tenets of the Washington Consensus from embarrassment and refutation by modifying a few of its less central policy prescriptions. Indeed, the new thinking reaffirms and even extends its neoliberal character in several important policy domains (such as the increased attention that is paid to the promotion of labour market flexibility). Harvard University economist Dani Rodrik (2002) has aptly coined the term 'Augmented Washington Consensus' to refer to work along these lines.

This book seeks to provide real alternatives to the Washington Consensus – augmented or otherwise – in the developing world. *Our goal is nothing short of 'Reclaiming Development' from the neoliberal orthodoxy that has dominated discussions of development policy during the last quarter of a century.* We explain how and why neoliberal policies have failed developing countries, and demonstrate that there exists a range of achievable and desirable policy alternatives.

We begin the book in Part I by presenting and rejecting the six major 'Development Myths' that are used to justify the neoliberal policies that have been pursued with such disastrous results in the developing world during the last quarter of a century (Chapters 1–6). Part II is the heart of the book. Here we provide activists, policymakers and students of development policy with an array of concrete policy options that are superior to their neoliberal counterparts. In these chapters we look specifically at policies towards trade and industry (Chapter 7), privatization and intellectual property rights (Chapter 8), foreign bank borrowing and portfolio and foreign direct investment (Chapter 9), domestic financial regulation (Chapter 10), and exchange rates and currencies, central banking and monetary policy, and government revenue and expenditure (Chapter 11). In each case, we explain why the neoliberal policy recommendations in these domains have failed, often with disastrous consequences for developing countries. We then counterpose an array of alternative policies that can promote faster economic development than can neoliberalism, while ensuring that it is equitable and sustainable.

We must emphasize at the outset that we present this range of proposals in the spirit of pluralism and humility. We do not share the hubris of neoliberals, and therefore do not argue that there is an ideal, single approach to 'good' policy. We hope that this work will contribute to the promising new search within developing countries, multilateral agencies, nongovernmental organizations (NGOs) and activist communities for alternatives to neoliberal policy regimes.

We hope that this book is an antidote to the defeatism found among many opponents of neoliberalism who do not challenge these policies, believing that there are no credible alternatives. We also hope that our book empowers those who seek concrete

4 Reclaiming Development

alternatives to neoliberal policy. Towards these ends, we present our ideas in a clear and accessible manner so that both busy policymakers and those with little formal training in economics can make use of this book. However, the book is not simply a 'beginners' guide' to development policy. Professional economists will also find that our arguments are firmly grounded – even if plainly argued – in frontier research in development economics.

Our greatest hope for this book is that it is useful, empowering and accessible. We hope that it stimulates discussion of the ways that development policies can be reclaimed by those seeking to promote rapid economic development around the world that is equitable, stable and sustainable.

Note

1. In particular, we are pleased that recent work by neoliberals recognizes that unrestrained flows of liquid international capital can lead to speculative bubbles and financial crises in developing countries.

Part I

Myths and Realities about Development

The chapters in Part I examine six distinct, but related, 'Development Myths'. These myths form the basis of today's conventional wisdom regarding the types of economic policies and institutions that are both appropriate and feasible for developing countries. This discussion serves as the backdrop for our discussion of economic policy alternatives in Part II.

Each of these chapters begins with a brief statement of a development myth as it is generally articulated ('The Myth'). This is followed by an explication of the arguments that advocates generally advance in support of the myth ('The Myth Explored'). Finally, each chapter concludes with a detailed refutation of the myth ('The Myth Rejected').

| **Myth 1**

'Today's wealthy countries achieved success through a steadfast commitment to the free market'

1.1 **The Myth**

Today's industrialized countries have prospered because of their steadfast commitment to free-market economic policies. Unfortunately, many policymakers in developing countries today have failed to learn this lesson, and remain committed to state interventionism. But the laws of economics and history cannot be denied, and this approach is doomed to failure.

1.2 **The Myth Explored**

> The rich countries prospered through free trade and free financial flows.

Many economists argue that countries like Britain and the USA became world economic leaders because of their vigorous commitment to free-market policies.[1] These policies promote market- rather than state-direction of trade and financial flows. This strategy minimizes the scope of government regulation while encouraging private ownership of resources, enterprises and even ideas.

In this view, nineteenth-century France lost ground to Britain as a dominant player on the world scene because of its notoriously

8   Reclaiming Development

meddlesome government. Similarly, the Japanese economy has suffered from slow growth over the last decade because its leaders
failed to liberalize the country's state led economy.

The folly of state intervention is most dramatically illustrated
by the failed interlude of trade protectionism in industrialized
countries in the early twentieth century. Following Britain's success with free trade during and since the eighteenth century, most
of today's industrialized countries had adopted free trade policies
by the 1870s. Free trade inaugurated an era of unprecedented
economic growth that extended until 1913.

Sadly, this free trade era ended with World War I and the
ensuing economic and political instability. In this context, governments ceded to pressures for protectionism. The Great Depression
exacerbated this trend: during the 1930s, governments erected a
variety of tariff barriers against one another and implemented
other 'beggar-thy-neighbour' strategies in a vain effort to promote
domestic growth and stability. The protectionist, nationalist direction of trade policy ultimately prolonged the Depression, undermined the world trading system, and fuelled the flames of fascism
in Europe. These economic, social and political tensions – the
consequence in part of the retreat from the market – contributed
significantly to the outbreak of World War II.

Today's industrialized countries returned to free-trade policies
following the end of World War II. Since then they have pursued
trade liberalization through the General Agreement on Trade
and Tariffs (GATT) and more recently through the World Trade
Organization (WTO). In parallel fashion, they also deregulated
and privatized their domestic industries. These initiatives have
promoted world prosperity, especially in developing countries.

A similar story applies to finance. Over the last two centuries or so, today's industrialized countries gradually learned
of the benefits of deregulated, market-mediated (domestic and
international) capital flows. 'Financial liberalization' has many
components, including market allocation of investment funds,
protection of investor rights and freedoms, and the maintenance

of transparency. The trend towards financial liberalization has been reversed from time to time, but today most industrialized countries are deeply committed to the market mediation of financial flows – domestically and internationally.

> Developing countries have suffered because of policymakers' proclivity to adopt interventionist economic policies.

With the attainment of independence, most developing countries adopted highly interventionist economic strategies. As a consequence, they have faced economic stagnation.

Interventionism had many components. Pursuing 'infant industry protection' and 'import-substituting industrialization' (ISI) policies, governments insulated domestic industries from foreign competition with steep tariffs, restrictive quotas and large subsidies. Governments also nationalized key industries, creating state-owned enterprises (SOEs), and heavily regulated private-sector firms. Moreover, governments manipulated investment by nationalizing banks, regulating domestic financial activities, and restricting cross-border capital flows.

Most developing countries maintained these interventionist policies until the early 1980s. By then, however, these policies were recognized to be a resounding failure. Infant industry protection had not achieved the objective of promoting internationally competitive mature industries. SOEs also fared poorly: state subsidies and insulation from market competition left them bloated, inefficient and dependent on the state. Financial markets were stunted, while financial institutions provided funds to otherwise nonviable firms. In addition, industrial and financial controls gave rise to widespread corruption, bureaucratic 'red tape', and a costly misallocation of entrepreneurial talents. Together, these policies induced huge budget deficits and international debts, rapid inflation and myriad economic dislocations.

The economic crisis that swept through the developing world in the 1980s was the direct result of these misguided policies.

10 Reclaiming Development

The crisis led policymakers to embrace free-market capitalism – and not a moment too soon.

1.3 **The Myth Rejected**

The 'secret' of their success: today's industrialized countries did not become rich through free trade and free financial flows.

An honest reading of the historical record shows that today's industrialized countries pioneered and relied upon myriad interventionist industrial, trade and financial policies in the early and often in the later stages of their own development (see Chapters 7–11 and Chang 2002). With respect to trade, Britain and the USA, the most strident free-trade missionaries in the world today, actively utilized protectionist policy during the early years of their development. Indeed, they exercised greater protection than even Germany and France, countries typically associated with trade protection and industrial regulation. In the eighteenth century, for instance, Britain introduced import protection and export promotion policies to challenge the industrial supremacy of the Netherlands and Belgium (see Chapter 7) – policies that Japan and others would utilize so effectively in the decades after World War II.

The prize for protectionism, however, goes to the USA! It had the most protected economy in the world between the mid-nineteenth century and World War II (only Russia, for a brief period in the early twentieth century, maintained a more protected economy). The USA was also the intellectual home of infant industry protection, a strategy later adopted so successfully by Germany and Japan (see Chapter 7).

Most of today's industrialized countries also used aggressive industrial policy to rebuild and modernize their economies after the devastation of World War II, even while they liberalized trade. Industrial policy played an especially important role in the post-World War II economic transformation of Japan, France, Norway,

Austria and Finland. State-owned enterprises were also important during this period in France, Austria and Norway. Indeed, even the USA relies upon industrial policy, though it is not identified as such. For example, massive state investment and support for research and development (R&D) in defence and pharmaceuticals and large agricultural subsidies are de facto industrial policies with significant private-sector spillovers.[2] The development of transistors, radar, computers, nuclear fission, laser technology and the Internet can be traced directly to defence-related subsidies by the federal government.

Industrialized countries also used a variety of interventionist financial policies during the post-World War II period, and to great effect. These countries suffered from incessant financial instability prior to World War II because many then had neither central banks nor effective financial regulations. The financial stability (and ensuing growth) of the post-World War II era was very much a product of the effective financial regulation that characterized this era.

During the post-World War II era, Japan and most continental European countries subordinated their financial sectors to the needs of industrial development and thereby achieved rapid industrial growth. For example, the French government (via the central bank which it controlled) ensured that industrial policy objectives were met by the financial system. The Japanese government (working through the central bank and the Ministry of Finance) ensured that strategic industrial sectors received sufficient finance at attractive prices.

As we shall see in Chapter 9, almost all industrialized nations maintained stringent controls on international capital movements from the end of World War II until about 1980. These policies, known as capital controls, were designed to promote economic development and to protect fragile economies from the instability caused by capital flight. The USA was nearly alone in its failure to maintain capital controls following World War II (except for a brief moment in the early 1960s). The absence of capital controls

12   Reclaiming Development

in the USA was largely the product of the country's unique status as the world's financial superpower.

Finally, even while proclaiming the virtues of the free market, policymakers in industrialized countries have been quite willing to intervene in and re-regulate markets to avert financial crisis and/or to protect national (or sectoral) interest. Indeed, the US government has acted to socialize financial and economic risk on many recent occasions. Examples include its rescue of the Chrysler Corporation in 1980, and the multi-billion-dollar, publicly funded bail-outs of the savings and loan banks in 1989, the hedge fund Long-Term Capital Management (LTCM) in 1998, and the airline industry in 2001. In each of these cases, the government was willing to sacrifice the discipline of free financial markets in order to promote financial stability and to restore investor confidence.

> The truth about developing countries: well-designed
> programmes of intervention explain most success stories.

As discussed in Chapter 2, the vast majority of developing countries performed far better in the post-World War II era of interventionism than in the post-1980 era of free-market policies. Indeed, the performance of developing countries during the interventionist era was impressive not only in an absolute sense, but also relative to the performance of today's industrialized countries at a comparable stage in their development.

The truly dismal period of developing country performance was prior to World War II. During this period, developing countries were often coerced into using extreme free-market policies by colonial powers or, when nominally independent, through treaties that deprived them of tariff autonomy and the right to have a central bank. The typical result was sluggish growth and even economic decline. Economic performance in developing countries only improved after World War II because independence in some countries and a supportive ideological climate enabled policymakers to pursue interventionist strategies.

This is not to say that state intervention always works. There are cases where state intervention failed spectacularly. But when we look at the most dramatic success stories, the record clearly shows that development success is strongly related to myriad types of interventionism. Indeed, except for the case of Hong Kong, the East Asian 'miracle' was engineered by activist 'developmental states' that aggressively promoted economic development and financial stability (see Woo-Cumings 1999). China and India have also developed successfully via strong state direction of economic affairs (see Chapters 5, 7–11).

Notes

1. This policy regime was then known as 'liberalism'. In its modern form it is called 'neoliberalism'. This concept is explored more carefully in Chapter 2.
2. Throughout the post-World War II period, between half and two-thirds of US R&D was supported by the federal government (Mowery and Rosenberg 1993: Table 2.3). In 1989, 46.4 per cent of US R&D was supported by the government, while only 16.4 per cent of Japanese R&D in the same year was government supported (Odagiri and Goto 1993: Table 3.3). This contrast is rather striking, especially given the widely held view of Japanese state interventionism.

Myth 2

'Neoliberalism works'

2.1 **The Myth**

Over the past two decades, those developing countries that adopted the neoliberal agenda have prospered, while those that continued to pursue state-directed economic models have stagnated. The lesson is clear: neoliberalism represents the sole path to development and prosperity.

2.2 **The Myth Explored**

> Neoliberalism has succeeded where other regimes have failed.

The term 'neoliberalism' refers to the contemporary adoption of the free-market doctrines associated with the classical 'liberal' economists of the eighteenth and nineteenth centuries (such as Adam Smith and David Ricardo). The term 'Washington Consensus' is often used synonymously with neoliberalism because the US government, the International Monetary Fund (IMF) and the World Bank, all based in Washington DC, are such forceful advocates of these reforms.[1] They have been joined in the campaign to spread neoliberalism by the governments and business communities of many industrialized countries, and by many reformers within developing countries as well.

Neoliberalism has three chief components. It elevates the role of markets (over governments) in economic governance and in mediating flows of goods and capital (through the elimination of price supports and ceilings, free trade, market-determined exchange rates, etc.); it enhances the role and scope of the private sector and private property (through privatization, deregulation, etc.); and it promotes a particular notion of 'sound economic policy' (through balanced budgets, labour-market flexibility, low inflation, etc.).

These policies represent the *only* path to economic prosperity for developing countries in today's globalized world economy. Neoliberalism has dramatically improved growth performance, raised living standards, and promoted democracy and transparency throughout the world during the last two decades when these policies have been in place.

> Two decades of neoliberalism demonstrate that it delivers results.

The neoliberal 'revolution' was motivated by the failure of the interventionist policies that were widely implemented from World War II through the 1970s. At the time, even while liberalizing international trade and financial flows, industrialized countries pursued Keynesian 'tax-and-spend' policies and heavily regulated their economies. Excessive government expenditure resulted in high inflation, low levels of savings, and discouraged private investment. High taxes, excessive social expenditure and extensive government regulation stifled private initiative. For their part, developing countries pursued other forms of interventionism, as we have seen. These policies, too, proved to be counterproductive and unsustainable.

The neoliberal revolution that began in the 1980s and that continues to unfold today has already generated tremendous benefits. The curtailment of the state has reduced budget deficits and inflationary pressures, and has promoted market competition, efficiency, private initiative and entrepreneurship. The incentives

16   Reclaiming Development

and opportunities introduced by neoliberalism have also promoted efficiency, savings, and domestic and foreign investment. Most importantly, neoliberalism has promoted rapid economic growth and improved living standards the world over.

Neoliberalism has also promoted democracy, good governance and sound economic policy in developing countries in several ways. First, the economic freedoms associated with the market economy undermine political autocracy and kleptocracy. Second, international investors generally shun countries with corrupt or autocratic regimes. Third, neoliberalism integrates governments and firms into the global community and thereby encourages the adoption of the norms of policy conduct and business practice associated with it.

But what are we to make of the series of financial crises that have rocked the developing world over the past two decades? These crises are evidence not of neoliberalism's failures but of the incompleteness of neoliberal reform. Crises indicate that governments continue to interfere in economic affairs – such as through government direction of credit to their 'clients', and through measures that insulate favoured investors from risk. The solution to this problem, then, is more neoliberalism, not less.

2.3   **The Myth Rejected**

> The record shows that neoliberalism has failed, even on its own terms. Neoliberalism has not delivered economic growth.

Putting the matter bluntly: roughly two decades of neoliberalism have failed miserably to generate economic growth. Harvard University economist Dani Rodrik (2002) cites dismal growth performance during the 1990s as the most damning evidence of the failure of neoliberalism. Only three countries, Argentina, Chile and Uruguay, grew faster during the neoliberal era of the 1990s than their historical average growth rates during the interventionist era of 1950–80. However, the Argentinean economy has since imploded, with devastating effects on its smaller neighbour Uruguay, largely because of the failure of its neoliberal policies. And Chilean success is at least partially attributable to 'non-orthodox' policies such as government subsidies to certain export industries (e.g. forestry) and, more importantly, to a stringent regime of capital controls during much of the 1990s (see Chapter 9.3).

In the industrialized countries, the annual growth rate of per capita income has fallen from about 3 per cent during the interventionist era of 1960–80 to 2 per cent during the neoliberal era of 1980–2000.[2] Developing countries have fared even worse. Their average annual per capita income growth slowed from 3 per cent during 1960–80 to 1.5 per cent during 1980–2000. Indeed, the median rate of per capita GDP growth in developing countries over the last two decades was zero. Most disturbing is the fact that the poorest developing countries (defined as countries with per capita GDP from $375 to $1,121) went from a modest 1.9 per cent rate of per capita GDP growth during the interventionist 1960s–80s to a *decline* of 0.5 per cent per year during the neoliberal era. In short, countries at every level of per capita GDP performed worse on average during the neoliberal era than in the two preceding decades.

Even these dismal statistics put too positive a spin on the achievements of neoliberalism. Growth rates in developing countries over the last two decades or so have been buttressed by the acceleration of economic growth in the two largest developing economies, namely China and India – countries that in no sense followed the neoliberal formula. During the neoliberal period, Latin America has virtually stopped growing, while sub-Saharan Africa has experienced negative growth, and many of the former Communist economies have simply collapsed. In Latin America and the Caribbean, for example, per capita GDP grew by only 7 per cent from 1980 to 2000. By contrast, per capita GDP for the same region grew by 75 per cent during 1960–80. The data for sub-Saharan African countries is even more startling: per capita GDP fell by about 15 per cent during 1980–2000, after having grown by about 34 per cent during 1960–80.

18 Reclaiming Development

To summarize: two facts make it impossible to accept the claim that neoliberalism promotes economic growth. The best performing developing economies in the world today are highly interventionist, and the economic performance of developing countries as a whole has been decidedly worse during the neo-liberal era than in the decades immediately preceding it.

> The growth failures of neoliberalism mean that it cannot even compensate for the other costs that it has introduced.

That neoliberalism does not deliver economic growth is just the beginning of the problem. Even worse is the fact that the anaemic growth achievements of this regime have been accompanied by numerous adverse consequences in other areas.

Neoliberals acknowledge that the transition to this regime induces short-term 'adjustment costs'. For instance, reductions in social spending may undermine living standards; reductions in government support for certain sectors may result in job losses; and so on. But neoliberals claim that these adjustment costs are transitory since the new environment provides attractive oppor-tunities for adaptable individuals and firms to generate greater wealth. Additionally, neoliberals claim that the growth dividend induced by neoliberalism gives governments a means to compen-sate those who have temporarily lost ground. These claims do not stand up to scrutiny.

First, neoliberalism introduces new problems and aggravates existing ones, such as an increased vulnerability to banking, cur-rency and generalized financial crises (Grabel 2002) and increased levels of inequality and poverty. These problems are long-lasting and hurt the majority of the population, especially in developing countries (see Chapters 7–11). Contrary to the claims of its advo-cates, neoliberalism is the root cause of these problems. Extending neoliberalism further cannot therefore be the solution.

Second, neoliberalism does not provide governments with the motivation or the means to compensate those who lose ground under this regime. This is the case for several reasons.

Development Myth 2 **19**

Neoliberalism is based on the premiss that the government bears minimal responsibility for social welfare since extensive social welfare policy would distort the incentives associated with the free market. The anti-inflationary bias of neoliberal policy also means that governments are not apt to engage in adequate social spending. Moreover, the groups that are disenfranchised economically by neoliberalism also generally lack sufficient political power to secure compensation from the government (DeMartino 2000). Even if appropriate political will for compensatory schemes existed, governments have few resources to expend for this purpose. This is because neoliberalism reduces the tax base, places a high priority on budget balance, and makes it difficult to tax internationally mobile firms and investors (see Chapter 11.3).

Neoliberalism aggravates inequality among and within nations.

Neoliberalism induces international unevenness and inequality rather than widespread growth. Most importantly, private capital flows tend to concentrate in those countries that have already inaugurated a virtuous cycle of growth, investment and rising productivity (see Chapter 9.1). Contrary to the neoliberal claim, foreign private capital inflows *follow rather than create rapid growth*. Taiwan, South Korea and China are exemplars of this process (and of the success of well-designed programmes of interventionism). Developing countries (especially the poorest of these) must therefore institute policies that initiate a sustainable growth path as a precondition for private capital inflows.

There are by now myriad studies demonstrating the clustering of productive economic activity and the associated concentration of private capital flows across the globe during the neoliberal period. Inward investment by multinational corporations (MNCs), termed foreign direct investment (or FDI), is representative of the broader trend. Contrary to economic theory, the majority of FDI is destined for capital-rich countries in the North rather than capital-poor countries of the South. In 2000, for instance, only

20   Reclaiming Development

15.9 per cent of total world FDI and 5.5 per cent of total cross-border investment in financial assets, termed portfolio investment (PI), reached the South. Moreover, those flows that do reach the South are extremely concentrated.[3] In 2002, for example, China alone received about 37 per cent of all North–South FDI, while the top ten destination countries together received 70 per cent of the developing country total. In contrast, the far poorer countries of sub-Saharan Africa, where the need is unarguably the greatest, received only 4.9 per cent of total North–South FDI in that year (see Chapter 9.1).

Neoliberalism has induced rising inequality among countries, partly as a result of this concentration of private capital flows. The UNDP finds that in 1960 the countries with the richest 20 per cent of the world's population had aggregate income 30 times that of those countries with the poorest 20 per cent of the world's population. By 1980, at the beginning of the neoliberal era, that ratio had risen to 45 to 1; by 1989, it stood at 59 to 1; by 1997, it had risen to 70 to 1 (UNDP, 2001, 1999). In the neoliberal era, then, inequality between the richest and the poorest countries nearly doubled. This divergence is particularly apparent when one looks at the situation of sub-Saharan African countries. In 1960, per capita income in sub-Saharan Africa was about 11 per cent of per capita income in industrialized countries. By 1998, it had fallen to half that figure (UNDP, 2001: 16).

The neoliberal revolution has also deepened inequality within countries. A thorough empirical study of 73 countries by Cornia (2003) finds that 53 of them experienced a surge in income concentration over the last two decades. In regard to particular regions, Cornia concludes that: 'this increase [in income concentration] was universal in the economies in transition, almost universal in Latin America and the OECD and increasingly frequent, if less pronounced in the South, Southeast and East Asia' (2000: 9). He concludes that much of this increase in inequality within nations is due to various aspects of neoliberal reform (most importantly, liberalization of capital flows, domestic financial and labour markets, and tax reform).[4]

It is particularly notable that income inequality has grown faster in countries that have more fully embraced the neoliberal ideal, such as the USA and UK, than in those that have not (UNDP, 2001: 18). In the UK, the income share of the top 1 per cent nearly doubled from 5.37 per cent to 9.57 per cent between 1979 and 1998 (Atkinson 2002). In his study of the US economy, Paul Krugman observes that: '1 per cent of families in the US receive about 16 per cent of total pretax income, and have about 14 per cent of after-tax income. That share has roughly doubled over the last 30 years, and is now about as large as the share of the bottom 40 per cent of the population' (Krugman 2002: 67). Krugman also notes (citing a study by the Congressional Budget Office) that, 'between 1979 and 1997, the after-tax incomes of the top 1 per cent of families rose 157 per cent, compared with only a 10 per cent gain for families near the middle of the US income distribution' (64). More striking is the growing gap in the USA between the very rich, the shrinking middle class and the very poor.

We can compare the US record of increased inequality with the experience of Sweden, a country that has retained a good measure of social-democratic economic governance even while opening its economy to international trade and capital flows during this period. Again quoting Krugman:

> The median Swedish family has a standard of living roughly comparable with that of the median US family: wages are if anything higher in Sweden, and a higher tax burden is offset by public provision of health care and generally better public services. And as you move further down the income distribution, Swedish living standards are way ahead of those in the US. Swedish families that are ... poorer than 90% of the population have incomes 60% higher than their US counterparts. And very few people in Sweden experience the deep poverty that is all too common in the US. One measure: in 1994 only 6% of Swedes lived on less than $11 per day, compared with 14% in the US. (76)

22   Reclaiming Development

> Poverty has risen in many regions of the developing world
> during the neoliberal era, and earlier progress in improving
> social conditions has been reversed.

Neoliberals often point out that the overall proportion of the
world's population that lives in severe poverty has fallen over the
last two decades. But they neglect to mention that this achievement is largely due to the strong economic performance of China
and India, two countries that pursue distinctly non-neoliberal
policies and collectively account for more than half of the world's
poor.

Beyond China and India, poverty levels (according to a variety
of measures) have risen in a great many countries during the
neoliberal era. Today, the UNDP (2002: 2) reports that 2.8 billion
people live on less than $2 per day, while 1.2 billion people live
on less than $1 per day. In sub-Saharan Africa alone, half of the
region's population is poorer now than in 1990 and 46 per cent
of the population lives on less than $1 per day (UNDP, 2001:
10; 2002: 17). In South Asia, 40 per cent of the population now
lives on less than $1 per day; the comparable figure is 15 per cent
in East Asia, the Pacific and Latin America (UNDP 2001: 10).
Moreover, progress in improving life expectancy and education
and in reducing infant mortality was slower for a large number of
countries during the neoliberal era as compared to the previous
two decades (Weisbrot et al. 2001).

> Neoliberalism does not promote democracy. Indeed, in some
> important respects it undermines accountability, pluralism and
> national autonomy.

Finally, on the level of politics, neoliberalism is not associated
with an increase in democracy or transparency. Evidence shows
that the relationship between neoliberalism and democracy is far
more complex than neoliberals recognize.

First, the market system is compatible with diverse political
structures, ranging from repressive to democratic regimes. It does

not necessarily serve as a corrosive on authoritarian regimes, as many neoliberals claim.

Second, global neoliberalism threatens democracy by granting global investors and corporations veto power over domestic policy choices that they oppose. A fundamental aspect of democratic governance entails the right of those affected by policy to participate meaningfully in decision-making. Under neoliberalism, however, owners of internationally mobile factors of production (particularly large investors and the wealthy) have secured increased 'veto power' over the legislative and policy domain (see Chapter 9). By affording these actors freedom to withdraw funds from those countries that pursue strategies that threaten their interests, global neoliberalism effectively erodes national policy autonomy (DeMartino 1999). This structural power need not be exercised to be effective; today large investors and firms can merely threaten to relocate as a means to block government and citizen initiatives that they oppose. Therefore the flight of investors, or even the threat thereof, serves as a powerful deterrent to expansionary or redistributive economic and social policies, and to policies that promote labour rights (including the right to form unions and bargain collectively).

Third, the increased frequency of financial crisis under neoliberalism has greatly increased the power of the IMF vis-à-vis national governments. IMF assistance comes with 'strings attached': critical domestic decisions are vetted by an institution that is dominated by the USA and serves the interests of the global financial community. Neoliberalism thus undermines pluralism and policy independence in developing countries.

Notes

1. Rodrik (2002) uses the term 'Augmented Washington Consensus' to reflect the numerous caveats that neoliberals now attach to this agenda, such as the need for good governance, anti-corruption measures, anti-poverty programmes, and, most notably, some control over

24   Reclaiming Development

liquid, international capital flows. Kuczynski and Williamson (2003) are an exemplar of this perspective. They emphasize that they do not reject the original Washington Consensus, but rather claim that 'the way forward is to complete, correct, and complement the [neoliberal] reforms of a decade ago, not to reverse them' (18). But, especially in practice, this new consensus still gives pride of place to widespread liberalization (especially in labour, currency and product markets) and fiscal discipline over other goals. This was demonstrated forcefully during the IMF's 2001–02 negotiations with Argentina and Brazil when it conditioned financial assistance on the traditional package of neoliberal reforms.

2. Data in this and the next paragraph are from Weisbrot et al. 2001. See also Chang (2002: ch. 4) on the growth failures of neoliberalism.

3. All data in this paragraph are taken from World Bank (various years).

4. For consistent findings on transition economies and Asia, see UNDP 1999: 36; for Latin America, where 83.8 per cent of the population live in countries with worsening inequality, see ECLAC 2002: 83.

Myth 3

'Neoliberal globalization cannot and should not be stopped'

3.1 **The Myth**

Globalization is an inevitable, unstoppable force that promises tremendous rewards. Policymakers, especially in developing countries, must learn to cope with and respond to globalization by embracing neoliberal economic policies if they are to promote economic security and prosperity.

3.2 **The Myth Explored**

Globalization is driven by technological progress.

Globalization is the result of the revolutions in communication and transportation that began in the nineteenth century. Starting with the invention of the telegraph and the steamship, technologies of transport and communication have progressed relentlessly, drawing various parts of the world ever closer.[1] It took the early US settlers several months to sail across the Atlantic in the early seventeenth century; it took several weeks for early steamships to make the crossing in the nineteenth century; and it takes only three hours for supersonic aircraft to traverse this distance today. Prior to the long-distance telegraph, it took five weeks to send a message from London to Bombay. Long-distance telegraphs

26   Reclaiming Development

reduced transmission time to minutes (Standgate 1999: 97), and the Internet has made communication almost instantaneous.

Each advance in communications and transport technology changes the nature of business and production. It is only natural that entrepreneurs would look beyond their national borders for profitable opportunities and new markets made accessible by new technologies. Transportation costs are so low today that Japan can import coal from Australia; Sweden can import furniture parts from India; and Europe can import bottled water from Canada. The Internet has increased the speed and efficiency of international business since it reduces the need for face-to-face contact among executives. Finnish firms can arrange to outsource their production to Taiwan and Chileans can export smoked salmon to Korea based upon deals arranged over the Internet, while Bangladeshi farmers can learn about pest management techniques through the World Wide Web.

In so far as globalization is the result of technological progress, efforts to slow or reverse it are futile and reactionary. Those who try to obstruct globalization today are caught up in the same naive and futile project that was undertaken by the English Luddites during the early days of the Industrial Revolution. The Luddites convinced themselves that they could frustrate industrialization and thereby protect their jobs and idealized rural communities by sabotaging machines.

Efforts to curtail globalization suffer from misplaced fears and self-interest. But to the degree that they are successful, these efforts to stall globalization necessarily reduce global living standards by preventing a more efficient allocation of resources. Even worse, anti-globalization strategies in high-income countries retard growth and perpetuate poverty in the developing world.

> Globalization makes it extremely costly, if not impossible, for countries to maintain anything but market-friendly, neoliberal economic policies.

The pressures and opportunities associated with globalization provide incentives for governments to pursue the 'right policies'

– that is, neoliberal economic policies (see Chapters 2 and 6). This argument is straightforward: the benefits of globalization are available only to countries that permit the free, market-mediated flow of goods and capital. Countries that restrict imports deprive themselves of the opportunity to purchase goods produced elsewhere in the world at attractive prices. This harms consumers, and undermines export performance by forcing domestic producers to utilize more costly domestic inputs in the production process. Moreover, countries that restrict investor or business freedoms (through tariffs, capital controls, excessive government regulations, etc.) will be pariahs in international financial markets. Investors will demand a premium on their funds to invest in such inhospitable countries, and these higher capital costs will cripple economic growth. Investors also shun countries that have lax fiscal or monetary management. This means that countries that seek to attract foreign investment must maintain a sound macroeconomic environment.

The choice, then, is clear. Globalization and neoliberal economic policies (hereafter 'neoliberal globalization') are essential to the promotion of high living standards and prosperity. While the transition to open markets and policy discipline may generate short-term pain (such as a temporary rise in unemployment), the long-term benefits of these strategies are immense. It is therefore unsurprising that policymakers in nearly all countries (save North Korea and a few others) have come to embrace these keys to prosperity.

3.3 **The Myth Rejected**

> Globalization is not the inevitable outcome of technological advances.

Historical evidence does not support the claim that advances in transportation and communications technologies necessarily induce globalization. These technologies have progressed almost

28 Reclaiming Development

continuously over the last two centuries, but the progress of globalization during this time has been highly uneven. For example, levels of economic globalization – measured in a variety of ways – were considerably higher in the late nineteenth century, when international commerce depended on steamships and telegraphs, than they were in the 1950s, 1960s and 1970s, when transportation and communications technologies were much further advanced.[2]

> Political decisions – rather than technology – are the primary driving force behind the pace and form of globalization. Technology merely defines the realm of possibilities.

The pace and form of globalization that prevail at any point in time are the result of deliberate policy choices. Thus the neoliberal globalization of the last two decades stems directly from government initiatives in industrialized and developing countries from the late 1970s and early 1980s, respectively. International institutions, such as the IMF and the WTO, have also played a critically important role in promoting policies that facilitate the rapid pace and neoliberal character of globalization in most developing countries today.

To be sure, technology is not a trivial player in the globalization process. Technology delimits what is possible, such as how quickly and under what conditions goods and finance can flow across national borders. But whether these flows will be permitted depends on political decisions in the realm of international trade and financial policy. For instance, since the 1980s the extent of international financial speculation has intensified dramatically. This development is not due to the advent of the Internet, as the technologies necessary for rapid flows of speculative finance (such as the telephone and the fax machine) existed prior to the 1980s. Speculation has become more prevalent because opportunities and incentives to speculate have been created by policies of financial liberalization.

Development Myth 3 **29**

> The link between globalization and neoliberalism can be
> broken.

While being critical of the neoliberal discourse on globalization,
we also reject the claim that globalization itself is at the heart
of many of the economic and social problems observed in developing countries. *It is the neoliberal form of globalization that is
being promoted so aggressively today – and not globalization itself – that
is chiefly responsible for the poor economic performance and the deterioration
of living standards in so many countries* (see Chapter 2).

Neoliberals maintain that success in a globalized world economy
depends on the creation of a neoliberal policy environment on the
domestic and international levels. Indeed, they claim that eventually
all countries will converge around this policy regime, since any
other regime will be severely punished by global markets.

These arguments are simply incorrect. Globalization is perfectly compatible with different degrees and patterns of openness (to trade and capital flows) at the national level. The 1950s
and 1960s combined rapid globalization with extensive economic
regulation, in developing and industrialized countries alike. Thus
globalization and neoliberalism are not necessarily two sides of
the same coin.

The argument that the competitive pressures fostered by globalization make it necessary for all countries to converge to the
same neoliberal economic model is not borne out by evidence
(as we will see in Chapters 5, 7–11; see also Berger and Dore
1996). A considerable degree of policy and institutional diversity
exists among industrialized countries today, despite the progress
of globalization. For example, Sweden, Austria, the Netherlands,
France and Germany have all maintained policies and institutional
arrangements that are quite distinct from those in the neoliberal
economies of the USA and the UK. Larger and/or richer developing countries – especially China, India, Taiwan and Malaysia
– have also managed to maintain non-neoliberal policy regimes.
To be sure, smaller and/or poorer developing countries confront

30   Reclaiming Development

more severe restrictions on their policy autonomy. But even these countries may enjoy greater policy autonomy than is generally recognized. Chile is an example of a developing country that pursued a generally neoliberal path in the 1990s, but nevertheless managed to maintain a rather stringent regime of capital controls (see Chapter 9).

In sum, the neoliberal globalization that has been emerging over the past several decades is but one form of globalization. *Different policy choices (particularly as concern trade and financial policies) can create a form of globalization that would not be so noxious to living standards and growth prospects in developing countries.* Numerous examples of such policy alternatives are provided in Part II of this book.

Notes

1. Regular transatlantic steamship service was inaugurated in 1838, but until the 1860s the ships mainly carried high-value goods (as do airplanes today). Steamships started to dominate sailing ships only from the 1870s (O'Rourke and Williamson 1999: 33–4). The first telegraph system was patented in 1837. The first successful long-distance telegraph transmission was made in the USA in 1844. The first successful transatlantic telegraph cable was laid in 1868 (Held et al. 1999: 335).
2. There are many measures of globalization. Frequently used measures include international trade or short-term international capital flows as a percentage of a nation's total economic activity, and the share of immigrants in total population.

Myth 4

'The neoliberal American model of capitalism represents the ideal that all developing countries should seek to replicate'

4.1 The Myth

By now it is clear that American neoliberalism has outperformed all other economic systems. Any lingering doubts about this matter were erased during the 1990s when the USA prospered while other economies faltered. The demise of these systems exposes the failure of all forms of 'statism' and heralds the inevitable convergence of all nations upon the American model that embraces neoliberalism and democracy.

4.2 The Myth Explored

> The 'new economy' of the 1990s reflects the dynamism and superiority of the US economic model.

During the 1990s the US economy experienced sustained economic and productivity growth, low unemployment and low inflation. The 2001 *Economic Report of the* [US] *President* (ERP: ch. 1) reports that from the first quarter of 1993 through the third quarter of 2000 real GDP grew at an average annual rate of 4 per cent – which was 46 per cent faster than the average rate from 1973 to 1993; productivity (i.e. output created per hour of work) of non-farm jobs grew at an average rate of 2.3 per cent per year, compared to an average of 1.4 per cent per year for the previous twenty years; the number of jobs increased by more than 22 million while

32   Reclaiming Development

the unemployment rate declined steadily (reaching 3.9 per cent in 2000, the lowest level in a generation); and core inflation (i.e. the rate of inflation excluding price increases in food and energy) remained at a tolerable 2–3 per cent. These achievements are evidence of a 'new economy' that was fuelled by the information and telecommunications technology revolution. It may even be that this new economy is not susceptible to the business cycles that had plagued capitalist development for centuries.

The USA was the natural launching pad for the new economy, given its innovation-promoting regulatory regime and the prevalence of market incentives. For example, intellectual property rights (IPRs) are well protected, business taxes are low, employee compensation is based on performance (rather than on seniority or favouritism), business transparency is promoted by the legal environment, and the government does not discourage private initiative through excessive expenditure.

While the 'old' mass production economy of the USA clearly stumbled in the 1970s and 1980s, the country has demonstrated that its flexible, competitive and privatized economic system is uniquely capable of generating new technologies and new forms of commerce. This type of dynamism and adaptability is the recipe for success in a world economy that is now characterized by globalization and driven by rapid technological progress (see also Chapters 1–3).

The uncertainties in the global political and economic environment that have followed the events of 11 September 2001 have taken a toll on the US economy, of course. But there is no cause for fundamental concern. History has proven the inherent resilience of the US economy. Indeed, the flexibility of the US economy has enabled it to emerge from any difficulties more quickly than the rigid and inefficient economies of Europe and Japan.

> The superiority of the US model is also evidenced by the failings of the economies of Continental Europe and Japan.

The recent experiences of Continental Europe and Japan confirm the desirability of American neoliberalism. The interventionist economies of Continental Europe have been plagued by slow growth and high unemployment since the 1980s. Fortunately, many of the region's economies have recently begun to undertake bold, American-style economic reform. European nations have begun to deregulate and privatize industry, open up to trade, capital and labour flows within the region, and pursue monetary discipline under the leadership of the new European Central Bank. As a consequence they have begun to show modest signs of economic recovery (with regard to improved investor confidence, growth, etc.).

In contrast, Japan's situation remains dire. The country has been stalled in recession for over a decade, a consequence of its overregulated economy. Unfortunately, Japanese policymakers appear unwilling to develop a plan to restore economic prosperity through radical deregulation.

The superiority of American neoliberalism is also demonstrated by the enviable performance of those countries that have patterned their economies on that of the USA, namely the 'Anglo-American economies' of the UK, Canada, New Zealand and Australia. All have performed impressively during the 1990s.

In sum, the record is clear: the neoliberal American model of capitalism outperforms all other economic models. It is uniquely positioned to respond to new technological challenges and to deliver growth and prosperity in today's world economy. Though the anti-market economic systems of Europe and East Asia never constituted an ideal, the present juncture finds them positively outdated (see also Chapter 5).

4.3 **The Myth Rejected**

> American triumphalism is based on wishful thinking rather than on a careful, objective analysis.

There are several reasons to reject claims for the superiority of US capitalism, particularly in relation to its performance in the 1990s. The case for exporting this model to the developing world is, in a word, underwhelming.

34   Reclaiming Development

There never was a new economy in the 1990s.[1]

Contrary to the claims of new economy enthusiasts, US economic performance during the 1990s was rather unimpressive. In fact, the US grew more slowly in the 'new-economy' 1990s than in the preceding periods. Focusing on the first several years of business upturns in successive decades, economist Dean Baker finds that the average growth rate of GDP from 1991 to 1995 was 2.7 per cent, while growth averaged 4.4 per cent from 1982 to 1986 and 4.8 per cent from 1970 to 1973 (Baker 2000). US economic growth was notable only during 1996–99 (as GDP growth averaged 4 per cent over the four years from 1995 to 1999). But these few years of strong growth in the latter portion of the 1990s only offset the anaemic growth of the preceding period. Moreover, Baker argues that the impressive growth in the late 1990s is partly an illusion stemming from a change in US government measurement techniques.

A similar story can be told of US productivity growth. The average annual rate of productivity growth was 1.9 per cent during the 1990s, compared to an average annual rate of close to 3 per cent in the twenty-five years that followed World War II and 1.4 per cent for the years 1973 to 1989. As with economic growth, productivity growth was only strong during the later years of the 1990s: productivity growth averaged 2.5 per cent from 1995 to 1999; and some of the apparent increase in productivity growth is attributable to changes in measurement. Baker's analysis of US performance during the 1990s concludes that claims for a new economy are empirically unsupported.

The 1990s boom did not benefit the lives of ordinary Americans.

US economic performance during the 1990s also looks quite different when one takes account of distributional issues (see also Chapter 2). The US stock market boom of the 1990s – itself a consequence of the new economy hype – redounded to the benefit of the wealthiest 20 per cent (and especially the wealthiest 1 per

Development Myth 4   **35**

cent) of the population, and provided only meagre benefits to the average American family (Wolff 2000). Similarly, the increasing inequality in US wages that began in the 1980s continued through the 1990s, as wage increases went disproportionately to the most affluent (Baker 2000).[2]

The economic boom of the 1990s did little to eradicate poverty.[3] Indeed, the US Census Bureau reported in June 2002 that the proportion of families classified as poor remained virtually unchanged between 1989 and 2000 (*New York Times,* 5 June 2002). In 2000, 9.2 per cent of US families were classified as poor, compared to 10 per cent in 1989.

> The collapse of the US stock market bubble of the 1990s reveals a disturbing pattern of corporate corruption and resource misallocation.

Throughout the 1990s, economists lauded the incentives associated with the US system of executive compensation as a spur to efficiency and rapid innovation. Corporate executives garnered extremely high salaries, stock options (which gave them the right, but not the obligation, to buy or sell stocks by a future date at an agreed-upon price) and other perks.

These compensation packages resulted in vast disparities between the compensation of executives and average workers within the same firm. For example, in 1970 the average inflation-adjusted annual compensation of the top one hundred chief executive officers (CEOs) in the USA was $1.3 million – 39 times the pay of an average worker. By 1999, the average compensation of the top one hundred CEOs had risen to $37.5 million, more than 1,000 times the pay of an average worker (Krugman 2002: 64).

These executive compensation packages represented a massive misallocation of resources as firms were managed with the objective of maximizing the short-term value of the stock options held by highly placed insiders (see Chapters 8.1 and 10). The financial and corporate environment of the 1990s also promoted myriad forms of corruption. The US corporate corruption and accounting

36 Reclaiming Development

scandals of 2002 revealed that many corporate executives, boards and external auditors were seduced by the huge rewards available through stock appreciation. They manipulated accounting and other information to fuel an unsustainable rise in stock prices.

> Many other industrialized countries performed at least as well as the USA and other Anglo-American economies during the 1990s.

US economic performance during the 1990s also fails to impress when one considers it in comparative perspective. Many other industrialized countries performed as well or better than the USA during the 1990s. For example, between 1990 and 2000, Ireland (with a growth rate of 6.8 per cent), Singapore (5.3 per cent), Norway (3.1 per cent), Australia (2.8 per cent), Portugal (2.6 per cent) and Finland (2.4 per cent) grew at least as fast as the USA, while many others, such as Denmark (2.3 per cent), the Netherlands (2.2 per cent), Spain (2.2 per cent) and the UK (2.2 per cent), grew almost as fast.

As a group, the Anglo-American economies did not fare terribly well during the 1990s. New Zealand and the UK were at the forefront of neoliberal reform during the last two decades. But these reforms seem to have had no discernible effect on their economic performance. Indeed, economic growth rates in the USA, UK and New Zealand were nearly identical during the neo-liberal era of 1980–2000 and the interventionist era of 1960–79 (see also Chapter 2). The neoliberal era did, however, bring with it a striking increase in inequality within these nations.

Notes

1. The data in this and the following paragraph are taken from Baker 2000.
2. US wage gains during the 1990s were quite modest. Baker (2002) reports that real hourly wages for typical US workers rose at an annual rate of 0.5 per cent from June 1990 to March 2001. Although

Development Myth 4 **37**

real hourly wages rose at an annual rate of 1.5 per cent from 1995 to 2001, they fell at an average rate of 0.4 per cent annually from 1990 to 1995.

3. Reform of the social welfare system in the USA (involving significant curtailment of transfer payments to the poor) also contributed to the stagnation in poverty levels in the 1990s.

[5]

World Development Vol. 32, No. 4, pp. 567–589, 2004
© 2004 Elsevier Ltd. All rights reserved
Printed in Great Britain
0305-750X/$ - see front matter

www.elsevier.com/locate/worlddev

doi:10.1016/j.worlddev.2003.10.007

Is Globalization Reducing Poverty and Inequality?

ROBERT HUNTER WADE *
London School of Economics and Political Science, UK

Summary. — Over the past 20 years or so India, China, and the rest of East Asia, experienced fast economic growth and falls in the poverty rate, Latin America stagnated, the former Soviet Union, Central and Eastern Europe, and sub-Saharan Africa regressed. But what are the net trends? The neoliberal argument says that world poverty and income inequality fell over the past two decades for the first time in more than a century and a half, thanks to the rising density of economic integration across national borders. The evidence therefore confirms that globalization in the context of the world economic regime in place since the end of Bretton Woods generates more "mutual benefit" than "conflicting interests." This paper questions the empirical basis of the neoliberal argument.
© 2004 Elsevier Ltd. All rights reserved.

Key words — globalization, poverty, inequality, neoliberalism, political economy of statistics, World bank

'Over the past 20 years the number of people living on less than $1 a day has fallen by 200 million, after rising steadily for 200 years' (James Wolfensohn, president of the World Bank, World Bank, 2002b).

'The *best evidence available* shows...the current wave of globalization, which started around 1980, has actually promoted economic equality and reduced poverty' (Dollar & Kraay, 2002; emphasis added).

'Evidence suggests the 1980s and 1990s were decades of declining global inequality and reductions in the proportion of the world's population in extreme poverty' (Martin Wolf, *The Financial Times*, 2002).

'[G]lobalization has dramatically increased inequality between and within nations' (Jay Mazur, US union leader, 2000).

1. INTRODUCTION

The neoliberal argument says that the distribution of income between all the world's people has become more equal over the past two decades and the number of people living in extreme poverty has fallen, for the first time in more than a century and a half. It says that these progressive trends are due in large part to the rising density of economic integration between countries, which has made for rising efficiency of resource use worldwide as countries and regions specialize in line with their comparative advantage. Hence the combination of the "dollar-Wall Street" economic

regime[1] in place since the breakdown of the Bretton Woods regime in the early 1970s, and the globalizing direction of change in the world economy since then, serves the great majority of the world's people well. The core solution for lagging regions, Africa above all, is freer domestic and international trade and more open financial markets, leading to deeper integration into the world economy.

Evidence from the current long wave of globalization thus confirms neoliberal economic theory—more open economies are more prosperous, economies that liberalize more experience a faster rate of progress, and people who resist further economic liberalization must be acting out of vested or "rent-seeking" interests. The world economy is an open system in the sense that country mobility up the income/wealth hierarchy is unconstrained by the structure. The hierarchy is in the process of being flattened, the North–South, core-periphery, rich country-poor country divide is being eroded away as globalization proceeds. The same evidence also validates the rationale of the World Trade Organization (WTO), the World

* I thank without implicating Sanjay Reddy, Michael Ward, Branko Milanovic, Ron Dore, David Ellerman, Martin Wolf, Timothy Besley, and James Galbraith; and the Institute for Advanced Study, Berlin, and the Crisis States Program, DESTIN, LSE, for financial support. Final revision accepted: 30 October 2003.

Bank, the International Monetary Fund (IMF) and other multilateral economic organizations as agents for creating a global "level playing" field undistorted by state-imposed restrictions on markets. This line of argument is championed by the more powerful of the centers of "thinking for the world" that influence international policy making, including the intergovernmental organizations such as the World Bank, the IMF and the WTO, also the US and UK Treasuries, and opinion-shaping media such as *The Financial Times* and *The Economist*.

The standard Left assumption, in contrast, is that the rich and powerful countries and classes have little interest in greater equity. Consistent with this view, the "anti-globalization" (more accurately, "anti-neoliberal") argument asserts that world poverty and inequality have been rising, not falling, due to forces unleashed by the same globalization (for example, union leader Jay Mazur's quote above). [2] The line of solution is some degree of tightening of public policy limits on the operation of market forces; though the "anti-neoliberal" camp embraces a much wider range of solutions than the liberal camp.

The debate tends to be conducted by each side as if its case was overwhelming, and only an intellectually deficient or dishonest person could see merit in other's case. For example, Martin Wolf of *The Financial Times* claims that the "anti-globalization" argument is "the big lie." [3] If translated into public policy it would cause more poverty and inequality while pretending to do the opposite.

This paper questions the empirical basis of the neoliberal argument. In addition, it goes beyond the questions to suggest different conclusions about levels and trends, stated in terms not of certainties but stronger or weaker probabilities. Finally it explains why we should be concerned about probably-rising world inequality, and how we might think about the neglected subject of the political economy of statistics.

2. THE REGIONAL COLLAGE

The growth rate of world GDP, measured in US dollars and at current exchange rates, fell sharply from around 5.5% in 1970–80 to 2.3% in 1980–90 to 1.1% in 1990–2000. [4] This is bad news, environmental considerations aside. But

Table 1. *GNP per capita for region as % of core's GNP per capita*[a]

Region	1960	1980	1999
Sub-Saharan Africa	5	4	2
Latin America	20	18	12
West Asia and North Africa	9	9	7
South Asia	2	1	2
East Asia (w/o China and Japan)	6	8	13
China	1	1	3
South	**5**	**4**	**5**
North America	124	100	101
Western Europe	111	104	98
Southern Europe	52	60	60
Australia and NZ	95	75	73
Japan	79	134	145
North (= core)	**100**	**100**	**100**

Source: Arrighi, Silver, and Brewer (2003).
[a] Based on World Bank data. GNP at current exchange rates.

it still grew a little faster than world population over the past two decades; and the (population-weighted) GDP of developing countries as a group grew a little faster than that of the high-income countries. On the other hand, regional variation within the global South is large. Table 1 shows the trends of regional per capita GNP to the per capita GNP of the "core" regions (with incomes converted to US$ at current exchange rates as a measure of *international* purchasing power). During 1960–99 the per capita incomes of sub-Saharan Africa, Latin America, and West Asia and North Africa fell as a fraction of the core's; South Asia's remained more or less constant; East Asia's (minus China) rose sharply; China's also rose sharply but from a very low base. The most striking feature is not the trends but the size of the gaps, testimony to the failure of "catch-up." Even success-story East Asia has an average income only about 13% of the core's. [5] It is a safe bet that most development experts in 1960 would have predicted much higher percentages by 2000.

The variation can also be shown in terms of the distribution of world income by regions and income percentiles. Figure 1 shows the regional distribution of people at each income percentile for two years, 1990 and 1999. Here incomes are expressed in "purchasing power parity" dollars (PPP$), [6] in order to measure,

IS GLOBALIZATION REDUCING POVERTY AND INEQUALITY?   569

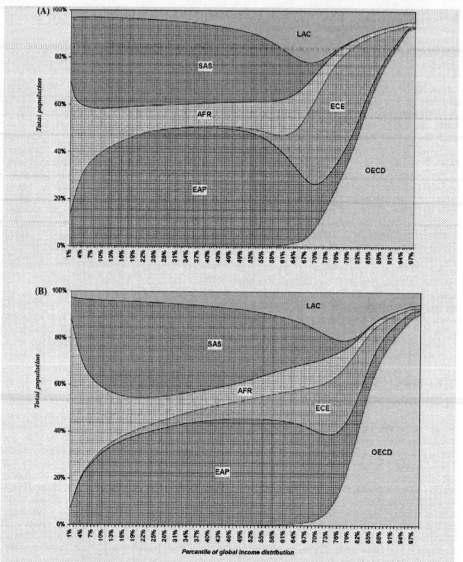

Figure 1. *World income distribution, by region, at each percentile of global income distribution: (A) 1990 and (B) 1999 (population at any particular income = 100) (Source: Dikhanov & Ward, 2003).*

notionally at least, *domestic* purchasing power. One sees the African collapse in the increased share of the African population in the bottom quintile; also the falling back of the Eastern and Central European populations from the second to the third quintile; and the rising

share of the East Asian population in the second quintile.

Figure 2 shows, in the top half, the world's population plotted against the log of PPP$ income, taking account of both between-country and within-country income distribution;

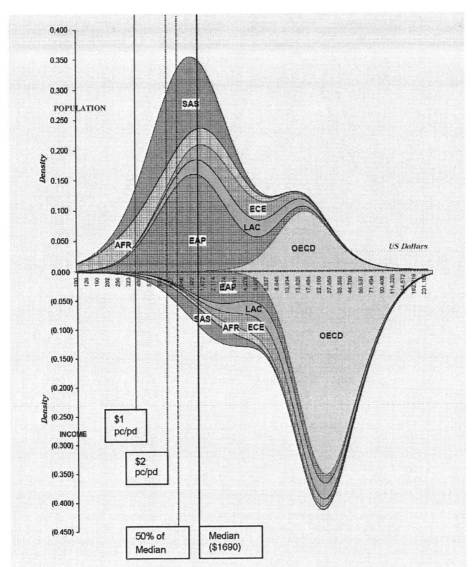

Figure 2. *World income distribution, by region: top half, distribution of world population against income; bottom half, distribution of world income against income, 1999 (Source: Dikhanov & Ward, 2003).*

and the breakdown by region. The bottom half shows the world's income plotted against income level, hence the share of income accruing to people at different income levels and in different regions. Residents of South Asia and East Asia predominate at income levels below the median, and residents of the OECD countries predominate at the top.

Finally, Figure 3 shows the movement in the bimodal shape of the overall PPP$ income-to-population distribution during 1970–99. The 1999 distribution has shifted forward compared

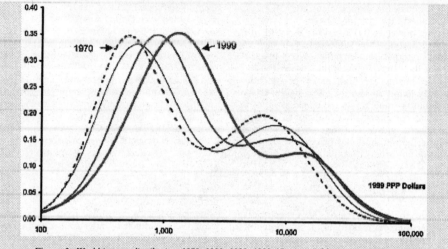

Figure 3. *World income distribution, 1970, 1980, 1990, 1999 (Source: Dikhanov & Ward, 2003).*

to the 1970 one, especially the lower of the two income humps, reflecting the arrival of large numbers of South and East Asians into the middle deciles of the world income distribution.

How does the collage—positive world per capita growth and wide divergence of economic performance between developing regions—net out in terms of global trends in poverty and inequality?

3. POVERTY

Figure 2 shows the two standard international poverty lines, $1 per day and $2 per day; and also the line corresponding to an income of 50% of the world's median income. Notice that even the higher $2 per day absolute poverty line is below the conventional "minimum" *relative* poverty line of half of the median. Notice too how small a share of world income goes to those on less than $1 per day, and how small a share of the income of the richest earners would be needed to double the income of the poorest.

Figures 1–3 are based on a data set on income inequality compiled by the United Nation's World Institute for Development Economics Research (WIDER).[7] But the standard poverty numbers—the ones normally used in discussions about the state of the world—come from the World Bank's data set. This is the source of the claims that, in the words of President James Wolfensohn, "Over

the past 20 years the number of people living on less than $1 a day has fallen by 200 million, after rising steadily for 200 years"[8] and "the proportion of people worldwide living in absolute poverty has dropped steadily in recent decades, from 29% in 1990 to a record low of 23% in 1998."[9] The opening sentence of the Bank's *World Development Indicators 2001* says, "Of the world's 6 billion people 1.2 billion live on less than $1 a day," the same number in 1987 and 1998.[10]

No ifs or buts. I now show that the Bank's figures contain a large margin of error, and the errors *probably* flatter the result in one direction.[11]

To get the world extreme poverty headcount the Bank first defines an international poverty line for a given base year by using purchasing power parity conversion factors (PPPs) to convert the purchasing power of an average of the official national poverty lines of a set of low-income countries into the US dollar amount needed to have the same notional purchasing power in the United States in the same year. In its first global poverty estimation this procedure yielded a conveniently understandable US$1 per day for the base year of 1985.[12] Then the Bank uses PPP conversion factors to estimate the amount of local currency, country by country, needed to have the same purchasing power in the same year as in the US base case. This gives an international extreme poverty line equivalent to US$1 per day, expressed in domestic currency. By way of illustration, Rs. 10 may have the same pur-chasing power in India in 1985 as US$1 in the United States in the same year, in which case India's international extreme poverty line is Rs. 10 per day. From household surveys the Bank then estimates the number of people in the country living on less than this figure. It sums the country totals to get the world total. It uses national consumer price indices to keep real purchasing power constant across time, and adjusts the international poverty line for each country upwards with inflation.

(a) *Large margin of error*

There are several reasons to expect a large margin of error, regardless of direction. First, the poverty headcount is very sensitive to the precise level of the international poverty lines. This is because the shape of income distribution near the poverty line is such that, in most developing countries, a given percentage change in the line brings a similar or larger percentage change in the number of people below it. Recent research on China suggests that a 10% increase in the line brings a roughly 20% increase in the poverty headcount.

Second, the poverty headcount is very sensi-tive to the reliability of household surveys of income and expenditure. The available surveys are of widely varying quality, and many do not follow a standard template. Some sources of error are well known, such as the exclusion of most of the benefits that people receive from publicly provided goods and services. Others are less well known, such as the sensitivity of the poverty headcount to the survey design. For example, the length of the recall period makes a big difference to the rate of reported expendi-ture—the shorter the recall period the higher the expenditure. A recent study in India suggests that a switch from the standard 30-day report-ing period to a seven-day reporting period lifts 175 million people from poverty, a nearly 50% drop. This is using the Indian official poverty line. Using the higher $1/day international line the drop would be even greater. [13] The point here is not that household surveys are less reli-able than other possible sources (for example, national income accounts); simply that they do contain large amounts of error.

Third, China and India, the two most important countries for the overall trend, have PPP-adjusted income figures that contain an even bigger component of guess work than for most other significant countries. The main sources of PPP income figures (the Penn World Tables and the International Comparison Pro-ject) are based on two large-scale international price benchmarking exercises for calculating purchasing power parity exchange rates, one in 1985 in 60 countries, the other in 1993 in 110 countries. The government of China declined to participate in both. The purchasing power parity exchange rate for China is based on gu-estimates from small, *ad hoc* price surveys in a few cities, adjusted by rules of thumb to take account of the huge price differences between urban and rural areas and between eastern and western regions. The government of India declined to participate in the 1993 exercise. The price comparisons for India are extrapolations from 1985 qualified by later *ad hoc* price sur-veys. The lack of reliable price comparisons for China and India—hence the lack of reliable evidence on the purchasing power of incomes across their distributions—compromises any statement about levels and trends in world poverty. [14]

Fourth, the often-cited comparison between 1980 and 1998—1.4 billion in extreme poverty in 1980, 1.2 billion in 1998—is not valid. The Bank introduced a new methodology in the late 1990s which makes the figures noncom-parable. The Bank has recalculated the poverty numbers with the new method only back to 1987. [15]

The change of method amounts to: (i) a change in the way the international poverty line was calculated from the official poverty lines of a sample of low- and middle-income countries (and a change in the sample countries), which resulted in, (ii) a change in the international poverty line from $PPP 1 per day to $PPP 1.08 per day, and (iii) a change in the procedure for aggregating, country by country, the relative price changes over 1985–93 for a standard bundle of goods and services.

We do not know what the 1980 figure would be with the new method. We do know however that the new method caused a huge change in the poverty count even for the same country in the same year using the same survey data. [16] Table 2 shows the method-induced changes by regions for 1993. Angus Deaton, an expert on these statistics, comments that "Changes of this size risk swamping real changes... it seems impossible to make statements about changes in world poverty when the ground underneath one's feet is changing in this way." [17]

Table 2. *1993 poverty rate, using old and new World Bank methodology*[a]

	Old poverty rate (%)	New poverty rate (%)
Subsaharan Africa	39.1	49.7
Latin America	23.5	15.3
Middle East/N Africa	4.1	1.9

Source: Deaton (2001).

[a] The poverty rate is the proportion of the population living on less than $1 a day.

(b) *Downward bias*

Further sources of error bias the results downward, making the number of people in poverty seem lower than it really is; and the bias probably increases over time, making the trend look rosier than it is. There are at least three reasons.

First, the Bank's international poverty line underestimates the income or expenditure needed for an individual (or household) to avoid periods of food-clothing-shelter consumption too low to maintain health and well-being. (Moreover, it avoids altogether the problem that basic needs include unpriced public goods such as clean water and access to basic healthcare.) The Bank's line refers to an "average consumption" bundle, not to a basket of goods and services that makes sense for measuring poverty (though "$1 per day" does have intuitive appeal to a Western audience being asked to support aid). Suppose it costs Rs. 30 to buy an equivalent bundle of food in India (defined in terms of calories and micronutrients) as can be bought in the United States with $1; and that it costs Rs. 3 to buy an equivalent bundle of services (haircuts, massages) as $1 in the United States, such services being relatively very cheap in developing countries. [18] Current methods of calculating purchasing power parity, based on an *average* consumption bundle of food, services and other things, may yield a PPP exchange rate of $PPP 1 = Rs. 10, meaning that Rs. 10 in India buys the equivalent average consumption bundle as $1 in the United States. But this is misleading because the poor person, spending most income on food, can buy with Rs. 10 only one-third of the food purchasable with $1 in the United States. To take the international poverty line for India as Rs. 10 therefore biases the number of poor downward.

We have no way of knowing what proportion of food-clothing-shelter needs the Bank's international poverty line captures. But we can be fairly sure that if the Bank used a basic needs poverty line rather than its present artificial one the number of absolute poor would rise, because the national poverty lines equivalent to a global basic needs poverty line would probably rise (perhaps by 30–40%). [19] A 30–40% increase in a basic-needs-based international poverty line would increase the world total of people in extreme poverty by at least 30–40%. Indeed a recent study for Latin America shows that national extreme poverty rates, using poverty lines based on calorific and demographic characteristics, may be more than *twice* as high as those based on the World Bank's $1/day line. For example, the World Bank estimates Brazil's extreme poverty rate (using its international poverty line) at 5%, while Economic Commission for Latin America, using a calories-and-demography poverty line, estimates the rate at 14%. [20]

In short, we can be reasonably confident that switching from the Bank's rather arbitrarily derived international extreme poverty line to one reflecting the purchasing power necessary to achieve elementary human capabilities would substantially raise the number of people in extreme poverty.

The second reason is that the Bank's new international poverty line of $1.08/day probably increases the downward bias, leading the Bank to exaggerate the decline in the poverty headcount between the years covered by the old methodology and those covered by the new one. The new international poverty line of $PPP 1.08 *lowers* the equivalent national poverty lines in most countries compared to the earlier $PPP 1 line. It lowers them in 77% of the 94 countries for which data are available, containing 82% of their population. It lowers the old international poverty line for China by 14%, for India, by 9%, for the whole sample by an average of 13%. [21] As noted, even a small downward shift in the poverty line removes a large number of people out of poverty.

Third, future "updating" of the international poverty line will continue artificially to lower the true numbers, because average consumption patterns (on which the international poverty line is based) are shifting toward services whose prices relative to food and shelter are lower in poor than in rich countries, giving the false impression that the cost of the basic consumption goods required by the poor is falling. [22]

All these problems have to be resolved in one way or another in any estimate of world poverty, whoever makes it. But the fact that the World Bank is the near-monopoly provider introduces a further complication. The number of poor people is politically sensitive. The Bank's many critics like to use the poverty numbers as one of many pointers to the conclusion that it has accomplished "precious little," in the words of US Treasury Secretary O'Neill; which then provides a rationale for tighter US control of the Bank, as in the statement by the head of the US Agency for International Development, "Whether the US way of doing things drives some multilateral institutions, I think it should, because, frankly, a lot of the multilateral institutions don't have a good track record." [23]

A comparison of two recent Bank publications suggests how the Bank's statements about poverty are affected by its tactics and the ideological predispositions of those in the ideas-controlling positions. *The World Development Report 2000/2001: Attacking Poverty* says that the number of people living on less than $1 a day *increased* by 20 million from 1.18 billion in 1987 to 1.20 billion in 1998. When it was being written in the late 1990s the key ideas-controlling positions in the Bank were held by Joe Stiglitz and Ravi Kanbur (respectively, chief economist and director of the *World Development Report 2000/2001*), not noted champions of neoliberal economics. [24] At that time the Bank was trying to mobilize support for making the Comprehensive Development Framework the new template for all its work, for which purpose *lack* of progress in development helped. Then came the majority report of the Meltzer Commission, for the US Congress, which said the Bank was failing at its central task of poverty reduction and therefore should be sharply cut back—as shown by the fact that the number of people in absolute poverty remained constant at 1.2 billion during 1987–98. [25] Now the Bank needed to emphasize progress. The next major Bank publication, *Globalization, Growth, and Poverty: Building an Inclusive World Economy*, claimed that the number of people living in poverty *decreased* by 200 million in the 18 years over 1980–98. [26] By this time Stiglitz and Kanbur were gone and David Dollar, a prominent Bank economist, was ascendant. He was chief author of *Globalization, Growth and Poverty.* [27]

(c) *Conclusions about poverty*

We can be fairly sure that the Bank's poverty headcount has a large margin of error in *all* years, in the sense that it may be significantly different from the headcount that would result from the use of PPP conversion factors based more closely on the real costs of living of the poor (defined in terms of income needed to buy enough calories, micronutrients and other necessities in order not to be poor). By the same token we should question the Bank's confidence that the trend is downward.

We do not know for sure how the late 1990s revision of the method and the PPP numbers alters the poverty headcount in any one year and the trend. But it is likely that the Bank's numbers substantially underestimate the true numbers of the world's population living in extreme poverty, and make the trend look brighter.

On the other hand, it is quite plausible that the *proportion* of the world's population living in extreme poverty has fallen over the past 20 years or so. For all the problems with Chinese and Indian income figures we know enough about trends in other variables—including life expectancy, heights, and other nonincome measures—to be confident that their poverty headcounts have indeed dropped dramatically over the past 20 years. If it is the case (as some experts claim) that household surveys are more likely to miss the rich than the poor, their results may *overstate* the proportion of the population in poverty. The magnitude of world population increase over the past 20 years is so large that the Bank's poverty numbers would have to be *huge* underestimates for the world poverty rate not to have fallen. Any more precise statement about the absolute number of the world's people living in extreme poverty and the change over time currently rests on quicksand.

4. INEQUALITY

The world poverty headcount could move in one direction while world inequality moved in the other. The neoliberal argument says that they have both dropped. [28] But in the past several years world income distribution has become a hot topic of debate in international economics and in sociology (much hotter than trends in world poverty). Disagreements about the overall inequality trend should not be surprising given the variation in regional economic performance—different ways of measuring emphasize different parts of the collage.

The only valid short answer to the question, "What is the trend of world income distribution?" is, "It depends on which combination out of many plausible combinations of measures and countries we choose." [29] Whereas we *could* get better data on the poor to the extent that the poverty headcount would command general agreement, there is no single best measure of world income inequality.

The choices include: alternative measures of income (GDP per capita converted to US dollars using market exchange rates or GDP per capita adjusted for differences in purchasing power across countries); alternative weightings of countries (each country weighted as one unit or by population); alternative measures of distribution (including the Gini or some other average coefficient, or ratios of the income of the richer deciles of world population to that of poorer deciles, or average income of a set of developing countries to that of a set of developed countries); alternatives sources of data on incomes (national income accounts or household surveys); alternative samples of countries and time periods.

We can be reasonably confident of the following six propositions.

Proposition 1. *World income distribution has become rapidly more unequal, when incomes are measured at market exchange rates and expressed in US dollars.*

No one disputes this. The dispute is about what the figures mean. Most economists say that exchange-rate-based income measures are irrelevant, and hence would dismiss the data in Table 1. GDP incomes should always be adjusted by PPP exchange rates to take account of differences in purchasing power, they say. [30] This makes a big difference to the size of the gap between rich and poor. As noted, the PPP adjustment is made by computing the relative prices for an average bundle of goods and services in different countries. The PPP adjustment substantially raises the relative income of poor countries. India's PPP GDP, for example, is about four times its market exchange rate GDP. The PPP adjustment thus makes world income distribution look much more equal than the distribution of market-exchange-rate incomes.

Market-exchange-rate-based income comparisons do suffer from all the ways in which official exchange rates do not reflect the "real" economy: from distortions in the official rates, exclusion of goods and services that are not traded, and sudden changes in the official exchange rate driven more by capital than by trade movements. Nevertheless, we should reject the argument that incomes converted via PPP exchange rates should always be used in preference to incomes converted at market exchange rates.

The practical reasons concern the weaknesses of the PPP numbers. Plausibly constructed PPP numbers for China differ by a factor of two. Estimates for countries of the former Soviet Union before the 1990s also differ by a wide margin; and India's differ too. So if incomes converted via market exchange rates do not give an accurate measure of relative purchasing power, neither do the PPP numbers for countries that carry heavy weight in world trends. Confidence in world PPP income distribution should be correspondingly limited.

Practical problems aside, PPP-adjustment is in principle preferable when one is interested in domestic purchasing power or, more generally, material well-being. We may however, be interested in income not only as a measure of material well-being. We may *also* be interested in income as a proxy for the purchasing power of residents of different countries over goods and services produced in other countries—for example, the purchasing power of residents of developing countries over advanced country products, compared to the purchasing power of residents of advanced countries over developing country products. If we are interested in any of the questions about the economic and geopolitical impact of one country (or region) on the rest of the world—including the cost to developing countries of repaying their debts, importing capital goods, and participating in international organizations—we should use market exchange rates.

The reason why many poor small countries are hardly represented in negotiations that concern them directly is that they cannot afford the cost of hotels, offices, and salaries in places like Washington DC and Geneva, which must be paid not in PPP dollars but in hard currency bought with their own currency at market exchange rates. In addition, the reason they cannot afford to pay the foreign exchange costs of living up to many of their international commitments—hiring foreign experts to help them exercise control over their banking sectors so that they can implement their part of the anti-money-laundering regime, for example—likewise reflects their low market-exchange-rate incomes. On the other hand, international lenders have not been lining up to accept repayment of developing country debts in PPP dollars, which would reduce their debt repayments by 75% or more in many cases.

These same "foreign" impacts feed back to domestic state capacity. For example, we should use market exchange rates to pick up the key point that the long-run deterioration in the exchange rates of most developing countries is putting those countries under increasing *internal* stress. When a rising amount of real domestic resources has to go into acquiring a given quantity of imports—say, of capital goods—other domestic uses of those resources are squeezed, including measures to reduce poverty, to finance civil services and schools and the like. This backwash effect is occluded in PPP calculations.

Hence we do need to pay attention to what is happening to market-exchange-rate world income distribution. It is widening fast.

The next four propositions refer to inequality of PPP-adjusted incomes, as an approximation to domestic purchasing power.

Proposition 2. *World PPP-income polarization has increased, with polarization measured as richest to poorest decile.*

The broad result is hardly surprising: the top 10% is comprised almost entirely of people living in the core countries of North America, western Europe, and Japan, where incomes have grown over the past 20–30 years, while a large chunk of the bottom 10% is comprised of African countries where incomes have stagnated or fallen. According to one study, the trend of richest to poorest decile goes like this: 1970—92, 1980—109, 1990—104, 1999—104. [31] Another study finds a jump in the ratio of 25% over 1988—93. [32] The change is made up of the top decile pulling sharply up from the median and the bottom decile falling away from the median. The polarizing trend would be much sharper with the top 1% rather than the top decile.

Proposition 3. *Between-country world PPP-income inequality has increased since at least 1980, using per capita GDPs, equal country weights (China = Uganda), and a coefficient like the Gini for the whole distribution.*

Of course, we would not weight countries equally if we were interested simply in relative well-being. But we would weight them equally—treat each country as a unit of observation, analogous to a laboratory test observation—if we were interested in growth theory and the growth impacts of public policies, resource endowments, and the like. We might, for example, arrange (unweighted) countries by the openness of their trade regime and see whether more open countries have better economic performance.

The same inequality-widening trend is obtained using a somewhat different measure of inequality—the dispersion of per capita GDPs across the world's (equally weighted) countries. Dispersion increased over the long period, 1950—98, and especially fast over the 1990s. Moreover, the dispersion of per capita GDP growth rates has also risen over time, suggesting wider variation in performance among countries at each income level. A study by the Economic Commission for Latin America using these dispersion measures concludes that there is "no doubt as to the existence of a definite trend toward distributive inequality worldwide, both across and within countries." [33]

Proposition 4. *Between-country world PPP-income inequality has been constant or falling since around 1980, with countries weighted by population.*

This is the result that the neoliberal argument celebrates. There are just two problems. First, exclude China and even this measure shows a widening since 1980; also exclude India and the widening is pronounced. Therefore, *falling income inequality is not a general feature of the world economy, even using the most favorable combination of measures.* [34]

Second, this measure—the average income of each country weighted by population—is interesting only as an approximation to what we are really interested in, which is income distribution among all the world's people or households regardless of which country they reside in. We would not be interested in measuring income inequality within the United

States by calculating the average income for each state weighted by population if we had data for all US households.

Proposition 5. *Several serious studies find that world PPP-income inequality has increased over a period within the past two to three decades, taking account of both between- and within-country distributions.*

Studies which attempt to measure income distribution among all the world's people show widely varying results, depending on things like the precise measure of inequality, the sample of countries, the time period, and the sources of income data. But several studies, which use a variety of data sources and methods, point to widening inequality.

Steve Dowrick and Muhammad Akmal make an approximation to the distribution of income among all the world's people by combining (population-weighted) between-country inequality in PPP-adjusted average incomes with within-country inequality. They find that world inequality widened over 1980–93 using *all of four* common measures of inequality over the whole distribution. [35]

Branko Milanovic uses the most comprehensive set of data drawn only from household income and expenditure surveys (it does not mix data from these surveys with data from national income accounts). He finds a sharp rise in world inequality over as short a time as 1988–93, using both the Gini coefficient and ratio (or polarization) measures. [36] Some of his findings are shown in Table 3. Preliminary analysis of 1998 data suggests a slight drop in inequality in 1993–98, leaving a large rise over 1988–98.

We have to be cautious about Milanovic's results partly because household surveys have the kind of weaknesses described above (though these weaknesses do not make them worse than the alternative, national income accounts, which have their own problems), and partly because even a 10-year interval, let alone

a five-year interval, is very short, suggesting that some of the increase may be noise.

Yuri Dikhanov and Michael Ward combine micro level household survey data with national income accounts, using the WIDER data set, a different statistical technique to the earlier authors, and a longer time period, 1970–99. They find that the Gini coefficient increased over this period from 0.668 to 0.683. [37]

Proposition 6. *Pay inequality within countries was stable or declining from the early 1960s to 1980–1982, then sharply and continuously increased to the present. 1980–82 is a turning point toward greater inequality in manufacturing pay worldwide.* [38]

Pay data have the great advantage over income data that pay data are a much less ambiguous variable, have been collected systematically by the United Nations Industrial Development Organization (UNIDO) since the early 1960s, and give many more observation points for each country than any data set on incomes. (The standard data set for world poverty and inequality, the World Bank's Deininger-Squire set, has few observation points for most of Africa, West Asia and Latin America during the 1980s and 1990s, requiring the analyst to guess the intervening years.) The disadvantage of pay data, of course, is that they treat only a small part of the economy of many developing countries, and provide only a proxy for incomes and expenditure. They are of limited use if our interest is only in relative well-being (though of more use if our interest is in the effects of trade, manufacturing innovation, etc.). But not as limited as may seem at first sight, because what is happening to pay rates in formal-sector manufacturing reflects larger trends, including income differences between countries and income differences within countries (since the pay of unskilled, entry-port jobs in manufacturing is closely related to the opportunity cost of time in the "informal" or agricultural sectors). [39]

Table 3. *World income distribution by households (1988 and 1993)*

	1988	1993	% Change
Gini	0.63	0.67	+6
Richest decile/median	7.28	8.98	+23
Poorest decile/median	0.31	0.28	−10

Source: Milanovic (2002a).

(a) China and India

With 38% of the world's population, China and India shape world trends in poverty and inequality. They have grown very fast over the past decade (India) or two (China), if the figures are taken at face value. China's average purchasing power parity income rose from 0.3

of the world average in 1990 to 0.45 in 1998, or 15 percentage points in only eight years.

We can be sure that world poverty and inequality are less than they would be had China and India grown more slowly. About any stronger conclusion we have to be cautious. First, recall that China's and India's purchasing power parity numbers are even more questionable than those for the average developing country, because of their nonparticipation in the international price comparisons on which the PPP calculations rest. Second, China's growth in the 1990s is probably overstated. Many analysts have recently been revising China's growth statistics downward. Whereas government figures show annual real GDP growth of 7–8% in 1998 and 1999 one authority on Chinese statistics estimates that the economy may not have grown at all. [40]

Even the Chinese government says that the World Bank has been overstating China's average income, and the Bank has recently revised its numbers down. Table 4 shows the Bank's estimates for China's average GNP in US$ for 1997–99 and the corresponding growth rates. The level of average (exchange rate-converted) income *fell* sharply during 1997–98, while the corresponding growth rate over 1997–98 was +6.4%. The Bank reduced China's per capita income partly because it believed that China's fast growth campaign begun in 1998 had unleashed a torrent of statistical falsification. In addition, the Chinese government arm-twisted the World Bank (especially after the allegedly accidental US bombing of the Chinese embassy in Belgrade in May 1999) to lower average income below the threshold of eligibility for concessional IDA lending from the Bank—not for cheap IDA loans but for the privilege extended to companies of IDA-eligible countries to add a 7.5% uplift on bids for World Bank projects. [41]

Table 4. *China's GNPPC and growth rate (1997–99)*[a]

	1997	1998	1999
GNPPC/PPP (US$)	3,070	3,050	3,550
GNPPC (US$)	860	750	780
Annual growth rate of GNPPC (%)	7.4	6.4	6.1

Source: World Bank, *World Development Indicators* (1999–2001).
[a] Note that each volume gives figures for only one year, so that the discrepancy can be seen only by compiling one's own table.

Over the 1990s China's annual growth rate is more likely to have been around 6–8% than the 8–10% of the official statistics. This one change lowers the probability that world interpersonal distribution has become more equal. [42]

We have to be cautious about going from China's fast growth to falls in world income inequality not only because China's growth rates and income level may be overstated but also because the rise in inequality within both China and India partly offsets the reduction in world income inequality that comes from their relatively fast growth of average income— though careful calculations of the relative strength of the two contrary effects have yet to be made. [43] China's surging inequality is now greater than before the Communists won the civil war in 1949, and inequality between regions is probably higher than in any other sizable country. The ratio of the average income of the richest to poorest province (Guangdong to Guizhou) rose from around 3.2 in 1991 (current yuan) to 4.8 in 1993, and remained at 4.8 in 1998–2001. [44] The corresponding figure for India in the late 1990s was 4.2, the United States, 1.9.

(b) *The United States and other Anglo political economies*

Canada excepted, all the countries of English settlement, led by the United States, have experienced big increases in income inequality over the past 20–30 years. In the United States, the top 1% of families enjoyed a growth of after-tax income of almost 160% over 1979–97, while families in the middle of the distribution had a 10% increase. [45] Within the top 1% most of the gains have been concentrated in the top 0.1%. This is not a matter of reward to education. Inequality has expanded hugely among the college-educated. Whatever the causes, the fact is that the United States is now back to the same level of inequality of income as in the decades before 1929, the era of the "robber barons" and the Great Gatsby. Income distribution in the United Kingdom grew more unequal more quickly than even in the United States during the 1980s, and is now the most unequal of the big European countries.

(c) *Country mobility*

How much do countries move in the income hierarchy? One study uses real GNP per capita data (GNP deflated in local currency to a common base year, then converted to dollars at the exchange rate for that base year), and finds a robustly trimodal distribution of world population against the log of GNP per capita during 1960–99. [46] The three income zones might be taken as empirical correlates of the conceptual zones of core, semi-periphery, and periphery. For the 100 countries in the sample, 72 remained in the same income zone over the whole period sampled at five yearly intervals (e.g., Australia remained in zone 1, Brazil in zone 2, Bolivia in zone 3). The remaining 28 countries moved at least once from one zone to another (e.g., Argentina from 1 to 2). No country moved more than one zone. (South Korea, Hong Kong and Singapore in 1960 were already in the middle, not low zone.) There are about as many cases of upward movement as downwards. Compared to the rate of potential mobility (each country moving one zone at each measurement date) the rate of actual mobility was 3%.

Of the 28 out of 100 countries that moved at least once between zones, about half had "stable" moves in the sense that their position in 1990 and 1999 was one zone above or below their position in 1960 and 1965. Greece moved stably up from 2 to 1, Argentina moved stably down from 1 to 2, El Salvador moved stably down from 2 to 3. As many countries moved stably up as down.

(d) *The absolute income gap*

Our measures of inequality refer to relative incomes, not absolute incomes. Inequality between developing countries as a group and developed countries as a group remains constant if the ratio of developing country income to developed country income remains at 5%. But this, of course, implies a big rise in the absolute size of the gap. The absolute gap between a country with average income of $1,000 growing at 6% and a country with average income $30,000 growing at 1% continues to widen until after the 40th year! China and India are reducing the absolute gap with the faltering middle-income states such as Mexico, Brazil, Russia and Argentina, but not with the countries of North America, Western Europe and Japan. Dikhanov and Ward's figures show that, overall, the absolute gap between the average income of the top decile of world population and the bottom decile increased from $PPP 18,690 in 1970 to $PPP 28,902 in 1999. [47] We can be sure that—a

seventh proposition—absolute gaps between people and countries are widening fast and will continue to widen for at least two generations.

(e) *Conclusions about inequality*

The evidence does support the liberal argument when inequality is measured with population-weighted countries' per capita PPP-adjusted incomes, plus a measure of average inequality, taking China's income statistics at face value. On the other hand, polarization has clearly increased. Moreover, several studies that measure inequality over the whole distribution and use either cross-sectional household survey data or measures of combined inequality between countries and within countries show widening inequality since around 1980. The conclusion is that world inequality measured in plausible ways is probably rising, despite China's and India's fast growth. The conclusion is reinforced by evidence of a quite different kind. Dispersion in pay rates within manufacturing has become steadily wider since the early 1980s, having remained roughly constant from 1960 to the early 1980s. Meanwhile, absolute income gaps are widening fast.

5. GLOBALIZATION

I have raised doubts about the liberal argument's claim that (a) the number of people living in extreme poverty worldwide is currently about 1.2 billion, (b) it has fallen substantially since 1980, by about 200 million, and (c) that world income inequality has fallen over the same period, having risen for many decades before then. Let us consider the other end of the argument—that the allegedly positive trends in poverty and inequality have been driven by rising integration of poorer countries into the world economy, as seen in rising trade/GDP, foreign direct investment/GDP, and the like.

Clearly the proposition is not well supported at the world level if we agree that globalization has been rising while poverty and income inequality have not been falling. Indeed, it is striking that the pronounced convergence of economic policy toward "openness" worldwide over the past 20 years has gone with divergence of economic performance. But it might still be possible to argue that globalization explains differences between countries: that more open economies or ones that open faster have a better record than less open ones or ones than open more slowly.

This is what World Bank studies claim. The best known, *Globalization, Growth and Poverty*, [48] distinguishes "newly globalizing" countries, also called "more globalized" countries, from "nonglobalizing" countries or "less globalized" countries. It measures globalizing by *changes* in the ratio of trade to GDP over 1977–97. Ranking developing countries by the amount of change, it calls the top third the more globalized countries, the bottom two-thirds, the less globalized countries. It finds that the former have had faster economic growth, no increase in inequality, and faster reduction of poverty than the latter. "Thus globalization clearly can be a force for poverty reduction," it concludes.

The conclusion does not follow. First, using "change in the trade/GDP ratio" as the measure of globalization skews the results. [49] The globalizers then include China and India, as well as countries such as Nepal, Côte d' Ivoire, Rwanda, Haiti, and Argentina. It is quite possible that "more globalized" countries are *less* open than many "less globalized" countries, both in terms of trade/GDP and in terms of the magnitude of tariffs and nontariff barriers. A country with high trade/GDP and very free trade policy would still be categorized as "less globalized" if its *increase* in trade/GDP over 1977–97 put it in the bottom two-thirds of the sample. Many of the globalizing countries initially had very *low* trade/GDP in 1977 and still had relatively low trade/GDP at the *end* of the period in 1997 (reflecting more than just the fact that larger economies tend to have lower ratios of trade/GDP). To call relatively closed economies "more globalized" or "globalizers" and to call countries with much higher ratios of

trade/GDP and much freer trade regimes "less globalized" or even "nonglobalizers" is an audacious use of language.

Excluding countries with high but not rising levels of trade to GDP from the category of more globalized eliminates many poor countries dependent on a few natural resource commodity exports, which have had poor economic performance. The structure of their economy and the low skill endowment of the population make them dependent on trade. If they were included as globalized their poor economic performance would question the proposition that the more globalized countries do better. On the other hand, including China and India as globalizers—despite relatively low trade/GDP and relatively protective trade regimes—guarantees that the globalizers, weighted by population, show better performance than the nonglobalizers. Table 5 provides an illustration.

The second problem is that the argument fudges almost to vanishing point the distinction between trade quantities and trade policy, and implies, wrongly, that rising trade quantities—and the developmental benefits thereof—are the consequence of trade liberalization.

Third, the argument assumes that fast trade growth is the major cause of good economic performance. It does not examine the reverse causation, from fast economic growth to fast trade growth. Nor does it consider that other variables correlated with trade growth may be important causes of economic performance: quality of government, for example. One reexamination of the Bank's study finds that the globalizer countries do indeed have higher quality of government indicators than the nonglobalizer countries, on average. [50] Finally, trade does not capture important kinds of "openness," including people flows and ideas

Table 5. *Trade-dependent nonglobalizers and less-trade-dependent globalizers*

	Exports/GDP			GNPRG 1988–99 (%)
	1990	1999	% Change	
Nonglobalizers				
Honduras	36	42	17	−1.2
Kenya	26	25	−0.04	0.5
Globalizers				
India	7	11	57	6.9
B'desh	6	14	133	3.3

Source: World Bank, *World Development Report 2000/01*, Tables 1 and 13.

flows. Imagine an economy with no foreign trade but high levels of inward and outward migration and a well-developed diaspora network. In a real sense this would be an open or globalized economy, though not classified as such.

Certainly many countries—including China and India—have benefited from their more intensive engagement in international trade and investment over the past one or two decades. But this is not to say that their improved performance is largely due to their more intensive external integration. They began to open their own markets *after* building up industrial capacity and fast growth behind high barriers. [51] In addition, throughout their period of so-called openness they have maintained protection and other market restrictions that would earn them a bad report card from the World Bank and IMF were they not growing fast. China began its fast growth with a high degree of equality of assets and income, brought about in distinctly nonglobalized conditions and unlikely to have been achieved in an open economy and democratic polity. [52]

Their experience—and that of Japan, South Korea and Taiwan earlier—shows that countries do not have to adopt liberal trade policies in order to reap large benefits from trade. [53] They all experienced relatively fast growth behind protective barriers; a significant part of their growth came from replacing imports of consumption goods with domestic production; and more and more of their rapidly growing imports consisted of capital goods and intermediate goods. As they became richer they tended to liberalize their trade—providing the basis for the misunderstanding that trade liberalization drove their growth. For all the Bank study's qualifications (such as "We label the top third 'more globalized' without in any sense implying that they adopted pro-trade policies. The rise in trade may have been due to other policies or even to pure chance"), it concludes that trade liberalization has been the driving force of the increase in developing countries' trade. "The result of this trade liberalization in the developing world has been a large increase in both imports and exports," it says. On this shaky basis the Bank rests its case that developing countries must push hard toward near-free trade as a core ingredient of their development strategy, the better to enhance competition in efficient, rent-free markets. Even when the Bank or other development agencies articulate the softer principle—trade liberal-

ization is the necessary direction of change but countries may do it at different speeds—all the attention remains focused on the liberalization part, none on how to make protective regimes more effective.

In short, the Bank's argument about the benign effects of globalization on growth, poverty and income distribution does not survive scrutiny at either end. And a recent cross-country study of the relationship between openness and income distribution strikes another blow. It finds that among the subset of countries with low and middle levels of average income (below $5,000 per capita in PPP terms, that of Chile and the Czech Republic), higher levels of trade openness are associated with *more* inequality, while among higher-income countries more openness goes with less inequality. [54]

6. CONCLUSION

It is plausible, and important, that the proportion of the world's population living in extreme poverty has probably fallen over the past two decades or so, having been rising for decades before then. Beyond this we cannot be confident, because the World Bank's poverty numbers are subject to a large margin of error, are probably biased downward, and probably make the trend look rosier than it really is. On income distribution, several studies suggest that world income inequality has been rising during the past two to three decades, and a study of manufacturing pay dispersions buttresses the same conclusion from another angle. The trend is sharpest when incomes are measured at market-exchange-rate incomes. This is less relevant to relative well-being than PPP-adjusted incomes, in principle; but it is highly relevant to state capacity, interstate power, and the dynamics of capitalism. One combination of inequality measures does yield the conclusion that income inequality has been falling—PPP-income per capita weighted by population, measured by an averaging coefficient such as the Gini. But take out China and even this measure shows widening inequality. Falling inequality is thus not a *generalized* feature of the world economy even by the most favorable measure. Finally, whatever we conclude about income inequality, absolute income gaps are widening and will continue to do so for decades.

If the number of people in extreme poverty is not falling and if global inequality is widening, we cannot conclude that globalization in the context of the dollar-Wall Street regime is moving the world in the right direction, with Africa's poverty as a special case in need of international attention. The balance of probability is that—like global warming—the world is moving in the wrong direction.

The failure of the predicted effects aside, the studies that claim globalization as the driver are weakened by (a) the use of *changes* in the trade/GDP ratio or FDI/GDP ratio as the index of globalization or openness, irrespective of level (though using the level on its own is also problematic, the level of trade/GDP being determined mainly by country size); (b) the assumption that trade liberalization drives increases in trade/GDP; and (c) the assumption that increases in trade/GDP drive improved economic performance. The problems come together in the case of China and India, whose treatment dominates the overall results. They are classed as "globalizers," their relatively good economic performance is attributed mainly to their "openness," and the deviation between their economic policies—substantial trade protection and capital controls, for example—and the core economic policy package of the World Bank and the other multilateral economic organizations is glossed.

At the least, analysts have to separate out the effect of country size on trade/GDP levels from other factors determining trade/GDP, including trade policies, because the single best predictor of trade/GDP is country size (population and area). They must make a clear distinction between statements about (i) levels of trade, (ii) changes in levels, (iii) restrictiveness or openness of trade policy, (iv) changes in restrictiveness of policy, and (v) the content of trade—whether a narrow range of commodity exports in return for a broad range of consumption imports, or a diverse range of exports (some of them replaced imports) in return for a diverse range of imports (some of them producer goods to assist further import replacement).

(a) *Should we worry about rising inequality?*

The neoliberal argument says that inequality provides incentives for effort and risk-taking, and thereby raises efficiency. As Margaret Thatcher put it, "It is our job to glory in inequality and see that talents and abilities are given vent and expression for the benefit of us all."[55] We should worry about rising inequality only if it somehow makes the poor worse off than otherwise.

The counterargument is that this productive incentive effect applies only at moderate, Scandinavian, levels of inequality. At higher levels, such as in the United States over the past 20 years, it is likely to be swamped by social costs. Aside from the moral case against it, inequality above a moderate level creates a kind of society that even crusty conservatives hate to live in, unsafe and unpleasant.

Higher income inequality within countries goes with: (i) higher poverty (using World Bank data and the number of people below the Bank's international poverty line);[56] (ii) slower economic growth, especially in large countries such as China, because it constrains the growth of mass demand; (iii) higher unemployment; and (iv) higher crime.[57] The link to higher crime comes through the inability of unskilled men in high inequality societies to play traditional male economic and social roles, including a plausible contribution to family income. But higher crime and violence is only the tip of a distribution of social relationships skewed toward the aggressive end of the spectrum, with low average levels of trust and social capital. In short, inequality at the national level should certainly be a target of public policy, even if just for the sake of the prosperous.

The liberal argument is even less concerned about widening inequality between countries than it is about inequality within countries, because we cannot do much to lessen international inequality directly. But on the face of it, the more globalized the world becomes, the more that the reasons why we should be concerned about within-country inequalities also apply between countries. If globalization within the current framework actually increases inequality within and between countries, as some evidence suggests, increases in world inequality above moderate levels may cut world aggregate demand and thereby world economic growth, making a vicious circle of rising world inequality and slower world growth.

Rising inequality between countries impacts directly the national political economy in the poorer states, as rich people who earlier compared themselves to others in their neighborhood now compare themselves to others in the United States or Western Europe, and feel deprived and perhaps angry. Inequality above moderate levels may, for example, predispose the elites to become more corrupt as they compare themselves to elites in rich countries. They may squeeze their own populations in order to sustain a comparable living standard, enfeebling whatever norms of citizenship have emerged and preventing the transition from an "oligarchic" elite, concerned to maximize redistribution upward and contain protests by repression, to an "establishment" elite, concerned to protect its position by being seen to operate fairly. Likewise, rapidly widening between-country inequality in current exchange rate terms feeds back into stress in public services, as the increasing foreign exchange cost of imports, debt repayment and the like has to be offset by cuts in budgets for health, education, and industrial policy.

Migration is a function of inequality, since the fastest way for a poor person to get richer is to move from a poor country to a rich country. Widening inequality may raise the incentive on the educated people of poor countries to migrate to the rich countries, and raise the incentive of unskilled people to seek illegal entry. Yet migration/refugees/asylum is the single most emotional, most atavistic issue in Western politics. Polls show that more than two-thirds of respondents agree that there should be fewer "foreigners" living in their countries. [58]

Rising inequality may generate conflict between states, and—because the *market-exchange-rate* income gap is so big—make it cheap for rich states to intervene to support one side or the other in civil strife. Rising inequality in market-exchange-rate terms—helped by a high US dollar, a low (long-run) oil price, and the WTO agreements on intellectual property rights, investment, and trade in services—allows the United States to finance the military sinews of its postimperial empire more cheaply. [59]

The effects of inequality within and between countries depend on prevailing norms. Where power hierarchy and income inequality are thought to be the natural condition of man the negative effects can be expected to be lighter than where prevailing norms affirm equality. Norms of equality and democracy are being energetically internationalized by the Atlantic states, at the same time as the lived experience in much of the rest of the world is from another planet.

In the end, the interests of the rich and powerful should, objectively, line up in favor of greater equity in the world at large, because some of the effects of widening inequality may contaminate their lives and those of their children. This fits the neoliberal argument. But the route to greater equity goes not only through the dismantling of market rules rigged in favor of the rich—also consistent with the neoliberal argument—but through more political (nonmarket) influence on resource allocation in order to counter the tendency of free markets to concentrate incomes and power. This requires international public policy well beyond the boundaries of neoliberalism.

The need for deliberate international redistribution is underlined by the evidence that world poverty may be higher in absolute numbers than is generally thought, and quite possibly rising rather than falling; and that world income inequality is probably rising too. This evidence suggests that the income and prosperity gap between a small proportion of the world's population living mainly in the North and a large proportion living entirely in the South is a structural divide, not just a matter of a lag in the South's catch-up. Sustained preferences for the South may be necessary if the world is to move to a single-humped and more narrowly dispersed distribution over the next century.

(b) *The political economy of statistics*

Concerns about global warming gave rise to a coordinated worldwide project to get better climatological data; the same is needed to get better data on poverty and inequality. The World Bank is one of the key actors. It has moved from major to minor source of foreign finance for most developing countries outside of Africa. But it remains an important global organization because it wields a disproportionate influence in setting the development agenda, in offering an imprimatur of "sound finance" that crowds in other resources, and in providing finance at times when other finance is not available. Its statistics and development research are crucial to its legitimacy. [60] Other regional development banks and aid agencies have largely given up on statistics and research, ceding the ground to the World Bank. Alternative views come only from a few "urban guerrillas" in pockets of academia and the UN system. [61] Keynes' dictum on practical men and long-dead economists suggests that such intellectual monopolization can have a hugely negative impact.

Think of two models of a statistical organization that is part of a larger organization working on politically sensitive themes. The "exogenous" model says that the statistics are produced by professionals exercising their best judgment in the face of difficulties that have no optimal solutions, who are managerially insulated from the overall tactical goals of the organization. The "endogenous" model says that the statistics are produced by staff who act as agents of the senior managers (the principals), the senior managers expect them to help advance the tactical goals of the organization just like other staff, and the statistics staff therefore have to massage the data beyond the limits of professional integrity, or quit.

Certainly the simple endogenous model does not fit the Bank; but nor does the other. The Bank is committed to an Official View of how countries should seek poverty reduction, rooted in the neoliberal agenda of trade opening, financial opening, privatization, deregulation, with some good governance, civil society and environmental protection thrown in; it is exposed to arm-twisting by the G7 member states and international nongovernmental organizations (NGOs); it must secure their support and defend itself against criticism. [62] It seeks to advance its broad market opening agenda not through coercion but mainly by establishing a sense that the agenda is right and fitting. Without this it would lose the support of the G7 states, Wall Street, and fractions of developing country elites. The units of the Bank that produce the statistics are partly insulated from the resulting pressures, especially by their membership in "epistemic communities" of professionals inside and outside the Bank; but not wholly insulated. To say otherwise is to deny that the Bank is subject to the Chinese proverb, "Officials make the figures, and the figures make the officials;" or to Goodhart's law, which states that an indicator's measurement will be distorted if it is used as a target. (Charles Goodhart was thinking of monetary policy, but the point also applies to variables used to make overall evaluations of the performance of multilateral economic organizations.) To say otherwise is equally to deny that the Bank is affected by the same pressures as the Fund, about which a former Fund official said, "The managing director makes the big decisions, and the staff then puts together the numbers to justify them." [63] But little is known about the balance between autonomy and compliance in the two organizations, or the latitude of their statisticians to adjust the country numbers provided by colleagues elsewhere in the organization which they believe to be fiddled (as in the China case, above). [64]

Some of the Bank's statistics are also provided by independent sources, which provide a check. Others, including the poverty numbers, are produced only by the Bank, and these are more subject to Goodhart's law. The Bank should appoint an independent auditor to verify its main development statistics or cede the work to an independent agency, perhaps under UN auspices (but if done by, say, UNCTAD, the opposite bias might be introduced). And it would help if the Bank's figures on poverty and inequality made clearer than they do the possible biases and the likely margins of error.

All this, of course, only takes us to the starting point of an enquiry into the causes of the probable poverty and inequality trends, [65] their likely consequences, and public policy responses; but at least we are now ready to ask the right questions. Above all, we have to go back to a distinction that has all but dropped out of development studies, between increasing returns and decreasing returns or, more generally, between positive and negative feedback mechanisms. The central question is why, at the level of the whole, the increasing returns of the Matthew effect—"To him who hath shall be given"—continues to dominate decreasing returns in the third wave of globalization.

NOTES

1. Gowan (1999).

2. Mazur (2000).

3. Wolf (2000).

4. International Monetary Fund (2003). The trend is, however, highly sensitive to the dollar's strong depreci-

ation in the 1970s and appreciation in the 1990s. When this is allowed for, the world growth rate may be closer to trendless.

5. In more concrete terms the number of hours of work it took for an entry-level adult male employee of McDonalds to earn the equivalent of one BigMac around 2000 ranged from: Holland/Australia/NZ/UK/US,

0.26–0.53 h; Hong Kong, 0.68 h; Malaysia/South Korea, 1.43–1.46 h; Philippines/Thailand, 2.32–2.2.66 h; China, 3.96 h; India, 8 h.

6. Purchasing power parity is a method of adjusting relative incomes in different countries to take account of the fact that market exchange rates do not accurately reflect purchasing power—as in the common observation that poor Americans feel rich in India and rich Indians feel poor in the United States.

7. The WIDER data set marries consumption from household surveys with consumption from national income accounts, and makes an allowance for (nonpublic sector) nonpriced goods and services.

8. World Bank (2002a) and World Bank (2002b, p. 30).

9. Wolfensohn (2001).

10. World Bank (2001b, p. 3). The $1 a day is measured in purchasing power parity. See also World Bank (2002c).

11. I am indebted to Sanjay Reddy for discussions about the Bank's poverty numbers (Reddy & Pogge, 2003a). See also Ravallion (2003), and Reddy and Pogge (2003b). In this paper I do not consider the additional problems that arise when estimating the impact of economic growth on poverty. See Deaton (2003).

12. The Bank also calculates a poverty headcount with $2/day, which suffers from the same limitations as the $1/day line.

13. Reported in Deaton (2001).

14. See Reddy and Pogge (2003a).

15. Also "[Since 1980] the most rapid growth has occurred in poor locations. Consequently the number of poor has declined by 200 million since 1980" (Dollar & Kraay, 2002, p. 125).

16. The new results were published in World Development Report 2000/2001 (World Bank, 2001a).

17. Deaton (2001, p. 128).

18. I take this example from Pogge and Reddy (2003).

19. The 25–40% figure is Reddy and Pogge's estimate, the range reflecting calculations based on PPP conver-

sion factors for 1985 and 1993, and for "all-food" and "bread-and-cereals" indices.

20. Also, Bolivia's extreme poverty rate according to the World Bank line was 11%, according to the ECLA line, 23%; Chile, 4%, 8%; Colombia, 11%, 24%; Mexico, 18%, 21% (ECLA, 2001, p. 51).

21. Reddy and Pogge (2003a).

22. This effect is amplified by the widespread removal of price controls on "necessities" and the lowering of tariffs on luxuries.

23. Gopinath (2002).

24. See Wade (2002a). It uses Stiglitz's firing and Kanbur's resignation to illuminate the US role in the Bank's generation of knowledge.

25. Meltzer Commission (2000). Meltzer later described the drop in the proportion of the world's population in poverty from 28% in 1987 to 24% in 1998 as a "modest" decline, the better to hammer the Bank (Meltzer, 2001).

26. World Bank (2002c). See Deaton (2002).

27. Dollar was ascendant not in terms of bureaucratic position but in terms of epistemic influence, as seen in the Human Resource department's use of him as a "metric" for judging the stature of other economists. When reporters started contacting the Bank to ask why it was saying different things about the poverty numbers—specifically why two papers on the Development Research Complex's web site gave different pictures of the trends—the response was not, "We are a research complex, we let 100 flowers bloom," but rather an assertion of central control. Chief economist Nick Stern gave one manager "special responsibility" for making sure the Bank's poverty numbers were all "coherent" (Stern to research managers, email, April 4, 2002).

28. Non-World Bank champions of the idea that globalization improves global income distribution include Martin Wolf of The Financial Times (Wolf, 2002b; source of the epigraph; Wolf, 2000, 2001a, 2001b); also Giddens, described by some as a leading social theorist of his generation (2002, p. 72), and Ian Castles, former Australian Statistician, who claims that "most studies suggest that the past 25 years have seen a reversal in the trend towards widening global inequalities which had been proceeding for two centuries" (Castles, 2001).

29. In addition to the studies referenced elsewhere I draw on: Firebaugh (1999), Jones (1997), Pritchett (1997), Quah (1997), UNDP (1999), Kanbur (2002), Korzeniewicz and Moran (1997, 2000).

30. A reviewer comments, "The idea of using market exchange rates to calculate international inequality is unbelievably stupid, and it is amazing that it still makes an appearance here. The UN had a commission of enquiry on this, which concluded unambiguously that using market exchange rates was wrong." But the World Bank continues to use market exchange rates, adjusted by the "Atlas" methodology, to calculate the per capita incomes that it then uses to rank countries by their degree of development; and hence as a criterion for its lending decisions. Member countries' voting shares in the Bank are based largely on their Fund quotas, which in turn are based largely on relative GDP at market exchange rates. So the Bank's practice does imply that it thinks that relative per capita incomes calculated through market exchange rates are meaningful proxies for well-being (and the practice has the benefit of holding down the voting share of developing countries). Moreover, as the text explains, incomes converted at market exchange rates do give meaningful measures of *international* purchasing power. Businesses making exporting and FDI decisions (auto makers, for example) pay more attention to relative incomes at market exchange rates than to PPP incomes.

31. Dikhanov and Ward (2003).

32. Milanovic (2002b).

33. ECLA (2002, p. 85). The dispersion of per capita GDP/PPP is measured as the average logarithmic deviation, the dispersion of growth rates as the standard deviation.

34. In an earlier debate with Martin Wolf I wrongly said that the result depends on both China and India. Wolf commented, "Here you argue that if we exclude China and India, there is no obvious trend in inequality. But why would one want to exclude two countries that contained about 60% of the world's poorest people two decades ago and still contain almost 40% of the world's population today? To fail to give these giants their due weight in a discussion of global poverty alleviation or income distribution would be Hamlet without the princ." (Wolf, 2002a). This misconstrues my argument.

35. Dowrick and Akmal (2001). They find that world inequality increased over 1980–93 using Gini, Theil, coefficient of variation, and the variance of log income.

36. Milanovic's (2002a) preliminary analysis of 1998 data and an associated reworking of 1988 and 1993 data has produced the following Gini coefficients (and standard deviations): 1988: 61.9 (1.8), 1993: 65.2 (1.8), 1998: 64.2 (1.9). The trend for the Theil coefficient is similar (personal communication, June 9, 2003). Sala-i-Martin (2002) finds a drop in both extreme poverty and inequality. His findings have been rejected in Milanovic (2002c) and Nye and Reddy (2003).

37. Dikhanov and Ward (2003).

38. See the work of James Galbraith and collaborators in the University of Texas Inequality Project, http://utip.gov.utexas.edu. Also, Galbraith (2002).

39. This is the answer to a reviewer's remark, "The work of Galbraith and his collaborators at Texas is essentially worthless for the purposes currently being discussed. We are interested in people's command over resources, not the earnings of people in work in the formal sector. The latter is transparently irrelevant in most of the poor countries of the world, including India and China."

40. See Kynge (2002) and Rawski (2002). As another example from Rawski's analysis, Chinese government figures show total real GDP growth of 25% during 1997–2000, whereas energy consumption figures show a drop of 13% (not all of which is likely to be due to replacement of inefficient coal-fired furnaces.) Rawski estimates the growth rate since 2000 has been about half the official rate. See further Waldron (2002).

41. World Bank sources who request anonymity. During negotiations for China's joining the WTO Chinese economists argued against the insistence of the United States and other rich countries that its average income be expressed in terms of purchasing power party—and hence that China should be under the same obligations as "middle-income" countries, tougher than those on "low-income" countries. This is another example of the politics of statistics.

42. In addition, taking account of even just the obviously big and roughly measurable environmental costs lowers China's official GDP by roughly 8%, India's, by 5%. See Hommann and Brandon (1995).

43. Evidence for rising inequality in India over the past two decades is set out in Jha (2000). Deaton agrees that inequality in India has been increasing "in recent years," and that consumption by the poor did not rise as fast as average consumption (Deaton, 2002).

IS GLOBALIZATION REDUCING POVERTY AND INEQUALITY?   587

44. Some sources give ratios of 7:1 in the early 1990s to 11:1 in the late 1990s. But these figures take Shanghai as the richest province. With Shanghai province = city as the numerator the ratio reflects not only regional disparity but also rural-urban disparity, and more specifically, the growth of a new Hong Kong within China (one whose average income is exaggerated because nonpermanent residents are not included in its population). For these points I thank Andrew Fischer, PhD candidate, Development Studies Institute, LSE.

45. Krugman (2002).

46. Babones (2002).

47. Dikhanov and Ward (2003).

48. World Bank (2002c).

49. In this Section I draw on the arguments of Rodrik (1999, 2001).

50. Besley (2002). Besley uses indicators such as press freedom, democratic accountability, corruption, civil rights.

51. Cf. "As they reformed and integrated with the world market, the 'more globalized' developing countries started to growth rapidly, accelerating steadily from 2.9% in the 1970s to 5% through the 1990s" (World Bank, 2002c, p. 36, emphasis added).

52. Rodrik (1999).

53. Wade (2003a [1990]).

54. Milanovic (2002b). Milanovic finds that in countries below the average income of about $PPP 5,000, higher levels of openness (imports plus exports/GDP) are associated with lower income shares of the bottom 80% of the population.

55. Quoted in George (1997).

56. Besley and Burgess (2003).

57. Lee and Bankston (1999), Hsieh and Pugh (1993), Fajnzylber, Lederman, and Loayza (1998) and Freeman (1996).

58. Demeny (2003).

59. Wade (2003b, 2003c).

60. Kapur (2002).

61. For a good example of a heterodox book from a corner of the UN system, see UNDP (2003). The WTO lobbied to prevent its publication.

62. Wade (2003d).

63. Gopinath (1999).

64. Key experts in the relevant statistical unit thought that colleagues had fiddled the China income numbers reported in Table 4, but their boss ignored their objections.

65. For discussion of causes see Wade (2002b, in press).

REFERENCES

Arrighi, G., Silver, B., & Brewer, B. (2003). Industrial convergence, globalization and the persistence of the North–South divide. *Studies in Comparative International Development, 38*(1), 3–31.

Babones, S. (2002). The structure of the world-economy, 1960–1999. In *97th annual meeting of the American Sociological Association*, Chicago.

Besley, T. (2002). Globalization and the quality of government. Manuscript, Economics Department, London School of Economics, March.

Besley, T., & Burgess, R. (2003). Halving world poverty. *Journal of Economic Perspectives, 17*(3), 3–22.

Castles, I. (2001). *Letter to The Economist*, May 26.

Deaton, A. (2001). Counting the world's poor: problems and possible solutions. *The World Bank Research Observer, 16*(2), 125–147.

Deaton, A. (2002). Is world poverty falling? *Finance and Development, 39*(2), 34. Available: http://www.imf.org/external/pubs/ft/fandd/2002/06/deaton.htm.

Deaton, A. (2003). Measuring poverty in a growing world (or measuring growth in a poor world). NBER Working Paper 9822. http://d.repec.org/n?u = Re-PEc:nbr:nberwo:9822&r = dev.

Demeny, P. (2003). Population policy dilemmas in Europe at the dawn of the twenty-first century. *Population and Development Review, 29*(1), 1–28.

Dikhanov, Y., & Ward, M. (2003). Evolution of the global distribution of income in 1970–99. In *Proceedings of the Global Poverty Workshop*, Initiative for Policy Dialogue, Columbia University. Available: http://www-1.gsb.Columbia.edu/ipd/povertywk.html.

Dollar, D., & Kraay, A. (2002). Spreading the wealth. *Foreign Affairs* (January/February), 120–133.

Dowrick, S., & Akmal, M. (2001). Explaining contradictory trends in global income inequality: a tale of two biasses. Faculty of Economics and Commerce, Australia National University, March 29. Available: http://ecocomm.anu.edu.au/people/info.asp?Surname = Dowrick&Firstname = Steve.

ECLA (2001). *Panorama social de America Latina 2000– 01*, ECLA (CEPAL), Santiago.

ECLA (2002). *Globalization and development*. ECLA, Santiago.

Fajnzylber, P., Lederman, D., & Loayza, N. (1998). What causes violent crime? Typescript, Office of the Chief Economist, Latin America and the Caribbean Region. World Bank, Washington, DC.

Firebaugh, G. (1999). Empirics of world income inequality. *American Journal of Sociology, 104*(6), 1597–1630.

Freeman, R. (1996). Why do so many young American men commit crimes and what might we do about it? *Journal of Economic Perspectives, 10*(1), 25–42.

Galbraith, J. K. (2002). A perfect crime: inequality in the age of globalization. *Daedalus* (Winter), 11–25.

George, S. (1997). How to win the war of ideas: lessons from the Gramscian right. *Dissent, 44*(3), 47–53.

Giddens, A. (2002). *Where now for new labour*. Cambridge: Polity Press.

Gopinath, D. (1999). Slouching toward a new consensus. *Institutional Investor, 1*(September), 79–87.

Gopinath, D. (2002). Poor choices. *Institutional Investor*, September 1, 41–50.

Gowan, P. (1999). *The global gamble*. London: Verso.

Hommann, K., & Brandon, C. (1995). The cost of inaction: valuing the economy-wide cost of environmental degradation in India. In *Modelling global sustainability conference*. United Nations University, Tokyo.

Hsieh, C. C., & Pugh, M. (1993). Poverty, income inequality, and violent crime: a meta-analysis of recent aggregate data studies. *Criminal Justice Review, 18*, 182–202.

International Monetary Fund (2003). *World economic outlook*. Database IMF, Washington, DC, April.

Jha, R. (2000). Reducing poverty and inequality in India: has liberalization helped? Available: http://www.wider.unu.edu/research/1998-1999-3.1.publications.htm.

Jones, C. (1997). On the evolution of world income distribution. *Journal of Economic Perspectives, 11*(3), 19–36.

Kanbur, R. (2002). Conceptual challenges in poverty and inequality: one development economist's perspective, WP2002-09, Dept. of Applied Economics, Cornell University, Ithaca, NY.

Kapur, D. (2002). The changing anatomy of governance of the World Bank. In J. Pincus & J. Winters (Eds.), *Reinventing the World Bank* (pp. 54–75). Ithaca, NY: Cornell University Press.

Korzeniewicz, R., & Moran, T. (1997). World-economic trends in the distribution of income, 1965–1992. *American Journal of Sociology, 102*(4), 1000–1039.

Korzeniewicz, R., & Moran, T. (2000). Measuring world income inequalities. *American Journal of Sociology, 106*(1), 209–214.

Krugman, P. (2002). For richer. *New York Times*, October 20.

Kynge, J. (2002). Pyramid of power behind numbers game. *Financial Times*, February 27.

Lee, M. R., & Bankston, W. (1999). Political structure, economic inequality, and homicide: a cross-sectional analysis. *Deviant Behavior: an Interdisciplinary Journal, 19*, 27–55.

Mazur, J. (2000). Labor's new internationalism. *Foreign Affairs, 79*(January/February), 79–93.

Meltzer, A. (2001). The World Bank one year after the Commission's report to Congress. In *Hearings before the Joint Economic Committee*, US Congress, March 8.

Meltzer Commission (United States Congressional Advisory Commission on International Financial Institutions) (2000). Report to the US Congress on the International Financial Institutions. Available: http://www.house/gov/jec/imf/ifiac.

Milanovic, B. (2002a). True world income distribution, 1988 and 1993. first calculations based on household surveys alone. *Economic Journal, 112*(476), 51–92.

Milanovic, B. (2002b). Can we discern the effect of globalization on income distribution? Evidence from household budget surveys. World Bank Policy Research Working Papers 2876. Available: http://econ.worldbank.org.

Milanovic, B. (2002c). The Ricardian vice: why Sala-i-Martin's calculations are wrong. Typescript, Development Research Group, World Bank. Available: www.ssrn.com.

Nye, H., & Reddy, S. (2003). Weaknesses of recent global poverty estimates: Xavier Sala-i-Martin and Surjit Bhalla. Available: www.socialanalysis.org.

Pogge, T., & Reddy, S. (2003). Unknown: the extent, distribution, and trend of global income poverty. Available: http://www.socialanalysis.org.

Pritchett, L. (1997). Divergence: big time. *Journal of Economic Perspectives, 11*(3), 3–17.

Quah, D. (1997). Empirics for growth and distribution: stratification, polarization, and convergence clubs. *Journal of Economic Growth, 2*(1), 27–57.

Rawski, T. (2002). Measuring China's recent GDP growth: where do we stand? Available: http://www.pitt.edu/~tgrawski.

Reddy, S., & Pogge, T. (2003a). How not to count the poor. Available: http://www.socialanalysis.org.

Reddy, S., & Pogge, T. (2003b). Reply to Ravallion. Available: http://www.socialanalysis.org.

Ravallion, M. (2003). Reply to Reddy and Pogge. Available: http://www.socialanalysis.org.

Rodrik, D. (1999). The new global economy and developing countries: making openness work. In *Policy Essay 24, Overseas Development Council*. Baltimore: Johns Hopkins University Press.

Rodrik, D. (2001). Trading in illusions. *Foreign Policy, 123*(March/April), 55–62.

Sala-i-Martin, X. (2002). The disturbing 'rise' in global income inequality. NBER Working Paper 8904,

April. Available: http://papers.nber.org/papers/w8904.

UNDP (1999). *Human development report 1999*. New York: United Nations.

UNDP (2003). *Making global trade work for people*. London: Earthscan.

Wade, R. H. (2002a). US hegemony and the World Bank: The fight over people and ideas. *Review of International Political Economy, 9*(2), 201–229.

Wade, R. H. (2002b). Globalisation, poverty and income distribution: does the liberal argument hold. In *Globalisation, Living Standards and Inequality: Recent Progress and Continuing Challenges* (pp. 37–65). Sydney: Reserve Bank of Australia.

Wade, R. H. (2003a [1990]). *Governing the market*. Princeton, NJ: Princeton University Press.

Wade, R. H. (2003b). The invisible hand of the American empire. *Ethics and International Affairs, 17*(2), 77–88.

Wade, R. H. (2003c). What strategies are viable for developing countries today. The WTO and the shrinking of development space. *Review of International Political Economy, 10*(4), 621–644.

Wade, R. H. (2003d). The World Bank and its critics: the dynamics of hypocrisy. *Studies in Comparative International Development*, in press.

Wade, R. H. (2004). On the causes of increasing world poverty and inequality, or why the Matthew Effect prevails. *New Political Economy, 9*(2).

Waldron, A. (2002). China's disguised failure: statistics can no longer hide the need for Beijing to instigate painful structural reforms. Financial Times, July 4.

Wolf, M. (2000). The big lie of global inequality. *Financial Times*, February 8.

Wolf, M. (2001a). Growth makes the poor richer: reversing the effects of globalization might increase equality as the critics claim, but it would be an equality of destitution. *Financial Times*, January 24.

Wolf, M. (2001b). A stepping stone from poverty. *Financial Times*, December 19.

Wolf, M. (2002a). Are global poverty and inequality getting worse? Yes: Robert Wade, No: Martin Wolf. *Prospect* (March), 16–21.

Wolf, M. (2002b). Doing more harm than good. *Financial Times*, May 8.

Wolfensohn, J. (2001). Responding to the challenges of globalization: Remarks to the G-20 finance ministers and central governors. Ottawa, November 17.

World Bank (1999). *World development indicators 1999*. Washington, DC: The World Bank.

World Bank (2000). *World development indicators 2000*. Washington, DC: The World Bank.

World Bank (2001a). *World development report 2000/2001, Attacking Poverty*. New York: Oxford University Press.

World Bank (2001b). *World development indicators 2001*. Washington, DC: The World Bank.

World Bank (2002a). *World development indicators 2002*. Washington, DC: The World Bank.

World Bank (2002b). *Global economic prospects and the developing countries 2002: making trade work for the world's poor*. Washington, DC: The World Bank.

World Bank (2002c). *Globalization, growth, and poverty: building an inclusive world economy*. New York: Oxford University Press.

[6]

New Political Economy, Vol. 9, No. 2, June 2004

Carfax Publishing
Taylor & Francis Group

On the Causes of Increasing World Poverty and Inequality, or Why the Matthew Effect Prevails

ROBERT HUNTER WADE

In the 1870s the American economist Henry George remarked that 'the association of poverty with progress is the great enigma of our times'. Today the enigma is well on the way to being solved. World poverty and income inequality have both fallen during the past 20 years, thanks in large part to the third great wave of 'globalisation' (rising economic openness and integration of national economies).[1] This, at least, is the claim of the neoliberal argument, which supports the optimism about globalisation that emanates from the pages of the World Bank, the International Monetary Fund (IMF), the World Trade Organization (WTO), *The Financial Times, The Economist* and other organs of 'thinking for the world'.

For example, the World Bank says that the number of people in extreme poverty (living on an income of less than US$1 a day in purchasing-power-parity [PPP] terms) has fallen in the past two decades for the first time in more than 150 years, from 1.4 billion in 1980 to 1.2 billion in 1998.[2] No ifs or buts. Or, in another version, the Bank says that 'the long trend of rising global inequality and rising numbers of people in absolute poverty has been halted and even reversed [since around 1980]'.[3] This reversal of the long trend is the 'net effect', says the Bank, of surging globalisation; as shown by the fact that the big falls in poverty and inequality—sufficient to reverse the long global trend—have occurred in the 'new globalisers', that is, countries that had the biggest increases in trade to Gross Domestic Product (GDP) in 1977–97 (the top one third in a sample of developing countries ranked by trade/GDP increase). The 'non-globalisers' (the countries in the bottom two thirds of the ranking) make little or no contribution to the reversal of trend.

The empirical evidence thus confirms the neoliberal predictions that openness is good and more openness is better, both at the level of the world economy and at the level of national economies. Those who oppose further liberalisation (including trade unions, sections of business) must be acting—wittingly or unwittingly—out of 'vested interests' or 'rent seeking', and the few marginal academics who argue against simply do not understand the theory. Those who

Robert Hunter Wade, Development Studies Institute, London School of Economics and Political Science, Houghton Street, London WC2A 2AE, UK.

ISSN 1356-3467 print; ISSN 1469-9923 online/04/020163-26 © 2004 Taylor & Francis Ltd
DOI: 10.1080/1356346042000218050

care for the general interest of nations, the world, and especially the poor, should ignore them. The mandates of the international financial institutions (including the IMF, the World Bank and the WTO) should continue to centre on the drive to liberalise markets and keep them free of restrictions (subject to environmental sustainability and protection of vulnerable groups like indigenous peoples); and they should receive public support provided that they stick to this agenda (though some neoliberals still regard them as 'socialist' and in need of shrinking or even closing down).

The underlying theory rests on the notion of comparative advantage—that in an open economy resources will move to their most efficient uses. It further assumes that decreasing returns prevail, that beyond a certain point additional inputs yield decreasing marginal returns. So, when a high cost, high wage, high saving economy (A) interacts through free markets with a low cost, low wage, low saving economy (B), capital tends to move from A to B in search of higher returns, and labour from B to A. This is good for 'world' poverty and inequality.

In a previous essay I argued that world poverty—the number of people living in extreme poverty, known as the poverty headcount—may be increasing; and that world income inequality may also be increasing.[4] This strikes at the heart of the neoliberal argument. It suggests that Henry George's enigma may be deepening; or, in more analytic terms, that at the level of world economy as a whole increasing returns in income generation—the positive feedback of the Matthew effect, 'To him that hath shall be given'—prevails over diminishing returns, despite the third wave of globalisation. For economics this is very bad news.

Leading theorist John Hicks considered introducing an assumption of increasing returns into economic theory in the late 1930s and drew back in alarm. 'It must be remembered that the threatened wreckage is that of the greater part of general equilibrium theory', he warned, because 'unless we can suppose ... that marginal costs generally increase with output at the point of equilibrium ... the basis on which economic laws can be constructed is shorn away'.[5] The need for determinate mathematical solutions bent economics—as the aspiring universal science of human behaviour—away from the study of increasing returns, not for any reason to do with the real world but because increasing returns are difficult to treat mathematically. But the framework thus constructed also bolstered economists' normative faith in free markets and distrust of the state. Now this evidence on poverty and inequality—and quite a lot of other evidence as well—challenges the normative faith as well as the conceptual apparatus.

Having indicated what is at stake I now summarise the earlier findings about levels and trends and then go on to talk about some of the bulldozer (not scalpel) causes.

World poverty and inequality

To get an overview of what we are talking about, consider Figure 1. It shows the distribution of the world's population by the average income of the country in which they live. It shows incomes measured at purchasing power parity and divides India and China into rural and urban sectors. We want to know the

164

Increasing World Poverty and Inequality

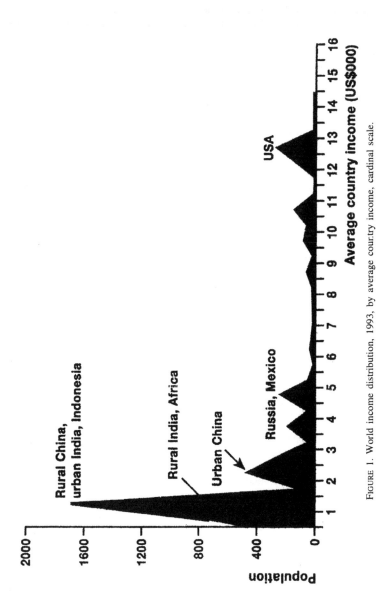

FIGURE 1. World income distribution, 1993, by average country income, cardinal scale.

Source: Branko Milanovic, 'True World Income Distribution, 1988 and 1993: First Calculations Based on Household Surveys Alone', *Economic Journal*, Vol 112, No. 476 (2002), pp. 51–92.

number of people living in extreme poverty and its trend, and the degree of inequality of income distribution and its trend.

On poverty the strong conclusion is that we must be agnostic about the poverty headcount—level and trend—because deficiencies in current statistics make for a large margin of error. The less strong conclusion is that the poverty numbers are higher than the Bank says, and the numbers have risen over the past two decades. On the other hand, it is plausible that the *proportion* of the world's population in extreme poverty has fallen in the past two decades. The margin of error would have to be huge for this not to have happened.

On income distribution the strong conclusion is that the only valid short answer to the question, 'What is the trend of world income distribution?', is: 'It depends'. It depends on the particular combination of measures, samples and data sets—for example, on the choice between (1) incomes measured at market exchange rates or in terms of PPP; (2) inequality measured in terms of average country incomes ('between-country' distribution) or in terms of both between-country and within-country distributions (that is, the distribution between all individuals or households in the world regardless of where they live); (3) countries weighted equally or by population; (4) inequality measured as an average across the distribution (such as the Gini coefficient) or as a ratio of top to bottom (such as top decile to bottom decile, or 'core' zone to 'peripheral' zone); and (5) national income distribution calculated from household surveys or national income accounts. There is no single 'best' combination. At least 10 combinations are plausible, and they yield different conclusions about magnitudes and trends.

One combination does indeed yield the neoliberal answer. It uses (1) PPP incomes, (2) average GDP, (3) countries weighted by population and (4) Gini or other average coefficient. World income inequality measured in this way very likely fell in 1980–2000.

There are just two problems. First, take out China and the falling disappears; take out India as well and the trend is clearly increasing. Hence falling inequality is not a generalised feature of the world economy in the third (post-1980) wave of globalisation, even using the most favourable combination. Second, this combination is not interesting because it ignores trends in distribution within countries. We would not be interested in a statement about US income distribution based on average state income weighted by state population if we had data on individuals or households.

From hereon the neoliberal argument fares even worse. World inequality is certainly increasing—fast—when incomes are measured in current exchange rates. But most economists say that this is irrelevant, because incomes should always be measured at purchasing power parity, not at market exchange rates. This is true in principle if we are interested in income as a proxy for well-being, though the margins of error in current measures of PPP-incomes (especially for China, India and the former Soviet Union before 1990) are probably not much less than those in market exchange rate-incomes. But we are often interested in income as a proxy for international purchasing power, because this is more relevant than PPP for measuring relative impacts of one part of the world on others, including the ability of one set of people (for example, in a developing country) to import, to borrow, to repay loans, and also to participate in international rule-making fora. The difficulty that developing country governments face in staffing offices in the rule-making centres and in hiring consultants and lawyers to advise them in international negotiations is directly related to the widening of inequality in market-exchange-rate terms, because they must pay in US dollars bought at current market exchange rates, not PPP-adjusted US dollars. Creditors have not been lining up to accept debt repayment in PPP-adjusted dollars.

Income inequality is also increasing when PPP-adjusted inequality is measured in terms of ratios of richer to poorer income deciles, which captures the idea of polarisation better than the Gini or some other average. The several other plausible combinations of measures yield more ambiguous results, more contingent on things like the time period and the countries included in the sample. But several recent studies, using different methodologies, different samples, different time periods, do find that world income inequality has risen in the period since the early 1980s.[6]

It is therefore disingenuous to say, *tout court*, that world income distribution has become more equal in the third wave of globalisation. More likely, a rising proportion of the world's population is living at the ends of the world income distribution and a rising share of the world's income is going to those at the top (see Figure 2). Most of the population of China and India are still at purchasing-power-parity incomes that put them in the bottom third, not the middle, of the distribution.

However, the whole discussion about inequality misleads by considering only relative incomes. Absolute income gaps between the West and the rest are widening even in the case of the fast growing countries like China and India, and are likely to go on widening for another half century. No one disputes this, but it is treated as a fact of no significance.

Country mobility

If we tip Figure 1 on its side to put income on the vertical axis we are led to wonder about forces in the world economy analogous to gravity and electromagnetic levitation, the first keeping the great mass of the world's population from rising up the income scale, the second keeping the 15 per cent in the states of the core from falling.

Studies of country mobility suggest that the rate of mobility up and down the scale is rather low. One study took the real Gross National Product (GNP) per capita of 100 countries between 1960 and 1999 and found a robustly trimodal distribution of world population against the log of GNP per capita.[7] The three income zones might be taken as empirical correlates of the conceptual zones of core, semi-periphery and periphery. Seventy-two of the countries remained in the same income zone over the whole period sampled at five yearly intervals (for example, Australia remained in zone one, Brazil in zone two, Bolivia in zone three). The remaining 28 countries moved at least once from one zone to another (for example, Argentina from one to two). No country moved more than one zone. (South Korea, Hong Kong and Singapore in 1960 were already in the

Robert Hunter Wade

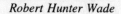

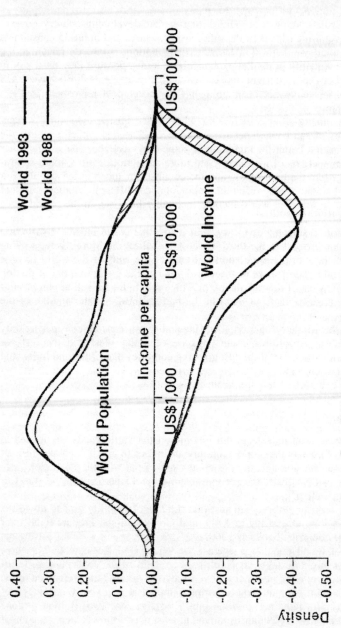

FIGURE 2. World income distribution, 1988, 1993, log scale.

Source: Based on Milanovic, 'True World Income Distribution'. *Note*: Includes between-country and within-country distributions; incomes measured at PPP, on log scale. Shaded areas indicate rising share of world population at the top end and the bottom end between 1988 and 1993 (top half), and rising share of world income accruing to people at the top end (bottom half).

Increasing World Poverty and Inequality

middle, not low zone.) There are about as many cases of upwards movement as downwards.

Fourteen countries had 'stable' moves in the sense that their position in 1990 and 1999 was one zone above or below their position in 1960 and 1965. Greece moved stably up from two to one, Argentina moved stably down from one to two, El Salvador moved stably down from two to three. As many countries moved stably up as down. When more than 80 per cent of countries ended the twentieth century in the same zone as they were in 40 years before, country immobility is the predominant fact. Unless one supposes, improbably, that country economic policies remained unchanged in the non-mobile countries, were 'good' in the countries that went up and 'bad' in the countries that went down, this suggests that forces other than good or bad policies had a powerful effect on country position and change in position.

The globalisation hypothesis

The neoliberal argument says that 'openness is a necessary—though not sufficient—part of modern economic growth', and that 'more open' economies perform better than 'less open'. The World Bank recently restated this argument in *Globalisation, Growth and Poverty: Building an Inclusive World Economy.*[8] Globalisation in the form of increasing openness of national economies to movements of goods, services, capital and skilled labour has been reducing world poverty and inequality, it says.

The obvious critique is that it is probably explaining the wrong trends. But, in addition, it loses credibility by measuring globalisation as the change in trade/GDP, irrespective of level. It ranks a sample of countries by the increases in trade/GDP over 1977–98; calls the top one third 'more globalised' or 'globalisers' or 'open', and the bottom two thirds 'less globalised' or 'non-globalisers'; calculates the economic performance of the two groups; finds that the former does better than the latter on several measures; and then concludes that liberalisation of trade policy drives the increase in trade/GDP and increase in trade/GDP drives better economic performance. 'Thus, globalisation clearly can be a force for poverty reduction', it says.[9]

The problems come together in the case of China and India. China and India have experienced relatively good economic growth performance over the past one (India) or two (China) decades, and their population size ensures that the world results are much affected by how they are classified. The Bank study classes them as 'more globalised' because they have experienced relatively fast increase in trade/GDP over 1977–98, and suggests that their relatively good economic performance, and that of the other globalisers, is due in large part to their fast increase in trade/GDP—though it adds that other 'reforms' (to strengthen property rights, rule of law and macroeconomic stability) also helped. 'As they reformed and integrated with the world market, the "more globalised" developing countries *started to grow rapidly*, accelerating steadily from 2.9 per cent in the 1970s to 5 per cent through the 1990s.'[10] The fact that China and India continued to have substantial trade protection and capital controls, and other market restrictions that run against the neoliberal economic policy pre-

169

Robert Hunter Wade

TABLE 1. Trade-dependent non-globalisers and less-trade-dependent globalisers

	Exports/GDP			GNP Annual Average Rate of Growth 1988–99 (%)
	1990	1999	% change	
Non-globalisers				
Honduras	36	42	17	− 1.2
Kenya	26	25	− 0.04	0.5
Globalisers				
India	7	11	57	6.9
Bangladesh	6	14	133	3.3

Source: World Bank, *World Development Report 2000/01*, Tables 1 and 13. The classification of countries comes from World Bank, *World Development Indicators* (World Bank, 2002).

scription of the World Bank, is glossed. All the attention is directed at the liberalisation, as though only the liberalisation could have helped their growth, not the remaining protection and other market restrictions, even though they both began to grow fast well before they undertook much trade liberalisation.

On the other hand, many economies that are very poor, slow growing, very open, with high trade/GDP are put in the category of 'non-globalisers', because their rate of increase over the past two decades was relatively low. This audacious use of language ensures that the 'non-globalisers' have worse performance than the 'globalisers'—including countries that remain relatively closed in terms of both restrictive trade policy and low trade/GDP.

Table 1 illustrates the problem. The two 'globaliser' countries have low exports/GDP but high growth; the two 'non-globaliser' countries have high exports/GDP but low growth.

When trade is used as a proxy for globalisation we should separate out the effect of country size on trade/GDP levels from other factors determining trade/GDP, including trade policies, because the single best predictor of trade/GDP is country size (population and area). We should make a clear distinction between statements about (1) levels of trade, (2) changes in levels, (3) restrictiveness or openness of trade policy, (4) changes in restrictiveness of policy and (5) the content of trade—whether a narrow range of commodity exports in return for a broad range of consumption imports, or a diverse range of exports (some of them replaced imports) in return for a diverse range of imports (some of them producer goods to assist further import replacement).

The problem, though, is not just 'increase in trade/GDP' as the measure; it is also the inattention to things other than trade. What about people flows, ideas flows? Imagine an economy with no foreign trade but high levels of inwards and outwards migration and a well-developed diaspora network. In a real sense this would be an open or globalised economy, though not classified as such. And what about the impact of the current, post-Bretton Woods framework or regime of the world economy, or what Gowan describes as the 'Dollar-Wall Street regime'; namely, the dominance of a debt money (rather than an asset money), the US dollar, and the dominance of private (rather than public) international financial markets centred on the USA?[11] Globalisation in this particular framework may have different effects than globalisation in an alternative framework.[12]

Structure and agency in global inequality

The development economics and modernisation theory of the 1950s to the 1970s would point to failure to industrialise as the likely cause of negative trends, on the assumption that (market-friendly) industrialisation is the vehicle to carry developing countries close to the prosperity of the developed world.

No. Taking manufacturing's share of GDP or of employment we find a remarkable convergence—developing countries as a group now have a bigger share than developed countries.[13] But each additional increment of manufacturing in developing countries is yielding less income over time. This is not what one would expect if manufacturing in developing countries was embedded in a dynamic capitalism. The failure of this prediction may help to explain why industrialisation has disappeared to the margins of the 'international community's' development agenda. The World Bank scarcely mentions it. In the Bank's eyes, development is about poverty alleviation, market access, good governance and environmental protection, not about capitalist industrialisation as such.

If failure to industrialise is not the culprit, what other factors might explain rising income inequality? A large part of the answer must relate to the determinants of the world location of qualitatively different activities (different in terms of their contribution to growth); in particular, the world location of activities subject to increasing returns and those subject to decreasing returns. We know that in the general case location patterns can be understood in terms of the relative strength of agglomeration and dispersion tendencies. We also know that there have indeed been powerful dispersion tendencies at work in 'manufacturing' as a whole; but that the dispersion has not yielded income convergence. To understand why, we must disaggregate the manufacturing value-chain and factor in the increasing dominance of finance in the advanced economies, and we also have to combine these 'structural' factors with considerations of 'agency'—the US 'primacy' strategy and certain design features of the architecture of the world economic order that came out of the strategy.

I consider the following: (1) 'sticky' locations for high value-added/increasing return activities; (2) decreasing returns in the middle levels of the manufacturing value chain; (3) continuing, perhaps even increasing, concentration of big multinational corporations on the markets of advanced economies; (4) financialisation of the advanced economies; (5) East Asia; (6) population growth; and (7) the US 'primacy' project and international regimes. With such a stretch the discussion is necessarily schematic. It is an overview on a cloudy day.

Sticky locations in increasing return activities

In the simple version of neoliberal theory, capital and technology move from high-income, high-cost zones to low-income, low-cost zones, and low-cost labour moves in the opposite direction. The result is convergence of factor

171

incomes, eventually. If this were the dominant trend in today's world—as dominant as in economic models—we should see falling poverty and inequality.

To understand the 'fact' of non-convergence—or uneven development, or failure of catch-up—we have to understand a general property of modern economic growth. Some kinds of economic activities and production methods have more positive effects on growth and productivity than others. They are activities rich in increasing returns (to scale, to agglomeration), in contrast to activities with decreasing returns. To oversimplify, increasing return activities are those characterised by falling marginal costs as output rises; they tend to have large unpriced 'spill over' benefits that can be captured by other firms in the locality (which therefore enjoy lower costs than otherwise); and they tend to yield higher value-added than diminishing return activities.

Countries and regions with higher proportions of increasing return activities enjoy higher levels of real incomes, in a virtuous circle; countries and regions with higher proportions of diminishing return activities have lower incomes, in a vicious circle. The central national-level development problem is to shift the resources of a national economy, at the margin, away from diminishing return activities and towards increasing return activities, away from the activities that Malthus wrote about and towards those that Schumpeter wrote about. As a first approximation, this means to shift resources out of agriculture and primary commodities and into manufacturing and related services (or into higher level processing of primary commodities).

To understand the paradox of substantial catch-up of developing countries as a group to developed country levels of manufacturing/GDP without a corresponding catch-up of income one has to start with the manufacturing value chain. The value chain is the sequence of operations that go to make final products, including research and development (R&D), design, procurement, manufacturing, assembly, distribution, advertising and sales. Thanks in part to the communications advances associated with globalisation, manufacturing value-chains have become spatially disarticulated, and value-added has 'migrated' to the two ends of the value chain—to R&D, design, distribution and advertising.[14] Activities within the value chain that are more subject to diminishing returns have been shifting to low wage zones while those more subject to increasing returns tend to stay at home.

In other words, the increasing returns/high value-added activities in manufacturing and in services continue to cluster in the high cost, high wage zone of the world economy, even when markets are working well (and not as a result of 'market imperfections'). German skilled workers cost more than 15 times to employ as Chinese skilled workers; yet Germany remains a powerful centre of manufacturing. Japanese skilled workers cost even more; yet Japan too remains a powerful centre of manufacturing, despite being only 700 km from Shanghai across the East China Sea.

Why, then, are locations sticky for the increasing return/high value-added activities? First, costs per unit of output may not be lower in the lower wage zone, because lower wages may be more than offset by lower productivity. In any case, the cost of employing people has fallen to a small proportion of total costs in automated assembly operations, often 10 per cent or less. As the

Increasing World Poverty and Inequality

technology content of many engineering products—such as vehicle parts and aircraft—becomes increasingly sophisticated, this raises the premium on the company keeping highly skilled workers to develop and manufacture these products; and one way to keep them is to pay them highly. The fact that wages are a small part of total costs means that higher wage payments do not have much effect on the net incentive to move to the low wage zone of the world economy.

Second, the 'capability' of a firm relative to its rivals (the maximum quality level it can achieve, and its cost of production) depends not only on the sum of the skills of its workforce, but also on the collective or firm-level knowledge and social organisation of its employees. In the case of increasing return/higher value-added activities much of this knowledge and social organisation is tacit, transferred mainly through face-to-face relationships—not transferred easily between people in different places in the form of machinery or (technical and organisational) blueprints.[15] The value of tacit knowledge typically increases as a share of total value even as the ratio of tacit to codified knowledge falls with computerisation. If a firm or plant were to move its increasing return activities to a lower wage zone and some of its employees were not mobile, the costs to the firm's capacity, including the loss of tacit knowledge, may outweigh the advantages of relocation.

Third, tacit knowledge transfer is bigger the shorter the physical and cultural distance; and some other forms of transactions costs fall in the same way. This is a powerful driver of spatial clustering in increasing return activities. Firms in a network of spatially concentrated input-output linkages can derive (unpriced) spill-over benefits from the presence of the other firms and supporting infrastructure. They all get access to nests of producers' goods and services, ranges of skills, people practised at adapting and innovating, and tacit knowledge—in short, to the external economies of human capital that are a major source of increasing returns to location in the high wage zone.[16] These spill-over benefits compound the tendency for any one firm not to move to a low wage zone, or to transplant only its low value added assembly activities by outsourcing or establishing subsidiaries while holding at home the core activities that depend on varied inputs, tacit knowledge, social contacts and closeness to consumers. Further, as skill shortages develop in the core and the supply of skilled people rises in the low wage zone, firms nowadays can remain rooted in the core because skilled people are increasingly crossing borders to find them.[17]

Firm immobility is reinforced by the fact that, for many products and services, quality and value added go up not continuously but in steps. (Ballbearings below a quality threshold are useless.) Getting to higher steps may require big investments, critical masses, targeted assistance from public entities, long-term supply contracts with multinational corporations seeking local suppliers. 'Normal' market processes—now fortified by WTO agreements that make many forms of industrial policy illegal[18]—can therefore prevent firms and countries in the low wage zone from transforming themselves into attractive sites for higher quality work.

The empirical significance of these effects is suggested by the fact that about two thirds of manufacturing output in the Organisation of Economic Cooperation and Development (OECD) is sold by one firm to another firm within the OECD. In addition, parent companies based in the OECD, especially in some of the biggest manufacturing sectors (including electronics and vehicles), have formed increasingly concentrated vertical production networks in which they put a rising proportion of routine manufacturing operations in lower tier suppliers in the low-wage zone, often locally-owned companies, while keeping control of the high value-added activities of proprietary technology, branding and marketing. They then use their market power and intense competition among the lower tier suppliers to extract more value-added from them. The lower tier suppliers are first to suffer in a recession.

This is not the end of the sticky location story. At the next round the greater wealth and variety of economic activities in the high wage zone—not to mention institutions that manage conflict and encourage risk-taking, such as legally guaranteed civil rights, social insurance, a legal system that supports limited liability, and socially more homogeneous populations—mean that the high wage zone can more readily absorb the Schumpeterian shocks from innovation and bankruptcies, as activity shifts from products and processes with more intense competition to those with less competition closer to the innovation end. There is less resistance to the 'creative destruction' of market processes, despite the fact that organising people to resist tends to be easier than in the low wage zone. Enron may go bankrupt, but there are plenty more companies to take on its business and employ its employees.

Diminishing returns in the middle rungs of the manufacturing value chain

Over the 1980s and 1990s many firms in the North moved the more labour-intensive parts of their value chains to low wage locations, and many analysts expected that the plants and firms in developing countries which undertook this work would be able to rise up the chain, undertaking progressively higher value-added work. (In apparel, this would mean moving from stitching of imported cut pieces, to cutting and stitching, to 'full package' production, including designs.)[19] They expected too that this upwards mobility would be developmentally nutritious; and that the trade flows associated with the expansion of North–South production networks would be as good for development as the arms-length trade assumed in the standard economic models.

The evidence suggests that plants and firms in the low wage zone have indeed moved up the chain—but the resulting increase in competition between low wage producers in the higher stages of manufacturing has caused a fall in returns at the higher stages.[20] One study of 'a decade's worth of hard data' found 'an almost uniform wage meltdown in the apparel industry in the Third World'.[21] The trends in apparel also apply in other assembly-intensive industries, including consumer electronics.

China is often held up as the prime example of an economy that has benefited massively from the expansion of production tied to Northern value chains. But in fact exports from foreign-funded-enterprises have yielded much less value-added for the national economy than the roughly equal value of exports from national firms, because the import content of the foreign-funded enterprises remains much higher.[22]

Increasing World Poverty and Inequality

Here is a microeconomic explanation of the macro trend to world-wide convergence of manufacturing but non-convergence of incomes. Each increment of manufacturing in developing countries is yielding less value-added in the South and more in the North.

In short, the several mechanisms described here—particularly the combination of spatial clustering of high value-added activities in the prosperous zone and the fall in returns to the middle stages of manufacturing as more Southern producers enter them—help to explain a stably divided world in which high wages remain high in one zone while low wages elsewhere remain low, even as the industrial-isation gap has closed. The important point is that well-functioning free markets in a highly economically globalised world produce, 'spontaneously', an equilib-rium division of activities between the high wage zone and the low wage zone that is hardly desirable for the low wage zone.

To spell out the causality further, one might hypothesise that rising levels of (especially manufacturing) trade to GDP raise the income share of the rich in low-income developing countries, who have education and control over critical trade-related services, while shrinking the share of the bulk of the population with minimal or no education. The consumption preferences of the rich lock the low-income countries into dependence on sophisticated imports from the high income countries, restricting the replacement of imports by national production that is a key to expanding prosperity rooted in diversifying production for the national economy rather than in narrow export specialisation for foreign markets. Oligopolistic industrial organisation in the high income zone reinforces the inequalities by supporting mark-up pricing, which generates falling terms of trade for the low wage zone.

Falling terms of trade facing developing countries are a major proximate cause of the persistence of the North–South divide. The prices of exports from developing countries, not only of primary commodities but also of manufactur-ing goods, have fallen sharply over the past two decades in relation to the prices of exports from developed countries, depressing the share of world income going to the low income zone[23] (see Figure 3). The harnessing of China's vast reservoirs of labour has particularly depressed the terms of trade for developing country manufactures. The sharp fall in the developing countries' manufacturing terms of trade soon after 1984 is largely due to China's dramatic entry into manufacturing exports. At a stretch, one could say that China's biggest export is deflation.

Regional, not global, focus of multinational corporations

Not only are multinational corporations based in the high cost zone keeping their high value-added activities in the high cost zone, they are also depending more, not less, on the high cost, high income zone for their sales. Contrary to the common idea of markets and firms becoming increasingly global, most of the Fortune 500 biggest multinational corporations depend for most of their sales on their home region, whether North America, the European Union, or East Asia (the 'Triad').[24] Less than a dozen are 'global' in their sales, even in the restricted sense of having 20 per cent or more of total sales (from parents and subsidiaries)

Robert Hunter Wade

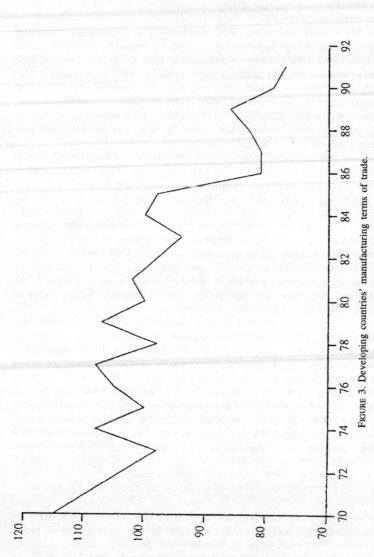

FIGURE 3. Developing countries' manufacturing terms of trade.

Source: Patrick Minford and others, 'The elixir of growth', *CEPR Discussion Paper*, No. 1165, May 1995.

Note: Ratio of developing countries' manufacturing export prices (US$) to developed countries' export prices of machinery, and transport equipment and of services (US$).

Increasing World Poverty and Inequality

in each of these three regions and virtually none depend to any significant degree on markets in developing countries outside of East Asia (more evidence of the skewness of world income distribution). Moreover, their focus on just one or two of the Triad regions intensified in the second half of the 1990s compared to the first half. The foreign operations of the multinationals became less profitable than their home-based operations in the second half of the 1990s, having been more profitable in the first half of the 1990s. The other side of this concentration of sales in one or two Triad regions is the concentration of the small proportion of total foreign private direct investment going to developing countries in only half a dozen; and most of it is for producing exports back to developed countries, not for sales in developing countries.

Briefly, multinational corporations are 'regionalising' more than 'globalising', and their regions do not include developing countries outside East Asia. They have correspondingly little interest in the economic development of developing countries.

Financiulisation of the economy

More distant causes of the likely poverty and income inequality trends lie in the transformation of capitalism from assembly lines to information manipulation, from manufacturing to finance. This places higher premiums on skills and education and penalises those without.

But at the top end of the world income distribution the sharp shift of world income towards the very richest families cannot be explained by returns to education. It relates more to the shift in corporate culture from a norm of 'earned differentials' to a norm of 'winner take all', such that senior management pay deals worth hundreds of times the pay of workers no longer provoke outrage.[25]

This in turn relates to the ascendancy of finance in the most powerful economies, or the 'financialisation of the economy' (FOE). Financialisation has occurred to the point where the financial sector is the pivot of the US and UK economies, interlocked with the other sectors in ways that tend to preserve its pre-eminence. For example, finance is institutionally interlocked with the richest third of households via stock-market-based pension funds, and normatively interlocked with the corporate sector via 'return on capital' as the chief measure of corporate performance.[26] The financial sector accrues very high value-added to the economies where it is dominant, because (retail financing aside) it faces only weak price competition, it operates world-wide with clients who, understanding little of the more esoteric of its products, are on the wrong side of 'asymmetrical information' and easily duped,[27] and is subject to the increasing returns of reputation. Furthermore, much of its income comes from transaction fees; so it gains from a regional bubble as it arranges the inflows of finance, and gains from the subsequent crash as it arranges the outflows.

The norms and institutional models that underpin the dominance of finance in the West are then 'internationalised' to the rest of the world, partly via the WTO, the IMF, the World Bank and some bilateral aid agencies. For example, under the banner of 'capital market development' the World Bank and the US Agency for International Development (USAID) are promoting mandatory public or private pension funds even in countries, like Kazakhstan, that lack accountants and adequate record keeping, let alone a stock market.[28] This open honey pot is a sure way to make finance the sector of choice for predatory national elites.

This is turn makes it less likely that developing country governments, often dominated or constrained by finance-based elites with easy exit options, will focus on development strategy—including long gestation projects that intensify the internal articulation of the national economy through import replacement, production diversification, technological upgrading, and the like. Finance in the driving seat erodes both economic citizenship and development strategy.

East Asia

Even about East Asia's ability to continue to defy economic gravity we should not get too optimistic. Only a miniscule portion of world R&D work is done in (non-Japan) East Asia. Virtually all of it continues to be done in the Triad countries of North America, Euroland and Japan. Even Singapore, which looks to be an Asian centre of R&D, does not do 'real' R&D; its R&D laboratories mostly concentrate on adapting products developed in North America and Europe for the regional market and listening in on what competitors are doing.[29] The much heralded 'globalisation of R&D' is really about movement within the high-income Triad.

China still relies heavily on foreign investment and imported components for its higher-tech manufactured output. Incoming foreign investment is still mainly seeking low-cost labour, tax breaks and implied promises of protection, as distinct from rapidly rising skills. Even its information technology engineering complex around Shanghai depends heavily on Taiwanese and other foreign know-how. Japanese alarm bells have been ringing at graphs showing Japan's personal computer exports to the USA falling as China's rise; but the figures conceal the fact that the computers are assembled in China using high value-added technology from Japan and elsewhere. Some of the technology is spilling into the heads of the millions of Chinese employees, almost certainly more than is occurring in other developing countries (China has 200 'technicians' per million people, using the UNESCO definition, compared to 108 in India, 30 in Thailand, 318 in South Korea and 301 in Singapore).[30] Nevertheless, if China is prevented by WTO rules from deploying the sorts of industrial policies used earlier in the capitalist economies of East Asia—used to generate productive 'rent-seeking' in activities important for the economy's future growth—it may remain for a prolonged period as an assembly platform for low value-added exports.

These qualifications should caution us about a scenario of declining world income inequality based on China's continued fast growth and transformation. But whether or not China does substantially upgrade the value-added of its exports, it will continue to cause a widening of income inequality between many other developing countries and the West. As it becomes the world centre for low-cost manufacturing it is knocking out competing producers in higher wage countries, such as Mexico and Brazil. At the same time it is boosting demand for agricultural and mining commodities from these countries. The result may be

Increasing World Poverty and Inequality

a spatial shift of 'comparative advantage', as developing countries outside of East Asia lose comparative advantage in manufacturing and resume their earlier specialisation as commodity suppliers, now not only to the West but also to China and the rest of East Asia. One analyst observed that a 'paradigm shift' may be underway as Latin America moves away from efforts at economic diversification back to its area of historic comparative advantage—agricultural and industrial commodities.[31] In the simple economic model that still informs development thinking, specialisation in line with comparative advantage will benefit (almost) everyone. The developmental consequences of Latin America moving back towards the role of commodity supplier dramatise the failures of the model to take account of real world increasing returns.

In short, the benign effects of free markets in spreading benefits around the world, as celebrated in the liberal argument, are probably offset by other tendencies, yielding divergence between, on the one hand, an increasing returns, high value-added, highly versatile and high wage zone and, on the other, a diminishing returns, low value-added, narrowly specialised and low wage zone—even as ratios of manufacturing to GDP, total trade/GDP, and manufacturing exports/total exports rise in the latter, and even as national income inequality in the high wage zone rises towards the level of inequality in the low wage zone.

Population growth

At the low-income end, population is growing many times faster than in the rich zone, raising the share of world population living in the low income zone (Figure 1). High-income zone natural population growth (excluding migration) is close to zero; low-income zone growth is around 2 per cent excluding China or around 1.5 per cent including China. With dreadful irony, some regions where high population growth used to be seen as a problem are now experiencing the opposite: AIDS is wiping out so many adults, including farmers, civil servants, judges, teachers and other professionals, that development is going backwards. But within sub-Saharan Africa this is mainly in the eastern and southern regions; the region as a whole continues to grow faster than any other at around 2.5 per cent and is likely to continue to do so because its young age distribution imparts high growth momentum. India, even as its population growth rate slows dramatically, will experience another 500–600 million people in the next 50 years, and will overtake China.

The US 'primacy' project and international regimes

The factors considered so far are to do with 'structures' or 'parameters', not agents. But agents also have an important role in the story. They have created rules, organisations, structures which help them to win. The US government was the primary architect of the international monetary system in place since the breakdown of the Bretton Woods system around 1970.[32] One of the key features of this regime is the use of a debt currency (rather than an asset currency)—the

179

Robert Hunter Wade

US dollar, not linked to gold—as the primary asset of foreign exchange reserves and the primary currency of international transactions. This feature has exempted the USA from the normal 'debtor's curse', whereby a country running sizeable current deficits must either devalue the currency or undertake aggregate demand contraction or both. On the contrary, the USA has the magical 'debtor's blessing', whereby the surplus countries on the other end of the US deficits continue to accumulate US dollar assets. Their central banks use surplus dollars to buy US Treasury Bills issued to finance the deficits, so that they in essence lend back to the USA the finance with which to cover the US deficits—the deficits themselves generate the finance with which to finance them, a kind of Says Law of deficits. Equally, they do not press the USA to lower the value of the dollar, because this would lower the competitiveness of their exports and the value of their existing reserves. Hence the USA does not have to contract aggregate demand. US interest rates are kept lower than otherwise by the inflow of foreign finance and the US dollar kept higher than otherwise. US firms are able (thanks to the high dollar) to buy up foreign assets cheaply and low US interest rates give them a stronger incentive to do so. The USA has more autonomy than any other state to set key parameters of aggregate demand in accordance with its own domestic conditions and not worry about the reactions of others. And—the bottom line—it continues to have more guns and butter than anyone else, because it faces softer trade-offs between more consumption, more investment and more military expenditure. If necessary, it can 'cash in' its military dominance for support from other states for its preferred international economic policies in a way that no other state can.

On the other hand, the Dollar–Wall Street regime, with its private (rather than public, through central banks) capital markets, puts pressure on the more successful developing countries—or those that have liberalised their capital account—to curb their growth rates so as to limit the risk of crisis triggered by sudden capital flight.

The Uruguay Round/WTO trade regime, under the banner of 'free trade and a level playing field', has tipped the playing field decisively in favour of the developed countries—as seen in the agreements about textiles, agriculture and intellectual property, and the prohibition of most of the 'performance requirements' that East Asian governments placed on foreign-invested firms, including local content and export requirements.[33] The pre-Uruguay Round norm of 'special and differential treatment' of developing countries—because they are developing—has more or less disappeared, replaced by the norm of 'reciprocity'. As a *Financial Times* editorial said, endorsing reciprocity as the obvious principle of fairness, 'they [developing countries] cannot have it both ways. *Unless developing countries … are ready to open their markets, it is unrealistic to expect industrialised ones to do so.* More to the point, liberalisation would do them good. The economics of trade, like freedom, are indivisible: there is not one set of rules for the rich and another for the poor'.[34]

Almost all the multilateral economic organisations with clout take it for granted that more market access is always better, that differences in market regulations between national markets are an undesirable obstacle to trade, that harmonisation should occur around 'international best practice', that poor countries should give high priority in terms of the use of scarce skills to meeting WTO conditions for market access.

The World Bank and the Fund have withdrawn support for industrial policies aimed at creating industries that replace imports and challenge established ones in the West—policies that might help to offset the centrifugal, polarising forces described earlier. On the other hand, their 'structural adjustment' programmes have forced adjusting countries to increase their exports quickly, and therefore to export unprocessed commodities; an effect reinforced by the tariff escalation in developed countries, which imposes higher tariffs on more processed products. The result is over-supply of commodities and falling terms of trade for commodity exporters, making a good deal for commodity consumers in rich countries.

Mongolia is a grim example. In 1991, following the break up of the Soviet Union, its government adopted a full-scale liberalisation package. Within five years its industrial sector, built up over 50 years, was almost wiped out. As people were driven back into (diminishing return) agriculture and herding, yields plunged. Its social indicators, which had been well above the norm for its per capita income, also plunged. The radically liberalising government did, however, wish to retain one industrial policy instrument, a tax on the export of raw wool (a measure the English king adopted in the 15th century, which accelerated the growth of the English textile industry). The Asian Development Bank announced it would hold up a loan until the government removed the export ban. The government obliged. More than 50 textile mills were closed. The Chinese now process virtually all of Mongolia's wool.[35]

At one remove, the development and stabilisation strategies of the multilateral economic organisations can be understood as instruments of the American 'primacy' strategy, which reached fruition during the Clinton administrations of the 1990s. Primacy refers not just to superordination, as in military and economic dominance; for superordination could be consistent with a range of political economies in other states. Rather, it refers to the establishment of a world economic order in which the political economy arrangements of other states are homogenised around an essentially Anglo-American political economic model, presented as the 'natural' kind of capitalism, analogous to Rousseau's Noble Savage. As the Noble Savage is corrupted by society, so natural capitalism is corrupted by politics and government 'intervention'. In *Time* magazine's paraphrase of the core belief of Allen Greenspan, chairman of the US Federal Reserve, 'markets are an expression of the deepest truths about human nature and ... as a result, they will ultimately be correct'.[36] This bedrock belief of American elites supports the post-Cold-War US 'enlargement' strategy. National Security Affairs Presidential Assistant Anthony Lake explained the strategy in 1993. During the Cold War, he noted, opening the rest of world's markets had to be balanced against containing communism—the 'containment' strategy. With the end of the Cold War,

> The successor to a doctrine of containment must be a *strategy of enlargement*, enlargement of the world's free community of market democracies. ... During the Cold War, even children

Robert Hunter Wade

understood America's security mission: as they looked at those maps on their schoolroom walls, they knew we were trying to contain the creeping expansion of that big, red blob. Today ... we might visualise our security mission as promoting the enlargement of the 'blue areas' of market democracies.[37]

The interesting questions are how the USA has been able to harness the multilateral economic organisations—meant to be cooperatives of states—to advance its national economic and security strategy with rather little opposition; and how the pursuit of the strategy has impacted on trends in world poverty and distribution.

Conclusions

If the number of people in extreme poverty may not be falling and if global inequality may be widening (in terms of several plausible measures, and emphatically in terms of absolute income gaps) we cannot conclude that globalisation—the spread of free-market relations within the current framework—is moving the world in the right direction, with Africa's poverty as a special case for international attention. The balance of probability is that—like global warming—the world is moving in the wrong direction.

Should we worry about rising inequality?

The neoliberal argument says that inequality provides incentives for effort and risk-taking, and thereby raises efficiency. We should not worry provided that it does not somehow make the poor worse off than otherwise. The counter-argument is that this productive incentive effect applies only at moderate levels of inequality. At higher levels, such as in the USA over the past 20 years, it is likely to be swamped by social costs. Aside from the moral case against it, inequality above a moderate level creates a kind of society that even crusty conservatives hate to live in, unsafe and unpleasant.

Higher income inequality within nations goes with: (1) higher poverty (using World Bank data and the number of people below the Bank's international poverty line);[38] (2) higher unemployment; (3) slower economic growth; and (4) higher crime.[39] Evidence from across US cities suggests that greater inequality is associated with higher rates of crime. The link to higher crime comes through the inability of unskilled men in high inequality societies to play traditional male economic and social roles, including a plausible contribution to family income. But higher crime and violence is only the tip of a distribution of social relationships skewed towards the aggressive end of the spectrum, with low average levels of trust and social capital. In short, inequality at the national level should certainly be a target of public policy, even if just for the sake of the prosperous.

The neoliberal argument is even less concerned about widening inequality

Increasing World Poverty and Inequality

between countries than it is about inequality within countries, because we cannot do anything directly to lessen international inequality. On the face of it, the more globalised the world becomes, the more that the reasons why we should be concerned about within-country inequalities also apply between countries. If globalisation within the current framework actually increases inequality within and between countries, as is consistent with a lot of evidence, increases in world inequality above moderate levels may cut world aggregate demand and thereby world economic growth, producing a vicious circle of rising world inequality and lower world growth.

Rising inequality between countries impacts directly on national political economy in the poorer states, as rich people who earlier compared themselves to others in their neighbourhood or nation now compare themselves to others in the USA or western Europe, and feel deprived and perhaps angry. Inequality above moderate levels may, for example, predispose the elites to become more corrupt as they compare themselves to elites in rich countries and squeeze their own populations in order to sustain a comparable living standard, enfeebling whatever norms of citizenship have emerged.

Likewise, rapidly widening between-country inequality in current exchange rate terms feeds back into stress in public services, as the increasing foreign exchange cost of imports, debt repayment and the like has to be offset by cuts in budgets for health, education and industrial policy.

Migration is a function of inequality, since the fastest way for a poor person to get richer is to move from a poor country to a rich country. Widening inequality may raise the incentive on the educated people of poor countries to migrate to the rich countries, and raise the incentive on unskilled people to seek illegal entry. Yet migration/refugees/asylum is the single most emotional, most atavistic issue in Western politics. Polls show that more than two thirds of respondents agree that there should be fewer 'foreigners' living in their countries.[40]

Again, widening between-country inequality may intensify conflict between states, and—because the market–exchange-rate income gap is so big—make it cheap for rich states to intervene to support one side or the other in civil strife. Rising inequality in market–exchange-rate terms—helped by a high US dollar, a low (long-run) oil price and the new intellectual property agreement of the WTO—allows the USA to finance the military sinews of its emerging empire more cheaply.

The effects of inequality within and between countries also depend on prevailing norms. Where power hierarchy and income inequality are thought to be the natural human condition, the negative effects can be expected to be lighter than where prevailing norms sanction equality and where the sense of relative deprivation is stronger. The significance for the future is that norms of equality and democracy are being energetically promoted by the prosperous democracies in the rest of the world, at the same time as the lived experience in much of the rest of the world belongs to another planet.

Moreover, all these effects may be presumed to operate in response to widening absolute income gaps even if relative income gaps are narrowing (and therefore inequality falling by our normal measures).

183

Development economics

If sizeable fractions of the world's population are to reach today's median income over the next half century we need to revisit the theory and prescriptions of development economics. It is one of the ironies of our time that during the great drive to mathematise economics in the 1940s to the 1970s increasing returns, cumulative causation and the like disappeared from the realm of high theory but remained in play in the sub-discipline of development economics (for example, in the ideas of the 'big push', 'unbalanced growth', 'industry first'); by contrast, since the 1980s, much work in the realm of high theory investigates the heterodox world of increasing returns, linkages, monopolistic competition and the like, while these ideas have more or less dropped out of the more applied variants of development economics. The dominant 'structural adjustment' pre-scriptions of the Bretton Woods organisations assume orthodox decreasing returns, stable equilibria and no significant non-market linkage effects. Some-times the same economists straddle both worlds, setting aside their knowledge of the heterodox world of increasing returns when they deal with development policy in order to hammer home the orthodox 'fundamentals' about efficient, rent-free markets assumed implicitly to operate in a world of diminishing return activities, and hence to be self-adjusting towards an optimal equilibrium.

Contemporary applied development economics teaches that (a) economic growth is a by-product of well-functioning markets; (b) countries should special-ise in line with their comparative advantage; and (c) countries should practise free trade, for free trade is Pareto optimal—the only issue of trade policy is how fast and in what sequence to move to free trade.

In the 1990s development economics has added to these 'fundamentals' a new concern with 'good governance' in the form of slimmed down, decentralised, corruption-free public sectors and participatory procedures for public invest-ments. The neoliberal development agenda—often called the Washington Con-sensus—takes as its central tasks the creation of (a) efficient, rent-free markets, (b) efficient, corruption-free public sectors able to supervise the delivery of a narrow set of inherently public services, and (c) decentralised arrangements of participatory democracy and civil society. The more these conditions are in place the more development and prosperity are expected to follow.

The argument flies in the face of the history of both the now advanced countries of western Europe and North America and the post-Second-World-War success stories. The history of development suggests, on the contrary, that deliberate, government-sponsored efforts to create 'rents' (returns above the normal market level) through various forms of infant industry nurturing—aimed in the first instance at replacing some current imports with local production and at shifting resources at the margin towards increasing return activities—is an almost-necessary condition.[41] Far from specialising in line with comparative advantage, successful developers have diversified their production base, right up to the per capita income of the lower levels of the World Bank's 'high income' countries.[42] They have not relied upon well-functioning markets to produce economic growth as a by-product, for the reason that markets are good at signalling relative profitability at the margin but bad at signalling the structural

Increasing World Poverty and Inequality

changes, the lumpy investments of the kind entailed by economic development. They have not practised free trade, by and large, and one can see on theoretical grounds why free trade may not be Pareto optimal—because free trade, by raising risk and volatility, can make everyone worse off by prompting resource owners to reallocate into lower risk, less productive activities; not to mention that, in the real world, IMF and World Bank programmes often require a cut-back in government transfer payments, and hence reduce the ability of the government to ensure that the gainers from the move to free trade really do compensate the losers.

We need to reintroduce a distinction that has dropped out of the development lexicon, between 'external' integration and 'internal' integration. In current usage 'integration' refers to integration of a national economy into world markets, and more external integration is assumed automatically to stimulate internal integration between wages, consumption and production, and between sectors like rural and urban, consumer goods and intermediate goods, and so on. Much evidence suggests, on the contrary, that deliberately engineered increases in internal integration can propel higher external integration, especially through the replacement of some current imports with national production, thereby generating demands for new kinds of imports.[43] Some import replacement occurs 'naturally' in response to transport costs, growing skills, shifting relative costs. The development experience of Latin America and Africa over the whole of the twentieth century suggests that regions that integrate into the world economy as commodity-supply regions are only too likely to remain stuck, their level of prosperity a function of access to rich country markets and (falling) prices for their narrow portfolio of commodities. Deliberate efforts to accelerate import replacement, or internal integration more broadly, can certainly go awry, as much experience in Latin America, Africa and South Asia shows. The response should be to do import replacement better, not less.

In the end the central development problematique must be less about how to alleviate poverty, sustain the environment, and establish rent-free markets and corruption-free public sectors, and more about how to create forms of capitalism able to generate rising mass living standards in the low wage zone of the world economy on the basis, mainly, of expanding domestic demand for domestic production. In this context, the rule of thumb is that an inefficient manufacturing sector is better than no manufacturing sector. For many economies (Mongolia is one), this is the choice, because an efficient manufacturing sector is nowhere in sight. It is remarkable how completely the issue of creating dynamic capitalisms has disappeared from the international development agenda. We need to re-engage with the issues that Malthus and Schumpeter were talking about.

Multilateral economic agreements

The question is how to reconfigure multilateral economic organisations so as to legitimise expanded 'special and differential treatment' for developing countries and dilute requirements for 'reciprocity', 'national treatment' and 'international best practice'. The rules of the international economic regime must allow developing countries to accelerate import replacement by measures such as

Robert Hunter Wade

tariffs, subsidies, preferential government procurement for national firms, and targeted efforts to develop supply links between subsidiaries of multinational corporations and local firms (preferably all made conditional on improved performance of the assisted industries), and to impose restrictions on capital flows at times of surges.[44] This is what developing country representatives in international economic organisations should be concerting their agendas around.

On the other hand, it is true that China's rise to the centre of low end manufacturing has hugely complicated any concerted action by developing countries. Mexico and Korea are now likely to line up with the USA and the other Group of 7 states in seeking various forms of protection against China's exports. The political line between developed and developing countries has become quite detached from the income line.

All this policy prescription assumes, of course, that the structure of the world economy is open enough to permit the upward mobility of large demographic masses. It assumes that nothing in the functioning of world capitalism in the Dollar–Wall Street framework precludes movement towards a unipolar distribution of world income and a shrinking of the gap between bottom and top, or pushes some demographic masses down the income scale as others rise. What is the evidence?

Notes

1. The first wave was 1870–1914; the second, 1945–80; the third, 1980 to the present. See World Bank, *Globalisation, Growth, and Poverty: Building an Inclusive World Economy* (World Bank/Oxford University Press, 2002).
2. James Wolfensohn, 'Foreword', *World Development Indicators 2002* (World Bank, 2002).
3. World Bank, *Globalisation, Growth and Poverty*, p. 50.
4. Robert Hunter Wade, 'Is Globalisation Reducing Poverty and Inequality?', *World Development*, Vol. 32, No. 4 (2004).
5. John Hicks, *Value and Capital* (Oxford University Press, 1946), pp. 84–5, 88–9. Hicks continued: 'We must be aware, however, that we are taking a dangerous step, and probably limiting to a serious extent the problems with which our subsequent analysis will be fitted to deal. Personally, however, I doubt if most of the problems we shall have to exclude for this reason are capable of much useful analysis by the methods of economic theory.' I thank David Ellerman and Philip Toner for the Hicks reference. See also Erik Reinert, 'Globalisation in the periphery as a Morgenthau Plan: the underdevelopment of Mongolia in the 1990s', in: Erik Reinert (ed.), *Globalisation, Economic Development and Inequality: An Alternative Perspective* (Edward Elgar, forthcoming 2004); and Philip Toner, *Main Currents in Cumulative Causation: The Dynamics of Growth and Development* (Palgrave Macmillan, 1999).
6. They include: Steve Dowrick and Muhammad Akmal, 'Explaining contradictory trends in global income inequality: a tale of two biases', Faculty of Economics and Commerce, Australia National University, (2001), available at: http://ecocomm.anu.edu.au/people/info.asp?Surname=Dowrick&Firstname-Steve; Branko Milanovic, 'True World Income Distribution, 1988 and 1993: First Calculations Based on Household Surveys Alone', *Economic Journal*, Vol. 112, No. 476 (2002), pp. 51–9; Branko Milanovic, *Can We Discern the Effect of Globalisation on Income Distribution? Evidence from Household Budget Surveys*, World Bank Policy Research Working Papers, No. 2876, 2002; and Yuri Dikhanov & Michael Ward, 'Evolution of the global distribution of income in 1970–99', *Proceedings of the Global Poverty Workshop* (2003), Initiative for Policy Dialogue, Columbia University, available at http://www-1.gsb. Columbia.edu/ipd/povertywk.html.
7. Salvatore Babones, 'The structure of the world-economy, 1960–1999', paper presented at 97th Annual Meeting of the American Sociological Association, Chicago, 2002.
8. World Bank, *Globalisation, Growth, and Poverty*. For more examples of this kind of analysis, see Francois Bourguignon *et al.*, *Making Sense of Globalisation: A Guide to the Economic Issues* (Centre for Economic Policy Research, 2002).

Increasing World Poverty and Inequality

9. World Bank, *Globalisation, Growth and Poverty*, p. 51.
10. *Ibid.*, p. 36. Emphasis added.
11. Peter Gowan, *The Global Gamble* (Verso, 1999).
12. It would be worth comparing the World Bank's set of 'globaliser' countries with Babone's set of seven countries out of 100 that went stably up one zone between 1960 and 1999. Do all of Babone's seven fall within the Bank's 'globalisers'?
13. Giovanni Arrighi, Beverly Silver & Benjamin Brewer, 'Industrial Convergence, Globalisation and the Persistence of the North–South Divide', *Studies in Comparative International Development*, Vol. 38, No. 1 (2003), pp. 3–31.
14. Gary Gereffi & Miguel Korzeniewicz (eds), *Commodity Chains and Global Capitalism* (Praeger, 1994).
15. I draw on John Sutton, 'Rich Trades, Scarce Capabilities: Industrial Development Revisited', Keynes Lecture, British Academy, October 2000. See also Ralph Gomory & William Baumol, *Toward a Theory of Industrial Policy-Retainable Industries*, C.V. Starr Center for Applied Economics, New York University, RR 92–54, December 1992; Michael Porter, 'Clusters and the New Economics of Competition', *Harvard Business Review*, Vol. 76, No. 6 (1998), pp. 77–90; Masahisa Fujita, Paul Krugman & Anthony Venables, *The Spatial Economy: Cities, Regions, and International Trade* (MIT Press, 1999); and Anthony Venables, 'Trade, geography and monopolistic competition: theory and an application to spatial inequalities in developing countries', in: Richard Arnott, Bruce Greenwald, Ravi Kanbur & Barry Nalebuff (eds), *Economics for an Imperfect World: Essays in Honour of Joe Stiglitz* (MIT Press, 2003), pp. 501–18.
16. Robert Lucas, 'On the Mechanics of Economic Development', *Journal of Monetary Economics*, Vol. 22 (1988), pp. 3–42.
17. I sat next to an Indian woman on a plane from London to Boston, who asked me whether she had to declare to Customs a 20 kilo bag of rice. I asked her why she was bringing such a large amount. She explained that she came from a village near Chennai (Madras), she worked as a programmer for a local software company, one day she received a letter from a Massachusetts software company offering her a job. She had never been to Delhi or Mumbai before, let alone America. She was bringing the rice as a subsistence cache while exploring for safe foods in America.
18. Robert Wade, 'What Strategies are Viable for Developing Countries Today? The WTO and the Shrinking of Development Space', *Review of International Political Economy*, Vol. 10, No. 4 (2003), pp. 621–44.
19. For example, Gary Gereffi, 'International Trade and Industrial Upgrading in the Apparel Commodity Chain', *Journal of International Economics*, Vol. 48, No 1 (1999), pp. 37–70.
20. Andrew Schrank, 'Ready-to-wear development? Foreign investment, technology transfer, and learning-by-watching in the apparel trade', mimeo, Department of Sociology, Yale University, November 2002.
21. Alan Tonelson, 'There's only so much that foreign trade can do', *Washington Post*, 2 June 2002.
22. See UNCTAD, 'China's accession to the WTO: managing integration and industrialization', in: *Trade and Development Report 2002: Developing Countries in World Trade* (UNCTAD, 2002), ch. 5.
23. ECLA, *Globalisation and Development* (ECLA, 2002), Box 2.1, p. 38.
24. Michael Gestrin, Rory Knight & Alan M. Rugman, *The Templeton Global Performance Index*, Templeton College, University of Oxford, 1999, 2000 and 2001, available at http://www.templeton.ox.ac.uk.
25. Paul Krugman, 'For richer', *New York Times*, 20 October 2002.
26. The financial sector is also among the biggest sources of political finance in the USA. On financialisation, see Robert Wade, 'The US role in the long Asian crisis of 1990–2000', in: Arvid Lukauskas & Francisco Rivera-Batiz, *The Political Economy of the East Asian Crisis and its Aftermath* (Edward Elgar, 2001), pp. 195–226; and Ronald Dore, *Stock Market Capitalism: Welfare Capitalism—Japan and Germany vs. the Anglo-Saxons* (Oxford University Press, 2000).
27. Frank Partnoy, *F.I.A.S.C.O: Blood in the Water on Wall Street* (Norton, 1997).
28. World Bank, *Averting the Old-Age Crisis*, Policy Research Report, Washington DC, 1994; and R. Holzmann & Joseph Stiglitz (eds), *New Ideas about Old Age Security* (World Bank, 2001).
29. Alice H. Amsden, Ted Tschang & Akira Goto, *A New Classification of R&D Characteristics for International Comparison (With a Singapore Case Study)*, Asian Development Bank Institute, Tokyo, December 2001.
30. UNCTAD, *Trade and Development Report*, p. 167.
31. Richard Lapper, 'China begins to exert its influence on Latin America', *Financial Times*, 26 September 2003.
32. Gowan, *The Global Gamble*.

Robert Hunter Wade

33. Also in services. See *Out of Service: The Development Dangers of the General Agreement on Trade in Services*, World Development Movement, London, March 2002; and Wade, 'What Strategies are Viable for Developing Countries Today?'.

34. 'WTO's yard a mess; developing countries need to embrace trade reforms, too', *Financial Times*, 8 August 2003. Emphasis added.

35. Reinert, 'Globalisation in the periphery'.

36. Joshua Cooper Ramo, 'The three marketers', *Time*, 15 February 1999.

37. National Security Affairs Presidential Assistant Anthony Lake, speech of 21 September, 1993. Emphasis added.

38. Timothy Besley & Robin Burgess, 'Halving World Poverty', *Journal of Economic Perspectives*, Vol. 17, No. 3 (2003), pp. 3–22.

39. Matthew Lee & William Bankston, 'Political Structure, Economic Inequality, and Homicide: A Cross-Sectional Analysis', *Deviant Behaviour: An Interdisciplinary Journal*, Vol. 19, No. 3 (1999), pp. 27–55; Ching Chi Hsieh & Mark Pugh, 'Poverty, Income Inequality, and Violent Crime: A Meta-Analysis of Recent Aggregate Data Studies', *Criminal Justice Review*, Vol. 18, No. 2 (1993), pp. 182–202; Pablo Fajnzylber, Daniel Lederman & Norman Loayza, 'What causes violent crime?', The World Bank, Office of the Chief Economist, Latin America and the Caribbean Region, processed 1998; and Richard Freeman, 'Why Do so Many Young American Men Commit Crimes and What Might We Do About It?', *Journal of Economic Perspectives*, Vol. 10, No. 1 (1996), pp. 25–42.

40. Paul Demeny, 'Population Policy Dilemmas in Europe at the Dawn of the Twenty-First Century', *Population and Development Review*, Vol. 29, No. 1 (2003), pp. 1–28.

41. Wade, 'Creating capitalisms', introduction to new printing of *Governing the Market* (Princeton University Press, 2003).

42. See Jean Imbs & Romain Wacziarg, 'Stages of Diversification', *American Economic Review*, Vol. 93, No. 1 (2003), pp. 63–86. There are interesting analytical questions about how to integrate the advantages of diversification (economic activity spreading more equally across sectors as per capita income rises, in one country) with the advantages of a rising ratio of increasing to decreasing return activities; and interesting policy questions about how and when to accelerate diversification with infant industry promotion policies.

43. Wade, *Governing the Market*. See also Jane Jacobs, *Cities and the Wealth of Nations: Principles of Economic Life* (Random House, 1984); Sanjaya Lall, *Competitiveness, Technology and Skills* (Edward Elgar, 2001); Ha-Joon Chang, *Kicking Away the Ladder: Development Strategy in Historical Perspective* (Anthem, 2002); and Linda Weiss, *The Myth of the Powerless State* (Polity, 1998).

44. Wade, 'What Strategies are Viable for Developing Countries Today?'.

[7]

The Economic Journal, **108** (*September*), 1463–1482. © Royal Economic Society 1998. Published by Blackwell Publishers, 108 Cowley Road, Oxford OX4 1JF, UK and 350 Main Street, Malden, MA 02148, USA.

GLOBALISATION AND THE RISE IN LABOUR MARKET INEQUALITIES*

Adrian Wood

1. Introduction

Since about 1980, in almost all developed countries, the gaps between skilled and unskilled workers in wages and/or unemployment rates have widened (OECD, 1997; Gottschalk and Smeeding, 1997; Murphy and Topel, 1997). This rise in inequalities has coincided with rapid globalisation – falling barriers to international economic transactions, particularly between developed and developing countries – and there are good economic reasons for believing that the association is causal. This section provides some historical perspective, section 2 outlines the theory, section 3 reviews the empirical evidence, and section 4 concludes, noting areas for further research and implications for policy. The paper covers only developed countries: the more varied recent changes in inequality in developing countries, to which globalisation has probably also contributed, are discussed in UNCTAD (1997) and Wood (1997, 1998).

The widened gaps in wages and unemployment rates show that the demand for skilled (relative to unskilled) labour has increased, relative to its supply. This recent shift must be viewed in a longer-term context, looking back over at least a century, during which both the relative demand for skilled labour and its relative supply have risen greatly. These secular increases in demand and supply, moreover, have been similar in magnitude, suggesting the existence of causal linkages between them: thus increases in income generated by rising employment of skilled workers gradually shift the education supply curve by relaxing budget constraints on households and governments; and increases in the supply of skilled labour gradually shift the demand curve, with rising employment of skilled workers creating needs and opportunities to hire even more skilled workers through externalities and by inducing skill-using technical progress (new products, new processes, and new forms of work organisation).

The response of the demand curve to supply shifts appears to be somewhat slower than the response of the supply curve to demand shifts, as a result of which there has been a modest secular downward tendency in the relative

* The writing of this paper was funded by the UK Economic and Social Research Council under award R000236878. It benefited greatly from discussions with Edward Anderson, Nick von Tunzelmann, Paul Tang, Joe Francois, Jonathan Haskel, Stephen Machin, Matthew Slaughter and others at the 1998 Royal Economic Society annual conference, and from the comments of Keith Bezanson, Lawrence Katz and Patrick Minford.

wages of skilled workers in all developed countries. However, the downward path has not been steady. In the United States, for example, in the late 19th and early 20th centuries, immigration of unskilled workers raised the relative wages of skilled manual workers, which then fell in the boom of the first world war and stagnated in the inter-war slump (Anderson, 1998), while the relative wage of college graduates declined sharply in the 1940s, but rose in the 1950s and 1960s, before being pulled down again in the 1970s by a surge in supply (Autor *et al.*, 1998).

In the past two decades, there has been another such deviation from the secular wage trend, in an upward direction, driven mainly by faster growth of relative demand for skilled workers. This is illustrated by Table 1, which refers to the relativities between college and high school graduates in the United States. On average over the four decades 1940-80, the relative supply of college graduates increased slightly faster than the relative demand for them, causing their relative wage to decline by 0.3% per year. By contrast, during 1980-96, their relative wage rose by 1.1% per year, as a result partly of slower supply growth (down by 0.7% per year, back to its 1940-70 trend rate, after the 1970s surge) and partly of faster demand growth (up by 1.2% per year). The acceleration of demand growth appears to have started in the 1970s, was most pronounced in the 1980s, and slowed in the 1990s.

The lesson from this excursion into history is that it is vital to think dynamically – in terms of acceleration or deceleration of secular upward trends in both the relative demand for and the relative supply of skilled labour, rather than in terms of comparative-static supply and demand curve diagrams (such as those in Wood, 1995, 1997). This lesson is particularly important for the interpretation of the debate between the 'trade' and 'technology' explanations of recent changes in inequality – and here let me simplify by temporarily assuming that trade (or more precisely, reductions in barriers to trade) and technology (or more precisely, skill-biased technical change) are strictly alternative and non-overlapping forces.

Thus, referring to Table 1, one can ask two different questions about the demand shift: the first is 'what explains the 4.0% rise in demand during 1980-96?'; the second is 'what explains the acceleration in the growth rate of demand from 2.8% in 1940-80 to 4.0% in 1980-96?' My answer to the first question is 'mainly technology', but my answer to the second question is

Table 1

Growth of college/high school relative wage, supply and demand, US 1940-96
(% p.a.)

	Relative wage	Relative supply	Relative demand
1940-80	−0.3	3.2	2.8
1980-96	1.1	2.5	4.0

Source: Autor *et al.* (1998, Table II, college-equivalent series, assuming an elasticity of substitution of 1.4).

'mainly trade'. These two different answers are consistent with each other, because they relate to two different questions. Moreover, the numbers in Table 1 make clear that it is the second question, rather than the first, that is relevant to explaining the rise in wage inequality, because if the rate of growth of relative demand had not accelerated after 1980, the rise in the relative wage of college graduates, even allowing for the deceleration of supply growth, would have been inconsequentially small (about 0.2% per year).

To put the point another way, my belief is that most (between two-thirds and three-quarters) of the *rise* in the relative demand for skilled labour during the past two decades was caused by the same force that had propelled it upward over the previous century, namely skill-biased technical change, loosely defined to include factoral and sectoral biases in production methods, product innovation and shifts in the composition of final demand. At the same time, however, I believe that most of the *acceleration* in the growth rate of the relative demand for skilled labour in the past two decades above its trend of the previous few decades, and hence the rise in labour market inequalities, was caused by globalisation.

The distinction between the rise in demand and the acceleration of demand growth has been neglected in research and writing on this subject (including my own, but with the honourable exceptions of Mishel *et al.*, e.g. 1997, and Autor *et al.*, 1998). The neglect of this distinction has caused some unnecessary disagreement. For example, many economists have concluded that most of the rise in the relative demand for skilled labour in the past two decades has been caused by skill-biased technical change (with which I agree), but have then inferred from this finding that trade cannot explain the recent rise in wage inequality, which does not necessarily follow (and with which I disagree). The scope for conflict between the trade and technology views is thus much narrower than is usually supposed, being confined to the causes of the *acceleration* of the rate of growth of the relative demand for skilled labour.

2. Theory

The effects of trade on wage inequality are usually analysed in a Heckscher-Ohlin model with skilled and unskilled labour as the two factors and North (developed) and South (developing) as the two countries. Trade with the South causes the North to specialise in the production of skill-intensive manufactures, in which it has a comparative advantage because of its relatively large supply of skilled labour, and to reduce production of labour-intensive manufactures. In the North, there is a rise in the relative price of skill-intensive goods and the relative demand for skilled labour, and a widening of the wage gap between skilled and unskilled workers, and vice versa in the South (for a fuller exposition of the theory, see Wood, 1995, 1997).

There is more than one way of modelling recent events in a Heckscher-Ohlin framework (as is discussed further in section 3), but the model which I think provides the most accurate simple description has falling trade barriers shifting the North from 'manufacturing autarky', in which it produces all the manufactures it consumes, to complete specialisation in the production of skill-intensive manufactures and reliance on imports from the South to supply its needs for labour-intensive manufactures. This change in output mix increases the average skill-intensity of Northern manufacturing, a tendency amplified by 'defensive innovation' (a non-Heckscher-Ohlin element), whereby firms faced with import competition from the South find new ways of producing with fewer unskilled workers, which enables them to fight off the imports, but still reduces their demand for labour (Wood, 1994, pp. 159-61). Employment in manufacturing thus shrinks, relative to non-traded services, while the displacement of unskilled workers drives down their relative wage (as in the US) or, if the relative wage is rigid (as in Europe), raises unskilled unemployment.[1]

The specialised trade equilibrium is a moving one, because of continuing reductions in barriers, of two main types. One involves the transfer of activities (mainly services) from the non-traded sector to the 'manufacturing' sector (which should be thought of as including traded services), as a result, say, of improvements in communications facilities or removal of legal obstacles to entering foreign markets. The labour-intensive activities that become tradable (for example, routine key-punching) are displaced by imports from the South, while the skill-intensive ones (for example, banking and insurance) expand through exports to the South. The second type of barrier reduction occurs within the traded sector and involves splitting up moderately skill-intensive production activities into their more skill-intensive parts, which remain (and expand) in the North, and their labour-intensive parts, which are moved or subcontracted to the South (a process known as 'outsourcing'). Both types of barrier reduction further reduce the relative demand for unskilled workers in the North.

This trade model, in which technical change also plays an important role (in reducing transport and communications costs, and through defensive innovation) can explain the recent widening of economic inequalities between skilled and unskilled workers in the North – though in some countries it is necessary to weave in another international strand, namely immigration, which has exacerbated the economic misfortunes of the least-educated workers in the United States (Borjas *et al.*, 1997). What this model does not explain, however, is why inequalities have widened also *among skilled workers*: increases near the top of the wage distribution have been particularly large, while the average skilled worker has gained much less (and in the US has lost in real terms); and the rise in inequality in the upper half of the wage distribution has persisted into the 1990s, while that in the lower half ceased in the late 1980s, at least in the US (Bernstein and Mishel, 1997). Shrinkage of unskilled employment in

---

[1] This distinction between the US and Europe is oversimplified (Nickell and Bell, 1996; Nickell, 1997). It is clear, however, that unskilled workers in most European countries are afflicted to a much greater extent than in the US by low employment rather than low wages (Blau and Kahn, 1996; Gottschalk and Smeeding, 1997). It is also clear that changes in institutions contributed to the widening of wage inequalities in both the US and the UK (Machin *et al.*, 1996; Fortin and Lemieux, 1997).

manufacturing, although workers with specific skills in labour-intensive sectors were also hurt, does not seem a sufficient explanation for this persistent widening of wage gaps among skilled workers.

In recent work, I argue that an important part of the 'trade' story is missed by the standard Heckscher-Ohlin assumption that the South always had the technical capability to produce the same range of goods as the North (Wood, 1998; Tang and Wood, 1998). Instead, I augment the Heckscher-Ohlin model by assuming that production of high-quality (including new) goods requires the involvement of a small category of 'highly-skilled' workers, most of whom reside in the North, which in consequence until recently had a near-monopoly of the world market for high-quality goods, from which all categories of Northern workers benefited. Over the past few decades, though, improvements in travel and communications facilities and in business organisation have made it economic to move part of the production of high-quality goods to the South, by enabling highly-skilled Northern-based workers to co-operate with Southern workers through frequent short visits bridged by telecommunication.

In other words, there has been an economically crucial reduction in barriers to the movement of (a small class of) *people*, in addition to the reduction in barriers to the movement of *goods*. This movement of people, it should be noted, is mainly temporary, intermittent, and short-run (as opposed to migration or long-term expatriate employment) and it includes movement of people's services (via telecommunication) as well as of their bodies. Like the movement of goods, moreover, this movement of people is not costless: indeed it is expensive, especially because a lot of time of the workers concerned is wasted (for example, in airport departure lounges). What has happened lately is just that this movement has become less expensive: to put it briefly, there has been a fall in 'co-operation costs', in addition to the fall in 'transport costs' emphasised in my Heckscher-Ohlin 'specialisation' story.[2]

The expansion of high-quality production in the South, as a result of the fall in co-operation costs, has raised the wages of highly-skilled workers by widening the market for their services, but has lowered the wages of all other Northern workers, by eroding their privileged access to production with highly-skilled workers. The wage differential in the North between highly-skilled and medium-skilled workers has thus increased. This theory remains to be tested, but it seems plausible: the falling costs, increasing convenience and rapid growth of business travel and communication are common knowledge, as is the steep rise in the earnings of internationally mobile business people: managers, designers, engineers and others with skills that are globally scarce. There is a technology strand in this story, too, since technical innovations have helped to reduce co-operation costs (and it casts a new light on the role of

---

[2] The transfer of labour-intensive Northern manufacturing to the South has been caused by reductions in both sorts of international transactions costs (a point dimly perceived in Wood, 1994, p. 172). In the model of Minford *et al.* (1997), this transfer is driven entirely by (in effect) falling co-operation costs.

1468   THE ECONOMIC JOURNAL   [SEPTEMBER

computers in the rise in wage inequality, since they are used by highly-paid people mainly for communication).

3. Evidence

Much empirical research has been undertaken over the past few years on the causes of the rise in labour market inequalities in developed countries, from which a consensus has emerged that globalisation is of minor importance, and that the main cause is skill-biased technical change (e.g. OECD, 1997; Cline, 1997, ch. 2). In this section, I review and reappraise the evidence, suggesting that most of it is, in fact, consistent with the hypothesis that the main cause of the rise in labour market inequalities is globalisation.

Country-level Panel Data Studies

There is of course a broad coincidence of timing between the rise in imports of manufactures from developing countries and the changes in developed-country labour markets. In addition, I showed in Wood (1994) that there is a clear inverse correlation across developed countries between rising import penetration ratios and falling shares of manufacturing in employment, which is hard to interpret in any way other than the former causing the latter. This analysis is extended by Saeger (1997) and Rowthorn and Ramaswamy (1998), who combine the time-series and the cross-country dimensions into a panel, and control for other influences, including North-North trade. Their results confirm that there is a robust relationship between rising Southern imports and falling employment in manufacturing.

The estimated magnitude of the impact is sensitive to specification, including choice of control variables. The lowest estimate is that of Rowthorn and Ramaswamy, who conclude that trade with the South accounted for about 20% of the fall in manufacturing employment in OECD countries during 1970-94. Saeger estimates the average contribution to have been 25-30% if time dummies are included in the regression, and about 50% without them (since they disguise the influence of rises in import penetration which were common to all countries, as may some of the other trended variables included in these regressions, such as per capita income and its square). The latter figure is similar to the lower-limit estimate in Wood (1994), whose central estimate is about 70%. The regressions of both Saeger and Rowthorn and Ramaswamy are probably underestimating by using import penetration as their measure of exposure to trade, thus neglecting defensive innovation (which reduces employment but keeps imports out).

Analysis of multi-country panel data with skill differentials as the dependent variable would in principle be more relevant, but in practice is harder, for lack of comparable time series across countries, and because widening differentials emerged in some countries mainly in wages and in others mainly in unemployment rates. In Wood (1994), I constructed a rough composite indicator of changes in relative wages and unemployment rates, and found it to be correlated across developed countries with increases in Southern import penetration. No further research of this type has been undertaken. However, OECD (1997, table 4.8), in an analysis of nine developed countries during 1970-90, finds a significant but slight positive relationship between the relative wage of skilled workers in manufacturing and a North-South trade price index. Dewatripont *et al.* (1998) find, in four European countries in 1988-91, a significant positive relationship between long-term unemployment and developing-country import penetration.[3]

Factor Content Calculations

Although imports of manufactures from developing countries have grown at a high rate over the last few decades, and passed the $500 billion mark in 1995, they remain a small fraction – about 3% – of Northern GDP (Fig. 1). It is widely agreed that this figure understates their impact on Northern labour markets, because the wages of Southern workers are lower than those of Northern workers (so that a dollar of imports embodies more labour than a dollar of Northern GDP), and because the imports are less skill-intensive than Northern GDP (so that the embodied labour is mainly unskilled). However, there is much disagreement about the magnitude of the understatement.

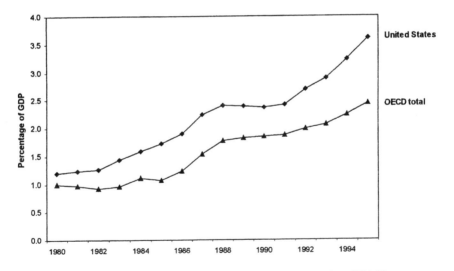

Fig. 1. *Southern-manufactured import penetration, current prices, 1980-95*
Source: OECD data (for details, see Wood and Anderson, 1998).

[3] This relationship disappears when they include sectoral dummies, which they interpret as meaning that the true cause was technology, but I interpret as a result of collinearity arising from systematic variation in the size of Southern import penetration ratios across sectors.

Many economists, including me, have tried to assess this magnitude by calculating the factor content of North-South trade. This involves estimating how much skilled and unskilled labour is used in producing the North's exports, and how much would have been used to produce its imports, with the difference between exports and imports being interpreted as the impact of trade on the demand for skilled and unskilled labour, by comparison with what it would have been in the absence of trade (or if trade had remained at some earlier lower level). The results depend crucially on the assumptions made in calculating the labour content of the hypothetical domestic production that would substitute for Southern imports.

The standard approach is to base the import calculation on current Northern sectoral labour coefficients, which invariably makes the impact of trade seem rather small. But this assumes that the imports in a given statistical category (say 'computers') are goods of the same type, and in particular of the same skill intensity, as those produced in the corresponding domestic sector, an assumption which is unreasonable for imports from developing countries. My alternative calculations (in Wood, 1994) assume instead that these imports are mainly 'non-competing' – labour-intensive items which are no longer produced on any significant scale in developed countries. This makes the effect of trade on the relative demand for skilled labour about ten times larger than in a standard factor content calculation (e.g. Wood, 1995, table 1).

Even this modified calculation in my judgement underestimates the impact of trade, for two reasons. The first is that it is confined to manufacturing, and thus omits the effects of trade in services and the indirect effects of trade on labour demand in non-traded sectors. The second is that it ignores defensive innovation: displacement of unskilled labour without increases in import penetration. There is no accurate way of measuring the size of either of these sources of understatement, but, on the basis of partial information, I guessed that each of them doubles the impact estimated by my factor content calculation, and hence concluded that expansion of trade with the South had, by 1990, raised the relative demand for skilled labour in the North by approximately 20%, mostly in the 1980s. This estimate is of the same general magnitude as the acceleration in relative demand growth of 1.2% per year during 1980-96 in table 1 above.

The theoretical validity of factor content calculations has been the subject of a lively debate (e.g. Krugman, 1995b; Leamer, 1996; Lawrence and Evans, 1997; Panagariya, 1998), but it is now broadly agreed that the type of calculation I made, comparing a situation of (specialised) trade with one of (manufacturing) autarky, can in principle yield roughly correct results. However, the way I did the calculation in practice continues to attract criticism (Lawrence, 1996; Cline, 1997): my assumptions about the extent of non-competing imports, the size of elasticities of substitution, and the upward adjustments for services and defensive innovation, are argued to make my estimates much too large. The assumptions were justified at length in Wood (1994) and further defended in Wood (1995). My 20% estimate is subject to a wide margin of error, but I still believe it to be of about the right magnitude.

Although it is now accepted that the results of standard factor content calculations are biased downward, there have been few other non-standard calculations.[4] A recent exception is the work of Borjas *et al.* (1997), who estimate the labour content of imports for the United States on the basis of domestic sectoral input coefficients at an earlier point in time (the assumption being that these would reflect the 'autarky' product mix). With a lag of 25 years – applying 1970 coefficients to 1995 imports – their estimate of the decline in the relative demand for high-school dropouts caused by expansion of trade with the South is similar in size to mine (for unskilled workers in all developed countries, unadjusted for trade in services or defensive innovation). However, they regard the assumptions involved as extreme, and prefer a more modest adjustment of the standard calculation.

Factor content calculations are usually made in a partial equilibrium framework, but the impact of trade on labour markets has been analysed also in general equilibrium models (Rowthorn, 1995; Krugman, 1995*a*; Robinson and Thierfelder, 1996; Minford *et al.*, 1997; Cardebat and Teiletche, 1997; Cline, 1997; Cortes and Jean, 1997*a*; Tyers *et al.*, 1997; Smith, 1998; Francois and Nelson, 1998). The specifications of the models vary, as do their simulations, and hence also their estimates of the size of the impact of trade with the South on relative wages. However, it appears that neglect of general equilibrium repercussions in itself does not much reduce the accuracy of factor content calculations. For example, Cline (1997) estimates that falls in transport costs and protection over the previous 20 years raised the relative wage of skilled workers in the US in 1993 by 10%.[5] This is broadly consistent with my estimate that the increase in manufactured imports from the South, allowing for direct and indirect trade in services, had by 1990 raised the relative demand for skilled labour by about 10% (the rest of my final 20% estimate arises from my 'doubling' assumption about defensive innovation).

Analyses of factor content raise an interesting question about the relative wages of men and women (Wood, 1994, pp. 269-70; Freeman, 1998; Freeman and Revenga, 1998). Since some sectors with conspicuously high Southern import penetration are female-intensive (garments, for example), it might be expected that women would suffer more than men from greater trade with the South. Thus the fact that the relative demand for females in the North has increased leads Freeman to doubt that trade can have caused the fall in the relative demand for unskilled labour. However, the North's imports of manufactures from the South are spread across a broad range of goods. Moreover, manufacturing was initially a male-intensive sector, relative to non-traded services, so that its contraction has tended to hurt males more than females.

---

[4] However, in a study of Spain, Minondo (1998) not only disentangles non-competing from competing imports, but also distinguishes among trade flows with different partners – Spain's imports being a mixture of highly skill-intensive goods from richer countries and labour-intensive goods from developing countries.

[5] This figure is from Cline's (1997, table 4.7) counterfactual experiment 4 with his TIDE model: his preferred estimate of the impact of trade is 6% (ibid., table 5.1).

1472   THE ECONOMIC JOURNAL   [SEPTEMBER

Changes in Relative Prices

In Heckscher-Ohlin theory, the changes in the relative wages of skilled and unskilled workers caused by greater exposure to trade are linked with (smaller) changes in the relative prices of skill-intensive and labour-intensive goods. This linkage has been the subject of much recent research. The main studies of the United States are cogently reviewed by Slaughter (1998): in the 1960s, there was little change in the relative prices of skill-intensive and labour-intensive goods; in the 1970s, the relative prices of labour-intensive goods fell; and in the 1980s, a fall in the relative domestic producer prices of labour-intensive goods is observed only if computers are omitted.[6] The time pattern of relative price changes does not match that of relative wage changes, particularly in the 1970s, when the relative price of labour-intensive goods fell and the relative wage of unskilled workers rose. In Europe, moreover, there was no general fall in the relative producer prices of labour-intensive goods, either in the 1970s or in the 1980s (Lawrence, 1996; Lücke, 1997; Neven and Wyplosz, 1998; Anderton and Brenton, 1998*a*).

There are three reasons, common to the US and Europe, why the linkage between relative price changes and relative wage changes is less clear-cut in reality than in Heckscher-Ohlin theory. One, discussed at length by Slaughter (1998), is the influence of intermediate inputs and of technical progress, for which most studies have made allowance. A second, also noted by Slaughter, is that the theory assumes that all factors are perfectly mobile among sectors, so that factor prices are always equal in all sectors, whereas in reality the sectoral specificity of capital and skills is likely to cause the adjustment of relative factor prices to relative product prices to be prolonged. For example, the fall in the relative wage of unskilled workers in the 1980s might be a lagged result of the fall in the relative price of labour-intensive goods in the 1970s. The first effect of price competition from the South was probably to reduce the profitability of labour-intensive Northern sectors, postponing the impact on the labour market (Wood, 1994, section 5.4), which, when it did emerge, initially caused wages to fall mainly in these particular sectors (e.g. Freeman and Revenga, 1998).

The third reason is that even four-digit sectoral data are too aggregated to pick up all relevant price changes. In the 1980s, the manufactured exports of the South diversified from mainly labour-intensive industries such as clothing and footwear into the labour-intensive interstices of almost every industry, which was accomplished partly by outsourcing. These detailed changes are not captured in sectoral producer price statistics. They are captured, however, in changes in the prices of imports relative to exports (or domestic output), both within sectors (Feenstra and Hanson, 1996; Anderton and Brenton, 1998*a*; Neven and Wyplosz, 1998) and between sectors which are mainly importers from the South and sectors which are mainly exporters to the South (OECD,

---

[6] Schmitt and Mishel (1996) get similar results for the 1980s, but find no clear relationship in either the 1960s or the 1970s. Pryor (1997) finds a decline in the relative prices of labour-intensive goods during 1970-90.

1997). They also show up as an improvement in the North's terms of trade in manufacturing with the South (Minford *et al.*, 1997; Wood, 1997).

The most likely cause of the difference between the United States and Europe in the behaviour of relative domestic producer prices, given that the changes in export and import prices are similar and clear-cut in both regions, is the greater rigidity of relative wages in Europe (where the deteriorating position of the unskilled was manifested mainly in higher unemployment). If relative wages cannot change, then neither can relative domestic producer prices, unless there is an induced change in the technology through which they are connected. With rigid wages, a shift in external supply thus causes a change not in relative domestic producer prices but in the composition of domestic output (Krugman, 1995*a*). A country with an artificially low relative wage for skilled labour thus specialises in a narrower range of goods at the top of the skill intensity spectrum than its relative endowment of skilled labour would otherwise dictate.

It is surprising that there is no more evidence of a fall in the relative producer price of labour-intensive goods in the UK than in other European countries, even though the UK, like the US and unlike other European countries, experienced a large rise in wage inequality. One possible explanation is that much of the rise in inequality in the UK in the 1980s was just the reversal of a temporary compression of relative wages by incomes policies in the 1970s (Wood, 1994, figs. A3.1, A4.1, A4.3). Even after the rise, the *level* of inequality in the UK in the mid-1980s was much less than in the US, and the real wages of its least-skilled workers higher (Gottschalk and Smeeding, 1997, fig. 1), indicating that the UK is a more typical European country than is sometimes suggested.

Changes in Sectoral Skill Intensity, Productivity and Employment

Many recent studies have analysed the cross-sectoral pattern of changes in skill intensity, productivity and employment, seeking relationships with trade variables, technology indicators and initial levels of skill intensity which might cast light on the relative importance of globalisation and skill-biased technical change in raising the relative demand for skilled labour, and also on the effects of trade on technical change, including defensive innovation. I will briefly review the findings of these studies, and then discuss their interpretation.

The rise in the relative demand for skilled labour, reflected in the share of skilled workers in sectoral wage bills or employment, has occurred mainly within sectors and firms (rather than by inter-sectoral shifts), is apparent in virtually all manufacturing industries and in non-traded sectors, and is correlated with technology indicators – computers, other capital goods, and R&D (Machin *et al.*, 1996; Berman *et al.*, 1997; Autor *et al.*, 1998; Haskel and Haden, 1998). The rises in skill intensity are also correlated across sectors with trade variables. Thus for US manufacturing in the 1980s, Feenstra and Hanson (1996, 1997) find a strong association with import shares, which they attribute to outsourcing, while Bernard and Jensen (1996) find a strong association with exporting, as do Autor et al. (1998). However, Freeman and Revenga (1998, p. 27) find no association, in 18 developed countries in the 1980s, between changes in import penetration and changes in the skill mix of employment in 49 manufacturing industries. These studies use data on trade with all partners, developed and developing.

Other studies focus on trade with developing countries. Lawrence (1998) finds no association across US manufacturing industries in the 1980s between changes in skill intensity and levels or changes of imports from the South. Desjonqueres *et al.* (1997) likewise find no association in ten developed countries and 16 manufacturing industries during 1970-90 between rises in Southern import penetration and in the skill intensity of employment. Nor do Dewatripont *et al.* (1998) for four European countries in the 1980s. In France, Germany and the United States in the 1980s, Cortes and Jean (1997*b*) find that increased import penetration raised skill intensity in manufacturing, but that there was no difference in this regard between imports from the South and from the North, and that the effect was small. OECD (1997), using data on manufacturing in nine developed countries during 1970-90, and a trade indicator based on prices rather than quantities, find that trade with the South increased the skill intensity of employment, but only slightly. In the UK textiles sector, Anderton and Brenton (1998*b*) find that Southern import penetration explains about one-third of the rise in the skill intensity of employment during 1970-83, with a smaller effect in the non-electrical machinery sector (and with neither trade prices nor Northern imports making any contribution).

Some studies have examined the relationship across manufacturing industries between rises in skill intensity and initial levels of skill intensity, hypothesising that greater exposure to trade with the South might cause more skill upgrading in initially less skill-intensive industries: the expected correlation is thus negative. In the US, the correlation in the 1980s is in fact weakly positive (Sachs and Shatz, 1994; Lawrence, 1998). Cortes *et al.* (1998) find a somewhat stronger positive correlation in France in 1977-93. However, Neven and Wyplosz (1998) find negative correlations in both France and Germany in 1976-90, while Haskel and Slaughter (1998) find that, in both the US and the UK, the correlation was positive in the 1980s but negative in the 1970s (which is consistent with the insignificant association found for the US over the whole period 1971-91 by Pryor, 1997).

Several studies relate variation in productivity growth across manufacturing industries to exposure to trade, and sometimes also to skill intensity. In the US, total factor productivity (TFP) growth tended to be faster in less skill-intensive industries in the 1980s (Sachs and Shatz, 1994), though there is no association with skill intensity over the whole period 1971-91 (Pryor, 1997). Feenstra and Hanson (1997) conclude that import penetration slowed TFP growth in less skill-intensive US industries in the 1980s. By contrast, Lawrence (1998) concludes that import penetration, particularly from the South, raised TFP growth in less skill-intensive US industries in the 1980s. Cortes and Jean (1997*b*) find, in the US, France and Germany in the 1980s, that import penetration had a substantial positive effect on growth of labour productivity, and that the effect was twice as big for imports from the South as for those from the North. In the UK, Greenaway *et al.* (1997) and Hine and Wright (1997) find that exposure to trade raised labour productivity growth, but not much, and with trade with the North having more effect than trade with the South, while Cameron *et al.* (1998) find that import penetration was associated with faster TFP growth.

Finally, many cross-manufacturing-industry studies have shown declines in employment over the past couple of decades to be correlated with increases in import penetration and with low skill intensity. Freeman and Revenga (1998) find a negative relationship between employment and import penetration in their large panel of countries and industries during 1978-90, though the effect is stronger for imports from the North than for those from the South.[7] Sachs and Shatz (1996) show that in the US in 1979-90 employment rose in skill-intensive manufacturing industries and fell in labour-intensive industries. Neven and Wyplosz (1998) also find large employment declines in labour-intensive industries in four European countries during 1976-90, but no simple association between changes in employment and in import prices. OECD (1997, chart 4.4) show that in all developed countries during 1980-90 employment in industries with high Southern import penetration fell relative to industries which export to the South, and that this relative employment shift was associated with an adverse relative shift in trade prices.

At first sight, the mass of sectoral evidence summarised in the preceding five paragraphs may seem confusing and inconsistent with the hypothesis that expansion of trade with the South explains most of the recent rise in wage inequality. However, if one stands back from it a bit, the picture becomes clearer-and more consistent with the globalisation hypothesis. Almost all the studies refer to variation across industries *within* the manufacturing sector, and thus miss the most important part of the globalisation story in the North, which concerns the relationship *between* manufacturing as a whole and the rest of the economy. Put simply, exposure to trade with the South caused the entire manufacturing sector to become much less unskilled-labour-intensive, through changes in product and activity mix and through defensive innovation. The resulting excess supply of unskilled labour in manufacturing was partly re-absorbed, largely in the service sector, through a fall in its relative wage (particularly in the US), and partly became unemployed (particularly in European countries with rigid relative wages).

This description of events is incompatible with the usual 'one-cone' version of the Heckscher-Ohlin model, in which the North is portrayed as an open diversified trading country affected by a change in relative world prices.[8]

---

[7] The effect is also stronger in the US than in Europe, which is surprising in view of the greater flexibility of US wages, but this result is sensitive to their choice of estimation technique.

[8] In particular, the change in world prices would not in general cause a shift of unskilled employment from manufacturing to non-traded services. It would not directly affect manufacturing output levels, and the indirect effects (via changes of technique within sectors, and via shifts of demand between traded and non-traded sectors in response to changes in the relative prices of traded and non-traded goods arising from the change in relative wages) might either expand or contract unskilled employment in services relative to manufacturing.

However, it is compatible with my preferred version of the Heckscher-Ohlin model, in which trade with the South is portrayed as having shifted the North from manufacturing autarky to complete (but moving) specialisation in skill-intensive items. The crucial difference is that in this latter version of the model, relative wages (insofar as they are flexible) are not tied to relative world prices, but determined by domestic factor demand and supply conditions. Thus the impact of trade occurs not through the 'Stolper-Samuelson' link between world prices and relative wages, but through changes in the sectoral composition of output, which alter the relative domestic demand for skilled labour.[9] (The displacement of unskilled labour from manufacturing into services can be modelled also in a non-Heckscher-Ohlin framework: Sachs and Shatz, 1996, 1998.)

If my theory is correct, the skill intensity of manufacturing (and traded services) should have risen relative to the skill intensity of (non-traded) services, as indeed it has – though it remains to be established that this shift was more than the continuation of a pre-existing trend (Wood, 1994, app. A2; Colecchia and Papaconstantinou, 1996; Cline, 1997, p. 138, citing unpublished work by Burtless; Greenhalgh *et al.*, 1998, table 1). Moreover, defensive innovation in manufacturing should have accelerated its rate of TFP growth relative to that of services, as is also evident (Wood, 1994, app. A2; Lawrence, 1996). Another fact consistent with this story is that the skill-intensity rise and employment fall in manufacturing in the US and the UK were most rapid in a short period (1979-83) during which the real exchange rates of both countries were over-valued (Schmitt and Mishel, 1996; Anderton and Brenton, 1998*b*). This adverse cost shock pushed a large part of each country's labour-intensive manufacturing off the edge of a cliff of comparative disadvantage on which it had been teetering for some time.

Trade-related pressures to reduce unskilled employment were common, in some degree, to all manufacturing industries, but the pressures and the outcomes varied from industry to industry in complicated ways. Employment shrank most in the initially least skill-intensive sectors, as the trade with the South story predicts, but exactly how this was accomplished depended on other characteristics of the sectors: some just shrank without changes in skill intensity or TFP (and experienced large increases in imports from the South); others switched to more skill-intensive product and activity mixes (but still experienced a rise in imports); and others shed unskilled labour by defensive innovation (and so experienced little rise in imports). All this was entangled with exogenous sectoral shifts in technology and product mix, and with changes in North-North trade, making the pattern extremely intricate. However, to understand what happened to the economy-wide relative demand for

---

[9] However, the shift from autarky to specialised trade does involve a change in *relative domestic* producer prices. For a fuller discussion of the differences between the two models, see Wood (1995) and Lawrence and Evans (1997). Lawrence and Evans also present a hybrid model, as do Robinson and Thierfelder (1996), in which relative wages are affected both by domestic demand and supply and by world prices, which is probably more accurate. However, it is convenient and in my view quite realistic to assume as a first approximation that the relative wage is strictly independent of relative world prices.

unskilled labour, it is not vital to explain what happened to individual manufacturing industries: what matters is the broad difference between manufacturing and services, which most recent research has overlooked (exceptions being Minford *et al.*, 1997; Cline, 1997; Sachs and Shatz, 1998; and Gregory *et al.*, 1998).

The choice between Heckscher-Ohlin models mentioned above greatly affects the analysis of defensive innovation. In the 'one-cone' model, adopted by Cardebat and Teiletche (1997) and Feenstra and Hanson (1997), the focus is on differences in TFP growth across manufacturing industries, with product prices given by world prices and hence infinitely elastic demand for each industry's output. Thus if exposure to trade with the South provokes innovation in labour-intensive industries, accelerating their TFP growth, it tends to raise the relative wage of unskilled workers – helping them, rather than compounding their problems. By contrast, in the 'specialised' model, defensive innovation, by accelerating skill-biased technical progress in manufacturing as a whole, hurts unskilled workers. More specifically, the trade-induced rise in the productivity of unskilled labour in manufacturing lowers the demand for unskilled labour, even though it also reduces the price of manufactures relative to non-traded services, because the elasticity of substitution in consumption between manufacturing and non-traded services is below unity. In reality, as in this model, the relative price of manufactures has fallen in the North (the current-price share of manufacturing in GDP has decreased relative to the constant-price share), and so has the demand for unskilled labour.

What can be inferred from the sectoral studies reviewed above about *exogenous* skill-biased technical progress, the main alternative explanation of the recent rise in wage inequality? That forces unrelated to North-South trade are at work cannot be doubted, because the demand for skilled labour has risen not only in Northern manufacturing but also in non-traded sectors and in many Southern manufacturing sectors (Berman *et al.*, 1997; Desjonqueres *et al.*, 1997). The conclusion of most of the sectoral studies, indeed, is that exogenous forces loosely grouped under the heading of skill-biased technical change account for most of the recent rise in the relative demand for skilled labour – for example, an average share of 70% for OECD manufacturing is suggested by Berman *et al.* This is consistent with my own view, set out in section 1 above, and with much other evidence, and should not be a matter of contention.

The crucial issue, which few studies have addressed, is instead whether the recent *acceleration* of the rate of growth of relative demand for skilled labour was caused by an exogenous *acceleration* of skill-biased technical progress. The search for direct evidence on this point has provoked disagreement. Mishel *et al.* (1997), using various technology indicators, find no evidence in the United States of an acceleration in the 1980s. By contrast, Autor *et al.* (1998) find an association between the rise in the relative wages of skilled workers and intensified use of computers, though they are cautious about the causal link from computers to wages, which is vigorously challenged by DiNardo and

Pishke (1997). Mixed results have emerged also from firm and plant level studies of the relationship between computer use and the demand for skills (e.g. Doms, Dunne and Troske, 1997; Haskel and Heden, 1998).

4. Conclusions

Did globalisation cause the rise in labour market inequalities? More precisely, was the recent acceleration of the long-term trend rise in the relative demand for skilled labour caused mainly by falling barriers to international transactions or mainly by unrelated changes in technology? The empirical evidence does not rule out either of these explanations, but on balance seems to me to give more support to the globalisation hypothesis. The country-level panel data studies and factor content calculations suggest that the impact of more trade with the South was big enough to explain the acceleration of demand growth; and the price studies and cross-sectoral studies of skill intensity, productivity and employment, though they do not actively support the globalisation hypothesis, are not inconsistent with it, either. There is plenty of evidence that skill-biased technical change has raised the relative demand for skilled workers, but much less evidence of an autonomous acceleration in its pace over the past two decades.

Further empirical research could help to resolve this issue. Three somewhat neglected areas in which more work would shed light on the causes of the fall in demand for unskilled workers in the 1980s are: (i) country-level panel data analysis, particularly with skill differentials in wages and unemployment rates as the dependent variable, and with price as well as quantity measures of exposure to trade among the independent variables; (ii) comparison of the sizes of demand shifts in traded and in non-traded sectors (which should permit, among other things, better estimates of the magnitude of defensive innovation); and (iii) closer scrutiny of the timing of the demand shift and of the relationship between changes in product markets, including prices and profitability, and in labour markets. Research in all these areas could either strengthen or weaken the 'trade' hypothesis, relative to the 'technology' hypothesis. Two other hypotheses also merit attention: changing macroeconomic conditions; and the North-North dimension of globalisation (UNCTAD, 1995; Marris, 1996; Dinopoulos and Segerstrom, 1998).

Another point of focus for further research should be the changing nature of the rise in labour market inequalities. Recent evidence suggests that the fall in demand for unskilled workers has slowed since the late 1980s, while inequality among skilled workers has continued to rise (Bernstein and Mishel, 1997; Autor *et al.*, 1998; Wood and Anderson, 1998). This shift raises some intriguing questions, particularly because there has been no obvious break in the growth of either trade or computerisation. Are we dealing with two phenomena with different causes (for example, trade explaining the fall in demand for the unskilled, and technology the rise in inequality among the skilled)? Or are these two different results of a single cause, which might be either globalisation or technical change, acting in a complicated way? To address these questions, we need to use models with more than two skill classes of labour. We probably also need to think more about real wages and about inter-country wage inequalities, as well as about inequalities within countries (Chui *et al.*, 1998; Wood, 1998).

Even harder to assess is how the impact of globalisation on inequalities, whatever its nature and size in the past, might change in the future. Some economists believe that the effects are largely over, others that they are largely still to come: the truth is probably somewhere in between. Policy barriers to international transactions have some way to fall, particularly in services and investment, but also in merchandise trade (e.g. the phase-out of the Multi-Fibre Arrangement, and trade liberalisation in South Asia). The technical potential for reduction of transport and communications costs is far from fully realised in many developing countries, and in developed countries, there is no slackening of the stream of ideas for taking advantage of low transport and communications costs to outsource labour-intensive activities in goods and services production, and to export skill-intensive services. However, the effects of future declines in international transactions costs will vary. For example, more outsourcing and trade in services will increase inequality in the North, but growth of labour-intensive manufactured exports from South Asia will not, since the North no longer competes in that market – the increases in inequality will occur in other developing countries (Wood, 1994, ch. 9).

As regards implications for policy, there is broad agreement between economists who attribute the recent rise in labour market inequalities mainly to globalisation (Wood, 1994; Rodrik, 1997; Leamer, 1998) and those who attribute it mainly to new technology (e.g. Lawrence, 1996; OECD, 1997). All favour better education and training, redistribution of income, and using taxes and public spending to raise the domestic demand for unskilled labour (see also Collins, 1998, and Memedovic *et al*, 1998). Almost none favour protection against imports from the South, but all see the risk of a political backlash against globalisation, which has caused most economists to err on the side of underestimating the impact of globalisation on inequality. My own view is that it is better to meet protectionists on their own ground, to concede that globalisation has increased inequality, and to explain that other sorts of policies provide a cheaper solution than protection. Northern governments have begun to implement these other policies, and in this regard the protectionists are inadvertently playing a socially useful role, by counterbalancing the reluctance of the skilled gainers from globalisation to pay the taxes needed to finance assistance to the unskilled or less-skilled losers.

Institute of Development Studies at the University of Sussex

References

Anderson, E. (1998). 'Globalisation and wage inequalities, 1870-1970.' Unpublished paper, Institute of Development Studies, University of Sussex.
Anderton, B. and Brenton, P (1998*a*). 'Trade with the NICs and wage inequality: evidence from the UK

and Germany.' Forthcoming in *Global Trade and European Workers* (ed. P. Brenton and J. Pelkmans), London: Macmillan.

Anderton, B. and Brenton, P. (1998*b*). 'Did outsourcing to low-wage countries hurt less-skilled workers in the UK?' Unpublished paper, National Institute of Economic and Social Research.

Autor, D., Katz, L. and Krueger, A. (1998). 'Computing inequality: have computers changed the labor market?' *Quarterly Journal of Economics*, forthcoming.

Berman, E., Bound, J. and Machin, S. (1997). 'Implications of skill-biased technological change: international evidence'. NBER Working Paper 6166.

Bernard, A. and Jensen, B. (1996). 'Exporters, skill upgrading and the wage gap.' *Journal of International Economics*, vol. 42, no. 1, pp. 3-32.

Bernstein, J. and Mishel, L. (1997). 'Has wage inequality stopped growing?' *Monthly Labor Review*, December, pp. 3-16.

Blau, F. and Kahn, L. (1996). 'International differences in male wage inequality: institutions versus market forces.' *Journal of Political Economy*, vol. 104, no. 4, pp. 791-837.

Borjas, G., Freeman, R. and Katz, L. (1997). 'How much do immigration and trade affect labor market outcomes?' *Brookings Papers on Economic Activity*, 1, pp. 1-85.

Cameron, G., Proudman, J. and Redding, S. (1998). 'Openness and its association with productivity growth in UK manufacturing industry.' Forthcoming in *Openness and Growth* (ed. J. Proudman and S. Redding), London: Bank of England.

Cardebat, J.-M. and Teiletche, J (1997). 'Salaires relatifs, commerce Nord-Sud et progrès technique.' *Revue Economique*, vol. 48, no. 5, pp. 1337-59.

Chui, M., Levine, P. and Pearlman, J. (1998). 'Winners and losers in a North-South model of growth, innovation and product cycles.' Unpublished paper, London Business School, University of Surrey and London Guildhall University.

Cline, W. (1997). *Trade and Income Distribution*. Washington DC: Institute for International Economics.

Colecchia, A. and Papaconstantinou, G. (1996). 'The evolution of skills in OECD countries and the role of technology.' STI Working Paper 1996/8, OECD.

Collins, S. (ed.) (1998). *Imports, Exports and the American Worker*. Washington DC: Brookings Institution Press.

Cortes, O. and Jean, S. (1997*a*). 'La concurrence des pays émergents menace-t-elle le travail des non-qualifiés en Europe?' In *Commerce Nord-Sud, Migration et Délocalisation* (ed. J. de Melo and P. Guillaumont), Paris: Economica.

Cortes, O. and Jean, S. (1997*b*). 'International trade spurs productivity.' In Francois *et al.* (forthcoming).

Cortes, O., Jean, S. and Pisani-Ferry, J. (1998). 'Trade with emerging countries and the labour market: the French case.' In Dewatripont *et al.* (1998).

Desjonqueres, T., Machin, S. and van Reenen, J. (1997). 'Another nail in the coffin? Or can the trade based explanation of changing skill structures be resurrected?' Unpublished paper, University College, London.

Dewatripont, M., Sapir, A. and Sekkat, K. (1998). 'Labour market effects of trade with LDCs in Europe.' In Dewatripont *et al.* (1998).

Dewatripont, M., Sapir, A. and Sekkat, K (1998). *Trade and Jobs in Europe: Much Ado about Nothing?* Oxford: Clarendon Press.

DiNardo, J. and Pishke, J.-S. (1997). 'The returns to computer use revisited: have pencils changed the wage structure too?' *Quarterly Journal of Economics*, vol. 112, no. 1, pp. 291-307.

Dinopoulos, E. and Segerstrom, P. (1998). 'A Schumpeterian model of protection and relative wages.' *American Economic Review*, forthcoming.

Doms, M., Dunne, T. and Troske, K. (1997). 'Workers, wages and technology.' *Quarterly Journal of Economics*, vol. 112, no. 1, pp. 253-90.

Feenstra, R. and Hanson, G. (1996). 'Foreign investment, outsourcing and relative wages.' In *Political Economy of Trade Policy: Essays in Honor of Jagdish Bhagwati* (ed. R. Feenstra, G. Grossman and D. Irwin), Cambridge MA: MIT Press.

Feenstra, R. and Hanson, G. (1997). 'Productivity measurement and the impact of trade and technology on wages: estimates for the US, 1972-90.' Working Paper 97-17, University of California at Davis.

Fortin, N. and Lemieux, T. (1997). 'Institutional changes and rising wage inequality: is there a linkage?' *Journal of Economic Perspectives*, vol. 11, no. 2, pp. 75-96.

Francois, J. and Nelson, D. (1998). 'Trade and wage linkages: general equilibrium linkages.' ECONOMIC JOURNAL, this issue.

Francois, J., Roland-Holst, D. and van der Mensbrugghe, D. (eds.) (forthcoming). *Globalisation and Employment Patterns: Policy, Theory and Evidence*. London: CEPR.

Freeman, R. (1998). 'Will globalisation dominate US labor market outcomes?' In Collins (1998).

Freeman, R. and Revenga, A. (1998). 'How much has LDC trade affected Western job markets?' In Dewatripont *et al.* (1998).

Gottschalk, P. and Smeeding, T. (1997). 'Cross national comparisons of earnings and income inequality.' *Journal of Economic Literature*, vol. 35, no. 2, pp. 633-87.

Greenaway, D., Hine, R. and Wright, P. (1998). 'Modelling the impact of trade on employment in the United Kingdom.' CREDIT Discussion Paper 97/11, University of Nottingham.

Greenhalgh, C., Gregory, M. and Zissimos, B. (1998). 'The impact of trade, technological change and final demand on the skills structure of UK employment' Unpublished paper, Institute of Economics and Statistics, Oxford.

Haskel, J. and Heden, Y. (1998). 'Computers and the demand for skilled labour: industry and establishment-level panel evidence for the UK.' Unpublished paper, Queen Mary and Westfield College, University of London.

Haskel, J. and Slaughter, M. (1998). 'Does the sector bias of skill-biased technological change explain changing wage inequality?' Unpublished paper, Queen Mary and Westfield College, University of London, and Dartmouth College.

Hine, R., and Wright, P. (1997). 'Trade and manufacturing employment in the United Kingdom.' In *International Trade and Labour Markets* (ed. J. Borkakoti and C. Milner), London: Macmillan.

Krugman. P. (1995*a*). 'Growing world trade: causes and consequences.' *Brookings Papers on Economic Activity*, 1, pp. 327-77.

Krugman, P. (1995*b*). 'Technology, trade and factor prices'. NBER Working Paper 5355.

Lawrence, R. (1996). *Single World, Divided Nations?* Paris: OECD Development Centre.

Lawrence, R. (1998). 'Does a kick in the pants get you going or does it just hurt? The impact of international competition on technological change in US manufacturing.' Unpublished paper, Harvard University.

Lawrence, R. and Evans, C. (1997). 'Trade and wages when nations specialise.' In Francois *et al.* (forthcoming).

Leamer, E. (1996). 'What's the use of factor contents?' NBER Working Paper 5448.

Leamer, E. (1998). 'In search of Stolper-Samuelson linkages between international trade and lower wages.' In Collins (1998).

Lücke, M. (1997). 'European trade with lower-income countries and the relative wages of the unskilled: an exploratory analysis for West Germany and the UK.' Working Paper 819, Kiel Institute of World Economics.

Machin, S., Ryan, A. and van Reenen, J. (1996). 'Technology and changes in skill structure: evidence from an international panel of industries.' CEPR Discussion Paper 1434.

Marris, R. (1996). *How to Save the Underclass.* London: Macmillan.

Memedovic, O., Kuyvenhoven, A. and Molle, W. (eds.) (1998). *Globalisation of Labour Markets: Challenges, Adjustment and Policy Response in the European Union and Less Developed Countries.* London: Kluwer Academic Publishers.

Minford, P., Riley, J. and Nowell E. (1997). 'Trade, technology and labour markets in the world economy, 1970-90'. *Journal of Development Studies*, vol. 34, no. 2, pp. 1-34.

Minondo, A. (1998). 'The impact of trade on middle-income countries' labour markets: the case of Spain.' Doctoral dissertation, Universidad de Deusto.

Mishel, L., Bernstein, J. and Schmitt, J. (1997). *The State of Working America.* New York: M. E. Sharpe.

Murphy, K. and Topel, R. (1997). 'Unemployment and nonemployment.' *American Economic Review*, vol. 87, no. 2, pp. 295-300.

Neven, D. and Wyplosz, C. (1998). 'Relative prices, trade and restructuring in European industry.' In Dewatripont *et al.* (1998).

Nickell, S. (1997). 'Unemployment and labor market rigidities: Europe versus North America.' *Journal of Economic Perspectives*, vol. 11, no. 3, pp. 55-74.

Nickell, S. and Bell, B. (1996). 'Changes in the distribution of wages and unemployment in OECD countries.' *American Economic Review*, vol. 86, no. 2, pp. 302-7.

OECD (1997). 'Trade, earnings and employment: assessing the impact of trade with emerging economies on OECD labour markets.' *Employment Outlook*, OECD.

Panagariya, A. (1998). 'Trade and wages: the content of factor content.' Unpublished paper, University of Maryland.

Pryor, F. (1997). 'The impact of foreign trade on the employment of unskilled US workers: some new evidence.' Unpublished paper, Swarthmore College.

Robinson, S. and Thierfelder, K. (1996). 'The trade-wage debate in a model with nontraded goods: making room for labor economists in trade theory.' TMD Discussion Paper 9, International Food Policy Research Institute.

Rodrik, D. (1997). *Has Globalisation Gone Too Far?* Washington DC: Institute for International Economics.

Rowthorn, R. (1995). 'A simulation model of North-South trade.' *UNCTAD Review*, pp. 35-66.

1482   THE ECONOMIC JOURNAL   [SEPTEMBER 1998]

Rowthorn, R. and Ramaswamy, R. (1998). 'Growth, trade and deindustrialisation.' IMF working paper, Research Department, International Monetary Fund.

Sachs, J. and Shatz, H. (1994). 'Trade and jobs in US manufacturing.' *Brookings Papers on Economic Activity*, 1, pp. 1-84.

Sachs, J. and Shatz, H. (1996) 'US trade with developing countries and wage inequality.' *American Economic Review*, vol. 86, no. 2, pp. 234-9.

Sachs, J. and Shatz, H. (1998). 'International trade and wage inequality in the United States: some new results.' In Collins (1998).

Saeger, S. (1997). 'Globalisation and deindustrialisation: myth and reality in the OECD.' *Weltwirtschaftliches Archiv*, vol. 133, no. 4, pp 579-608.

Schmitt, J. and Mishel, L. (1996). 'Did international trade lower less-skilled wages during the 1980s? Standard trade theory and evidence.' Technical Paper, Economic Policy Institute.

Slaughter, M. (1998). 'What are the results of product-price studies and what can we learn from their differences?' Unpublished paper, Dartmouth College.

Smith, A. (1998). 'The labour market effects of international trade: a computable general equilibrium model.' In Dewatripont et al. (1998).

Tang, P. and Wood, A. (1998). 'Globalisation, co-operation costs and wage inequalities.' Unpublished paper, Netherlands Planning Bureau and Institute of Development Studies, University of Sussex.

Tyers, R., Duncan, R. and Martin, W. (1997). 'Trade, technology and labour markets: general equilibrium perspectives.' In Francois et al. (forthcoming).

UNCTAD (1995, 1997). *Trade and Development Report*. Geneva: UNCTAD.

Wood, A. (1994). *North-South Trade, Employment and Inequality: Changing Fortunes in a Skill-Driven World*. Oxford: Clarendon Press.

Wood, A. (1995). 'How trade hurt unskilled workers.' *Journal of Economic Perspectives*, vol. 9, no. 3, pp. 57-80.

Wood, A. (1997). 'Openness and wage inequality in developing countries: the Latin American challenge to East Asian conventional wisdom.' *World Bank Economic Review*, vol. 11, no. 1, pp. 33-57.

Wood, A. (1998). 'An augmented Heckscher-Ohlin theory of globalisation and wage inequalities.' In Francois et al. (forthcoming).

Wood, A. and Anderson, E. (1998). 'Does Heckscher-Ohlin theory explain why the decline in demand for unskilled labour in the North first accelerated and then decelerated?' Unpublished paper, Institute of Development Studies, University of Sussex.

[8]

Feasible Globalizations

DANI RODRIK

W E WANT ECONOMIC INTEGRATION to help boost living standards. We want democratic politics so that public policy decisions are made by those that are directly affected by them. And we want self-determination, which comes with the nation-state. This chapter explains why we cannot have all three things simultaneously. The political "trilemma" of the global economy is that the nation-state system, democratic politics, and full economic integration are mutually incompatible. We can have at most two out of the three. Because global policymakers have yet to face up to this trilemma, we are headed in an untenable direction: global markets without global governance.

I argue instead for a renewed "Bretton-Woods compromise": preserving some limits on integration, as built into the original Bretton Woods arrangements, along with more global rules to handle the integration that can be achieved. Those who would make a different choice—toward tighter economic integration—must face up to the inevitable choice: either tighter world government or less democracy.

The strategy pursued by the leaders of the world economy underwent a subtle but important shift sometime in the 1980s. During the first four decades after the Second World War, international policymakers had kept their ambitions in check. They pursued a limited form of economic internationalization, leaving lots of room for national economic management. Successive rounds of multilateral trade negotiations made great strides, but focused only on the most egregious of national barriers and excluded large chunks of the economy (e.g., agriculture, services, and "sensitive" manufactures such as garments). In capital markets, restrictions on currency transactions and financial flows remained the norm rather than the exception. This Bretton Woods/GATT regime was successful because its architects subjugated international economic integration to the demands of national economic management and democratic politics.

This has changed drastically during the last two decades. Global policy is now driven by an aggressive agenda of "deep" integration: elimination of *all* barriers to trade and capital flows. The results have been problematic in terms of both economic performance (relative to the earlier postwar decades) and political legitimacy. The simple reason is that deep economic integration is unattainable in a world where nation states and democratic politics still exert considerable force.

Thus, the title of this essay—"feasible globalizations"—suggests two ideas. First, that there are inherent limitations to how far we can push global economic integration. It is not feasible (nor is it desirable) to maximize what Keynes called "economic entanglements between nations."[1] Second, that within the array of feasible globalizations, there are many different models to choose from. Each of these models has different implications for whom we empower and whom we don't, and for who gains and who loses.

We need to recognize these two facts in order to make progress in the globalization debate. One implication is that we need to scale down our ambitions with respect to global economic integration. Another is that we need to do a better job of writing the rules for a "thinner" (that is, less ambitious) version of globalization.

My argument about the limits to globalization isn't self-evident. It rests on several building blocks. First, markets need to be embedded in a range of non-market institutions in order to work well. These institutions create, regulate, stabilize, and legitimize markets, all functions that are crucial to the performance of markets..

The second and much widely less appreciated point is that there is no simple or unique correspondence between these functions and the form of the institutional infrastructure. American-style capitalism differs greatly from Japanese-style capitalism; there is tremendous variety in labor-market and welfare-state institutions even within Europe; and low-income countries often require heterodox institutional arrangements if they are to succeed at development.

Third, this institutional diversity is a significant impediment to full economic integration. Indeed, now that formal restrictions on trade and investment have mostly disappeared, regulatory and jurisdictional discontinuities created by heterogeneous national institutions constitute the most important barriers to international commerce. Deep integration would require removing these transaction costs through institutional harmonization—an agenda on which the World Trade Organization has already embarked. However, because institutional diversity performs a valuable economic (as well as social) role, this is a path full of dangers.

Fortunately, there are feasible models of globalization that would generate significantly more benefits than our current version—and a much more equitable distribution of those benefits. Toward the end of this chapter, I'll discuss a modification of global rules that would produce particularly powerful results: a multilaterally negotiated temporary visa scheme that would allow a broader mix of skilled and unskilled workers from developing nations to enter the developed world. Such a scheme would create income gains greater than all of the items on the WTO negotiating agenda taken together, even if the increase in cross-border labor flows was relatively small.

Markets and Nonmarket Institutions

The paradox of markets is that they thrive best not under *laissez-faire* but under the watchful eye of the state. Here is how historian Jacques Barzun describes the extensive regulatory apparatus in place in Venice at the height of its wealth and power around 1650:

> There were inspectors of weights and measures and of the Mint; arbitrators of commercial disputes and of servants and apprentices' grievances; censors of shop signs and taverns and of poor workmanship; wage setters and tax leviers; consuls to help creditors collect their due; and a congeries of marine officials. The population, being host to sailors from all over the Mediterranean, required a vigilant board of health, as did the houses of resort, for the excellence of which Venice became noted. All the bureaucrats were trained as carefully as the senators and councilors and every act was checked and rechecked as by a firm of accountants (Barzun 2000: 172).

What made Venice the epicenter of international trade and finance in seventeenth-century Europe was the quality of its public institutions. The same can be said of London in the nineteenth century and New York in the second half of the twentieth.

It is generally well understood that markets require nonmarket institutions—at the very least, a legal regime that enforces property rights and contracts. Without such a regime, markets cannot exist in any but the most rudimentary fashion. But the dependence of markets on public institutions runs deeper. Markets are not self-regulating, self-stabilizing, or self-legitimizing. As Adam Smith complained, businessmen seldom meet together without the conversation ending up in a "conspiracy against the public." In the absence of regulations pertaining to antitrust, information disclosure, prudential limits, public health and safety, and environmental and other externalities, markets can hardly do their job correctly. Without a lender-of-last-resort and a public fisc, markets are prone to wild gyrations and periodic bouts of underemployment. And without safety nets and social insurance to temper risks and inequalities, markets cannot retain their legitimacy for long.

The genius of capitalism, where it works, is that it has managed to continually reinvent its institutional underpinnings, with innovations that include central banking, stabilizing fiscal policy, antitrust and regulation, social insurance, and political democracy.

However, creating, regulating, stabilizing, or legitimizing markets are *functions* that need not map into specific institutional *forms*. Consider property rights, for example. What is relevant from an economic standpoint is whether current and prospective investors have the assurance that they can retain the fruits of their investments, not the precise legal form that this assurance takes. China is an extreme but illustrative example. It has managed to provide investors with this assurance despite the complete absence of private property rights. It turns out that institutional innovations in the form of the Household Responsibility System and the Township and Village Enterprises have served as functional equivalents of a private-enterprise economy. How else can we explain the tremendous burst in entrepreneurial activity that has taken place in China since the reforms of the late 1970s?

By contrast, many countries, such as Russia during the 1990s, fail to provide investors with effective control rights over cash flow, even though private property rights are nominally protected.

The variety of legal and social forms among today's advanced 3countries underscores the point. The United States, Europe, and Japan are all successful societies. Each has enjoyed a period of vogue among economists and social scientists: Scandinavia was everyone's favorite in the 1970s; Japan became the model to emulate in the 1980s; and the United States was the undisputed king of the 1990s. Yet none of these models can be deemed a clear winner in the contest of "capitalisms"; each has produced comparable amounts of wealth over the long term.

Nonetheless, their institutions in labor markets, corporate governance, regulation, social protection, and banking and finance all differ greatly. Furthermore, despite much talk about convergence in recent years, there have been few real signs of it. Financial systems (and to a much lesser extent corporate governance regimes) have tended to move toward an Anglo-American model. But labor marker arrangements (as measured by union membership or collective bargaining coverage rates) have actually diverged.[2]

There are good reasons for the resistance of national institutions to convergence. For one thing, societies differ in the values and norms that shape their institutional choices. To take an obvious example, Americans and Europeans tend to have different views as regards the determinants of economic outcomes;

compared to Americans, Europeans put greater weight on luck and smaller weight on individual effort.[3] Europeans correspondingly favor extensive redistribution and social protection schemes. Americans, for their part, tend to focus on equality of opportunity and tolerate much larger amounts of inequality.

There is a second, subtler reason for the absence of convergence in institutional arrangements: Different elements of a society's institutional configuration tend to be mutually reinforcing. Consider, for example, how Japanese society provides its citizens with social protection. Unlike Europe, the Japanese government does not maintain an expensive welfare state financed by transfers from taxpayers. Instead, social insurance has been provided in the postwar period through a combination of elements unique to Japanese-style capitalism: lifetime employment in large enterprises, protection of agriculture and small-scale services ("mom-and-pop" stores), government-organized cartels, and regulation of product markets.

All of these affect other parts of the institutional landscape. One implication of these arrangements is that they strengthen "insiders" (managers and employees) relative to "outsiders" (shareholders). This necessitates a particular corporate governance model. In Japan, "insiders" have traditionally been monitored and disciplined not by shareholders but by banks (Aoki 1997). In the United States, by contrast, the prevailing model of shareholder-value maximization privileges profits over the interests of insiders and other stakeholders. But the flip side is that profit-seeking behavior is constrained by the toughest antitrust regime in the world. It is difficult to imagine governments in Europe or Japan humiliating their premier high-tech company as the United States has done with Microsoft.

With such mutual dependence among the different parts of the institutional landscape, anything short of comprehensive change can be quite disruptive and is therefore difficult to contemplate in normal times. The result is what economists call "path dependence" or "hysteresis": if the institutional setup performs reasonably successfully (and often even when it does not), it gets locked in.

The last major category of reasons for institutional diversity has to do with the special needs of developing nations. Sparking and maintaining economic growth often requires institutional innovations that can depart significantly from American or Western ideals of best practice. Consider China again, the most spectacular case of success in the developing world in the last quarter century. A western-trained economist advising China in 1978 would have advocated a complete overhaul of the socialist economic regime: private property rights in land, corporatization of state enterprises, deregulation and price liberalization, currency unification, tax reform, reduction of import tariffs and elimination of quantitative restrictions on imports. China undertook few of these, and those that it did take on (such as currency unification and trade liberalization) were delayed for a decade or two after the onset of high growth. Instead, the Chinese leadership devised highly effective institutional shortcuts. The Household Responsibility System, Township and Village Enterprises, Special Economic Zones, and Two-Tier Pricing, among many other innovations, enabled the Chinese government to stimulate incentives for production and investment without a wholesale restructuring of the existing legal, social, and political regime.[4]

The Chinese experience represents not the exception, but the rule. Transitions to high growth are typically sparked not by comprehensive transformations that mimic best-practice institutions from the West but by a relatively narrow range of reforms that mix orthodoxy with domestic institutional innovations. South Korea and Taiwan since the early 1960s, Mauritius since the early 1970s, India since the early 1980s, and Chile since the mid-1980s are all examples of this strategy.[5]

INSTITUTIONAL DIVERSITY VERSUS DEEP INTEGRATION

When economists talk about obstacles to global economic integration, they typically have in mind things like import tariffs, quantitative restrictions on trade, multiple currency practices, restrictive regulations on foreign borrowing and lending, and limitations on foreign ownership. The past few decades have witnessed unparalleled reduction in such barriers; all have been eliminated or slashed across the globe. With these textbook impediments gone, one would have expected national economies to become seamlessly integrated with each other. But, to their surprise, economists have discovered that economic integration remains seriously incomplete.

To be sure, the volume of cross-border trade and investment flows has increased enormously in recent decades. Yet when measured against the benchmark of *national* markets, international markets remain highly fragmented. A well-known study calculated that the volume of trade between two Canadian provinces is twenty times larger than that between a province and an adjacent United States (McCallum 1995: 615–23). While later academic studies have reduced this large differential, they all confirm that national borders strongly depress economic exchange (Anderson and van Wincoop 2001).

A different strand of the literature has focused on a related phenomenon trade economists call "missing trade." It seems that the flow of "factors" (such as labor and capital) embodied in trade falls far short of what standard theories of comparative advantage predict. In other words, given the very large differences in relative factor endowments across countries and the apparent absence of formal trade barriers, there is much less trade in "factor services" than there should be.[6]

202   *Dani Rodrik*

From an economic standpoint, what matters is not the volume of trade as much as the degree of price convergence across national markets. Here, too, the results have been disappointing. Prices of tradable commodities often diverge substantially across national markets, even after the effects of indirect taxes and retail costs are eliminated from the comparison. Moreover, when prices do converge to a common level, it happens slowly, over several years.[7] All of these pieces of evidence point to the same conclusion: National borders continue to act as serious impediments to economic exchange, even though formal trade barriers have all but disappeared.

Surprisingly, much the same is true in capital markets. In a world of free capital mobility, households would invest in internationally diversified portfolios, and the location of enterprises would not affect their access to financing. In reality, financial markets are subject to a large amount of "home bias." Investments in plant and equipment are constrained by the availability of domestic savings, and portfolios remain remarkably parochial (Tesar and Werner 1998). Even in periods of exuberance, *net* capital flows between rich and poor nations fall considerably short of what theoretical models would predict. And in periods of panic, which occur with alarming frequency, capital flows from North to South can dry up in an instant. Global foreign exchange markets may turn over $1.5 trillion in a single day, but any investor who acts on the assumption that it's all one big capital market out there and that national borders don't matter would be in for a big surprise—sooner rather than later.

How do these border barriers arise? We are now in a position to link this discussion with the concept of institutional diversity. Institutional and jurisdictional discontinuities serve to segment markets just as transport costs or import taxes do. In effect, national borders, and the institutional boundaries that they define, impose a wide array of transaction costs.

These transaction costs arise from various sources. Most obviously, contract enforcement is more problematic across national boundaries than it is domestically. Domestic courts may be unwilling—and international courts may be unable—to enforce a contract signed between residents of two different countries. This problem is particularly severe in the case of capital flows, as financial contracts inevitably involve a *promise* to repay. Thus, a key reason why more capital does not flow to poorer countries is that there is no good way such a promise can be rendered binding across national jurisdictions (short of resorting to the gunboat diplomacy of old).

Often, contracts are implicit rather than explicit, in which case they require either repeated interaction between the parties or side constraints to make them sustainable. Within a country, implicit contracts are often embedded in social networks which provide sanctions against opportunistic behavior. One of the things that keep businessmen honest is fear of social ostracism. The role played by ethnic networks in fostering cross-border trade and investment linkages (for example, among the Chinese in Southeast Asia) suggests the importance of group ties in facilitating economic exchange (Casella and Rauch 1997). But such ties are hard to set up across national borders in the absence of fortuitous ethnic and other social linkages.

Transaction costs also result from national differences in regulatory regimes and in the rules of doing business—informal as well as legal. That such differences raise the cost of buying, selling, and investing across national boundaries is one of the most frequent complaints heard from businessmen around the world. Indeed, these differences are increasingly to blame for trade conflicts. When the United States blames Japan's retail distribution practices for keeping Kodak out of the Japanese market, or when it lodges a complaint against the EU in the WTO because of Europe's ban on hormone-treated beef, the issue is the impact that different styles of regulation have on international trade. Conversely, developing nations have won WTO judgments against the United States, centering on gasoline standards and fishing regulations enacted pursuant to the U.S. Clean Air Act and the U.S. Endangered Species Act, on the grounds that these regulations were harmful to their sales of gasoline and shrimp, respectively.

Conflicts like these have forced trade negotiators to focus on harmonizing such regulatory differences away. A major victory in the Uruguay Round of GATT was the Agreement on Trade Related Aspects of Intellectual Property Rights (TRIPs), which established a minimum patent length requirement. In the area of international finance, a similar push is under way through the promulgation of a series of codes and standards on corporate governance, capital adequacy, bank regulation, accounting, auditing, and insurance.

Many economists have concluded that the way forward is to offset the centrifugal forces created by institutional boundaries through international agreements, harmonization, and standard setting. But as I have argued earlier, diversity in national institutions serves a real and useful purpose. It is rooted in national preferences, sustains social compacts, and allows developing nations to find their way out of poverty. Eliminating this diversity might not be beneficial even if it were possible.

The Political Trilemma of the Global Economy

The discussion of this trilemma draws heavily on Rodrik 2000. The inevitable tradeoffs are illustrated in figure 8.1, which shows what I call The Political Trilemma of the Global Economy. The key point is that the nation-state system,

204   *Dani Rodrik*

deep economic integration, and democracy are mutually incompatible. We can have a full measure of, at most, two out of these three. If we want to push global economic integration much further, we will have to give up either the nation state or democracy (that is, mass politics). If we want to maintain and deepen democracy, we will have to choose between the nation state and international economic integration. And if we want to keep the nation state, we will have to choose between democracy and international economic integration.

Why is this so? Consider a hypothetical perfectly integrated world economy in which national borders do not interfere with exchange in goods, services, or capital. Transaction costs and tax differentials would be minor; convergence in commodity prices and factor returns would be almost complete. Is such a world compatible with the nation-state system? Can we maintain the nation-state system while ensuring that national jurisdictions—and the differences among them—do not hamper economic transactions? Possibly, if nation states were to focus above all on becoming attractive to international markets. In that case, national jurisdictions would be geared toward maximizing international commerce and capital mobility. Domestic regulations and tax policies would be either harmonized according to international standards, or structured to mini-mize any hindrance to international economic integration. And the only public goods provided would be those compatible with integrated markets.

It is possible to envisage a world of this sort. In fact, many commentators believe we actually live in it. Many governments today do compete in pursuing policies that they believe will earn them market confidence and attract trade and capital inflows: tight money, small government, low taxes, flexible labor legis-lation, deregulation, privatization, and general openness. These are the poli-cies that make up what Thomas Friedman (1999) has aptly termed the Golden

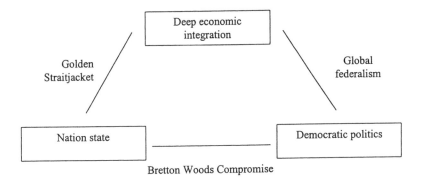

FIGURE 8.1 *The political trilemma of the world economy*

Straitjacket. However, the price of maintaining national sovereignty while markets become international is that politics has to be exercised over a much narrower domain. Friedman writes (1999: 87):

As your country puts on the Golden Straitjacket, two things tend to happen: your economy grows and your politics shrinks. . . . [The] Golden Straitjacket narrows the political and economic policy choices of those in power to relatively tight parameters. That is why it is increasingly difficult these days to find any real differences between ruling and opposition parties in those countries that have put on the Golden Straitjacket. Once your country puts on the Golden Straitjacket, its political choices get reduced to Pepsi or Coke—to slight nuances of tastes, slight nuances of policy, slight alterations in design to account for local traditions, some loosening here or there, but never any major deviation from the core golden rules.

The crowding out of democratic politics is reflected in the insulation of economic policymaking bodies (central banks, fiscal authorities, and so on); the disappearance or privatization of social insurance; and the replacement of developmental goals with the need to maintain market confidence. Once the rules of the game are set by the requirements of the global economy, domestic groups' access to, and their control over, national economic policymaking is necessarily restricted.

No country went farther down this path in the 1990s than Argentina, which looked for a while like the perfect illustration of Friedman's point. Thus, Argentina's ultimate collapse carries an important lesson for this discussion.

Argentina undertook more trade liberalization, tax reform, privatization, and financial reform than virtually any other country in Latin America. It did everything possible to endear itself to international capital markets. Obtaining an investment-grade rating—the ultimate mark of approval by international markets—became the Argentine government's first priority.[8] Why did international investors nonetheless abruptly abandon the country as the decade was coming to a close?

The financial markets did not fear any lack of commitment by the political leadership to repay foreign debt. Indeed, during the course of 2001 President de la Rúa and economy minister Cavallo abrogated their contracts with virtually all domestic constituencies—public employees, pensioners, provincial governments, bank depositors—to ensure their ability to pay 100 percent of their obligations to foreign creditors. What ultimately sealed Argentina's fate in the eyes of financial markets was not what Cavallo and de la Rúa were doing, but what the Argentine people were willing to accept. Markets grew skeptical that the Argentine congress, provinces, and common people would continue to tolerate the policy of putting foreign obligations before domestic ones. And in the end, the markets were proven correct. After a couple of days of mass protests and riots just before Christmas, Cavallo and de la Rúa had to resign.

So Argentina's lesson has proved to be a different one than Friedman intended. Mass politics casts a long shadow on international capital flows, even when political leaders single-mindedly pursue the agenda of deep integration. In democracies, when the demands of foreign creditors collide with the needs of domestic constituencies, the former eventually yield to the latter. In time of crisis, democracy escapes from the Golden Straitjacket.

A conceivable alternative would be to drop nation states rather than democratic politics. This is the solution dubbed "global federalism" in figure 8.1. Global federalism would align jurisdictions with markets and remove border effects. In this scenario, politics would not wither: instead, it would relocate to the global level.

This is the United States model expanded on a global scale. Although there are some differences in regulatory and taxation practices among the American states, the presence of a national constitution, national government, and federal judiciary ensures that U.S. markets are truly national. The European Union, while very far from a federal system at present, is headed broadly in the same direction. Under global federalism, national governments would not necessarily disappear, but their powers would be severely circumscribed by supranational legislative, executive, and judicial authorities.

If this sounds unlikely, it is. The historical experience of the U.S. shows how tricky it is to establish and maintain a political union among states that have major differences in their institutional arrangements. One such difference—slavery—came close to destroying the United States. Today, the uncertain development of political institutions within the EU and the persistent complaints about their democratic deficits reflect the same kinds of difficulties, which persist even though the EU encompasses nations at similar income levels and with similar historical trajectories. Thus, global federalism is at least a century away.

The third and final option is to sacrifice the goal of deep economic integration. I term this the Bretton Woods compromise. The essence of the Bretton Woods-GATT regime was that countries were free to dance to their own regulatory tune so long as they removed a number of border restrictions on trade and generally did not discriminate among trade partners.[9] They were allowed (indeed encouraged) to maintain restrictions on capital flows, since Keynes and the other architects of the postwar economic order regarded a system of free capital flows as incompatible with domestic economic stability.

Under this regime, although impressive trade liberalization was undertaken during successive rounds of GATT negotiations, many barriers remained in place. Services, agriculture, and textiles were effectively left out of the negotia-

tions. Various clauses in the GATT (on anti-dumping and safeguards, in particular) permitted countries to erect trade barriers when their industries came
under severe competition from imports. And developing country policies were
effectively left outside the scope of international discipline.

Until the 1980s, these loose rules left enough space for countries to follow
divergent paths of development. Western Europe chose to integrate separately
and to erect an extensive system of social insurance. Japan developed its own
distinctive brand of capitalism, combining a dynamic export machine with
large doses of inefficiency in services and agriculture. China grew by leaps and
bounds once it recognized the importance of private initiative, even though it
flouted every other rule in the guidebook. Much of the rest of East Asia relied on
industrial policies that have since been banned by the WTO. And until the late
1970s, scores of countries in Latin America, the Middle East, and Africa generated unprecedented economic growth rates by following import-substitution
policies that insulated their economies from the world economy.

The Bretton Woods compromise was largely abandoned in the 1980s as the
liberalization of capital flows gathered speed and trade agreements began to
break through national borders. We have since been trapped in an uncomfortable and unsustainable zone somewhere between the three nodes of figure 8.1.
Neither of the alternatives to the Bretton Woods compromise provides a real
way forward. The Golden Straitjacket may be feasible, but it is not truly desirable. Global federalism may be desirable, but it is not feasible.

Therefore, if the principal locus of democratic politics is to remain the nation state, we have no choice but to settle for a thin version of globalization—to
reinvent the Bretton Woods compromise for a different era.

ALTERNATIVE GLOBALIZATIONS: THE CASE OF LABOR MOBILITY

Global economic rules are not written by Platonic philosopher-kings, or even by the
present-day pretenders to that status, the academic economists. If WTO agreements
were truly about "free trade," they could all be replaced with a single sentence: "Trade
shall be free." The reality, of course, is that politics plays a role in WTO agenda setting and rule making, and those with power get more out of the system than those
without it. Nonetheless, advocates of globalization often present their position with
an air of inevitability, as if it has a natural logic that only economic illiterates would
reject. Recognizing that there is a multiplicity of feasible globalizations—as there is
a multiplicity of institutional underpinnings for capitalist economies—would have
an important liberating effect on our policy discussions.

So what kind of globalization should we strive for? There are important choices to be made. Consider the following thought experiment. Imagine that the negotiators who recently met in Doha to hammer out an agenda for world trade talks really meant it when they said that the new round of GATT would be a "development round," that is, one designed to bring maximum benefit to poor countries. What would they have focused on? Increasing market access for developing country exports? Reform of the agricultural regime in Europe and other advanced countries? Intellectual property rights and public health in developing nations? Rules on government procurement, competition policy, environment, or trade facilitation?

The answer is none of the above. In all these areas, the benefits to developing countries are slim at best. The biggest bang by far would lie in something that was not even on the agenda at Doha: relaxing restrictions on the international movement of workers. This would produce the largest possible gains for the world economy, and for poor countries in particular.

We know this because of a basic principle of economics: *The income gains that derive from international trade rise with the square of the price differentials across national markets.* What does this mean? Compare the treatment of markets in goods and financial assets, on the one hand, with that of markets for labor services on the other. The removal of restrictions on markets for goods and financial assets has narrowed (though it has not eliminated) the price differentials in these markets. Remaining price differences rarely exceed 2 to 1. By contrast, markets for cross-border labor services are still very restricted. Consequently, wages of similarly qualified individuals in the advanced and low-income countries often differ by a factor of 10 or more. Applying the economics principle enunciated above, liberalizing cross-border labor movements could be expected to yield benefits that are roughly 25 times larger than those that accrue from liberalizing the flow of goods and capital!

It follows that even a minor liberalization of international labor flows would create gains for the world economy that are much larger than the combined effect of all the post-Doha initiatives under consideration. Consider, for example, a *temporary* work visa scheme that would allow skilled and unskilled workers from poor nations to work in the rich countries for three to five years, to be replaced by a new wave of inflows upon return to their home countries. Even if the workers involved amounted to no more than 3 percent of the rich countries' labor force, a back-of-the-envelope calculation indicates that such a system would easily yield $200 billion annually for the citizens of developing nations. That is vastly more than the existing estimates of the gains from the

Critical Perspectives on Globalization

current trade agenda. The positive spillovers that the returnees would generate for their home countries—the experience, entrepreneurship, investment, and work ethic they would bring back with them and put to work—would increase these gains even further. Equally important, the economic benefits would accrue directly to workers from developing nations. We would not need to wait for trickle-down to do its job.

So relaxing restrictions on cross-border flows through temporary work contracts and other schemes has a compelling economic logic. But is it politically feasible? Probably not. Such flows might hurt workers in advanced countries, especially low-skill workers. Worries about crime and other social problems (as well as racism) have made immigration unpopular in many rich countries. And some might fear that increased labor flows could enhance the threat of terrorism in our post–September 11 world.

Yet the political factors at work are subtler than is commonly supposed. Imports from developing countries—which are, in economic terms, nothing other than inflows of embodied labor services—create the same downward pressure on rich country wages as immigration, and that has not stopped policymakers from bringing trade barriers down. The bias toward trade and investment liberalization (and against increased labor flow) is certainly not due to domestic politics. The typical voter in the advanced countries is against both immigration *and* imports: less than 20 percent of Americans and Britons favor unrestricted imports, about the same as the fraction that believe immigration is good for the economy. In any case, a well-designed scheme of labor inflows could address many of the social and economic worries among citizens in the host countries. For example, we can imagine aligning the skill mix of guest workers with that of the natives, allowing in no more than one construction worker or fruit picker, say, for every physician or software engineer.

Thus, substantial liberalization of trade and investment has taken place not because it is popular among voters, but because the beneficiaries (mainly multinational firms and financial enterprises) have organized successfully and become politically effective. By contrast, increased labor flows have no well-defined constituency in the advanced countries. When a Turkish worker enters the European Union or a Mexican worker enters the United States, the ultimate local beneficiaries can't be identified in advance. Only after the worker lands a job does his employer develop a direct stake in keeping him in the country. This explains why, for example, the U.S. federal government devotes a large amount of resources to border controls to prevent *hypothetical* immigrants from coming in, while it does little to deport employed illegals or fine their employers once they are actually inside the country. The same principle also explains why the rare relaxations on labor restrictions come about only in response to pressure from well-organized interest groups such as agricultural producers or Silicon Valley firms.

The lesson? Political constraints can be malleable. Economists have remained excessively tolerant of the political realities that underpin restrictions on international labor mobility, even as they continually decry the protectionist forces that block further liberalization of an already very open trading system.[10]

To ensure that labor mobility produces benefits for developing nations, it is imperative that the regime be designed in a way that generates incentives for return to home countries. While remittances can be an important source of income support for poor families, they are generally unable to spark and sustain long-term economic development. Designing contract labor schemes that are truly temporary is tricky, but it can be done. There need to be clear incentives for all parties—workers, employees, and home and host governments—to live up to their commitments. One possibility would be to withhold a portion of workers' earnings until return takes place. This forced saving scheme would ensure that workers would come back home with a sizeable pool of resources to invest. In addition, there could be penalties for home governments whose nationals failed to comply with return requirements. For example, sending countries' quotas could be reduced in proportion to the numbers that fail to return. That would increase incentives for sending government to do their utmost to create a hospitable economic and political climate at home and to encourage their nationals' return.

In the end, it is inevitable that the return rate will fall short of 100 percent. But even with less than full compliance, the gains from reorienting our priorities toward the labor mobility agenda would remain significant.

CONCLUSION

I have highlighted two shortcomings of current discussions of globalization. First, there's too little appreciation of the fact that economic globalization is necessarily limited by the scope of desirable institutional diversity at the national level. Under current political configurations and economic realities, deep integration is impossible.

Second, there are many models of feasible globalization, each with different economic implications. As my discussion of labor mobility illustrates, we are not focusing currently on the areas of economic integration with the biggest potential gains.

The hopeful message is that it is possible to squeeze much additional mileage out of globalization, while still remaining within the boundaries of feasibility I have identified

ACKNOWLEDGMENT

The author is grateful to Michael Weinstein for very helpful suggestions.

ENDNOTES

1. Keynes 1933 used this phrase in an essay written in the midst of the Great Depression, in which he appeared to have given up on free trade altogether: "I sympathize with those who would minimize, rather than those who would maximize economic entanglements between nations. Ideas, art, knowledge, hospitality and travel should be international. But let goods be homespun whenever it is reasonable and conveniently possible, and above all let finance be primarily national."

.2. On the limited convergence in effective patterns of corporate governance, see Mayer 2000; Khanna, Kogan, and Palepu 2001. On divergence in labor market institutions, see Freeman 2000.

3. For an analysis of differences in attitudes toward inequality, see Alesina, di Tella, and MacCulloch 2001.

4. See the discussion of "transitional institutions" in Yingyi Qian (forthcoming).

5. This is why studies such as Dollar and Kraay 2001, which purport to show that "globalizers" grow faster than "non-globalizers," are so misleading. The countries used as exemplars of "globalizers" in these studies (China, India, Vietnam) have all employed heterodox strategies, and the last conclusion that can derived from their experience is that trade liberalization, adherence to WTO strictures, and adoption of the "Washington Consensus" are the best way to generate economic growth. China (until recently) and Vietnam were not even members of the WTO, and together with India, these countries remain among the most protectionist in the world.

6. The standard reference on this is Trefler (1995: 1029–1046).

7. For example, Bradford (2000: table 2) estimates that domestic prices of motorcycles and bicycles exceed world prices by 100% in the U.K., 76% in Belgium, and 60% in Germany. See also the survey by Rogoff(1996: 647–68).

8. The much-maligned currency board system, originally aimed at stopping inflation, eventually became part of this same strategy. A government that was prevented from printing money, it was felt, would be more attractive to foreign investors.

9. John Ruggie has written insightfully on this, describing the system that emerged as "embedded liberalism." See especially Ruggie 1983.

212   *Dani Rodrik*

10. Characteristically, two recent books by prominent academic defenders of free trade pass over the question of labor mobility entirely. See Bhagwati 2002 and Irwin 2002.

REFERENCES

Alesina, Alberto, Rafael di Tella, and Robert MacCulloch. 2001. "Inequality and Happiness: Are Europeans and Americans Different?" National Bureau of Economic Research Working Paper 8198, Cambridge, MA (April).

Anderson, James E. and Eric van Wincoop. 2001. "Gravity with Gravitas: A Solution to the Border Puzzle." National Bureau of Economic Research Working Paper 8079, Cambridge, MA (January).

Aoki, Masahiko. 1997. "Unintended Fit: Organizational Evolution and Government Design of Institutions in Japan." In M. Aoki et al., eds. *The Role of Government in East Asian Economic Development: Comparative Institutional Analysis*. Oxford: Clarendon Press.

Barzun, Jacques. 2000. *From Dawn to Decadence: 500 Years of Western Cultural Life.* New York: Perennial.

Bhagwati, Jagdish. 2002. *Free Trade Today*. Princeton: Princeton University Press.

Bradford, Scott. 2000. "Paying the Price: The Welfare and Employment Effects of Protection in OECD Countries." Economics Department, Brigham Young University. Unpublished paper (December).

Casella, Alessandra and James Rauch. 1997. "Anonymous Market and Group Ties in International Trade," National Bureau of Economic Research Working Paper W6186 (September).

Dollar, David and Aaart Kraay. 2001."Trade, Growth, and Poverty" (Development Research Group, The World Bank), unpublished paper (March).

Freeman, Richard. 2000. "Single Peaked vs. Diversified Capitalism: The Relation Between Economic Institutions and Outcomes," National Bureau of Economic Research Working Paper 7556, Cambridge, MA, February 2000.

Friedman, Thomas L. 1999. *The Lexus and the Olive Tree*. New York: Farrar Strauss Giroux.

Irwin, Douglas A. 2002. *Free Trade Under Fire*, Princeton: Princeton University Press.

Keynes, John Maynard. 1933. "National Self-Sufficiency." *Yale Review*.

Khanna, Tarun. Joe Kogan, and Krishna Palepu. 2001. "Globalization and Corporate Governance Convergence? A Cross-Country Analysis." Harvard Business School, unpublished paper (October).

Mayer, Colin. 2002. "Corporate Cultures and Governance: Ownership, Control, and Governance of European and US Corporations." Said Business School, Oxford University, unpublished paper (March). 2002.

McCallum, John. 1995. "National Borders Matter: Canada-U.S. Regional Trade Patterns." *The American Economic Review* 85, no. 3. (June): 615–23.

Qian Yingyi. Forthcoming. "How Reform Worked in China." In Dani Rodrik, ed. *In Search of Prosperity: Analytic Narratives on Economic Growth*. Princeton: Princeton University Press.

Rodrik, Dani. 2000. "How Far Will International Economic Integration Go?" *Journal of Economic Perspectives* (Winter).

Rogoff, Kenneth S. 1996. "The Purchasing Power Parity Puzzle." *Journal of Economic Literature* 34, no. 2 (June).

Ruggie, John. G. 1983. "International Regimes, Transactions, and Change: Embedded Liberalism in the Postwar Economic Order." In Stephen D. Krasner, ed. *International Regimes*, Ithaca: Cornell University Press.

Tesar, Linda and Ingrid Werner. 1998. "The Internationalization of Securities Markets Since the 1987 Crash." In R. Litan and A. Santomero, eds. *Brookings-Wharton Papers on Financial Services*. Washington DC: The Brookings Institution.

Trefler, Daniel. 1995. "The Case of the Missing Trade and Other Mysteries." *The American Economic Review* 85, no. 5. (December).

[9]
Globalization for Whom?[1]

Time to change the rules – and focus on poor workers

Dani Rodrik

Globalization has brought little but good news to those with the products, skills, and resources to market worldwide. But does it also work for the world's poor?

That is the central question around which the debate over globalization – in essence, free trade and free flows of capital – revolves. Antiglobalization protesters may have had only limited success in blocking world trade negotiations or disrupting the meetings of the International Monetary Fund (IMF), but they have irrevocably altered the terms of the debate. Poverty is now *the* defining issue for both sides. The captains of the world economy have conceded that progress in international trade and finance has to be measured against the yardsticks of poverty alleviation and sustainable development.

For most of the world's developing countries, the 1990s were a decade of frustration and disappointment. The economies of sub-Saharan Africa, with few exceptions, stubbornly refused to respond to the medicine meted out by the World Bank and the IMF. Latin American countries were buffeted by a never-ending series of boom-and-bust cycles in capital markets and experienced growth rates significantly below their historical averages. Most of the former socialist economies ended the decade at *lower* levels of per-capita income than they started it – and even in the rare successes, such as Poland, poverty rates remained higher than under communism. East Asian economies such as South Korea, Thailand, and Malaysia, which had been hailed previously as 'miracles,' were dealt a humiliating blow in the financial crisis of 1997. That this was also the decade in which globalization came into full swing is more than a minor inconvenience for its advocates. If globalization is such a boon for poor countries, why so many setbacks?

Globalizers deploy two counter-arguments against such complaints. One is that global poverty has actually decreased. The reason is simple: while *most* countries have seen lower income growth, the world's two largest countries, China and India, have had the opposite experience. (Economic growth tends to be highly correlated with poverty reduction.) China's growth since the late 1970s – averaging almost 8 per cent per annum per capita – has been nothing short of spectacular. India's performance has not been as extraordinary, but the country's growth rate has more than doubled since the early 1980s – from 1.5 per cent per capita to 3.7 per cent. These two countries house more than half of the world's poor, and their experience is perhaps enough to dispel the collective doom elsewhere.

The second counter-argument is that it is precisely those countries that have experienced the greatest integration with the [29] world economy that have managed to grow fastest and reduce poverty the most. A typical exercise in this vein consists of dividing developing countries into two groups on the basis of the increase in their trade – 'globalizers' versus 'non-globalizers' – and to show that the first group did much better than the second. Here too, China, India, and a few other high performers like Vietnam and Uganda are the key exhibits for the pro-globalization argument. The intended message from such studies is that countries that have the best shot at lifting themselves out of poverty are those that open themselves up to the world economy.

How we read globalization's record in alleviating poverty hinges critically, therefore, on what we make of the experience of a small number of countries that have done well in the last decade or two – China in particular. In 1960, the average Chinese expected to live only 36 years. By 1999, life expectancy had risen to 70 years, not far below the level of the United States. Literacy has risen from less than 50 per cent to more than 80 per cent. Even though economic development has been uneven, with the coastal regions doing much better than the interior, there has been a striking reduction in poverty rates almost everywhere.

What does this impressive experience tell us about what globalization can do for poor countries? There is little doubt that exports and foreign investment have played an important role in China's development. By selling its products on world markets, China has been able to purchase the capital equipment and inputs needed for its modernization. And the surge in foreign investment has brought much-needed managerial and technical expertise. The regions of China that have grown fastest are those that took the greatest advantage of foreign trade and investment.

But look closer at the Chinese experience, and you discover that it is hardly a poster child for globalization. China's economic policies have violated virtually every rule by which the proselytizers of globalization would like the game to be played. China did *not* liberalize its trade regime to any significant extent, and it joined the World Trade Organization (WTO) only last year; to this day, its economy remains among the most protected in the world. Chinese currency markets were *not* unified until 1994. China resolutely refused to open its financial markets to foreigners, again until very recently. Most striking of all, China achieved its transformation without adopting private-property rights, let alone privatizing its state enterprises. China's policymakers were practical enough to understand the role that private incentives and markets could play in producing results. But they were also smart enough to realize that the solution to their problems lay in institutional innovations suited to the local conditions – the household responsibility system, township and village enterprises, special economic zones, partial liberalization in agriculture and industry – rather than in off-the-shelf blueprints and Western rules of good behavior.

The remarkable thing about China is that it has achieved integration with the world economy *despite* having ignored these rules – and indeed because it did so. If China were a basket case today, rather than the stunning success that it is, officials of the WTO and the World Bank would have fewer difficulties fitting it within their worldview than they do now.

China's experience may represent an extreme case, but it is by no means an exception. Earlier successes such as South Korea and Taiwan tell a similar story. Economic development often requires unconventional strategies that fit awkwardly with the ideology of free trade and free capital flows. South Korea and Taiwan made extensive use of import quotas, local-content requirements, patent infringements, and export subsidies – all of which are currently prohibited by the WTO. Both countries heavily regulated capital flows well into the 1990s. India managed to increase its growth rate through the adoption of more pro-business policies, despite having one of the world's most protectionist trade regimes. Its comparatively mild import liberalization in the 1990s came a decade *after* the onset of higher growth in the early 1980s. And India has *yet* to open itself up to world financial markets – which is why it emerged unscathed from the Asian financial crisis of 1997.

By contrast, many of the countries that *have* opened themselves up to trade and capital flows with abandon have been rewarded with financial crises and disappointing performance. Latin America, the region that adopted the globalization agenda with the greatest enthusiasm in the 1990s, has suffered rising inequality, enormous volatility, and economic growth rates significantly below those of the post-World War II decades. Argentina represents a particularly tragic case. It tried harder in the 1990s than virtually any country to endear itself to international capital markets, only to be the victim of an abrupt reversal in 'market sentiment' by the end of the decade. The Argentine strategy may have had elements of a gamble, but it was solidly grounded in the theories expounded by US-based economists and multilateral agencies such as the World Bank and the IMF. When Argentina's economy took off in the early 1990s after decades of stagnation, the reaction from these quarters was not that this was puzzling – it was that reform pays off.

What these countries' experience tells us, therefore, is that while global markets are good for poor countries, the rules according to which they are being asked to play the game are often not. Caught between WTO agreements, World Bank strictures, IMF conditions, and the need to maintain the confidence of financial markets, developing countries are increasingly deprived of the room they need to devise their own paths out of poverty. They are being asked to implement an agenda of institutional reform that took today's advanced countries generations to accomplish. The United States, to take a particularly telling example, was hardly a paragon of free-trade virtue while catching up with and surpassing Britain. In fact, US import tariffs during the latter half of the nineteenth century were higher than in all but a few developing countries today. Today's rules are not only impractical, they divert attention and resources from more urgent developmental priorities. Turning away from world markets is surely not a good way to alleviate domestic poverty – but [30] countries that have scored the most impressive gains are those that have developed their *own* version of the rulebook while taking advantage of world markets.

The regulations that developing nations confront in those markets are highly asymmetric. Import barriers tend to be highest for manufactured products of greatest interest to poor countries, such as garments. The global intellectual-property-rights regime tends to raise prices of essential medicines in poor countries.

But the disconnect between trade rules and development needs is nowhere greater than in the area of international labor mobility. Thanks to the efforts of the United States and other rich countries, barriers to trade in goods, financial services, and investment flows have now been brought down to historic lows. But the one market where poor nations have something in abundance to sell – the market for labor services – has remained untouched by this liberalizing trend. Rules on cross-border labor flows are determined almost always unilaterally (rather than multilaterally as in other areas of economic exchange) and remain highly restrictive. Even a small relaxation of these rules would produce huge gains for the world economy, and for poor nations in particular.

Consider, for example, instituting a system that would allot temporary work permits to skilled and unskilled workers from poorer nations, amounting to, say, 3 per cent of the rich countries' labor force. Under the scheme, these workers would be allowed to obtain employment in the rich countries for a period of three to five years, after which they would be expected to return to their home countries and be replaced by new workers. (While many workers, no doubt, will want to remain in the host countries permanently, it would be possible to achieve acceptable rates of return by building specific incentives into the scheme. For example, a portion of workers' earnings could be witheld until repatriation takes place. Or there could be penalties for home governments whose nationals failed to comply with return requirements: sending countries' quotas could be reduced in proportion to the numbers who fail to return.) A back-of-the-envelope calculation indicates that such a system would easily yield $200 billion of income annually for the citizens of developing nations – vastly more than what the existing WTO trade agenda is expected to produce. The positive spillovers that the returnees would generate for their home countries – the experience, entrepreneurship, investment, and work ethic they would bring back with them – would add considerably to these gains. What is equally important, the economic benefits would accrue directly to workers from developing nations. There would be no need for 'trickle down.'

If the political leaders of the advanced countries have chosen to champion trade liberalization but not international labor mobility, the reason is not that the former is popular with voters at home while the latter is not. They are *both* unpopular. When asked their views on trade policy, fewer than one in five Americans reject import restrictions. In most advanced countries, including the United States, the proportion of respondents who want to expand imports tends to be about the same or lower than the proportion who believe immigration is good for the economy. The main difference seems to be that the beneficiaries of trade and investment liberalization have managed to become politically effective. Multinational firms and financial enterprises have been successful in setting the agenda of multilateral trade negotiations because they have been quick to see the link between enhanced market access abroad and increased profits at home. Cross-border labor flows, by contrast, usually have not had a well-defined constituency in the advanced countries. Rules on foreign workers have been relaxed only in those rare instances where there has been intense lobbying from special interests. When Silicon Valley firms became concerned about labor costs, for example, they pushed Congress hard to be allowed to import software engineers from India and other developing nations.

It will take a lot of work to make globalization's rules friendlier to poor nations. Leaders of the advanced countries will have to stop dressing up policies championed by special interests at home as responses to the needs of the poor in the developing world. Remembering their own history, they will have to provide room for poor nations to develop their own strategies of institution-building and economic catch-up. For their part, developing nations will have to stop looking to financial markets and multilateral agencies for the recipes of economic growth. Perhaps most difficult of all, economists will have to learn to be more humble! [31]

Dani Rodrik '79 is Hariri professor of international political economy at the Kennedy School of Government and author of 'The New Global Economy and Developing Countries: Making Openness Work.'

Notes

Numbers in square brackets relate to page numbers in the original article
* Reprinted from Harvard Magazine. For copyright and reprint information, contact Harvard Magazine, Inc. at www.harvardmagazine.com

[10]

2

By Nancy Birdsall

Secure and equitable markets demand political institutions.
. . Markets are the domain of competition; politics, the domain
of collective action.
Luiz Carlos Bresser-Pereira, Getulio Vargas Foundation, Sao Paulo, Brazil

My remarks today are about globalization, its asymmetries between rich and poor, and because of its asymmetries, the need to rethink our global development architecture. I will be talking mostly as an economist this afternoon, but my real theme is that integration of the global economy is outpacing the development of a healthy global polity.[1] The globalization of markets can and has brought mutual benefits to the rich and poor alike. But it is only through better global politics that the values and rules critical to a secure and just world will be realized, and it is only then that the full benefits of a global market will be available to all.

Put another way, good global politics is critical to the battle against global poverty and unrealized human development, and to a more just and fair as well as a more stable and prosperous global economy.

By globalization I mean the increasing integration of economies and societies, not only in terms of goods and services and financial flows but also of ideas, norms, information and peoples. In popular use, however, the term globalization has come to mean the increasing influence of global market capitalism or what is seen as the increasing reach of corporate and financial interests at the global level.

A debate continues to rage about the merits and demerits of market-led globalization for the poor. On one side of the debate are most mainstream economists, the United Nations, the World Bank and the other international financial institutions, most finance ministers and central bank governors in poor as well as rich countries, and most professional students of development. All of these generally argue that globalization is not the culprit in any increase in world poverty and inequality. It is, after all, the people least touched by globalization, living in rural Africa and South Asia, who are the poorest in the world. On the other side of the debate are most social activists, members of non-profit civil society groups who work on environmental issues, human rights, and relief programs, most of the popular press, and many sensible, well-educated observers. To them, the issue seems self-evident. Globalization may be good for the rich, that is the rich countries and the rich within countries, but it is bad news for the poorest countries, and especially for the poor in those countries.

The furious debate about the merits and demerits of globalization for the poor boils down to a debate about the current distribution of economic and political power in the world, and the

---

[1] This is how Gus Speth put it at the Carter Center Forum.

3

question of whether the outcome of that distribution of power is just or fair, that is whether it provides for equal opportunities to those who are poor and, in global affairs, relatively powerless.[2] On this score, I believe it is time for the first group (Ravi Kanbur's Group A economists and finance ministers) to internalize the arguments of the second group (Kanbur's Group B activists and civil society types), and recognize the need for an improved global politics, in which more democratic and legitimate representation of the poor and the disenfranchised in managing the global economy mediates the downside of more integrated and productive global markets.

I begin by setting out two views of the facts about the effects of globalization on world poverty and inequality. The bottom line: globalization is not the cause, but neither is it the solution to world poverty and inequality. Then I explore why and how the global economy is stacked against the poor, making globalization asymmetric, at least up to now. I conclude with some ideas about a new agenda of good global politics, an agenda to shape a future global economy and society that is less poor and less unequal -- not only because it is more global and competitive, but also because it is more fair and more politically representative.

Section 1. Globalization, Poverty and Inequality: Two Views

For most developing countries, postwar integration began only in the 1980s. Prior to the 1980s, though developing countries participated in some multilateral trade agreements, they did so essentially via special preferences that permitted them to retain relatively high levels of protection of their own markets. In the 1980s, however, and with increasing depth in the 1990s, most developing countries took steps to open and liberalize their markets. Along with reduction and elimination of tariffs and non-tariff barriers came fiscal and monetary reforms, privatization, deregulation, elimination of interest rate ceilings and other changes in the financial sector, and in the 1990s opening of capital markets a package that came to be known as the Washington Consensus. Liberalization of markets and accompanying, often socially painful structural change, was encouraged and supported by the IMF, the World Bank, and the U.S. Treasury, including with large loans typically conditioned on countries' adopting and implementing agreed policies. The increasing reliance on markets in the developing world, and in the 1990s in the countries of the former Soviet empire, is with good reason seen as part and parcel of the globalization process. And because of the conditioned loans, many of today's protesters see the turn to the market – and thus to global capitalism -- as imposed on the developing countries. (This is so even though, ironically, the international loans generally were disbursed even when agreed conditions were not implemented.)

With the growing influence of markets in the last two decades have come changes in the levels of global inequality and of world poverty. Over the last 100 years, global inequality by

---

[2] Kanbur (2001) notes that the debate may be due to different perspectives between economists and social activists in terms of aggregation and time horizon. That is true. The additional view behind these notes is that their major difference in perspective, however, may well be that the second group is concerned primarily with fairness (as opposed to economic efficiency) and with the apparently disproportionate role of power in the design and implementation of the rules of the global economy.

4

most measures has been increasing. The ratio of the average income of the richest to the poorest country in the world increased from 9 to 1 at the end of the 19th century to about 30 to 1 in 1960, to more than 60 to 1 today.[3] So the average family in the U.S. is 60 times richer than the average family in Ethiopia or Bangladesh (in purchasing power terms). The century-long increase in inequality is the result of a simple reality. Today's rich countries, which were already richer 100 years ago (primarily as a result of the Industrial Revolution), have been blessed with economic growth and have gotten a whole lot richer. Today's poorer countries, mostly in Africa, which were poor to start with, have not grown much if at all.

Global inequality is high, but not necessarily rising

However, in the last two decades, the picture has changed somewhat. Some countries, including China and its smaller neighbors in East Asia and more recently India, have grown at faster rates than the already rich countries. It is difficult to imagine incomes in those countries ever fully converging to that typical in rich countries. It would take China and India almost a century of growth at faster rates even to reach current U.S. levels. Still, there has been some catching up of income between the advanced industrialized economies and some developing countries – what economists call convergence.[4]

Rapid growth in India and China turns out to be key to the decline of world poverty in the last decade. The percentage of the world's population that is poor (using the World Bank's poverty line of $1 a day in 1985 dollars) declined between 1987 and 1998 from about 25 percent to 21 percent using World Bank figures, and the absolute number from an estimated 1.2 to 1.1 billion.[5] The declines in poverty in India and China are key to the overall worldwide decline. Elsewhere in the developing world, including in Africa, Latin America and other parts of Asia, and in the transitional economies of the former Soviet Union, the absolute numbers of poor rose.[6]

Recent studies combine data on differences across countries in average incomes with household data on incomes within countries to produce a "world" distribution of income, in which figuratively speaking, individuals or households around the world are lined up by income in a single unified ranking, and each person (or household) has the same weight in the distribution, independent of whether he or she lives in a small or large country. This is probably the best measure in terms of human welfare of what has been happening in the last couple of decades.

World inequality measured this way is incredibly high – greater than inequality within Brazil and South Africa, the highest inequality countries in the world, where the richest 20 percent of households are about 25 times richer than the poorest 20 percent. And over the last

---

[3] Pritchett (1995).
[4] Cline (2002); Sala-I-Martin (2002); Bhalla (2002), among others.
[5] Bhalla (2002) claims that the decline in India has been underestimated, and that the number of world poor has fallen more, to about 600 million.
[6] Between 1990 and 1998 the number of poor rose by an estimated 59.3 million in Africa; 26.7 million in South Asia; and 10.5 million in Central Asia and Eastern Europe (World Bank 2001).

5

100 years, it has been increasing, because those differences in historic rates of growth between what have become today's rich and poor countries have dominated this "world" distribution. However in the last 20 years, with the rapid growth of India and China, that trend also has been moderated, and increases in world inequality have slowed. The world distribution as I have described it of course gives much greater weight to these high population countries. As a result, if we compare not changes in average incomes between the richest and poorest countries, but changes in average incomes between the initially 20 percent richest and 20 percent poorest individuals in the world (say about two decades ago), we find that world inequality, though incredibly high, has been leveling off in this recent era of "globalization".[7]

Changes in inequality within countries have not made much difference to this overall story. Income inequality has been increasing steadily in the United States since the early 1970s, though the increase did level off finally in the last couple of years. In the last two decades, income inequality increased in China, where phenomenal income growth has been heavily concentrated in urban areas; in most countries of Eastern Europe and the former Soviet Union, where growth has been minimal and the current poor are worse off than they were before the fall of Communism; and in Mexico, Panama and Peru in Latin America, where it rose during the low-growth years of the 1980s and failed to decline with the return to modest growth in the 1990s. On the other hand, it would be an exaggeration to say that rising inequality within countries has been the norm, or to associate it specifically with increasing global integration. In most countries, income inequality has simply not changed, and in a few, including Japan, Canada, and Italy among industrialized countries, and Bangladesh, Ghana and the Philippines, it appears to have declined.

So at the world level, it is fair to say that poverty is declining and inequality is not increasing, even though that is not the case within many countries. Today's global inequality is mostly a matter of differences between rich and poor countries in past rates of growth. That brings us back to the main argument of globalization's proponents. It is countries that have successfully entered the global market and participated in globalization that have grown most. In the past, that included Japan, beginning in the Meiji era between 1868 and 1912; the poorer countries of Western Europe during the 19th century and then again during the post World War II period of European integration; and among the developing world in the postwar era, the so-called miracle economies of East Asia in the three decades before the 1998 financial crisis. More recently, it has included China, India, and in addition Bangladesh, Brazil, Malaysia, Mexico, Mozambique, the Philippines, Thailand, Uganda and Vietnam.[8] Poverty remains highest in the countries (and regions) and for peoples that are marginal to global markets,

---

[7] See Sala-I-Martin (2002) and Cline (2002b) for this result using alternative measures of inequality. These studies all compare incomes across countries in purchasing power parity terms. Milanovic (2002) reports a slight increase in the world distribution between 1988 and 1993, but the difference he reports is not statistically robust. Wade (2001) sets out technical counterarguments to the mainstream view that world inequality has leveled off. He notes that by most definitions and measures, except for the "world distribution" in PPP terms, inequality has increased.

[8] Dollar and Kraay (2001). Even though income inequality within some of these countries failed to decline or even increased (China especially), their average growth has brought their populations as a whole closer to the income of the rich countries, reducing world inequality.

6

including many in Africa, some in South Asia, and among people, the rural populations of China, India, and Latin America. To the extent that globalization has "caused" increasing inequality, it is not because some have benefited a lot – a good thing – but because others have been left out of the process altogether.

Globalization is not the solution

Globalization is not the cause but neither is it the solution to continuing miserable poverty and haunting inequality at the global level. Consider first the plight of a large group of the poorest countries, including many in Africa. Highly dependent on primary commodity and natural resource exports in the early 1980s, they have been "open" for at least two decades, if openness is measured by their ratio of imports and exports to GDP. But unable to diversify into manufacturing (despite reducing their own import tariffs) they have been victims of the decline in the relative world prices of their commodity exports, and have, literally, been left behind.[9] These countries have not been xenophobic or in any way closed to the global economy. But despite rising exports, tariff reductions, and economic and structural reforms including greater fiscal and monetary discipline and the divestiture of unproductive state enterprises, they have been unable to increase their export income, have failed to attract foreign investment, and have grown little if at all.[10]

Many of these countries in sub-Saharan Africa, as well as Haiti, Nepal, and Nicaragua, seem trapped in a vicious circle of low or unstable export revenue, weak and sometimes predatory government, inability to cope with terrible disease burdens (the HIV/AIDS pandemic being only one recent and highly visible example), and failure to deliver the basic education and other services to their children that are critical to sustainable growth. Their governments have made, from time to time, fragile efforts to end corruption, to undertake economic reforms, and, more to the point, to enter global markets. But, caught in one variety or another of a poverty trap, "globalization" has not worked for them. For these countries, success in global markets might be a future outcome of success with growth and development itself, but it does not look like a good bet as a key input.

For the better-off emerging market economies globalization has failed to work on another dimension. For them global trade has been generally a boon, but global financial markets pretty much a bust. In the last decade, Mexico, Korea, Thailand, Indonesia, Russia, Brazil, Ecuador, Turkey and this year Argentina were all hit by financial crises triggered or made worse by their exposure to global financial markets. For these countries the benefits of global financial markets

---

[9] Birdsall and Hamoudi (2002) argue that the use of the trade/GDP ratio to represent policy openness is misleading as many of Dollar and Kraay's (2001) "non-globalizers" are commodity-dependent exporters with limited import protection.

[10] The problems of these countries have often been compounded by the concentrations of wealth and the internal conflicts over control of their natural resources to which they seem so prone. Of course, there are many possible reasons for stalled growth; in many commodity-dependent countries: poor governance, civil conflicts, high disease burdens and bad geography.

7

have been heavily offset by their increased risks. Because their local financial markets are less resilient, and local and foreign creditors more wary, they are much more vulnerable than their industrial country counterparts to the panicked withdrawal of capital typical of bank runs. Particularly troubling is the growing evidence that the financial instability associated with open capital markets is especially costly for the working poor and the emerging middle class, and tends to exacerbate inequality within countries.[11] In Turkey, Argentina and Mexico, with repeated bouts of inflation and currency devaluations in the last two decades, the ability of those with more financial assets to move them abroad, often simultaneously acquiring bank and corporate debt that is then socialized and paid by taxpayers, has been disequalizing – and certainly appears unfair. In parts of Asia and in much of Latin America, inequality increased during the boom years of high capital inflows in the mid-1990s as portfolio inflows and high bank lending fueled demand for assets such as land and stocks, which were beneficial to the rich.

In both regions the poor and working class gained the least during the pre-crisis boom, and then lost the most, certainly relative to their most basic needs, in the post-crisis bust. The high interest rates to which the affected countries resorted to stabilize their currencies also had a redistributive effect, hurting most small capital-starved enterprises and their low-wage employees. The bank bailouts that often follow financial crises create public debt that is seldom equally shared; public debt implies a transfer from taxpayers to rentiers. China and India have kept their capital markets relatively closed, and survived relatively well the financial crises of the late 1990s compared to Mexico, Argentina and Thailand. Success in trade is good for growth and that benefits the poor, but rapid and near-complete opening of capital markets, heavily pushed by the IMF and the U.S. Treasury throughout the 1990s, is not so simple in its effects.[12] It is no wonder that social activists are suspicious of corporate and financial influence in global markets.

A third problem with "globalization" has been the link between market reforms and the potential for new and costly rounds of corruption. Privatization and liberalization of financial markets in the absence of adequate regulatory institutions and banking standards and supervision invite corruption; Russia is only the most visible example. Open capital markets make it easier for corrupt leaders to burden their own taxpayers with official and private debt while transferring resources to their own foreign bank accounts. Unregulated markets make money laundering and tax evasion easier, and raise the costs asymmetrically for poor countries to defend their own tax systems. Globalization and global capital markets are not the underlying cause of all these problems, but like an occasion of sin they increase the likelihood that human failings will corrupt the system, usually at a cost to the poor and powerless.

Section 2: Unequal Opportunities: The Global Economy is Stacked Against the Poor

Not all the suspicions of the activists are necessarily warranted. But they are right in one important respect. Globalization is not necessarily the solution to high levels of poverty and

---

[11] Birdsall (2002).

[12] Among others Stiglitz (1999), and Easterly, Islam and Stiglitz (2000) emphasize this point, for developing countries in general and for the poor within them.

8

inequality; indeed the relatively benign *outcomes* of globalization up to now belie unfair *opportunities* in an unfair global economy. Let me suggest three ways in which the global economy sustains or worsens unequal opportunities.

- The market *works*; in the global market game, those without the right training and equipment inevitably lose;

- the market *fails*; in the global economy, negative externalities raise new costs for the vulnerable and compound the risks faced by the already weak and disadvantaged;

- in the global game, economic power matters more than ever across countries; it is natural that the rich and powerful can influence the design and implementation of global rules to their own advantage.

The market works

Globalization is shorthand for global capitalism and the extension of global markets. Markets that are bigger and deeper reward more efficiently those who already have productive assets: financial assets, land, physical assets, and perhaps most crucial in the technologically driven global economy, human capital. This is true not just across people but across countries too. The economic return to healthy and stable country institutions is huge. Countries that are already ahead – with stable political systems, secure property rights, adequate banking supervision, reasonable public services, and so on – are better able to cope with market-driven changes in world prices. I mentioned above that many countries heavily dependent on commodity exports seem caught in a poverty trap. But that has not been the case for countries that entered the global economy with the "asset" of strong political and social institutions (e.g. Australia, Chile, Norway). Their pre-existing institutional assets explain much of why 80 percent of all foreign investment occurs among the industrialized countries while just 0.1 percent of all U.S. foreign investment went to sub-Saharan Africa last year.[13]

In short, countries caught in an "institutional poverty trap" will not necessarily benefit from a healthy global market. Of course there is nothing necessarily permanent about a poverty trap. Like poor and uneducated people, with the right rules and some help from friends, countries can escape welfare dependency. But more on that below.

At the individual level, the best example of how healthy markets can generate unequal opportunities is the rising returns throughout the world to higher education. The effect of having a university education compared to secondary education or less has been increasing for years everywhere. This is true despite the fact that more and more people are going to university. In the global economy, with the information and communications revolution, the supply of university-educated people has not been keeping up with ever-increasing demand. In the United

---

[13] UNCTAD (2001).

9

States the highly educated have enjoyed healthy earnings gains for three decades, while those with high school education or less have suffered absolute wage losses. Similarly in Latin America, between 1991 and 1995, the period of intense liberalization, the wage gap between the skilled and unskilled increased for six of seven countries for which reliable wage data are available. In Eastern Europe, with the fall of Communism, the wage difference between those with and without post-secondary education has widened considerably.[14] Just about everywhere in the world (Cuba, China, Kerala state in India, all socialist entities being exceptions) education reinforces initial advantages instead of compensating for initial handicaps.

Rising wage gaps in open and competitive markets should not surprise or alarm us; they may be a short-term price worth paying for higher long-run sustainable growth. They create the right incentives for more people to acquire more education, in principle eventually reducing inequality. The same can be said for the development of institutions at the country level. Many poor countries have responded to global opportunities by strengthening the rule of law, building and strengthening democratic processes, and investing in public health and education. But just as poor families need resources as well as incentives to educate their children, so poor countries need resources as well as reforms to build their institutions.

The global market for skilled and talented people is another example of how markets can hurt the already weak. In today's global economy the highly skilled are highly mobile. Indian engineers can quadruple their earnings by moving from Kerala to Silicon Valley, and Indian Ph.D. biochemists from Delhi to Atlanta or Cambridge. For the individuals concerned, this is a good thing, and eventually this brain drain can generate offsetting remittances and return investments if the institutional and policy setting in India and other poor countries improves.[15] In the short run, however, it makes the task of poorer countries, trying to build those institutions and improve those policies, tougher. The annual loss to India of its brain drain to the U.S. is estimated at $2 billion, about equal to all the foreign aid it receives.[16] The farmers and workers whose taxes finance education in poor countries are subsidizing the citizens of the rich countries -- whose tax revenues are boosted by the immigrants' contributions (and whose cultures by the way are also greatly enriched).

The efficiency gains and increased potential for growth of a global market economy are not to be disdained. But in modern market economies, there is a well-defined social contract that tempers the excess inequalities of income and opportunity that efficient markets easily generate. The social contract may not be perfect, but it exists at the national level. Progressive tax systems provide for some redistribution, with the state financing at least minimal educational opportunities for all and some social and old age insurance. At the global level, there is no analogue. Statements of social and economic rights in the United Nations, and relatively minor transfers of financial and technical resources from rich to poor countries are as close as we have come to managing a global social contract. Ironically, one problem with the World Bank, a

---

[14] For more on the United States see Levy (1999) or Cline (trade and inequality); on Latin America see Duryea and Szekely (1998); on Eastern Europe see Terrell (2001); on Mexico author's calculations.

[15] Kapur (*forthcoming*).

[16] UNDP (2001) and UNDP India (1998).

10

lightning rod for anti-globalization protests, may not be that it is too powerful, but that it is too weak to manage a global social contract.

The market fails

Markets fail in many domains. Global markets compound the risks and costs of market failures for the weak. What is true at the local level, where local polluters do not internalize the costs of their pollution, obtains at the global level, and often in spades. The rich countries that have historically emitted the highest per capita greenhouse gas emissions have imposed costs on the poor. As the biggest polluter in per capita terms, the United States is imposing costs not only on its own future citizens, but also on the children and grandchildren of the world's poor, who are much less likely to have the resources to protect themselves from the effects.

Financial contagion across countries, affecting even those emerging market economies with relatively sound domestic policies, is another example of how market failures can affect the already vulnerable asymmetrically. The problem the emerging market economies of Latin America and East Asia face in global financial markets has not only brought instability and reduced growth; it has affected their capacity to develop and sustain the institutions and programs they need to protect their own poor. With global market players doubting the commitment of non-industrialized countries to fiscal rectitude at the time of any shock, countries are forced to resort to tight fiscal and monetary policy to reestablish market confidence, just when in the face of recession they would ideally implement macroeconomic measures to stimulate their economies. The (procyclical) austerity policies that the global capital market demands of emerging market are the opposite of what the industrial economies implement – such as reduced interest rates, unemployment insurance, increased availability of food stamps and public works employment – fundamental ingredients of a modern social contract. We know that the effects of unemployment and bankruptcy can be permanent for the poor; in Mexico, increases in child labor that reduced school enrollment during the 1995 crisis were not reversed, implying some children did not return to school when growth resumed.[17]

The risks of global warming and the problems of global financial contagion are only two examples of market failures that entail asymmetric costs and risks for poor countries and poor people. The same can be said of contagious disease that crosses borders, of transnational crime, and of potentially beneficial but risky new technologies such as genetically modified foods. Similarly, poor countries that protect global resources such as tropical forests and biological diversity are paying the full costs but are unable to capture the full benefits of these global goods. Within countries, governments temper market failures through regulations, taxes and subsidies, and fines; and they share the benefits of such public goods as public security, military defense, management of natural disasters and public health through their tax and expenditure decisions. Ideally the latter are made in a democratic system with fair and legitimate representation of all people, independent of their wealth. In nations, such political systems

---

[17] Szekely (2001).

11

seldom work perfectly (as the proponents of campaign finance reform in the U.S. would argue). In the global community, a comparable political system just barely exists.

Economic power influences global rules and their implementation

Trade is the best and thus the worst and most costly example for the poor. In general, political constraints in rich and powerful countries dominate the design of global rules. The resulting protection of agriculture and textiles in the U.S. and Europe locks many of the world's poorest countries out of potential markets. Because these are the sectors that could generate jobs for the unskilled, rich country protection, through tariffs and subsidies, hurts most the poor.[18] The recent initiative of the European Union to eliminate all barriers to imports from the world's 49 poorest countries, and the African Growth and Opportunity Act in the U.S. are steps in the right direction. But since the countries that can benefit make up only a minuscule proportion of all world production, they represent very small steps indeed. And even those modest initiatives were watered down considerably by domestic political pressures, and include complicated rules that create uncertainty and limit big increases in poor country exports.

Political constraints also affect the way already agreed trade rules are implemented. The process of complicated negotiations and dispute resolution puts poor and small countries with limited resources at a disadvantage. The use of anti-dumping actions by U.S. producers, even when they are unlikely to win a dispute on its merits, creates onerous legal and other costs to current producers in developing countries, and chills new job-creating investment in sensitive sectors. About one-half of anti-dumping actions are initiated against developing country producers, who take up 8 percent of all exports.[19] Even the Bush Administration, with the right rhetoric on free trade, could not resist the pressure of the U.S. steel industry to invoke anti-dumping legislation.

International migration is governed by rules that are also stacked against the developing countries, and in particular against the poor and unskilled in those countries. Permanent migration is small relative to the past because higher-income countries restrict immigration. In the last 25 years, only 2 percent of the world's people have changed their permanent country residence, compared to 10 percent in the 25 years before WWI.[20] Yet more movement would reduce world inequality considerably, as did the tremendous movements of Europeans to the Americas in the 19th century.[21] An auto mechanic from Ghana can at least quintuple his income, just by moving from Ghana to Italy; as can a Nicaraguan agricultural worker, by moving to Arizona. During the recent boom in the information technology sector, the United States established a special program to allow highly skilled workers to enter with temporary visas – a good thing, no doubt, for the individual beneficiaries, but also an implicit tax on the working taxpayers in poorer countries who helped finance the education of those emigrants, and another example of the capacity of the already rich to exploit their power.

---

[18] World Bank (2001).
[19] Author's calculations based on World Trade Analyzer and Finger and Schuknecht (1999).
[20] Dollar and Kraay (2002).
[21] O'Rourke and Williamson (1999).

12

What about intellectual property rights? Because knowledge is not an excludable good, it makes sense to compensate for the resulting market failure through intellectual property rights. At the global level, those rights are now regulated by the WTO, under what is called the TRIPS, or trade-related intellectual property rights agreement. Intellectual property rights ideally balance society's gains from incentives for invention with the benefits of access to resulting products. But it is highly debatable whether the current international regime has achieved an appropriate balance in the poorest developing countries, where the minimum 20-year patent period under TRIPS implies higher costs for many products – the most notorious example being now in the area of AIDS anti-virals with little likelihood of local creation of new products.

In fact the WTO rules allow countries to issue compulsory licenses for the production and importation of patented products, under certain circumstances. The U.S. issues compulsory licenses to mitigate the monopoly power, and Canada before signing NAFTA regularly issued compulsory licenses for the domestic production of patented pharmaceuticals. But implementation of this aspect of TRIPS has been affected by the imbalance of power. U.S. pharmaceutical firms have systematically pressured the United States Trade Representative to threaten extra-WTO sanctions against countries threatening to use compulsory licensing. Under tremendous pressure from civil society groups in the case of AIDS drugs, the U.S. has desisted from bringing formal actions against South Africa and more recently Brazil. But Thailand is still under pressure, and for other less visible health problems business as usual puts the weak at a disadvantage against the strong.

Economic power also affects the rules and the conduct of those rules by the international institutions. The International Monetary Fund is the world's institution meant to help countries manage macroeconomic imbalances and minimize the risks of financial shocks. But in the 1990s, the IMF was too enthusiastic about developing countries' opening their capital accounts. This is only one example where the IMF and the World Bank have been insufficiently humble in their recipes and probably all too heavily influenced by their richer members. Even if the policies supported have made sense – and I believe for the most part they have – the reality is that those who advocate them have no real accountability to the people in developing countries most affected by them. For one thing, developing countries are poorly represented, at least in the voting structure of these institutions.

Conclusion: A New Agenda of Good Global Politics

That poverty is declining worldwide and inequality after a century is leveling off is not a sign that all is well in our new globalized economy. Proponents of market-led globalization need to recognize that the global economy, even if it is not causing more poverty and inequality, is not addressing those global problems either, and is ridden with asymmetries that add up to unequal opportunities. Social activists need to insist on the reform not the dismantling of the limited institutions for managing globalizations downside. Both groups need to join forces in pushing a new global agenda, aiming for a new global politics to accompany the global economy. They need to focus on the good political arts – of arguing, persuading, compromising and cooperating

13

in collective action for the commonweal.

A global social contract

Statements of social and economic rights in the United Nations, and relatively minor transfers of financial and technical resources from rich to poor countries are as close as we have come to anything like a global social contract. Anyone arriving from another planet into our highly unequal global economy would have to conclude that rich countries have no interest at all in doing anything much to help the poor in poor countries – surprisingly given what could be their enlightened self-interest in a more secure and prosperous global economy. The logic of a global social contract is clear, but it cannot be constructed out of nothing. As is the case within countries, a social contract involves some transfers – for investments in the human capital and the local institutions that can ensure equal opportunities for the poor.

The business of foreign aid is more effective and sensible than in the Cold War era, but more can be done to make it competitive, effective, and better channeled to those countries with the greatest need and reasonable capacity to use resources well. The program of official debt relief is an admission that past aid to the poorest countries has not worked. It should also be a first step in a larger reinvention of the foreign aid business – away from tied aid, multiple and onerous standards of different donors, and conditionality that doesn't work, and toward a more generous but more disciplined system.[22] At the same time, the need to do better should not be an excuse for the rich countries' minimal spending on foreign aid. With many poor countries consolidating reforms, and with Cold War misuse of aid behind us, the ability to spend resources well now far exceeds the available amounts. Domestic social contracts, in the form of public transfers for investing in education, health, housing and so forth, and for social safety net programs such as unemployment insurance and disability and taxpayers financed welfare and pensions programs, usually amount to more than 10 percent of GDP. Foreign aid for a global social contract is below 0.5 percent of rich countries' combined GDPs.

Most important, the global and regional institutions we have that are the world's most obvious mechanisms for managing a global social contract need to be reformed, not dismantled. It is ironic that the World Bank and the IMF have been the lightning rod for anti-globalization protests. It may be not that they are too powerful but too limited in their resources and insufficiently effective to manage a global contract that would bring equal education, health and other opportunities to the poor in poor countries. Making them more representative and more accountable to those most affected by their programs, and thus more effective, has to be on the agenda of better global politics.

Addressing global market failures

The returns to spending on global public goods that benefit the poor have been extraordinarily high. This is the case of tropical agricultural research, public health research and

---

[22] Birdsall and Williamson (2002); Easterly (2002).

disease control, and the limited global efforts to protect regional and global environmental resources. These global programs need to be financed by something that mimics taxes within national economies. The IMF is now proposing a new approach to sovereign bankruptcy that might make the costs of financial crises less great for poor countries and poor people. Global agreements on bankruptcy procedures, on reducing greenhouse gas emissions, on protecting biodiversity and marine resources, on funding food safety and monitoring public health are all development programs in one form or another – because they reduce the risks and costs of global spillovers and enhance their potential benefits for the poor.

Just global rules and full and fair implementation

Reducing protection in rich country markets belongs on the agenda of all those fighting for global justice and the elimination of world poverty. Many developing countries are at an unfair disadvantage in global trade and other negotiations, and they need transfers from rich countries simply to effectively participate. This is especially the case for smaller and poorer countries.

Rich counties should make increasing efforts to open their doors to unskilled and not just skilled immigrants, allocating resources at home to ease the adjustment of native workers through job training. The rules governing international migration are notably illiberal. Even within political constraints, much more could be done by the rich countries in their own interests to make immigration regimes more sensible and more consistent with their overall policies in support of developing countries a part of their overall development policy. Sharing of tax receipts of skilled immigrants across sending and receiving countries is one example. Another is the effort to reduce the transaction costs of remittances. These could help offset the perverse effects of the brain drain on poor countries.

It is time to revisit the delicate problem of balancing public health needs with the benefits of an international regime of intellectual property rights. There is plenty of scope to do this within current WTO rules.

In general the developing countries should be more fully and fairly represented in international institutions; this is especially the case in the international financial institutions, whose policies and programs are so central to their development prospects.

*   *

Those concerned with global justice – whether Kanbur's Group A economists and finance ministers or Group B activists – face a daunting problem of global collective action. They need to make a common agenda, for a global social contract that would make meaningful investments in economic opportunities for the poor possible; for global rules and regimes in trade, foreign investment, property rights and migration that are more fair; and for global institutions that are more representative and accountable to the poor as well as the rich. In practical terms that means working together in the short run to build a more level playing field in

15

global governance. It means reforming rather than undermining the existing global institutions, so they can manage the downside of globalization, reduce its asymmetry, and provide for a more equal world because it is more just. The two groups need to come together in insisting that a new global development architecture be based on good global politics and not just expanded global markets.

16

References:

Bhalla, Surjit S. (2002). "Imagine There is No Country: Globalization and its Consequences for Poverty, Inequality and Growth" (processed).
See: http://www.oxusresearch.com/downloads/imagine2002.PDF

Birdsall, Nancy. (2002). "A Stormy Day on an Open Field: Asymmetry and Convergence in the Global Economy." Paper presented at "Globalisation, Living standards and Inequality: Recent progress and continuing challenges," a conference hosted by the Group of 20, Australian Federal Reserve Bank and Australian Treasury. Sydney, Australia.
See: http://www.cgdev.org

Birdsall, Nancy and Amar Hamoudi. (2002). "Commodity Dependence, Trade, and Growth: When "Openness" is Not Enough." Center for Global Development, Working Paper No. 7.
See: http://www.cgdev.org/wp/cgd_wp007.pdf

Birdsall, Nancy and John Williamson with Brian Deese. (2002). Delivering on Debt Relief: From IMF Gold to a New Development Architecture. Washington, D.C.: Center for Global Development and Institute for International Economics.
Cline, William. (2002). "Financial Crises and Poverty in Emerging Market Economies" Center for Global Development, Working Paper No. 8.
See: http://www.cgdev.org/wp/cgd_wp008.pdf

        (2002b). "Convergence versus Divergence in International Income Levels" in Trade Policy and Global Poverty. (Draft)

Diwan, Ishac. (2002). "Debt as Sweat: Labor, financial crises, and the globalization of capital" Washington, D.C.: World Bank.
See: http://www.worldbank.org/wbi/B-SPAN/docs/diwan.pdf

Dollar, David and Art Kraay. (2001, June). "Trade, Growth, and Poverty." World Bank, Macroeconomics and Growth Group Working Paper, No. 2615.
See: http://www.worldbank.org/research/growth/pdfiles/Trade5.pdf

Dollar, David and Art Kraay (2002, January/February) "Spreading the Wealth" *Foreign Affairs* pg

Duryea, Suzzane and Miguel Szekely. (1998) "Labor Markets in Latin America: A supply side story" Paper prepared for the annual meeting of the Inter-American Development Bank, Cartagena.

Easterly, William. (2002). "The Cartel of Good Intentions: Markets vs. bureaucracy in foreign aid" Center for Global Development, Working Paper No. 4.

17

See: http://www.cgdev.org/wp/cgd_wp004_rev.pdf

Easterly, William, Roumeen Islam and Joseph Stiglitz. (2000, April). "Shaken and Stirred: Explaining Growth Volatility," Proceeding of Annual World Bank Conference on Development Economics. Washington D.C.: World Bank pp 191-211.
See: http://www.worldbank.org/research/growth/growth%20volatility%20jan%202000.html

Finger, J. Michael and Ludger Schuknecht "Market Access Advances and Retreats: The Uruguay Round and Beyond" World Bank, Working Paper.
See: http://econ.worldbank.org/docs/959.pdf

Kanbur, Ravi. (2001). "Economic Policy, Distribution and Poverty: The Nature of Disagreements." *World Development.* 29 (6) pp. 1083-1094.

Kapur, Davesh. (Forthcoming). Global War: The Global Competition for Talent Washington D.C.: Center for Global Development.

Levy, Frank. (1999) The New Dollars and Dreams: American Incomes and Economic Change. New York: Russell Sage Foundation

Milanovic, Branko. (2002). "True World Income Distribution, 1988 and 1993: First Calculations Based on Household Surveys Alone." World Bank, Policy Research Working Paper 2244.
See: http://www.worldbank.org/poverty/inequal/abstracts/recent.htm

Pritchett, Lant (1995). "Divergence Big Time" World Bank, Policy Research Working Paper 1522.

O'Rourke, Kevin H. and Williamson, Jeffrey G. (1999). Globalization and History-Evolution of a Nineteenth-Century Atlantic Economy, Cambridge, Mass: The MIT Press.

Sala-i-Martin, Xavier (2002). "The World Distribution of Income (estimated from Individual Country Distributions)" National Bureau of Economic Research, Working Paper 8933.

Inter-American Development Bank. (1999). Facing up to Inequality in Latin America 1998-1999 Report on the Economic and Social Progress in Latin America. New York: Oxford University Press.

Stiglitz, Joseph. (1999). "Foreward" to Global Economic Prospects in Developing Countries: Beyond Financial Crisis. Washington D.C.: International Bank for Reconstruction and Development/The World Bank.
See: http://www.worldbank.org/prospects/gep98-99/foreword.htm

Terrell, Katherine. (2000). "Worker Mobility and Transition to a Market Economy: Winners and

18

Losers." In Nancy Birdsall and Carol Graham (Ed.) New Markets, New Opportunities: Economic and Social Mobility in a Changing World. Washington D.C.: The Brookings Institution.

United Nations Conference on Trade and Development. (2001).World Investment Report 2001. New York: United Nations

United Nations Development Programme. (2001). Human Development Report 2001: Making New Technologies Work for Human Development. New York. Oxford University Press.

United Nations System India. (1998). "Annual Report of the Resident Coordinator for India." Delhi, India: United Nations. See: http://www.un.org.in/rc/rc98/overview.htm

Wade, Robert (April 26, 2001). "Winners and Losers" *The Economist*.

World Bank (2001). World Development Report: Attacking Poverty. New York: Oxford University Press

     (2001b). Global Development Finance: Building Coalitions for Effective Development Finance. Washington, D.C.: World Bank.

[11]

Reforming International Financial Architecture

Jane D'Arista

This former government economist presents a bold plan for international financial reform when most of her colleagues propose no more than incremental change.

THE sudden crises that flattened East Asian economies in 1997 profoundly shook confidence in the international financial system. Plunging asset prices and steep currency devaluations rekindled concerns about the system's inherent stability and its effects on economic and human development. Responses to the crisis—and to subsequent disorders in Russia, Brazil, and other nations—called into question the capacity of existing public and private institutions to redress such swift, far-reaching meltdowns.

Since the events of 1997, proposals for reforming the financial system have regularly punctuated public discussions of the global economy. But, so far, neither these discussions nor a series of official multilateral initiatives have produced even modest changes in global finance or the monetary infrastructure on which it rides. During 1999, the momentum for re-

---

JANE D'ARISTA is director of programs at the Financial Markets Center. Previously, she taught at the graduate program in International Banking Law Studies at the Boston University School of Law and served as chief finance economist for the Subcommittee on Telecommunications and Finance of the House Energy and Commerce Committee. Before that, she served for five years as an international analyst at the Congressional Budget Office and for twelve years as a staff member of the House Banking Committee. Her publications include The Evolution of U.S. Finance *(M.E. Sharpe, 1994).*

Challenge, vol. 43, no. 3, May/June 2000, pp. 44–82.
© 2000 M.E. Sharpe, Inc. All rights reserved.
ISSN 0577–5132 / 2000 $9.50 + 0.00.

form dissipated, despite the persistence of powerfully desta-bilizing features in the global system and the likelihood of future crises.

The most worrisome feature is, in many respects, the most deeply ingrained. After the worldwide removal of regulatory constraints, market forces have assumed a dominant role in the international monetary and payments system. With the ascen-dancy of liberalization as a governing paradigm for financial enterprise, the role of the public sector has been cut down if not cut out. As a result, what the public sector alone can do—man-age liquidity, launch countercyclical initiatives, and respond to crises at the international level—has become far less effective than in the past. Financial liberalization also poses a substantial threat to the sovereignty of nations, particularly those with emerging economies that stand most exposed to the punishing judgments of unrestrained market forces.

Ultimately, remedying these problems will require that the public sector reconstitute its powers to promote stability and growth in the global economy while enhancing the rights of in-dividual countries to shape their own economic, social, and po-litical outcomes. The following three proposals suggest a framework through which old and new institutional arrange-ments could help reinvigorate these powers and rights.

- The first proposal puts forward a plan for establishing a public international investment fund for emerging markets. Structured as a closed-end mutual fund, this investment vehicle would address the problems that have emerged with the extraordinary growth in cross-border securities invest-ment transactions in the 1990s. The proposal advocates a role for the public sector in managing those problems so that private portfolio investment—now the dominant chan-nel for flows into emerging markets—can promote steady, sustainable growth rather than the boom-and-bust cycles that so far have been its primary contribution.[1]

- The second proposal recommends a new allocation of special drawing rights (SDRs), the international reserve asset issued by the International Monetary Fund (IMF). Issuing a new round of SDRs would provide substantial short-term relief from the debt burdens that aggravate imbalances in nations' access to international liquidity and perpetuate policies favoring lower wages, fiscal and monetary austerity, and deflation.[2]

- The third proposal articulates an alternative to the privatized, dollar-based international monetary system that is a root cause of global instability and market failure. The proposal describes an international transactions and payments system managed by a public international agency in which cross-border monetary exchanges can be made in each country's own currency. This critical feature would help governments and central banks conduct effective economic policies, including countercyclical initiatives, at a national level. Equally important, it would allow all countries—not just a privileged few—to service external debt with wealth generated in their domestic markets. Thus it would help end the unsustainable paradigm of export-led growth that now governs the global economy.[3]

Creating a Public International Investment Fund for Emerging Markets

The Rise of Foreign Portfolio Investment

Of all the profound changes that shook the global financial order during the past two decades, none has had more dramatic

effects than the rise of securities markets as the principal chan-
nel for private international investment flows. After World War
II, international bank loans had been the preeminent medium
for these flows. But, beginning in the 1980s, three interrelated
developments gradually established the supremacy of foreign
portfolio investment.

First, patterns of saving and investment underwent a major
shift in major industrialized countries. Increasingly, individuals put their savings in pension plans and other institutional
pools that invest those funds directly in securities rather than
placing them in the hands of intermediaries such as depository
institutions. In Canadian, German, Japanese, and U.K. financial
markets, assets of institutional investors doubled or nearly
doubled as a percentage of gross domestic product (GDP) from
1980 through 1994. In the United States, the share of total finan-
cial-sector assets held by institutional investors rose from 32
percent in 1978 to 54 percent in 1998 as the share of depository
institutions fell from 57 percent to 27 percent. (See Table 1.)

The rapid growth of these assets helped fuel a boom in cross-
border investments. International transactions in bonds and
equities among the G-7 countries rose from 35 percent of combined gross domestic product in 1985 to 140 percent of combined GDP in 1995.[4]

The explosion in cross-border securities transactions was aided
and abetted by a second key event—the dismantling of controls
on capital movements by rich, poor, and middle-income countries alike. The United States took the lead in 1974, removing
controls that had been imposed in the 1960s to halt capital outflows: the interest equalization tax on issues of foreign securities in U.S. markets, restrictions on transfers of funds by U.S.
multinational corporations to their foreign affiliates, and limits
on new foreign lending by U.S. banks.

In 1979, the United Kingdom eliminated controls on capital

Table 1

Assets of Institutional Investors

	1980	1988	1990	1992	1995
In billions of U.S. dollars					
Canada	93	257	326	376	493
Germany	165	443	627	764	1,113
Japan	244	1,459	1,650	1,972	3,035
United Kingdom	345	992	1,208	1,432	1,790
United States	1,607	4,316	5,221	7,183	10,501
Total	2,454	7,466	9,031	11,727	16,932
As percentage of GDP					
Canada	35	52	57	66	87
Germany	20	37	42	43	46
Japan	23	50	56	54	59
United Kingdom	64	118	124	137	162
United States	59	88	95	119	151

Sources: International Monetary Fund, *International Capital Markets*, 1995; Bank of International Settlements, *68th Annual Report*, 1997–98, June 1998.

outflows, and other European countries repealed limits on both outflows and inflows (such as reserve requirements and taxes on foreign borrowing) over the following decade to comply with the timetable set for unification and the implementation of the European Monetary System. Ending capital controls also became a prerequisite for membership in the Organization for Economic Cooperation and Development (OECD), which prompted their removal by Mexico and Korea in the 1990s. Under pressure from the U.S. government and foreign investors, other emerging market countries also lifted restrictions on inflows in the 1990s.

In many countries, the wholesale removal of capital controls took place against the backdrop of a vast privatization of state enterprise. The wave of privatization extended from the Thatcher government in England to the restructuring of centrally planned economies, and it generated more securities issues in a wider range of national markets than in any previous period. This third critical development ensured the rise of portfolio investment worldwide. As cross-border securities transactions mushroomed in volume and scale, national capital markets expanded accordingly, markets grew more integrated worldwide, and capital mobility accelerated.

Portfolio Investment Flows and Macroeconomic Leverage

For most of the 1980s, America reigned as the primary recipient of foreign portfolio investment—initially as a result of easy fiscal and tight monetary policies that drove up real interest rates and the value of the dollar. As the third world debt crisis (triggered in part by those same policies) stretched across the decade, debt service payments provided a large, continuing source of inflows to the United States.

But the end-of-decade recession that sapped demand and depressed asset prices in the United States and other industrialized countries caused investors to redirect funds into developing economies. Between 1989 and 1993, private investment flows into emerging markets multiplied more than twelve times over as a percentage of total foreign securities investment by industrial countries.

From a distance, this pattern superficially resembled earlier ebbs and flows in post–Bretton Woods economic and financial activity. During the 1970s, for example, rapid oil-price increases produced recession and falling interest rates in industrialized countries, which set the stage for a wave of private lending to developing countries.

But international investment in the early 1990s differed from preceding periods in at least two important ways. First, developing countries absorbed a much larger volume of funds in much less time than ever before. As unrestrained foreign portfolio investment poured into national markets, it bid up the prices of

D'Arista

Table 2

Capital Flows to Developing Countries (in billions of U.S. dollars)[a]

	All developing countries	Asia	Western hemisphere	Other developing countries[b]
1977–82				
Total net capital inflows	183.0	94.8	157.8	−69.6
Net foreign direct investment	67.2	16.2	31.8	19.2
Net portfolio investment	−63.0	3.6	9.6	−76.2
Bank lending & other	178.8	75.0	116.4	−12.6
1983–89				
Total net capital inflows	61.6	116.9	−116.2	60.9
Net foreign direct investment	93.1	36.4	30.8	25.9
Net portfolio investment	45.5	9.8	−8.4	44.1
Bank lending & other	−77.0	70.7	−138.6	−9.0
1990–94				
Total net capital inflows	625.5	195.3	203.8	226.4
Net foreign direct investment	224.6	116.8	68.8	39.0
Net portfolio investment	324.6	36.9	184.4	103.3
Bank lending & other	76.2	41.7	−49.6	84.1
1995–98				
Total net capital flows	618.9	143.7	276.6	198.6
Net foreign direct investment	482.7	217.5	169.9	95.3
Net portfolio investment	225.5	9.0	114.4	102.1
Bank lending & other	−89.4	−82.8	−7.9	1.3

Source: International Monetary Fund, *International Capital Markets*, 1995 and 1999 editions.
[a] Flows exclude exceptional financing.
[b] Includes countries in Africa, Eastern Europe, and the Middle East. Excludes capital exporting countries such as Kuwait and Saudi Arabia.

financial assets at unprecedented rates. Aggregate capital flows to Mexico from 1990 to 1993 totaled $91 billion, an amount equal to one-fifth of all net inflows to developing countries in those years (Table 2). Two-thirds of the net inflow was portfolio investment, most of it channeled into a bubbling Mexican stock market, which rose 436 percent between 1990 and 1993.

Second, the opening of financial markets to massive flows of foreign portfolio capital exposed countries to short investment horizons and hair-trigger investor judgments. Rather than residing as long-term assets on the books of banks, developing-nation investments became overnight guests on the constantly changing balance sheets of pension funds, mutual funds, and hedge funds. Freed from restrictions on entry or exit, institutional investors could now shuffle their investments in bonds and equities from market to market in response to cyclical developments that raised and lowered returns—a privilege that subtly but inexorably weakened the impact of countercyclical monetary policies.

As the notion of "hot money" entered the popular lexicon, central bankers discovered that the increasingly potent interest- and exchange-rate effects of capital flows were undermining their ability to control credit expansion and contraction. By lowering interest rates to revive economic activity, monetary authorities were likely instead to precipitate or intensify capital outflows and reduce credit availability in their national economy. By raising interest rates to cool economic activity, central banks would attract foreign inflows seeking higher returns. If large enough, the inflow might stimulate rather than suppress borrowing and lending.[5]

The danger of these procyclical pressures manifested itself with a vengeance in the mid-1990s, as industrialized countries pulled out of recession and increased their demand for credit. After skyrocketing from $29 billion to $142 billion between 1990 and 1993, the net value of annual foreign portfolio investment flows by U.S. residents fell to $50 billion in 1994. The Federal Reserve played a decisive role in this reversal by initiating what became a seven-step monetary tightening in March 1994 and narrowing the spreads between U.S. and emerging market debt issues.

As these spreads narrowed, equity prices fell in Mexico and other emerging markets, eroding their value as collateral for bank loans. Meanwhile, an appreciating peso lowered the cost of imported consumer goods and hammered Mexico's export sector, pushing the country's current-account deficit to a whopping 8 percent of GDP by the final quarter of 1994. As new foreign investment in private securities diminished, the Zedillo government attempted to finance the deficit by issuing dollar-indexed, short-term debt—so-called *tesobonos* that promised to protect their holders against the possibility of currency devaluation.

Though temporarily effective, this response only increased Mexico's vulnerability to a loss of confidence by foreign investors. Amid a series of political shocks and mounting concern over the country's dwindling international reserves, domestic and foreign investors began to take flight, forcing Mexico to devalue the peso in December 1994. Ultimately, the *tesobono* overhang contributed to the cost of a $50 billion bailout orchestrated by the Clinton administration.

In the wake of the peso crisis, many emerging market countries took measures to counter the propensity of heavy investment inflows to inflate exchange rates (thereby eroding the competitiveness of export sectors) and increase the volatility of capital markets (thereby heightening the vulnerability of their financial systems). According to the IMF, these remedial mea sures included increases in bank reserve requirements, increased exchange rate flexibility, and the imposition of exchange controls. In 1995, the Bank for International Settlements (BIS) reported widespread agreement that short-term financial transactions should not be free from controls until developing nations could ensure the soundness of their financial systems.

This agreement, however, ran up against a far more powerful consensus in Washington. Leading American financial firms, the Democratic administration, the Republican Congress, the Federal Reserve, the IMF, and elite opinion makers all continued to press for unimpeded financial liberalization, insisting that greater freedom for capital movements was the solution, not the problem. Portraying capital inflows as wholly beneficial, these influential advocates claimed that mass outflows were an inevitable response to bad policies and an acceptable tool of market discipline.

As the 1994 Mexican crisis subsequently replayed itself in different forms throughout the world, the shortsightedness of this Washington consensus became clearer. When capital raced out of East Asia, Russia, Brazil, and other emerging markets in successive waves of panic, the ripple effects on exchange rates, asset values, commodity prices, employment, incomes, and financial systems brought the global economy to its knees.

Though partial recovery has begun, it is likely to take many years for these damaged national economies to repair their losses. And despite its role as the principal engine of recovery, America—with its bubbling equity prices, large current-account deficits, and unsustainable consumer debt burdens—may be increasingly susceptible to harsh judgments by the liberalized financial system that the U.S. policy elite has imposed on the rest of the world.

Taming Portfolio Investment Flows to Emerging Markets

With the phenomenal growth of institutional investors' assets, foreign portfolio capital could provide urgently needed financing for long-term economic expansion in developing countries. To achieve this beneficial result, however, emerging-market nations need portfolio investment inflows that are sizable, stable, and disciplined by the standards of public purpose.

Chile has been fairly successful in using capital controls to moderate unwanted effects. During the 1990s, Chile required foreign investors to hold securities for a year or more and Chilean companies to maintain reserve requirements on direct borrowing abroad. Similarly, Korea imposed strict limits on foreign borrowing by domestic companies for many years before its recent liberalization. Such controls may be fine as far as they go. But they don't go far enough toward accomplishing the dual task of injecting long-term private capital into emerging markets while deterring the destructive fluctuations in asset prices and exchange rates associated with procyclical surges in foreign portfolio flows.

One innovation that might be equal to this task is a closed-end investment fund for emerging market securities. Such a fund could issue its own liabilities to private investors and buy stocks and bonds of private enterprises and public agencies in a wide spectrum of developing countries. Both the number of countries and the size of the investment pool would be large enough to ensure diversification. The fund's investment objectives would focus on the long-run economic performance of enterprises and countries rather than on short-term financial returns. Selecting securities in consultation with host governments would help the fund meet these objectives.

Unlike open-end mutual funds, which must buy back an unlimited number of shares whenever investors demand it, closed-end investment pools issue a limited number of shares that trade on a stock exchange or in over-the-counter markets. This key structural difference makes the holdings in closed-end portfolios much less vulnerable to the waves of buying and redemptions that sometimes characterize open-end funds. Thus, a closed-end fund would provide emerging markets a measure of protection by allowing the prices of shares in the fund to fluctuate without triggering destabilizing purchases and sales of the underlying investments.

To further balance the goals of market stability and economic dynamism, the closed-end fund should possess a solid capital cushion. Between 10 and 20 percent of the value of shares sold to investors should be used to purchase and hold government securities of major industrial countries in amounts roughly proportional to the closed-end fund shares owned by residents of those countries. These holdings would provide investors a partial guaranteed return, denominated in their own currencies, and the government securities would explicitly guarantee the value of the fund's capital. This double-barreled guarantee would moderate investors' concerns about potential risk.

Creating one or more closed-end funds on this model would reduce the need for capital controls, especially in countries that choose to accept foreign portfolio investment solely through this vehicle. The closed-end fund would have several additional benefits. It would help pension plans in developing and developed countries to diversify their portfolios while minimizing country risk and transactions costs. And it would help institutional investors in developing countries to share the cost of information and collectively combat the lack of disclosure by domestic issuers in these markets.

Despite the potential for promoting growth and stability, private investors are unlikely to inaugurate a closed-end fund on their own. For better or worse, these investors approach all markets with narrow interests, limited time horizons, and a demonstrated willingness to externalize the costs of unsustainable economic activity and unstable financial markets through expensive, ad hoc, public-sector bailouts. Therefore, like the modern public-purpose market innovations in the United States that began with the Reconstruction Finance Corporation in the 1930s and culminated in the development of the secondary mortgage market in the 1970s, governments must take the lead in laying institutional groundwork for a closed-end fund.

These arrangements need not reinvent the wheel. Just as the structural mechanisms and potential assets of an emerging economy's closed-end fund already exist in the marketplace, so the capacity for managing such a fund falls well within the reach of an existing public institution. Indeed, this management function is wholly consistent with the World Bank's mandate to facilitate private investment in developing countries. Moreover, the bank's experience in issuing its own liabilities in global capital markets would expedite the start-up of a closed-end fund.

Like other Bretton Woods institutions, the World Bank ought to operate in a far more open, accountable, and responsive fashion. Managing a closed-end fund would not in itself fully accomplish these goals. But it could play a substantial part in realigning the bank's program with the powers and functions enumerated in its charter. Properly structured (no small feat), the fund could make a significant down payment on the democratic deficits that characterize governance and policy-making at international financial institutions.

Issuing a New Allocation of SDRs

In the unsettled aftermath of the cold war, Western responses to Russia's financial collapse spoke volumes about the political economy of U.S. leadership. In April 1999, the International Monetary Fund agreed to resume lending to Russia in return for renewed commitments to fiscal and banking reform. At the insistence of U.S. and European officials, however, the IMF declined to provide cash and arranged merely to transfer monies from one account to another to prevent default on Russia's outstanding debt to the fund. The accounting was creative, but it replicated the same technique used during the third world debt crisis of the 1980s: piling debt on debt by capitalizing interest payments.

Compare the thrust of these policies to the reconstruction effort following World War II. Then, the United States rebuilt Europe and Japan with Marshall Plan grants amounting to 2 percent of annual GDP. By using U.S. taxpayers' money to purchase U.S. goods, Marshall Plan beneficiaries recycled funds back into the U.S. economy, helping to prevent the usual pattern of postwar recession. In addition to promoting mutual growth, the arrangement manifested a deeper understanding that nagging debts make enemies, not friends.

Now, of course, the United States is in no position to repeat its midcentury largesse. America has become a debtor nation and provides stimulus to the global economy by going deeper into debt as it buys goods from others. And the United States, like other debtors, is beginning to express its enmity toward those from whom it borrows to buy.

So what's a poor hegemonist to do? The United States can still make war with taxpayers' money but finds it increasingly difficult to tap that source for lending, let alone grants. But more loans are not what Russia or any country trying to recover from financial crises needs. Nor does the world need the brand of medicine Alan Greenspan prescribed in an April 1999 speech to the World Bank.

Addressing the subject of "Currency Reserves and Debt," the Fed chairman proposed that emerging-market nations adopt an "external balance sheet rule" patterned on the ideal balance-sheet configurations of the private international financial institutions that are their creditors. The rule for emerging-market countries would be to preserve a cushion of foreign exchange reserves while carefully managing the average maturity of foreign debt. Despite its ostensible emphasis on debt management for the sake of "private-sector burden-sharing," Greenspan's proposal simply reinforces the current paradigm that binds virtually every developing country to some combination of austerity, foreign borrowing, and export-led growth.[6]

What the world needs instead is a dose of Marshall Plan–like creativity to remove debt's stranglehold on the global economy. One of the few existing resources available to this effort is the special drawing right, designed in the 1960s to deal with prospective global liquidity crunches. The following modest proposal describes how a new allocation of SDRs could contribute to solving current problems.

SDRs: Some Background

Special drawing rights are assets created by the IMF to supplement existing international reserves. The pool of existing reserves includes gold, member nations' positions in the IMF, and financial assets denominated in foreign currencies (foreign exchange reserves).

Under a system created in 1969, the IMF allocates SDRs to member countries in proportion to their quota—their share of membership dues and voting power—in the fund. SDRs are valued in relation to a basket of five currencies and serve as the unit of account in which all fund transactions and obligations are denominated. Member countries' obligations to and claims on the fund also are denominated in SDRs.

SDRs may be used as reserve assets by a member country in exchange for another country's currency in cases where the former needs to finance a balance-of-payments deficit and the latter has a strong balance-of-payments position. Such transactions can take place at the direction of the fund or through the mutual consent of the two countries. In addition, SDRs can be used in swap arrangements, loans, and the settlement of other financial obligations among member countries and between member countries and the fund.

Although the fund's Articles of Agreement state the intention of "making the special drawing right the principal reserve asset in the international monetary system," this has not occurred. The last allocation of SDRs took place in 1981, and the cumulative value of total allocations is a modest SDR 21.4 billion or about $28 billion. By contrast, outstanding official foreign exchange reserves totaled $1.6 trillion at year-end 1997.

Why a New Allocation Now?

A 1987 IMF staff report affirmed that SDR allocations could serve as "a 'safety net' to cope with an international financial emergency of limited, though uncertain, duration." Today, widening imbalances in the global economy have created a liquidity crisis for countries with 40 percent or more of the world's population. In the absence of a true international lender of last resort, SDRs represent the single instrument in place at the global level to address the problem.

Given the unprecedented amount of IMF resources already committed to crisis-ridden member countries, new sources of funding are urgently needed. In theory, the IMF could obtain these funds by borrowing in private markets. But member-country taxpayers would still remain the guarantor of IMF obligations. And the IMF would simply perpetuate the worst features of its current crisis-response operations if it reloaned privately raised funds to affected countries.

Debt owed to the IMF is no different than debt owed to the private sector in terms of the pressure it puts on countries to export their way out of massive loan obligations. New SDR allocations provide a uniquely benign alternative to bailout loans that compound the underlying inequities—not to mention the destructive trade practices, anti-Western resentments, and growing inducements to violence—inherent in a global system organized around foreign currency–denominated debt. (See Table 3.)

How a New SDR Allocation Should Be Structured

By issuing a new allocation of SDRs, the IMF could accomplish three objectives. First, it could provide badly needed debt relief. Second, it would permit countries to shift from an export-led growth paradigm toward fostering deeper, stron-

D'Arista

Table 3

Debt and the Crisis Countries: Total External Debt ($ billions, year-end 1996)

Emerging markets	$2,095
Russia	125
The Asian Five	459
Indonesia	129
Korea	158
Malaysia	40
Philippines	41
Thailand	91

Sources: International Monetary Fund, *World Economic Outlook and International Capital Markets: Interim Assessment* (December 1998).

ger internal markets. Third, it could foster conditions for a resumption of growth in developing countries and in the global economy.

Ideally, new allocations should be directed only to highly indebted poor countries (HIPCs) and to those nations that have been hit hardest by the effects of financial crises. But changing the IMF's Articles of Agreement to direct allocations to particular countries would surely be contentious and time-consuming. On the other hand, a general allocation based on quotas—a system that would distribute almost half the newly issued SDRs to G-7 countries—could be done quickly, if agreed to by 85 percent of the IMF Board.[7]

In any event, allocations for debt relief should supplement the so-called equity allocations (adopted in April 1997 but not yet ratified) for countries that had not become members of the IMF when the last SDR allocations were made during 1979–81. Allocations to HIPCs should be sufficiently large to enable them to pay off public and private external debt. Allocations to other countries should be used to repay public debt and a needed portion of private debt.

In the case of Russia, allocations should cover all debt incurred by the former USSR. In repaying private debt, SDR recipients would exchange the drawing rights with central banks of strong-currency countries for foreign exchange to pay off private lenders.

In addition, recipient countries should retain a portion of the new drawing rights as reserves to back a resumption of domestic bank lending. Adding reserves to their central banks' balance sheets would increase the countries' liquidity, enable monetary expansion, and thereby allow domestic banks to lend at reasonable rates of interest. (See Table 4.)

The current reliance on high interest rates to attract foreign capital and raise currency values suppresses growth in crisis-battered countries. Borrowers can't earn enough to repay their loans; hobbled banking systems drain public resources; credit crunches deter, rather than spur, new infusions of capital by foreign and domestic investors.

Moreover, unless newly allocated SDRs are also employed as domestic financial reserves, the export-led development paradigm inevitably will continue. Absent an injection of liquidity in domestic markets, hard-hit countries must struggle to earn the reserves needed to rebuild financial systems capable of bankrolling job creation and income growth in the real sector. Under the prevailing system, increased exports provide their only way to earn those reserves.

What a New Allocation Can't Accomplish

Issuing a new allocation of SDRs for use by a selected group of countries would provide badly needed relief for battered regions and the global economy. However, SDRs will not become the principal reserve asset in the international monetary system and will not provide a long-term solution to embedded global imbalances or growing financial fragility.

Table 4

Highly Indebted Poor Countries: A Profile

Number of countries	41
Share of world's population	20 percent
Per capita annual income	less than $925
Total debt	$221.0 billion
U.S. government's share	$6.8 billion
Owed to private creditors	$55.2 billion
Owed to other governments and multilateral financial institutions	$159.0 billion
Ratio of debt to annual exports	250 percent
Debt service in 1997	$8.0 billion
Share of budgetary revenues and expenditures (average)	60 percent

Source: International Monetary Fund, *HIPC Initiative: Perspectives on the Current Framework and Options for Change,* April 2, 1999. Data are for 1995 except as noted.

The SDR was designed for a system in which the preponderance of international liquidity was created, controlled, and distributed among and between central banks and the fund. With the collapse of the Bretton Woods system in 1971 and the private financial sector's emerging dominance over international liquidity-creation, the SDR was marginalized at birth. At present, the SDR is a hybrid instrument issued by a credit institution. Neither the SDR nor the fund is adequate to the role of governing liquidity. That role requires the explicit structure of a bank of issue.

The 1987 IMF staff report on the role of the SDR correctly called for "better international control of international liquidity and thus for making more active use of the reserve system for international stabilization policy conducted by the international community." Given the dominance of uncontrolled financial markets over trade flows and real-sector activity, stabilizing the global economy requires a full-scale revival of public-sector influence over the creation of international liquidity.

Creating an International Clearing System

From the Mexican peso crisis through the collapse of Long-Term Capital Management, every defining event in international finance during the 1990s has been rooted in a silent, if commanding, reality: The global system of monetary relations isn't really a system at all. At the dawn of a new millennium and in the face of enormous economic dislocation, the fate of the world's money and, inevitably, the welfare of its people depend upon a web of privatized arrangements unaccountable to any larger public purpose.

During the past quarter-century, these anchorless arrangements effectively displaced the postwar foreign exchange system fashioned at Bretton Woods in response to devastating currency instability in the previous decade. Despite giving rise to an unprecedented era of economic growth and stability, the Bretton Woods system broke down in the face of its own flaws, rapid technological change, concerted ideological pressures, and sustained efforts to create lucrative spot, forward, and futures markets in freely floating currencies.

Western governments began yielding to these pressures when President Nixon ended the convertibility of dollars into gold and subsequently allowed the dollar exchange rate to float in response to changes in global supply and demand for the U.S. currency. These actions effectively signaled the end of any stable basis for the international monetary system. During the next two and a half decades, governments acquiesced to the growth of an unregulated offshore Eurodollar market that usurped the role of public institutions in recycling OPEC surpluses and eventually forced the rollback of financial regulation in national markets. Meanwhile, the privatized international monetary system expanded in both scope and volume. Increasingly, market participants grew to depend on over-the-counter derivatives markets to offset the volatility created by the abandonment of exchange- and interest-rate controls and the weakening of other monetary policy tools.

Despite the problems associated with these trends, establishment debate over monetary matters remains narrow, generally contenting itself with rehashing the relative merits of fixed versus floating exchange-rate regimes. The Clinton administration did propose that the International Monetary Fund provide foreign central banks more reserves to preclude traders' bets against their national currencies. But experience clearly shows that these kinds of injections only reassure investors if coupled with policies that constrain economic growth. When growth falters, the resources invariably wind up as profits for speculators. Modest, well-intentioned adjustments to the prevailing international monetary arrangements are not capable of restoring financial stability or facilitating sustainable economic activity. A new system of currency relations is needed.

Key Features of the Clearing System

To succeed, this new system must possess three essential attributes. First, it must enable national governments and central banks to reclaim from financial markets their sovereign capacities to conduct appropriate national economic policies. Second, it must promote the ability of governments and central banks to employ effective countercyclical policies at a national level. And third, it must support a symmetrical relationship between the creation of real wealth and the servicing of financial liabilities, regardless of the country of origin or currency of the creditor.

An international clearing agency (ICA) functioning as a clearinghouse and a repository for international reserves should be the keystone for this new system of monetary relations. Although its creation would demand significant collaboration among nations, such an institution would not be a supranational central bank. It would not issue a single global currency. Indeed, it would not issue currency at all. That would remain the prerogative of national central banks. But, by providing a multinational structure for clearing payments, it would enable countries to engage in international trade and financial transactions in their own currencies.

The proposed international clearing agency would hold debt securities of its member nations as assets and their international reserves as liabilities. Those assets and liabilities would allow the ICA to clear payments between countries. Exchange rates would be readjusted within a set range and over a set period of time in response to changes in levels of reserves held by the ICA. These periodic adjustments would reflect the valid role of market forces in shaping exchange rates through trade and investment flows. But speculators would no longer dominate the process.

The ICA's asset and liability structure also would allow it to conduct open market operations on an international basis, much as the Federal Reserve and other central banks do at the national level. By conducting these operations, the ICA would help smooth changes in international reserves caused by imbalances in trade or investment flows. For example, if a nation was experiencing excessive capital inflows, the ICA could help the national central bank absorb liquidity by selling its own holdings of that country's government securities to residents in the national market. In the case of a country experiencing excessive capital outflows, the ICA could assist the national central bank in supplying liquidity by buying government securities from residents in the national market and augmenting that country's supply of international reserves.

Thus, its ability to create liquidity would allow the ICA to act as a global lender of last resort—a role that neither the International Monetary Fund nor any other existing institution is structured to play effectively. In this capacity, the ICA could also help countries counter the effects of political shocks, commodity price gyrations, and natural disasters on international payments.

Membership in the ICA would be open to national central banks of all participating countries, and branches of the clearinghouse would conduct operations in every major financial center in order to implement its critical role in international payments. The institution would fund its operations with earnings from the government securities on its balance sheet. Like the Federal Reserve System, the ICA would remit to the issuers of those securities (e.g., the U.S. Treasury, in the case of America) annual earnings in excess of its expenses.

Like national central banks, the ICA should be equipped with a highly skilled transactional, policy, and legal staff attuned to market dynamics and alert to the needs of commercial banks and other financial institutions. However, the ICA's mandate must focus on the interests of people and their institutions of self-government. Unlike national central banks such as the Fed, the ICA should not include commercial banks and other financial institutions among its primary constituents nor as members of its advisory committees.

To guard against becoming a clubhouse for creditors or unrepresentative elites, the new ICA must level the central bank playing field upward. ICA eligibility standards should require member central banks to demonstrate genuine accountability to citizens in their own countries. The ICA itself would hew to tough disclosure and reporting standards that equal or exceed the best practices of government agencies (not just monetary authorities) worldwide.

Population as well as economic output would determine participating nations' governing power within the ICA. For example, the executive committee in charge of the agency's operations and policy should be appointed on a rotating basis, with the requirement that its members represent countries that, in the aggregate, constitute over half the world's population and over half its total output. To ensure diverse inputs into policy deliberations, the ICA's staff and advisory bodies would represent a variety of regions, occupations, and sectors and include constituencies who are frequently overlooked in the formulation of national policy.

While the ICA's independent directors would be the coequals of national central bank officials, their obligations and perspective must be mega-economic in scope. In seeking to influence the course of national economic policy, the ICA would operate primarily through persuasion and negotiation rather than resorting to unilateral exercise of its financial leverage in the open market. However, with a super-majority or consensus of member countries, the ICA would have the ability to redirect national policy in the long-term economic interests of all.

This aspect of the ICA's operations may seem radical, even with an unprecedented degree of transparency and accountability built in. In fact, it is far less radical and far more respectful of national sovereignty than financial markets' existing capacity to override national policy goals and undermine democratic institutions. Moreover, numerous precedents exist for international efforts to reshape economic policy in one country in the interests of global stability and widely shared prosperity. Among the most visible and recent precedents are attempts by the other six members of the G-7 to redirect the course of Japan's macropolicy.

Main Benefits of the Clearing System: Developing Countries

Restoring to the public sector its historic role as facilitator and guardian of the international payments system would have deep and lasting benefits. A stable regime of currency relations is key to reversing incentives in the current global economic system for lower wages and the export of goods and capital on ruinous terms.

In effect, an ICA would eliminate over-the-counter foreign exchange activities of large multinational banks, ending the wasteful reign of the vast ($1.5 trillion daily volume) foreign exchange casino and curbing the volatile movements in currency values that frustrate real economic activity. The new ICA would bar speculators from raiding the world's currency reserves by requiring that those reserves be held by the agency and by periodically using changes in reserve levels to determine adjustments in exchange rates.

In such a system, no individual or firm could accumulate sufficient foreign exchange balances to influence the value of a currency. And allowing only authorized participants access to a national payments system would radically diminish the ability of individuals, firms, or unregulated havens to initiate or encourage off-market transactions. Most important, by requiring each country to pay for cross-border transactions in its own currency, an ICA-based system would allow national governments and central banks to focus on the needs of the domestic economy.

The current system requires that cross-border financing for development results in debt, most of which is not denominated in local currencies and cannot be serviced with local-currency income from domestic economic activity. Since external debt is denominated in foreign currencies, only export sales provide a means to earn the foreign exchange necessary for servicing it. During the past several decades, the debt-service imperative has relentlessly refocused international economic competition around labor costs rather than broader measures of comparative advantage.

At the same time, the spread of financial liberalization has exposed developing nations to the promise and perils of export strategies financed by hot money. Moreover, a deregulated environment dominated by portfolio investment flows fosters powerful, built-in incentives for austere monetary and fiscal policies in all nations—and corresponding disincentives for expansionary policy.

Today, the deflationary consequences of these trends have come home to roost. Emerging-market investment manias, the downward pull on global wages, and debtor nations' forced export of goods and capital have fostered huge global imbalances in productive capacity and effective demand. Volatile movements in the foreign exchange casino compound the deflationary effect.

An international clearing system would help right these imbalances in several ways. If the ICA had been in existence for the past several years, it could have helped prevent the inflation of asset bubbles in Mexico, Thailand, Korea, and other developing countries. These nations initially encouraged capital inflows in order to augment national savings and build the foreign exchange reserves needed to import production inputs and service external debt. But, in many cases, emerging markets were overwhelmed by the volume of funds seeking outsized returns—and subsequently flattened by the wholesale withdrawal of those funds.

By preemptively absorbing some of the excess liquidity flooding into these countries, an ICA could have helped moderate their booms and prevent their busts. Emerging markets will still need foreign capital in order to develop. But by alleviating their need to build up foreign exchange reserves, the ICA's new monetary regime would allow developing countries to more effectively control capital flowing through their borders. Equally important, these nations will be able to turn their attention to developing broader, more diversified domestic markets for goods and services.

If, alternatively, a newly minted ICA had inherited the Asian crisis of pervasive asset bubbles and speculative attacks, it could have offset huge capital outflows by buying the beleaguered governments' securities and making sensible, incremental adjustments to their reserve positions. By making those adjustments, the ICA would have eliminated the precipitous change in currency values that drove up the cost of external debt for businesses in the affected countries.

In its capacity as a liquidity-absorber and liquidity-provider, the ICA would give nations greater freedom to run prudent expansionary policies based on their domestic needs. However, since exchange rates would be determined by a clearly articulated set of ICA rules as well as underlying trade and investment flows, the agency would not provide a blank check or unconditional safety net for wrongheaded policies. Moreover, the ICA's ability to help mop up excess liquidity or provide new liquidity would obviate the need for capital controls, which have proven to be of only limited and temporary effectiveness.

Main Benefits of the Clearing System: Industrialized Countries

Perhaps most important, the ICA would not benefit only developing nations. It would also be a boon to the industrialized world, especially the United States.

Despite its huge liabilities to foreign public and private investors, America's lack of foreign exchange reserves has caused barely a ripple of concern. Some say that continued use of the dollar as the dominant international reserve and transactions currency gives the United States the equivalent of a platinum credit card that allows it to buy a great deal more than it sells to the rest of the world and run up debts on which it never has to pay principal, only interest. Perhaps, optimists suggest, foreign investors will be willing to perpetuate this arrangement forever.

Perhaps. But more likely, the dollar's status as money of choice imposes costs as well as conferring benefits on America. Whether issued by U.S. or foreign institutions, dollar-denominated debt increases the pressure on U.S. markets to absorb the goods that generate income needed to service that debt—to function as a

perennial buyer of last resort. These pressures compel growing
trade deficits as peremptorily as would the most rigid command-
and-control economic plan. U.S. workers and firms in export-
oriented sectors pay the price. And so do their counterparts who
compete with imports for domestic sales.

At the same time, the worldwide proliferation of dollar holdings as central bank reserves and in private hands has resulted
in enormous capital inflows into the United States. These flows
not only pushed the U.S. current account into deficit but also
transferred U.S. financial assets to foreign owners, making us
more vulnerable to sudden swings in market sentiment about
the dollar. What flows in can flow out.

In a privatized international monetary system where economic
performance provides the measure of a store of value, it is unclear how long other nations will continue to use the currency
of an economy that remains a chronic net international debtor.
Given the interdependence of national and global financial markets and the scale of U.S. liabilities to the rest of the world, a run
on the dollar similar to the run in 1979 could produce global
turmoil that dwarfs the dislocations of 1997–98. On the other
hand, under the current monetary regime, preserving confidence
in the dollar and all other currencies requires policies with a
solidly deflationary bias—another, if perhaps slower, road to
the same destination.

That's why Americans, as much as anyone, would benefit from
genuine reform of the international monetary system.

The Rules of the Game for an International Clearing System

The term "rules of the game" refers to the practices and conditions that nations accept as the framework for participating in
an international payments system. At the national level, such

practices may be informally adapted to international transactions, as under the gold and gold-exchange standards, or may formally conform to multinational agreements, such as Bretton Woods. But any international monetary system that involves public-sector institutions requires adherence to certain conventions. The rules of the game for the ICA system include the following:

- All cross-border payments would be made in the payer's domestic currency.

- Commercial banks in member countries would be required to accept checks denominated in any other member country's currency. ("Commercial banks" means any financial institution that is part of a country's payments system.)

- Commercial banks in member countries would be required to present foreign-currency-denominated checks to their national central banks for payment. Payment would be made by crediting individual banks' reserve accounts to provide support for the creation of a domestic currency deposit of equal value. Thus, commercial banks would not be permitted to hold foreign currency deposits or make foreign currency payments.

- National central banks in member countries would be required to present all foreign-currency-denominated payments received by their national commercial banks to the International Clearing Agency for payment. Foreign currency payments received by the ICA would be processed through credits and debits to member countries' international reserve accounts. Thus, all international reserves would be held by the ICA.

- International reserves would constitute bookkeeping entries on the asset side of the balance sheet of national central banks and on the liability side of the balance sheet of the ICA. The value of these reserves would reflect the aggregate value of all member countries' currencies—a comprehensive basket—rather than the value of individual currencies involved in specific transactions.

• National central banks would be required to accept all checks denominated in their currencies and finalize payment by debiting the domestic reserve accounts of the originating banks.

In summary, international payments would take place through the simultaneous debiting and crediting of (a) reserve accounts held by commercial banks with their national central banks and (b) the reserve accounts of national central banks held with the international clearing agency. No payments would be made directly between national central banks, nor would national central banks provide foreign currency to private-sector financial and nonfinancial institutions. All international reserves would be held by the international clearing agency and denominated in a weighted basket of currencies.

This structure would not prevent nonresidents from holding domestic currency assets or deposits in a national market, nor would it prevent foreign financial institutions from acting as authorized intermediaries for lending and investing transactions in the domestic currency within a national market. It would, however, restrict the use of a currency in transactions outside its national market, since only banks holding reserves with national central banks could accept payments in foreign currency or make payments to nonresidents in the domestic currency. In other words, this framework would effectively disband and prevent the re-creation of external financial structures like the Eurodollar and Euroyen markets, which have become the main impediment to effective implementation of monetary policy and financial regulation by national authorities.

The Transactional Framework for an International Clearing System

The transactional work of the international clearing system begins when a check is written in country B to pay for goods, services, or investments purchased in country A. The buyer pays in his own currency. The seller deposits the foreign currency check in her own bank account. Her bank deposits the foreign currency check in its national central bank and receives a credit to its reserve account, which enables it to create a domestic currency deposit for the seller equivalent to the foreign currency she received.

Country A's central bank then submits the foreign currency check to the international clearing agency and receives a credit in that amount to its international reserve account. The ICA, in turn, submits the check to country B's central bank and accepts payment for it by debiting country B's international reserve account. The final step in the process comes when country B's central bank submits the check to the buyer's bank and debits that institution's reserve account—exactly as the Fed and other central banks currently clear checks on a domestic basis. The check is then canceled and returned to the buyer.

During the course of a day, this kind of transaction would be repeated many times and involve many buyers and sellers in a number of countries. At the end of the day, however, countries A and B might end up in the same place as in the solitary transaction described in the above figure. Both the international reserves and domestic bank reserves of country A have increased while the international and domestic bank reserves of country B have declined. In the event of such symmetrical transactions, the ICA's balance sheet would reflect a shift in reserves. But neither the ICA's total assets and liabilities—or, therefore, global liquidity—would change, as indicated by the balance of payments effects shown in the series of pluses, minuses, and zeros below the line in Figure 1.

Reforming International Financial Architecture

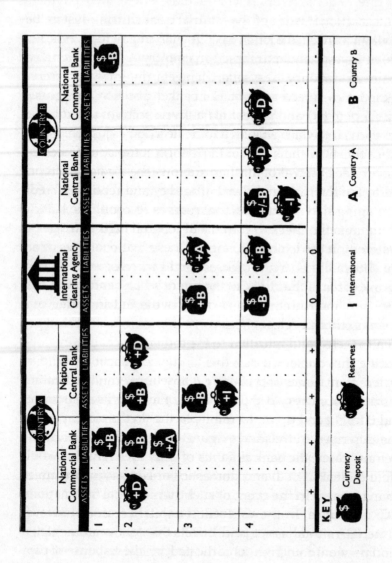

Figure 1. Clearing Function.

Within the international clearing system, all member countries' international reserves will fluctuate as a result of payments
for international trade and investment transactions—just as they
do today. However, the job of the ICA will be to manage these fluctuations through a system of appropriate exchange rates determined
at the inauguration of the system. Changes in international reserves
that exceed an agreed-upon band in either direction (*e.g.*, plus or
minus 5 percent) and persist for a given amount of time (e.g.,
more than 30 days) would signal the need for adjustments. Figure 2 shows how the ICA would perform these adjustments.

Blocks one and two of this figure show the stock of assets and
liabilities of the ICA before and after the transactions in Figure
1. Assuming that changes in the reserves of countries A and B
are large enough and have persisted long enough to trigger an
adjustment in the exchange rates of these two countries, block
three shows the ICA's response. It will increase or reduce its
holdings of these countries' government securities to bring their
values into line with the values of the two countries' reserves at
the new exchange rates.

Again, these adjustments would produce no change in global
liquidity. However, if the ICA had to buy additional government
securities from residents of country A or sell government securities
to residents of country B in the process of making its adjustments,
the agency's actions would reinforce the economic impacts of
changes in reserve levels and exchange rates on these countries.

In most cases, the central banks of countries A and B would
be able to deal with the expansionary or contractionary effects
of changes in exchange rates in ways that promote their national
policy objectives. In the absence of capital controls, however,
the interest-rate and asset-price effects that follow an exchange-
rate adjustment could reinforce the procyclical response of capital flows. If flows become excessive and shocks occur, the ICA
could prevent or moderate further exchange-rate realignments

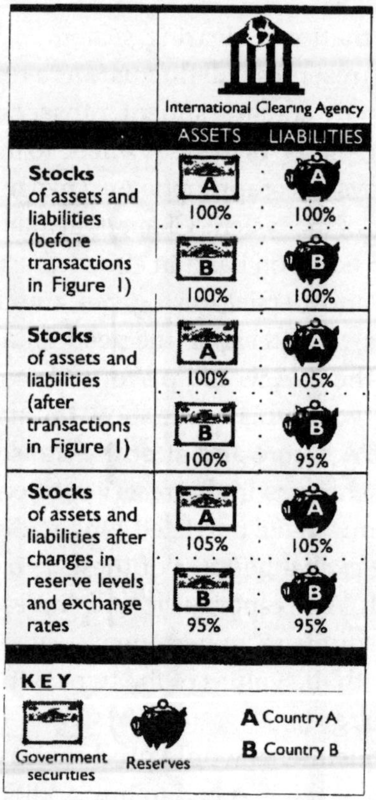

	International Clearing Agency	
	ASSETS	LIABILITIES
Stocks of assets and liabilities (before transactions in Figure 1)	A 100%	A 100%
	B 100%	B 100%
Stocks of assets and liabilities (after transactions in Figure 1)	A 100%	A 105%
	B 100%	B 95%
Stocks of assets and liabilities after changes in reserve levels and exchange rates	A 105%	A 105%
	B 95%	B 95%
KEY		
Government securities Reserves		**A** Country A **B** Country B

Figure 2. **Exchange Rate Adjustment**

by adjusting the international reserve holdings of one or more countries, as shown in Figure 3.

Again, block one shows the effects of the transactions in Figure 1 on the stocks of assets and liabilities of the ICA and the central banks of countries A and B. The international reserves of country B have fallen by 5 percent while those of country A have risen by 5 percent. The resulting decline/increase in domestic bank reserves puts contractionary/expansionary pressure on the domestic economy in the two countries.

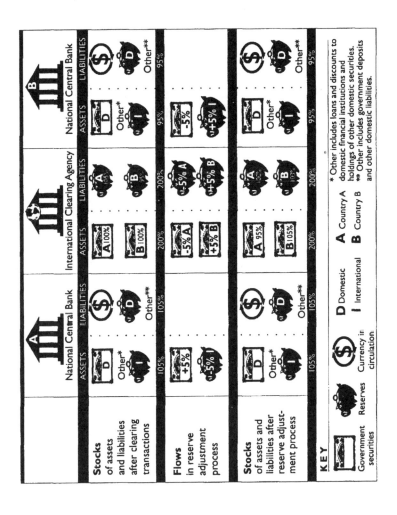

Figure 3. Adjustment in Reserve Holdings

To cushion the impact of these pressures, the ICA reduces country A's reserves by selling some of its holdings of country A's government securities to its central bank and accepting payment for them by debiting its international reserve account (see block two). At the same time, the ICA buys country B's government securities from its central bank and pays for them by crediting its international reserve account (also depicted in block two). As block three shows, these reserve adjustments alter the composition of assets and liabilities at the two central banks and the ICA—but do not change the aggregate level of assets and liabilities or alter international liquidity.

These transactions give the two central banks additional capacity to wrestle with the effects of international transactions on their domestic economies and financial sectors. The additional capacity does not guarantee a successful result. But it does enable national monetary authorities to use open market operations and other policy tools to cope more effectively with falling employment, rising prices, or other domestic trends.

As Figure 3 suggests, the ICA's transactional framework enables the agency itself to conduct open-market operations at the international level to reinforce national policy objectives, to stabilize global markets in ordinary circumstances, or to act as a lender of last resort in crisis situations. Figures 4a and 4b outline the transactions involved in the conduct of international open-market operations by the ICA.

The ICA would conduct international open market operations much as a central bank does in its national market by buying or selling government securities directly from or to residents of that country (block one, Figures 4a and 4b). When the ICA buys government securities, it would write a check denominated in the currency of that country for deposit in a commercial bank, which would submit the check to the country's central bank and receive credit in its reserve account (blocks two and three, Fig-

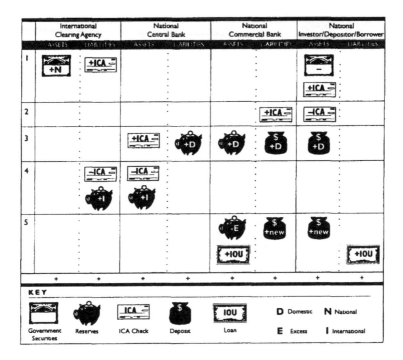

Figure 4a. International Open Market Operations (Expansionary)

ure 4a). The potential expansionary effects of the transaction are shown as increases in the assets and liabilities of both the central bank and the commercial bank.

The real expansion takes place after the central bank submits the check to the ICA and is paid with an increase in its international reserve account (block four, figure 4a). At this point, the commercial bank actually has excess reserves to make new loans that will expand economic activity (block five, Figure 4a). As the series of pluses below the line indicate, the increase in international and domestic reserves produces an increase in global liquidity.

If the ICA sold government securities to a resident of a member country, it would receive a check drawn on a commercial

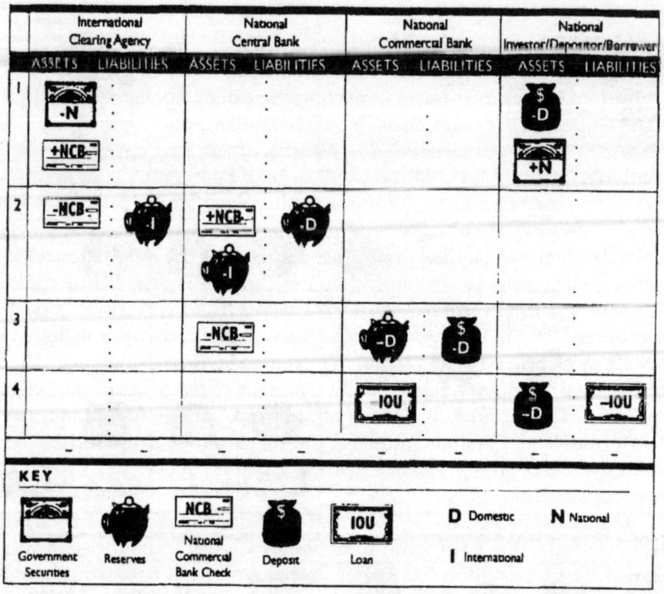

Reforming International Financial Architecture

International Clearing Agency		National Central Bank		National Commercial Bank		National Investor/Depositor/Borrower	
ASSETS	LIABILITIES	ASSETS	LIABILITIES	ASSETS	LIABILITIES	ASSETS	LIABILITIES
1 -N +NCB						$ -D +N	
2 -NCB -I		+NCB -D -I					
3		-NCB		-D $ -D			
4				IOU		$ -D -IOU	

KEY

Government Securities   Reserves   National Commercial Bank Check   Deposit   Loan   IOU

D Domestic   N National   I International

Figure 4b. International Open Market Operations (Contractionary)

bank in the domestic currency (block one, Figure 4b), present the check to the country's central bank, and accept payment by debiting the central bank's international reserve account (block two, Figure 4b).

The loss of international reserves (assets) by the national central bank would automatically reduce its liabilities (domestic reserves). But the loss would be absorbed initially by the commercial bank on which the check had been drawn (block three, Figure 4b). The reduction in the commercial bank's reserves and deposits would help rein in credit (block four, Figure 4b) and lower the volume of economic activity. As the series of minuses below the line indicate, this tightening mechanism would shrink global liquidity.

Notes

1. The proposal for a closed-end investment fund was originally offered in a presentation to a conference on macroeconomic policy sponsored by the United Nations Development Program and China's State Planning Commission in Beijing in 1995. It was subsequently included in a series of working papers for the Project on International Capital Markets and the Future of Economic Policy sponsored by the Center for Economic Policy Analysis at the New School for Social Research (available at www.newschool.edu/cepa). Sources for the data include the Bank for International Settlements, *Annual Report* (various issues); the International Monetary Fund, *International Capital Markets* (various issues); and the Bureau of Economic Analysis, U.S. Department of Commerce, *Survey of Current Business* (various issues).

2. The proposal for a new allocation of SDRs was previously published in *FOMC Alert*, May 18, 1999. Much of the factual material on SDRs is drawn from the March 1987 International Monetary Fund study, *The Role of the SDR in the International Monetary System*. The discussion also benefited from "Adequacy of Liquidity in the Current International Financial Environment," a paper prepared by Aziz Ali Mohammed for the Group of Twenty-Four in April 1999.

3. The proposal for an international clearing system was previously published in *FOMC Alert*, December 22, 1998. In that version, the proposed clearinghouse was called a central bank. I am grateful to Nancy C. Alexander for suggesting that it be renamed. The international clearing agency proposed here would not issue a transactions currency that could be used by the general public. It would, however, create a non-national reserve asset similar to bancor, the reserve asset included in John Maynard Keynes's clearinghouse proposal offered at the Bretton Woods conference. And, similar to a proposal by U.S. Treasury official Harry Dexter White at Bretton Woods, the proposed agency would have the power to conduct open-market operations. The analysis of the problems inherent in a dollar exchange standard is indebted to the work of Robert Triffin. There are debts as well to Walter Russell Mead's essay, "American Economic Policy in the Antemillennial Era" (*World Policy Journal* [fall 1989]), which introduced the concept of a "mega-economic" perspective.

4. Cross-border transactions data for the G-7 countries exclude the United Kingdom because of the uniquely international nature of its financial markets.

5. In other cases, hiking interest rates may fail to attract foreign funds to finance a current-account deficit or halt a drain on reserves if investors are not convinced the rate is high enough or will be maintained long enough to sustain the inflow and prevent a fall in the exchange rate.

6. Alan Greenspan, "Currency Reserves and Debt" (remarks before the World Bank Conference on Recent Trends in Reserves Management, Washington, DC, April 29, 1999).

7. David Lipton of the Carnegie Endowment for International Peace has suggested that a large general allocation be used to create a pool of funds to defend the international financial system in time of dire threat. Lipton's proposal constitutes a sensible use of SDRs allocated to countries that do not need debt relief or access to international liquidity.

To order reprints, call 1-800-352-2210; outside the United States, call 717-632-3535.

B The Sustainability Critique

[12]

Globalizing Rights?

Susan George

In this essay I shall try to explain why neoliberal globalization is incompatible with the globalization of human rights. This incompatibility is neither an aberration nor a temporary inconvenience which will improve with time but a built-in feature of the system.

Let me start by defining terms. What do I mean by globalization? Some people see it entirely in terms of technology. Globalization may have been given a decisive push by the information revolution, but computers and the internet didn't cause it. Similarly, purely economic definitions of globalization are inadequate even though it's quite true that cheap capital, information, and transport have been vital to its success.

If more intense international exchange of goods, services, and finance were all there is to it, one could argue that globalization has been with us since the Romans, the Italian Renaissance bankers, and the British Empire. Nor is globalization defined by the capacity of transnational corporations to produce, ship, and assemble anything anywhere or that of financial organizations to move money at the speed of light. We need a political definition as well and this in turn is linked to the end of the Cold War.

The Cold War had two major political consequences. First, no place in the world could be judged unimportant because even the most obscure and destitute country could become

SUSAN GEORGE

the scene of superpower rivalry. Second, the West had to maintain the postwar welfare state since it could not do less for its citizens than the Soviet Union did for its people. With the fall of the Wall, the situation has changed radically. Now that there is only one superpower, plenty of places in the Third World have sunk back into destitution and obscurity—think of Somalia! Similarly, the welfare state has come under permanent threat.

We all use the word 'globalization'; it figures in the titles of countless seminars, conferences, and lectures and has been repeated so often that we tend to accept it uncritically. Allow me to suggest that by doing so, we become victims of a particularly successful ideological hijacking of language because the word 'globalization' gives the impression that all people from all regions of the globe are somehow caught up in a single movement, an all-embracing phenomenon and are all marching together towards some future Promised Land.

I would argue that precisely the opposite is the case, that the term 'globalization' is a trap because it masks rather than reveals present reality and is convenient shorthand for *de facto* exclusion. It has nothing to do with the creation of a single, somehow integrated and unified world, nor with a process from which all earth's inhabitants will somehow benefit. Rather than encompassing everyone in a collective march towards a better life, globalization is a process that allows the world market economy to 'take the best and leave the rest'.

Now something about rights. Many people think of human rights exclusively in terms of torture, political prisoners, or massacres of civilians. All such horrors must be fought and Amnesty International has always stood courageously in the avant-garde of this battle. Let us not forget, however, that the framers of the 1948 Universal Declaration of Human Rights

16

GLOBALIZING RIGHTS?

took a much broader view of the issue and devoted their attention to the choices of society with regard to the *just distribution of material and non-material advantages*. The notion of 'just distribution' includes inequalities both within and between nations; the shares allotted to different social classes in particular societies and also the disparities between rich and poor at the international level.

The Universal Declaration of Human Rights actually defined a collective ethics and laid down standards for a rights-based society which consciously chooses to respect the dignity of every human being so that no one is left out. An ethical, rights based society would be one in which Article 25 of the Universal Declaration of Human Rights would fully apply. Part of Article 25 reads as follows:

Everyone has the right to a standard of living adequate for the health and well-being of himself and of his family, including food, clothing, housing and medical care and necessary social services and the right to security in the event of unemployment, sickness, disability, widowhood, old age or other lack of livelihood.

Let me also remind you of John Rawls's classic work *A Theory of Justice*. Rawls says that before choosing the principles that should govern society, you should first imagine that society from the point of view of someone who is ignorant of his or her own place in it; someone who has no idea of his birthplace or status, nor of the talents and opportunities with which he or she will be gifted in life. You would then choose a world in which, according to Rawls, 'social and economic inequalities are arranged so that they are to the greatest benefit of the least advantaged'.

The Universal Declaration does not aim for complete equality and it certainly isn't compatible with a political

17

SUSAN GEORGE

system based on some form of coercive collectivism, or state socialism as it existed in Eastern Europe—quite the contrary. An ethical, rights-based society is one in which each person is guaranteed a decent and dignified material livelihood and opportunities for personal attainment, but is also guaranteed freedom of expression, of political association, of worship, and the like. So the realization of human rights clearly requires a democratic form of government as well.

If this is the case, then I hope to convince you that *globalization as I've defined it is directly opposed to human rights*. Why? Because globalization has inexorably transferred wealth from the poor to the rich. It has increased inequalities both within and between nations. It has remunerated capital to the detriment of labour. It has created far more losers than winners.

None of these statements is ideological and all are easy to prove. At the level of world wealth distribution, the United Nations Development Programme's annual Human Development Reports document the increase of rich–poor disparities, year after year. One of the most striking images is the well-known 'champagne-glass graph' which shows that the top 20 per cent of humanity now captures 86 per cent of all wealth (compared to 70 per cent 30 years ago), while the bottom 20 per cent has seen its already meagre portion of this wealth reduced to just 1.3 per cent.

Whole regions are being left out of the globalization process, including most of Africa, large parts of Asia and Latin America, and many regions within the supposedly rich countries themselves. Repeated financial crises exacerbate this trend towards radically unequal development.

Overall, the North–South differential was about 2 to 1 in the eighteenth century and 30 to 1 in 1965. It's now over 70

18

GLOBALIZING RIGHTS?

to 1 and rising. The comparison between the billionaires and the billions is also striking, even though it's not a scientific comparison. The top 225 fortunes in the world amount to a total of over 1,000 billion dollars (a trillion dollars). This sum is roughly equivalent to the annual revenues of the 2.5 billion poorest people in the world, about 42 per cent of the entire global population. The three richest people in the world have a collective fortune greater than the total Gross Domestic Product of the 48 poorest countries in the world.

Naturally, not everyone in poor countries is poor, nor is everyone in rich countries rich. If we look at wealth disparities within nations as opposed to global disparities between North and South, we discover the same tendencies towards greater inequality. Some 30 or 40 years ago, an American corporate Chief Executive Officer received salary and benefits roughly 40 to 60 times greater than his average employee. That was already a large spread. Today's CEO routinely receives 200–300 times as much as the average company employee.

If you were already among the haves—roughly the top 20 per cent of a given society—then you have benefited from globalization. If you were further down the social ladder, statistically you have lost. Twenty years of neoliberal policies—structural adjustment programmes in the South and in Eastern Europe; and Reaganite or Thatcherite policies in the North—have resulted in huge transfers of wealth from the bottom of society to the top. They have also caused a 'hollowing out' of the middle classes. Here are a few quotes from the *UNCTAD 1997 Trade and Development Report* to make this point:[1]

19

SUSAN GEORGE

In the 1990s, income inequality has increased sharply from relatively low levels in the former socialist countries of Eastern Europe and also in China.
[This is also true in Latin America and in many OECD countries, particularly the US, Britain, Australia, and New Zealand.]

A recurrent pattern of distributional change in the 1980s was an increase in the income shares of the rich, which was almost invariably associated with a fall in the income shares of the middle class. For many countries, this was a reversal of trends before 1980 . . .

An important feature of these patterns is the degree of synchronization in the timing of distributional changes in countries with very different economic structures and cultures. *Synchronized shifts can be taken as an indicator that income inequality trends are increasingly being influenced by forces common to all the countries, i.e. forces which are global in character* . . . This phenomenon [of rising inequality despite, in some cases, growth] appears to be related to a sudden shift in policies giving a much greater role to market forces.

Hundreds of empirical studies document the huge increases in revenue shares at the top of society, the stagnation of wages and the growth of inequality—UNCTAD's data are based on 2,600 such studies.

Advocates of globalization point to the unprecedented creation of wealth in the past decade. Aside from the fact that much of this wealth is fictitious, mere poker chips in the casino economy, globalization has also created unprecedented numbers of losers. One reason is that the most powerful transnational corporations employ very few people relative to their size and are constantly downsizing their staffs. The top 100 corporations have over $4,000 billion ($4 trillion) in sales and account for over 15 per cent of world product yet they employ fewer than 12 million people worldwide. These companies, between 1993 and 1996, increased their sales by 24 per

20

GLOBALIZING RIGHTS?

cent yet still managed to reduce their workforce by 0.5 per cent during the same period.[2]

It would be foolhardy to count on global corporations to provide jobs or job security. Even if one includes in the calculations the jobs they create indirectly, these companies employ less than 1 per cent of the world's available workforce. Most foreign investment doesn't lead to job creation either, quite the contrary. Depending on the year, between two-thirds and three-quarters of all so-called foreign direct investment is not devoted to new, so-called 'greenfield' investment but to mergers and acquisitions which almost invariably destroy jobs.

There are also loser nations. Raw material producers, including once powerful oil exporters, are pitted against each other, all exporting a fairly narrow range of products, yet are obliged to increase exports to pay off their debts. According to the most recent World Bank projections, downward pressure on prices will continue for all raw materials—affecting energy, minerals and metals, foods and beverages. This should hardly come as a surprise to the World Bank: with the IMF it has been the principal organizer of a world in which producers are forced to create gluts and can only watch as commodity prices drift lower and lower on world markets. The more they produce, the greater their poverty.

For a long time, many people believed that the Asian Tiger model could be generalized and would prove that globalization could work for everyone. Aside from the obvious fact that the four original tigers—Taiwan, Korea, Singapore, Hong Kong—have a population of only 65 million and the equally obvious fact that not everyone can win in the export markets, the financial crisis has shown how fragile the gains of the tigers really were. They too have learned what it is to become victims of competition.

21

SUSAN GEORGE

What about losers at the individual level? What, exactly, does it mean for a person to be a loser in a globalized world economic system; to be among the 'rest' in a system that takes the best and leaves the rest?

Neoliberalism and the kind of globalization it has spawned are entirely based on competition. This means that ordinary people, even skilled people, have little or no protection. Anyone can be ejected from the system at any time—for reasons of illness, pregnancy, age, perceived failure, or for no particular reason at all. We could ask one of the victims of those *Newsweek* once labelled as 'Corporate Killers', like Mr Albert Dunlap, affectionately known as Chainsaw Al. This celebrated downsizer wrote a book titled *Mean Business* in which he explains how heartlessness pays off. It was very satisfying to me, and I'm sure to all other lovers of poetic justice, to learn that Chainsaw Al had himself been sacked last summer. But at least he was honest and made no bones about the fact that competition is brutal and violent.

To learn what it means to be a loser, we could also ask the homeless and the unemployed in Europe, or one of the 40 million Americans with no health insurance, or perhaps an ordinary Mexican. After the 1994–5 financial crisis and devaluation in Mexico, 28,000 small and medium sized businesses failed and half the Mexican population dropped below the poverty line. Sixty per cent of Mexicans are now reckoned as poor. A year or two ago, the Asian Tigers were the World Bank's poster children. Today, literal starvation has returned to Indonesia. A sharp increase in suicides has taken hold in Korea and Thailand where workers no longer see any hope. They kill themselves and their families: locally, these deaths are known as 'IMF suicides'. In Russia, life-expectancy rates for men have plummeted by seven years in less than a decade,

22

GLOBALIZING RIGHTS?

an unheard-of occurrence in the twentieth century. Africa and its populations are virtually dropping off the map.

Unfortunately, no one responsible for the forward march of globalization has a clue what to do with the losers. But it's clear that the creation of untold numbers of unprotected, excluded people has profound implications for politics. It will necessarily shape all our lives and will pose stark choices. And it will naturally force organizations like Amnesty to step beyond their traditional boundaries.

For centuries, the central question of politics was who rules whom. Everything revolved around hierarchy and everyone knew exactly his or her place in that hierarchy. You sought favours from those above while dispensing them to those below you. This order began to break down in the eighteenth century and since then, particularly since the Second World War, the central question of politics has been who gets what share of the pie. Groups vie with other groups, petitioning governments more or less peacefully in order to increase their share.

But I would submit that politics in the twenty-first century will not be primarily about either of these questions, although naturally, aspects of both hierarchy and pie-sharing will remain. The really big, central question will be a quite different one.

If neoliberal globalization is allowed to endure, politics will concern primarily the deadly serious issue of survival. This is the bottom-line issue of human rights: who has a right to live and who does not? Do people who contribute nothing to the market economy either as producers or consumers—and one can easily foresee that there will be hundreds of millions of such people—do such people have the right to survive and to live decently or not? I am talking

23

SUSAN GEORGE

about the kind of radical exclusion from the economic system which results in death.

My book *The Lugano Report*[3] is posited on a deep fear of the answer to that question—who has a right to survive? We are already witnessing in everyday life a radical separation between the 'best and the rest'. The people I call the fast castes, the transnational elites, are moving ever-upwards, leaving more and more slow, defenceless, rooted people behind.

How can we guarantee the human rights of those that globalization leaves behind? This is the same as asking what obligations, if any, have the fast castes to the slow ones, the best to the rest? This is the ethical question that needs to be tackled. The highly educated, highly skilled people of today will, on the whole, reap more material rewards from the world economy than any previous highly skilled and highly educated generation. This is because the system, so long as it continues on its present course, will necessarily continue to move money and power to the top. I believe that this power will, more and more, include power over life and death.

In other words, this advantaged young generation will have to decide how to deal with the losers or how to avoid having losers to begin with. Every ethical system has grappled with the fundamental problem of the nature of our obligations to other people. The Universal Declaration of Human Rights, now 50 years old, is merely the latest in a long series of answers to the solemn question, 'What do we owe to others?' Every world religion has replied with variations on a single theme. In Christianity it's called the Golden Rule: Do unto others as you would have others do unto you. Though good individuals of all religious persuasions have scrupulously observed this rule, I can think of no time in the entire history of humanity when it has been collectively practised, though

24

GLOBALIZING RIGHTS?

some societies have obviously come closer than others and in modern times the welfare state has perhaps come closest of all.

One response of society to this question I personally find not only spurious but dangerous, although my view may well be considered controversial. As exclusion and loser-hood and collective disasters increase, they give rise to collective humanitarian impulses. In France, we have the Restaurants du Coeur, soup kitchens catering to indigents throughout the winter months. You all know about the action of Médecins sans Frontières—Doctors without Borders—in the Third World.

Far be it from me to criticize charitable volunteerism or donations, but it's still fair to say that charity for the system's losers will never cause them to be included in the social and economic system itself. The point is not charity for the excluded but the defence and the creation of an inclusive society in which people have rights, including the right to belong, as defined in Article 25 previously cited. The virtue required to create such a society is not charity but solidarity, which is not a one-way street but a two-lane highway; it is based on reciprocity. It also requires political choice, human organization, and hard work rather than following the lazy way, which is to allow markets to make all our social choices for us.

Another answer to the ethical question was given by the great Chinese sage Lao-tzu who concludes his timeless Tao-te Ching with these words: *'Above all, do not compete.'* Lao-tzu saw a great truth. Competition is at the root of many social ills, but his advice in the context of neoliberal globalization is about as welcome as saying 'Above all, do not breathe.'

We could also look to another source, the father of modern capitalism, Adam Smith. Not everyone remembers that Smith

25

SUSAN GEORGE

was a Professor not of Economics but of Moral Philosophy.
He wrote a book called *The Theory of Moral Sentiments*
which ought to be read in tandem with *The Wealth of
Nations*. In this book, Smith develops the notion of what he
calls 'fellow-feeling', which is basically the human instinct for
fairness and justice. Adam Smith also believes we necessarily
refrain from certain actions because we have great regard for
the 'good opinion of others'; we respect those Smith calls the
'spectators' who observe, or could observe, our behaviour.
Here is a short passage from *The Theory of Moral Sentiments*:

> In the race for wealth, honours and preferment [a man] may run as
> hard as he can and strain every nerve and muscle in order to outstrip
> all of his competitors. But if he should jostle or throw down any of
> them, the indulgence of the spectators is entirely at an end. It is a
> violation of fair play which they cannot admit of.

Smith could thus not imagine that competition would lead to
exclusion—in his words, we would not 'jostle and throw
down' other people because natural, built-in, human ethical
impulses and the desire for the good opinion of the 'spectators' would prevent such an outcome. Smith's ideas may
have been valid in the eighteenth-century England of the
Enlightenment, when capitalism was mostly local and people
were rooted in their communities, but these ideas seem sadly
outdated today.

Globalization as now conceived places in direct competition people who will never meet, so that, as Thomas Hobbes
said, 'Every man is enemy to every man'. Such competition
creates the well-known 'race to the bottom' with regard to
labour rights and environmental standards as countries compete for foreign direct investment. Everyone is at the mercy of
his neighbours who may be able to provide the same labour

26

or product or service or raw material at a lower cost, regardless of the social and human consequences.

In neoliberal doctrine, however, competition is the central value and always seen as a virtue. It is good and necessary that all people, firms, regions, and nations compete because this is supposed to lead to optimum allocation of resources whether physical, natural, financial, or human.

Furthermore, in neoliberal doctrine, the problem of 'jostling and throwing down' other people and excluding them does not even arise because the goal and the obligation of industrial, service, or financial firms is to 'increase shareholder value'. Since this obligation is central, and by definition ethical, it follows that whatever increases shareholder value is good and whatever decreases it is bad. In such a scenario, there is no room for obligations to staff, to suppliers, to the community, or to the nation in which one happens to be located.

From these central principles of neoliberal virtue—competition and the obligation to increase shareholder value—one can derive secondary principles which characterize this ethical universe.

One such secondary principle is that *capital must have total freedom to cross borders*, whereas labour is rooted and cannot migrate freely. Capital can therefore seek out the best conditions for its employment, whereas people cannot.

Taxation should be avoided as far as possible because it reduces profits and shareholder value. *The Economist* says that in the past 20 years or so, taxes on capital and self-employment in Europe have dropped from 50 per cent of total receipts to under 35 per cent; in the United States, taxes on corporations are down from 27 per cent to 17 per cent of the total. According to the US Treasury, three-quarters of foreign businesses in the US pay no taxes at all. Transfer pricing or creative

27

SUSAN GEORGE

accounting, still according to the Treasury, results in losses estimated at anything from $12 to $50 billion annually in revenues.

Even the IMF is alarmed. Emerging market economy countries often give companies extraordinary tax concessions which the beneficiaries then use with their home countries to extract tax reductions there as well. The IMF calls this well-orchestrated process 'tax degradation, whereby some countries change their tax systems to raid the world tax base and export their tax burden'.[4]

In the political context, a system based on solidarity as opposed to charity, a rights-based system as opposed to an unregulated market free-for-all and competition, translates as taxation with redistribution to the less privileged. It requires the creation and maintenance of services including health care and education to which all citizens have access. When mobile international capital escapes taxation, as it increasingly does, it makes social protection much more difficult to pay for. It places heavy downward pressure on rights people thought they had won once and for all. Virtually all the gains of the past 50 years, if not the past century and a half, are suddenly up for grabs. Governments are trying to wind down their commitments and of course they also tax local salaries, wages, and consumption more heavily to make up for the loss caused by tax degradation.

Another principle of neoliberal doctrine is that *the private should always take precedence over the public and the state should stay out of business's way.* Government should confine its activities to creating a favourable climate for the proper operation of markets and to its judicial, police, and defence functions. This concept is sometimes referred to as the 'night watchman state'.

But this is a contradiction, since business invariably profits

28

GLOBALIZING RIGHTS?

from state expenditure: public schools supply it with literate, productive personnel; road and rail transport brings that personnel to work; the health care system keeps employees in good shape, etc. However, as already noted, someone else is expected to pay for these conveniences. National taxpayers are also supposed to pay for the bailout of firms like Crédit Lyonnais, Chrysler, the Savings and Loans, the Japanese banks, etc. According to neoliberal doctrine, the welfare state is bad and wasteful when it provides allocations to citizens, but good when it provides them to businesses that have made disastrous mistakes.

A further principle derived from the principle of competition is that *one person's crisis is another person's opportunity for enrichment.* In competitive market terms, behaviour based on solidarity would be the height of foolishness. Rival firms and nations must, rather, seize their own advantage. The recent Asian crisis, arguably caused or at least worsened by the sudden withdrawal of volatile foreign capital, has resulted in windfalls for global business. *The International Herald Tribune* reported recently how foreign investors are 'snapping up' Thai and Korean companies and banks. Not surprisingly, these purchases are expected to result in 'heavy layoffs'.[5]

In other words, the result of years of work by thousands and thousands of Thais and Koreans is being transferred into foreign corporate hands. Many of those who laboured to create that wealth have already been, or soon will be, left on the pavement. This is clearly 'jostling and throwing down' on a huge scale, yet under the principles of competition and maximizing shareholder value, such behaviour is seen not merely as normal but as virtuous.

I could go on, and in particular would have liked to discuss environmental rights and obligations to the earth, but that is

29

SUSAN GEORGE

outside the scope of this essay. Let me sum up here: I see little hope for the losers, little hope for an ethics of solidarity and human rights so long as our economy is based exclusively on the values of competition, shareholder value, and profit maximization, and not on human needs, fulfilment, and inclusion.

But I don't want to end on such a depressing and pessimistic note. Let me at least try to recommend remedies that do not require the utter demise of world capitalism, an objective not even I am utopian enough to propose, or at least not yet. I don't even want capitalism to reach the terminal crisis it seems so bent on attaining because of the enormous human suffering it would create—I've already given a few examples of human costs from Asia, Mexico, and Russia. What rights-based rules would be in the longer-term interest of a stable society, without which markets—and indeed capitalism itself—can't work properly? Now I'm entering the realm not of what is, but of what ought to be.

The first rule is to *stop deifying the market.* The market can do many things well and should be allowed to do those things without hindrance. But it makes no sense to expect the market to make ethical choices for society. Only politics can do that. Democratic politics should decide what role the market should play, as a servant, not a master. The market is not God and it is not its job to dictate rules to society. Oscar Wilde reportedly said, 'Socialism is all very well but it takes too many evenings.' Well, democracy does too, and someone, preferably everyone, has to put in those evenings.

The second rule is *look to the well-being of the system as a whole, not simply that of the top 20 per cent or the profits of firm X, Y, or Z.* Cancer of the body occurs when certain cells want all the resources and space for themselves and multiply until they

30

GLOBALIZING RIGHTS?

devour the whole body, which means that the cancerous cells die too because they have killed their host.

Marxists say it's not possible to change the rules, that capitalism will always engender its own crises, that its own avidity, greed, and iron laws will be its undoing. The daily papers seem to bear them out—look at the way the present unregulated system creates financial crisis; look at the way anarchic investment is creating huge overcapacity in production; look at the way the obsession with downsizing and reducing labour costs is getting rid of potential customers. Henry Ford said, 'I pay my workers so they can buy my cars' but his capitalist wisdom breaks down at the international level.

If the Marxists are right and the neoliberal, globalized system is incapable of policing itself, then we are on the road to the global accident. If such an accident occurs, human rights, including the right to survive, will be the first casualties. How does one avoid such a dire outcome? This is the test of neoliberal globalization. Can it recognize that the current model will necessarily produce and exacerbate poverty, crime, social exclusion, and conflict?

The Masters of the Universe, the leaders of globalization, have met in Davos in 2001 under the auspices of the World Economic Forum. Their self-declared objective is to 'shape the global agenda' and their themes at Davos, because they're getting more and more scared, were 'Responsible Globalization' and 'Governing Globalization'. So they may be pulling back from triumphalism, but they didn't get far. Let's write their governing charter for them.

They *should take the lead in designing equitable international taxation systems*, including a Tobin Tax on all monetary and financial market transactions and taxes on transnational

SUSAN GEORGE

corporation sales on a pro-rata basis. By that I mean that if you
sell 15 per cent of your goods in France, you pay 15 per cent
of your taxes, at a flat worldwide fee, in France, end of story.
The first brokerage house that proposes to tax its own transactions will get the kind of public relations boost money can't
buy. The receipts should be applied to reducing the North–
South gap and to applying Article 25 of the Universal Declaration throughout the world.

*Legitimate businesses and banks should be begging governments to
get rid of tax havens and so-called fiscal paradises* like the Caymans,
Gibraltar, etc. Whatever helps criminals, particularly the drug
economy, is harmful to the system as a whole and who knows
better than business, their lawyers, and their consulting firms
how to close the loopholes?

*Business should accept that it has responsibilities not just to share-
holders but to employees, suppliers, and the communities and nations
where it is located, as well as to the environment.*

Let me sum up now. The neoliberal model has been deliberately designed by mostly Western economists, Western politicians, international financial institutions, corporate and
banking leaders—in other words, the sorts of people who met
in Davos. Their claim that everyone will eventually benefit
from their model is demonstrably false. Their system is a vast,
planetary experiment which I deeply fear is going to blow up.
That's the bad news.

The good news is that neoliberal globalization is not the
natural and normal condition of mankind and it has not been
put in place by God or by supernatural decree. What human
beings have designed, human beings can reshape and reform.
They can seek to restore power to communities and states
while working to institute democratic rules and fair distribution at the international level. They can recognize that busi-

32

GLOBALIZING RIGHTS?

ness and the market have their place, but it can't take up the entire space of human existence.

Further good news is that there is plenty of money sloshing around out there and a tiny fraction, a ridiculous, infinitesimal proportion of it would be enough to provide a decent life to every person on earth, to supply universal health and education, to clean up the environment and prevent further destruction to the planet, to close the North–South gap. In other words, it is well within the realm of human possibility, right now, to apply Article 25.

I suppose for me the basic philosophical issue is whether or not human systems, particularly the one we are living in now, are rational. Is this system capable of saving itself and the rest of us with it, or is it like a small child which, left alone with a box of matches, will set fire to the house? I can't answer this question, but what I do feel sure of is that this generation will be the last to get a shot at solving the problem, because if not the system will generate increasingly dramatic crises, collapse under its own weight, and take us all down with it.

So in a sense, it's the same old refrain that has to be brought up to date: 'We must love one another or die.'[6] That is, ultimately, the *raison d'être* of Amnesty and I am proud to have been a part of the Oxford Amnesty Lecture Series.

33

ENDNOTES

Notes to Chapter 1

1. Part two, ch. iii. The 2,600 income distribution observations have been 'filtered to give high-quality data', including 682 observations from 108 countries.

2. Calculated from data on the top 100 transnational corporations in *United Nations, World Investment Report 1998* and *World Investment Report 1995.*

3. Susan George, *The Lugano Report* (London: Pluto Press, 1999).

4. Both cited in Howard M. Wachtel, 'The Mosaic of Global Taxes', published in French in *Le Monde Diplomatique,* October 1998.

5. 'Amid Restructuring, Seoul Predicts a Surge in Investment' and 'Foreigners Buy Record Total of Thai Assets', *International Herald Tribune,* 5 January 1999.

6. [Editor's note]: W. H. Auden's celebrated line is from 'September 1 1939', a poem he subsequently disavowed (he later pointed out that one had to die in any case). It can be found in E. Mendelson (ed.), *The English Auden: Poems, Essays and Dramatic Writings 1927–1939* (London: Faber, 1977), pp. 245–7.

[13]

WAR AGAINST NATURE AND THE PEOPLE OF THE SOUTH

Dr. Vandana Shiva

Vandana Shiva is a physicist, founder and president of the Research Foundation for Science Technology and Ecology, and one of India's leading activists. She played a key role in the famous Chipko movement to save the Himalayan forests and now works on behalf of India's farmers, trying to resist the introduction of globalized industrial agriculture and biotechnology into Indian food production. She is a member of the Board of Directors of the International Forum on Globalization, and was a recipient of the Right Livelihood Award (also known as the alternative Nobel Peace Prize). Her most recent book is Biopiracy: The Plunder of Nature and Knowledge *(Boston: South End Press, 1997).*

In this paper, Shiva describes how the transformation of peasant agriculture in India to a globally industrialized model has reduced food security, threatened local businesses and biodiversity, driven farmers off their lands, and opened the door for global corporations to take over the nation's food processing. Shiva then examines the forces driving the globalization of agriculture, including the agribusiness giants and two of the WTO agreements these firms have promoted: the agreements on agriculture and intellectual property rights.

SHIVA

Supporters of globalization often claim that this process is natural, inevitable, and evolutionary and one that is bringing prosperity and growth, embracing us all and knitting us into a Global Village. Only by participating in global markets, they say, can Third World people get access to jobs and better lives. In reality, globalization is not a natural process of inclusion. It is a planned project of exclusion that siphons the resources and knowledge of the poor of the South into the global marketplace, stripping people of their life-support systems, livelihoods, and lifestyles.

Global trade rules, as enshrined in the World Trade Organization (WTO) Agreement on Agriculture (AOA) and in the Trade Related Intellectual Property Rights (TRIPs) agreement, are primarily rules of robbery, camouflaged by arithmetic and legalese. In this economic hijack, the corporations gain, and people and nature loose.

The WTO's overall goal of promoting "market competition" serves two functions. Firstly, it transforms all aspects of life into commodities for sale. Culture, biodiversity, food, water, livelihoods, needs, and rights are all transformed and reduced to markets. Secondly, the destruction of nature, culture, and livelihoods is then justified on the basis of the rules of competition. Policy makers attack ethical and ecological rules that sustain and maintain life, claiming that they are "protectionist" barriers to trade. In reality, the WTO does not reduce protectionism; it merely replaces protections for people and nature with protections for corporations.

The global reach of corporations to take over the resources of the poor of the Third World is made possible not just by reduction and removal of tariffs, one of the goals of the WTO. It is facilitated by the removal of ethical and ecological limits on what can be owned as private property and what can be traded. In this way, globalization is completing the project of colonization

War against Nature and the People of the South

that led to the conquest and ownership of land and territory. Biological resources and water, the very basis of life's processes, are being colonized, privatized, and commodified.

Agriculture, which is still the primary livelihood for three-quarters of humanity, and which is as much a cultural activity as an economic one, is also threatened by "trade liberalization," driven both by the structural adjustment programs of the World Bank and the IMF, and by the WTO's Agreement on Agriculture.[1] The globalization of food and agriculture systems, in effect, means the corporate takeover of the food chain, the erosion of food rights, the destruction of the cultural diversity of food and the biological diversity of crops, and the displacement of millions from land-based, rural livelihoods. Global free trade in food and agriculture is the biggest refugee creation program in the world, far exceeding the impact of Kosovo. It is equivalent to the ethnic cleansing of the poor, the peasantry, and small farmers of the Third World.

GLOBALIZATION OF INDIA'S AGRICULTURE

TRADE AND INVESTMENT LIBERALIZATION have led to a dramatic transformation of agriculture in India that has had a devastating impact on peasant farmers. These policies have brought about:

- a shift in production from food to export crops that has reduced food security
- a flood of imports that have wiped out local businesses and diversity and
- an opening for global corporations to take over the control of food processing.

SHIVA

A. SHIFT TO EXPORT CROPS
Cotton: Seeds of Suicide

Economic globalization is leading to a concentration of the seed industry, the entry of global corporations into agriculture, the increased use of pesticides, and, finally, increased debt, despair, and sometimes suicide among small farmers. Capital-intensive, corporate-controlled agriculture is being spread into regions where peasants are poor but, until now, have been self-sufficient in food. In the regions where industrial agriculture has been introduced through globalization, higher costs are making it virtually impossible for small farmers to survive.

The new export-oriented policies that are part of agricultural globalization have led to a shift in India from the production of food crops to commodities for exports, such as cotton. Cotton cultivation has expanded even into semiarid areas such as Warangal in Andhra Pradesh, where farmers traditionally grew paddy, pulses, millets, oilseeds, and vegetable crops. Enticed by promises that cotton would be like "white gold," yielding high profits, farmers in Warangal have nearly tripled the amount of land used for cotton production in the past decade, while slashing production of traditional food grains like jawar and bajra.

However, what these farmers have learned is that while cash crops like cotton may fetch higher prices, they also demand a higher level of expenditure. Under corporate pressure, farmers have largely switched from planting open-pollinated seeds, which can be saved by farmers, to hybrids that need to be purchased every year at a high cost. Because hybrids are very vulnerable to pest attacks, pesticide use has also increased. Expenditures on pesticide in the district went up from $2.5 million for the entire decade of the 1980s to $50 million in 1997—a 2,000 percent increase. For poor peasants, this cost could be borne only through debts.[2]

Because trade liberalization had also led to budget cutbacks

94

War against Nature and the People of the South

on extension and withdrawal of low-interest credit from cooperatives and public sector banks, peasants have had to take
high-interest loans from the same companies that sell them
hybrid seeds and pesticides. Thus, the corporations have become
money lenders, extension agents, seed suppliers, and pesticide
salesmen rolled into one. As a result, peasants have become
buried under the weight of unpayable debt. This financial stress
is blamed for an epidemic of suicides in Warangal district. More
than 500 farmers took their own lives in 1998, and the suicides
have continued in 1999.

In the regions where high costs of industrial agriculture
introduced through globalization are already pushing farmers to
suicide, Monsanto has tried to introduce genetically engineered
cotton seeds. While the argument used to promote these crops
in the Third World is that they will increase yields, trials have
shown a decrease in yields and an increase in the use of pesticides.[3] In protest, farmers in Andhra Pradesh and Karnataka have
uprooted the genetically engineered cotton, and the Research
Foundation for Science, Technology, and Ecology has filed a case
in the Supreme Court to stop the introduction of these genetically
engineered crops in Indian agriculture.[4] The case is based on the
belief that genetic engineering would introduce new ecological
and economic risks that Third World peasants cannot afford.[5]

Shrimp Factories
The shift from a "food first" to an "export first" policy is justified
on grounds of food security, because export earnings are supposed
to pay for food imports. In fact, export-oriented agriculture has
reduced food security by encouraging a shift from small-scale,
sustainable production to large-scale, non-sustainable industrial
production. It also brings changes in ownership over natural
resources and means of production, from small autonomous pro-
ducer/owners to large corporate and commercial interests. Peasants

SHIVA

are displaced from farming, while commercial interests take over land for industrial-scale production of export commodities such as shrimp, flowers, vegetables, and meat. These enterprises often have negative environmental impacts, creating further hardship for local communities.

The transformation of shrimp farming in India is a prime example of the social and environmental costs of industrial agriculture. While small-scale, indigenous shrimp farming has been sustainable over centuries, shrimp exports require the establishment of factory farms for shrimp production. Each acre of a shrimp farm needs 200 "shadow acres" for absorbing the ecological costs of factory farming of shrimp. "Shadow acres" are the units required to supply resources to and absorb the waste from a particular economic activity.

Shrimp farming is so damaging because it requires enormous quantities of fish to be caught at sea for shrimp feed, most of which is converted to waste that is poured into the sea, polluting the water and damaging mangroves. Shrimp farming also destroys coastal agriculture because the shrimp factories require the pumping of seawater into the ponds for shrimp production. This causes salinization, reducing drinking water supplies and destroying trees and crops near the factories.

These costs undermine the claims that shrimp exports are a major source of economic growth. For each dollar earned by corporations through exports of shrimp to consumers in the United States, Europe, and Japan, an estimated $10 worth of damage is done to India's natural resources and local economic income. This includes the destruction of mangroves, water, agriculture, and fisheries.[6]

Shrimp factories have met with stiff resistance in India. In December 1996, local communities and environmental groups won a case in the Indian Supreme Court to ban industrial shrimp farming. However, the shrimp industry received a stay order, and

War against Nature and the People of the South

continues to operate.[7] On May 29, 1999, four fishermen were killed when they protested against the commercial shrimp operators called the "shrimp mafia" in the Chilka lake in Orissa.

This tragedy illustrates how the inequalities aggravated or generated by export-oriented agriculture can also lead to violations of human rights and subversion of law and order. Trade can only be increased by taking resources away from people's subsistence and survival. When people attempt to defend their human right to work and live, commercial interests that gain from exports often work with the state apparatus to crush people's movements. Many people lose what little they have. In the most extreme cases, such as that of the Orissa fishermen, they pay for exports with their lives.

Other Export Crops: Costs Exceed Earnings
Like shrimp exports, flower, meat, and vegetable exports have costs that often far exceed the earnings generated. Large scale meat exports, for example, have an external "shadow" cost that is ten times higher than export earnings. This is due to the former ecological contribution of livestock in small-scale agriculture, now on the wane.

Particularly in developing countries, livestock are not just meat on legs. Animals are the primary source of fertilizer in the form of organic manure. They also generate energy for farm operations, by plowing, and by helping with agro-processing; for example, with edible oil extraction via animal-driven "ghanis." Livestock in India help produce $17 million worth of milk, and $1.5 billion worth of food grain; they also provide $17 million worth of energy.[8] If the animals are slaughtered, all of these benefits are lost. In the case of one export-oriented slaughterhouse alone, meat exports earned $45 million, whereas the estimated contribution of the slaughtered animals to the economy if they had been allowed to live was $230 million.[9]

SHIVA

In the case of flowers, countries must import plant material, pesticides, greenhouse equipment and pay for consultants. India spent Rs. 13.7 billion in foreign exchange to import inputs for floriculture and earned only Rs. 0.3 billion from flower sales, thus having a net drain of Rs. 10 billion on scarce foreign change.[10]

If the resources used for floriculture had been allocated for food production, India would have produced four times more food than it could buy on global markets using earnings from flower sales. In terms of national food security, export-oriented agriculture therefore destroys more than it creates.

Under the pressure of so-called "liberalization" policies, food prices have doubled and the poor have had to cut their consumption in half. Prices have increased because food has been exported, creating domestic scarcity, at the same time that food subsidies have been withdrawn. As a housewife in Bombay stated "we are eating half of what we used to after food prices doubled in the last year. Even dal is a luxury now. After milk prices increased, I stopped buying milk as well." [11]

Export-oriented agriculture is also creating an agricultural apartheid, with the Third World being asked to stop growing food staples and instead grow luxury products for the rich North. Production of food staples is now concentrated in the United States, and in the hands of a few multinational seed companies and grain trading companies.

B. IMPORTS: DIVERSITY DESTROYED

AS COUNTRIES ARE FORCED to destroy their agricultural systems to grow and export commodities, both cultural diversity and biological diversity disappear. Diverse cereals, oilseeds, and legumes are displaced by soybeans from the United States. While exports destroy local food systems by diverting resources and changing ownership patterns, imports also destroy food systems by hijacking markets.

War against Nature and the People of the South

In August 1999, there was a case of mustard oil adulteration that was restricted to the city of Delhi, but affected all local brands of oil. In response, the government banned mustard oil, the main cooking oil in North India, and removed all restrictions on edible oil imports.[12] Soybean and soy oil imports were liberalized or deregulated. Within one growing season, millions of oilseed-producing farmers growing mustard, groundnut, sesame, and niger had lost the market for their diverse oil seed crops. Liberalized imports of soybeans have destroyed the entire edible oil production and processing in India. Millions of small mills have closed down. Prices of oilseeds have collapsed and farmers cannot even recover what they have spent on cultivation. Sesame, linseed, and mustard have started to disappear from the fields as cheap, subsidized imports of soybeans are dumped on the Indian market. These imports totaled three million tons in one year (a 60 percent rise compared to earlier years) and cost nearly $1 billion, thus worsening the country's balance of payments situation.[13]

U.S. soybeans are cheap not because of cheap production but because of subsidies. The price of soybeans is $155 a ton, and this low price is possible because the U.S. government pays $193 a ton to U.S. soybean farmers, who would not otherwise be able to stay in production given the low commodity prices. This government support is not really a farmer subsidy; it is an indirect corporate subsidy. As heavily subsidized soybeans flooded India's domestic market, prices crashed by more than two thirds. The local oil processing industry, from the small-scale "ghanis" to larger mills, started to close down. Domestic oilseed production declined, and domestic edible oil prices crashed. Groundnut prices went down by 3 percent from Rs. 48 per kilogram to Rs. 37 per kilogram. Meanwhile, some farmers protesting against the collapse of their markets were shot and killed.

SHIVA

C. CORPORATE CONTROL OF PROCESSING AND PACKAGING

GLOBAL AGRIBUSINESS is now attempting to take over food processing by making fresh, locally produced food appear backward, and stale food clothed in aluminum and plastic appear "modern." Industrial processing and packaging was first applied to edible oils, destroying the livelihoods of millions of oil mill operators and small farmers because of imported soybeans. An attempt is now being made to take over the wheat economy.

Wheat is called *"kanak,"* the word for gold in North India. The Indian wheat economy is based on decentralized, small-scale local production, processing, and distribution systems. Wheat and flour *(atta)* provide livelihoods and nutrition to millions of farmers, traders *(artis)*, and local mill operators *(chakki wallas)*.

The decentralized, small-scale, household-based economy of food production and processing is huge in aggregate. It generates millions of livelihoods while ensuring that fresh and wholesome food at accessible prices is available to people. Moreover, such production and processing has no negative environmental impacts.

Millions of Indian farmers grow 6,050 million tons of wheat every year.[14] Most of this is bought as wheat by consumers from the local corner store *(kirana)* and taken to the local *chakki walla*. A chain of *artis*, or traders, bring the wheat from the farm to the local shops.

It is estimated that more than 3.5 million family-run *kirana* shops supply wheat to Indian consumers. More than 2 million small neighborhood mills produce fresh flour. In addition, flour is also produced by millions of women working at the household level. The rolling pin *(belan)* used for making *"rotis"* has always been a symbol of women's power. It is often mistakenly said that only 2 percent of food is processed in India. This is because officials ignore women's work in the home and the contribution of this work to the national economy.

War against Nature and the People of the South

While 40 million tons of wheat is traded, only 15 million tons is purchased directly as *atta* because Indians love freshness and quality in food. Less than 1 percent of the consumed *atta* carries a brand name because Indian consumers trust their own supervision of quality at the local *chakki* better than a brand name attached to stale, packaged flour.

This decentralized, small-scale economy based on millions of producers, processors and traders works with very little capital and very little infrastructure. People are the substitute for capital and infrastructure. However, such a people-centered economy impedes large-scale profits for big agribusiness. They are therefore eyeing the Indian wheat economy to transform it into a source of profits.

In an industry report entitled *"Faida"* (profit), the hijack of the wheat and atta supply by global agribusiness is described as the "wheat opportunity in India." Their plan is based on making farmers directly dependent on agribusiness corporations for purchase of inputs such as seeds, destroying local seed supply, and displacing the local *artis* or traders and destroying the local *chakki wallas*.

The destruction of millions of livelihoods, of the local decentralized economy, and of people's access to fresh and cheap *atta*, is described as "modernization of the food chain." In the Third World, packaged food is described as the food of the rich, even though the rich in industrialized countries in fact eat fresh food, while the poor are forced to eat heavily processed and packaged food.

Packaging is not "modernization," but rather an obsolete aspect of a non-sustainable economy that uses packaging and brand names as a way to displace the more efficient and cheaper system through which people can get food processed locally in front of their eyes and hence ensure quality and freshness.

India's wheat and *atta* economy is complex and highly developed, but global agribusiness defines it as underdeveloped because the big players like Cargill and Archer Daniels Midland (ADM) do not control it. As the *Faida* report states, "The Indian wheat sector is currently at a nascent stage of development. Despite its importance, the industry is at a very early stage of improvement."

The main criterion used to declare India's wheat economy underdeveloped is that the global corporations are missing from the scene. Underdevelopment is the absence of corporate control. "Development" is then defined as equivalent to the corporate hijack of the economy.

A decentralized, locally controlled, and small-scale system is defined as "nascent" and "underdeveloped," while monopolized food systems are defined as "developed." The hijack of the food system is thus made to appear as the "natural evolution" from small to big. Freshness and wholesomeness are defined as "low technology." Impure, stale flour with a brand name is defined as "high quality." This distorted attitude is reflected in a section of the *Faida* report that states, "As a result of the inadequate technology used by the millers, the shelf life of flour in India is typically 15 to 20 days. This is very short when compared to the six months to a year achieved in the United States." What the report fails to recognize is that the brand name players have no choice but to ensure a longer shelf life, given the huge distances between the factory and the markets.

The highest level of Orwellian doublespeak is being used to accomplish the hijack of wheat from Indian farmers and processors. Decentralization is defined as *fragmentation*. But *centralization* is defined as *integration*, even though decentralized, locally controlled systems are highly integrated while centrally controlled systems are based on disintegration of ecosystems and local economic communities.

Agribusiness has already started to try to get Indian con-

War against Nature and the People of the South

sumers to doubt their own quality control systems and trust the brand names. They see a potential corporate-controlled market that would generate RS. 3,000 *crore* or RS. 10 billion of profits through sale of packaged, brand name wheat. The corporate agenda for India is to introduce monopolies in wheat such as those of Cargill and ADM, and in seed such as those of Monsanto, Novartis, Dupont, and Zeneca. These seed corporations demand monopolistic intellectual property rights to seed, forcing farmers to pay royalties while also controlling other inputs. This trend is moving the country toward an agricultural economy in which only a small number of people are involved—and only as tractor drivers and pesticide sprayers. All other functions of farmers—as maintainers of biodiversity, stewards of soil and water, and seed breeders—are destroyed.

The *Faida* report claims that 5 million jobs will be "created" by the takeover of the food chain by global corporations. However, it is well known that giant firms often invest in technology that is used to displace people. For example, ADM owns 200 grain elevators, 1,900 barges, 800 trucks, and 130,000 railcars to transport and store wheat. The number of jobs generated by ADM is not significant, however, because the company uses pneumatic blowers to load and unload grain and other technologies to lower labor costs.

Moreover, if one takes into account the 20-30 million farmers, 5 million *chakki wallas*, 5 million *artis*, 3.5 million *kirana* shops, and the households dependent on them, at least 100 million people's livelihoods and sustenance will be destroyed by the industrialization of the wheat economy alone.

SHIVA

THE DRIVING FORCES BEHIND
GLOBALIZATION OF AGRICULTURE

A. THE AGRIBUSINESS GIANTS

AGRIBUSINESS GIANTS HAVE DRIVEN the process of globalization in their efforts to gain control over the world's agricultural economy, from selling seeds and other inputs, to trading commodities, to processing food.

One of the most ominous developments in the past decade has been the merger of chemical, pharmaceutical, biotechnology and seed companies to create what they call "Life Sciences" corporations. A more accurate name would be "Death Sciences" corporations because they produce genetically engineered, herbicide-tolerant seeds that lock farmers into dependence on chemical inputs, destroy biodiversity, and render agriculture more vulnerable. These corporations are also genetically engineering sterile seed, through what is called "Terminator Technology," so that farmers cannot save seed and are forced to buy seed every year.[15]

Monsanto is the world's largest biotechnology corporation. It controls large parts of the soybean and cotton seed supply through patents and through having acquired seed companies across the world, including Dekalb, Agracetus, Asgrow, Calgene, Holden, Delta and Pine Land, MAHYCO, Rallis, and the seed division of Cargill.

Commodities trading is also highly concentrated and becoming more so. U.S.-based Cargill, already the world's largest grain trader, recently merged with the second largest grain trading corporation, Continental Grain. Cargill also processes and distributes agricultural, food, financial, and industrial products and has approximately 80,600 employees in more than 1,000 locations in 65 countries and business activities in 130 more. Cargill controls over 70 percent of the world's trade in cereals.

War against Nature and the People of the South

Cargill's presence in India is also extensive. In 1998, Cargill became the biggest exporter of protein meal from India—having exported 300,000 tons. It also exported 10,000 tons of non-basmati rice. During 1999, it has procured 10,000 tons of wheat. It has entered into an agreement with the Punjab Government to procure wheat and rice, develop grain handling and storage facilities, and enter into contract farming of wheat. It already has its own pier in Jamnagar.

B. THE WTO AGREEMENT ON AGRICULTURE
ALL OVER THE WORLD, structural adjustment and trade liberalization have already driven millions of farmers off the land because of rising costs of production and collapsing prices of commodities. Instead of supporting policies that help farmers survive, WTO rules are driving small farmers to extinction and ensuring that agriculture is controlled by global corporations.

The Agreement on Agriculture (AOA) of the WTO is a rule-based system for trade liberalization of agriculture that was pushed by the United States in the Uruguay Round of the GATT. However, these rules are the wrong rules for protecting food security, nature, and culture. Instead, they are perfectly shaped for the objective of corporate rule over our food and agriculture systems.

The AOA rules apply to countries, even though it is not countries or their farmers that engage in global trade in agriculture but global corporations like Cargill. These firms gain from every rule that marginalizes farmers by removing support from agriculture. They gain from every rule that deregulates international trade, liberalizes exports and imports, and makes restrictions of exports and imports illegal. Market openings through the AOA are therefore market openings for the Cargills and Monsantos.

The outcome of negotiations for the AOA should not be surprising, because global agribusiness corporations held tremendous influence over the negotiations. In fact, the U.S. delegation was

SHIVA

led by Clayton Yeutter, a former Cargill employee.

There are three components to the AOA:

* Domestic Support
* Market Access
* Export Competition

Domestic Support

The WTO clauses on "Domestic Support" demand commitment to reduce domestic "support" to producers by 20 percent of the country's 1986-1988 level by 1999. For developing countries, this has been reduced to 13 percent to be implemented over ten years.

Support is defined by a formula called the Aggregate Measure of Support (AMS). The AMS calculates all domestic support policies that are considered to have a significant effect on the volume of production. The AMS is nothing more than a device to anesthetize the public so that no one senses the hihack of food systems by corporate power. Through an extremely complicated and confusing system of "amber box," "green box," and "blue box" labeling, the WTO regime makes it difficult for citizens, policy makers, and governments to figure out what is really happening. Policies that do have a substantial impact on the patterns and flow of trade are classified as the "amber box" policies and are subject to reduction. These include budgetary outlays, foregone revenue, and payments at national and sub-national levels. Policies that are not deemed to have a major effect on production and trade are classified as the "green box." Policies that fall in between are called the "blue box."

There is a false assumption that these rules on Domestic Support will reduce subsidies for industrial agriculture and global trade, making small farmers and the Third World more competitive and leading to prices that reflect the true cost of production. This is not true for a number of reasons. The articles on Domestic Support target only a small fraction of subsidies in

War against Nature and the People of the South

agriculture. For example, reduction of the "amber box" policies under AMS directly affects farmers, because these only address prices at the first point of sale. Additional subsidies enjoyed by global agribusiness and trading interests, such as subsidies for investment, fertilizer, marketing, and infrastructure, are all exempted. Thus, WTO rules allow support for corporations but not for farmers.

Other examples of how corporate, industrialized agriculture is given advantages through this box system are as follows:

♦   The allowable "green box" policies include "producer retire-
    ment" programs, "resource (land) retirement programs,"
    environmental programs, marketing information, and infra-
    structure. The subsidy for producer retirement must be
    conditional on total and permanent retirement of the recip-
    ients from marketable agriculture production. Thus, farmers
    can get assistance to leave farming, but not for staying active
    as producers. The farmers also have no say in what happens
    to the land they leave. The subsidy for resource retirement
    must be conditional on retiring land from marketable agri-
    cultural production for at least three years, and in the case of
    livestock, on its slaughter or permanent disposal. For the
    most part, these "green box" policies will affect only farmers
    in affluent countries, since these governments are more able
    to pay for them.
♦   "Blue box" policies can include measures such as direct pay-
    ments to farmers and land set-aside. These policies are
    allowed as long as the supports are "de-coupled" from pro-
    duction supports. This implies that direct payments can be
    provided to support incomes of farmers, and that the overall
    cost of production will not be reflected in the price of com-
    modities. In effect, these exclusions imply that incomes of
    farmers in industrialized countries will be directly paid by
    governments, and will not be influenced by trade. On the

other hand, since incomes of Third World farmers are derived from production and trade, and not from direct income support from governments, Third World farmers will be totally vulnerable to changes in global trade patterns and international prices of agricultural commodities.

According to the AOA, India does not need to reduce its subsidies because India's AMS is below 10 percent (based on 1986-88 period), therefore India does not have a total AMS reduction commitment under the agreement. In fact, India's AMS is negative. However, agricultural subsidies related to water and power are being removed under World Bank adjustment policies. Thus, the support to farmers is declining, whereas the support and subsidies to industries providing inputs for agriculture are increasing. For example, the subsidies for Urea increased from Rs. 16.7 billion in 1996-97 to Rs. 20 billion budgeted for 1997-98. Trade liberalization has, therefore, left India with an additional burden just for subsidies for chemical fertilizers. The politics of subsidies in the WTO is therefore clearly weighted in favor of industry and northern agribusiness and against farmers, especially those of the Third World.[16]

Market Access

The WTO agreement on the import of food is entitled "market access" and is covered by Part III, Articles 4 and 5 and Annexure 3. All signatory countries must convert quantitative restrictions and other non-tariff measures into ordinary customs duties. This is referred to as "tariffication." Countries have to provide minimum market access, beginning with 1 percent of the domestic consumption in the first year of the implementation period, to be increased in equal annual installments to 2 percent at the beginning of the fifth year. After that, it has to be increased to 4 percent. "Market access opportunities" are defined as "imports as a percentage of the corresponding domestic consumption."

War against Nature and the People of the South

Customs and other duties on imports are to be reduced by 36 percent (24 percent for developing countries) to facilitate imports at cheaper prices. Customs and other duties shall not exceed one-third of the level of the customs duties, i.e., these duties will be calculated on the basis of the difference between the import price and the trigger price. (The trigger price is the average of 1986 to 1988 prices.) Removal of quantitative restrictions on imports of agricultural commodities is a major goal of trade liberalization.

While the governments of Third World countries are busy meeting schedules, calculating AMS, and fighting disputes, the corporations are taking over their agricultural systems. Arithmetic has been made a mode of conquest and a source of distraction in the WTO. Government energy is focused on the arithmetic of dismantling, and corporate energy is focused on the politics of takeover.

According to the UN's Food and Agriculture Organization (FAO), as a result of trade liberalization measures, Africa's food import bill will go up from $8.4 billion to $14.9 billion by the year 2000. For Latin America and the Caribbean, the value of increased imports is $0.9 billion. For the Far East, the import bill will increase by $4.1 billion. For the Near East, the import bill will increase to $27 billion and the trade gap will widen from US$11 to US$19 billion by the year 2000.[17]

Export Competition
Articles 8-11 of the AOA deal with exports under the title "Export Competition." The official justification for the AOA is the removal of export subsidies that have facilitated the sale of large European Union and U.S. surpluses on the world market. The main elements of the export subsidy commitments are as follows:
♦   Export subsidies, measured in terms of both the volume of subsidized exports, and in terms of budgetary expenditure on subsidies, have been capped.

SHIVA

♦ Developed countries are committed to reducing the volume of subsidized exports by 21 percent and the expenditure on subsidies by 36 percent, both over a six-year period (1995-2000).

♦ For developing countries, the reduction commitments are 14 percent and 24 percent for volume and expenditure respectively, while the implementation period (1995-2004) lasts ten years rather than six. However, governments of developing countries can continue to subsidize the cost of marketing exports of agricultural products including handling, upgrading, and other processing costs and the costs of international transport and freight. The costs of internal transport and freight charges on export shipments can continue to receive subsidies.

♦ The agreement precludes export bans even in years of domestic shortages.

While the liberalization of exports was justified by the argument that Northern agricultural markets would open up to India, India's exports to Europe have actually declined from 13 percent to 6 percent. One of the reasons for this is because high subsidies and protectionist barriers are still largely maintained in the North. Thus, trade liberalization is a uni-directional phenomenon that opens markets in the South for Northern business and corporations but closes markets in the North for trade from the South.

Direct export subsidies of $14.5 billion will still be allowed under the AOA. The export subsidies that are allowed to developing countries are not subsidies to Third World farmers or the poor, because farmers do not export, companies do. They are subsidies that go to commercial and corporate interests, since it is northern agribusiness corporations which are expanding in the Third World, the exempted export subsidies for developing countries are again export subsidies to global corporations. Third World governments are, therefore, allowed to support global corporations but not their farmers and the poor since they can continue to subsidize transport, processing and marketing.

War against Nature and the People of the South

Transnational corporations therefore gain both from northern subsidies and southern subsidies under WTO rules. Further, northern subsidies to agribusiness have not been touched. Since the WTO was established, the United States has expanded export credit and marketing promotion programs. Even IMF loans to Third World countries have been used for export subsidies to U.S. agribusiness.

Dan Glickman, U.S. secretary of Agriculture, has stated, "The main reason we have not lost more exports to Asia is because the [U.S. Department of Agriculture] extended U.S. $2.1 billion in export credit guarantees. Without IMF actions another $2 billion in agricultural exports would have been at great risk in the short-term and far larger amounts in the long term."[18]

The 1996 U.S. Farm Bill mandated $5.5 billion for export promotion. An additional $1 billion was granted for promoting sales to "emerging markets." Another $90 million has been allocated for Market Access Programs which go to food and agriculture corporations for product promotion abroad.

WTO rules are for preserving and enhancing corporate subsidies and withdrawing support to farmers and rural communities whether they refer to Domestic Support, Market Access or Export Competition. Protection of farmers' livelihoods, food security, and sustainable agriculture requires major changes in the AOA.

Upcoming Review of the AOA
The United States has already announced that further liberalization of agriculture will be its top priority at the WTO Ministerial meeting in Seattle. However, the AOA does provide an opportunity to challenge this approach, which is a requirement (Article 20) that parties review the Agreement.

While Article 20 lays out the requirement for a review, the preamble of the Agreement provides an opening for challenging the current AOA on the basis of food security and environmental concerns. The preamble, in part, states:

Commitments under the reform program should be made in an equitable way among all Members, having regard to non-trade concerns, including food security and the need to protect the environment; having regard to the agreement that special and differential treatment for developing countries is an integral element of the negotiations, and taking into account the possible negative effects of the implementation of the reform program on least developed and net food-importing countries.

Recommendations regarding the AOA review:

1. The primary non-trade concerns identified in the AOA preamble are food security and sustainability. The impact of trade liberalization on both has been negative. On this basis, an exemption clause should be introduced in the WTO that allows countries to keep agriculture outside trade liberalization rules, allows them to support their agriculture and environment, and allows national sovereignty over policies for food security and sustainability.

2. The reviewed and amended AOA should have only two roles after agriculture has been exempted on food security grounds. Firstly, to remove export subsidies in all forms, including the disguised subsidies in export guarantee and credit schemes, investment, and transport. It is not the support at domestic levels that creates the problem of dumping. It is a combination of export subsidies and forced imports. If export subsidies were removed and countries were allowed to maintain quantitative restrictions for food security, not just for balance of payments purposes, domestic support would not translate into dumping and consequent destruction of local markets and local livelihoods.

3. The second important role of the AOA should be to prevent monopolies such as those enjoyed by Cargill in trade and those enjoyed by Monsanto in seeds. Consolidation and

War against Nature and the People of the South

integration at all levels has led to monopoly conditions both at the level of inputs and at the level of food processing and distribution systems. Anti-monopoly, anti-trust laws should be introduced in agriculture.

4. The review process should include the following steps:

♦   Freeze on all further trade liberalization of agriculture and on implementation of current rules.

♦   Two-year review of impact of trade liberalization on food security and sustainability.

♦   Exempt agriculture from trade liberalization on the grounds of food security and sustainability and introduce anti-monopoly clauses.

Need for a New Paradigm

For these proposals to be realized, we need to build a movement around a new paradigm for food and agriculture that identifies trade liberalization itself as the cause of environmental degradation and loss of livelihoods for the poor in the South. Even where exports are possible, they are often at heavy social and ecological cost to commodities from the South. Therefore, the rules of the WTO must change and imports and exports should not be forced and food and agriculture must be removed and exempted from the "discipline" of free trade so that it can serve the objectives of food security and environmental protection.

Trade cannot, and must not be made the highest objective to govern food systems because this implies rule of trading interests i.e., the rule of global corporations. Corporations view food as a source of profits, not a source life and livelihoods. Because their profits can grow only by destroying livelihoods and self-provisioning systems of seed production and food production, globalization of trade in agriculture implies genocide. Revising free trade logic is necessary if life of humans and other species is to be protected.

Protection of domestic agriculture needs to be recognized as a food security imperative, and WTO rules should not undermine food security by destroying local agriculture and food systems through subsidized dumping. Putting up tariff barriers to genocide is a moral imperative.

Third World countries are now locked into growing export crops because of debt and balance of payment crises. Their exports should be facilitated through fair trade arrangements, i.e., trade that is not based on environmental destruction and displacement of small peasants and destruction of local food economies. Fair trade will not be ensured by the free trade rules of market access of WTO which can be forced on the South but not on the North. It needs a spirit of solidarity and rules of cooperation. Genocidal market competition needs to be replaced by ethical trading, fair trade, and new rules of North-South cooperation. We need to build a movement to allow countries to exclude food and agriculture from free-trade arrangements, so that ecological and social justice concerns can be the basis of how food is produced, distributed, and consumed.

C. TRIPS AND BIOPIRACY

IN ADDITION TO THE AOA, the WTO threatens Third World food and agriculture through the Trade Related Intellectual Property Rights (TRIPs) agreement, which was introduced during the Uruguay Round of GATT. This agreement sets enforceable global rules on patents, copyrights, and trademarks. TRIPs rules extend to living resources, so that genes, cells, seeds, plants, and animals can now be patented and "owned" as intellectual property.[19] As a result, developing countries are being forced to reorganize their production and consumption patterns to allow monopolies by a handful of so-called "Life Sciences" corporations that are in reality peddlers of death.

War against Nature and the People of the South

History of Intellectual Property Rights

To understand the flaws of TRIPs, it is important to know that this agreement is essentially the globalization of western patent laws that historically have been used as instruments of conquest. The word "patents" derives from "letters patent"—the open letters granted by European sovereigns to conquer foreign lands or to obtain import monopolies. Christopher Columbus derived his right to the conquest of the Americas through the letter patent granted to him by Queen Isabel and King Ferdinand.[20]

In the United States, patent laws were originally a patchwork of state laws that did not offer protection for the patentee outside the state in which it had been granted. This changed in 1787, when members of the Constitutional Convention institutionalized a national statute. The politicians were convinced that a single federal patent law would serve the fledgling nation and its inventors far more effectively than the existing state patents. One outcome was that broad patents were granted in the United States for steamboats—in spite of the steam engine having been invented and patented by James Watt in Scotland fifteen years before.

The United States has continued to ignore the pre-existence and use of inventions in other countries when granting patents. Thus, paradoxically, a legal system aimed at preventing "intellectual piracy" is itself based on legitimizing piracy. This system is codified in Section 102 of the U.S. Patent Act of 1952, which denies patents for inventions that are in use in the United States but allows patents for inventions in use in other countries unless they have been described in a publication. If, for example, someone in Europe were operating a machine and you, in good faith, independently and without knowledge of its existence, developed your own invention that was essentially the same machine, that fact would not prevent you from obtaining a patent in the United States.

In addition, the United States has created unilateral instruments such as clause Special 301 in its Trade Act to force other

SHIVA

countries to follow its patent laws. Thus, a country that depended on borrowed knowledge for its own development of industrial power has acted to block such transfer of knowledge and technology to other countries.

Introduction of TRIPs

During the Uruguay Round of the GATT, the United States introduced its flawed patent system into the WTO, and thus imposed it on the rest of the world. U.S. corporations have admitted that they drafted and lobbied on behalf of TRIPs. As a Monsanto spokesman said, "The industries and traders of world commerce have played simultaneously the role of patients, the diagnosticians, and prescribing physicians."

TRIPs not only made intellectual property rights (IPR) laws global geographically, but also removed ethical boundaries by including life forms and biodiversity into patentable subject matter. Living organisms and life forms that are self-creating were thus redefined as machines and artifacts made and invented by the patentee. Intellectual property rights and patents then give the patent holder a monopolistic right to prevent others from making, using, or selling seeds. Seed saving by farmers has now been redefined from a sacred duty to a criminal offence of stealing "property." Article 27.3 (b) of the TRIPs agreement, which relates to patents on living resources, was basically pushed by the "Life Science" companies to establish themselves as Lords of Life.

The chemical companies of the world have bought up seed and biotechnology companies and reorganized themselves as Life Science corporations, claiming patents on genes, seeds, plants and animals. Ciba Geigy and Sandoz have combined to form Novartis; Hoechst has joined with Rhone Poulenc to form Aventis; Zeneca has merged with Astia; Dupont has bought up Pioneer HiBred; and Monsantio now owns Cargill seeds, DeKalb, Calgene, Agracetus, Delta and Pine Land, Holden, and

War against Nature and the People of the South

Asgrow. Eighty percent of all genetically engineered seeds planted are Monsanto's "intellectual property." And Monsanto owns broad species patents on cotton, mustard, soyabean— crops that were not "invented" or "created" by Monsanto but have been evolved over centuries of innovation by farmers of India and East Asia working in close partnership with biodiversity gifted by nature.

There are three perversions inherent in patents on living material:

1. Ethical perversion

This refers to the claim that seeds, plants, sheep, cows, or human cell lines are nothing but "products of the mind" "created" by Monsanto, Novartis, Ian Wilmut or PPL. Living organisms have their intrinsic self-organization, they make themselves, and hence cannot be reduced to the status of "inventions" and "creations" of patent holders. They cannot be "owned" as private property because they are our ecological kin, not just "genetic mines."

2. Criminalization of Saving and Sharing Seeds

The recognition of corporations as "owners" of seed through intellectual property rights converts farmers into "thieves" when they save seed or share it with neighbors. Monsanto hires detectives to chase farmers who might be engaging in such "theft."

3. Encourages Biopiracy

"Biopiracy" is the theft of biodiversity and indigenous knowledge through patents. Biopiracy deprives the South in three ways:

◆ It creates a false claim to novelty and invention, even though the knowledge has evolved since ancient times. Thus, biopiracy is intellectual theft, which robs Third World people of their creativity and their intellectual resources.

◆ It diverts scarce biological resources to monopoly control of corporations, depriving local communities and indigenous practitioners. Thus, biopiracy is resource theft from the

SHIVA

poorest two thirds of humanity who depend on biodiversity for their livelihoods and basic needs.

♦ It creates market monopolies and excludes the original innovators from their rightful share of local, national, and international markets. Instead of preventing this organized economic theft, WTO rules protect the powerful and punish the victims. In a dispute initiated by the United States against India, the WTO forced India to change its patent laws and grant exclusive marketing rights to foreign corporations on the basis of foreign patents. Since many of these patents are based on biopiracy, the WTO is in fact promoting piracy through patents.

Over time, the consequences of TRIPs for the South's biodiversity and southern people's rights to their diversity will be severe. No one will be able to produce or reproduce patented agricultural, medicinal, or animal products freely, thus eroding livelihoods of small producers and preventing the poor from using their own resources and knowledge to meet their basic needs of health and nutrition. Royalties for their use will have to be paid to the patentees and unauthorized production will be penalized, thus increasing the debt burden.

Indian farmers, traditional practitioners, and traders will lose their market share in local, national and global markets. For example, recently the U.S. government granted a patent for the anti-diabetic properties of karela, jamun, and brinjal to two non-resident Indians, Onkar S. Tomer and Kripanath Borah, and their colleague Peter Gloniski. The use of these substances for control of diabetes is everyday knowledge and practice in India. Their medical use is documented in authoritative treatises like the "Wealth of India," the "Compendium of Indian Medicinal Plants" and the "Treatise on Indian Medicinal Plants."

If there were only one or two cases of such false claims to invention on the basis of biopiracy, they could be called an error.

War against Nature and the People of the South

However, biopiracy is an epidemic. Neem, haldi, pepper, harar, bahera, amla, mustard, basmati, ginger, castor, jaramla, amaltas and new karela and jamun have all been patented. The problem is not, as was made out to be in the case of turmeric, an error made by a patent clerk. The problem is deep and systemic. And it calls for a systemic change, not case-by-case challenges.

Some have suggested that biopiracy happens because Indian knowledge is not documented. That is far from true. Indigenous knowledge in India has been systematically documented, and this in fact has made piracy easier. And even the folk knowledge orally held by local communities deserves to be recognized as collective, cumulative innovation. The ignorance of such knowledge in the United States should not be allowed to treat piracy as invention.

The potential costs of biopiracy to the Third World poor are very high since two thirds of the people in the South depend on free access to biodiversity for their livelihoods and needs. Seventy percent of seed in India is saved or shared farmers' seed; 70 percent of healing is based on indigenous medicine using local plants.

If a patent system that is supposed to reward inventiveness and creativity systematically rewards piracy, if a patent system fails to honestly apply criteria of novelty and nonobviousness in the granting of patents related to indigenous knowledge, then the system is flawed, and it needs to change. It cannot be the basis of granting patents or establishing exclusive marketing rights. The problem of biopiracy is a result of Western-style IPR systems, not the absence of such IPR systems in India. Therefore, the implementation of TRIPs, which is based on the U.S.-style patent regimes, should be immediately stopped and its review started.

The survival of the anachronistic Art. 102 of the U.S. Patent Law thus enables the United States to pirate knowledge freely from other countries, patent it, and then fiercely protect this stolen knowledge as "intellectual property." Knowledge flows freely into the United States but is prevented from flowing freely out of the United States. If biopiracy is to stop, then the U.S. patent laws must change, and Article 102 must be redrafted to recognize *prior art* of other countries. This is especially important given that U.S. patent laws have been globalized through the TRIPs agreement of the WTO.

Upcoming Review of TRIPs

In 1999, Article 27.3 (b) of the TRIPs agreement is scheduled to come up for review. This is the article that most directly impacts indigenous knowledge because it relates to living resources and biodiversity. In the year 2000, countries can also call for an amendment of TRIPs as a whole.

The review and amendment of TRIPs should begin with an examination of the deficiencies and weakness of western-style IPS systems. Instead of being pressured, as India has been, to implement a perverse IPR system through TRIPs, developing countries should lead a campaign in the WTO for review and amendment of the system. In the meantime, these countries should freeze the implementation of TRIPs. While TRIPs implementation is frozen, they should make domestic laws that protect indigenous knowledge as the common property of the people, and as a national heritage.

The implementation of the Convention on Biological Diversity (CBD) enables us to do this. Because CBD is also an international treaty, protecting indigenous knowledge via a Biodiversity Act does not violate international obligations. In fact, removing the inconsistencies between TRIPs and CBD should be an important part of the international campaign for the review and amendment of TRIPs.

Piracy of indigenous knowledge will continue until patent laws directly address this issue, exclude patents on indigenous

War against Nature and the People of the South

knowledge and trivial modifications of it, and create sui generis systems for the protection of collective, cumulative innovation.

The protection of diverse knowledge systems requires a diversity of IPR systems, including systems that do not reduce knowledge and innovation to private property for monopolistic profits. Systems of common property in knowledge need to be evolved for preserving the integrity of indigenous knowledge systems on the basis of which our everyday survival is based.

Neither TRIPs nor the U.S. patent law recognize knowledge as a "commons," nor do they recognize the collective, cumulative innovation embodied in indigenous knowledge systems. Thus, if indigenous knowledge is to be protected, then TRIPs and U.S. patent laws must change. Nothing less than an overhaul of western-style IPR systems with their intrinsic weaknesses will stop the epidemic of biopiracy. And if biopiracy is not stopped, the every day survival of ordinary Indians will be threatened, as over time our indigenous knowledge and resources will be used to make patented commodities for global trade. Global corporate profits will grow at the cost of the food rights, health rights, and knowledge rights of one billion Indians, two thirds of whom are too poor to meet their needs through the global market place.

Patents on indigenous knowledge and uses of plants is an "enclosure" of the intellectual and biological commons on which the poor depend. Robbed of their rights and entitlements to freely use nature's capital because that is the only capital they have access to, the poor in the Third World will be pushed to extinction. Like the diverse species on which they depend, they too are a threatened species.

Citizens' Movements
"No patents on life" movements and movements against biopiracy are already strong in the North and South. These citizens initiatives need to be the basis of the TRIPs to exclude life from

SHIVA

patents and IPR monopolies. In India, Navdanya (the movement
for conservation of native seeds) has catalyzed broad-based
alliances for food freedom and seed freedom with farmers'
groups, women's groups, and environmental groups. The Bija
Satyagraha or Seed Satyagraha is the non-cooperation movement against patents on life, genetic engineering of crops and
corporate monopolies in agriculture. The "Jaiv Panchayat" movement or the Living Democracy movement focuses on the
protection of all species and for local democratic control on biodiversity and indigenous knowledge.

   During Freedom Week, August 9-15, 1999, the Living Democracy movement from more than 500 village communities sent
notices to biopirates such as W.R. Grace, which has claimed the
use of neem as pesticide as its invention; Monsanto, whose sub-
sidiary Calgene has patents on mustard and castor; and RiceTec,
which has a patent on basmati. Notices have also been sent to
the WTO for overstepping its jurisdiction because under traditional legal systems and under the Indian Constitution, the local
community (*gram sabha*) is the highest competent authority on
matters related to biodiversity.

   Another peoples' organization, *Hamara Roti, Hamara Azadi* (Our
Bread, Our Freedom), brings together environmentalists, women,
farmers, workers, and students. The coalition is increasing awareness of corporations such as Monsanto and Cargill, which are
trying to control Indian agriculture and are destroying millions of
livelihoods in food production and food processing, destroying
the rich biological and cultural diversity of our agricultural and
food systems, and destroying the ecologically sustainable consumption patterns. On August 13, 1999, protestors at the Delhi
offices of Monsanto and Cargill demanded that the corporations
divest from India and stop their ecocide and genocide.

   The TRIPs agreement has an impact on biodiversity and thus
subverts our democratic rights to our biodiversity and indige-

War against Nature and the People of the South

nous knowledge. Biodiversity should stay in the hands of local communities. This is a right recognized in our traditions and enshrined in our Constitution. The WTO is destroying our democratic decision-making structures by forcing the government to undo the Panchayati rights of the people in decentralized democratic structures through the implementation of TRIPs. Our campaign for the review of TRIPs will be to designate the *gram sabha*, or local community, as the competent authority for the defense of biodiversity and the protection of indigenous knowledge as collective and cumulative innovation.

CONCLUSION

THE REAL MILLENNIUM ROUND for the WTO is the beginning of a new democratic debate about the future of the earth and the future of its people. The centralized, undemocratic rules and structures of the WTO that are establishing global corporate rule based on monopolies and monocultures need to give way to an earth democracy supported by decentralization and diversity. The rights of all species and the rights of all peoples must come before the rights of corporations to make limitless profits through limitless destruction.

Free trade is not leading to freedom. It is leading to slavery. Diverse life forms are being enslaved through patents on life, farmers are being enslaved into high-tech slavery, and countries are being enslaved into debt and dependence and destruction of their domestic economies.

We want a new millennium based on economic democracy, not economic totalitarianism. The future is possible for humans and other species only if the principles of competition, organized greed, commodification of all life, monocultures and monopolies, and centralized global corporate control of our daily

SHIVA

lives enshrined in the WTO are replaced by the principles of protection of people and nature, the obligation of giving and sharing diversity, and the decentralization and self-organization enshrined in our diverse cultures and national constitutions.

The WTO rules violate principles of human rights and ecological survival. They violate rules of justice and sustainability. They are rules of warfare against the people and the planet. Changing these rules is the most important democratic and human rights struggle of our times. It is a matter of survival.

War against Nature and the People of the South

FOOTNOTES

1. Vandana Shiva, "Globalization of Agriculture and the Growth of Food Insecurity," Report of International Conference on Globalization, Food Security and Sustainable Agriculture, RFSTE, 1996.
2. Vandana Shiva and Afsar H. Jafri, "Seeds of Suicide: The Ecological and Human Costs of Globalization of Agriculture," RFSTE, 1998.
3. Vandana Shiva, Afsar H. Jafri & Ashok Emani, : "Globalization and The Threat to Seed Security: The Case of Transgenic Cotton Trials in India," EPW, March 1999).
4. Ibid.
5. Supreme Course Case, RFSTE, Writ Petition No.71,1999.
6. Vandana Shiva, "Betting on Biodiversity: Why Genetic Engineering Will Not Feed the Hungry," RFSTE, 1998.
7. Vandana Shiva and Gurpreet Karir, "Towards Sustainable Aquaculture: Chenmmeenkettu," RFSTE, 1997.
8. Vandana Shiva , Afsar H. Jafri and Gitanjali Bedi, "The Ecoomic Cost of Economic Globalization: The Indian Experience," RFSTE, 1997.
9. Maneka Gandhi, "The Crimes of Al-kabir," People for Animals Newsletter, May 1995).
10. Vandana Shiva (Ed), "Globalization and Agriculture," SAGE Publications (forthcoming).
11. "Urban poor find food hard to come by," Times of India, 9 July 1999.
12. Vandana Shiva, "Mustard or Soy? The Future of India's Edible Oil Culture," Navdanya, 1998
13. Ibid.
14. CII & McKinsey, FAIDA, 1998.
15. "Monsanto: Peddling "Life Sciences" or "Death Sciences?" RFSTE, 1998.
16. WTO Trade Policy Review India, WT/TPR/S/33WTO.
17. Contract Agreement of Bioseed Research India Private Limited.
18. "Inside U.S. Trade," Release No. 008998, Remarks of Secretary, Dan Glickman, 1998, Agricultural Outlook, Washington D.C., February 23, 1998.
19. Vandana Shiva, Biopiracy: The Plunder of Nature and Knowledge, South End Press, USA 1997 and RFSTE, New Delhi, 1998.
20. Ibid.

[14]

The Environmental Cost of
Economic Globalization

Simon Retallack

Advocates of economic globalization claim that it is instrumental to ecological sustainability on the grounds that it makes environmental protection more affordable and desirable. In reality, however, the natural environment is one of the greatest casualties of economic globalization, which is accelerating the depletion of the planet's natural resource base and the exhaustion of its carrying capacity for wastes at the same time as preventing adequate mitigating action from being taken.

Simon Retallack is managing editor of The Ecologist's *special issues and is co-director of the Climate Initiatives Fund – a grant-making foundation dedicated to accelerating efforts to mitigate climate change. He graduated in government from the London School of Economics and was a researcher at the London-based think-tank Demos. He was also a visiting fellow at the International Forum on Globalisation in San Francisco, for which he has recently edited and cowritten a report on the environmental impact of economic globalization. He writes and speaks regularly on climate and trade related issues.*

The importance of the natural world, in intrinsic terms and for human life, is fundamental. Without it, we cannot survive. Yet we have sufficiently divorced ourselves from it to become capable of devising an economic system that is destroying it.

The revolutionary set of policies that has been implemented to create the global economy has brought into play new rules and dynamics that are incompatible with environmental protection. In particular, creating increasingly global and unfettered markets for trade and investment has significantly increased the destructive impact of economic activity upon the Earth, exhausting the world's natural resource endowment and ecological carrying capacity at such a voracious rate as to jeopardize the planet's ability to support generations to come.

To make matters worse, the new rules and dynamics of economic globalization have simultaneously led to the holding back or removal of regulations and taxes designed to protect the natural environment, just when they are most needed. The principal economic actors of today, corporations, are thus increasingly able to operate free of constraints. In the process, economic accountability, democracy and the possibility of democratically achieved environmental protection are being seriously eroded.

As a result, we now face chronic, uncontrolled global crises in deforestation, biodiversity loss, climate change, fisheries depletion, soil loss, land degradation and freshwater depletion. Perilously, economic globalization is pushing the Earth beyond its limits.

THE IMPACT OF LIBERALIZING TRADE AND INVESTMENT

National barriers to trade and investment have been dramatically reduced around the world in the past 20 years, following the adoption of IMF and World Bank SAPs across the developing world, the sweeping to power of neo-liberal governments in the North, the creation of free trade areas in Europe and North America, and the implementation of successive rounds of GATT (see Chapter 10).

As a result, FDI by transnational corporations in developing countries grew twelvefold between 1970 and 1992 (*World Investment Report 1996*, 1996). It then almost trebled between 1992 and 1997, rising to US$149 billion out of a worldwide FDI total of US$400 billion – itself nearly double the total for 1994 (*World Investment Report 1996* and *1998*, 1996; 1998). The opening of markets worldwide to foreign imports and the promotion of exports has caused a similar explosion in the volume of world trade, whose value has grown from US$380 billion in 1950 to US$5.86 trillion in 1997: a fifteenfold increase (*World Economic Outlook October 1997*, 1997; see also *Financial Statistics Yearbook*, 1997; *International Financial Statistics*, 1998).

The boom in world trade and investment that has resulted from economic globalization has contributed to a number of very specific ecological problems.

For trade to take place, it requires transportation. Given that current means of transportation are driven by fossil fuels – that when combusted release various harmful gases into the air including greenhouse gases – the increase in transport that has necessarily accompanied the increase in world trade has led directly to increased air pollution and global climate change (see Chapter 20). The same process has also led to increased bioinvasion – a primary cause of species extinction by which species from distant ecosystems are transported in the cargoes or ballasts of ships, planes and trucks to new places with often catastrophic results for local biodiversity.

Many endangered species are further threatened by another consequence of trade liberalization. The removal of border controls on trade – as, for example, within the European single market – and increased trade-related transport across North American and other international borders have seriously hindered the task of preventing illegal traffic in endangered species. The same processes have made it much harder to prevent illegal trade in hazardous wastes and in banned chlorofluorocarbons (CFCs) that play a leading role in destroying the ozone layer.

But trade liberalization is perhaps most serious because of its overall ecological impact. Because of the tearing down of barriers to trade, corporations – whose primary goal is to expand in order to increase their stock market value and profits for shareholders – are able to access two important new markets. The first is a vast new market of consumers, to whom they can sell a corresponding increase of manufactured products by persuading them, through advertisements, that commodity consumption brings satisfaction. And the second is a vast new market for natural resources to meet production for these new consumer markets and to continue to satisfy the high consumption levels of industrialized countries.

Consequently, products, technologies and lifestyles that were previously confined to industrialized countries, and that when used or followed are often highly polluting, are now exported and sold worldwide. That is the case, for example, of the motor car, whose numbers have increased from a few thousand worldwide in 1900 to 501 million today (cited by Brown and Flavin in *State of the World 1999*, 1999, p6). Since the opening of markets to foreign imports, car ownership has been booming in most industrializing countries. South Korea and Thailand, for instance, witnessed annual car growth rates of 25 and 40 per cent respectively in the early 1990s (Matthews and Rowell, 1992, p6). The result is crippling air pollution in urban centres and more greenhouse gas emissions, seriously exacerbating climate change.

Meanwhile, the unceasing flow of products that corporations sell to their traditional home markets, and the increasing flow to the new consumer markets that are opened to them by trade liberalization, require that a correspondingly unceasing and increasing flow of raw materials is produced. Metals must be mined from the ground to be converted into cars; trees must be felled to be converted into paper, packaging and furniture; oil and coal must be mined to be converted into electricity; fisheries are exploited for fish products; and soils are mined for cash crops. With the removal of barriers to exports and imports, those natural resources, many of which are non-renewable, are now accessible on a scale that they never were before. They are available to be purchased to meet corporate production needs, explaining in part, at least, why there has been an eighteenfold increase in the global consumption of materials (including minerals, metals, wood products and fossil-fuel-based materials) since 1900 (cited by Gardner and Sampat in *State of the World 1999*, 1999, pp43–49).

The consequence is much more rapid resource exploitation. Mineral and metal extraction is leaving an ever larger and more damaging environmental footprint, from the generation of vast quantities of pollution and waste to the destruction of huge tracts of land. Mining now strips more of the Earth's surface each year than natural erosion by rivers (cited by Gardner and Sampat in *State of the World 1999*, 1999, pp43–49). Global fish-stock depletion and deforestation have reached devastating levels, with overfishing now threatening most major commercial fishing grounds, and logging for wood products threatening more than 70 per cent of the world's large intact virgin forests (Bryant et al, 1997). The production of cash crops for export is also causing severe and unsustainable ecological damage, including soil erosion, land degradation from overgrazing, desertification, water depletion, chemical contamination, biodiversity loss and deforestation.

Yet, economic globalization ensures that this damage takes place. The imperative to export is the necessary outcome of the dismantling of export and import barriers; the logic of free trade is based on specialization according to comparative advantage; and the quest to earn foreign exchange is to pay off debts to Northern banks. Were it not for the resulting drive to export, we can be sure that most of the natural resources from which primary products are derived would not be exploited to the extent that they are. In 1990, all of the diamonds produced in Botswana, for example, were for export; 99 per cent of the coffee produced in Burundi; 93 per cent of the bananas grown in Costa Rica; 83 per cent of the cotton cultivated in Burkina Faso; 71 per cent of the tobacco produced in Malawi; half of the tress felled for timber in Malaysia; and half of Iceland's fish catch – all for export (cited by French in *Costly Tradeoffs, Reconciling Trade and the Environment*, 1993, p12).

Economic globalization further ensures increased natural resource depletion by dismantling barriers to foreign investment, enabling corporations engaged in resource extraction – either as primary commodity exporters or to meet their own manufacturing needs to expand their operations around the world. Thus, transnational corporations such as Exxon–Mobil and Shell of the oil industry; Rio Tinto Zinc and BHP of the mining industry; Mitsubishi and Boise Cascade of the logging industry; Pescanova and Arctic-Tyson Foods of the fishing industry; Vivendi SA and Suez Lyonnaise des Eaux of the water industry; and Cargill and Monsanto of the food industry have expanded their operations to the four corners of the Earth. In a world with fewer barriers to investment, any business with sufficient capital, technology and expertise can haul away as much oil, gas, minerals, timber, fish, water and food, among other natural resources, as it wants. When the resources of one area have been thoroughly depleted, businesses simply move on to another. The consequence is massive and often permanent ecological damage.

That damage does not end with the extraction of primary commodities: processing them into more and more manufactured goods is also often highly polluting. It requires large quantities of energy, mostly in the form of fossil fuels, contributing to air pollution and climate change. In the US, for example, material processing and manufacturing alone claimed 14 per cent of the country's energy use in 1994 (cited by Gardner and Sampat in *State of the World 1999*, 1999, p48). Manufacturing also involves the use of large quantities of chemicals. As an exponentially rising number of manufactured products are made and exported worldwide, the annual world production of synthetic organic chemicals has increased enormously. From 7 million tons in 1950, chemical production has grown to nearly a billion tons today and is generating huge amounts of hazardous waste in the process (cited by Karliner in *The Corporate Planet*, 1997, p16). The consequences are a significant decrease in biodiversity and a horrifying growth in cancer rates. A white male in the US today, for example, is twice as likely to get cancer as his grandfather (Davis et al, 1994; cited in *Rachel's Hazardous Waste News*, 14 April 1994).

Economic globalization not only promotes these trends by stimulating increased commodity production for export. By liberalizing investment, it permits corporations to expand industrial production around the world, increasing the scale of ecological problems such activities cause. Thus, we have witnessed the global expansion of the computer, car, steel, paper, plastic, chemical and oil refining industries – all of which generate significant quantities of hazardous waste, with serious implications for public health and biodiversity.

Investment liberalization also permits Northern-based corporations which are engaged in activities that are so ecologically harmful that they incur heavy financial cleanup penalties, or are illegal in most industrialized countries, to continue to engage in them wherever in the world environmental laws or their enforcement are lax (see Chapter 12). Many cases have been documented in which particularly hazardous operations have relocated from the North to escape strict and costly environmental standards. They include producers of asbestos, benzidine dyes, ozone-destroying CFCs, certain pesticides such as DDT, as well as lead and copper smelters, and some mineral processors (Leonard, 1988). A number of serious environmental problems are thus perpetuated with devastating implications for public health and biodiversity.

Similarly appalling problems are caused by the disposal of increased municipal waste arising from the increased volume of consumer products and packaging entering markets worldwide, and the expansion of the industrial way of life that is taking place with the opening of markets to trade. The increased use of waste disposal methods such as incineration and landfill, pollutes more water supplies, leaches more mercury, generates more methane (a powerful greenhouse gas), and fills the air we breathe with more cancer-causing dioxins.

The tearing down of barriers to trade and investment around the world clearly contributes to all of these problems by providing growth-oriented corporations with unprecedented access to consumers and raw materials, and by maintaining the unsustainable industrialized way of life beyond its natural limits while extending it to the rest of the world.

If the consequent rising tide of ecological destruction is to be halted, the task of strengthening environmental regulations is more urgently needed than ever. Yet another key feature of economic globalisation is *de*regulation. The competitive dynamic that economic globalization creates, and the new trade rules of the global economy principally administered by the WTO, are causing governments around the world to roll back and hold back legislative and fiscal measures designed to protect the natural environment. Constraints on ecologically destructive corporate activity are thus being removed, just when they are needed most.

THE IMPACT OF GLOBAL COMPETITION

As the economy and corporate activity have become global, democratic government has remained nationally based, enabling corporations to function increasingly beyond the reach of public accountability and control, with very serious implications for the possibility of achieving the level of environmental protection that is so desperately needed.

In their battles to thwart environmental regulations or taxes, corporate executives tell regulators that if environmental costs, whether real or perceived, are imposed on them, they will be forced to reflect them in the price of their goods. Because their goods must compete in a global market with goods that do not carry such environmental costs, their company, they claim, will be at a systematic competitive disadvantage and, over time, will go out of business, shedding precious jobs. If that strategy fails, corporations can use the ultimate threat: to use their new freedom – created by the dismantling of barriers to trade and investment – to relocate to another country with less onerous environmental regulations or enforcement (see Chapter 12).

Governments in both the industrialized and the industrializing world have proven utterly susceptible to such arguments and threats. Once their countries are part of the global economy, they are invariably desperate to attract inward investment to generate jobs, facilitate the transfer of new technologies that improve productivity and increase economic growth and hence GDP. They are also invariably intimidated or bought off by the enormously increased wealth and economic power of transnational corporations that has resulted from economic globalization. The assets and sales of the largest transnational corporations are now far in excess of the GNP of most countries in the world. Indeed, 51 of the largest 100 economies in the world (excluding banking and financial institutions) are now corporations (cited by Karliner in *The Corporate Planet*, 1997, p5).

As corporations use their new strength and mobility in the global economy to exert political influence, notably by playing off states and communities against one another to leverage optimum investment conditions, a global 'race to the bottom' has been initiated, in which standards fall towards the level of the most desperate. Many environmental protections have been overturned or left unenforced and countless others prevented from seeing the light of day – all so that national companies remain or feel they remain competitive in the global economy, and foreign corporations are induced to invest.

Leading the drive to deregulate are developing countries. Whether prompted by IMF–World Bank structural adjustment programmes or unilateral governmental initiatives, the aim is the same: to be competitive enough to attract and retain foreign investment. And for developing countries such as India, this has meant rolling back environmental laws. Prohibitions against siting industrial facilities in ecologically sensitive areas have been removed and conservation zones stripped of their status so that cement plants, bauxite mines, prawn aquaculture and luxury hotels can be built. Forestry regulations have been relaxed for the pulp and paper industry, fisheries controls weakened for fishing transnationals, and mining laws watered down for mining corporations (Karliner, 1997, p146).

An increasing number of developing countries are going even further to sacrifice their natural environments on the altar of global competitiveness. They are creating hundreds of so-called 'free-trade zones', usually situated near key communications centres within their countries, and in which lax environmental enforcement is part of a package of measures designed to establish 'ideal' investment climates for foreign corporations. In the process, whole regions are being ecologically decimated. A particularly notorious free-trade zone is located on the Mexican side of the border with the US and is populated by more than 3400 factories known as *maquiladoras* (see Chapter 12). In China too, *maquiladora*-type zones have sprung up in the provinces of Guandong and Fujian, where low wages and lax environmental controls are attracting billions of dollars of investment.

The competitive pressures of the global economy also undermine ecological best practice in developing countries. Agriculture is a good example. Enormous volumes of staple crops – such as wheat, maize and rice – are grown for export in the North, in monocultures, with the aid of very high and unsustainable levels of chemical and mechanical inputs, as well as genetic engineering technology, and are benefitting from huge subsidies and economies of scale. With the dismantling of import barriers, these crops now flood markets in developing countries, fatally undercutting small-scale, low-input agriculture that is unable to compete. The more ecologically sustainable system of agriculture therefore goes to the wall. And the only way left for farmers in those countries to compete is to imitate the system of agriculture of their industrialized world competitors – with further devastating consequences for the natural environment. As Mexico's agriculture minister, Romarico Arroyo, recently said, with 25 per cent of Mexican corn imports now genetically modified, 'if we don't put genetic engineering to use, it will be difficult for us to compete', despite the damage to Mexican biodiversity that could result (cited in Tricks and Mandel-Campbell, 1999).

The forces of market competition undermine ecological best practice in developing nations in another way. Many such countries have slashed budgets dedicated to protecting the environment, since reducing non-commercial expenditure to lower the tax burden and increase competitiveness is often a condition of receiving an IMF–World Bank SAL. To cite two examples: the budget for the Mexican environmental protection agency was cut by 60 per cent in real terms between 1986 and 1989 (cited by Bello in Mander and Goldsmith, 1996, p283); and in 1998, Brazil's environment budget was cut by 66 per cent, and funds dedicated to protecting the Amazon rainforest were reduced from US$61.1 million to US$6.4 million (Steven Schwartzman, Environmental Defence Fund, Washington, DC).

If that were not enough, some industrializing countries will go even further to placate the gods of competitiveness and foreign investment. As an advertisement placed in *Fortune* magazine by the Philippine government has said: 'To attract companies like yours. . . we have felled mountains, razed jungles, filled swamps, moved rivers, relocated towns. . . all to make it easier for you and your business to do business here' (cited by Korten, 1995, p159).

To compete, as industrialized nations must in the global economy, with such countries and, which is still more often the case, with states at similar levels of economic development, they too have pursued deregulation programmes with serious consequences for environmental protection. The Reagan administration, for example, set up a taskforce on regulatory relief, headed by Vice-President George Bush, that was heavily involved in weakening, rolling back and obstructing environmental, consumer and worker safety protections. In 1989, during the Bush administration, Vice-President Quayle's council on competitiveness undertook the same work. The council was active in opening up half of American protected wetlands for development, and tabling over 100 obstructive amendments to the EPA's implementation proposals for the 1990 Clean Air Act (according to Public Citizen's Congress Watch). In the mid 1990s, another frenzy of environmental deregulation began, undertaken this time by the Republican-controlled US Congress led by House Speaker Newt Gingrich. It took place, in part at least, as a result of pressure from corporations using powerful new weapons available to them in the global economy.

In 1995, for example, transnational timber corporation Boise Cascade used the threat of relocating some of its operations to Mexico to try to water down US environmental standards. Its threat was credible because earlier that year it had closed mills in Oregon and Idaho and set up production in Guerrero, Mexico, to exploit lax environmental regulations and other new investment 'opportunities' fostered there by NAFTA. 'How many more mills will be closed,' Boise Cascade spokesman Doug Bertels told the *Idaho Statesman*, 'depends on what Congress does' (case and quote cited by Karliner, 1997, p154). It can be no coincidence that that same year, Congress passed the Timber Salvage Rider, designed to make US timber producers more competitive by opening up US national forests to deregulated logging at subsidized prices.

The drive to maintain economic competitiveness in industrialized countries extends beyond the overturning of existing regulations. It is also preventing governments from raising sufficient taxation from business and channelling that revenue into environmental programmes. If direct or indirect taxation is hiked, either industrial competitiveness is reduced, or corporations use their new-found global mobility in the world economy to relocate to tax havens or lower-tax countries. Either way, government revenues, that urgently need to be invested in renewable energy and energy efficiency technologies, public transport, forest regeneration or environmental cleanup operations, are significantly reduced.

THE IMPACT OF THE HARD RULES OF THE GLOBAL ECONOMY

If any environmental protections survive the onslaught of competitive deregulation, many are now vulnerable to being struck down by the WTO and the 'hard' rules of the global economy that the WTO is primarily responsible for enforcing. The principal purpose of these rules and of the WTO is to eliminate barriers to trade. Because many national and international environmental laws and agreements often restrict trade in some way, the WTO has the power to override, weaken, eliminate or prevent them from ever being drawn up. Under the rules, when there is a conflict, free trade effectively takes precedence over all other considerations – including that of protecting the natural environment.

Officially, global trade rules do allow for the adoption or enforcement of measures 'necessary to protect human, animal or plant life or health' and those 'relating to the conservation of exhaustible natural resources' (Article XX of GATT). But such measures must run the gauntlet of impossible legal hurdles created by a host of trade rules and rulings before these provisions can apply, rendering them virtually meaningless.

For example, no environmental measure is allowed if it is 'applied in a manner which would constitute a means of arbitrary or unjustifiable discrimination between countries where the same conditions prevail' or if it represents 'a disguised restriction on international trade' (Article XX of GATT). The same rule also states that no measures designed to conserve exhaustible natural resources are permissible unless they 'are made effective in conjunction with restrictions on domestic production or consumption' (cited by Shrybman, 1999, p22). No measure can, in fact, discriminate among foreign producers, or between foreign and domestic producers of a 'like' product (Articles I and III of GATT). In addition, no environmental measure affecting trade will be judged legitimate unless it is proved to be both 'necessary' and 'the least trade restrictive' way to achieve the conservation or environmental goal it is seeking (Article 2.2 of the WTO Agreement on Technical Barriers to Trade) (cited by Shrybman, 1999, p82). Moreover, no standards on food safety, biotechnology, pesticides, and plants and animals generally that affect trade are allowable unless an international scientific consensus is reached that such standards are scientifically justified, according to risk assessment (as stated by various articles of the WTO Agreement on the Application of Sanitary and Phytosanitary Measures).

All of these highly restrictive conditions provide enormous scope for subjective interpretation – scope that the biased nature of the WTO dispute resolution process has ensured is exploited fully in the interests of asserting the primacy of free trade over all environmental considerations (see Chapter 16).

In every case to date, WTO rules which restrict the ability of governments to implement policies that might even indirectly interfere with trade have been given expansive interpretation by WTO tribunals. Extremely narrow interpretation, meanwhile, has been given to provisions that might create space for environmental exceptions to free trade. That explains why every environmental or conservation measure that has been ruled upon so far by the WTO, and GATT before it, has been shot down. It also explains why the mere threat or possibility of WTO action has been sufficient to persuade many countries to change their laws voluntarily to be 'WTO compliant'. Under this so-called 'chilling effect', countless existing or prospective measures that are vital to environmental protection are either under threat or are no longer even considered by governments.

Among a whole raft of environmental controls that are now at risk because of world trade rules are those that apply to exports. Exports controls can be an important tool for conserving and protecting important and scarce natural resources, such as forests, fish and water, particularly when larger and larger volumes of these 'resources' are being exploited for global export. When governments have imposed export bans on raw materials to promote conservation and local employment in the past, such as the Canadian ban on the export of raw logs and unprocessed fish, they have had an immediate and obvious impact on the rate of resource exploitation (Shrybman, 1999, p60).

Such policies, however, are illegal under GATT–WTO rules, and tribunal rulings have confirmed that. The 1908 Canadian Fisheries Act prohibiting the export of unprocessed salmon and herring, for example, was struck down by a GATT panel, following a US challenge in 1986 designed to secure a larger share of Canada's valuable fisheries resources for its own domestic canning industry.

GATT–WTO rules also prevent the adoption of effective controls on imports, with serious implications for environmental laws and regulations. Quotas or bans on imports are forbidden, as is any discrimination among foreign producers and between foreign and domestic producers of a 'like' product – including through tariff policy. That means that no distinction can be made between products that look alike, even if the methods used to manufacture or produce them differ. Given that many goods and commodities are produced, grown, harvested and extracted in ways that seriously harm the natural environment, outlawing the ability to discriminate against goods that are produced in such ways removes an essential tool for achieving ecological sustainability (see Chapter 16).

We thus have a lose–lose situation for environmental protection. If governments only allow products to enter domestic markets on condition that they conform to domestic environmental production standards, such behaviour can be found in breach of GATT rules and banned by the WTO. That is exactly what has happened to key clauses of the US Marine Mammal Act that blocked imports of tuna caught in ways that kill dolphins, and to key clauses of the US Endangered Species Act restricting imports of shrimp caught without devices that reduce sea turtle deaths. If, on the other hand, governments allow imports of products that do not meet domestic environmental production standards, as is now the case with regard to tuna and shrimp in the US, those standards will clearly be undermined and domestic producers who abide by them (and whose goods are consequently often more costly) undercut and potentially forced out of business.

Given that the laws involved in both the tuna–dolphin and shrimp–turtle cases could be considered as part of attempts to fulfil the goals of multilateral environment agreements (MEAs) to protect endangered species, such as CITES, each ruling and the logic that lay behind it has serious ramifications for MEAs. Most MEAs contain trade instruments that can require other countries to change their policies and practices in pursuit of global environmental goals. Most, for example, either discriminate against 'like' products according to how they are made or where they are from, or generally restrict imports or exports in some way. Under GATT–WTO rules, most MEAs could thus be challenged.

As Steven Shrybman, director of the West Coast Environmental Law Foundation, explains, MEAs such as CITES, the Montreal Protocol and the Basel Convention violate GATT rules banning the use of quantitative trade controls, since each of these MEAs seeks to control or ban trade in endangered species, ozone-depleting chemicals and hazardous wastes respectively. By allowing different rules to be applied to foreign and domestic producers, these MEAs also violate the GATT requirement for 'national treatment'. The Basel Convention and CITES, for instance, seek respectively to restrict international trade in waste and endangered species, but do not regulate domestic trade or consumption. CITES and the Montreal Protocol also violate GATT rules by discriminating between 'like' products, according, respectively, to whether or not a product comes from a country where a particular species is threatened or is a full party to the protocol (Shrybman, 1999, pp20–21).

At least seven other MEAs, including the UN's Convention on Climate Change and the Kyoto Protocol, contravene GATT and WTO rules and are hence at risk, according to the World Wide Fund for Nature (WWF) (WWF press release, 4 October 1999). The threat posed is serious, especially since a proposal by the European Union that MEAs should override WTO rules was rejected by the WTO's committee on trade and the environment.

The only standards the WTO is keen to recognize are those international ones shaped by industry that it can use to overturn or lower national environmental standards. The harmonizing down of environmental and food standards in that way is the purpose of two WTO agreements – one on technical barriers to trade (TBT) and the other on the application of sanitary and phytosanitary measures (SPS).

Under the TBT agreement, national environmental laws are defined as 'technical barriers to trade' (also referred to as 'non-tariff barriers') and must be replaced with international standards where such standards have been established. Rather than harmonizing upward and thus improving protection everywhere, a lowering of standards usually results, since the process of reaching a consensus among governments subject to heavy industry lobbying often results in adopting the lowest common denominator. Worse, under the TBT agreement, such standards place a ceiling on environmental regulation, but no floor. Already, TBT provisions have been used to undermine or threaten a number of environmental regulations (see Chapter 16).

The WTO's SPS agreement – governing standards on food safety, biotechnology, pesticides and plants and animals generally – sets even stricter conditions for governments seeking to maintain or introduce any national standards that surpass weak, industry-shaped international ones recognized by the WTO. Governments must, in effect, demonstrate that an international scientific consensus has been reached in support of the proposition that their higher standards are scientifically justified, according to risk assessments. Absence of such a consensus constitutes proof that the protection is not justified and that it therefore constitutes an illegal barrier to trade. This rule is in fundamental contradiction to the precautionary principle – based on the premise that it is safer not to wait for complete scientific justification to take action to prevent potentially harmful effects, because scientific proof and complete scientific consensus can take years to establish, if at all.

The precautionary principle lies behind the EU's ban on the sale and import of beef from cattle treated with artificial growth hormones, which EU studies show increase both the risk of illness in treated animals and in humans who consume them. Even though the ban applies to domestic and foreign products alike, following a complaint from the US and Canada – the principal exporters of hormone-treated beef – two WTO panels ruled that the ban is illegal because it has been taken in advance of scientific certainty (which is forbidden under WTO provisions).

The panel would only accept the standard for artificial hormones in meat adopted by the Codex Alimentarius Commission in 1995, which stated that such meat was safe. The Codex standard, however, is highly controversial. It was set under undue industry influence (140 of the world's largest multinational food and agrochemical companies participated in Codex meetings held between 1989 and 1991 alone), and instead of being arrived at through consensus, it resulted from a vote of a bare majority of 33 countries in favour, 29 against and 7 abstentions (Greenpeace US study cited by Korten, 1995, p179). In these circumstances, the adoption of the European ban seems all the more legitimate. But for the WTO, the EU lacked sufficient scientific proof and it ruled that the ban would consequently have to be eliminated, or else the imposition of trade sanctions would follow. (To date, the EU has refused to comply with the WTO ruling and the ban thus remains in place, although the US and Canada – the two countries most affected by the ban – have been authorized by the WTO to impose tariffs on imports of European produce to the sum of US$128 million.)

The implications of that ruling for other regional or national health or environmental standards around the world are extremely serious. The EU ban on imports of certain genetically modified foods and crops could yet be threatened. Further conflict and further environmental damage are likely.

The prospects for national environmental protections will only become worse if, as proposed, during the next round of world trade talks, the WTO adopts the investment measures that featured in the proposed multilateral agreement on investment (MAI) that was defeated at the OECD in 1998. Under MAI-type investment rules, for example, national regulations preventing corporations with bad environmental track records from investing domestically could be forbidden. Laws requiring new investors to meet certain environmental conditions, such as having to transfer environmentally sound technology, could be banned. And foreign corporations could be given the power to sue national governments directly for monetary compensation if they believed government policies, including environmental or public health laws, 'expropriated' or undercut their future profits.

A clear indication of the devastating consequences such rules would have for regional, national and local environmental regulations can by gauged from the application of identical rules under NAFTA. A recent case is particularly illustrative. In 1996, the Canadian government introduced legislation banning the import and interprovincial transport of MMT – a neurotoxin used as a fuel additive that causes irreparable damage to vehicle pollution control systems, thereby increasing emissions of harmful gases such as carbon monoxide, carbon dioxide and hydrocarbons. As soon as the law was proclaimed, the only North American manufacturer of MMT, the US multinational Ethyl Corporation, sued the Canadian government for US$350 million in damages. It argued that the Canadian law violated national treatment rules of NAFTA and constituted an expropriation of Ethyl's Canadian investments. It even claimed that merely by introducing and debating the bill, the Canadian government harmed Ethyl's international reputation, thereby 'expropriating' part of its future profits. Lawyers advised the government that it would lose under NAFTA rules, and so the ban on MMT was repealed and millions of dollars and an apology were provided in compensation.

That outcome has set a terrifying precedent. According to Steven Shrybman, in its wake, 'More than one trade lawyer from the corporate sector has warned that there will be many more such suits as their clients make more frequent use of their rights under these investment treaties to "harass" governments contemplating regulatory initiatives the corporations oppose' (Shrybman, 1999, p134). The adoption of NAFTA-style investment rules by the WTO would therefore have disastrous consequences.

The logic that underlies such rules is nothing less than suicidal. Unless their adoption by the WTO is fully rejected, and unless the *current* rules of the WTO are changed, we can fully expect the list of essential environmental laws struck down in the name of free trade to grow ever longer – further emasculating democracy and crippling the ability of societies everywhere to address effectively the environmental and social crises of modern times.

CONCLUSION

At the core of the problem that economic globalization poses for the environment is the issue of scale: the transformation of economic activity from the small and local to the large and global, a change that underlies nearly all definitions of globalization. It is often referred to as *delocalization*: the uprooting and displacement of activities and relationships that until recently were local, into networks of activities and relationships whose reach is distant or worldwide (Gray, 1998, p57; Giddens, 1990, p64). The fundamental problem with that transformation when it is applied to economic activity is that it ends up violating the basic rules of environmental sustainability *and* sound economics.

Environmental sustainability requires economic accountability, which is best ensured at a local level. In a local economy, when a locally owned investment damages the environment, the investor and his or her local community are more likely to be immediately aware and directly affected by it. And as the local community is more likely to know or have access to that investor, it has a strong incentive and capacity to force the investor to address the problem rapidly. In a global economy, in contrast, power is detached from responsibility and those who take decisions are separated from those who are affected by them, thus ensuring that environmental problems continue unabated.

Economic globalization, moreover, increases the scale of environmental damage to a global level by extending the industrial market model throughout the world to vast swathes of the planet where it had never previously existed. Yet the global economy cannot expand indefinitely if the ecosystems on which it depends continue to deteriorate. If it attempts to do so, the planet will become uninhabitable. In the words of the United Nations *Global Environmental Outlook* report for the year 2000, 'The present course is unsustainable and postponing action is no longer an option' (UNEP, 1999).

Ultimately, we cannot live, and our economies cannot function, without a healthy natural environment. So if we are serious about giving our children a future, more of the same is not an option: fundamental reform is our only alternative.

References

Bello, Walden (1996), 'Structural Adjustment Programs: "Success" for Whom' in J.
    Mander and E. Goldsmith (eds) *The Case Against the Global Economy and for a
    Turn Towards the Local*, San Francisco: Sierra Club Books
Brown, I. and C. Flavin (1999), 'A New Economy for a New Century' in *State of the
    World 1999*, Washington, DC: Worldwatch
Bryant, D , D Nielsen and L. Tangley (1997), *The Last Frontier Forests*, Washington,
    DC: World Resources Institute
Davis, D. I. et al (1994), 'Decreasing Cardiovascular Disease and Increasing Cancer
    Among Whites in the United States from 1973 through 1987', *Journal of the
    American Medical Association*, vol. **271**(6) (9 February). As quoted in *Rachel's
    Hazardous Waste News*, Environmental Research Foundation, no 385 (14 April)
French, Hilary (1993), *Costly Tradeoffs: Reconciling Trade and the Environment*,
    Washington, DC: Worldwatch
Gardner, G. and P. Sampat (1999), 'Forging a Sustainable Materials Economy' in *State
    of the World 1999*, Washington, DC: Worldwatch
Giddens, A. (1990), *The Consequences of Modernity*, Cambridge: Polity Press
Gray, J (1998), *False Dawn: the Delusions of Global Capitalism*, London: Granta
    Books
Karliner, J. (1997), *The Corporate Planet: Ecology and Politics in the Age of
    Globalization*, San Francisco: Sierra Club Books
Korten, David C. (1995), *When Corporations Rule the World*, London: Earthscan
    Publications Ltd
Korten, David C. (1995), *When Corporations Rule the World*, New York: Kumarian
    Press
Leonard, H. J. (1988), *Pollution and the Struggle for the World Product*, Cambridge:
    Cambridge University Press
Matthews, D. and A. Rowell (1992), *The Environmental Impact of the Car*,
    Washington, DC: Greenpeace
Shrybman, S. (1999), *A Citizen's Guide to the World Trade Organization*, Ottawa and
    Toronto: The Canadian Centre for Policy Alternatives and James Lorimer and Co
Tricks, H. and A. Mandel-Campbell (1999), 'Mexico's Farming Habits Under Pressure
    from Transgenics', *Financial Times* (12 October)

[15]

Technologies of Globalization

Jerry Mander

Chapters elsewhere in this book present evidence of the multiple harms caused by biotechnology, robotics, global computer networks, global television, the production and dumping of toxics, and industrial expansion. All of these technologies and processes are intrinsic aspects of a globalized economy. Given the evidence, however, we still hesitate to draw conclusions about the political drift of modern technologies. We cling to the idea that technologies are 'neutral', just as we like to think of science as 'value free' – that it is only a matter of access. This chapter argues that the very idea that technology is neutral is itself not neutral, as it leads to passivity regarding technology's onrush and unconsciousness about its role in the globalization process.

Jerry Mander is the president of the International Forum on Globalization (IFG), which is an alliance of 60 organizations in 20 countries providing public education and campaigns on global economic issues. He is also the programme director for the Foundation for Deep Ecology and a senior fellow at the Public Media Centre, a non-profit advertising company working only for environmental and social causes. In the 1960s Mander was president of a major San Francisco advertising company before turning his talents to environmental campaigns throughout that decade. In 1971 Mander formed the United States' first non-profit advertising agency, Public Interest Communications, for environmental, community and social action groups. He was also director of the Elmwood Institute, an ecological think-tank. His books include Four Arguments for the Elimination of Television *(1977) and* In the Absence of the Sacred *(1991). He holds a graduate degree (MS) from Columbia University's Business School in international economics.*

It is commonplace nowadays to hear new technologies described as 'revolutionary', but rarely do we learn whether the revolution is right-wing or left. This is especially true of the most dominant technologies and those with the greatest impact. Automobiles, television and computers, for example, have so enveloped society that we scarcely remember a world before they existed. Society accepts the onrush of these technologies with alarming passivity, and without any systematic consideration of the social and political changes they bring with them. Indeed,

46 *Engines of Globalization*

despite calling the technologies revolutionary, we rarely acknowledge that they have any political implications, such as the way they accelerate the globalization process. The great technology critic Langdon Winner has written that 'all artifacts have politics', meaning that each technology has predictable social, political, and environmental outcomes. He says: 'The most interesting puzzle of our times is that we so willingly sleepwalk through the process for reconstituting the conditions of human existence. . . In the technical realm we repeatedly enter into a series of social contracts, the terms of which are revealed only after the signing' (Winner, 1986).

Two decades earlier, Marshall McLuhan made surely one of the most important and importantly misunderstood comments of the century when he said 'the medium is the message' (1964). He meant that the most significant aspects of technology lie not in their apparent content (the transportation that a car provides or the news programme that the television supplies) but in the systemic changes that they catalyse. The questions we need to learn to ask include the following. How does the technology change work, family life, leisure, art? How does it alter our experience of everyday life? How does it change our concepts of self, community, politics, nature, time, distance? How does it influence how we learn, what we know, and what we are capable of knowing? What are its implications for human health and disease, and the environment? How does it reorganize power arrangements in society? For instance, does it centralize power or decentralize it? Does it serve to homogenize cultures or, on the contrary, to maintain diversity? Who gains and who loses?

Why hasn't our society developed a process of articulating and evaluating the totality of the effects caused by technology and then voting upon them before they become so pervasive that they become extremely difficult to dislodge? Indeed, certain technological inventions change society far more dramatically than do any of the political figures we vote for. Our total immersion in computers, for example, has and will continue to revolutionize our experience of life far more than whether our president is Republican or Democrat. But there is no congressional vote on this; there are no popular referenda. Even in this most democratic of societies, we have no process for decision-making about technology and little practice in evaluating it. We have only the market to make our decisions for us, and that process is profoundly skewed, as we will see.

How did things get this way? There are dozens of possible explanations, but I will only cite three main points.

The first has to do with the information climate about technology. It is a melancholy fact that in our society the first waves of descriptions about new technologies invariably come from the corporations and scientists who invent and market these technologies and who have much to gain by our accepting a positive view. Their descriptions are invariably optimistic, even utopian, and are supported by hundreds of millions of dollars in advertising and public relations. The 'Green Revolution' will solve global hunger. Nuclear power will solve the world's energy problems and provide clean, safe, cheap, inexhaustible energy. Television will unify global consciousness and bring peace and understanding everywhere. The microcomputer revolution will bring all the information in the world to every person merely by the striking of a key.

One could find similarly optimistic statements for every new technology that comes along. Those who emit such statements have nothing to gain from our learning the possible negative consequences of these new commodities, so we are left with a constant stream of best-case scenarios and virtually no counter-vailing voice. As we have discovered, however, many manufacturers and industries – including nuclear, chemical, auto, cigarette and tobacco – are aware of the serious negative outcomes of their technologies, but choose not to share these with the public and often hide them even from investigative inquiry.

Over the century since the Industrial Revolution, wave after wave of techno-utopian visions have so immersed us in positive expectations that the development of new technologies has become virtually synonymous with the general advance-ment of society. It is only long after a technology has entered into general production and has gained an important role in everyday life that we begin to perceive its adverse effects on humans or nature. Even then, the proposed solutions usually consist of creating new generations of technology designed to fix the problems of the old. Thus the wave rolls on to the next technical generation.

A second factor explaining our utter passivity to technology is that, when we do attempt to analyse the virtues of a particular technology, we do so in personal terms. The car drives us where we need to go in relative comfort and convenience. The television is often entertaining and informative. The airplane shrinks the globe; we can be anywhere on Earth in hours. The computer edits, stores data, hooks us to other like-minded people, speeds up our work, and permits us to 'publish' our viewpoints to a potentially vast audience. All technology is useful or entertaining, or else we'd have no interest in it in the first place. But to base our ultimate conclusions about technology mainly on our personal experience leaves out the social, political and ecological dimensions; in other words, it overlooks the effects on everything but ourselves. What are the other consequences of high-speed travel? Is a smaller world better? Who else benefits from global computer networks?

In our individualistic society, we are not practised in making judgements beyond our personal experience, but it is just that practice – seeking the systemic or holistic effects – that will help us evaluate the positive and negative aspects of specific technologies. The question then is not how or whether technology benefits us but who benefits most and what outcomes are involved.

This brings us to the third and, I think, most important reason for our passivity about technology – the blinding notion that technologies are neutral, that the only thing that matters about them is who is in control, that they have no intrinsic qualities which inevitably produce certain ecological or political outcomes. It may be one of the most important survival skills of our times to

48   *Engines of Globalization*

break with this idea. Every technology has a predetermined political drift, and it is critical that we perceive that and make our judgements and adjustments accordingly.

To help clarify this point, I'll use two familiar examples of energy technologies: nuclear power and solar power. Both of these technologies will light the lamps in your house and run the refrigerator, the television and the computer. But there the similarities end.

INTRINSIC BIAS IN ENERGY TECHNOLOGIES

When a society decides to use nuclear power, it commits itself to many additional outcomes besides the delivery of the energy itself. To build and operate nuclear power plants requires a large, highly technical, and very well-financed infrastructure. It's not something that people in your neighbourhood can get together and decide to do. It can only be done by huge, centralized institutions. Without such institutions, nuclear power could not exist.

Nuclear power also depends upon substantial military protection against possible terrorist attacks, or thefts of dangerous ingredients. And nuclear energy produces a terrifying waste product, some of which needs to be stored safely someplace for as long as 250,000 years – a technical task that is still not solved – requiring techno-scientific–military care and protection for all that time, something no society could guarantee. This also preempts many choices that might otherwise be available for future generations. For example, what if, a few centuries down the road, a society wishes to re-establish agrarianism and low-impact technology as its primary *modi operandi?* It would still have to monitor the dangerous wastes from centuries earlier and maintain a technical capability for doing it. So, nuclear power today predetermines much about the form of future society.

Solar power, on the other hand, has entirely different intrinsic characteristics. The technology is so simple and inexpensive that my sons and I and a few friends could probably install solar units on most of the houses in our neighbourhood, without backing from any centralized financial interests. We would require no military to protect the units; there would be very negligible dangerous waste product; and the technology would not predetermine the shape of any future society.

So it would be fair to say that nuclear power is an appropriate technology for an industrialized, mass society such as ours, organized around large central military and financial systems. Solar power is more appropriate for societies made up of small communities, catering to local markets, with very low environmental impact.

What is important to note is that the significant features of each of these rival technologies are *intrinsic* to them. If the authors in this book were somehow put in charge of the world's nuclear power plants, we would surely have to operate them in more or less the same way as they are presently being run, albeit perhaps with a higher degree of caution. But all of the major implications of nuclear power – financial, military and environmental – would remain, because they are determined by the technology itself. So it is truly preposterous to argue that either of these technologies is neutral, when both are intrinsically predisposed to produce dramatically divergent outcomes.

That kind of comparative *systemic* technological analysis should have occurred long before our society made any of its choices about which energy technologies to employ. Other energy sources such as coal, gas, oil, and biomass should also have been included in a comprehensive comparison, long before corporate marketing interests were able to exert their persuasive influence. In the end, the question becomes: what kind of technology relates to what kind of society?

Consider the case of the automobile.

REFERENDUM ON THE AUTO

What would have happened if a systemic analysis of the automobile had been offered to the public at the time of its invention? It's not as if most of the negative effects were not known ahead of time, for businesses spend enormous sums researching both the market potential of their product and the possible downside disasters. Businesses don't like surprises. Indeed, an excellent study of the level of awareness of certain technologies' impacts at the time of their invention can be found in the *Retrospective Technology Assessment* reports financed by the National Science Foundation and managed by the Massachusetts Institute of Technology.

When Henry Ford and others first promoted the automobile before the turn of the 20th century, the technology was described, as usual, solely in 'best-case' terms. Automobiles would bring a 'revolutionary' new era of personal freedom and democracy in the form of private transportation that was fast, clean (no mud or horse manure) and independent. But what if people had been told that the car would bring with it the modern concrete city? Or that the car would contribute to cancer-causing air pollution, to noise, to global warming, to solid waste problems and to the rapid depletion of the world's resources? What if it had been reported that for production efficiency the private car would eventually be manufactured by a small number of giant corporations that would acquire tremendous economic and political power? That these corporations would create a new mode of mass production – the assembly line – which in turn would cause worker alienation, physical injury, drug abuse and alcoholism? That these corporations might conspire to eliminate other means of popular transportation, including trains? That the automobile would facilitate suburban growth with its intolerable impact on landscapes? What if we had known that 30,000 people would die annually in car accidents? What if the public had been forewarned of the unprecedented need for oil that the private car would create, and that horrible wars would be fought over oil supplies? What if the public had realized that automobiles and roads would redesign even the most exotic societies into forms and behaviour very much like ours? That cities such as Bangkok and Kathmandu would increasingly feel like Manhattan at rush hour?

Would a public informed of such outcomes have decided to proceed with developing the private automobile? Would the public have still thought it a good thing?

I really cannot guess whether a public so well informed and given the chance to vote would have voted against cars. Perhaps not. But the public was not so informed.

If such a debate about the automobile had occurred in the public realm, there surely would have been more support for public transport, and we surely would not have seen quite the proliferation of private cars and public roads. Some countries and locales might have prohibited private cars completely and thereby retained their indigenous social, cultural, biological and geographical characteristics.

TV: THE CLONING OF CULTURES

Several contributors to this book have described aspects of the globalization and homogenization of values, culture, and consciousness that cultural exports of Western films, fashion, music, and television have introduced (see Chapters 14 and 15). With the new trade agreements effectively suppressing the remaining ability of individual nations to resist such cultural invasions, the process of cultural cloning is accelerating, but it has been advancing for some while.

Because of the advent of satellite television in the 1970s and 1980s, more than 75 per cent of the global population now has access to daily television reception. People living in remote parts of Borneo or in the Himalayas or in the tundras of Siberia are watching nearly identical programmes, mostly produced by Western corporate interests, all of it expressing Western values and imagery, instigating enormous cultural change.

I had the chance to observe this process up close during a visit to the Mackenzie River Valley of the Northwest Territories of Canada in the mid 1980s. I was invited there by the Native Women's Association, which expressed deep concern about the sudden changes caused by the recent introduction of satellite television into their communities.

The Mackenzie Valley stretches south from the Arctic Circle and runs 2400 kilometres to the Great Slave Lake. If you're not familiar with the area, let me remind you of the Russian nuclear satellite that fell from orbit some years ago. It was feared it would fall on Paris or New York or Tokyo, so there was a great relief when it fell on what was described in the press as 'an icy unpopulated wasteland'.

To call this area unpopulated only confirms how invisible native people are to the mass media because it is actually populated by 26 communities of Dene Indians and Inuit (Eskimo) peoples – about 20,000 people in all – who have lived there successfully for 4000 years. To this day they speak 22 native tongues, mostly as a first language. In many of these places, the traditional economy of hunting, ice fishing and dog sled travel has survived, largely because the Canadian government had little interest in the area. But when oil was discovered in the 1960s, oil workers were needed, and the government decided it was time that the natives be turned into Canadians.

Television is the normal instrument of choice for such cultural conversion. The government offered each of the 26 communities free satellite dishes and television sets; most communities accepted, but not all.

When I arrived in Yellowknife, the capital city of the Northwest Territories (population then 9000; the only town with paved streets and cars), the weather was 40 degrees Celsius below zero. The women who greeted me told me they were at first pleased about television. Dene and Inuit communities are often hundreds of kilometres from each other, without any connecting roads. Communication between these places was difficult: dog team, radio and airplane. 'Until recently it didn't matter,' I was told by the Dene Nation communications director, Cindy Gilday. 'Most of the communities have been self-sufficient for centuries, but now the government is changing things so fast, it's important for people to know what's going on.'

Television had seemed a logical advance in communications, but it had not lived up to its potential. As with most indigenous and developing world locales where television is just arriving, the programmes are not produced locally, but come mostly from the US or other Western countries. Sixty per cent of the programmes in the Northwest Territories were from the US, including *Dallas*, *Edge of Night*, *Happy Days*, and *The Six Million Dollar Man* (and, lately, CNN). Gilday said:

> 'There's only one hour per week of local shows, and rarely does that have anything to do with native people, though we're the majority population here. . . We can already see that TV has had a devastating effect, especially in the villages out in the bush. The effect has been to glamorize behaviours and values that are poisonous to life up here. Our traditions have a lot to do with survival. Community cooperation, sharing, and non-materialism are the only ways that people can live here. But TV always presents values opposite to those.'

Many of the women I met were schoolteachers, and they said that when television came to the villages they saw an immediate change. The children immediately lost interest in the native language; they wanted only to learn Canadian English. Now the children want all kinds of new things like cars; yet most of the communities have no roads. They don't want to learn how to fish on the ice or go hunting anymore. 'But worst of all is what it's doing to the relations between the young and the old,' I was told by the women. 'TV makes it seem like the young people are all that's important, and the old have nothing to say. And yet in our cultures, the old people are the ones who tell the stories and teach the kids how to be Indians.'

Most important of all, the women said, was that TV had put a stop to storytelling. It used to be that the old people would sit each evening in the corner of the house, telling the children ancient stories about life in the North. Through that process, the elders had been the windows through which the younger generation could see their own past and traditions; it was how the children could sense their own Indian roots. It was also an educational system teaching how to survive in such a harsh place. The women were horrified that the process was being interrupted by television. They saw it as the death of their culture. Gilday told me:

> 'You have to realize that most people still live in one- or two-room houses. The TV is going all the time, and the little kids and the old people are all sitting around together watching it. They're watching something totally alien, and they're not hearing the stories anymore; they don't want to be Indians now. They hate being Indians.
>
> They want to be Canadians and Americans. . . It's so crazy and so awful. Nobody ever told us that all this would be coming in with TV. It's like some kind of invasion from outer space or something. First it was the government coming in here, then those oil companies and now it's TV.'

With satellite television now bringing *Dallas*, *The Edge of Night*, and *The Oprah Winfrey Show* to 75 per cent of the world population, the process just described in the Mackenzie Valley is happening globally. Television technology is clearly the most efficient instrument ever invented for global cultural cloning, and it is the pathbreaker for what follows: cars; paved roads; Western franchise foods; economies converted from self-sufficiency to corporate export; frantic and stressful lifestyles; loss of traditional skills; immersion in computers, walkmans, and CD ROMs; and so on.

One can certainly argue that the benefits of modernization are well worth the sacrifice, even when the sacrifice is not apparent at the time of the change and comes as a shocking surprise. In fact, it is the ultimate rationalization for the entire Western development ethic that the sacrifice of cultural and biological diversity is worth what is gained, even if every place on Earth begins to look like Bakersfield, California. That viewpoint notwithstanding, we should become exquisitely aware of the nature of the bargain and give ourselves the freedom and the opportunity to conclude that, on balance, it may be a losing proposition for everyone.

Television is one technology that does live up to the promises proposed by its inventors: it produces a unified global consciousness. But is that good?

THE COMPUTER REVOLUTION

The computer revolution is an odd kind of revolution, because every corner of society, including those that normally disagree fiercely with each other on most issues, is in agreement on this one: they all think it's good. The engineers and the artists; the Al Gores and the Newt Gingriches; corporations and their anti-corporate counterparts; conservatives and liberals – all are dazzled by images of computer-driven utopias, though it's possible they have slightly different utopias in mind.

Most of my own friends and colleagues share this utopian expectation. My writer friends wonder how it is even possible to write books without a computer, though several writers in history – from Shakespeare to Hemingway to Atwood to Illich – are known to have done it. Even now, there are those who write books by longhand (Edward Goldsmith and Wendell Berry, among them). And there is the impressive fact that 400,000 generations of human beings got through their days without computers. It has been done.

'That is not the point,' my friends say. They argue that I fail to appreciate how 'empowering' computers can be (a popular way of describing them these days) and how they can help us organize against the corporate juggernaut. Computers bring real power back to the individual, and the cybernet helps us build new alliances with like-minded radicals sitting at their terminals, using e-mail and web pages to spread news and mobilize battles. By such analyses, computers seem clearly to be in service of 'progressive', democratizing, decentralizing tendencies.

The more esoteric among my colleagues like to invoke the views of influential *Wired* magazine editor Kevin Kelly, who has described a new 'revolutionary' political structure that he feels microcomputation has wrought. 'The correct symbol of today is no longer the atom,' he says, 'it's the net.' The political centre has been wiped out, and a revolutionary structure has replaced it. This is leading to a new decentralized worldview that 'elevates the power of the small player' and promotes heterogeneity. It also leads to a new kind of pure democracy and an 'incipient technospiritualism' (Kelly, 1994).

Kelly is right on the 'technospiritualism' point, though frankly I prefer the old kind of spiritualism that requires no mediation through machines. As for the main idea that the old political centre has been eliminated and that our new net or web politics brings us computer-enhanced democracy run through cyberspace, let me ask: should we call it *virtual democracy*? As Richard Barnet

54   *Engines of Globalization*

and John Cavanagh point out in Chapter 4 on the casino economy, the giant
financial institutions of today could not exist on their present scale if there were
no computers. Computers are their global nervous systems; their way of keeping
track of billions of moving parts, keeping them synchronized and moving in the
same direction for central purposes. Richard Sclove of the Loka Institute put it
this way:

> *'For all the hype in the media about how the new technologies will
> enhance democracy, what we are getting is not individual empow-
> erment but a new empowerment for multinational corporations
> and banks, with respect to workers, consumers, and political systems.'*
> (Sclove, 1994).

In fact, it is my opinion that computer technology may be the single most important instrument ever invented for the acceleration of centralized power. While
we sit at our PCs editing our copy, sending our e-mail and expressing our
cyberfreedoms, the TNCs are using their global networks, fed by far greater
resources. They are able to achieve not only information exchange but concrete
results that express themselves in downed forests, massive infrastructural
development, destruction of rural and farming societies, displacement of millions
of people and domination of governments. In a symbiotic embrace with other
technologies of rapid economic development, they operate on a scale and at a
speed that make our own level of cyberempowerment pathetic by comparison.
Speaking in traditional political terms, the new telecommunications technologies
assist the corporate, centralized, industrialized enterprise (the 'right'?) far more
efficiently than the decentralized, local, community-based interests (the 'left'?),
which suffer a net loss.

So much for elevating 'the power of the small player'.

. . .

I have been describing a few macro effects of computers. It is relevant to mention
a few other dimensions: the role computer production plays in creating the toxic
crises of the industrial and developing worlds; the role of computer-based
surveillance technologies in corporations to measure and objectify worker
performance; and the manner in which microcomputation has sped up and
amplified the power of the military technologies of the advanced industrialized
nations. This was already obvious in the infamous 'launch-on-warning' phenomenon of the old Cold War and the 'smart bombs' of the hotter and more recent
US–Iraq war, where mass killing by automated bombs left human beings (save
for those at the receiving end) free of dirty-handed engagement in the killing
process.

Then there is the simple dimension of speed. E F Schumacher told us that small is beautiful, but one could also make the case that *slow* is beautiful, especially in preserving the natural world. Computers speed up communications exchanges over long distance, a quality that is most advantageous to the large centralized institutions we have been describing in this book. Of course, it also offers a speedup for resistance movements, but that speedup is mainly to keep pace with the high-speed activity of corporations.

Has there been a net gain? In political terms, I think not. In environmental terms, surely not. To ensure the survival of nature, everything, especially development and especially people, must slow down and synchronize with the more subtle and slower rhythms of the natural world. In our cyber-walkman-airplane-fax-phone-satellite world, we are so enclosed within a high-speed technical reality that the values and concerns of nature tend to become opaque to our consciousness.

THE COMPUTER AS IT AFFECTS EDUCATION AND SOCIETY

Portland State University Professor of Education C A Bowers has been focusing on the way computer usage affects the basic ecological and political values of the people who use them. Bowers makes the case that the advance of computers is contributing to a loss of ecological sensitivity and understanding, since the very process of using computers, particularly educating through computers, effectively excludes an entire set of ideas and experiences that earlier had been the building blocks for a developing connection with the Earth. Bowers opposes the use of computers in primary and secondary education, saying that they change the way. children's minds process information and affect not only what they know but what they are capable of knowing – that is, computers alter the pathways of children's cognition. Newly immersed in data-based forms of knowledge and limited to information transmissible in digital form, our culture is sacrificing the subtle, contextual, and memory-based knowledge gleaned from living in a nature-based culture, meaningful interactive learning with other humans, and an ecologically based value system (Bowers, 1993).

So, by accepting computers so completely for schools, says Bowers, our society also accepts a massive cultural transformation, leaving human beings altered in predictable ways. McLuhan said that we turn into the technologies that we use. And so, says Bowers, the more we use the computer and the more it is used globally, the stronger its culturally homogenizing effects and the greater likelihood that our new globalized digital culture will be less concerned about the disappearance of nature.

Richard Sclove adds this final political point:

> 'People are using telecommunications to establish [virtual] social bonds that are completely unrelated to territorial relations or face-to-face acquaintance. I might now have a lively social life with people in Amsterdam but not a clue about what's going on with my neighbour next door. Spending one's life on-line, with little direct experience of the natural world – without sensuous knowing – debases our willingness to act with responsibility toward the environment. . . The ultimate political risk comes down to this: to the extent that virtual community takes over for face-to-face community, we get a mismatch between bonds of social affiliation, which are non-territorial, and political systems, which are territorial. How do political jurisdictions govern when the citizens within those boundaries have nothing to do with each other or with the realities of the place?'

MEGATECHNOLOGY

It is not only individual technologies which need systemic ideological consideration, but what they combine to achieve. For example, as recently as two decades ago it was possible to speak about two different parts of the planet as distinct places with distinct cultures, living habits, conceptual frameworks, behaviours and power arrangements. It was also possible to speak of distinctly different geographies. And one could sensibly speak about individual technologies as if they were distinct from one another: television as opposed to computers; lasers as opposed to satellites.

However, technological evolution has brought us to the point where such distinctions among cultures, places, systems of organization and technological forms are being wiped out under the homogenization drives of a much larger technical juggernaut. Telecommunications, highspeed computer technology, satellite systems, robotics, lasers and other new technologies have made possible, practical and inevitable an interlocked worldwide communication system that enables corporate actors to perform globally with unprecedented speed and efficiency. In such a system corporations themselves are an intrinsic part of the technical machine. In fact, they are technical forms, too, inventing the machines that operate on this global scale and in turn being spawned by them in an accelerating symbiotic cycle.

Finally, there is one more technical form to complete the picture: the recently restructured global economic system itself, which is specifically designed to overcome resistance to the megatechnological homogenization drive.

The big trade agreements are an intrinsic part of the global technical structure; in fact, they are the 'consciousness' of the megadevelopment, megatechnological, monocultural model that encircles the globe and permeates our lives.

In such a context, democracy has a difficult future. In fact, democracy is already suffering its greatest setback, as a direct result of this *de facto* conspiracy of technical structures, technologies themselves and corporate purposes, all within the Western development paradigm. Understanding of that entire set of forces – *megatechnology* – must be grasped quickly. Otherwise we will be led blind and powerless through a destruction of nature, culture and diversity beyond anything that has preceded it.

Individual technologies have defined roles to play. Television serves as the worldwide agent of imagery for the new global corporate vision; computers are the nervous system that facilitates the setup of new global organizations; trade agreements wipe out resistance; telecommunications provide instant capital and resource transfer; genetics and space technologies expand the world market into the new wilderness areas – the internal cell structure of living creatures and the far reaches of untrammelled space. Together, these and other technologies combine to form the new technosphere that is anathema to democracy and diversity.

The answer to the trend is, of course, to work to reverse it, and to bring real power back to the local community, while supporting communities, cultures and nations who attempt to stand in the way of the juggernaut.

References

Barnet, Richard and Ronald E. Mueller (1974), *Global Reach: The Power of the Multinational Corporations*, New York: Simon and Schuster

Berry, Wendell (1987), *Sex, Economy, Freedom and Community*, New York: Pantheon Books

Bowers, C. A. (1993), *Education, Cultural Myths, and the Ecological Crisis: Toward Deep Changes*, Albany, NY: State University of New York Press

Goldsmith, Edward and Nicholas Hildyard (1990), *The Earth Report No. 2*, London: Mitchell Beazley

Kelly, Kevin (1994), *Out of Control: The Rise of Neo-Biological Civilizations*, New York: Addison-Wesley

Schumacher, E. F. (1989), *Small is Beautiful: Economics as if the Earth Really Mattered*, New York: Harper and Row

Sclove, Richard (1994), From a workshop at the International Forum on Globalization, San Francisco, publication forthcoming

Winner, Langdon (1986), *The Whale and the Reactor*, University of Chicago Press

[16]

A World Environment Organisation: The Wrong Solution to the Wrong Problem

Peter Newell

1. INTRODUCTION

⊤HIS paper is a response to the debate about the possible need for a World Environment Organisation (WEO). There has been increasing attention to the question of reform of international environmental institutions, both at a policy level, with debates provoked by leading figures such as former WTO director Ruggerio and former Executive-Secretary of the Biodiversity Convention, Calestous Juma,[1] as well amongst scholars of the environment.[2]

The starting point for a discussion of reform of the global environmental architecture should be an enquiry into the causes of the ineffectiveness of current arrangements. This can form the basis of an assessment of the viability of alternative institutional configurations and the likelihood that they will increase levels of environmental protection. In much of the debate on a WEO, the question posed is either how to improve coordination between existing regimes or how to create a counter-weight to the WTO. The assumption underlying these concerns is that the structure of contemporary institutions and their inter-relationships are the source of ineffective environmental policy. The actual causes of environmental degradation and the processes that generate it are often not discussed in this regard. This is what sets the paper by Whalley and Zissimos (this issue) apart from much of the other literature in this area. They take improved environmental outcomes as the goal and relate the lack of progress, to date, to the failure of existing regimes to bring about the internalisation of environmental externalities. Their proposal is for a deal-brokering body that promotes internalisation by

PETER NEWELL is from the Institute of Development Studies, University of Sussex. A shortened version of this paper appears in *Global Environmental Politics* Vol. 1 No. 1. Support for this research from the MacArthur Foundation is gratefully acknowledged.

[1] Calestous Juma (6 July, 2000), *Financial Times*.
[2] See special issue of *Global Environmental Politics* Vol. 1 No. 1 and Biermann (2000).

facilitating financial transfers in exchange for commitments to protect the environment.

The argument made here is, firstly, that many of the criticisms made of the existing architecture are misplaced while ignoring other key faults and, secondly, that the means of operationalising a WEO are problematic and may exacerbate existing problems, particularly for developing countries. Contributions to the debate from von Moltke and Calestous Juma have challenged those calls for a WEO which take the limits of existing institutional arrangements as their starting point. I concentrate here on Whalley and Zissimos's notion that the current approach to environmental cooperation is the problem and which warrants the creation of a WEO, as it seeks to address the underlying causes of ineffective international action on the environment. I argue that while the goal of internalisation is worth pursuing, their current proposal is unlikely to make much progress in delivering it because of misplaced assumptions about the existing political order and the ability of a deal-brokering WEO to remedy the problems they identify.

2. THE WEO APPROACH

There are many types of WEO that have been proposed, often as a counter-weight to the WTO in balancing trade with environmental objectives on the world stage. Indeed, the recent interest in a WEO from the WTO is driven by the desire of trade officials to remove environmental problems from their mandate, which they feel are not adequately or properly addressed by a trade body. WEO proposals are cast in this light and therefore generate enormous concern amongst environmentalists, many of whom are not in favour of creating a new and separate global environmental agency, but rather wish to see the WTO's mandate restricted to traditional trade concerns rather than *any* potentially trade discriminating activity, which inevitably includes environmental standards.

Many proposals take as their starting point existing weaknesses in the way the UN addresses global environmental problems. The reasons advanced for establishing a new environmental agency include (i) improving coordination and reducing fragmentation between the UN's treaties and agencies working on environmental issues to reduce duplication of activities and capitalise on positive issue-linkages; (ii) strengthening the enforcement mechanisms in existing environmental treaties; (iii) promoting the transfer of environmental technologies and finance to developing countries. However, according to former Executive-Director of the Convention on Biodiversity, Calestous Juma, the reasons cited for the UN's lagging environmental efforts are misplaced. He argues, for example, that:

A WEO: THE WRONG SOLUTION TO THE WRONG PROBLEM 661

The claim that consolidating existing international organisations will result in a stronger and more effective organisation runs counter to the experiences of modern institutions which are decentralising their operations. ... Environmental problems are diverse in character and require more specialised institutional responses.[3]

In advocating a WEO, Biermann's comment that:

It does not seem theoretically difficult to demarcate the responsibilities of a new international organisation,

overlooks the practical implications behind, and bureaucratic turf-wars that would frustrate, any attempt to collapse a loosely connected and discrete set of regimes and institutions into one overarching global body. Mitchell argues, in addition, that the real problem with the current approach to international environmental regulation is not the lack of institutional capacity, but an absence of will to address environmental issues, 'a problem that cannot be solved simply by making institutional changes.'[4]

The proposal by Whalley and Zissimos has a different emphasis, focusing on the issue of internalisation, traditionally understood to mean internalising the costs of environmental degradation at source and removing 'spillover' effects. The notion behind this approach, that market failures are responsible for poor levels of environmental protection and that creating markets for environmental goods is the most efficient and effective way to provide them, resonates with contemporary concerns with the provision of public goods at the global level.[5]

These assumptions also underpin discussions about emissions trading in the climate change regime. Such approaches have been criticised on a number of grounds, including their failure to address issues of equity, so that those who pollute most can buy themselves out of trouble while demanding changes in those countries without the economic clout to resist them. It is also questionable whether long-term sustainable development is being advanced by conferring upon pollution-absorbing activities the same status as efforts to check pollution at source. While in global net terms it may not make a difference where the saving is made, in terms of creating incentives for the largest polluters to address their own contribution to the problem, it certainly does.

The argument here is that while internalisation may be an appropriate goal, it is questionable how far this can be successfully brought about by a new global body engaging in deal brokering, whereby environmental commitments are exchanged for financial payments overseen by a WEO. This is so for a number of reasons. Firstly, there is the issue of the limits of such action at the international level. Most of the policy instruments we have for bringing about a degree of internalisation that seek to institutionalise a polluter-pays emphasis, such as taxes, exist at

---

[3] Calestous Juma (6 July, 2000), *Financial Times*.
[4] Ron Mitchell, intervention, Harvard debate on WEO (23 April, 1999).
[5] See Kaul, Grunberg and Stern (1999) and Heal (1999).

national and regional levels. There are reasons for this. States are reluctant to cede authority to a higher body with powers to penalise polluters. Attempts by the EU to acquire such powers for environmental ends have repeatedly failed.[6] Where there has been some progress with proposals for other market mechanisms at the international level, such as tradeable pollution permits, it is tentative and there is still concern over criteria for allocation and terms of enforcement, as the climate change negotiations illustrate. Importantly for WEO advocates that propose to bypass drawn-out decision-making processes through fast-track deal-brokering, permit-trading has only come near to fruition because it has evolved alongside a serious discussion of rules, procedures and penalties, and any trading that does take place will be within ceilings established by the type of science-driven standards that they consider to be one of the brakes on more effective action.

We should also recall that it is not the purpose of multilateral environmental agreements (MEAs) to bring about internalisation themselves. They set the goals and describe the means by which governments can initiate their own action on a particular issue. At the international level, the focus is on exchange of information, the establishment of principles and procedures by which an agreement can operate and policy areas where there is a clear international dimension such as technology transfer and aid, aimed at enforcing the agreement through side-payments. Concrete policy measures to achieve internalisation are potentially economically costly and politically difficult and, for this reason, tend to be made at the national level.

Agreeing and resolving property rights issues, which WEO proponents concede is critical to the functioning of the organisation, is also very difficult at this level. Even a cursory reading of the history of international environmental cooperation reveals a string of unresolved disputes concerning property rights over global public goods.[7] Rights to the use and protection of Amazonian rainforests, Antarctica and the deep-sea bed show that rights of access in the global commons are strongly contested and that the record of attempts to address them at the international level has been poor. If money is to be exchanged for the protection of resources, as envisaged in deals promoted by a WEO, entitlements would have to go well beyond an agreement not to exploit resources or to respect the ownership claims of others. Strong conditions would have to be imposed, the limits of which are discussed below. It is unclear how a WEO would make more progress than has been achieved to date in resolving these issues.

Given that property rights are a crucial precondition for any constituency to be involved in deal brokering, deals will be confined to areas where property rights are alleged to be clear, such as forests. Even here, however, there remain enormous tensions that a WEO could not, and should not, address around who has

---

[6] Grant, Matthews and Newell (2000).
[7] See for example Vogler (1996).

A WEO: THE WRONG SOLUTION TO THE WRONG PROBLEM 663

a title to the land, how much it is worth and who will retain the money for its stewardship on behalf of the North. Just to give one hypothetical example; who would get the money from a deal in which the EU bought up an area of Brazilian rainforest for a sum agreed by the Brazilian government, which has a very questionable entitlement to negotiate away the land of the people that inhabit the rainforests, and who are unlikely to be consulted about the deal? Are those who occupy and depend upon the land for their livelihoods likely to see the benefits of the deal and, therefore, feel any incentive to protect it in the way they would be obliged to under the WEO deal?

This example is from an issue area where trading should, in theory at least, be less problematic. Yet there would have to be clear evidence that a WEO would provide value-added outcomes in each of the issue-areas where there currently exists a carefully negotiated regime, if it is to represent an advance on the existing system of environmental governance. As Biermann notes 'many environmental problems do not fit neatly into [this] concept of insufficient global markets in environmental goods', where it is difficult to envisage bilateral market deals. The limited ability of the international community to determine and resolve property rights issues, means that it is likely that deals would be unworkable in all but a handful of uncontroversial areas, where there is political and financial will on both sides and where property rights are both clear and undisputed.

At a more fundamental level, there is likely to be a strong challenge to the notion that environmental resources are only as valuable as the OECD bidder that wants to pay for them. There has been a profound questioning of 'willingness to pay' as a formula for establishing the worth of environmental goods.[8] It assumes, by implication, that those without financial resources either do not care, or do not care enough about the environment to pay for it. It also assumes a certain 'willingness to accept' environmental damage by those whose environmental assets are not of interest to those with the capital to protect them. This has important implications for the scope and effectiveness of the WEO. Being driven by issues that are of interest to those with the capital to engage in deal-brokering, the body would be in danger of targeting a narrow range of environmental problems. Given this, the title *World* Environment Organisation may be an inflated description for a body dealing in reality with a small number of issues, involving a small number of parties.

3. THE LIMITS OF ENVIRONMENTAL AID AS A SOLUTION

Essentially what proposals for a WEO amount to is environmental aid with conditionalities that require action in exchange for the release of a sum of capital.

---

[8] Jacobs (1994).

664   PETER NEWELL

In assessing the value of creating a new institution to oversee these exchanges, we need to take account of what has been learnt already about environmental aid. Though financial transfer institutions for the environment have a relatively short history, there have been a number of attempts to assess their effectiveness; to establish the conditions in which they work and do not work.[9] This section of the paper briefly draws attention to those lessons that have a bearing on debates about the organisation and effectiveness of a WEO.

Debt-for-nature swaps perhaps provide the clearest parallel with the sort of deal-brokering activities suggested for a WEO. Despite initial optimism, the deals were both small in scale and had very little impact on deforestation and biodiversity conservation, with the principal expected sponsors (governments, MDBs and commercial banks) being reluctant to put up the resources for these schemes. Participation in the swaps was minimal with just eleven NGOs and three governments providing the $49.3 million that was spent on debt for nature swaps between 1987 and 1993.[10] Jakobeit argues:

> The funds mobilised were not sufficient to stem the many root causes of deforestation and rapid loss of biodiversity on the national scale.[11]

Although the schemes permitted NGOs to pinpoint hectares of forest being protected in the South by the dollars of concerned citizens, the swap was unable to affect the economic root causes that led to deforestation 'outside of small restricted areas'.[12] There is a danger that deals sponsored by a WEO would have the same effect; reducing complex problems to financial negotiations which allow the sponsoring institution in the North to present the deal as a 'win-win' situation for all parties, while doing very little to advance the internalisation of environmental externalities.

The Global Environment Facility also shares an important parallel with the WEO. The rationale behind its *modus operandi* is similar to the proposed WEO, in that it provides grants to compensate developing countries for undertaking activities costly to them, but which generate global environmental benefits. The GEF has suffered from being viewed as a Northern dominated institution, given its links with the World Bank and its project focus on issues that are regarded as principally Northern concerns such as climate change and biodiversity conservation. The GEF experience suggests that focus on global commons issues makes it very difficult to gain the allegiance of nationally and locally focused Southern actors whose cooperation it must have to fulfil its mandate.[13] The privileging of rich country environmental problems over local problems in

---

[9] Keohane and Levy (1996).
[10] Franz (1996, p. 379).
[11] Jakobeit (1996, p. 139).
[12] ibid., p. 145.
[13] Connolly (1996, p. 336).

A WEO: THE WRONG SOLUTION TO THE WRONG PROBLEM 665

developing countries in the way funding is prioritised, will be a key obstacle to effectiveness and the widespread and proactive participation of developing countries in the WEO.

The progress the GEF has made, however, is put down to the provision of aid for meeting principle and target-driven goals, as established by the Conventions which it supports, which are not foreseen in the WEO model proposed. Similarly, key to the relative success of the ozone fund under the Montreal Protocol was the fact it had a 'well elaborated, finite, contractual mechanism' for channelling funding to projects aimed at phasing out ozone-depleting substances in LDCs.[14]

Other lessons from the history of environmental aid include, firstly, the importance of the backing of powerful sponsors. Yet the combination of shrinking of aid budgets, the reluctance of governments to set aside new and additional funds for environmental aid (as demonstrated at the Rio conference)[15] and the isolationist chord in contemporary US politics, may pose a serious threat to the funding base of the proposed WEO.

Secondly, conditionality, which is required for the operation of WEO-style deals, is difficult to operationalise and enforce. Recipient governments often have stronger incentives to renege on their commitments than funding agencies have the capacity to enforce them. Particularly in economies that are highly dependent on resource-extraction activities (as many developing countries are), strong industrial interests with close links to government are likely to resist attempts to conserve resources. The failure to encourage action to prevent logging, for example, is attributed to the fact that:

> when the logging industry is part of the government coalition, as in Indonesia, funders cannot persuade governments to implement genuine reform.[16]

In circumstances such as these, 'buying reform' does not work in the absence of support from influential domestic constituencies and

> attempts to employ financial transfers to persuade recipients to pay more attention to the environmental externalities of domestic practices failed.[17]

Clearly then, just getting the incentives right at the global level will not be enough.[18]

Thirdly, capacity and enforcement are key to implementation of environmental initiatives. While the WEO envisaged may avoid some of the problems associated with acting upon often vaguely-worded commitments in international agreements, basic problems of lack of capacity to oversee commitments and to ensure

---

[14] DeSombre and Kauffman (1996, p. 90).
[15] Robins (1998, pp. 189–212).
[16] Connolly (1996, p. 21).
[17] ibid., p. 334.
[18] Keohane (1996).

666   PETER NEWELL

active and reliable chains of command exist between government (or whomever brokers a deal) and local level implementers, remain.

Enforcing conditions that take a long time to implement is particularly difficult. The time-lag issue is an important one given the possible tension between the relatively short-term scales of funding for deals and the extended period of time required for complex reforms. This creates an incentive towards highly visible projects with short-term returns, rather than those which will produce lasting benefits even after funding ceases.

The overall lesson from these experiences is that institutions have to be realistic about what they can achieve. As Connolly argues:[19]

> Financial transfers alone will save neither the ozone layer nor the Brazilian rainforest. Achieving such objectives will depend on the interest and ability of affected actors to attract and make effective use of other, more substantial resources.

Where the success of donor efforts

> depends solely on environmental conditionality or the simple linkage of financial transfers with environmental reforms, overall effectiveness will be quite low.[20]

4. ADVANTAGE TO THE SOUTH?

Given current patterns of production and consumption, the goal of bringing developing countries on board in global deal-brokering that drives Whalley and Zissimos's proposal seems misplaced if improved environmental outcomes is the goal. With the exception of newly and emerging industrialised countries such as Brazil, China and India, that will undoubtedly contribute considerably to future environmental degradation, but are already active players in existing regime arrangements, most developing countries contribute very little to the problems that a WEO is intended to address. Under the North-South formula for trading proposed, the South would be cast as a sink, a protector of resources which it can be 'bribed' to safeguard for the benefit of the North, which is not expected under these deals to do anything to address its own contribution to the problems, other than raise sums of money to transfer to developing countries. Yet the starting point for any serious discussion about internalisation has to be reforms in patterns of production and consumption that create environmental problems. We should also acknowledge that even those issues which a WEO could, in theory, address such as deforestation and species conservation, where developing countries have an important role to play, are driven, in part, by Northern demand for cheap timber and products derived from endangered species.

---

[19] Connolly (1996, p. 327).
[20] ibid., p. 337.

A WEO: THE WRONG SOLUTION TO THE WRONG PROBLEM 667

An additional concern is that, as it is currently conceived, the WEO may serve to entrench many of the problems that developing countries face. It may be the case that some Southern governments would support the creation of a WEO, on the basis that it would generate fresh sources of revenue and, in the WTO's preferred version of the WEO, remove from the trade organisation's ambit the discussion of trade-related environmental standards which may be used to discriminate against Southern exports. However, it would do little to address the exclusionary nature of global policy-making on the environment, which means that Southern concerns are rarely adequately represented. Under the WEO scheme, the allocation and exploitation of global commons resources would be privatised, subject to deals between those who steward the resources and are in a position to claim the financial benefit for their protection, and those with the capital to afford this protection. Whilst all are affected by the decisions made within the body, only those managing the resources, or with the finances to buy them, get a say in whether and how they are protected. This is a further step away from democratic management of the world's resources for the benefit of all. The bilateral nature of the proposed deal-brokering would indeed heighten the leverage that donors have over recipients. In practice, therefore, while as a result of WEO deals, we may have heavily guarded areas of protected rainforest and conservation zones of healthy elephant populations, projects which have enormous symbolic and emotive value, environmental problems that are not of interest to wealthy sponsors would continue unabated.

Proposals for a WEO overlook the reasons behind the South's alleged lack of interest in environmental protection, which is not supported by a review of environmental regimes from climate change to biodiversity, where developing countries have been in favour of legally-binding protection while the North has resisted restrictions. Aside from potential conflicts with pressing development objectives and the lack of capacity to implement the terms of agreements that often exists, the principal reason many developing countries are reluctant to accept the sort of environmental obligations they demand of the North is because these are problems historically created by the North which it has the primary responsibility to address. While deal-brokering may bypass debates on principles and science in the earliest stages of regime design, it is likely to have to address these basic issues if it is to make progress on the issue of internalisation and not be seen as a new instrument of private Northern control, bypassing the principal channels through which the developing world has sought to express its views on these issues to date, namely through UN fora.

5. A DIFFERENT VIEW OF INTERNALISATION

Explaining why international environmental cooperation is not more effective means looking at the causes of environmental degradation. When the disjuncture

668   PETER NEWELL

between the structures of production and consumption that generate existing environmental problems and the nature of exiting regime arrangements is placed at the centre of analysis, it is easier to determine reasons for the under-performance of existing governance structures. Current international regimes treat environmental problems as disconnected management problems that can be subject to coordinated control through scientific and technological cooperation. The industrial processes and actors that create these problems are rarely identified as being implicated, such that most regime arrangements do not question business-as-usual development practices. This inevitably gives rise to the narrowly-focused, piecemeal approach to environmental cooperation that WEO advocates decry.

Viewed this way, the failure of international cooperation is to target those actors and processes that create the problems that regime arrangements set out to address. Attempts by NGOs to include language in environmental agreements about consumption and production have met with rebuttals by leading industrialised nations.[21] Similarly, talk of regulating the pollutative activities of multinational enterprises, who by the International Chamber of Commerce's own estimates are responsible for a large percentage of global emissions, have met with resistance.[22] Powerful industrial lobbies, increasingly globally organised, have expended vast financial and political resources in ensuring that outcomes at the international level have not gone further, that their core activities remain unaffected by the sceptre of global regulation.[23]

Internalisation can never be achieved when policy in areas such as trade, energy and transport, with enormous ecological impacts, proceeds without restraint or account of its ecological impacts. This pattern is reproduced at both the national and international level. Internationally, failures of coordination across regimes mean that the goals and possible net gains from agreements on climate change, for example, are reduced to nothing because the WTO, at the same time, negotiates rounds of trade liberalisation which will increase emissions of CO_2 well beyond the savings carefully negotiated in the climate treaties (by increasing the volumes of goods transported over larger distances). Similarly, while we talk of the need to promote higher standards of environmental protection amongst firms, there is simultaneously discussion within the OECD of a Multilateral Agreement on Investment (MAI) that will allow companies to challenge national and local governments seeking to raise social and environmental standards in the name of non-discrimination against foreign investors.[24]

---

[21] Chatterjee and Finger (1994).
[22] According to the Business Council for Sustainable Development's (BCSD) own figures, 'Industry accounts for more than one third of energy consumed world-wide and uses more energy than any other end-user in industrialised and newly industrialising economies'. See Schmidheiny (1992, p. 43).
[23] Newell and Paterson (1998).
[24] Picciotto and Mayne (1999).

A WEO: THE WRONG SOLUTION TO THE WRONG PROBLEM 669

This is a function both of the nature of decision-making and bureaucratic power imbalances within government and the privileging of certain goals over others. The increasingly global nature of the economy makes it additionally difficult for governments, even if they wanted to, to discipline those market actors that contribute to environmental problems. Recognising this issue, however, is central to understanding the current failure of internalisation and has to be the starting point for strategies that seek to advance this goal. It is highly questionable, therefore, how far internalisation can be achieved at the international level, or through the WEO currently proposed. The key to internalisation, to changing the behaviour that generates environmental harm, is giving industries the right incentives to reduce pollution, to adopt best available technologies (BATs), and to maintain high standards wherever they invest. It is about building up government capacity to enforce standards and monitor enforcement so that polluters have the right balance of incentives and disincentives to practise environmentally responsible investment.

6. CONCLUSION

Instead of rushing to develop a new global architecture for the environment, we need to reflect on how far environmental problems, even allegedly global environmental problems, can best be addressed at the international level. Negotiations are costly, time-consuming and slow to achieve outcomes. This, indeed, is the appeal attributed to the WEO in its minimalist form, as a small-scale, low-maintenance, deal-brokering body. International processes are exclusionary (often with little effective participation from Southern delegations), complex (often mired in technical scientific and legal disputes), and resource and labour-intensive (which further limits the participation of poorer nations). Because of this, they tend to be driven by Northern delegations with the resources to attend all the meetings, and the armies of scientific and legal advisors to track the process and shape it according to their interests.

There is a serious need to rethink how we address global environmental problems. The mistake would be to 'go global' without considering other alternatives. More appropriate may be proposals to promote coherent, inclusive forms of multi-level environmental governance. Rather than assume the international level is the place to start, applying the principle of subsidiarity would encourage us to look to regional and national policy-processes as a starting point and only move decision-making upwards when the nature of the problem genuinely requires it. Many problems are not truly global at all. Climate change is caused primarily by OECD countries that could address it without relying on the participation of many developing countries, if they had the political will to do so. For developing countries, the preference may be for national and regional level initiatives where they have a stronger voice, where policies and programmes can more adequately reflect their interests and concerns. The added value of international cooperation for many LDCs is the provision of aid, technology transfer and other means of building capacity which *can* usefully be provided through multilateral fora. This is not a rejection of international cooperation therefore. It is a plea to be clear about what an international institution can and cannot achieve.

There is a case for a more rational use of the existing architecture in terms of exploiting fruitful cross-issue linkages, establishing more clearly defined divisions of labour between existing organisations that build on their respective strengths, but avoid duplication of activities.[25] Von Moltke suggests linking treaties that address issues that are closely related such as the Convention on Biological Diversity (CBD) and Ransar Conventions, for example. We also need to manage the relationship between trade and environment regimes in ways that do not just require the latter to be subordinate to the former (in which case internalisation will have failed) and to promote the proactive involvement of developing countries in global environmental debates.

Criticising the mechanisms that are currently in place, as if they have been chosen for the efficacy in solving environmental problems, rather than because of the economic and political purposes they serve, however, leads us to draw misplaced conclusions about the problem and appropriate alternatives. We need to be clear, therefore, about why international environmental cooperation is not delivering more effective environmental outcomes. The existing system of global environmental governance is undoubtedly not bringing about the internalisation of environmental externalities, but until the biggest polluters are forced to internalise the environmental costs they impose on the rest of society, no amount of institutional tinkering will improve the environment.

REFERENCES

Biermann, F. (2000), 'The Case for a World Environment Organisation', *Environment*, **42**, 9, 22–31.
Chatterjee, P. and M. Finger (1994), *The Earth Brokers: Power, Politics and World Development* (London: Routledge).
Connolly, B. (1996), 'Increments for the Earth: The Politics of Environmental Aid', in R.O. Keohane and M.A. Levy (eds.), *Institutions for Environmental Aid* (MIT Press, Cambridge, Massachusetts and London, England).

---

[25] There is potential for the Commission on Sustainable Development (CSD) to perform this function in providing overviews and assessments of existing agreements and the interplay between them, even if it is not currently engaged in the latter task. Mitchell concurs that the challenge is to identify gaps, overlaps and synergies and help other organisations solve the problems without adding tiers of hierarchy to what we already have (23 April, 1999, Harvard debate on WEO).

A WEO: THE WRONG SOLUTION TO THE WRONG PROBLEM 671

DeSombre, E.R. and J. Kauffman (1996), 'The Montreal Protocol Multilateral Fund: Partial Success Story', in R.O. Keohane and M.A. Levy (eds.), *Institutions for Environmental Aid* (MIT Press, Cambridge, Massachusetts and London, England),

Fairman, D. (1996), 'The Global Environment Facility: Haunted by the Shadow of the Future', in R.O. Keohane and M.A. Levy (eds.), *Institutions for Environmental Aid* (MIT Press, Cambridge, Massachusetts and London, England).

Fairman, D. and M. Ross (1996), 'Old Fads, New Lessons: Learning from Economic Development Assistance', in R.O. Keohane and M.A. Levy (eds.), *Institutions for Environmental Aid* (MIT Press, Cambridge, Massachusetts and London, England).

Franz, W.E. (1996), 'Appendix: The Scope of Global Environmental Financing – Cases in Context', in R.O. Keohane and M.A. Levy (eds.), *Institutions for Environmental Aid* (MIT Press, Cambridge, Massachusetts and London, England).

Grant, W., D. Matthews and P. Newell (2000), *The Effectiveness of EU Environmental Policy* (Basingstoke: Macmillan).

Heal, G. (1999), 'New Strategies for the Provision of Global Public Goods: Learning from International Environmental Challenges', in I. Kaul, I. Grunberg and M. Stern (eds.), *Global Public Goods: International Cooperation in the Twenty-first Century* (Oxford: Oxford University Press).

Jacobs, M. (1994), 'The Limits of Neoclassicalism', in M. Redclift and T. Benton (eds.), *Social Theory and the Global Environment* (London: Routledge).

Jakobeit, C. (1996), 'Nonstate Actors Leading the Way: Debt-for-Nature Swaps', in R.O. Keohane and M.A. Levy (eds.), *Institutions for Environmental Aid* (MIT Press, Cambridge, Massachusetts and London, England).

Kaul, I., I. Grunberg and M. Stern (eds.) (1999), *Global Public Goods: International Cooperation in the Twenty-First Century* (Oxford: Oxford University Press).

Keohane, R.O. (1996), 'Analyzing the Effectiveness of International Environmental Institutions', in R.O. Keohane and M.A. Levy (eds.), *Institutions for Environmental Aid* (MIT Press, Cambridge, Massachusetts and London, England).

Keohane, R.O. and M.A. Levy (eds.) (1996), *Institutions for Environmental Aid* (MIT Press, Cambridge, Massachusetts and London).

Newell, P. and M. Paterson (1998), 'Climate for Business: Global Warming, the State and Capital', co-authored with Matthew Paterson, *Review of International Political Economy*, **5**, 4 (Winter).

Picciotto, S. and R. Mayne (eds.) (1999), *Regulating International Business: Beyond Liberalization* (Basingstoke: Macmillan).

Robins, N. (1998), 'Competitiveness, Environmental Sustainability and the Future of European Union Development Cooperation', in J. Golub (ed.), *Global Competition and EU Environmental Policy* (London and New York: Routledge), 189–212.

Vogler, J. (1996), *The Global Commons: A Regime Analysis* (Sussex: John Wiley and Sons).

[17]

Melanesia, the Banks, and the BINGOs: Real Alternatives are Everywhere (Except in the Consultants' Briefcases)

Nicholas G. Faraclas

Globalization for Corporations, Not for People

Corporate globalization is presented to us as inevitable. But must we accept as an inevitable fact of life the mortgaging of the lives of future generations of entire nations in the form of debt to the banks and the profiteers who invented corporate globalization? Corporate globalization is discussed in the media as if it were a natural phenomenon. But can the most massive transfer of wealth in the history of humanity from the poor to the rich sponsored by the World Bank/International Monetary Fund (WB/IMF or 'the Bank') and enforced by the World Trade Organization (WTO) under the agenda of corporate globalization be considered natural? We are told that corporate globalization is the next logical step in the evolution of the world economy. But is there anything natural or logical about the premature death of our planet, which corporate globalization looks certain to bring about?

There is nothing natural, normal or inevitable about either corporate globalization or the 'alternatives' to it proposed by the WB/IMF, bilateral aid agencies, the Big International Non-Governmental Organizations (BINGOs) and the rest of the development establishment. Despite what the media, governments, schools, churches and economists say, human beings did not always live like this. Your ancestors and mine had control over their productive and reproductive processes, which they utilized to serve the interests of their communities as a whole, rather than those of a small minority. In fact, it is only in a few aberrant societies and only during the past few thousand years that the land, work, communities and cultures that once were controlled by all and used to satisfy the needs of all were enclosed, appropriated, diverted and distorted to feed the insatiable greed of a system that serves profits, not people. Unfortunately, these aberrant societies have perfected the technologies of illusion, addiction and death in such a way as to impose their system of profit and domination on most of the peoples of the earth.

Melanesia and Alternatives to Corporate Globalization

Indigenous Melanesians make up more than 95 per cent of the 4.5 million inhabitants of Papua New Guinea, the Solomon Islands and Vanuatu. The constitutions of the three nations recognize the power of indigenous peoples and their customary laws over the 90 per cent of their national territory that has not yet been registered under 'western'-style land legislation. In most of the rest of the world, the collective power over land that all of humanity once enjoyed has long ago been ceded to the state, in exchange for a few individual land-ownership rights. This has not yet happened to the vast majority of the indigenous peoples of Melanesia, who consequently enjoy the full food, housing, employment and land security that not so long ago all humans enjoyed. While the remarkable developmental achievements of traditional Melanesian societies fill transnational companies and WB/IMF consultants with bewilderment or disgust, they have the potential to inspire the rest of us to reconstruct our collective pasts and take back control over our common futures.

The battle over alternatives to corporate globalization is indeed a crucial one, but it will not be fought with money or guns or political machines. Instead, it will be fought with ideas, beliefs and community work. We ignore this fact at our own peril. The multinational companies certainly do not ignore it. Before land and labour can be enclosed in the interests of profit, people's minds and beliefs need to be enclosed. For this reason, there are more missionaries per capita in Melanesia than anywhere else on the earth today. Melanesians do not yet believe that it is normal for one person to have enormous wealth and another to have nothing, for people to be forced into suffocating sexual roles or nuclear families, or for someone else to control their land or their labour. But the combined forces of missionary preaching and company advertising that have invaded even the most remote villages are preparing yet another indigenous nation for submission to a patriarchal God who demands blind obedience, addiction to substances that require wage slavery to obtain, and the expropriation and exploitation that inevitably follow.

Popular Education, Alternative Pasts and Alternative Futures

At present, the debate over corporate globalization is effectively dominated by the profit system, working through international agencies such as the WB/IMF which are wholly dedicated to the propagation of the gospel of neo-liberal economics. The WB/IMF has quite successfully enlisted governments to adopt and implement its vision of corporate globalization, while at the same time co-opting non-governmental organizations to articulate its vision of 'alternatives' to corporate globalization. Until we can seriously consider alternative pasts, it is useless to talk about alternative futures. Unless we can effectively reconstruct our own pasts in our own interests, how will we be able to avoid constructing futures that serve only to feed the insatiable greed of the forces which are leading us all to misery and our planet to destruction?

This battle over alternatives must first be inspired by a reawakened memory that things do not have to be this way, then waged with our abundant power to resist and reject the 'alternatives' that are being presented to us now, and finally won with the boundless creativity that we as communities have to influence our futures in our own interests. To accomplish all of this, popular education and awareness are essential. It is not insignificant that among all the 'alternatives' currently being put forward by the preponderant majority of international agencies and BINGOs, few include a programme of genuine popular education or critical awareness. Popular education begins with communities collectively identifying their problems in a radical way, then critically analysing the causes of their problems, and finally formulating transformational solutions to their problems, using their own knowledge, resources and labour as much as possible. Because they lack these essential components, we can say that almost all of the 'alternatives' that are being presented to us today are not alternatives at all, just 'kinder, gentler' ways to sacrifice more land, more labour and more lives to the God of profit.

Corporate Globalization and Recolonization

In order to understand corporate globalization, we need to understand why the Bank and the WTO are promoting it as 'Our Future'. The great depression and the Second World War severely weakened the ability of the dominant classes of the North (especially those of Northern Europe and the United States) to extract profit from the lands and peoples of the Majority World, whether from the militant, unionized workforce of the 'First World', from the socialist states of the 'Second World', or the newly independent nations of the 'Third World'. It should be noted that I consider the Majority World to transcend national boundaries, i.e. most of Brixton and the Bronx are part of the Majority World. The WB/IMF was set up in the 1940s to remedy this situation. Its first major mission, which occupied it until the late 1960s, was to help reconstruct the former colonial powers and their war-ravaged economies.

Colonial economies, though, cannot exist without empires. Therefore, in the 1970s and 1980s the WB/IMF shifted its focus to its second main task, the recolonization of the world. But this form of colonization would not repeat the mistakes of the administrative type of colonialism practised by European governments on their dependent territories in the South since the fifteenth century. Instead, it would follow the much more efficient and insidious debt-driven model imposed since the nineteenth century by British and American banks on the nominally independent states of Latin America. The success of this strategy was phenomenal. By the early 1990s, the neo-liberal advisers from Washington could be said to have seized effective economic and administrative control over nearly every nation of Asia, Africa, Latin America, the Pacific and Eastern Europe.

The system that the WB/IMF and the WTO serve can never be satisfied. It must consume ever greater amounts of land, resources and labour to generate ever increasing rates of profit and regular record highs on the stock markets, or it collapses. Ultimately, it is a system that favours no one. Whatever it can get away with in the colonies, it eventually imposes on the metropoles, and vice versa. So while the WB/IMF was forcing the South to accept structural adjustment, Thatcher, Reagan and their neo-liberal clones such as Blair and Clinton have been imposing similar 'austerity programmes' first on the working classes of Britain and the United States, then eventually on all but a small minority of the peoples of Northern Europe, Japan, Australia and Aotearoa/New Zealand.

So the recolonization of the South is inextricably connected to the repauperization of the North; this is the essence of the corporate globalization which has been codified and made legally binding on all governments under the provisions of the WTO. Corporate globalization has dismantled the welfare state in the former 'First World', state socialism in the former 'Second World', and state sovereignty in the former 'Third World'. All of these worlds are being merged into one global configuration that pits an ever growing majority forced to live in misery against an ever shrinking minority 'enjoying' relative privilege behind barbed-wire fences. Distinctions between North and South and among nation-states are breaking down, with rapidly expanding pockets of Majority World 'underdevelopment' springing up in the former metropoles and corresponding enclaves of Minority World 'development' establishing themselves in the former colonies.

From Arrogance to Feigned Contrition: the Bank's Response to the Movement against Corporate Globalization

Over the past fifty years, an increasingly vocal and articulate movement has emerged in opposition to corporate globalization and the institutions that push it. Up until the massive protests at Seattle in 1999 and Prague in 2000, the WB/IMF systematically and categorically ignored these voices. But now that the WB/IMF's mission has largely been accomplished, some acknowledgement and even some tactical use can be made of such criticisms. It was possible for Robert McNamara to apologize for the WB's lending policies under his presidency only once the majority of the world's population, their children and their children's children had already been effectively enslaved by the debt mechanism unleashed by these same policies. When the WB was still lending money to reconstruct Japan and Germany after the war, these countries were allowed to default on debts and some of their debts were forgiven. But even after McNamara's admission of gross mismanagement at the Bank, no country in the South has been able to benefit from such forgiveness. The highly publicized plans for limited debt 'relief' are so restricted and require such complete capitulation to the most draconian form of neo-liberal adjustment that they do not merit consideration here.

The latest, heavily censored *World Development Report*s published by the Bank constitute the closest thing to an apology that can be expected from such a completely unaccountable institution for the unbridled attack that the WB/IMF has made over the past two decades on all forms of state services (excepting police, defence forces, prisons and subsidies for multinational 'investors', of course). In these reports, the Bank has glossed over the structural adjustment-induced 'misery factor' which played a major role in pushing Bosnia, Burundi and Rwanda over the edge. But now that the state has imploded in Liberia, the Democratic Republic of the Congo, Somalia and Sierra Leone under the unbearable pressure of structural adjustment combined with the legacy of the WB/IMF-supported dictatorships of Doe, Mobutu, Barre and the Freetown 'elite', the Bank has been forced to backtrack and take a more moderate position on the potential role of the state.

In this way, Africa has extracted a bitter-sweet revenge for being more or less written off the WB/IMF's development agenda in past editions of the *Report*. But it makes little difference in the final analysis; just as the Bank crucified the state, so it can resurrect it to do its bidding. Now that the governmental apparatus in the great majority of countries is directly or indirectly accountable to the WB/IMF (rather than to their people) and legally bound to structural adjustment under the WTO, the state has become a valuable tool in the extraction of labour and resources for the transnational companies who ultimately determine WB/IMF and WTO policy.

Much more threatening to the forces of corporate globalization is the emergence during the past decade of a very effective system of traditional

Fighting the New Colonialism   **72**

clan-based self-governance by the people of Somaliland (the former British-administered area in the north of what eventually became Somalia). Despite the fact that Somaliland has one of the best functioning and least corrupt governments in Africa, it has been ostracized by the farcical collection of agencies, governments, BINGOs, and media conglomerates that the companies sell to us as the 'international community'. With a civil service of only 6000 for a population of more than 2 million, no debt, and negligible dependence on the poisonous addiction that is otherwise known as bilateral and multilateral 'aid', Somaliland proves that indigenous systems of government can achieve peace, respect for human rights, and relative prosperity by making the national-state subservient and effectively accountable to a diverse collection of profoundly democratic local-level political and economic structures (Prunier 2000: 14).

The Bank's Defence of Corporate Globalization

As the mountain of evidence attesting to the disastrous consequences of structural adjustment can no longer be ignored, the Bank is finally responding. One response is that the WB/IMF acted with the best of intentions, but corrupt governments were to blame for the problems. Another contends that the plans were made correctly in Washington, but that they were implemented incorrectly on the ground by incompetent governments.

These arguments can be easily refuted by the long list of hopelessly corrupt and incompetent regimes which have been actively supported by the Bank, the longer list of regimes who were corrupted or further corrupted either by the type of money given by the Bank or by the way in which it was given, and the shorter list of relatively competent regimes who seriously attempted to be transparent and accountable to their people, but who were effectively boycotted by the Bank because they didn't adhere to the neo-liberal orthodoxy which has assumed the status of religious dogma in the WB/IMF and the WTO. Because the Bank has set itself up as the gatekeeper for nearly all bilateral and multilateral assistance, its blockades have swept these latter governments into the dustbin of history, with the help of an unsavoury group of mercenaries and Contras assembled by northern governments to defend the interests of the profiteers who call the shots in Washington, Paris, London and Tokyo.

When all other defences fail, WB/IMF officials use the ultimate justification for their policies, namely that there was no possible alternative to their intervention, and if they hadn't acted, things would have been much worse. Under normal circumstances it would be very difficult to argue against such an assertion, given the fact that the proponents claim to have complete knowledge of events past and future in several parallel universes. But in this case, we need only to cite the WB/IMF's sister UN organization UNICEF, which attributes 500,000 childhood deaths per year directly to WB/IMF structural adjustment programmes, not to mention the millions who have perished indirectly through the withdrawal of food subsidies and health services, the victims of the rapid rise in violence, war and genocide that accompanies structural adjustment, and so on. The WB is a profit-making institution. Current debt payments on loans made or brokered by the Bank are responsible for a net outflow of capital from the overwhelming majority of countries in the South to profiteers in the North. It doesn't take a clairvoyant to see that a simple cancellation of part or all of this debt would have landed us in a happier world than the one that neo-liberal economists present to us as 'the way it always was, the way it inevitably has become, and the way it will always be'.

From Marginalization to Co-optation: NGOs and the 'Alternatives Trap'

The WB/IMF is not only responding to criticism, however; it is re-cuperating it and utilizing it to co-opt and buy off its critics. Over the past few years, the WB/IMF has actually come to dominate debates on corporate globalization, not merely by defending the corporate globalist position, but by actively intervening in the construction of arguments on 'both sides' of the question. While the International Monetary Fund still boldly advocates corporate globalization in its pure 'unmanaged' form, the World Bank is putting forward a set of 'alternatives' which amount to nothing more than 'managed' versions of corporate globalization. The hard-line position of the IMF and the revisionist position of the WB create a false polarization that becomes very seductive to erstwhile critics who crave the short-term financial and political advantages of co-operating with the Bank. In Melanesia and elsewhere, transnational mining companies and the World Bank are now entering into partnerships with BINGOs such as WWF, the global environment network, to create 'alternative' programmes in tropical regions which are heavily impacted by mineral and timber extraction. Upon closer examination, however, these programmes turn out to be nothing but band-aid operations that put a 'human face' on the wholesale destruction of communities and habitats.

The World Bank is now funding smaller indigenous NGOs in countries like Papua New Guinea to show that they recognize that NGOs too have a role to play (in carrying out structural adjustment!). More than US$15 million for credit schemes (the flavour-of-the-month, since Grameen), portable sawmills, and the like is flooding into local communities. The WB managed to introduce the funding mechanism in the most divisive way possible, by buying off two prominent NGO leaders to head up two competing facilities for NGO involvement in a WB/IMF-sponsored 'Poverty Alleviation Programme'. The predictable splits over involvement with the Bank occurred in the organizations and networks which had placed their trust in these leaders. Of course, those NGOs that decided to take the money aligned themselves with the two different camps and came to blows over their competing claims.

Several existing NGOs which have financial management problems have put aside their scruples and taken the WB money. For them, the money is a new 'fix', allowing them to put off dealing with the crisis until it grows to such proportions that it destroys them. A significant portion of this money will go to 'mushroom NGOs' that formed only because the funds were available. Most of the money that will not be misused outright will go into 'alternative income generation' which usually means the setting up of one or a few individuals (mostly young men) as local businesspeople, who will disrupt traditional egalitarian political and economic mechanisms, and propagate relations of domination in their communities by becoming the local dispensers of beer, abusers of women and silencers of critics.

Just as it did when it tempted governments to take loans in the 1970s and 1980s, the WB/IMF is now waving money in the faces of NGOs, and a distressing number of former WB/IMF critics are taking the bait. Of course, the Bank will claim in a few years' time that the disintegration of the NGO movement in Papua New Guinea and the rampant corruption and financial mismanagement which followed this reckless disbursal of funds was in no way encouraged or abetted by the WB/IMF! Meanwhile, the 'mushroom NGOs' become the fifth column of the WB/IMF within the NGO movement and the 'local businesspeople' become the shock troops of the profit system within their communities.

Since the WB/IMF has embarked on the alternatives business, it is positioning itself as an 'expert' on the subject. When critics confront the Bank, they are immediately challenged to produce an alternative. This is the ultimate trap. No real alternatives to corporate globalization could ever be designed by the WB/IMF, programmed by governments, brainstormed in the headquarters of BINGOs, or even collectively formulated by indigenous local NGOs. When the Bank asks its critics to come up with alternatives, it is asking them to replicate the relations of domination that keep communities from articulating and implementing their own alternatives, rather than the 'alternatives' that the 'experts' from outside propose for them. The only real alternatives to corporate globalization involve processes of critical, radical and transformational community awareness, analysis and mobilization, not ready-made solutions to unanalysed problems.

Melanesia, Popular Education and Reclaiming the Abundance of Subsistence

The development establishment has reserved its last desperate weapon for those who have managed to avoid the alternatives trap and propose instead popular education processes as the basis for the emergence of real alternatives. The claim is that the popular education process has no basis in the past or the present, but only as part of some utopian dream. In fact, nothing could be further from the truth, and the evidence is to be found everywhere, once we begin to challenge received notions of how it was, is and will be.

In Melanesia, over 1500 languages are spoken by at least that many different ethnic groups. Each of these groups constitutes a society distinct from the others in countless ways, but there are some commonalities that unite them. In general, these societies have traditionally shunned extreme accumulation of wealth, have striven for collective decision-making, have recognized women's power over their own productive and reproductive processes, and have utilized an economy based on subsistence to create an abundance that ensures all of their members food, housing, employment and land. None has opted for the nuclear family, strait-jacketed sexual roles or profit-making as a positively valued social activity. Most importantly, however, these societies have maintained control over their own history, their mechanisms for dealing with problems in the present, and their vision for the future. Critical and democratic identification, analysis and resolution of problems by communities have been the norm rather than the exception in Melanesia. These incredibly significant achievements have been attained by each society in its own unique manner, without forced assimilation or conquest.

In Melanesia we have living evidence of what feminist archaeologists in Europe (Gimbutas 1991) and zoologists working with primates such as the bonobos in Central Africa (McKie 1997: 25) are discovering: that patriarchal society based on violence, repression, scarcity and domination is most probably a very recent phenomenon in human history, establishing itself without conquest or threat of conquest in only one or perhaps a few human populations. The society of domination that neo-liberal economists present to us as normal is therefore quite the opposite. Because they sustain themselves through illusion (like the stock market) and mass addiction (like consumerism) and because they propagate themselves through conquest and technologies of death, societies of domination are the antithesis of any but the most warped concept of what could be considered to be 'natural' or 'evolutionarily advantageous' to our species.

In other words, for all but a short moment of human existence on the

Fighting the New Colonialism 76

planet and in all but a handful of societies, all of our ancestors lived in the abundance of subsistence, in open societies which co-existed in relative peace, fostering and celebrating tremendous diversity, individuality and creativity. This is the past that we can all reclaim, if we dare to reject the version of history that portrays the loss by the vast majority of humanity of our power over our land, labour, communities, history and sense of possibilities during the past few thousand years as some sort of 'progress' into the 'light' from some dark and evil 'primitive' pre-history. We reclaim this past not to idealize it or to try mechanically to replicate it, but to use it as an inspiration for the reinterpretation of the present and the foundation for building a future for people, not for profit.

Resistance and Alternatives to Globalization are Everywhere

Equipped with this re-reading of our past, the present becomes abundantly rich with evidence for resistance to domination and possibilities for transcending it. Despite the fact that a WB/IMF-sponsored genocide has been practised against them, the peoples of West Papua continue to resist and reclaim their power over the land, just as indigenous peoples do worldwide. Despite the mass murder of millions of women as 'witches' to consolidate the patriarchal system in Europe and to make possible the imposition of that system on the rest of the world through missionization and colonization, women everywhere continue to reclaim control over their bodies. In order to survive as a human being in the neo-liberal universe, we are compelled to commit acts of resistance at nearly every moment and constantly to subvert the control that the profit system exerts over our minds, our labour and our lives.

When we remove the blinders of the limited 'alternatives' that the development establishment presents to us as the only possible choices for the future, a vast and almost limitless array of possibilities is open to us. The sense of such possibilities has allowed the indigenous peoples in Melanesia to develop and practise thousands of different but equally effective systems which guarantee equal access to the abundance of subsistence, collective decision-making, equitable relations between the sexes and so on. And this is the future that we can all claim, if we only dare.

References

Gimbutas, Marija (1991) *The Civilization of the Goddess: The World of Old Europe*, San Francisco, CA: Harper.

McKie, Robin (1997) 'Monkey business as science', *Guardian Weekly*, 3 August 1997, p. 25.

Prunier, Gerard (2000) 'Somalia reinvents itself', *Le Monde Diplomatique*, April, p. 14.

[18]

What Really Keeps Our Cities Alive, Money or Subsistence?

Veronika Bennholdt-Thomsen

No matter what question arises about the future of our cities, the first reaction from all sides is usually: Can we afford it? How much is it going to cost? One would almost think that our cities live from money. But don't they actually live far more from the activities of the people in them as they lead their daily lives, at work and play? This 'economy of daily well-being' has very little to do with money but a lot to do with human care and human contact; that is, with what we sociologists call interaction. In this case, people are not concerned with each other on some abstract level; their interaction is realized in material terms and given permanence through this. Included within this culture and economy of everyday life is child-care and caring for young and for old people and the subsistence labour of mothers and some fathers; but it also embraces the purpose behind the paid labour performed by the woman at the market stand and by the financial broker, who both earn money in order to pay for food, drink, clothes and accommodation, i.e. to pay for their subsistence.

However, on our modern scale of values, the purpose of this everyday process of human encounters, together with the social interconnection and integration which accompany them, is receding further and further into the background and being replaced by money *as a value in itself*. For us, money stands for subsistence, and the fact that it is merely a means of exchange is forgotten. These means have themselves come to epitomize the securing of the essentials of life.

The fixation with money as opposed to *people* with all their abilities, wishes and needs is closely allied to the fixation with wage-labour or, to be more exact, with the relationship between wage-labour and capital. We court capital as if wages and salaries kept us alive. Yet, today more than ever, this seems a questionable assumption. It goes without saying that in the future, as now, we will be responsible for ensuring our own and our children's survival and the smooth running of our lives together. It seems more than unlikely, however, that the majority of us will be able to do this by means of an income derived from wages or salaries, and on the level of those currently earned by skilled labour in Germany even less so.

Notwithstanding, at all levels of government, from local to national, everyone behaves as if full conventional employment for all were purely a question of the right policies. This is known in Germany as *Standortpolitik*: the term refers to policy decisions aimed at attracting investment to a particular location. The greater the financial volume of the enterprise or project thus enticed, the better it is supposed to be for all concerned, true to the principle that when the economy is thriving, everyone else is too.

This attitude is what I call 'money orientation', in the name of money orientation, subsistence orientation is systematically neglected. This is by no means an attitude that is typical only of or even mainly of the political administration; instead, it is an extremely widespread, indeed a cultural phenomenon of our society at the dawn of the third millennium. It is not things of immediate usefulness that have the highest value, but the money with which you can, supposedly, buy any useful thing, and much more besides. We no longer believe in natural growth, but in monetary growth, which is equated with economic growth. As everyone knows, the central criterion of economic growth is the gross national product, in which everything bought and sold in a country is expressed in terms of a sum of money. So a war, for example, makes an excellent contribution to economic growth.

It is only very slowly starting to dawn on us just how one-dimensional and ideologically-laden this concept of 'economy' is. What I hope to do here is shed a little more light on the general gloom, with specific reference to the economic life of the city.

Globalization, Liberalization, Privatization: The Demands of Big Capital

Since the 1980s economic and social life in our cities has been subjected to drastic changes. One visible expression of this is to be found in the large shopping centres, supermarkets and shopping malls which have sprung up everywhere, at the expense of a great many smaller and medium-sized retail outlets, even bigger shops that were not members of chains. The latter have all had to shut their doors to business.

This development did not take place all on its own, but is to a considerable extent the result of political and administrative decisions and priorities. One of the arguments trotted out most often has been that this sort of development would create jobs. This may be so, but how many jobs have been destroyed by other shops and businesses having to close? And what *kinds* of jobs have been promoted by deciding in favour of the big investor? Wage-labour jobs, exactly. But what kind of wage-labour can be seen as preferable to the independence of running a small business, as is apparently the case here? The big retailers, the Aldis and Schleckers, together with the McDonalds, Pizza Huts and Unilever-Nordsee fast-food chains have introduced insecure jobs with 'flexibilized' hours and few benefits, and established such poor working conditions as a norm, in Germany as elsewhere.

One justification sometimes heard is that decision-makers had no choice but to decide in favour of big investors and projects, since no small businesses could be found to supply the services needed in a given part of town. When I consider just how much effort it takes and has always taken in some places simply to (re)establish a weekly farm produce market in the face of stringent conditions imposed by the local administration, compared to the ease with which the infrastructure for a large supermarket is provided, I find this argument somewhat difficult to swallow. Rather, this kind of convenient mainstream attitude is an attempt to justify the almost compulsive repetition of the same kind of irresponsible behaviour. First of all the small shops and businesses were overwhelmed by supermarkets, Do It Yourself (DIY) stores and various other chains, then the gigantic shopping centres mushroomed on greenfield sites on the outskirts of town, and now the big investors are moving back into the city centres, where new, so-called shopping halls, shopping streets and centres for 'shopping experiences' are being created. A good example of this latest trend is the planning currently under way in Germany for the redesigning of downtown railway stations and the areas surrounding them as commercial centres.

Under these conditions it goes without saying that there needs to be some radical rethinking about how, for example, people can be given the chance of setting up small, independent businesses again.

When the small get elbowed out by the huge, we are often told: 'That's just the way things are.' After all, in a free market economy, competition rules, and in the so-called free-market play of one force against another, the cheaper, better and more efficient supplier is going to win the day. So the argument goes. This claim, however, is patently untrue; in view of the massive support which the large-scale projects enjoy in reality, it is simply untenable. For example, in Bielefeld, the city in northern Germany where I live, the transformation of the railway station building into a shopping centre will be financed up to 90 per cent by public funds, i.e. our taxes. The result, however, will belong to the privatized Railway Inc. (Bahn AG), which then will charge high rents to small shop-owners. That means they pay twice, while 90 per cent of the construction expenditures will be presented as a gift to the railway company. The fact is that over the last fifteen years, negotiated and backed at the political level, the course has quite deliberately been set in favour of big capital. We can inform ourselves about it every day in the newspapers and on TV, if we want to. So it is not the natural growth processes of free-market mechanisms that are ruining the smaller businesses, but deliberate political favouritism towards the big ones.

This course is being pursued at all levels. On the level of the International Monetary Fund and the World Bank, whose structural adjustment programmes force the governments of countries in the South to adopt policies that favour the big international banks, traders and manufacturers operating on the world market, as opposed to policies which would provide for the basic needs and social security of their own populations. And on the level of the General Agreement on Tariffs and Trade (GATT) talks, later part of the World Trade Organization (WTO), which since 1986 have included the agricultural sector in world-wide free trade, allowing the highly subsidized American agri-industrialist grain farmer to compete with the African peasant with a small sorghum crop in the free play of forces on the local African market for staple foods.

We find ample evidence of these same tendencies in the policies of the Organization for Economic Cooperation and Development (OECD) which designed and negotiated the Multilateral Agreement on Investment (MAI) as well as in the directives of the EU, whose agricultural policies have invariably targeted small and medium-scale farming operations for elimination. Its subsidies are for the agri-businessmen and factory farms; they only harm genuine peasants. Subsidies are paid per hectare, for instance. If you have a lot, you get a lot. Small and medium-scale farms cannot compete with the low prices that agri-industrialists are able to offer thanks to their high subsidies. And although the reasons why peasant production is dying out are more than well-known, the latest EU agricultural policies, outlined in the Agenda 2000, make no attempt whatsoever to address this crucial problem.

Between 1980 and 1993, the German government drastically lowered the tax rate paid by businesses on their profits from 33.6 to 18.3 per cent. At the same time, social welfare has been cut back, employment has been 'flexibilized' and the tax burden on employees has risen considerably (Klauss 1997: 12). It remains to be seen whether the Social Democrat–Green coalition currently in power will be willing or able to alter this course of events. And not every business is the same. Large companies, who can easily move production to less expensive venues offshore, pay only 28–30 per cent of business taxes collected by the government, whereas medium-sized businesses contribute about 66 per cent to the total revenue levied. Especially at present, despite the fact that the German export economy is booming, even the most hesitant hints that the re-distribution of wealth from the bottom to the top might be halted are greeted by big businesses with indignant threats to leave the country.

As profits continue to grow in Germany, so does unemployment. This phenomenon has been christened 'jobless growth' – a misleading phrase given the German use of the word 'job' to denote badly paid short-term contracts with poor social insurance, since 'jobs' in this sense are exactly what are on the increase, while secure and better-paid occupations and work situations are disappearing in a massive wave of rationalization.

The Urban Service Metropolis

But what has all this got to do with cities and their future?

To start with, cities are the places in whose conference halls and offices the policies I have been outlining are devised and set in motion. Or more accurately, the metropolises are where these developmental trends originate. Indeed, they have been designed specifically for this purpose, with tower blocks, motorways, airports, congress halls, shopping malls, leisure parks, hotel complexes and trade fair pavilions laid on for the international business community and political jet-set. These metropolitan trappings are now being aped by medium-sized cities and towns as well.

Cities, furthermore, repeat the pattern of globalization policies internally. The city is no longer regarded as the place where people of different ages, classes and genders make their lives together. Instead, cities are modelled on business concerns, as 'City Incorporated'.

For example, a municipality in the federal state of Hessen recently voted to build the latest shopping centre on the outskirts of town, despite the fact that permission for the project had long since been refused on economic and city planning grounds. But the big new supermarket would then have been built in the neighbouring town, and nobody wanted that, on account of the competition and the loss of revenue it would have entailed. For years, according to Wolfram Elsner, economic incentives at the municipal level have taken the form of 'prophylactic undercutting' to increase competitiveness; in the municipalities, just as at the national level, war has been waged with enticing offers to attract the big investor (Elsner 1998: 780). Presents are made of building sites, development costs are covered by the public purse, municipal building authorities devote the majority of their time to the projects of big investors, whose safety and hygiene requirements are met by public services. It is no wonder that the municipal coffers are empty.

Would it perhaps not be more appropriate if local development policies focused on those who, in terms of economic structure, offer genuine commitment to the locality instead? What about the corner shop, the small restaurant, the plumber, the joiner, all the small trade businesses and shops which do not summarily pack up and go somewhere else whenever it suits them, or suddenly decide to invest their capital in a more profitable sector. These kinds of businesses provide jobs for life and that is why those who own them or work in them have a strong attachment to the local community.

Instead of supporting small economic units, however, one has the impression that municipal and state officials are hindering them. Butcher shops in Germany are a case in point. The stringent conditions they have to fulfil may well be appropriate for a sausage factory, but in the context of a small butcher's business they smack suspiciously of ruinous chicanery. For example, butchers are charged from 200 to 300 deutschmarks for each chemical analysis of their premises by the health authorities, whose ridiculously convoluted regulations include the elimination of all right angles on work surfaces! It is common knowledge that most cases of food poisoning do not originate with small local producers or retailers. Bovine Spongiform Encephalitis (BSE or mad cow disease), the potential perils of genetically modified (GM) foodstuffs, and contamination with pesticides are the results of large-scale industrial production for world markets by chemical multi-nationals and food factories.

Twenty years ago, there were 168 butcher shops serving the 300,000 inhabitants of Bielefeld. Today only twenty-six are left. Those people who have lost their small businesses over the last ten to twenty years must find it a particularly bitter irony that the mushrooming 'Market Centres' (usually Americanized as 'Centers') being built by big investors are made to simulate artificially the look and feel of small businesses, albeit with the use of badly paid part-time employees or else with a new kind of pseudo-self-employment, namely by people who 'lease' the business franchise, and have to work most of the time to pay the lease. They are playing at older-style city or small-town business, without delivering the use value that this kind of business structure once really had for town dwellers. Instead, they offer articles for the yuppie consumer whose career has been made possible only by the destruction of the authentic, socially functional city.

Instead of changing course, however, the trend now is to sell off the municipal 'family silver'. For example, in a very small rural town in eastern Westphalia in the north-west of Germany, 3 ha of communal land were recently sold to reduce the municipality's debt. This example demonstrates very clearly how economic values are being rapidly and drastically reshuffled. The land sold was originally common land to which all inhabitants of the rural village had access and which provided grazing for their geese and small livestock. This meant that they were able to secure an appreciable part of their subsistence themselves. In the bigger towns and cities common land is also being sold off. To attract the big investors, common public property such as municipal land, revenues and services are handed over to big private enterprises. Related to this phenomenon are the recent campaigns to force certain population groups out of particularly chic shopping streets, sanitizing them for the use of the more well-heeled consumers. In Cologne railway station, for example, the public toilets have been taken over by an enterprise called (in German) McClean. Now one has to pay 2 deutschmarks to use the facilities, four times the amount that one used to hand over to the local toilet cleaner.

For a few years, it seemed that the strategy of giving preferential treatment to the rich and big business in order to swell the municipal coffers to such an extent that everyone benefited from the trickle-down effect was paying off; but this has not lasted long. In a recent report on city development in Frankfurt, Martin Wentz (1996), the head of the municipal planning department, wrote the following: 'For 30 years of prosperity, the fact that the economically stronger population, tradespeople and small businesses were leaving in a steady stream was accepted almost with goodwill.' Frankfurt was meant to become *the* financial centre for big banks and corporations, but obviously not a city to live in. 'Today, all the negative effects, culminating in the severely limited financial powers of the city of Frankfurt on Main, are apparent.' The same report suggests an innovative concept of city planning as a possible way out of the situation. Phrases such as '*combined use* – of flats, offices and small businesses', '*combination* – of types of buildings', 'spatial *separation* of functions' (emphasis added) dominate in this document. Summarized in one sentence, this means: 'In future, city planning as development policy *also* has to concentrate on keeping and binding together both *human* AND economic resources, if the *variety* and the functionability of the city is to be retained' (*Frankfurter Rundschau*, 2 February 1996).

In our growth-oriented culture, however, the imagination to see how this could happen seems to be lacking. As in so many other undeniably critical analyses which warn us about the urgency of adopting alternative approaches to urban planning, the recommendations for Frankfurt in the end amounted to nothing more than *Standortpolitik* once again, i.e. renewed efforts to attract big capital in order to create jobs.

Subsistence Orientation in Today's City

If our cities are to have a future shaped by urban community life and not by the profit motives of big business, then we need to shift from a money orientation to a subsistence orientation, i.e. to a system of values that looks first at the direct use of things and relationships in everyday life, and holds this to be more important than money. A subsistence orientation incorporates a world-view that seeks immediacy and satisfaction: having enough to eat, warmth, a roof over one's head and pleasure in being satisfied – in other words, one that values leisure and rejects the eternal nagging cry of 'have to' and the unremitting struggle against a contrived scarcity of resources that we believe we have to wage in order to fulfil the insatiable and imaginary needs that we have been talked into thinking that we have.

Unlike both the socialist and capitalist approaches, the subsistence orientation is not a model, or a Utopia, or a dream of a golden age, but a concept of action aimed at setting new and different processes in motion. Subsistence orientation is a plea for a re-orientation, a fresh look at relations and the setting of different priorities in decision-making. It could be applied equally well by WTO negotiators, heads of municipal building departments, city councillors and the woman and man in the street, if they based their thinking and actions on the following five principles:

1. Priority is given to the useful, to what is needed.
2. Small has priority over big.
3. Personal relationships are better than anonymous ones.
4. Decentralized solutions are better than centralized ones.
5. The local takes precedence over the international.

The word 'subsistence' means 'existing through oneself' and refers to 'the characteristic of independence', as Erika Märke has observed (1986: 138f). It also has a lot to do with providing for oneself, and self-determination.

Anyone who thinks a subsistence orientation should be banished 'to the stone age' or 'to the Middle Ages' or to the Third World, because in our developed society we have allegedly outgrown both self-provision and worries about subsistence, has failed to recognize that subsistence does not disappear, but rather changes through history and takes different forms in different contexts. At the start of the twenty-first century, subsistence looks different from the way it did twenty centuries ago or even fifty years ago. Subsistence in the city takes on forms that are different from those that it adopts in the country. Subsistence displays different characteristics in households with children than it does in childless households. But no matter when, where, or who practises it, subsistence means providing for oneself.

Subsistence refers to the manner in which people produce their own lives and reproduce them day by day, as well as to how and to what degree they hold these processes in their own hands in terms of material, substance and society. In the course of the twentieth century, though, we have relinquished our own control over these processes more and more. Absurdly enough, current political efforts to create jobs, allegedly in order to assure the subsistence of working people, are in fact the cause of ever-increasing insecurity about subsistence. This is because by 'jobs', only waged or salaried jobs are meant. No longer does anyone think in terms of small, self-employed tradespeople, independent retailers and other businesses, nor of associations of small independent businesses in the form of co-operatives, for example. Instead, everyone assumes that the only options are big companies and wage labour. Self-employment and *providing for oneself* in terms of supporting oneself, of 'earning one's living' rather than profit maximization, are dismissed as positively uneconomic; something to be prevented and destroyed. The net result is a population at the mercy of the commercial interests of big business. Everything, all the necessities of daily life – food, services, labour power, communication and even social contacts – are transformed into commodities marketed and sold to us by the big corporations.

When I speak of a 'subsistence orientation', this dismissive response often ensues: 'Oh, yes, money is bad all right, and we should get rid of it. But a complex society like ours can't function without money, so we have to bow to its mechanisms.' This is pure nonsense. First of all, we do without money and *do things* without money every day: in the care that a mother gives to her children, in relationships between friends and neighbours, in everyday acts of helpfulness and in providing for the young and the old. Honorary positions, clubs and associations and all sorts of other non-remunerated initiatives are indeed the most dynamic elements of our society.

Second, it *is* possible to organize exchange without money, even in complex societies. Maybe not in the entire global society at once, or even in an entire country, but locally and regionally. Here I am thinking of 'exchange circles' (in which people exchange services, skills and produce with a local currency which excludes interest) which are thriving in many German cities, even without the governmental support that they deserve.

However, my main point here is a different one. I contend that the heart of the problem lies in how we deal with money, rather than in money itself. In face-to-face relations and within local exchange networks reciprocity and the relationship itself are the important factors in the use of money. The bigger the enterprise, the more everything is handled in the manner of a supermarket, and the more anonymous are the relations of exchange, the greater is the power of the money per se. Therefore, one market is not the same as another. In southern Mexico, I did research in a town of 100,000 inhabitants in a region throughout which the peasants, fishers, tradeswomen and craftspeople determine their prices according to who is in front of them; their criteria are the extent of their social bonds with that person, and whether he or she owes them a favour or not. The result is not economic chaos (as many economists might predict) but a vibrant and thriving economy (see Bennholdt-Thomsen 1994).

In our cities, we do not need supermarkets and bogus marketplaces. Instead, we need small businesses, shops run by their owners and a real marketplace open to all. There are enough experts and interested individuals to transform the reality of our cities along the lines mentioned above, to put these into practice too; but the plans of prospective founders of very small businesses are frustrated by conditions imposed at the political level – conditions such as having to provide parking, separate toilet facilities for men and women and stringent hygiene rules, as well as a heavier tax burden than large-scale businesses. This is the case in Germany and the EU in any event. It is also becoming increasingly difficult to access loans, with the growing tendency of banks to reject applicants from medium-sized businesses out of preference for lending to large businesses, especially in the investment, insurance and pensions sectors instead.

The Wuppertal Institute has correctly ascertained that whereas the big corporations have rationalized away large numbers of jobs over the past decade, small and medium-sized enterprises have been creating new ones. Smaller businesses are in fact still regarded as the nation's trade school, where apprentices are ably prepared for the future. In September 2000 the institute organized a conference on small and medium-sized businesses. However, once again, genuinely small self-run enterprises were ignored since the conference was open only to businesses with more than fifty employees. Is even the Wuppertal Institute, an organization espousing the idea of sustainable economic activity, unable to free itself from the fixation on wage-labour and profit maximization? In our society, too, there is a sufficient number of people who want to exchange their money for the necessities of living on the market, and no more. These people deal with money in a different way. In market relations that follow a subsistence logic, reliability is more important to those involved than the anonymous race for profits, and more important than being able to shop as cheaply as possible (see Bennholdt-Thomsen and Mies 1999: 109–23).

Small-scale enterprises that approach the market from a subsistence perspective have an important role to play in the resolution of many of the environmental and social problems that we currently face. For a time, the market for organic products functioned according to this subsistence logic in Germany. Now, however, this sector is being appropriated by supermarket chains, and the struggle for market shares has begun in organic farming and sales of organic produce. Thus organic produce has become an important new source of profit for the factory farms, once again to the detriment of the small corner store, the small-scale farmer and the environment.

One kind of private property is not necessarily the same as another. The current wave of privatization occasioned by the policy of globalization, liberalization and privatization (GLP) views private property as the basis for profit maximization. The private property of small tradespeople and others with small businesses, small-scale farmers and home-owners, however, is the basis for their subsistence. To paraphrase the saying from Greek medicine, 'It's the size of the private property (the dose) that makes the poison'.

The belief in size, in profit maximization and wage-labour does indeed poison social relations in our cities. This is not only true in the sense that the small are being progressively expropriated by the ongoing preferential treatment of the large, but the community as such is being dispossessed and thus destroyed. Municipal land that up to now has provided space for allotments, for example, is being sold off to big investors; in other words, common land is being privatized. The same is happening to public rooms. More and more German municipalities are transforming the administration of the rooms and halls in schools, kindergartens and other public buildings into a business with a commercial cost–benefit analysis. When no lessons are taking place in them, the rooms are to be rented out. From the subsistence perspective, though, such rooms are clearly common spaces to which the whole community should have access without paying. What our cities need is not more money, but more life. Land and rooms should be deprivatized and communalized; i.e. instead of a state or a central administration decreeing what happens to them, the neighbourhood and local community should determine how they are used and administer them themselves. The dynamic element in our cities, the guarantor of social peace, is not going to be profit maximization, but social solidarity. The many-sided ways of being dependent on one another, including the market and money relations *within* the community, are the true life blood of our cities.

Those municipalities which have declared themselves MAI-free have understood this, too, at least in part. One major reason for their dissidence is the proposed regulation that any preferential conditions aimed at promoting one's own economy must, according to the draft MAI document, be made available to international corporations as well. Any conditions relating, for example, to environmental protection or rules pertaining to the creation of employment opportunities in a given city or even to aesthetic considerations, such as the height of buildings for instance, do *not* have to be fulfilled by foreign investors, in so far as they deviate from international standards. Otherwise one would be committing protectionism, *the* ultimate sin against GLP (see Mies and Werlhof 1998).

Summary

Below I would like to catalogue the elements which could give our cities a subsistence orientation in the form of ten criteria. These criteria are based on self-provision and self-determination, and will be listed starting with the smallest living unit, then going on to the neighbourhood, then to the whole city and finally to the level of the region.

1. In relation to accommodation, subsistence orientation means having the space for production for everyday needs, instead of being forcibly attached to the consumption machine: i.e. space for the storage and the tools required for home production, and also for mementos – a place with enough space for life, including life lived over the years.

2. Living also includes one's living environment. Inge Meta Hülbusch (1981) has called this relationship *Innenhaus und Außenhaus* (inside/inner-house and outside/outer-house). Here I mean that for genuine use-value and real satisfaction, more than just four walls are needed for the act of living. Also necessary is an environment in which, for example, a child experiences and becomes familiar with her or his world, or in which neighbourhood can be developed. The 'complementarity of inner–outer' is, according to a study conducted by Libor Schelhasse and Sonja Nebel (1998) in various conurbations in the South, the most important basis for securing the economy of everyday life. One of the biggest problems of our growth economy culture, however, lies in the fact that we have forgotten just how much people need social contacts in order to be happy – the family, the neighbourhood, the part of town they live in, their circle of friends and the daily culture of interaction in the city.

3. One important element of subsistence-oriented production to be found in our cities is what John F. C. Turner (1976) identified in the so-called 'popular quarters' in Mexico City. He shows how important it is particularly for people with low incomes to build for themselves, or else to be able to make decisions about how their own four walls, and above all the 'outer house', should look. Such houses can be far better adapted to the vagaries of life than the well-intentioned but dreadful designs that typify so much of state-controlled public housing. Above all, though, subsistence-oriented housing is geared to community life and economic exchange in the quarter, thus allowing the development of far more reliable social structures than those arising from paid labour (see Douthwaite and Diefenbacher 1998).

4. Subsistence-oriented production in the city is made up of many small

businesses. The International Labour Organization (ILO) in fact actually calls for official support for the smallest of the small, the so-called informal sector, also known as the shadow economy, not only in the countries of the South, but in those of the North as well (*Frankfurter Rundschau*, 29 May 1999). The ILO's argument is that without jobs, even if people are kept going with public handouts, the cities will collapse. And since formal employment in the form of waged work is nowhere in sight, the ILO urges the regulation of informal jobs instead of discrimination against them.

5. A similar recommendation is made by John F. C. Turner. With increasing deregulation and retreat of the state from any form of responsibility towards its citizens, it is particularly interesting that this recommendation comes from a man who calls himself an anarchist. He says that the poorer we are or become, the more important it is to have proscriptive rules to support and stimulate the creation of a self-regulating form (Turner 1976). Here he is appealing to the state to guarantee freedoms and spaces for the community instead of hastening ahead with privatization for the benefit of transnational corporations. Turner advocates a process I have called 'Communalization', by which I mean the protection and the re-creation of common land and spaces.

6. The elements of an urban economic structure sketched out here also fit in very well with the ideas of feminist city-planners and architects. For them a desirable city structure is one which allows a mixture of functions and uses, as opposed to 'monofunctionality' to the point where nothing is left but vast, stark residential landscapes with no infrastructure, 'which, besides the lack of opportunity for communication, also mean long, to some extent additional (e.g. driving the children around, etc.) trips for shopping and other chores' (Hünlein 1993: 118). A mixture of functions and uses is necessary too if work in the house, in paid employment and in the family are to be combined.

7. The social location we are speaking about in subsistence orientation closely resembles the female point of view *vis-à-vis* city planning. This is no coincidence, since it is women who are responsible for subsistence in our society. Conversely, though, this gender-specific separation of responsibilities as propounded in the dominating discourse is exactly what leads to an understanding of economy as resembling a permanent state of war. Because capitalist patriarchy first assigns loving and caring specifically to women as their duty within our society, and then makes the loving and caring work of women invisible with regard to the purported 'real economy', it becomes 'legitimate' to run that economy like a war, because these vital functions are being looked after 'elsewhere'.

With the concept of subsistence orientation this separation, an unfortunate division we have in our heads, can be overcome. What are labelled

Subsistence in Practice **230**

'women's concerns' are in reality the subsistence concerns of the society as a whole (see Schreyögg, n.d.: 3f).

8. Subsistence orientation and community orientation, i.e. an orientation to social context and community ties instead of to economic competition, are closely linked. Community orientation cannot be created idealistically; it needs an object, some kind of base material. And just as love in the family is 'produced' by a good meal or a warm blanket, so social closeness comes about through the exchange of things, including goods, that are necessary for daily well-being.

9. Subsistence-oriented urban economic life would not mean doing without technology. Rather, the implications are that in nearly everything related to technology, 'e.g. public utilities', decentralization is to be given preference; exactly the opposite of the present trend. The resuscitation of urban subsistence technologies is an urgent task.

10. The city cannot survive without the countryside. To secure the subsistence of the city and to consolidate the urban economy, it is essential for the city to become integrated on a regional level, not tethered to international business, as is increasingly the case. The city would draw its supplies from the region and vice versa, thus strengthening the regional market; small and middle-sized farms would continue to exist, and the cultural landscape would be preserved.

(Translated from German by Patricia Skorge)

References

Bennholdt-Thomsen, Veronika (ed.) (1994) *Juchitán – Stadt der Frauen*, Reinbek: Rowohlt.

Bennholdt-Thomsen, Veronika and Maria Mies (1999) *The Subsistence Perspective: Beyond the Globalized Economy*, London: Zed Books.

Douthwaite, Richard (1996) *Short Circuit. Strengthening Local Economies for Security in an Unstable World*, Dublin, Liliput Press.

Douthwaite, Richard and Hans Diefenbacher (1998) *Jenseits der Globalisierung. Handbuch für lokales Wirtschaften*, Mainz: Grünewald (adapted German version of Douthwaite 1996).

Elsner, Wolfram (1998) 'Die Zukunft unserer Städte und Regionen. Städte und Regionen im Konkurrenzkampf und die Kehrseiten des Neuen Regionalismus', *WSI Mitteilungen*, 11, pp. 778–86.

Hülbusch, Meta Inge (1981) *Innenhaus und Außenhaus*, Schriftenreihe der Organisationseinheit Architektur–Stadtplanung–Landschaftsplanung, Schriftenreihe 01, no. 033, 2nd edn, Kassel.

Hünlein, Ute (1993) 'Regionalplanung – Frauen mischen sich ein! Ein Werkstattbericht über die Arbeit der Regionalplanungsgruppe FOPA Rhein-Main e.V.', *Frei.Räume, Streitschrift der feministischen Organisationen von Planerinnen und Architektinnen, FOPA e.V.*, 6, pp. 115–20.

What Really Keeps Our Cities Alive?   **231**

Klauss, Martin (1997) *Politik für mehr Reichtum. Daten und Anmerkungen zur Entwicklung von Reichtum und Armut in Deutschland*, Freiburg: CfS.

Märke, Erika (1986) *Ein Weg aus der Abhängigkeit. Die ungewisse Zukunft des informellen Sektors in Entwicklungsländern*, Heidelberg. Forschungsstatte der Ev. Studiengemeinschaft, 1986.

Mies, Maria and Vandana Shiva (1993) *Ecofeminism*, London: Zed Books.

Mies, Maria and Claudia von Werlhof (1998) *Lizenz zum Plündern. Das Multilaterale Abkommen über Investitionen (MAI). Globalisierung der Konzernherrschaft – und was wir dagegen tun können*, Hamburg: Rotbuch.

Schelhasse, Libor and Sonja Nebel (1998) *Komplementarität Innen – Aussen. Kennzeichen einfachen Wohnens in Ballungsräumen des Südens*, Munster, LIT Verlag

Schreyögg, Friedel (n.d.), 'Beteiligung von Gleichstellungsstellen an der Stadt- und Bauplanung', in *Deutscher Städtetag, Frauen verändern ihre Stadt, Beratungsergebnisse der Kommission 'Frauen in der Stadt' und der Fachkommission 'Wohnungswesen' des Deutschen Städtetages zur Wohnungspolitik*, n.p., pp. 3–6.

Turner, John F. C. (1976) *Housing by People. Towards Autonomy in Building Environments*, London: Marion Boyars.

Wentz, Martin (1996) 'Die Zukunft des Städtischen. Wohnen, Arbeiten, Verkehr und Freizeit: die Entwicklungsplanung der Stadt Frankfurt am Main für die nächsten Jahrzehnte', *Frankfurter Rundschau*, 2 February 1996.

C   Gender and Globalization

[19]

Feminist Economics **9(2–3)**, 2003, 163–183

GLOBALIZATION AND WOMEN'S PAID WORK: EXPANDING FREEDOM?

Christine M. Koggel

ABSTRACT

In *Development as Freedom*, Amartya Sen takes expanding freedom to be the primary end and the principal means of development. I discuss his emphasis on women's agency as central to development theory and practice and the strategies he advocates for enhancing it. Recent work in feminist economics and postcolonial studies tests Sen's complex account of freedom. Further levels of complexity need to be added when we examine how global forces of power interact with local systems of oppression in ways that often limit women's freedom. This argument rests on an analysis of how globalization affects a domain of freedom that is a central concern for Sen, that of increasing women's freedom to work outside the home as a way of strengthening their agency. Attending to elements missing in Sen's account will enhance freedom in women's lives.

KEYWORDS
Amartya Sen, globalization, freedom, agency, women's paid work, postcolonial feminist studies

INTRODUCTION

Globalization has reshaped many issues: international relations, population growth, development, human rights, the environment, labor, healthcare, and poverty, among others. It has increased our awareness of the profound ways in which policies and practices in one region can affect the livelihoods of people in other regions, and even in the world as a whole. Recent research in ethics explores the implications of globalization as it affects these and many other areas of inquiry. Some of the products of this philosophical inquiry are the evolution of a language of human rights; attempts to formulate a global ethic; accounts of cross-cultural judgment and interpretation; and research on development ethics. In this context, feminist economics and Third World, postcolonial, and global studies have been vitally important for highlighting the need to be aware of power relations at both the global and local levels when providing accounts of development processes and

Feminist Economics ISSN 1354-5701 print/ISSN 1466-4372 online © 2003 IAFFE
http://www.tandf.co.uk/journals
DOI: 10.1080/1354570022000077935

ARTICLES

policies.[1] These theorists argue that many of these processes and policies
have had a detrimental impact on women in domains such as the
workplace, education, and healthcare, and in terms of their social,
political, and economic status and participation. This work is reshaping
both the conceptual terrain of these issues and the policies being framed
by national and international organizations.

Amartya Sen opens *Development as Freedom* by acknowledging this global
context of increasingly close linkages of trade, communication, and ideas
across countries and the conditions of "unprecedented opulence" and
"remarkable deprivation, destitution, and oppression" that coexist both
within countries and across rich and poor countries (Amartya Sen 1999: xi).
In fact, Sen provides a rather dismal picture of contemporary life:
"persistence of poverty and unfulfilled elementary needs, occurrence of
famines and widespread hunger, violation of elementary political freedoms
as well as of basic liberties, extensive neglect of the interests and agency of
women, and worsening threats to our environment and to the sustainability
of our economic and social lives" (Sen 1999: xi). A central goal of
development theory and policy is to address these problems that are made
all the more stark (and some would say even sustained) by the
unprecedented opulence in other parts of the world. Sen's solution is to
take the expansion of freedom or the removal of various types of
unfreedoms "both as the primary end and as the principal means of
development" (Sen 1999: xii). Development, he writes, "consists of the
removal of various types of unfreedom that leave people with little choice
and little opportunity of exercising their reasoned agency" (Sen 1999: xii).
Sen further argues that giving *women* freedom to exercise their agency
should be a key goal of development policy:

> The extensive reach of women's agency is one of the more neglected
> areas of development studies, and most urgently in need of correction.
> Nothing, arguably, is as important today in the political economy of
> development as an adequate recognition of political, economic and
> social participation and leadership of women. This is indeed a crucial
> aspect of 'development as freedom.'
>
> (Sen 1999: 203)

Before proceeding, I want to clarify my approach by making two points.
First, as shown in the section that follows, Sen provides a complex account
of the interconnectedness of various kinds of freedom. He argues that
increasing women's freedom to work outside the home is crucial for
increasing their freedom in domains such as the home, healthcare,
education, reproductive control, and social and political life. Clearly,
women's long and continued exclusion from the workforce has limited
their freedom, and Sen's work in drawing connections between the
freedom to work and other sorts of freedoms is important not only to

GLOBALIZATION AND WOMEN'S PAID WORK

development theory but to feminist theory more generally. My argument is not that women's workforce participation should not be promoted or that increasing their freedom in this domain does not have a positive impact on their freedom in other domains. Rather I raise questions about whether paid employment necessarily increases women's freedom and agency in all places and, specifically, under conditions of globalization. Second, there has been a longstanding debate about whether paid work necessarily improves the status and material standard of women and the circumstances that make this situation more or less likely. This debate has encompassed related issues such as the family wage and the double shift.[2] In this paper, I discuss some of these nonliberating aspects, but my focus is on women's paid work in the current context of globalization. If not entirely absent in Sen's account, power and oppression are not sufficiently recognized as factors of inequality in women's lives that are relevant to the kinds of policies required, at both the global and local levels, for increasing women's freedom and agency.

I. WOMEN'S AGENCY AND WELL-BEING

Sen understands freedom to be the end as well as the means of development, in the sense that progress is evaluated in terms of whether freedoms are enhanced and whether enhancing freedom is effective for achieving development:

> [d]evelopment has to be more concerned with enhancing the lives we lead and the freedoms we enjoy. Expanding the freedoms we have rea- son to value not only makes our lives richer and more unfettered, but also allows us to be fuller social persons, exercising our own volitions and interacting with – and influencing – the world in which we live.
>
> (Sen 1999: 14–15)

According to Sen, development theorists need to view various kinds of freedom (political, economic, and social) as inextricably interconnected, and they also need to know about the empirical connections that obtain when policies that limit freedom in one domain decrease freedoms in other domains: "[e]conomic unfreedom can breed social unfreedom, just as social or political unfreedom can also foster economic unfreedom" (Sen 1999: 8). Paying attention to kinds and levels of freedom, argues Sen, allows us to be sensitive to the ways in which human diversity and the particularities of social practices and political contexts affect one's ability to satisfy basic needs, perform various human functions, and live lives reflective of human flourishing.

Another vital aspect of Sen's theory of development is that he shifts the focus from people as patients of development to people as agents of development processes and change:

165

ARTICLES

... this freedom-centered understanding of economics and of the process of development is very much an agent-oriented view. With adequate social opportunities, individuals can effectively shape their own destiny and help each other. They need not be seen primarily as passive recipients of the benefits of cunning development programs. There is indeed a strong rationale for recognizing the positive role of free and sustainable agency.

(Sen 1999: 11)

In Chapter 8 of his *Development as Freedom*, Sen distinguishes strategies for promoting women's well-being from strategies that promote women's agency. The former is welfarist in the sense that women are treated as the passive recipients of policies designed to remove inequalities and achieve better conditions for them. An agency approach takes women to be active agents who themselves promote and achieve social and political transformations that can then better the lives of both women and men. Sen acknowledges that the two approaches overlap, since agency strategies have the goal of removing inequalities that affect women's well-being and well-being strategies need to draw on women's agency to effect real changes. However, Sen argues that distinguishing the two is important because treating a person as an agent is fundamentally different from treating him or her as a patient: "[u]nderstanding the agency role is thus central to recognizing people as responsible persons: not only are we well or ill, but also we act or refuse to act, and can choose to act one way rather than another" (Sen 1999: 190).

Sen views the promotion of women's agency as vital not only for improving the economic and social power of women, but for challenging and changing entrenched values and social practices that support gender bias in the distribution of basic goods such as food and healthcare and in the treatment of women and girls within families. He then makes the strong claim that the "changing agency of women is one of the major mediators of economic and social change, and its determination as well as consequences closely relate to many of the central features of the development process" (Sen 1999: 202).

On the face of it, feminists could hardly quarrel with Sen's emphasis on the promotion of women's agency as a way of enhancing their well-being. After all, what better way for well-being to be measured than to have it within women's control as active agents and placed in the context of women's lives? Yet Sen's account of agency involves more than giving women the power to make their own decisions regarding reproduction or childcare, to change the gendered division of labor, and to improve female access to healthcare in their own social and political contexts. He uses empirical studies to substantiate and defend particular policies for increasing women's freedom and agency. He argues that agency in the

GLOBALIZATION AND WOMEN'S PAID WORK

above-mentioned domains is integrally connected with freedoms in other domains such as the freedom to work outside the home: "freedom in one area (that of being able to work outside the household) seems to help foster freedom in others (enhancing freedom from hunger, illness, and relative deprivation)" (Sen 1999: 194).

Sen notes that in general terms, empirical data show that women's well-being is strongly influenced by "women's ability to earn an independent income, to find employment outside the home, to have ownership rights and to have literacy and be educated participants in decisions inside and outside the family" (Sen 1999: 191).[3] These abilities are aspects of agency in that women are *doing* things and making choices that then give them voice, social standing, independence, and empowerment. In Sen's own words on the case of paid employment:

> ... working outside the home and earning an independent income tend to have a clear impact on enhancing the social standing of a woman in the household and the society. Her contribution to the prosperity of the family is then more visible, and she also has more voice, because of being less dependent on others. Further, outside employment often has useful 'educational' effects, in terms of exposure to the world outside the household, thus making her agency more effective.
>
> (Sen 1999: 192)

My purpose is not to critically analyze the data Sen uses or all of the policies he suggests, but to focus on the connection he makes between promoting women's workforce participation and increasing their agency. For, as soon as we note that doing paid work outside the home is a key policy in his account, we are led to ask: does this necessarily increase women's agency and well-being? What factors might affect the outcome? Among possible factors could be whether women's paid work is located inside or outside the home; whether they have sole responsibility for domestic work in addition to their paid work; whether they work in the formal or informal sector; whether other family members have control over their income; whether the labor market permits high or low earnings; and whether jobs provide safety and leave provisions or control over conditions of work. These factors, which vary from location to location, have an impact on women's agency in local contexts as well as in the global context of multinational corporations. My aim is to examine global factors in more detail to understand how multinational corporations, for example, operate in specific local contexts in ways that sometimes enhance, but often limit, women's freedom and agency. The central question in my analysis thus becomes: is Sen's account sufficiently discerning of the ways in which global forces of power and local systems of oppression operate and interact in ways that limit women's freedom and agency even when they have paid work?

167

II. WOMEN'S PAID WORK AND THE GLOBAL CONTEXT

Sen's account, as noted, is rooted in empirical analysis, sensitive to the particularities of issues and policies, appreciative of diverse human needs and abilities, and responsive to various social conditions and political contexts. Yet there is reason to worry that there is still something missing, particularly when we examine the issue of women's workforce participation in the context of globalization. A good place to draw out the implications of this examination is with Chandra Mohanty's work. She examines both the local and the global aspects of oppressive conditions in women's lives. Thinking globally means being aware of the ways in which women's work is shaped by the contemporary arena of global corporations, markets, and capitalism. She notes:

> Third-World women workers (defined in this context as both women from the geographical Third World and immigrant and indigenous women of color in the U.S. and Western Europe) occupy a specific social location in the international division of labor which *illuminates* and *explains* crucial features of the capitalist processes of exploitation and domination. These are features of the social world that are usually obfuscated or mystified in discourses about the 'progress' and 'development' (e.g., the creation of jobs for poor, Third-World women as the markers of economic and social advancement) that is assumed to 'naturally' accompany the triumphal rise of global capitalism.
>
> (Chandra Mohanty 1997: 7, her emphasis)

Mohanty's description of discourses about progress and development suggests that providing women with jobs *may* be as inadequate a measure of economic and social advancement as are increases in the GNP or income levels. One of the reasons for this, according to Mohanty, is global capitalism itself and the processes of exploitation and domination generated by it.

Multinational corporate executives and financial institutions are motivated by increasing profits and decreasing costs, not by improving women's workforce participation or their freedom and agency. The drive to decrease costs means that particular women are recruited into specific kinds of jobs, but it does not mean that these women have choices that effectively change their levels of freedom. However, I want to temper the strong connection that Mohanty makes between global capitalism and exploitation by suggesting that women's paid work in a global context has mixed effects. It can provide opportunities for work not otherwise available to women in specific contexts, but it can and often does provide less than ideal work conditions. The complexity of factors relevant to a description of global corporations and their operations in specific locations means that opportunities for and conditions of work can change in both the short

168

GLOBALIZATION AND WOMEN'S PAID WORK

and long term. Yet while Mohanty can be said to ignore the positive aspects of global markets and corporations, she does pay attention to the details of women's lives at the local level. Her account, therefore, makes room for a more complex and sophisticated analysis (than she herself provides) of the sorts of global and local factors that can determine the kind of impact that increased workforce participation has on women's freedom and agency.

Mohanty, and the work of feminist economists on which she draws, rejects ahistorical and universal accounts of experiences shared by women, whether Third World women or all women in the workforce, and instead allows commonalities to emerge from detailed descriptions of the lives of working women in specific social contexts. Thus measuring women's increased participation in the workplace does not give us the whole story about the effect on their well-being or agency. For a fuller picture, we need to take account of the many barriers to women's freedom and agency, even when their participation in the workforce is permitted or increased, by examining not only the global context, but also the embeddedness of women's work in localized social practices and political institutions. Recognition of various forces of power at the global level is never far away in the analysis of the local.

Two of Mohanty's studies provide useful leads. In the first, Mohanty uses Maria Mies's work to analyze local systems of oppression affecting the working lives of the lace-makers of Narsapur in Andhra Pradesh, a state in south India. The second considers implications of Mohanty's discussion of electronics workers in the First World context of the Silicon Valley in California (USA) and demonstrates how multinational corporations often make use of gendered and racialized meanings in particular locations in ways that can limit rather than increase women's freedom and agency in the workplace and other domains. Highlighting local factors in the first example and global factors in the second serves to illustrate features of each. However, the descriptions also show that the local and the global cannot but intersect in the contemporary context of globalization.

The account of women's agency that emerges from these descriptions is inherently complex. Local and global factors and their interactions are not static, but are subject to changes in markets, economic conditions, labor demands, and so on. Whether change is possible depends on various factors, including the entrenchment of local gender norms, as illustrated by the example of lace-making in Narsapur. Moreover, even as women experience negative effects on their freedom in the workplace, there can be changes in gender norms and improvements in other spheres of women's lives, as illustrated by the example of electronics workers. A proper assessment of whether women's freedom and agency is improved or diminished needs these complex descriptions of local and global factors and their intersections in particular locations at particular times.

ARTICLES

As Maria Mies describes it, understanding the exploitative working conditions of the lace-makers in Narsapur requires understanding the power exercised by social norms in this location. Beliefs about women's proper sphere and the devaluation of their activity in the home, entrenched in this region's cultural practices, are not easily eliminated when women are allowed to "work." For the lace-makers, caste and gender work to transform beliefs about women's unequal status and power in a private sphere into a hierarchical ordering in which women's work in the production of lace is conceptualized as "leisure activity" with little pay, and where the products and proceeds of this industry are controlled by men. Mies demonstrates that the expansion of the lace industry into the global market "led not only to class differentiation within particular communities (Christians, Kapus) but also to the masculinization of all nonproduction jobs, especially of trade, and the total feminization of the production process. ... Men sell women's products and live on the profits from women's work" (Maria Mies 1982: 10). This gendered division of labor coupled with the conceptualization of lace-making as leisure, rather than as work, means that women have no control over their work hours or conditions of work, or even the proceeds of their "leisure" activity. In addition to their labor-intensive work of caring for families and maintaining households, they work six to eight hours a day making lace in confined spaces with poor lighting and little pay. Furthermore, this "leisure activity" is perceived as befitting the women's membership in a caste that promotes women's seclusion in the home as a status symbol. These women are both perceived as and perceive themselves as being of higher status than women who belong to castes of poor peasants or agricultural laborers. These local beliefs about proper gender and caste roles, and women's isolation from one another (because they are home-based), converge to prevent lace-makers from organizing to improve their conditions. They also cause the women themselves to cling to these symbols of higher status, even though women agricultural laborers of lower castes earn "considerably more in the course of a year than the lace workers" (Mies 1982: 15).

At the very least, this description tempers optimism about substantive gains to these women's freedom and agency, in either the private or public sphere, when they are permitted to join the workforce. What makes the case of lace-makers particularly problematic is that no one, not even the workers themselves, perceive them to be in the workforce. The conditions of their work are not only a function of globalized markets in lace, but also of their home-based work that makes them virtually invisible. The number of women dispersed throughout homes in many areas is high, and yet they do not count in labor statistics, where workers are those who earn a living outside the home. It is the men who control the industry and do the visible activities of buying and selling. In this example, the local details matter for an analysis of work and of *this* gendered and caste division of labor in which

GLOBALIZATION AND WOMEN'S PAID WORK

all the power is in the hands of those who control the markets, the capital, and the returns from the sales.[4] Here women are placed at the lowest and least visible part of the chain of a global industry and market in lace. Counting them as workers in local and international statistics on labor could of course make them visible in terms of numbers, but this in itself cannot change women's oppressive work conditions, for which other strategies would be needed, as discussed in Section III. Indeed, entrenched beliefs about gender and caste shape these women's lives in ways that limit their freedom and agency well beyond factors that could easily be measured in statistical reports on labor. Having "paid work" may do little to promote women's agency if work is inside the home and invisible and if income is appropriated by male heads of households.

The case of women workers in the Silicon Valley in California is different in that these women do perceive themselves to be workers and are also perceived to be so by others. Mohanty (1997) reports that in the 1980s, 80 to 90 percent of the laborer jobs on the shop floor of electronics factories in the Silicon Valley were held by women, half of which again were held by Asian immigrant women. She explains that Third World women's over-representation was the result of their being targeted and recruited into these underpaid jobs. The explanation, she notes:

> lies in the redefinition of work as temporary, supplementary, and un-skilled, in the construction of women as mothers and homemakers, and in the positioning of femininity as contradictory to factory work. In addition, the explanation also lies in the specific definition of Third-World, immigrant women as docile, tolerant, and satisfied with substandard wages.
>
> (Mohanty 1997: 18)

Diane Elson and Ruth Pearson's (1981) early research on women workers in the electronics industry of Southeast Asia throws light on the widespread beliefs within these industries about differences in the innate capacities of men and women and their income needs.

> Women are considered not only to have naturally nimble fingers, but also to be naturally more docile and willing to accept tough work dis-cipline, and naturally more suited to tedious, repetitious, monotonous work. Their lower wages are attributed to their secondary status in the labor market which is seen as a natural consequence of their ability to bear children.
>
> (Diane Elson and Ruth Pearson 1981: 149)

Evidence shows that these widespread beliefs about women play a role at all levels of upper and middle management, human resource departments, immediate supervisors, husbands and relatives, and the women themselves in ways that explain the recruitment of Asian immigrant women into jobs in

ARTICLES

California's Silicon Valley as well as the conditions of work that obtain in them. The effect of defining this work as temporary, unskilled, and tedious legitimizes entrapping these women into low-paying jobs, in which work conditions prevent them from engaging in union activity, political struggle, or collective action, activities that could change the exploitation and domination they face. Such systems of oppression that utilize gender and racial stereotypes structure the meaning and conditions of work for these electronic factory workers – and potentially, global perceptions as well.

Elisabeth Fussell's (2000) study of the rise of the female maquiladora labor force in Tijuana, Mexico, shows how multinational corporations operate in Third World countries to keep production costs and wages lower than in First World countries, often because of less rigid labor laws. Fussell points out that since the 1970s, "when global trade began to intensify, new production and labor-control technologies and competition between low-wage production zones combined to make the cost of labor the most variable component of production" (Elisabeth Fussell 2000: 60). To attract multinational corporations and under pressure through NAFTA, the Mexican government implemented policies such as the dismantling of independent labor unions and the lowering of maquiladora wages to the "lowest of developing countries with strong export marketing sectors" (Fussell 2000: 64).

In Tijuana, Mexican women, who are already perceived and perceive themselves as secondary wage earners supplementing men's wages, become ready suppliers of low-wage labor. Fussell defends feminist economists who have argued that there is deterioration rather than improvement in women's opportunities and agency precisely because "maquiladora employers attract a sector of the female labor force with low levels of human capital and a great need for stable employment which willingly accepts the low wages offered by the maquiladoras" (Fussell 2000: 63). The opportunities in this area, in other words, are restricted to a specific segment of women workers – those able to run the smallest risk of losing their jobs. As Fussell points out, "[b]eing 25 or older, having a child younger than 5, and having less than a primary level of education increase women's probability of maquiladora employment" (Fussell 2000: 73). These women are perceived to be and have proved to be docile and accepting of the challenges demanded by tedious assembly processes. They are less likely to risk losing their jobs through labor resistance than those who are more qualified and more likely to demand higher wages and better working conditions. Fussell argues that if there was ever any potential to improve the lives of women in Mexico by providing them with jobs, it has been "lost to the search for low wages and a flexible labor force" (Fussell 2000: 60). One could argue that the maquiladoras hire precisely those most in need of employment, those who would otherwise be worse off. Yet the descriptions of recruitment and work conditions highlight the ways in

GLOBALIZATION AND WOMEN'S PAID WORK

which corporate interests conspired to "take advantage of women's disadvantages" (Fussell 2000: 75) and "diminished the earnings potential of women employed in the maquiladoras" (Fussell 2000: 76).

In the abstract, maquiladoras provide job opportunities and promote national economic development. They fit the description of places that integrate women into the workforce, a goal that Sen argues is a way of increasing women's freedom and agency. However, a closer examination of how multinational corporations, with a vested interest in maximizing profits and minimizing costs, use entrenched meanings of gender and class casts doubt on the promise of workforce participation as necessarily improving the well-being or agency of these women.[5] In Sen's terms, these women would *seem* to be passive actors rather than active agents seeking to change their work conditions. If we question the motivations of corporate employers who seek to maximize gains by utilizing specific features of labor markets in Third World countries, then we must also question whether these women are truly the recipients of policies designed to remove inequalities and achieve better working conditions. We need to know about these factors at both the local and global levels to make proper assessments of the effects on women's freedom and agency, including factors that can have positive effects.

So far I have concentrated on the negative effects that global markets and multinational corporations can have on women's freedom and agency in particular locations. Global and local factors change, sometimes in ways that can improve women's work conditions. Tighter labor markets, for example, can give workers in some places at some times more bargaining power to negotiate improved wages and better working conditions. As Linda Lim points out, "more and more men are being employed by newly established maquiladoras (export-oriented factories), which are unable to recruit sufficient women due to the export industry boom and resultant tightening labor market in this region" (Linda Lim 1990: 108). More recently, there are reports that many of these factories in the Tijuana belt are closing as multinationals find cheaper labor elsewhere.[6] These are factors that could change the analysis provided in the studies by Fussell and Elson and Pearson. But there is also more serious criticism of these studies.

Lim emphasizes that these studies only focus on the negative impact of these jobs on women's freedom and agency: "feminists who see patriarchy and gender subordination as crucial underpinnings and inevitable consequences of all capitalism refuse to recognize any benefits to women in the Third World from employment in export factories, insisting that such employment intensifies rather than alleviates their gender subordination" (Lim 1990: 116). She adds:

> The predominant stereotype is that First World multinational factories located in the Third World export-processing zones employ mostly

173

ARTICLES

young, single, female rural – urban migrants, who are ruthlessly
exploited in harsh factory environments where they suffer long hours,
poor working conditions, insecure, unhealthy, and unsafe jobs, and
wages so low that they are not even sufficient to cover individual subsistence.

(Lim 1990: 111)

Lim does not claim that poor working conditions do not exist in some
areas. They were particularly evident when export factories were
established. Rather, she makes two points. The first is that changes to
labor and market demands can change workforce composition. The second
point is about the "tendency to generalize from ... observations in one
particular location at one time" (Lim 1990: 113), a tendency that often
ignores the ways in which women are changing their lives even as they
experience the negative impact of work conditions. Lim defends a dynamic
historical approach, one that highlights the importance of being sensitive to
changes in local and global factors when reading accounts of women's
work. She has us pay attention, for example, to the ways in which *having*
employment, where none was available previously, affects "women workers'
lives and their position in and relations with their families" (Lim 1990:
114). This dynamic approach endorses an account of women as agents,
who, in the process of interacting with and reacting to changing local and
global factors, themselves reshape meanings and therefore change the
conditions of their own lives.

Pearson has responded to Lim's critique by agreeing that her
collaborative work with Elson failed to acknowledge the force of a dynamic
approach:

in our desire to pursue the implications for gender positioning of the
new geography of women's labour we were ignoring the ways in which
that experience continually reformulated specific women's gender
identities and the ways in which women were active agents in the interaction between capital accumulation and traditional forms of gender
identities.

(Ruth Pearson 1998: 180)

This concession does not reject descriptions of the negative impact of
multinational corporations in places like Tijuana, but it recognizes the
importance of avoiding homogenizing, static, and generalized approaches.
María Fernández-Kelly demonstrates these principles when she reports her
experiences of applying for jobs and working inside maquiladoras. She
argues that even as women have limited potential to change the conditions
of their work, they are challenging and changing "conventional mores and
values regarding femininity" (María Fernández-Kelly 1997: 215) that have
prevailed in Mexican society.

GLOBALIZATION AND WOMEN'S PAID WORK

III. LESSONS FOR DEVISING POLICY

Generally, enabling women to work outside the home increases their freedom in other domains. Sen's analysis appears to show that there are improvements in domains such as women's access to healthcare, education, and birth control when women are allowed to enter the workplace. But what lessons can be learned from the detailed descriptions of what women's work is actually like? One is that descriptions of women's work in particular contexts complicates Sen's general strategy of advocating work outside the home. If agency enables women to make choices and *do* things that then give them voice, social standing, independence, and empowerment in both the public and private spheres, then care is needed in advocating for women's work participation as a sure way of increasing their freedom and agency. Another lesson is that we must pay attention to the global and the local, as well as to the impact of the global on the local. The weaving together of the analyses by Mohanty, Mies, Fussell, Pearson, Elson, and Lim provides a two-pronged critique of Sen's account. These consist of the local and global, and the critique requires tracing the interconnections between global forces of power and local systems of oppression to achieve a more extensive analysis of women's freedom and agency than that provided by Sen.

Consider, for instance, the local factors of power and oppression and their frequent shaping by global forces. Multinational corporations have relatively easy entry into most countries in the world, and they often shape freedom and agency at the local level. While capital and multinational corporations are highly mobile, labor is much less so. Also, labor is often key in maximizing profits and minimizing costs, which explains why multinational corporations seek to move quickly across borders at the expense of the relative immobility of labor. The maquiladoras in Tijuana illustrate how these features of local labor markets are employed by multinational corporations. They also illustrate how gender, race, and class are understood, defined, and used in specific locations to meet local and global demands for labor. Multinational corporations can determine not only who gets to work and what work they do, but also the social norms and the perceptions regarding workers and work itself. Unlike the lace-makers in South India, maquiladora women in Mexico are perceived to be and perceive themselves to be workers, but they are secondary wage workers with little or no freedom to choose the kind of jobs they want and little or no agency to change their working conditions. This is not to deny some of the benefits. Rather an awareness of the complex features of local and global conditions helps us recognize what spaces women have to negotiate and implement policies that alleviate the negative effects on their freedom and agency. For example, women workers who challenge conventional norms of femininity are also positioned to challenge the double shift of

175

ARTICLES

adding work outside the home to caring for children by, for example, pressing for daycare facilities. These changes can in turn positively affect freedoms in other areas such as health and education.

Other examples of women's work point to features of importance at the local level. Apart from conservative social norms, such factors as high unemployment, environmental disasters, persistent poverty, political corruption, civil unrest, and the absence of labor protection laws can all affect the exploitation of workers by local employers. Accounting for these factors would temper Sen's claim that there is a strong or inevitable link between increasing women's workforce participation and increasing their levels of freedom and agency in domains such as the home, reproductive decisions, and the equitable distribution of food, healthcare, and education within families.

Also, global forces of power often interact with local conditions in ways that shape levels of freedom and agency at the local level. Increasing women's freedom through work outside the home can fail as a general policy if pre-existing local conditions are disadvantageous. This is particularly likely where multinational corporations can prevent workers from organizing, challenging, and changing oppressive and exploitative work conditions. It can also fail as a general policy if the interests of multinational corporations, trade agreements such as NAFTA, or the rise and fall of its currency, rather than the interests of its least advantaged citizens, dictate the host government's policy. Again, I do not deny the importance of increasing women's freedom to work. Rather, I emphasize that recognition of the complex, unpredictable effects of these forces on the lives and conditions of women in particular regions is missing in Sen's account.

If transformations are to be truly in terms of increasing women's agency, we need to contextualize them by looking at the particular activities of multinational corporations and their disempowering effects on people in specific contexts. We need to know about the particularities of gender inequalities and injustices and the ways in which race, class, ethnicity, and so on intersect, shape, and sustain relations of power. Such detailed descriptions would reveal that advocating increased workforce participation is not sufficient for a meaningful improvement of women's freedom and agency in all places, and that there may be losses to freedom in some domains even as freedom may be increased in others. Analyses and critiques need to be multi-pronged and conducted at both local and global levels, and policies need to be multifaceted if genuine improvements to women's freedom and agency are to be obtained.

Descriptions of women's work at the local level also highlight the importance of acting locally so that power is transferred to those affected by oppressive norms and practices. Sen supports the idea that control of work needs to be in women's hands. He strongly advocates the promotion of

GLOBALIZATION AND WOMEN'S PAID WORK

women's agency and provides examples of the successful organizing and managing of businesses and bank loans by women in India (Sen 1999: 200–2). The Self-Employed Women's Association (SEWA), for example, has succeeded in enabling thousands of Indian women to "cut out some middleman activity and to command higher prices for their products in local, regional, and international markets" (Marilyn Carr, Martha Chen, and Jane Tate 2000: 138).[7] But the work of SEWA involves more than this, as Sen notes when he writes that it has been "most effective in bringing about a changed climate of thought, not just more employment for women" (Sen 1999: 116). Further, I would argue that the work of grassroots organizations such as SEWA illuminates how theory and policy need to be multifaceted to be effective. It shows that grassroots organizations themselves need to be vigilant about the ways in which the policies they advocate or put in place can be used, undermined, or reshaped by markets and corporate interests at the global level or even by their own governments.

Governments, for example, might promote women's employment when they need workers (say, as dictated by global markets), but these programs can be quickly withdrawn with shifts in global market conditions or in the local economy. Women's freedom to work can disappear when a multinational corporation decides to move its factories to minimize costs or to avoid government policies detrimental to its profit-maximizing interests. Women's freedom to work can also decline under pressure from religious and cultural groups or through a change in government. Or, women's work can be made invisible or rendered irrelevant in standard accounts of economic participation. These factors and many others need to be taken into account in devising strategies for increasing women's freedom and agency via employment.

At the global level, as suggested earlier, bodies such as the International Labor Organization (ILO) have a role to play in shaping policy regarding work conditions as well as in defining who counts as a worker by revising data-gathering procedures. Sen describes the ILO as the "custodian of workers' rights within the United Nations system" (Sen 2001: 33). He discusses his own work with the ILO and calls on it to implement an approach that is sensitive to diverse needs and context, but at the same time global and universalist:

> A universalist understanding of work and working relations can be linked to a tradition of solidarity and commitment. The need for in- voking such a global approach has never been stronger than it is now. The economically globalizing world, with all its opportunities as well as problems, calls for a similarly globalized understanding of the priority of decent work and of its manifold demands on economic, political and social arrangements.
>
> (Sen 2001: 43)

177

ARTICLES

While the role that organizations such as the ILO can play in formulating
these policies is clearly important, we need to be clear about what is really
needed for a globalized understanding, particularly when it involves
women's work. As Lourdes Benería's (1982) research shows, women's
"work" is often invisible or not valued because it does not fit the model of
commodity production and market exchange that has dominated
economic analysis. Economic analysis can, of course, be improved by
better data, and Benería claims that some progress has occurred in terms of
gathering data that interprets women's work as economic activity rather
than leisure or private sphere activities. This includes housework,
subsistence agricultural work, and home-based work (Lourdes Benería
1982: 120). But better economic analysis also needs a link with more
gender-sensitive policies. The case of lace-makers in India nicely illustrates
Benería's point that women's work and their participation in economic
activities can be performed without ever leaving the home. As noted earlier,
this work is perceived as leisure activity, even though women are carrying
the double burden of domestic work and making products for the global
market, all in a private sphere where their work is invisible and the returns
from it are controlled by men. Features of the global market in lace and
their interaction with this local system lead to this work neither increasing
women's participation in the public sphere nor enhancing their freedom
and agency in the private sphere. But this example also illustrates why
simply improving the definitions of work and the collection of data on labor
is not enough. Policies will not work if they are too general, rely too heavily
on the power and goodwill of international organizations, or are not
combined with local strategies for challenging the gendered, racialized,
and class divisions of labor.

Carr, Chen, and Tate advocate four interrelated and multidirectional
strategies in the case of home-based work: (1) research and statistical
studies "to document the number, contribution, and working conditions of
home-based workers and to assess the impact of globalization on them"; (2)
action programs "to help home-based workers gain access to – and bargain
effectively within – labor and product markets (both local and global)"; (3)
grassroots organizations "to increase the visibility and voice of home-based
workers and other women workers in the informal sector"; and (4) policy
dialogues "to promote an enabling work and policy environment for home-
based women workers" (Carr, Chen, and Tate 2000: 137). They give
substance to their policy proposals by describing the work of several
women's organizations, SEWA, HomeNet, and the United Nations
Development Fund for Women (UNIFEM), whose work at both local and
global levels illustrates their strategy. In 1997 these organizations formed a
coalition, Women in Informal Employment: Globalizing and Organizing
(WIEGO), "comprised of grassroots organizations, research institutions,
and international development agencies concerned with improving the

GLOBALIZATION AND WOMEN'S PAID WORK

conditions and advancing the status of women in the informal sector" (Carr, Chen, and Tate 2000: 141).

Strategies that make use of the resources of national and international bodies to counteract disempowerment and exploitation experienced by women will be important. Especially in contexts where very large percentages of the female labor force are in the low-paying end of the informal sector, we need grassroots organizing not only for assessing and minimizing the negative impact of multinational corporations and global markets on women's work, but also for putting mechanisms in place to protect earnings at the local level. SEWA, for example, has a system that protects informal sector savings from being appropriated by husbands or other family members. Grassroots organizations can put pressure on national and international organizations to implement or change labor laws that exclude women from being protected from the exploitative working conditions. For such policies to be effective, then, as Sen rightly argues, national and international bodies need to be committed to enhancing well-being and quality of life. But they also need to engage in multifaceted strategies and policies that generate meaningful improvements to women's agency and freedom in particular contexts.

IV. CONCLUSION

Sen rightly argues that allowing people "the freedom to lead lives that they have reason to value" means removing unfreedoms such as malnutrition, premature morbidity, disease, unemployment, and political oppression. Sen urges those interested in alleviating the suffering caused by conditions of poverty, famine, and the destruction and degradation of the environment to attend less to income levels, GDP measures, technological advancements, and industrialization, and more to helping an individual live a healthy, meaningful life. In the face of the objection that Sen's account is too complex and perhaps difficult to embrace as anything other than an ideal,[8] I have defended its complexity and argued for engaging with even greater levels of complexity. Informed discussion of development processes and policies must include accounts of global forces of power and their intersection with and utilization of local systems of oppression. These factors are particularly evident in the area of women's work and have a direct impact on women's freedom and agency in this and other domains. Taking these factors into account expands the discussion of freedom in *Development as Freedom* and identifies further barriers to women's freedom and agency in addition to those that Sen highlights.

There is no single effect of economic globalization on women's participation in the workforce or on their freedom and agency. Sen concentrates on the positive impact of women's increased workforce participation on their freedom and agency. I do not dispute such a

ARTICLES

potential positive impact, but the potential negative impact must also be recognized. Women's freedom and agency are not always improved when they enter the workforce, and merely increasing women's workforce participation is not an adequate development policy. The dynamic relationship between grassroots activities and national and international policy shows how women's agency can effect positive change, even as women grapple with the negative effects of local and global conditions on their lives.

Christine M. Koggel, Department of Philosophy, Bryn Mawr College,
101 N. Merion Avenue, Bryn Mawr, PA 19010-2899, USA
e-mail: ckoggel@brynmawr.edu

ACKNOWLEDGMENTS

I am grateful to the anonymous reviewers, to the three guest editors of this Special Issue, and to the participants of the Oxford Workshop (September 11–13, 2002) for their many useful comments and suggestions. Ingrid Robeyns' feedback and support, Jane Humphries' attention to background literature, and Bina Agarwal's detailed comments and input were especially important to this process. I would also like to thank all those who raised challenging questions at conferences where earlier drafts of this paper were presented, particularly Jay Drydyk, Sue Campbell, Kai Nielsen, Nelleke Bak, Colin Macleod, Sue Sherwin, and David Crocker. Lastly, Andrew Brook's close critical reading and attention to detail can always be counted on and is appreciated.

NOTES

[1] Postcolonial feminist literature is growing rapidly. In this paper, I especially use insights from Jacqui Alexander and Chandra Mohanty (1997) and Uma Narayan and Sandra Harding (eds. 2000). From these collections, papers by Chandra Mohanty (1997), Lorraine Code (2000), Uma Narayan (2000), and Ann Ferguson (2000) have been particularly useful.

[2] Important feminist literature on the topic of women's paid work and its effects on women's status and roles in the private and public spheres includes: Beatrice Leigh Hutchins and Amy Harrison Spencer (1907), Jane Humphries (1977), Elizabeth Roberts (1984), Jane Lewis (1986), and Janet Sayers, Mary Evans, and Nanneke Redclift (1987). In important research on the nonliberating aspects of paid work, S. Charusheela (forthcoming) argues that bargaining models tend to assume the perspective of privileged women and fail to consider work that has not been empowering for women of color, working-class women, ethnic minorities, or Third World women. I am indebted to Jane Humphries for alerting me to this research on paid work.

[3] I am grateful to Bina Agarwal for pointing out that Sen mentions factors such as property ownership in passing and that his main emphasis has been on women's

GLOBALIZATION AND WOMEN'S PAID WORK

employment, which is the focus of this paper. See, however, Bina Agarwal (1994) on the significance of control over property in enhancing women's agency and well-being.

[4] In a study of home-based work in domains such as fashion garments, nontraditional agricultural exports, and shea butter, Carr, Chen, and Tate argue that among the most disadvantaged of all workers in a global context are women who produce from their homes. They ask, "[w]hat greater contrast could there be – in terms of market knowledge, mobility, and competitiveness – than that between a large transnational company and a home-based woman producer?" (Marilyn Carr, Martha Chen, and Jane Tate 2000: 125).

[5] In the introduction to a special issue of *Feminist Economics* on globalization and gender, Benería, Floro, Grown, and MacDonald counter the argument that women's greater access to jobs generates gender equity with evidence that suggests that "gender inequality stimulated growth and that growth may exacerbate gender inequality" (Lourdes Benería, Maria Floro, Caren Grown and Martha MacDonald 2000: xi).

[6] The changing composition of the maquiladora workforce is substantiated by Verónica Vázquez García (per. com. 2002), who reports that men from rural areas of Mexico are being recruited. Kai Nielsen (per. com. 2002) has raised the point that lower labor costs in other regions are now resulting in the closing down of maquiladoras in Tijuana.

[7] SEWA, founded in India in 1972, has a membership of over 250,000 women and "has provided a range of services (financial, health, child care, and training) to its members." The work of SEWA is more important for the example it sets than for the number of women it reaches. More recently, SEWA has led an international movement of women workers and negotiated with international trade union federations and the International Labor Organization to recognize informal sector workers (Carr, Chen, and Tate 2000: 139).

[8] See, for example, Paul Seabright (2001).

REFERENCES

Agarwal, Bina. 1994. *A Field of One's Own: Gender and Land Rights in South Asia*. Cambridge, UK: Cambridge University Press.

Alexander, M. Jacqui and Chandra Talpade Mohanty. 1997. "Introduction: Genealogics, Legacies, Movements," in M. Jacqui Alexander and Chandra Talpade Mohanty (eds.) *Feminist Genealogies, Colonial Legacies, Democratic Futures*, pp. xiii–xlii. New York: Routledge.

Benería, Lourdes. 1982. "Accounting for Women's Work," in Lourdes Benería (ed.) *Women and Development: The Sexual Division of Labor in Rural Societies*, pp. 119–47. New York: Praeger.

——. 1999. "Globalization, Gender and the Davos Man." *Feminist Economics* 5(3): 61–83.

——, Maria Floro, Caren Grown, and Martha MacDonald. 2000. "Introduction: Globalization and Gender." *Feminist Economics* 6(3): vii–xviii.

Carr, Marilyn, Martha Alter Chen, and Jane Tate. 2000. "Globalization and Home-Based Workers." *Feminist Economics* 6(3): 123–42.

Charusheela, S. Forthcoming. "Empowering Work? Bargaining Models Reconsidered," in Drucilla Barker and Edith Kuiper (eds.) *Towards a Feminist Philosophy of Economics*. London: Routledge.

Code, Lorraine. 2000. "How to Think Globally: Stretching the Limits of Imagination," in Uma Narayan and Sandra Harding (eds.) *Decentering the Center: Philosophy for a Multicultural, Postcolonial, and Feminist World*, pp. 67–79. Bloomington, IN: Indiana University Press.

ARTICLES

Elson, Diane and Ruth Pearson. 1981. "The Subordination of Women and the Internationalisation of Factory Production," in Kate Young, Carol Wolkowitz, and Roslyn McCullagh (eds.) *Of Marriage and the Market: Women's Subordination in International Perspective*, pp. 144–66. London: CSE.

Ferguson, Ann. 2000. "Resisting the Veil of Privilege: Building Bridge Identities as an Ethico-Politics of Global Feminisms," in Uma Narayan and Sandra Harding (eds.) *Decentering the Center: Philosophy for a Multicultural, Postcolonial, and Feminist World*, pp. 189–207. Bloomington, IN: Indiana University Press.

Fernández-Kelly, María Patricia. 1997. "*Maquiladoras*: The View from Inside," in Nalini Vasvanathan, Lynn Duggan, Laurie Nisonoff, and Nan Wiegersma (eds.) *The Women, Gender and Development Reader*, pp. 203–15. London: Zed Books.

Fussell, Elisabeth. 2000. "Making Labor Flexible: The Recomposition of Tijuana's Maquiladora Female Labor Force." *Feminist Economics* 6(3): 59–79.

García, Verónica Vázquez. Personal communication. 12 September 2002.

Harding, Sandra. 2000. "Gender, Development, and Post-Enlightenment Philosophies of Science," in Uma Narayan and Sandra Harding (eds.) *Decentering the Center: Philosophy for a Multicultural, Postcolonial, and Feminist World*, pp. 240–61. Bloomington, IN: Indiana University Press.

Humphries, Jane. 1977. "Class Struggle and the Persistence of the Working-Class Family." *Cambridge Journal of Economics* 1(3): 241–58.

Hutchins, Beatrice Leigh and Amy Harrison Spencer. 1907. *A History of Factory Legislation*. Rev. edn. Westminster, UK: P. S. King & Son.

Lewis, Jane (ed.). 1986. *Labour and Love: Women's Experience of Home and Family, 1850–1940*. Oxford, UK: Blackwell.

Lim, Linda Y. 1990. "Women's Work in Export Factories: The Politics of a Cause," in Irene Tinker (ed.) *Persistent Inequalities: Women and World Development*, pp. 101–19. New York: Oxford University Press.

Mies, Maria. 1982. "The Dynamics of the Sexual Division of Labor and Integration of Rural Women into the World Market," in Lourdes Benería (ed.) *Women and Development: The Sexual Division of Labor in Rural Societies*, pp. 1–28. New York: Praeger.

Mohanty, Chandra Talpade. 1988. "Under Western Eyes: Feminist Scholarship and Colonial Discourses." *Feminist Review* 30(Autumn): 61–88.

——. 1997. "Women Workers and Capitalist Scripts: Ideologies of Domination, Common Interests, and the Politics of Solidarity," in M. Jacqui Alexander and Chandra Talpade Mohanty (eds.) *Feminist Genealogies, Colonial Legacies, Democratic Futures*, pp. 3–29. New York: Routledge.

Nielsen, Kai. Personal communication. 28 September 2002.

Narayan, Uma. 2000. "Essence of Culture and a Sense of History: A Feminist Critique of Cultural Essentialism," in Uma Narayan and Sandra Harding (eds.) *Decentering the Center: Philosophy for a Multicultural, Postcolonial, and Feminist World*, pp. 80–100. Bloomington, IN: Indiana University Press.

Pearson, Ruth. 1998. "'Nimble Fingers' Revisited: Reflections on Women and Third World Industrialization in the Late Twentieth Century," in Cecile Jackson and Ruth Pearson (eds.) *Feminist Visions of Development: Gender Analysis and Policy*, pp. 171–88. London: Routledge.

Roberts, Elizabeth. 1984. *A Woman's Place: An Oral History of Working-Class Women 1890–1940*. Oxford, UK: Blackwell.

Sayers, Janet, Mary Evans, and Nanneke Redclift (eds.). 1987. *Engels Revisited: New Feminist Essays*. London: Tavistock.

Seabright, Paul. 2001. "The Road Upward: *Development as Freedom*." *New York Review of Books* 48(5): (March 29), 41–3.

GLOBALIZATION AND WOMEN'S PAID WORK

Sen, Amartya. 1980. "Equality of What?" in S. M. McMurrin (ed.) *Tanner Lectures on Human Values* 1: pp. 195–220. Cambridge, UK: Cambridge University Press.

——. 1990. "Gender and Cooperative Conflicts," in Irene Tinker (ed.) *Persistent Inequalities: Women and World Development*, pp. 123–49. New York: Oxford University Press.

——. 1992. *Inequality Reexamined*. Cambridge, MA: Harvard University Press.

——. 1995. "Gender Inequality and Theories of Justice," in Martha Nussbaum and Jonathan Glover (eds.) *Women, Culture and Development: A Study of Human Capabilities*, pp. 259–73. Oxford, UK: Clarendon Press.

——. 1999. *Development as Freedom*. New York: Anchor Books.

——. 2001. "Work and Rights," in Martha Fetherolf Loutfi (ed.) *Women, Gender and Work: What is Equality and How do We Get There?*, pp. 33–44. Geneva: International Labour Office.

[20]

Locating Globalization: Feminist (Re)readings of the Subjects and Spaces of Globalization*

Richa Nagar
Department of Women's Studies, University of Minnesota,
Minneapolis, MN 55455
nagar001@tc.umn.edu

Victoria Lawson
Department of Geography, Box 353550, University of Washington,
Seattle, WA 98195-3550
lawson@u.washington.edu

Linda McDowell
Department of Geography, University College London, 26 Bedford Way,
London WC1H 0AP, UK
l.mcdowell@geog.ucl.ac.uk

Susan Hanson
School of Geography, Clark University, Worcester, MA 01610
shanson@clarku.edu

Abstract: The literatures on economic globalization and feminist understandings of global processes have largely remained separate. In this article, our goal is to bring them into productive conversation so that research on globalization can benefit from feminist engagements with globalization. In the first section, which focuses on the conceptual challenges of bringing the economic globalization literature into conversation with feminist analysis, we identify several key exclusions in that literature and propose parallel inclusions that a feminist reading of globalization suggests. Our suggested inclusions relate to the spaces, scales, subjects, and forms of work that research on economic globalization has largely neglected. The second section takes up several key themes in the large body of feminist research on global economic processes, which is also largely absent from the economic globalization literature: the gendering of work, gender and structural adjustment programs, and mobility and diaspora. In the final section, we address the implications of feminist epistemologies and methodologies for research on economic globalization. Here we argue for grounded, collaborative studies that incorporate perspectives of the south as well as the north and that construct understandings of place and the local, as well as space and general global processes; we point to the coconstitution of different geographic scales and highlight the need for studies that cut across them. The article demonstrates how a feminist analysis of globalization entails far more than recognizing the importance of gender; it requires substantial rethinking of how to conceptualize, study, and act in relation to economic globalization.

Key words: economic globalization, feminist geography.

* The authors collaborated fully in conceptualizing, writing, and revising this article, and we wish to acknowledge the pleasures and enrichments of this collaboration. Following an ancient feminist custom, we chose to list the authors in order of age. We thank the reviewers and David Angel for helpful comments on an earlier draft.

The literatures on economic globalization and feminist understandings of global processes have, for the most part, remained separate (Koffman and Youngs 1996; Marchand and Runyan 2000a are key exceptions). Our goal is to bring these two literatures into productive conversation so that research on globalization can benefit from feminist theoretical, epistemological, methodological, and empirical engagements with globalization. We begin by noting that globalization is not new. Political and economic relations at the global scale have long histories, rooted in colonialism, imperialism, and the discourses and practices of the development industry (Escobar 1995; Katz 2001). The recent outpouring of work on globalization has emphasized globalizing tendencies in the discourses and practices of corporate actors, in global financial and trade flows, in transnational networks of activists, and in the rescaling of governance (through treaties and institutions, such as the World Trade Organization (WTO), North American Free Trade Agreement, the European Union, and the International Monetary Fund (IMF)). This body of research has linked globalization to the historically specific (post-1989) hegemony of neoliberal discourse that is reworking nation-state power and the rhetorics and practices of development. In this article, we call attention to a large body of feminist work on gender and global processes that complements many of these insights but has been neglected in the literature on economic globalization.

The article is organized into three sections that discuss (1) theoretical and conceptual issues, (2) feminist empirical work, and (3) epistemological and methodological issues. Because these three topics are closely intertwined, the organization reflects a matter of emphasis, not a strict partitioning. In the first section, which focuses primarily on the conceptual challenges faced by bringing the economic globalization literature into conversation with feminist analysis, we identify several key exclusions in the economic globalization literature and propose parallel inclusions that a feminist reading of global-

ization suggests. Our focus is on what each inclusion can bring to globalization research. In the second section, we examine some of the major themes in the large body of empirical work on gender and global processes that the literature on economic globalization has not yet absorbed. In the final section, we address the implications of feminist epistemologies and methodologies for research on economic globalization. Joan Scott (1989, 680), a feminist historian, pointed out that the writing of women's history raised the question of who has the power to produce "social consensus about the meanings of truth." She asked, "By what process have men's actions come to be considered a norm, representative of human history, generally, and women's actions overlooked, or consigned to a less important, particularized arena?" (Scott 1993, 242). We raise similar questions about the writing of economic globalization: How is it that only certain parts of the process have entered the lexicon while others remain neglected? How are understandings of economic globalization diminished as a result of this neglect? Scott's question points to "the politics of knowledge production" (Scott 1993, 236) and underscores the inseparability of epistemology from conceptual and empirical issues.

A number of cross-cutting themes, which reflect our feminist position, run throughout this article. The only other explicitly feminist treatment of gender and globalization of which we are aware, Marchand and Runyan's (2000a) *Gender and Global Restructuring*, proposes that gender analysis is well suited for developing understandings of globalization that go beyond the narrowly economistic renditions that are characteristic of the mainstream economic globalization literature.[1] What are some of the hallmarks of a feminist approach that render it

[1] Marchand and Runyan's (2000a) edited collection develops complementary arguments about gender and global restructuring; however, their work differs from ours in that geographic scale and concepts of place are not central to the book's message.

so useful in analyzing global processes? Briefly, the themes that thread through all three sections of this article reflect these hallmarks: the recognition that gender is "a focal point both of and for [global] restructuring" (Marchand and Runyan 2000b, 18); a focus on power relations at various geographic scales; a suspicion of binaries or dualisms and a corollary preference for understanding connections and interdependencies, which feminists often refer to as relational analysis (see, e.g., Alexander and Mohanty 1997) or relational thinking (Marchand and Runyan 2000b); a concern for justice; the need to comprehend the cultural construction of difference and boundaries; and a desire to build grounded, contextual understandings of global processes.[2] Particularly in its focus on gender and its concern for grounded, contextual, empirical work, feminist analysis differs from other critical approaches, such as Marxism, which may share with feminism an interest in, for example, power relations and justice.

The contemporary focus in feminist scholarship on the ways in which globalization both connects women into networks across varied spaces and plays on and reconstitutes differences among them, as well as inequalities between women and men, has, we believe, been influenced by the coincidence of a number of material and theoretical shifts. Such shifts include the impact of the mobility and movement of Third World women to the West on feminist scholarship and the women's movement; the

growing visibility of "women's" issues on a global stage (e.g., international conferences on women's health, reproductive rights, women and war, violence, rape, and refugees); the significance of women's empowerment as an agent of development; the theoretical refocus among geographers from analyses at local, regional, or national scales to a multiscalar focus on the connections, relations, and processes across cultures that constitute geographic unevenness; and, finally, the continuing insistence that feminism, as a movement and a theoretical position, is about a serious engagement with the possibilities for transforming inequalities, about connecting women's struggles in different places, about mobilizing across cultural and national borders, and about building solidarity among women. In this last point, feminist work differs from postmodernist analysis in its continuing commitment to progressive ideals of justice and ethics, democracy and equality, albeit in ways that involve challenges to conventional liberal definitions of justice (Young 1990; Hartsock 2001).

Theorizing Economic Globalization: Toward a More Inclusive Account

A number of authors in geography and related fields have critiqued the literature on economic globalization, but, for the most part, these critiques have not seriously engaged feminist thinking. In this section, we seek to build a framework for a conversation between those who are critiquing economic globalization scholarship and feminists who have developed a large body of work on gender and global processes. Both the critiques we engage and our own feminist analysis take as a backdrop celebratory renditions of globalization from boosters, such as Toffler and Toffler (1995), Ohmae (1990, 1995), Fukuyama (1992), and Gingrich (1995). For these authors, "globalization is conceptualized as an inevitable leap into friction-free flows of commodities, capital, corporations, communication, and

---

[2] Despite our outline of some key features of feminist analyses of globalization, feminism as a body of scholarship is distinguished by its epistemological and methodological pluralism. The theorization of gender as a performance, for example, is not necessarily accepted by or relevant to all forms of feminist work. Indeed, Wiegman (2000, 356) suggested that "the impossibility of coherence [is] the central problematic and most important feature of feminism as a knowledge formation in the contemporary academy." For analysts of globalization, this lack of coherence is both an exhilarating and daunting challenge.

consumers all over the world. . . . Eroding away fixed in-state places into fluid un-stated places now preoccupies the neo-liberal managers of globalizing enterprises" (Luke and Tuathail 1998, 76).

Critiques of globalization complicate this celebration of a borderless world of flows, assertions of the end of the nation-state, and the imminent unbundling of territorial sovereignty. Scholars have critically examined new spatialities of power; assertions about the flows, flexibility, borders, and fixities of globalization; shifting scales of governance; and the shifting terrains and rhetorics of geopolitics (Herod, Tuathail, and Roberts 1998; Castells 2000; Giddens 2000; Greider 1997; Mittelman 2000; Kelly 1999; Luke and Tuathail 1998). This is a rich and important literature, and we aim to extend these critiques by pointing out that they tend to deal with (1) economic processes in the formal sector, (2) only certain places and scales, and (3) only certain actors. Our feminist analysis identifies these biases as underlying three key exclusions in the globalization literature; in the rest of this section, we discuss each of these exclusions, along with the parallel inclusions that a feminist analysis suggests. In describing the inclusions we advocate, we draw upon feminist work on gender and global processes—work that is discussed in greater detail in the second section.

Exclusions and Inclusions

Exclusion 1: Casual and informal spheres (of economies, cultures, and politics).

Although many of the critiques of globalization begin from geopolitical and cultural perspectives (e.g., Herod, Tuathail, and Roberts 1998; Thrift 1998; Castells 2000; Kelly 1999; Koffman and Youngs 1996), they focus primarily on public and formal spheres of economy and politics. These spheres encompass corporations, national political arenas, multilateral institutions, the production and dissemination of knowledge, and global media (Kelly 1999). This emphasis on the formal spaces of globalization is funda-

mentally masculinist in its exclusion of the economic, cultural, and political spheres (often casual or informal) that operate in households and communities; in daily practices of caring, consumption, and religion; and in networks of alternative politics where women's contributions to globalization are often located. We see these informal spheres as key sites for understanding globalization processes in their own right because of their crucial roles in society and because it is precisely these spheres and activities that underwrite and actively constitute the public spheres of globalization. As Nancy Folbre (2001, vii), an economist, noted, "Markets cannot function effectively outside the framework of families and communities built on values of love, obligation, and reciprocity."

Much of the analyses of globalization foregrounds a limited set of public sphere, economic and political processes (see, e.g., Bello, Cunningham, and Rau 1994; Korten 2001; Greider 1997). For example, political-economy critiques understand the rise of globalization's current form as a series of structural shifts in the form of late-modern capitalism, underwritten by the breakup of the Bretton Woods system of exchange-rate controls, fallout from the OPEC crisis, internationalization of manufacturing and finance, and the reframing of governance through international institutions, such as the IMF, World Bank, and WTO (Korten 2001; Mittelman 2000). These events are linked to crises of capitalist accumulation in the West, and economic globalization is represented as the next (perhaps inevitable) iteration of Eurocentric capitalist development. This focus on formal-sector economic processes reinscribes the centrality of corporations, markets, and financial and development institutions even as they are critiqued and, in so doing, neglects gendered processes that are taking place in other sites and alternative circuits such as households, communities, cooperatives, and transnational networks (Hotch 2000; SEEDS 2000; Sparke forthcoming).

We advocate starting from these informal spheres in which women and men are marginalized under global capitalism as a strategic way to reveal how informal economies of production and caring subsidize and constitute global capitalism through cheapening production in sweatshops and homework (Mitter 1986; Beneria and Roldan 1987; Lawson 1995, 1999). Gender is central to the operation of this subsidy. First, as profitability crises encourage restructuring, a series of spatial shifts (from factory to sweatshop to home) and ideological shifts (from family-wage work to poorly paid feminized work) cheapen production costs for global investors and producers. Although these processes take particular forms in specific places, feminist research has illustrated the ways in which cultural ideologies of domesticity, femininity, masculinity, and sexuality play out in defining who works where and for what rewards (Lawson 1995, 1999; Hanson and Pratt 1995; Pringle 1989; McDowell and Court 1994).

Melissa Wright's (1997) work illustrates how a discourse of "disposable women" has underwritten the success of *maquiladora* production in Ciudad Juarez, Mexico. Transnational firms have sought a large number of women, who are constructed, through discourses of femininity, as being in the workforce only temporarily and as working for "lipstick" (as opposed to a family wage). Because these female workers are discursively constructed as temporarily in the labor force, firms have not invested in educating, training, and promoting them. Their resultant low wages and dead-end jobs, justified through the gender ideologies that they are working only for their own amusement or for "pin money" and that they will soon leave the workforce for family reasons, reinforce the notion that they are disposable women and, in the process, justify their low wages in the service of global capital accumulation. In their detailed study of work in Worcester, Massachusetts, Susan Hanson and Geraldine Pratt (1995) demonstrated the power of the same processes in delineating economic opportunity in older industrialized places in the north. Processes of gendering shape who has access to various forms and sites of work, and, at the same time, the reworking of gender shapes the range of potential forms that global restructuring can assume.

A gendered analysis of globalization would reveal how inequality is actively produced in the relations between global restructuring and culturally specific productions of gender difference. In a similar fashion, neoliberal states are subsidized through the informal provision of housing, food, health care, and education. As neoliberal states withdraw from the provision of social services, this work is most often assumed by women in the feminized spheres of household and community. Women's disproportionate role in social reproduction is intelligible only in relation to gendered ideologies of caring and domesticity (Moser 1987; Folbre 2001). Despite the centrality of gender to these reworked forms of capitalism, feminist analyses of global restructuring processes have been neglected.

A closely related point is that studies of globalization focus on some networks and types of flows (technological, financial, corporate, trade, and production) and not others (e.g., activists who are concerned about environmental and health issues and transnational networks of indigenous and women's groups). In debating the very existence of globalization, authors focus on volumes of trade, investment, and migration flows across the globe as key indicators (e.g., Hirst and Thompson 1996; Smith 1997; Greider 1997; Weiss 1997; Kelly 1999). Scholars also debate the nature of globalization through attention to the existence of qualitative shifts in the relations among markets, states, and territories but still focus on the functional integration of economic activities across the globe (Kelly 1999). Castells (2000, 1) termed this the age of informationalization and globalization in which "a technological revolution, centered around information, transformed the way we think, we produce, we consume, we trade, we manage, we communicate, we live, we die, we make war, we make love. . . . Space and time, the material foundations of human experience, have been transformed, as the space of flows dominates the space of places."

Instead of seeing the spaces of globalization as consisting only of formal economic and political spheres and being constituted only by abstract flows, we advocate analyses that attend to the relations between and among flows emanating from different places and circuits (e.g., the linkages among debt repayments, state withdrawal from the provision of health care, and the rise of neighborhood clinics or relations between global media and transnational movements of indigenous identity formation). We argue that analyzing the interdependencies between formal and informal circuits of globalization can reveal the ways in which globalization depends on both gendered processes of marginalization and emergent processes of gendered resistance. For example, feminist scholarship has illustrated how global indebtedness, structural adjustment policies, and the hegemony of neoliberal development strategies have directly intensified women's triple roles in production, reproduction, and community management (Beneria and Feldman 1992; Marchand and Runyan 2000a). Even as women's poverty has deepened under these globalized regimes, women have often collectivized their gendered work, such as the provision of food and struggles for community infrastructure. In some cases, their collective work politicizes their roles and gives rise to local activism in response to globalization (Jelin 1991; Lind 2000). Without attention to how people experience globalization processes in their communities and homes, these politics do not come into view, and our understanding of globalization is incomplete. Much research on globalization has either paid scant attention to gendered experiences of globalization (see, e.g., Hirst and Thompson 1996) or has argued that globalization is leading to the incorporation and emancipation of women (see, e.g., Giddens 2000, 72–74; 83–84).

Even those who highlight the importance of discourse to the processes of globalization have focused on certain public-sphere discourses to the neglect of other discourses (as in Thrift 1998). Nonetheless, we value this work on the cultural and discursive production of globalization because these discourses have legitimized neoliberal policies and politics and so have reproduced the political conditions for globalization itself. As Kelly (1999, 380) argued, "by constructing a particular vision of global space and the 'place' of individuals, national economies and so on within it, it has been argued that the idea of globalization forms part of the rhetoric to legitimize certain political strategies. Thus . . . globalization can also be seen as a myth, a construction, a discourse."

For example, global institutions, such as the IMF and World Bank, have reframed debates over development in terms of neoliberal doctrine and are opening economies around the world to the freer flow of capital and commodities (Kelly 1999; Piven 1995). Scholars have also analyzed the discourses of globality that are promulgated by the private sector, business schools, and management gurus. These practices construct a historically and culturally specific, but intensely powerful spatial and political imaginary (Thrift 1998; Scholte 1996). Seeing globalization as socially constructed—rather than as an inevitable, inexorable, materialist process—is valuable because it opens up space for alternative readings of globalization. Nonetheless, these analyses remain focused on a top-down, global sphere of corporate strategies, managerial practices, geopolitical discourses, and the global economy.

We argue, along with Roberts (2001) and Gibson-Graham (1996), that research and discourses on globalization are peculiarly masculinist in that they serve to construct the spaces, scales, and subjects of globalization in particular ways. Specifically, discourses of global capitalism continue to position women, minorities, the poor, and southern places in ways that constitute globalization as dominant. Images of passive women and places (frequently southern, but also deindustrialized places in the north) are constructed and simultaneously serve to construct discourses of globalization as capitalist, as Western-centric, and as the only possible future for the "global economy." The result is "capitalist myopia," by which researchers assume that global capitalism is all encompassing and they cannot see, or consider salient, other noncapitalist, nonpublic spheres and actors.

Inclusion 1: Attention to casual and informal spheres (of economies, cultures, and politics).

This shift in focus enables analyses of the linkages between multiple spaces and subjects. Inclusion 1 is twofold. First, we consider how gendered processes that devalue certain waged jobs and certain groups of workers, as well as the work of caring for households and communities, serve to underwrite and constitute global-ization. Second, we theorize the openings that can arise from the crucial insight that economic globalization is not inevitable but, rather, a contingent and constructed discourse about capitalism.

First, the central questions and problem-atics of globalization research shift when we begin from the standpoints of marginalized people and economic spheres. In particular, such a shift reveals the ways in which contemporary globalization is intimately tied to gendered and racialized systems of oppression. Nancy Hartsock (2001) argued that understanding the situation of women is a key strategic move in grasping the dynamics of capitalism in a global context. She noted that theorizing from women's lives and experiences of work and oppression helps us see some fundamental dynamics that support global capitalism. These dynamics include

the devaluing of jobs, the shift from full time to part time, the shift from jobs with upward mobility to dead end jobs, the increasing infor-mality/casualization of the labor force—all are related to the feminization of employment in these jobs. I would want to stress that femi-nization of the labor force refers both to the increasing numbers of women in these jobs—especially the low-end jobs. But it also refers to the feminization of anyone who holds one

of these jobs—i.e., making them powerless, invisible, super-exploited. (p. 14)

We build from her insights to argue the importance of considering diverse subjects whose social location within cross-cutting relations of difference (age, ethnicity, race, gender, and so forth) shape their experiences of globalization. It is precisely the *relations between* high-skill and low-skill work, between formal and casualized economies, between production and caring work, between globalized and marginalized places (in south and north) that have allowed global capitalism to assume its contemporary forms (Hartsock 2001; Krause 1996; Mittelman 2000; Sassen 1998). Our feminist approach builds a relational understanding of global capitalist processes through an analysis that starts from the lives of those who are marginalized by globalization—and the informal spheres that are key to their lives. This analysis not only reveals how multiple oppressions constitute the contemporary system, but also suggests new openings for change.

Second, recognizing that globalization is a contingent and constructed discourse opens up the possibility of different read-ings of and responses to globalization. Our feminist approach theorizes that globalized capitalisms are historically and culturally contingent and engage with people in places to generate diverse and contradictory outcomes. Feminist scholarship has high-lighted conflictual interactions among capitalist economic restructuring, house-holds, and the state. Women and men in marginalized places engage in complex and contradictory ways with globalized capi-talisms (Ong 1987; Kondo 1990; Lim 1983; Mohanty 1991a, 1991b). This work has revealed how neoliberal austerity has reworked class processes and transformed gender relations and identities in households (Beneria and Feldman 1992; Beneria and Roldan 1987; Lawson 1995).

Victoria Lawson's (1995, 1999) work in Ecuador, for example, demonstrated that faced with a crisis of profitability, garment manufacturers who had previously employed factory workers shifted to subcontracting work to women homeworkers. In the context of a historic compromise between the state and patriarchal labor unions, women had been excluded from factory work and unions. As a consequence of these exclusions and powerful gendered discourses about women's "primary responsibilities," women now constitute a nonunion, cheap workforce that enables companies to elide the state-union compromise. At the same time, we should not assume that these new forms of work result in uniformly oppressive and subordinating experiences within the household. As several homeworkers remarked during in-depth interviews, they felt reaffirmed as independent and powerful people, as household heads, as mothers who were successful in keeping their families together. Even as the new source of homework serves the interests of garment producers and so facilitates economic globalization, the gender identities of the women in this study had shifted as the women came to feel empowered through their access to an income independent from other household members (Lawson 1995).

When we view economic globalization from the standpoint of women's lives, we uncover the complex and contradictory ways in which globalization reworks class processes and positions in ways that expand women's entrepreneurship and their political activism (Mies 1982; Tiano 1994). In response to deteriorating conditions of work in established firms in the United States (which can be linked to increasing competition associated with global markets), many women and men are turning to self-employment and entrepreneurship. Because, as we briefly noted earlier, women and men are positioned differently within the family and within the workplace, gender shapes these processes of business creation in interesting ways (Hanson 2001). We touch upon three of these ways here. First, many who leave waged or salaried employment to start their own businesses explain that an important motivation for doing so is the desire to create a better workplace, not only for themselves, but also for those whom they

employ; it is not surprising, in view of women's generally inferior labor market position, that this desire is more likely to motivate women's entrepreneurship than men's. Second, one of the specific ways that women business owners (to a far greater degree than male business owners) improve working conditions is to provide greater time-space autonomy and flexibility; that is, the owners and their employees have more choice than they had in their previous jobs in deciding the times and places of paid work and caring work. Often women seek this greater time-space flexibility as a way to achieve some kind of balance between their paid employment and their unpaid work in the family because women's reproductive labor does not diminish with their business ownership. Third, because new businesses emerge out of people's labor market experiences, which are not only gender specific but also largely anchored in the places where people start their new businesses, women's and men's businesses have different impacts on the places in which they are located. Hanson (2000) showed that women-owned businesses are particularly important to the survival and re-creation of Worcester, Massachusetts, as it struggles to redefine itself after deindustrialization. Only through attention to the interdependencies between formal and informal, paid and unpaid labor do we see how globalization is reshaping women's and men's lives in this place, as well as the place itself, which is not a major destination for global capital.

Similarly, Lind's (2000) research in Ecuador illustrates how women activists are remaking their claims on the state in the context of neoliberal austerity. Lind argued that women's organizations are not merely passive recipients of neoliberal policies; rather, they challenge both the masculinist exclusion of women's claims as citizens and the neglect of women's particular concerns, such as the provision of social welfare (see also Radcliffe and Westwood 1993; Pearson 2000). Feminist research has revealed that corporate attempts to situate regions, governments, and workforces as passive recipients of corporate domination are met by a range of responses that are framed in diverse cultural contexts and that may resist, accommodate, or acquiesce to the script of passivity and control. We argue that these blind spots in much of the research on economic globalization result from the exclusion not only of casual and informal spheres, but also of key spaces, places, scales, and actors through which globalization is lived, created, and acted upon in different historical and geographical settings.

Exclusion 2: Certain spaces, places, and scales.

The second element of our feminist engagement with existing critiques of research on globalization concerns the ways in which the spaces and scales of globalization are framed. Specifically, this research has emphasized abstract spaces of globalization; certain scales, such as the supranational or the nation-state (as in Koffman 1996); or certain public or formal spaces and sites, such as institutions, corporations, regions, and global cities (as in Sassen 1998; Thrift 1998). We examine not just which places and scales are included or excluded, but also how they are included or excluded. We challenge the ways in which certain places are constructed as marginal (for example, southern places and deindustrialized places in the north) and as passive recipients of, or as irrelevant to, globalization. The focus of much globalization research is major cities in advanced economies, with their reach and networks extending from the West sometimes to reach non-Western places (Sparke 2001). Southern places are constructed (if they even appear) in this literature as mere recipients of globalization, rather than as being able to act on and transform this global complex. Much of the literature on globalization engages in a double marginalization: Women are sidelined, as is gender analysis more broadly, and southern countries are positioned as the feminized other to advanced economies. In Herod, Tuathail, and Roberts's (1998) book, the case studies cover the United States, Australia, Canada, and France, along with globalized spaces. Sassen (1998) deals

with global cities, most of which are located in OECD countries, and Cox's (1997) edited collection focuses on the scales of globalization and questions of territorialization while emphasizing corporations and flows of commodities, capital, and information (the chapters by Herod and Low are exceptions). Accordingly, these important volumes continue to construct the south and deindustrializing places in the north as the passive, victimized, or invisible "other" to global spaces and processes. We argue that research on globalization would be substantially enhanced by attention to critical development studies' research on gender and on the feminization of southern countries (and deindustrialized spaces in the north). We discuss this surprising lack of engagement more fully in the second section.

Globalization research has also emphasized certain scales (especially those of the nation-state and supra- or multinational organizations) but ignored others. Much work on globalization has, ironically, reinscribed the centrality of nation-states by conceptualizing globalization processes as they relate to nation-state spaces, thereby excluding other crucial scales of analysis (as argued by Sassen 1998; Escobar 2001). These conceptualizations frequently frame the nation-state as subordinate, but even so, this focus on the nation-state encourages the neglect of other scales, such as the household, community, and body (Mountz 2001; Hyndman 2001). This global-national focus reinforces notions of space as discrete, bounded, and separate and works against imagining transnational connections or the salience of processes emanating from finer scales, such as communities, local organizations, and households (Escobar 2001). It also works against the notion that the scales of globalization are socially constructed, relational, and open to reframing. As Kelly (1999, 381–82) stated:

> To speak of local, regional, national, or even global processes is meaningless—social relations are in fact played out across scales rather than confined within them. Consequently, it makes little sense to privilege any scale as a

primary referent for analyzing particular social processes. . . . Establishing in this way that scale can be viewed as both constructed and political enables us to think about globalization in a different light.

Inclusion 2: Spaces and scales of globalization as multiple, intersecting, and socially and politically constructed.

Building on our arguments about the relations among economic, political, and cultural spheres of globalization, we advocate thinking of multiple geographic scales as they are socially constructed and politically charged (Kelly 1999; Cox 1997). Hyndman (2001) pointed out that feminist analysis incorporates a multiplicity of scales that are both larger and smaller than the nation-state, including the body and supranational organizations. We consider not only a broader range of scales as relevant to globalization (including transnational, community, household, and bodily scales), but also how scales are conceptualized in relation to social, political, and cultural processes. Cindi Katz (2001, 1214) argued for a topographical research approach that "carr[ies] out a detailed examination of some part of the material world, designed at any scale from the body to the global, in order to understand its salient features and their mutual broader relationships." Our analysis of globalization recognizes the particularities of places, but also traces the ways in which they are deeply interconnected with processes of globalization, to reveal "a local that is constitutively global" (p. 1214).

Sassen (1998) focused on processes of globalization at the supranational scale and the ways in which they instantiate gender in complex ways. With others (Sparke and Lawson 2001; Agnew 1999; Roberts 1997) Sassen noted that globalization has unbundled sovereignty with the rise of governance without government in the supranational sphere; this unbundling of sovereignty has complex effects with key implications for gender. On the one hand, the rise of transnational governance (Gupta 1998; Ong 1999) has strengthened the claims of powerful

actors (such as global corporations, global financial markets, international institutions, and treaties), opening vulnerable economies and pushing a large number into casualized work—with the poor, women, and minorities disproportionately represented in these marginal sectors (e.g., Lawson 1999; Sassen 1998). On the other hand, this reworking of sovereignty has challenged a historically masculinist framing of sovereignty at the nation-state scale. As both Sassen (1998) and Hyndman (2001) pointed out, nation-state sovereignty claimed that national territory is immune to international law. With globalization and the reworking of sovereignty, the state is no longer the exclusive representative of its population in the international arena; nongovernmental sectors and transnational networks of activists—including women's groups and feminist organizations—are also active players now (Escobar 2001; Radcliffe 2001; Sassen 1998). This rise of transnational civil society, and the role of feminist organizations within it, creates new openings for women to have visibility and political voice (Roberts 1997; Kelly 1999; Mittelman 2000; Pearson 2000).

We emphasize that globalization processes are embedded in community and household scales. Recent feminist scholarship by geographers has illustrated "how attention to processes at multiple geographical scales allows us to understand the nuanced ways in which neocolonial relations of power and political economic structures of domination and subordination combine to shape gendered politics of inequalities, difference, and resistance" in specific communities (Nagar 2000, 685). Similarly, Afshar and Barrientos (1999, 6) contended that

[T]he impact of globalization on women has often been complex and contradictory, both in terms of their "inclusion" and "exclusion." To be understood it needs to be analyzed *not only at the global* but also at the *local and household levels* [italics added]. Feminists have been disaggregating the specificities of women's experiences in the context of the global process, but this work has yet to find its way into much of the core debate over globalization.

Feminist scholars have shown how the emergence of transnational religious and popular discourses have produced new racialized and class-based sexual and labor practices at local and communal scales, giving rise to new geographies of exploitation and struggle. Analyses that recognize spaces, places, and scales inhabited by embodied and socially embedded actors allow for engagement with a series of critical social practices that are dramatically reshaped by global processes. A few examples follow.

Focusing on a village in central eastern Sudan, Katz (2001, 1215) offered "a noninnocent topography of globalization and its entailments in one place as a vehicle for developing a gendered oppositional politics that moves across scale and space." She wrote:

> Without romanticizing the local scale or any particular place, I want to get at the specific ways globalization works on particular grounds in order to work out a situated, but at the same time scale-jumping and geography crossing, political response to it. Tracing the contour lines of such a "counter-topography" to other sites might enable the formation of new political-economic alliances that transcend both place and identity and foster a more effective cultural politics to counter the imperial, patriarchal, and racist integument of globalization. (p. 1216)

Rachel Silvey (2001) analyzed similar multiscaled political responses in examining how Islam shapes the experiences and practices of Indonesian domestic laborers working in Saudi Arabia. She located women's shifting sense of power and religious subjectivities by engaging simultaneously with the policies and attitudes of the Indonesian state, the working conditions in Saudi Arabia, and the sociopolitical activism of domestic workers on their return to Indonesia.

Pratt (1999) and Richa Nagar (2000) explored further connections among transnational migrations, "discursive geographies"

(Pratt 1999), and gendered and racialized subjectivities. Pratt, for example, looked at how three discursive constructions of "Filipina" as "supplicant pre-immigrant"; as inferior "housekeeper"; and, within the Filipino community, as "husband stealer"— work to structure Filipinas' labor market experiences in Vancouver. Pratt's analysis demonstrates what poststructuralist theories of subject and discourse analysis can bring to theories of labor market segmentation and how material geographies of survival and resistance are often written into popular discourses.

Finally, Nagar analyzed the racially charged religious debate over *Mut'a* (temporary marriage) in a South Asian Shiite community in Tanzania, where the increasing economic prosperity of Shiite businessmen since the liberalization of trade in the 1980s and 1990s has led to the development of intimate ties with Islamists in Iran, as well as with South Asian Shiites in the United States, the United Kingdom, Canada, Pakistan, and India. Nagar (2000, 661) extended analyses of difference, sexuality, and postcolonialism by demonstrating how "(a) processes at local, national, and transnational scales intersect to define the heterosexist communal norms that regulate women's bodies in a particular context; (b) the ways in which women confront, defend, or negotiate the terms of this regulation; and (c) the implications of this regulation for women of different backgrounds in a place where gender hierarchies are enmeshed with religious, racial, and class-based distinctions." In all these examples, feminist research on the intersectionality of processes at multiple scales (global, national, community, household, and so on) has revealed how diverse social practices, ideologies of gender, and the shifting power of the subjects of globalization are restlessly being reworked.

As Nagar's research illustrates, the body is also a key site for understanding gender and globalization. Globalization processes occur in concert with a range of changing meanings of gender roles and identities and struggles over masculinity and femininity

(NACLA 2001). In this context, the body is constituted as "a multidimensional and complex object of political struggle—a 'cultural battleground' on which a wide array of issues are fought out" (NACLA 2001, 12). These struggles occur over issues of the commodification of sexuality and desire (Franco 2001; Hodge 2001) and reproductive rights as emblematic of women's citizenship and self-determination (Lamas 2001). Salzinger (2001) showed how a discourse of femininity sustained on the shop floor shapes gendered, disciplined workers inside the *maquiladora*. Gender identities and performances are constructed in the context of labor-control strategies in the factory, and women learn to manipulate male supervisors by deploying their desirability to avoid some aspects of strict managerial control (see also Oglesby 2001; Wright 1997).

In the cities of advanced industrial countries, the discourse of an embodied deferential femininity is a significant part of the restructuring of local economies and the growth of low-wage, low-status, often casual jobs, for which women are seen as ideal recruits. Bourgois (1995) and McDowell (2002) showed how the impact of this discourse constructs young men as unsuitable workers, disadvantaged by their gender and a specific embodied performance of a macho working-class masculinity. The dramatic rise in women-owned businesses in these countries (e.g., from 5 percent of all privately owned U.S. businesses in 1972 to 34 percent in 1992) can be seen, in part, as a resistance to the discourse that valorizes deferential femininity and construes entrepreneurship as a masculine activity, most appropriate for fashioning self-made men. In all these sites and spaces of globalization, the form and character of economic globalization can be fully understood only by attention to gendered social relations, discourses, and processes.

Exclusion 3: Certain subjects and actors.

The actors of economic globalization are frequently conceptualized as formal polit-

ical and economic institutions, such as corporations and multilateral and financial institutions (World Bank, IMF, WTO), and national governments (Greider 1997; Herod, Tuathail, and Robert 1998). Broadly speaking, people as subjects are absent from globalization research, including the critiques we mentioned at the outset of this section; instead, these institutions are the ones with power over the global economy, as is evident in Greider's (1997, 24–25) characterization of four competing power blocks:

> The biggest, most obvious loser . . . is *labor*. . . . *National governments*, likewise, have lost ground . . . most governments have become mere salesmen . . . *multinational corporations* are, collectively, the muscle and brains of this new system, the engineers who are designing the brilliant networks of new relationships. . . . [The] principles [of *finance capital*] are transparent and pure: maximizing return on capital without regard to national identity or political and social consequences. (italics added)

By characterizing corporations and finance capital as consciously engineering the global economy, Greider turned institutions into actors such that processes of trade and investment appear to have agency, if not conspiratorial power. In addition to conflating institutions with people, this focus on formal institutions foregrounds the specific roles that certain people (e.g., managers, not workers) play in those institutions, rather than examining the multiple and cross-cutting aspects of subjectivity and identity that shape people's experiences of globalization.

Some critical analyses of globalization do attend to the people in institutions, but these people are often conceptualized as one-dimensional individuals, categorized as "global managers" and "business gurus" (as in Thrift 1998). As Roberts (2001, 25) pointed out, globalization processes operate through the construction of these masculinist subjects (such as global managers), who are conceptualized as powerful actors who view markets and workers as objects to be controlled. Hence, even when people are incorporated into the analysis, they are elite agents of capital, acting in universal fashion in the service of globalization. Andy Herod (1997, 1998) broadened these conceptualizations by providing situated analyses of the ways in which organized labor has interacted with processes of globalization. His work emphasizes the contingent nature of capital-labor relations, varying from cooperative to conflictive, depending on time and place. It also points to some workers whose agency has influenced the integration of the global economy in various ways. Herod's focus on unionized workers, however, neglects those who are excluded from the labor movement (such as domestic workers, immigrants, and undocumented workers) and neglects the diverse ways in which these individuals engage with globalization in different realms of their lives (as family members, community members, and so on). One-dimensional renditions of people in globalization obscure the multiple oppressions that differentiate subjects in relation to production, politics, and daily life (Hartsock 2001; Roberts 2001; Gibson-Graham 1996).

Even those who consider gender relevant to understanding globalization frequently reduce their analyses to discussions of women as passive victims in poor countries (e.g., Krause 1996). Mittelman (2000, 76), for example, argued that "although there may seem to be nothing particularly masculinist about the ideology of globalization, its specific articulation with gender ideology *sustains the marginalization of women* . . . [T]he gender division of labor is actually one of the factors that makes globalization possible" (italics added). Mittelman's work is important in that it highlights the ways in which subjects of globalization are always embedded in gender relations. His analysis, however, does not engage with women as subjects per se, constructs women as victims, and reduces gender to women. Constructing women as universally exploited by global capital and neoliberal policies obscures the ways in which gendered subjects in particular historically and geographically specific places engage in

complex and contradictory experiences of, and in response to, global processes (see the next section for an elaboration of this point). We argue that richer and more complex understandings of globalization will emerge if analysts conceptualize its subjects as people who are embedded in social relations of gender, class, race, and so on, as well as in multiple networks for coping with, reforming, or resisting global processes (including unions, feminist organizations, and environmental social movements).

Inclusion 3: Analyses that incorporate subjects and actors that the economic globalization literature has neglected and that view these actors' subjectivities as multiple and contextual.

We agree with Herod (1997, 192) that economic geography would benefit from a more sustained engagement with situated agents: "[W]hereas economic geographers have traditionally relied on understanding the dynamics of capital to explain patterns of economic geography (e.g., theory of the firm, circuits of capital circulation, capital switching, and the like), [the preceding] analysis suggests the need to take labor's role in actively creating geographies much more seriously." We take a similar stance in advocating a focus on the lives of people who are marginalized by globalization to reveal the complex and contradictory ways in which people engage with global processes. This stance resonates with the work of scholars who have focused on an emergent bottom-up politics in resistance to the violences of globalization and have argued that a recomposition of civil society is emerging (Roberts 1997; Falk 1995; Mittelman 2000). Although this work makes a key contribution by foregrounding a "people-level globalization" (Mittelman 2000), it focuses on people who are engaged in political organizations and so emphasizes only resistance. A grounded, feminist approach starts from the lives of a variety of people with diverse relationships to globalization, including unorganized workers, undocumented immigrants, and those who are not involved with political movements. This broadened view attends to the range of social locations (gender, class, ethnicity, race, and sexuality) that refract globalization processes and to the multiple ways in which globalization is lived, created, accommodated, and acted upon in different historical and geographic settings.

Our Inclusion 3 challenges the ways in which certain actors—both individual and collective—are ignored or constructed only as passive victims of global processes or agents of resistance. One example comes from Hanson's (2000, 2001) study of owners of small business in a U.S. Rust Belt city; through their strong commitment to a particular, somewhat marginalized, place, these entrepreneurs are resisting globalization while simultaneously participating in global networks. Another example from the industrialized world is McDowell's (2000a, 2002) study of the impact of economic and social change, especially the decline of the manufacturing sector, in two localities in England, where she is investigating the opportunities that poorly educated young white men face as they finish compulsory schooling. As Katz (1998) and Bourgois (1995) have documented in New York City, working-class youths face declining labor market opportunities in inner-city neighborhoods but are culturally ill-equipped for employment in the service sector. Their attitudes of bravado and machismo often disqualify them from the only jobs there are—"feminized" service jobs that demand docile and deferential attitudes and performances. Young women in these localities, on the other hand, see their labor market opportunities expanding, albeit in low-status and poorly paid occupations. Thus, the combination of global economic restructuring and local "structures of feeling" and social networks are recasting gender relations among working-class young people to the disadvantage of men, leading some commentators to identify a contemporary "crisis of masculinity" (Clare 2000, McDowell 2000b).

A third example is that of Nagar and Raju (forthcoming), who view women's nongovernmental organizations (NGOs) in India as complex actors that are shaped by processes at multiple geographic scales, on the one hand, and by interlocking hierarchies of gender, class, caste, and religion, on the other hand. The authors connect the interwoven processes of empowerment and disempowerment in poor women's lives with the ways in which pressures from international donors have increasingly led to reshaping organizational structures, hierarchies, and agendas through mainstreaming and professionalization. Such changes, however, are laden with immense contradictions and possibilities. Also, the foreclosing of some political spaces is often accompanied by the emergence of new ones that enable NGOs to address issues of social and structural violence in innovative and highly contextualized ways.

Our Inclusion 3 highlights the complexities and contradictions that are inherent in actors' relationships to globalization. In the next section, we present a thematic overview of feminist research in critical development studies that highlights the ways in which global processes can be liberating as well as exploitative, empowering as well as disempowering, and transforming as well as reinforcing of patriarchal structures and gender relations. Recognizing such complexities and contradictions is central to a feminist epistemology, a point we explore more fully in the final section.

Feminist Research on Global Processes

In many ways, feminist interventions in critical development studies and transnational organizing over the past two decades can be seen as a long-term intellectual and political struggle over the same exclusions and inclusions that we detailed in the preceding section. Although much of this literature has been produced by nongeographers and hence does not explicitly reflect a geographic sensibility, its engagements with the politics of development, globalization, and empowerment have necessarily begun from the vantage point of those peoples and places that have been the most marginalized by global capitalist processes. Slowly but surely, these feminist studies have reshaped the terrain of development—at both the discursive and policy levels—by deeply politicizing notions of work; placing households, shop floors, hospitals, schools, weekly markets, and diasporic networks in direct relationship with corporations, markets, banks, and development institutions; engaging with people's lived experiences of globalization in all their contradictions; and revealing that these erased and neglected voices and spaces are by no means passive or simply victimized, but actively engaged in struggles over access to resources and the very definitions of *development, progress, empowerment,* and *justice.*

Because of the considerable overlap between globalization and development, one may expect these contributions to be equally visible in research on globalization. Sadly, however, there is an odd disconnect between the literatures on economic globalization and development, with the result that these critical feminist understandings are often absent from or, at best, muted in academic discussions of globalization. Here, we seek to connect the economic globalization community with the large body of feminist research on global processes.[3] Rather than provide a comprehensive review of what is a large literature, we highlight the nature of these contributions. Since the late 1980s, feminist scholars have developed powerful critiques of the neocolonial discourses on women and development (Mohanty 1991a, 1991b; Ong 1987; Parpart and Marchand 1995) and iden-

tified "lapses into foundationalism and essentialism in (Western) feminist texts on 'Third World' women" (Marchand 1995, 58). These discussions have sensitized feminist researchers to the problems of universal, ahistorical, and decontexualized generalizations about women's oppressions and have inspired more grounded analyses of the historically and geographically specific ways in which patriarchal discursive practices intersect with subsistence agrarian production and industrial capitalism in a globalizing world (Gordon 1996; Stitcher and Parpart 1990).

We consider feminist analyses that have emerged over more than a decade from a variety of sociopolitical locations and struggles on such subjects as international divisions of labor; informal economies and feminization of poverty; gender bias in structural adjustment/neoliberal economies; gender and social reproduction as women provide services to households and communities when the state withdraws from social reproduction; gender and mobility, including internal and transnational migrations, refugees, and international sex workers; and popular protests and transnational feminisms. Our review divides these topics into three themes that are the most pertinent to research on globalization: the gendering of work, gender and structural adjustment programs (SAPs), and mobility and diasporas.

The Gendering of Work

The gendering of work is one of the many areas in which feminists have used a grounded approach to examine how subjectivity is drawn upon and contested in shaping context-specific relationships between "globalized" capital and "localized" labor. Diane Wolf (1992) highlighted the contradictions and complexities of industrial capitalist proletarianization through the lives and voices of Javanese "factory daughters," and Chandra Mohanty (1997) illustrated how global processes of capitalism use local ideologies and gendered identities for their own ends. Naturalized assumptions about

---

[3] Some scholars have begun to consider the intersections and disjunctures between critical development studies and research on globalization (see, e.g., Slater (1992), Watts (1993), Gupta (1998), Escobar (1995), and Ong (1991)). Even in these studies, however, work on gender and development remains largely neglected. In addition, the proliferation of discourses on globalization and transnationalism—in both the mainstream and feminist literatures—has tended to crowd out analyses of the theory, praxis, and politics of development.

work and the worker are constructed around "notions of appropriate femininity, domesticity, (hetero) sexuality, and racial and cultural stereotypes" (Mohanty 1997, 6). Mohanty discussed (inter alia) Maria Mies's (1982) study of home-working lace makers in Narsapur to show how capitalists mobilized the ideology of women as housewives to define lace makers as nonworkers and to label their lace making for corporations as a leisure activity. Carla Freeman (2000, 3) explored the interconnected "dialectics of globalization/localization, production/consumption, and gender/class" through the everyday lives of pink-collar informatics operators in Barbados. She showed how the work process in informatics is imbued with notions of appropriate femininity and how dress and feminine image-making make workers' experiences simultaneously burdensome and pleasurable; she also tied their engagement in the formal informatics sector directly to a range of practices in the informal economy. This literature vividly illustrates that both the subjects of globalization (Exclusion 3) and the scale of the body (Exclusion 2) are central to the gendered processes of globalized work.

Research on flexible labor regimes has focused on the feminization of the transnational industrial force and its implications for workers' struggles in the "periphery." In contrast to Fordism, flexible accumulation draws on female and minority workers and involves, as Aihwa Ong (1991, 280) stated, "local milieus constituted by the unexpected conjunctures of labor relations and cultural systems, high-tech operations and indigenous values." Ong further argued that the means of labor control extend beyond the workplace into community life and that workers' resistance is "more often linked to kinship and gender than to class" (p. 281).

Recent feminist scholarship has expanded these ideas by highlighting the intersections across geographic scales, ranging from the bodily to the global, and across what are often problematically labeled "independent" spheres (formal/informal) and sectors (economy, culture, politics)—interdependencies that we discussed in Inclusion 1.

Research on home-based work, for example, shows how competition in international markets is increasingly pushing national companies to resort to flexible home-based subcontracting arrangements (Beneria and Roldan 1987; Mitter 1986; White 1994; Lawson 1995). The specific ways in which women, men, and children are drawn into these arrangements, however, are centrally shaped by communal discourses of religion, honor, respectability, and machismo; by the workings of state and legal structures at the local level; by the specific ways in which the public-private dichotomy is reproduced and reified; and by the forms of cooperation that emerge between unions and community groups (Prugl and Boris 1996; Mirchandani 1998). Similarly, Cravey (1998) analyzed how gender and class intersect in the transformation of Mexican industrial strategy, from one focused on import substitution to a neoliberal export orientation based on transnational investment. Cravey showed how microscale negotiations over the gender division of labor within households and neighborhoods influenced global and regional dynamics and was also shaped by national policies and global competition.

Gender and Structural Adjustment Programs

Perhaps no other issue has triggered a wider dialogue among feminist scholars and activists around the globe than SAPs (Dalla Costa and Dalla Costa 1993; Elson 1994; Emeagwali 1995; Sparr 1994). Indeed, critical interrogation of SAPs is one of the key areas in which feminist analysts have extended globalization research by demonstrating how new gendered understandings of globalization processes are intertwined with neoliberal discourses and policies. These studies also allow us to apprehend how globalization discourses legitimate neoliberal policies that redefine the positions of individuals and nations within the global context and how this legitimacy, in turn, serves the material processes of globalization (Kelly 1999). At the same time, they demonstrate that such relationships among discourses, policies, and processes are historically—not naturally or necessarily—produced and that alternative spaces can be created for progressive forms of globalization.

Among the salient themes in the discussion of SAPs are the relationships between social reproduction and international debt policies and among SAPs, governmental strategies, and market-led growth. In *Paying the Price* (Dalla Costa and Dalla Costa 1993, 1), several contributors likened the SAPs to "capital's first phase of 'primitive accumulation.'" Caffentzis (1993, 31) noted:

> [The World Bank] and other financial agencies have managed the debt crisis in such a way as to create a strikingly Malthusian situation, characterized by the presence of "positive" and "negative" checks: famines, war, and disease, generated by falling incomes, reduced health services and changes in land tenure and cropping. Indeed, the African body, especially the female body, has been attacked ... in ways similar to those in which the European proletariat in the "transition to capitalism" was terrorized by witch hunts, plagues of syphilis, the "price revolution," famines and war. The outcome of this campaign cannot be presented in traditional economic indices: GNP, interest rates or foreign exchange values. At best we can look at demographic statistics and note that, starting in 1982, there has been a reversal in the post-colonial decline in African mortality.

Social reproduction has thus become the "primary and therefore fundamental terrain for the restructuring needed in a new phase of accumulation" (Dalla Costa and Dalla Costa 1993, 1–2).

Diane Elson (1994) argued that in explicitly relying on price changes and market forces as the instruments for reallocating resources, architects of SAPs overlook their implicit reliance on a supply of unpaid female labor to enable the reallocation of paid labor. She pointed to the need for alternative policies that focus not simply on retargeting public expenditures and extending marketing opportunities more effectively to women, but on redressing

power inequalities by restructuring market relationships, political and bureaucratic relations, and relationships within households. This discussion, along with rich ethnographic studies of the kind undertaken by Gracia Clark (1994), illustrates the point we made in Inclusion 1, namely, that globalization needs to be understood in terms of gendered and racialized, culturally specific systems of oppression and struggles to negotiate and redefine those systems. Feminist work has helped to highlight how oppressions constitute globalization and how revealing these oppressions can lead to new openings and understandings about agency.

Although analyses of SAPs have often highlighted the increasing burdens on poor women, feminist scholarship has also challenged the idea of women as mere victims. Afshar and Barrientos (1999) criticized globalization research for either ignoring the unequal impact that globalization has had on women or simplistically viewing women as victims of globalization. They advocated research on how globalization can both empower and disempower women; how patriarchal power structures have been transformed, rather than erased, by globalization; and how new forms of resistance emerge as women are increasingly integrated into the global production process. The contributors demonstrated how local and global processes that help reshape formal and informal sectors of the economy are also linked with the remaking of fractured states and religious ideologies and varied articulations of women's agency. In so doing, they advanced previous work on the intersections among politicized religion, nationalisms, and women's activism in postcolonial contexts (see Moghadam 1994; Afshar 1996; Jeffery and Basu 1998). Rai (1999) addressed these interrelationships by exploring how women street vendors oppose, subvert, negotiate, and cooperate with various forms of the Indian state. Phalke (1999) looked at the intersections between patriarchy and modernity to understand the right-wing mobilization of Hindu women in India, and Afshar (1999) examined how Islamification and women's reconstruction of Islamic discourses in Iran have been shaped by the interactions between global policies and local specificities. Similarly, El-Mikawy (1999) demonstrated how conservative and populist counterreaction to globalization in Egypt has reified women's role as mothers but undermined their public role as civic partners.

Mobility and Diasporas

The new feminist literature on mobility and diasporas captures similar cultural, political, and economic complexities. Researchers in various parts of the world have analyzed how morality, religion, state ideologies, and colonial and postcolonial histories both enmesh with economic policies to shape gendered mobilities and subjectivities, production relations, and consumer aspirations in migrants' lives and sustain existing social hierarchies (Nagar 1998; Radcliffe 1990; Silvey 2000). This research has addressed another gap in the literature on globalization, which has largely ignored migrants and their networks; to the extent that migrants have been considered, they are conceptualized primarily as workers, rather than as complex, political subjects.

Some of the most creative feminist engagements with questions of mobility, ideology, subjectivity, and struggle are represented in emerging research on global sex work. Kempadoo's (2001) collaborative research with feminist scholars and practitioners in Colombia and Cuba identified the participation of women as sex tourists as an important part of the late twentieth-century Caribbean landscape and proposed an interrogation of the recolonizations shaped through the global tourism industry. By highlighting how Caribbean women and men are both subject to eroticizing, sexualizing fantasies and exploitation, and how sex tourists—both male and female—use the Caribbean as a place to consolidate or redefine their own cultural identities, these researchers have shown the limitations of feminist analyses that rely solely on masculine hegemony as an explanation for prostitution and sex work. Instead, they have

emphasized that sexual labor has been historically, culturally, and socially organized and how these specificities allow for a multiplicity of sexualized and gendered categories, identities, and dependencies. This research moves us beyond the essentialist notions of the prostitute and the client and "starkly [illustrates] the global repositioning that is occurring between postindustrial and postcolonial societies, where Black and Brown bodies become (or continue to be) the sites for the construction of (white) North American and Western European power, wealth, and well-being" (Kempadoo 2001, 58).

Questions of mobility and subjectivity have also resonated in feminist discussions on global democracy and social movements. Eschle (2001, 210–11) considered the work of "black and Third World feminists," such as Grewal, Anzaldua, Alexander, and Mohanty, who theorized the effects of *"enforced* mobility on a global scale" and "[drew] attention to the pain and trauma of processes of displacement and marginality that have been evacuated from more abstracted postmodern accounts." At the same time, these theorists have evoked strategies for reformulating subjectivity by drawing attention to the gendered and raced migrant subject whose location "disrupts the home/abroad and the margin/center constructs for more complex positionings" (Grewal 1994, 235) and whose rootedness in the "borderlands" is shaped by resistance to racist dualisms and to ethnocentric attempts to impose linguistic fixity (Anzaldua 1987, 1990).

By placing questions of mobility and subjectivity at the center, such feminist interventions emphasize how economic dimensions of contemporary globalization processes are thoroughly entangled with the ways in which the same processes reconstitute and reinvigorate preexisting social hierarchies (Alexander and Mohanty 1997). Furthermore, feminist theorists (e.g., Eisenstein 1997; Eschle 2001) have reminded us that globalizing reconfigurations of space, time and territoriality have coercive effects and occur unevenly, with much of the world continuing to live according to slow rhythms, embedded within territories, and with others forcibly displaced. Further, feminist accounts attempt to re-embed ostensibly supra-territorial and "hypermobile" interactions within material social relations, revealing interconnections with recognizable, territorially located, and socially stratified places and processes, as well as opportunities and dangers for people depending on their location and embodiment . . . . [Finally, globalization] allows for the subversive possibility of women seeing beyond the local to the global. This move puts male privilege clearly in view [as] never before. It also enables the construction of transborder identifications and organizations in response. (Eschle 2001, 187)

Eschle blended these insights with those of Newland (1988); Pietila and Vickers (1994); and coalitions, such as Women Living Under Muslim Laws, on anticapitalist organizing below and across the state and on transformatory change through coalition politics. She proposed a "skeptical and strategic approach to the state and state system" as an "appropriate way of understanding the dilemmas of transnational feminist organizing" (p. 215). In so doing, she advanced the pioneering analyses in feminist international politics that have conceptualized feminist activism in relation to gendered divisions of violence, labor, and resources and have specifically considered the combined impact of gender hierarchies and globalization on democracy (Enloe 1988; Pettman 1996; Peterson and Runyan 1999; Peterson 1995).

Taken as a whole, then, feminist research in development studies has provided grounded and contextual understandings of globalization by highlighting the ways in which gender—as a social category that is thoroughly interwoven with race, class, religion, and other axes of social difference— has been central to reworked forms of capitalism and to resistance. A major strength of this work is its ability to mediate analytically between larger structural processes and finer-scaled contextual reali-

ties in ways that underscore the complex workings of political economic and sociocultural processes at scales ranging from the body and the household to the local, national, and transnational. These approaches allow us to look at the intricacies of labor, identity, and agency and to explore the messy ways in which empowerment and disempowerment, production and reproduction, exploitation and pleasure remain thoroughly entangled with each other. In so doing, they have rejected simplistic generalizations that cast globalization as either totally victimizing or completely liberatory and have illuminated the subtle ways in which power relations, interdependencies, negotiated constructions of femininity and masculinity, and multilayered politics of difference constitute the everyday politics and realities of globalization.

We are curious why so little conversation has taken place between the feminist research reviewed in this section and the mainstream literature on economic globalization. And why is gender and development marginalized even within feminist work on globalization and transnationalism? We argue that these disconnects reflect conceptual, epistemological, and methodological differences between the two approaches, which make conversation difficult. Starting with the lives of marginalized people, rather than with the nation or the global economy, not only animates new questions, analyses, and insights on globalization, but has far-reaching methodological and epistemological implications. Although the literature reviewed here deals implicitly with questions of methodology and epistemology, we believe that an explicit engagement with these concerns lies at the heart of a feminist retheorizing of economic globalization. As the next section reveals, it is only through such an engagement that the politics of knowledge production on globalization can be recast and recentered on the voices, scales, and spaces of hitherto marginalized subjects.

Feminist Epistemologies and Methodologies

In this section, we consider the implications of feminist epistemologies and methodologies for understandings of economic globalization, recognizing that in the preceding sections we have already touched on many of the points that we explicitly address here. We take for granted a certain awareness of key debates among feminists, both feminist geographers and other social scientists, in recent years—about situated knowledges, critical social science, ethnocentrism, and the impact of postmodernism. In thinking about feminist epistemologies in the context of research on economic globalization, we aim to build on earlier critiques of the specificity of Western social science, especially in its Anglo and Anglo-American forms; we lay out a series of connections between recent work in feminist and geographic scholarship to show how current interests in both bodies of work in differentiation and variation among people and places has led to a coincidence of approaches. These feminist-inspired approaches—which take seriously issues of gender, scale, and politics—involve modes of knowledge creation that differ substantially from the ways in which analysts have sought understandings of economic globalization to date. As in the previous sections on conceptual issues and empirical work, our hope here is to generate productive conversation between the feminist and the economic globalization literatures.

Both feminist work and work in the mainstream of geography reflect a growing acknowledgement of the uneven nature of globalization and an interest in exploring its specificities in particular locations, whether households, firms and organizations, or localities. Some geographers have also shown an expanding interest in the interconnections between economic processes and social and cultural formations. Thus, through a common focus on globalization, analysts have begun to ask questions about the ways in which global flows—of capital, labor, information, and ideas—connect

and affect specific social and spatial formations in places that are distinguished by particular histories and geographies. These specificities result in differentiated forms of gender relations that are transformed by but also affect global shifts. This recognition of the connections between what is often called the global and the local is a striking feature of recent feminist work, particularly of scholarship from the peripheries, not the center, and by women of color and scholars in the south. Because global processes affect structures of domination in ways that often result in deepening patterns of inequality, the particular effects of globalization and the prospects of struggling against them are matters of huge theoretical and political concern.

Propositions

Next, we set out a series of propositions or arguments outlining the implications of feminist epistemologies for research on globalization.

Proposition 1: Capitalism must be analyzed as a set of social relations that are mediated through the simultaneous operation of gendered, sexualized, and racialized hierarchies.

That globalization clearly strengthens and deepens capitalist social relations means that capitalism must be increasingly placed at the center of analyses of globalization. As Alexander and Mohanty (1997, xvii) argued, "global realignments and fluidity of capital have simply led to further consolidation and exacerbation of capitalist relations of domination and exploitation"; what they termed "processes of recolonization" challenge and recast global relations of domination formed under previous regimes. Research, therefore, needs to examine the specific cultural, political, economic, and social consequences of the transformation of particular historical circumstances as different places are drawn into the social relations of globalization in different ways. It must also examine changing circumstances in the various arenas of everyday life from the perspective of participants who are differentiated by gender, sexuality, and racialization and so are drawn into or excluded from new social processes in particular ways. For example, studies of how new labor forces are assembled must clarify how gender and ethnicity are linked as well as how potential workers are positioned in the social relations of reproduction. Because production is not generic in its recruitment and organization of labor, "we must incorporate into our reading of the labor process the simultaneous processes of the culture of production and the production of culture" (Freeman 2000, 51).

Thus, in this emphasis on the impact of capital flows and the dominance of capitalist social relations, studies must incorporate the specificity of place and the differential impact of capitalist social relations. This point leads to Proposition 2.

> *Proposition 2: Analyses of globalization from the perspectives of both the south and the north are crucial, focusing on place and on the local, as well as on space and general globalizing processes and their coconstitution.*

Our insistence on bringing attention to the often-neglected subjects, scales, and places of globalization in the periphery, rather than in the center, resonates with Arturo Escobar's (2001) call for a reconceptualization of globalization in which close attention is paid to the role of place and local knowledges. Escobar followed J. K. Gibson-Graham (1996) in arguing against capital centrism, as it is often defined and theorized, as Eurocentric, thus excluding the possibilities of other ways of theorizing globalization. Capital-centric approaches currently privilege not only class relations but also Western knowledge about globalization processes; they also privilege spatialities of globalization that place the nation-state—a product of Western imperialism—at the center. Escobar argued that other stories can be told, stories from marginalized places that emphasize differences rather than similarities, diversity rather than homogeneity. As

he noted, "The erasure of place is a reflection of the asymmetry that exist[s] between the global and the local in much contemporary literature on globalization, in which the global is associated with space, capital, history, and agency while the local, conversely, is linked to place, labor, and tradition—as well as with women, minorities, the poor, and one might add, local cultures" (2001, 155–56). This challenge to reconceptualize the places of globalization and to work against the erasure of other readings from women, minorities, and the south is central to a feminist epistemology. A focus on places—on grounded analysis—has often been constructed, however, as marginal in theoretical and epistemological debates in geography, partly through its very localization. It is crucial to challenge the claims of the center, of capital-centrism and Eurocentrism that are the privileged, authoritative terrain of global-speak, as well as to insert into analyses of globalization a focus on the connections between production and the institutions of employment and reproduction, bodies, households, and communities. As we argued in the previous sections, there is still a great need for wider acceptance of long-term feminist arguments that production and reproduction must be analyzed in tandem. This point leads to Proposition 3, regarding work on the local and the particular:

> *Proposition 3: We recover place, but not to celebrate experience or the local per se, but rather to "reveal a local that is constitutively global" (Katz 2001, 1214).*

We draw on Cindi Katz's (2001) concept of topography, which builds on Massey's (1994) now-classic work on the constitution of place, to argue for research that moves beyond place as unique, self-contained, or victimized to place as an entry point for developing a relational approach to globalization that "situates places in their broader context and in relation to other geographic scales, offering a means of understanding structure and process. Indeed, my project is driven here by the notion that producing a critical topography makes it possible to excavate the layers of process that produce particular places and to their intersections with material social practices at other scales of analysis" (Katz 2001, 1228). Resolutely material, these countertopographies also reveal the contour lines that relate distinct locales to one another through their experience of particular social practices. As we noted in the first section, this reading of places as embedded and intimately related through globalization processes can lay the groundwork for building a gendered oppositional politics that moves across space and scale. As Alexander and Mohanty (1997, xix) have argued, feminist scholars stress issues of "power, history, memory, relational analysis, justice (not just representation), and ethics as central to our analysis of globalization." Therefore, we advocate the following proposition:

Proposition 4: Collaborative research must be undertaken with subjects of globalization in peripheralized places.

This proposition is linked to Hartsock's (2001) argument, reviewed in the first section, about the strategic potential of starting from the lives of those who are marginalized to understand the operation of global capitalism. Grounded, place-based, collaborative research is part of reimagining and retheorizing globalization and development. Appadurai (2000) argued for the significance of what he termed "grassroots globalization" on the basis that people in peripheralized places articulate diverse readings and social mobilizations regarding globalization. These visions articulate strategies and visions on behalf of the poor who strive for a democratic and autonomous standing with respect to various forms of global power. Appadurai suggested that Western academic research needs to engage seriously with alternative readings and strategies for engaging globalization, rather than continue to produce the hegemony of Western social science research practices that center Western academic norms of "scientific," often discipline-bounded, knowl-

edge production within research universities.

These norms of citation, value freedom, and replicability raise difficult questions for public intellectuals in the periphery, and Appadurai asked if we can imagine ways to internationalize social science research in this context. In other words, he proposed "a deeper consideration of the relationship between knowledge of globalization and the globalization of knowledge" (Appadurai 2000, 13). Appadurai argued for engaging with scholars from other cultures to debate what counts as new knowledge, what commitments of judgment and accountability should be central to critical studies on globalization. Using case studies from the writings of Third World scholars and developing collaborative research on globalization may produce new kinds of knowledge and pedagogy. Taking seriously the institutions, vocabularies, and horizons of globalization from below will require Western academics to step back "from the obsessions and abstractions that constitute our own professional practice to seriously consider the problems of the global everyday" (Appadurai 2000, 17–18). The inclusions we called for in the first section make explicit connections between political economy and localized struggles around identity politics. We argue for the importance of body, place, and transnational as scales of an alternative, feminist analytic of globalization.

On the basis of these propositions, we advocate building richly grounded work that develops intricate understandings across a multiplicity of scales. This work will involve collaborative case studies that tell different stories about globalization from the south and West and that do not privilege a singular theorization of dominant Western capitalism. In this way, the research will work against the erasures of marginalized peoples and places. In terms of methodological strategies, we are in sympathy with recent work in anthropology and sociology that has developed an approach that has been variously termed multisited or global ethnography, which is interested in analyzing the connections between and among places; in travel as well as dwelling; and in the flows of ideas, people, or money (Burawoy et al. 2000; Clifford 1997; Kaplan 1996; Marcus 1998).

Although all methodological strategies depend, to some extent, on the aim of the research in question, we advocate close attention to interconnections—whether between the arenas of waged work and the household, between economic and cultural processes, between the spatially distinctive parts of a multinational organization, or between nation-states and international institutions. To give just one example of an area in which future research needs to highlight such interconnected processes, we advocate building ethnographies of institutions of globalization and development (such as corporations, the World Bank, and the IMF) as well as place-based studies to reveal the emergence of new forms of governance, to understand the contingencies and vulnerabilities that drive different forms of global capital, to uncover the wide variety of power-knowledge regimes at work within the multiple institutions of globalization, and to understand the power of these actors in the contemporary period so as to envision a politics of opposition.

Conclusion

Building a feminist analysis of globalization is not simply a matter of recognizing the importance of gender in processes of economic globalization. A feminist understanding of globalization requires substantial conceptual, analytical, and epistemological shifts; it opens up new questions regarding what is appropriately included under the rubric of economic globalization and in any litany of probable causes or salient consequences. As Marchand and Runyan (2000b, 18) put it, global restructuring "entails reworkings of the boundaries between and meanings of femininity and masculinity, which are intimately related to the shifting boundaries and meanings of private and public, domestic and international, local and global." A feminist analysis dramatically expands the scope of "the

economic" in economic globalization by drawing attention to the inseparability of activities in the formal and informal, paid and unpaid, productive and reproductive spheres. While it appreciates the material dimensions of globalization, a feminist analysis also insists on the importance of cultural and political meanings (e.g., of femininity and masculinity, work, justice, and activism). Feminism's central concern with gender necessarily entails an engagement with power and the complex ways in which power works at multiple geographic scales, including those of the body and the household. A feminist analysis further emphasizes human agency and therefore calls attention to the resilience and creativity with which people and communities survive, accommodate to, and resist global processes. In short, we contend that research on globalization should attend to the cultural construction of difference; to productive and caring activities conducted outside the formal economy and its institutions; and to a diverse range of spaces, scales, and subjects. In doing so, it must theorize and engage with questions of intersectionality in the production, reproduction, and constitution of globalized spaces, places, and spheres of human activity.

We advocate research that both pays close attention to geographic and historical context and yields insights that are portable and hence applicable in other contexts; we do not see these two desiderata as incompatible. Rather, clarifying precisely how certain processes are related to specific contexts (when context includes linkages among diverse geographic scales) and carefully spelling out the nature of connections in a particular context illuminates which of the insights gained from one context (e.g., a case study of a Pakistani village) may be usefully employed in analyzing a similar problem in another context. Only by undertaking a large number of richly contextual studies that cut across many geographic scales will analysts be able to appreciate which aspects of any particular process or place usefully illuminate circumstances in a different time and place. In the second section, we described the burgeoning feminist literature on globalization that has begun this process of building a body of theory from carefully contextualized accounts. In contrast to conventional studies of economic globalization, these feminist studies begin with the lives of people, often those who have been marginalized by globalization. They insist on a relational analysis that highlights complexity and interdependencies without compromising a commitment to social equity, justice, ethics, and democracy. While such studies begin at the local scale, they do not assume that explanation lies only at this level.

A feminist analysis therefore fundamentally changes the nature of understandings of economic globalization. Above all, it entails a shift from a straightforward, linear, master narrative toward diverse and possibly conflicting accounts. These feminist accounts will motivate questions of whose and which accounts are to be believed—which accounts should count as knowledge? As Joan Scott (1989, 681) pointed out in the context of history, "Written history both reflects and creates relations of power. Its standards of inclusion and exclusion, measures of importance, and rules of evaluation are not objective criteria but politically produced conventions." In our view, the feminist approaches we have outlined here will greatly enrich understandings of economic globalization; they will also highlight that knowledge production is a political process and, we hope, generate lively debate. The first step is to initiate a conversation between these two realms of scholarship—feminist analysis and economic globalization.

References

Afshar, H., ed. 1996. *Women and politics in the Third World.* New York: Routledge.

———. 1999. The impact of global and the reconstruction of local Islamic ideology, and assessment of its role in shaping feminist politics in post-revolutionary Iran. In *Women, globalization and fragmentation in the developing world*, ed. H. Afshar and S. Barrientos, 54–76. London: Macmillan.

Afshar, H., and Barrientos, S., eds. 1999. *Women, globalization and fragmentation in the developing world.* London: Macmillan.

Agnew, J. 1999. The new geopolitics of power. In *Human geography today*, ed. D. Massey, J. Allen, and P. Sarre, 173–93. Cambridge, U.K.: Polity Press.

Alexander, M. J., and Mohanty, C.T. 1997. Introduction: Genealogies, legacies, movements. In *Feminist genealogies, colonial legacies, democratic futures*, ed. M. J. Alexander and C. T. Mohanty, xiii–xlii. New York: Routledge.

Anzaldua, G. 1987. *Borderlands/La Frontera: The new mestiza.* San Francisco: Aunt Lute Books.

———. 1990. La conciencia de la mestiza: Toward a new consciousness. In *Making face, making soul/Haciendo caras: Creative and critical perspectives by feminists of color*, ed. G. Anzaldua, 377–89. San Francisco: Aunt Lute Books.

Appadurai, A. 2000. Grassroots globalization and the research imagination. *Public Culture* 12:1–19.

Bello, W.; Cunningham, S.; and Rau, B. 1994. *Dark victory: The United States, structural adjustment, and global poverty.* Oakland, Calif.: Food First.

Beneria, L., and Feldman, S., eds. 1992. *Unequal burden: Economic crises, persistent poverty, and women's work.* Boulder, Colo.: Westview Press.

Beneria, L., and Roldan, M. 1987. *The crossroads of class and gender: Industrial homework, subcontracting and household dynamics in Mexico City.* Chicago: University of Chicago Press.

Bourgois, P. 1995. *In search of respect: Selling crack in el barrio.* Cambridge, U.K.: Cambridge University Press.

Burawoy, M.; Blum, J. A.; George, S.; Gille, Z.; Gowan, T.; Haney, L.; Klawiter, M.; Lopez, S. H.; and Riain, S. O.; and Thayer, M. 2000. *Global ethnography.* Berkeley: University of California Press.

Caffentzis, C. G. 1993. The fundamental implications of the debt crisis for social reproduction in Africa. In *Paying the price: Women and the politics of international economic strategy*, ed. M. Dalla Costa and G. F. Dalla Costa, 15–41. London: Zed Books.

Castells, M. 2000. *End of millennium.* Oxford, U.K.: Blackwell.

Clare, A. 2000. *On men: Masculinity in crisis.* London: Chatto and Windus.

Clark, G. 1994. *Onions are my husband: Survival and accumulation by West African market women.* Bloomington: Indiana University Press.

Clifford, J. 1997 *Routes: Travel and translation in the late twentieth century.* Cambridge, Mass.: Harvard University Press.

Cox, K. 1997. *Spaces of globalization.* New York: Guilford Press.

Cravey, A. 1998. *Women and work in Mexico's maquiladoras.* Lanham, Md.: Rowman and Littlefield.

Dalla Costa, M., and Dalla Costa, G. F., eds. 1993. *Paying the price: Women and the politics of international economic strategy.* London: Zed Books.

Eisenstein, Z. 1997. Women's publics and the search for new democracies. *Feminist Review* 57:140–67.

El-Mikawy, N. 1999. The informal sector and the conservative consensus: A case of fragmentation in Egypt. In *Women, globalization and fragmentation in the developing world,* ed. H. Afshar and S. Barrientos, 77–90. London: Macmillan.

Elson, D. 1994. Structural adjustment with gender awareness? *Indian Journal of Gender Studies* 1:149–67.

Emeagwali, G. T., ed. 1995. *Women pay the price: Structural adjustment in Africa and the Caribbean.* Lawrenceville, N.J.: Africa World Press.

Enloe, C. 1988. *Does khaki become you? The militarization of women's lives,* 2d ed. London: Pandora Press.

Eschle, C. 2001. *Global democracy, social movements and feminism.* Boulder, Colo.: Westview Press.

Escobar, A. 1995. *Encountering development.* Princeton, N.J.: Princeton University Press.

———. 2001. Culture sits in places: Reflections on globalism and subaltern strategies of localization. *Political Geography* 20:139–74.

Falk, R. 1995. *On human governance: Toward a new global politics.* University Park: Pennsylvania State University Press.

Folbre, N. 2001. *The invisible heart: Economics and family values.* New York: New Press.

Franco, J. 2001. Bodies in contention. *NACLA Report on the Americas* 34:41–5.

Freeman, C. 2000. *High tech and high heels in the global economy: Women, work, and pink-collar identities in the Caribbean.* Durham, N.C.: Duke University Press.

Fukuyama, F. 1992. *The end of history and the last man.* London: Hamish Hamilton.

Gibson-Graham, J. K. 1996. *The end of capitalism (as we knew it).* Oxford, U.K.: Blackwell.

Giddens, A. 2000. *Runaway world.* New York: Routledge.

Gingrich, N. 1995. *To renew America.* New York: HarperCollins.

Gordon, A. 1996. *Transforming capitalism and patriarchy: Gender and development in Africa.* Boulder, Colo.: Lynne Reiner.

Greider, W. 1997. *One world, ready or not.* New York: Simon and Schuster.

Grewal, I. 1994. Autobiographic subjects and diasporic locations: Meatless days and border-lands. In *Scattered hegemonies: Post-modernities and transnational feminist practices,* ed. I. Grewal and C. Kaplan, 231–54. Minneapolis: University of Minnesota Press.

Gupta, A. 1998. *Postcolonial developments. Agriculture in the making of modern India.* Durham, N.C.: Duke University Press.

Hanson, S. 2000. Recreating place. Paper presented at the annual meeting of the Association of American Geographers, Pittsburgh, Penn., 4–8 April.

———. 2001. Gender, place, and entrepreneurship. Paper presented at the annual meeting of the Association of American Geographers. New York, 27 February–3 March.

Hanson, S., and Pratt, G. 1995. *Gender, work and space.* London: Routledge.

Hartsock, N. 2001. Domination, globalization: Towards a feminist analytic. Paper presented at the Inkrit Conference on Domination and Ideology in High Tech Capitalism, Berlin, 24–27 May.

Herod, A. 1997. Labor as an agent of globalization and as a global agent. In *Spaces of globalization,* ed. K. Cox, 167–200. New York: Guilford Press.

———. 1998. Of blocks, flows and networks: The end of the cold war, cyberspace, and the geo-economics of organized labor at the *fin de millenaire.* In *Unruly world: Globalization, governance and geography,* ed. A. Herod, G. Tuathail, and S. Roberts, 162–95. London: Routledge.

Herod, A.; Tuathail, G.; and Roberts, S. 1998. *Unruly world: Globalization, governance and geography.* London: Routledge.

Hirst, P., and Thompson, G. 1996. *Globalization in question: The international economy and the possibilities of governance.* Cambridge, U.K.: Polity Press.

Hodge, G. D. 2001. Colonization of the Cuban body: The growth of male sex work in Havana. *NACLA Report on the Americas* 34:20–3.

Hotch, J. 2000. Classing the self-employed: New possibilities of power and collectivity. In *Class and its others*, ed. J. K. Gibson-Graham, S. Resnick, and R. Wolff, 143–61. Minneapolis: University of Minnesota Press.

Hyndman, J. 2001. Re-stating feminist geography. A research agenda. Paper presented at the annual meeting of the Association of American Geographers, New York, 27 February–3 March.

Jeffery, P., and Basu, A. 1998. *Appropriating gender: Women's activism and politicized religion in South Asia*. New York: Routledge.

Jelin, E., ed. 1991. Family, household and gender relations in Latin America. London: Kegan Paul.

Kaplan, C. 1996. *Questions of travel: Postmodern discourses of displacement*. Durham, N.C.: Duke University Press.

Katz, C. 1998. Disintegrating developments: Global economic restructuring and the eroding ecologies of youth. In *Cool places: Geographies of youth cultures*, ed. T. Skelton and G. Valentine, 130–44. London: Routledge.

———. 2001. On the grounds of globalization: A topography for feminist political engagement. *Signs: Journal of Women in Culture and Society* 26:1213–34.

Kelly, P. 1999. The geographies and politics of globalization. *Progress in Human Geography* 23:379–400.

Kempadoo, K. 2001. Freelancers, temporary wives, and beach-boys: Researching sex-work in the Caribbean. *Feminist Review* 67:39–62.

Koffman, E. 1996. Feminism, gender relations and geopolitics: Problematic closures and opening strategies. In *Globalization: Theory and practice*, ed. E. Koffman and G. Youngs, 209–37. London: Pinter.

Koffman, E., and Youngs, G. 1996. *Globalization: Theory and practice*. London: Pinter.

Kondo, D. 1990. *Crafting selves*. Chicago: University of Chicago Press.

Korten, D. 2001. *When corporations rule the world*. Bloomfield, Conn.: Kumarian Press.

Krause, J. 1996. Gender inequalities and feminist politics in global perspective. In *Globalization: Theory and practice*, ed. E. Koffman and G. Youngs, 225–37. London: Pinter.

Lamas, M. 2001. Standing fast in Mexico: Protecting women's rights in a hostile climate. *NACLA Report on the Americas* 34:36–40.

Lawson, V. 1995. Beyond the firm: Restructuring gender divisions of labor in Quito's garment industry under austerity. *Society and Space* 13:415–44.

———. 1999. Tailoring is a profession, seamstressing is just work! Resiting work and

reworking gender identities among artisnal garment workers in Quito. *Environment and Planning A* 31:209–27.

Lim, L. 1983. Capitalism, imperialism and patriarchy: The dilemma of Third-World women workers in multinational factories. In *Women, men and the international division of labor*, ed. J. Nash and M. P. Fernandez-Kelly, 70–91. Albany: State University of New York Press.

Lind, A. 2000. Negotiating boundaries: Women's organizations and the politics of restructuring in Ecuador. In *Gender and global restructuring. Sightings, sites and resistances*, ed. M. Marchand and A. Runyan, 161–75. London: Routledge.

Luke, T., and Tuathail, G. 1998. Global flow-mations, local fundamentalisms, and fast geopolitics. In *Unruly world: Globalization, governance and geography*, ed. A. Herod, G. Tuathail, and S. Roberts, 72–94. London: Routledge.

Marchand, M. H. 1995. Latin American women speak on development: Are we listening yet? In *Feminism/postmodernism/development*, ed. M. H. Marchand and J. L. Parpart, 56–72. London: Routledge.

Marchand, M., and Runyan, A. S. 2000a. *Gender and global restructuring: Sightings, sites, and resistances*. New York: Routledge.

———. 2000b. Introduction—Feminist sightings of global restructuring: Conceptualizations and reconceptualizations. In *Gender and global restructuring: Sightings, sites, and resistances*, ed. M. Marchand and A. S. Runyan, 1–22. New York: Routledge.

Marcus, G. E. 1998. *Ethnography through thick and thin*. Princeton, N.J.: Princeton University Press.

Massey, D. 1994. *Space, place and gender*. Minneapolis: University of Minnesota Press.

McDowell, L. 2000a. Learning to serve? Young men's labour market aspirations in an era of economic restructuring. *Gender, Place and Culture* 7:389–416.

———. 2000b. The trouble with men? Young people, gender transformations and the crisis of masculinity. *International Journal of Urban and Regional Research* 24:201–9.

———. 2002. Masculine discourses and dissonances: Strutting "lads," protest masculinity, and domestic respectability. *Environment and Planning D: Society and Space* 20:97–119.

McDowell, L., and Court, G. 1994. Missing subjects: Gender, power, and sexuality in merchant banking. *Economic Geography* 70:229–51.

Mies, M. 1982. *The lacemakers of Narsapur: Indian housewives produce for the world market*. London: Zed Books.

Mirchandani, K. 1998. Shifting definitions of the public-private dichotomy: Legislative inertia on garment homework in Ontario. *Advances in Gender Research* 3:47–71.

Mittelman, J. 2000. *Globalization syndrome*. Princeton, N.J.: Princeton University Press.

Mitter, S. 1986. *Common fate, common bond: Women in the global economy*. London: Pluto Press.

Moghadam, V. M., ed. 1994. *Identity politics and women: Cultural reassertions and feminisms in international perspective*. Boulder, Colo.: Westview Press.

Mohanty, C. T. 1991a. Cartographies of struggle: Third World women and the politics of feminism. In *Third World women and the politics of feminism*, ed. C. T. Mohanty, A. Russo, and L. Torres, 1–47. Bloomington: Indiana University Press.

———. 1991b. Under Western eyes: Feminist scholarship and colonial discourses. In *Third World women and the politics of feminism*, ed. C. T. Mohanty, A. Russo, and L. Torres, 51–80. Bloomington: Indiana University Press.

———. 1997. Women workers and capitalist scripts: Ideologies of domination, common interests, and the politics of solidarity. In *Feminist genealogies, colonial legacies, democratic futures*, ed. M. Jacqui, A. Mohanty, and C. Mohanty, 3–29. New York: Routledge.

Moser, C. 1987. The experience of poor women in Guayaquil. In *Latin America: Sociology of "developing societies,"* ed. E. Archetti, P. Cammack, and B. Roberts, 305–20. London: Monthly Review Press.

Mountz, A. 2001. Embodying the nation-state: Gendered narratives of human smuggling. Paper presented at the annual meeting of the American Association of Geographers, New York, 27 February–3 March.

NACLA. 2001. The body politic. Gender in the new world order. *NACLA Report on the Americas* 34:12–45.

Nagar, R. 1998. Communal discourses, marriage and the politics of gendered social boundaries among South Asian immigrants in Tanzania. *Gender, Place and Culture* 5:117–39.

———. 2000. Religion, race and the debate over Mut'a in Dar es Salaam. *Feminist Studies* 26:661–90.

Nagar, R., and Raju, S. Forthcoming. Women, NGOs, and the contradictions of empowerment and disempowerment. *Antipode*.

Newland, K. 1988. From transnational relationships to international relations: Women in development and the international decade for women. *Millennium: Journal of International Studies* 17:507–16.

Oglesby, E. 2001. Machos and machetes in Guatemala's cane fields. *NACLA Report on the Americas* 34:16–17.

Ohmae, K. 1990. *The borderless world: Power and strategy in the interlinked economy*. New York: Harper and Row.

———. 1995. *The end of the nation state: The rise of regional economies*. New York: Free Press.

Ong, A. 1987. *Spirits of resistance and capitalist discipline: Factory women in Malaysia*. Albany: State University of New York Press.

———. 1991. The gender and labor politics of postmodernity. *Annual Review of Anthropology* 20:279–309.

———. 1999. *Flexible citizenship*. Durham, N.C.: Duke University Press.

Parpart, J. L., and Marchand, M. H. 1995. Exploding the cannon: An introduction and conclusion. In *Feminism/postmodernism/development*, ed. M. H. Marchand and J. L. Parpart, 1–22. London: Routledge.

Pearson, R. 2000. Moving the goalposts: Gender and globalization in the twenty-first century. *Gender and Development* 8:10–19.

Peterson, V. S. 1995. Reframing the politics of identity: Democracy, globalization and gender. *Political Expressions* 1:1–16.

Peterson, V. S., and Runyan, A. S. 1999. *Global gender issues*, 2d ed. Boulder, Colo.: Westview Press.

Pettman, J. J. 1996. *Worlding women: A feminist international politics*. London: Routledge.

Phalke, J. 1999. Right-wing mobilization of women in India: Hindutva's willing performers. In *Women, globalization and fragmentation in the developing world*, ed. H. Afshar and S. Barrientos, 38–53. London: Macmillan.

Pietila, H., and Vickers, J. 1994. *Making women matter*, 2d ed. London: Zed Books.

Piven, F. F. 1995. Is it global economics or neo-laissez-faire? *New Left Review* 213:107–14.

Pratt, G. 1999. From registered nurse to registered nanny: Discursive geographies of Filipina domestic workers in Vancouver, B.C. *Economic Geography* 75:215–36.

Pringle, R. 1989. *Secretaries talk: Sexuality, power, and work*. New York: Verso.

Prugl, E., and Boris, E. 1996. Introduction. In *Homeworkers in global perspective: Invisible*

284 ECONOMIC GEOGRAPHY

no more, ed. E. Boris and E. Prugl, 3–18. New York: Routledge.

Radcliffe, S. 1990. Ethnicity, patriarchy and incorporation into the nation: Female migrants as domestic servants in Peru. *Environment and Planning D: Society and Space* 8:379–93.

———. 2001. Development, the state, and transnational political connections: State and subject formation in Latin America. *Global Networks* 1:19–36.

Radcliffe, S., and Westwood, S., eds. 1993. *"Viva": Women and popular protest in Latin America*. New York: Routledge.

Rai, S. 1999. Fractioned states and negotiated boundaries: Gender and law in India. In *Women, globalization and fragmentation in the developing world*, ed. H. Afshar and S. Barrientos, 18–37. London: Macmillan.

Roberts, S. 1997. Geo-governance in trade and finance and political geographies of dissent. In *Unruly world: Globalization, governance and geography*, ed. A. Herod, G. Tuathail, and S. Roberts, 116–34. London: Routledge.

———. Forthcoming. Global strategic vision: Managing the world. In *Globalization and governmentalities*, ed. R. Perry and B. Maurer. Minneapolis: University of Minnesota Press.

Salzinger, L. 2001. Making fantasies real: Producing women and men on the Maquila shop floor. *NACLA Report on the Americas* 34:13–19.

Sassen, S. 1998. *Globalization and its discontents*. New York: New Press.

Scholte, J. A. 1996. Beyond the buzzword: Towards a critical theory of globalization. In *Globalization: Theory and practice*, ed. E. Koffman and G. Youngs, 43–57. London: Pinter.

Scott, J. W. 1989. History in crisis: The others' side of the story. *American Historical Review* 94:680–92.

———. 1993. Women's history: New perspectives on historical writing. In *American feminist thought at century's end*, ed. L. Kauffman, 234–57. London: Blackwell.

SEEDS. 2000. *Women street vendors: The road to recognition*. New York: Population Council, New York.

Silvey, R. M. 2000. Diasporic subjects: Gender and mobility in South Sulawesi. *Women's Studies International Forum* 23:501–15.

———. 2001. Moral migrations: Gender, Islam and activism among West Java's transnational laborers. Paper presented at the annual meeting of the Association of American Geographers, New York, 27 February–3 March.

Slater, D. 1992. Theories of development and the politics of the post-modern: Exploring a border zone. *Development and Change* 23:283–319.

Smith, N. 1997. The satanic geographies of globalization: Uneven development in the 1990s. *Public Culture* 10:169–89. .

Sparke, M. 2001. Forthcoming. Networking globalization: A tapestry of introductions. *Antipode*.

Sparke, M., and Lawson, V. Forthcoming. Geoeconomics: Entrepreneurial geographies of the global-local nexus. In *The handbook of political geography*, ed. J. Agnew, K. Mitchell, and G. Tuathail. Oxford, U.K.: Blackwell.

Sparr, P., ed. 1994. *Mortgaging women's lives: Feminist critiques of structural adjustment*. London: Zed Books.

Stitcher, S., and Parpart, J. L. 1990. Introduction. In *Women, employment and family in the international division of labor*, ed. S. Stitcher and J. L. Parpart, 1–9. Philadelphia: Temple University Press.

Thrift, N. 1998. The rise of soft capitalism. In *Unruly world: Globalization, governance and geography*, ed. A. Herod, G. Tuathail, and S. Roberts, 25–71. London: Routledge.

Tiano, S. 1994. *Patriarchy on the line. Labor, gender and ideology in the Mexican maquiladora industry*. Philadelphia: Temple University Press.

Toffler, A., and Toffler, H. 1995. *Creating a new civilization: The politics of the third wave*. Atlanta, Ga.: Turner.

Watts, M. 1993. Development I: Power, knowledge, and discursive practice. *Progress in Human Geography* 17:257–72.

Weiss, L. 1997. Globalization and the myth of the powerless state. *New Left Review* 225:3–27.

White, J. 1994. *Money makes us relatives*. Austin: University of Texas Press.

Wiegman, R. 2000. Object lessons: Men, masculinity, and the sign *women*. *Signs: Journal of Women in Culture and Society* 26:355–88.

Wolf, D. L. 1992. *Factory daughters: Gender, household dynamics, and rural industrialization in Java*. Berkeley: University of California Press.

Wright, M. 1997. Crossing the factory frontier: Gender, place, and power in the Mexican maquiladora. *Antipode* 29:278–302.

Young, I. M. 1900. *Justice and the politics of difference*. Princeton, N.J.: Princeton University Press.

Moving the goalposts:
Gender and globalisation in the twenty-first century

Ruth Pearson

Development institutions saw their work challenged by those working on gender and development in the last third of the twentieth century. Ruth Pearson argues that the new century will witness an assertion of the global relevance of gender in development, and see gender analysis applied in new contexts, and to men as well as women.

Talk of globalisation is all the rage at the beginning of the new millennium. Some see it as the beginning of a new era which promises integration and development for all, with technology, investment, and trade overcoming geographical and economic isolation. Others understand globalisation as the acceleration of an on-going process of economic polarisation, in which more 'developed' regions get richer and richer, while countries in the periphery (particularly in sub-Saharan Africa, most of Latin America, parts of south and south-east Asia, and the former Soviet Union) become further impoverished and politically unstable, with little prospect of catching up and developing alongside the more prosperous parts of the world.[1]

Certain phenomena — including the HIV/AIDS pandemic, environmental degradation, pollution, global warming, civil and national conflict and insecurity — affect people throughout the world. It is also clear that the ability of individual states to challenge the larger forces emanating from beyond their frontiers is diminishing, and people from poorer and less developed regions are particularly vulnerable.

What does globalisation mean?

Globalisation is a term that has a broad and elastic meaning, denoting the process in which economic, financial, technical, and cultural transactions between different countries and communities throughout the world are increasingly interconnected, and embody common elements of experience, practice, and understanding.

However, many commentators focus only on the economic aspects of globalisation. For instance, the Secretary-General of UNCTAD defined it as 'a process whereby producers and investors increasingly behave as if the world economy consisted of a single market area with regional or national sub-sectors, rather than a set of national economies linked by trade and investment flows' (UNCTAD 1996, 6, cited in Panos 1999).

This focus on the economic aspect of globalisation reflects the extraordinary concentration of international trade, investment, and financial flows in recent years. There are many indicators of this: for example, foreign direct investment in production facilities has expanded twenty-fold in recent decades, from US$21.5 billion in 1973, to US$400 billion in 1997 (Panos 1999, 2). Transnational corporations (among the main instruments of globalisation of production) are now responsible for 80 per cent of foreign direct investment, and directly employ up to 50 million people in Export Processing Zones throughout the world (ibid.). Although this is only a fraction of the world's workforce, together with sub-contractors and allied services it represents a sizeable, and increasing, proportion of global employment and production.

Globalisation of trade and investment has also been accompanied by a rapid growth in financial flows across national borders for investment and speculation in commodities including financial products and currencies. The integration of world financial markets has become a very significant feature of the modern world economy. The Asian financial crisis in 1997/8, which started in Thailand and spread to Malaysia, Indonesia, and Japan, revealed the extent to which national economies and financial systems are interlinked one with another. On another side of the world, rather than cut off financial assistance to Russia in the face of the chronic instability of its economy, the World Bank and the IMF have offered additional short- and medium-term financial assistance in order to prevent financial crisis spreading to other parts of an increasingly interdependent world economy.

Technological change, associated with the so-called 'third industrial revolution'[2] has been at the heart of many changes in the world economy. The first of these is the ability of international corporations to operate on a scale that increasingly transcends national and regional borders. The scale and range of international transactions would not have been possible without the technology of electronic transfer and calculation of transactions. New technology has made possible the co-ordination of production and trade internationally, often from metropolitan centres, so that locally based sectors such as

fruit, flowers, and vegetable production are now co-ordinated on a global scale to serve markets all over the world. Second, the production of the semi-conductor (micro-chip) and its applications in computers and telecommunications have had significant effects on global trade and production. A range of new electronics components and equipment for military, production, and consumption markets, are now being developed and marketed in different parts of the world. Third, new computer and tele-communications technologies including the worldwide web have facilitated the spread of a whole range of new services and processes such as data entry, e-commerce, consumer-service call centres, and enter-tainment and leisure services, implying that neither production nor consumption of these services need be constrained by geographical boundaries or distance.

A key aspect of globalisation which is associated with these widespread economic and technical changes is the well-marked trend of international and national movements of populations. These have resulted not merely in growing urbanisation, but specifically in the creation of 'world cities' (Sassen 1991), starting with the global financial centres of New York, London, and Tokyo, followed by Paris, Frankfurt, Zurich, Amsterdam, Los Angeles, Sydney, and Hong Kong, and now including the 'mega-conurbations' of Mexico City, San Paolo, Buenos Aires, Bangkok, Tapai, and Bombay (Sassen 1998)[3].

The existence of these cities — literally 'concrete' manifestations of globalisation — reflects another very significant aspect of the contemporary world, that of increasing inequalities. Over the past 20 years, the share of income received by the poorest fifth of the world's population has dropped (from 2.3 per cent to 1.4 per cent), while the proportion taken by the richest fifth has risen. By the mid 1990s, in sub-Saharan Africa 20 countries had lower incomes per head in real terms than they had in the late

Critical Perspectives on Globalization

1970s (Giddens 1999). Within global cities, the same kind of inequalities coexist: the rich and well educated have lifestyles that reflect the advantages of global growth. Large numbers of low-paid workers — many of whom are migrants from poorer countries and regions — produce high-quality goods for consumption by their high-living neighbours, while others provide personal services for them.

As well as the diminishing spatial segregation between rich and poor, and the growth of metropolitan and peripheral communities, a combination of global communications technology, and marketing and advertising techniques have produced global patterns of consumption and tastes. These are transcending local customs and resource allocations. For example, the universal demand for certain kinds of sports and leisure wear — Nike trainers or Levi's jeans, or 'fast' or 'convenience' foods such as McDonald's hamburgers and Nestlé baby milk — is created by global practices rather than local priorities. The creation of global demand for such products can often distort local expenditure patterns, and create tensions and frustrations — or worse — for millions of people.

The implications of globalisation for women: a gender analysis

In looking at globalisation from a gender perspective, we need not only to find out how, and in what ways, women or men win or lose in the globalisation process, and to trace the (often nefarious) impact of globalisation on women. We also need to map out the different aspects of the globalisation process, and view each of these aspects through the lens of gender analysis. Only if we do this will we gain detailed insights into women and men's livelihood struggles. These insights will enable us to create policies, organisations, and institutions that will further the process

of sustainable human development for families, neighbourhoods, and countries in the twenty-first century.

A gender perspective on contemporary globalisation however, must be framed in terms of the historical reality of international economic and social policies in the 1980s and 1990s. This era was dominated by economic policies designed to compel indebted developing countries to restructure their economies and become solvent within the world economy. These policies, collectively known as structural adjustment packages, were the price demanded by the World Bank and the IMF in exchange for extending financial assistance and credit to such countries (Watt 2000). But the packages were based on economic models that were indifferent to gender divisions in household and national economies, and ignored the needs of populations for health and education services as the foundation for human resource development, and the family requirements for unpaid reproductive labour involved in child nurturing, care of the sick, disabled, and elderly, and community management (Elson 1995).

It is perhaps most straightforward to trace the economic implications of globalisation for women in terms of the employment generated by the expansion of global trade and production. As has been long acknowledged, the majority of the workforce in the new sectors producing consumption goods and services for global markets are women — in clothing and sportswear, in electronics components and consumer goods, in data entry facilities and financial services call centres, in fruit orchards and flower farms (UN 1999). Tourism, another by-product of economic internationalisation, also provides a high proportion of jobs for women. However, across these sectors, the evidence is that women are still largely confined to lower-paid occupations. Indeed, a feature of contemporary globalisation is the trend towards the flexibilisation of labour, including part-time, casual, and informal-sector jobs (including home-based work), and women are over-represented in all these sectors (UN 1999). In rural areas, evidence suggests that women still perform the bulk of tasks in subsistence agriculture. Meanwhile, increasing commercialisation of agriculture, as well as landlessness and impoverishment have meant that women as well as men have had to develop a portfolio of income-earning activities, including petty trade, services and artisan production, to meet the increasing cost of household survival. Surviving is a task made all the more difficult by the global trend towards user charges on basic social services, including education and health care.

In many ways, women have become the ideal 'flexible' workers in the new global economy, in the sense that their widespread incorporation into global labour markets has given them little security or bargaining power in relation to wages, working conditions, and entitlements to non-wage benefits and publicly provided reproductive services such as child care, elderly care or unemployment benefits or pensions (Pearson forthcoming). Moreover, the global features of the modern world economy have meant that new employment opportunities are vulnerable to externally induced economic crisis. The collapse of the south and east Asian economies a few years ago left many former women factory workers unemployed: reports indicate that 10,000 women workers in South Korea were laid off every day, while those whose earnings wholly or partially supported their families' survival had to face reductions in real wages of up to 100 per cent within a six-month period (Panos 1999). Women workers within the·global economy are also vulnerable to the fact that their working conditions are often unregulated and unprotected. For example, there is much evidence that electronics workers suffer a range of hazards to their health, including

their reproductive health, while the health of women working in seasonal export agriculture is harmed by chemical fertilisers and pesticides, and those working on computer terminals can suffer from repetitive strain injury and radiation effects (Pearson 1995).

Women's employment has been a key aspect of recent changes in global production and trade, particularly in labour-intensive manufacturing such as electronics, garments, and sportswear (Pearson 1998), data entry (Pearson and Mitter 1993; Dunn and Dunn 1999) and teleservices (Reardon 1999; Mitter 1999). Yet, there is evidence that ongoing technical change may actually override the reasons why women have become the preferred labour force in many industries. For example, automated fabrication and assembly can replace women's dextrous and accurate labour on electronics assembly lines; the worldwide web could replace call centres; and direct computer entry can replace data entry employment.[4] The fact that the demand for women's employment may decrease in this way in the coming decades highlights the structural problems women face in obtaining access to the technical skills and training required for their full participation in the new knowledge-based economy[5] that is such a key feature of globalisation.

Other aspects of globalisation also interlock with economic need to present problems and vulnerabilities for women. The growth of the international transport, tourism, and entertainment industries has fuelled demand for the trafficking of women for sexual services. Rising numbers of sex workers — legal, semi-legal and illegal — are an acknowledged aspect of the global reach of services and markets, which should not be overlooked in any analysis of globalisation (Pettman 1996).

While globalisation has resulted in women's increasing involvement in production and paid employment, most are retaining their primary responsibility for reproductive activities in an increasing unstable world. The rising participation of women in waged labour destroys any illusion that men have a unique role as family breadwinners, and this requires a difficult adjustment for current and future generations of men. At the same time, there is little evidence that men are significantly taking on more of what has traditionally been women's domestic labour, causing stress and conflict in many households (Koch Laier 1997). In situations where traditional sources of employment and income generation are no longer available, many men — and some women — are forced to migrate to other parts of the country or even to other countries and continents, splitting families and communities. While globalisation is challenging women in terms of increased and changing participation in the paid economy, there is no doubt that men's roles are also being challenged by globalisation processes; these are causing increasing polarisation in terms of access to education, training, and employment, and high levels of migration, separating men from their families and communities. The economic and social trends outlined above leave many women unsupported in their challenge to make a living and bring up their children.

The internationalisation of tastes referred to earlier places women and men living in poverty in the centre of a global consumption nexus, mediating between children whose demands are formulated through international media and imagery, and limited economic resources. A manifestation of the gendered nature of such global tastes lies with the hegemony of football as the world sport *par excellence* — primarily (though not solely) a masculine activity with a multi-billion-dollar spin-off industry of clothing, equipment, media, and communication products. Women and girls too are subject

to the relentless global marketing of fashion clothing and accessories, and 'modern', Western-style furniture and décor. Internationalisation of consumption not only reinforces and expands a gendered demand for consumption spending, which may itself cause inter-gender and intergenerational conflict, particularly in households with limited incomes, but also puts additional strain on women who are most frequently the individuals required to balance the competing demands on household budgets (Engle 1995).

Response or resistance to globalisation: the role of the international women's movement

Women's perspectives and gender issues have been increasingly prominent on the international stage since the First United Nations Conference in Mexico City in 1975 marked the start of the UN Decade for Women 1976–85. However, the debates of the Mexico City meeting were firmly rooted in a pre-global order of national and international politics.

One response to the increasing level of economic globalisation is the attempt to regulate international trade and investment through the activities of transnational bodies such as the World Trade Organisation (WTO). However, as the events surrounding the WTO negotiations in Seattle in December 1999 indicate, the terms on which the global economy is to be regulated are being fought out not just between national governments and representatives of transnational corporations (TNCs) and labour organisations, but also by a large range of organisations from across the spectrum of civil society. In a sense, the response to the Seattle trade talks reflects the multi-dimensional nature of globalisation, and the difficulties of trying to contain its forces within a purely economic and technical sphere.[6]

The quarter of a century since the Mexico City meeting has witnessed an internationalisation of feminist activism, asserting that economic and technical issues must be seen in their social and political context. Over the last years of the 20th century, women's organisations and lobby groups emerged as the transnational political actor *par excellence*. Women's perspectives have not been limited to the quinquennial United Nations meetings on women and development meetings, but have been central to key international conferences on the environment (Rio in 1992), human rights (Vienna, 1993), population (Cairo, 1994) and social development (Copenhagen, 1995). Globalisation of technology, and of economic regulation and production has afforded opportunities to the international women's movement to insist that women's perspectives are central to international policy and governance. They have resulted in important acknowledgements at international fora of the interlinked nature of economic, social, and political change, including the importance of environmental management for sustainable livelihoods; women's human right to freedom from violence in the home and the public sphere; the need for reproductive rights being mainstreamed into population and family planning policy; and the central importance of unpaid work in the family and community for the economic wellbeing of the public economy.

This mainstreaming of gender concerns in international policy fora has resulted in the formulation and reform of laws, ensuring that it is more than mere lip service to politically correct opinion. For example, the recognition that women have the right to freedom from violence and bodily integrity as a basic human right has been translated into the addition of rape as an international war crime, and several war trials following the conflicts in the Balkans and in Rwanda have concretely reflected this change in public policy.

Global feminist action has also resulted in changes of policy on the part of international development bodies. An example here is the current international concern about the exclusion of women and girls from employment, education, and health care in Afghanistan. Both aid agencies and international organisations have reiterated their commitment to the principle of equitable development, and negotiations for development assistance in Afghanistan have centred on issues of equitable access and resources for women and men (Emmott 1999). The broader issue of the rise of fundamentalism all over the world — and the control on women's lives, education, and marriage exercised in the name of adherence to religious texts — is also being challenged on the grounds of universal human rights of women.

International solidarity between women in different parts of the world is being assisted greatly by the new communications technologies associated with globalisation. For instance, there is a new campaign against the practice of female genital mutilation (FGM), supported by Womankind Worldwide, a UK-based NGO. FGM is a practice rationalised in the name of culture and tradition, but which has long been contested by African women in the continent and in the diaspora. The Womankind Worldwide programme is building on this opposition by facilitating the creation of an international coalition of women's groups from a range of African countries and Northern countries. It is using the world wide web to share experiences, knowledge of health and legal practices and devise strategies for advocacy and awareness campaigns).[7]

A further illustration of the current incorporation of gender concerns at a global policy level is the current discussions at the IMF and the World Bank on the proposed Global Standard for Social Policy. Proposals for this draw on the 1995 United Nations Social Summit in Copenhagen and its

Platform for Action. They cover general principles in the following four areas: achieving access to basic social services; enabling all men and women to attain secure and sustainable livelihoods, and decent working conditions; promoting systems of social protection; and fostering social integration[8] (Norton 1999). Although such discussions are at a very early stage, they reflect a recognition of the interconnectedness of production and reproduction, which has been the basis of gender analyses of the global economy over the past 30 years. This recognition itself reflects the growing realisation on the part of economic policy-makers that they cannot continue to limit their policy analysis to the formal employment sector, but instead have a responsibility for the majority of producers in the developing world, who work in self-employed, family-based or informal forms of labour and therefore fall outside formal systems of social protection.

The problems for women arising from their incorporation into the global economy are real and ever-present. But so, too, are initiatives seeking to extend guarantees of the ILO's Core Labour Standards to all international production and global trade. While the internationalisation of global consumption patterns will continue to accentuate the pressure on women responsible for making family budgets viable, international consumer pressure has also been responsible for a range of initiatives including Voluntary Codes of Conduct to safeguard the working conditions of workers involved in the production of a range of consumer products including sportswear, clothing, and fruit and vegetables. While such initiatives cover both men and women some of the most far reaching Codes of Conduct are those drawn up by and for women workers. These cover non-wage benefits, sexual harassment, security and safety of employment, and serve as a model for other workers in global production chains (Seyfang 1999).

The challenges for gender of globalisation

There are many who have reacted against the global incorporation of gender issues into the NGO and development agenda, contending that it reflects a Western imperialist bias and indicates opposition to appropriate local social relations and practices. However, the robustness of the challenge on gender issues from feminist activists and gender and development policy-makers to development policy and institutions in the last third of the twentieth century indicates that its relevance transcends the local. The indications are that the new century will witness an assertion of the global relevance of gender in development not just by gender advocates, but by development institutions and organisations concerned with meeting the challenges of globalisation (Sen 1997); extending the application of gender analysis to men as well as women, and encouraging the creative application of gender-equitable policies to new generations and contexts.

While the constraints and inequalities produced by economic and technological globalisation will provide the backdrop necessary for international and local campaigning, advocacy, and policy design and implementation, they also offer the opportunities for new and appropriate initiatives. I will conclude by mentioning a project recently initiated in a small British provincial town, Norwich. Called 'Moving the Goalposts', it has as its objective the promotion of girls' football in an area around Mombasa in Kenya.[9] It seeks to provide training for local girls, links with girls' and community football projects in Norwich through educational and fund-raising activities, and ultimately through international exchange visits and tournaments. This was an initiative that came in the wake of the Woman's Football World Cup in 1999, which attracted a great deal of international intention, but it was also inspired by an existing girls' football team of some years' standing in Kilifi, eastern Kenya. In seeking to empower young women in both Kenya and the UK, the project demonstrates a fresh and innovative approach to gender and development. It offers the opportunity to capture the interest of an entire new generation in a new context, promote international understanding and learning, and use global communications in a positive way. Such a project is the product of internationalisation — of sport, of media, of communications and product markets — and an example of how women's activism and imagination can be used to subvert the gendered stereotypes of international sport. It may not have the weight of the international sports and leisure industry behind it, but it provides an indication of the fluidity of gender relations in a global world, and the sense that there is everything to play for.

Ruth Pearson is Professor of Development Studies, University of Leeds, Leeds LS2 9JT, UK. E-mail: r.pearson@leeds.ac.uk

Notes

1 The various academic and political positions on globalisation and its implications in different regions are well covered in Lechner, Frank J and Boli, John (eds) (2000) *The Globalization Reader*, Blackwell Publishers, Oxford.

2 The 'third industrial revolution' refers to the great changes in production technology that followed the development of micro-electronics and biotechnology, leading to the production of a range of new products, as well as to their incorporation into existing products such as cars and television sets. The application of micro-electronic and computer technology to telecommunications has further revolutionised a range of production processes, and catalysed the development of new products and services such as mobile telephones and the worldwide web. Most importantly, it has made possible not just international communications, but international control and dispersion of production and services.

3 For further discussion of world cities and globalisation see leGates, RT and Stout, F (eds) (1996) *The City Reader*, Routledge, UK.

4 A call centre is a relatively new and fast-growing kind of production sité where service functions are carried out over the telephone, for a range of enterprises including sales, banking and financial services, inland revenue (tax) offices, airline and travel companies. Telephone interaction replaces (or less commonly complements) face-to-face interaction with the customer. Call centres are offices, usually fairly large in scale, and may operate for a single operation or handle teleservices for a range of contractors. See Richardson (1999). Further information can be found on http://www.callcentreworld.com/

5 The knowledge economy refers to the increasing displacement of physical labour (usually men's) and manually dextrous and docile labour (usually women's, required in sectors such as micro-electronic assembly, garments, food production, data-entry, and tele-services) with technically trained and qualified labour, predominantly male. See World Bank 1999.

6 For more discussion on the WTO, see the *Globalization Reader*, op cit (note 1).

7 Website: http//www.womankind.org.uk /cpgfgm.htm. For more information on Womankind Worldwide see Resources section, p 115.

8 Social protection refers to systems (usually run by the state) of social security and income support for the unemployed, the elderly and the sick. Social integration refers to the combating of social exclusion (a term increasingly used to denote not only economic poverty, but exclusion from opportunities in the labour market, education and services).

18   *Gender and Development*

9 This project is organised by a local women's group who have applied to the UK National Lottery for funding. A current fundraising activity is a so-called 'bootlink' in which local (to Norwich) football-playing girls are encouraged to donate second-hand football boots and other kit to be donated to the much poorer teams in Kenya.

References

Blumberg, RL, Rakowski, CA, Tinker, I and Monteon, M (eds) (1995) *Engendering Wealth and Well-being: Empowerment for global change*, Westview Press.

Dunn, L and Dunn, HS (1999) *Employment, Working Conditions and Labour Relations in Offshore Data Service Enterprises: Case studies of Barbados and Jamaica*, Multinational Enterprises Programme Working paper No 86 ILO, Geneva.

Emmott, S (1999) 'Personnel management in a time of crisis: experience from Afghanistan' in Porter F, Smyth, I and Sweetman, C (eds) (1999) *Gender Works: Oxfam experience in policy and practice*, Oxfam GB, Oxford.

Engle, P (1995) 'Father's Money, Mother's Money, and Parental Commitment: Guatemala and Nicaragua' in Blumberg et al. (eds) (1995).

Elson, D (1995) *Male Bias in the Development Process*, Manchester University Press.

Giddens, A (1999) *Runaway World: How globalisation is re-shaping our lives*, Profile Books, London.

Koch Laier, J (1997) 'Women's Work and the Household in Latin America: A Discussion of the Literature', CDR Working Paper 97, Centre for Development Research, Copenhagen.

Norton, A (1999) 'Can there be a Global Standard for Social Policy? The Social Policy Principles as a Test Case', ODI Briefing Paper (draft), October.

Mitter, S (1999) 'Globalization, Technological Changes and the Search for a New Paradigm for Women's Work', *Gender, Technology and Development*, 3:1.

Mitter, S and Bastos, M-I (eds) (1999), *Europe and Developing Countries in the Globalised Information Economy: Employment and distance education*, Routledge, UK.

Panos (1999) *Globalisation and Employment: New opportunities, real threats* (1999), Panos Briefing No 33 May (Panos briefings can be obtained from PANOS 9 White Lion Street, London, N1 9PD, UK. Tel +44 (0)20 7278 0345; e-mail: panoslondon@gn.apc,org; website: http://www.oneworld.org/panos/

Pearson, R (1995) 'Gender perspectives on health and safety in information processing: Learning from international experience', in Mitter, S and Rowbotham, S (eds) (1995) *Women Encounter Technology: Changing Patterns of Employment in the Third World*, Routledge, UK.

Pearson, R (Dec 2000, forthcoming) 'All Change? Women, men and reproductive work in the global economy', in *European Journal of Development Research*.

Pettman, J (1996) 'An international political economy of sex?', in Kofman, E and Youngs, G (eds) *Globalization: Theory and Practice*, Pinter, London.

Reardon, G (1999) 'Telebanking: Breaking the logic of spatial and work organisation', in Mitter, S and Bastos, M-I (eds) (1999).

Richardson, R (1999) 'Call centres and the prospects for export-oriented work in the developing world', in Mitter, S and Bastos, M-I (eds) (1999).

Sassen, S (1991) *The Global City: New York, London and Tokyo*, Princeton University Press.

Sassen, S (1998) *Globalization and its Discontents*, The New Press.

Sen, G (1997) 'Globalization in the 21st Century: Challenges for civil society', University of Amsterdam Development lecture 1997. Available from the Institute for Development Research Amsterdam (IDRA), University of Amsterdam, Plantage Muidergracht 12, 1018 TV Amsterdam, The Netherlands; e-mail: j.r.muller@frw.uva.nl

Seyfang, G (1999) 'Private Sector Self-Regulation for Social Responsibility: Mapping codes of conduct', Working Paper No 1, Research Project on Ethical Trading and Globalisation, Overseas Development Group, UEA, December.

UN (1999) *1999 Survey on the Role of Women in Development: Globalization, Gender and Work*, UN Division for the Advancement of Women, Department of Economic and Social Affairs, New York.

Watt, P (2000) *Social Investment and Economic Growth: A strategy to eradicate poverty*, Oxfam GB, Oxford.

World Bank (1998) *Knowledge for Development: World Bank Report 1998/9*, Washington DC.

[22]

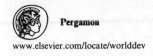

Pergamon

www.elsevier.com/locate/worlddev

World Development Vol. 28, No. 7, pp. 1231–1238, 2000
© 2000 Elsevier Science Ltd. All rights reserved
Printed in Great Britain
0305-750X/00/$ - see front matter

PII: S0305-750X(00)00024-3

Secular Changes in the Gender Composition of Employment and Growth Dynamics in the North and the South

KORKUT ERTÜRK
University of Utah, Salt lake City, USA

and

WILLIAM DARITY, JR. *
University of North Carolina at Chapel Hill and Duke University, Durham, North Carolina, USA

Summary. — In a simple theoretical exercise, the paper shows that gender relations matter in the standard analysis of trade liberalization and economic growth. It utilizes a model with the two differential equations, phase diagram technique which enables us to examine the cumulative interaction between economic growth and changes in the female share of employment. The model shows that changes in the gender composition of employment caused by a new global division of labor between the North and the South can thwart the economic benefits customarily associated with trade liberalization in both regions. © 2000 Elsevier Science Ltd. All rights reserved.

Key words — trade liberalization, gender relations, female share of employment, North and South

1. INTRODUCTION

The push toward trade liberalization in developing countries has been a salient aspect of the international economy since the early 1980s. It is by now widely recognized that these policies had asymmetric gender effects in many of the countries where they were implemented. For instance, numerous case studies from the developing world have shown that the adverse welfare effects of structural adjustment policies on women in poverty, one of whose main objectives has invariably been trade liberalization, were more severe than their impact on poor men. [1] Mainstream economists have uniformly maintained, however, that trade liberalization and integration with the world economy in general, benefit all countries involved both in the North and the South, promoting convergence in per capita levels of income among countries at different levels of development. [2] It has also been argued that increased openness to the world economy tends to reduce all kinds of discriminatory labor market practices, including those based on gender (Black & Brainerd, 1999).

In contrast, research by nonmainstream economists suggests that gender inequalities in pay and working conditions generally have remained persistent in the face of increased female participation in paid employment following trade liberalization in developing countries (Standing, 1999). More recently, the focus of attention among some feminist economists has shifted onto exploration of possible feedback effects of gender inequalities on economic performance at the macro level. [3] It is argued that gender inequalities, and more broadly gender relations, can have ramifications for macroeconomic variables at the national and as well as at the level of international economy. For instance, a wide body of evidence suggests that gender inequalities have

* The authors are grateful to Ingrid Palmer, the editors and two anonymous referees for their helpful comments and encouragement.

played an important role in foreign direct investment flows and in the export-led growth performance of many of the newly industrializing countries. [4]

The objective of this paper is to contribute to this literature by means of a simple theoretical exercise that highlights the importance of taking gender relations into consideration in the standard analysis of trade liberalization and economic growth. We develop a heuristic framework for further research on the possible gender feedback effects at the macro level. Using a simple two-equation model, the paper looks at the implications of the possible interaction between economic growth and changes in the gender composition of the labor force.

Based on the premise that gender relations on growth dynamics differ between countries at different levels of development, we find that benefits from trade liberalization between the North and the South can be offset by changes in the female share of employment caused by a new global division of labor brought about by changing trade relations. Thus, the conclusion of the exercise is that gender relations possibly can thwart the economic benefits customarily associated with trade liberalization.

The following discussion is organized into two sections: the model and its conceptual background are discussed in Section 2; its assumptions and dynamic properties are evaluated in Section 3.

2. THE MODEL

The conceptual orientation and the assumptions we employ in the model draw from a stylized reading of the empirical trends reported in the gender and development literature. The discussion focuses on two of the channels through which gender relations can affect long-term economic growth: (a) unpaid female labor within the household shoulders the social cost of reproducing the labor power in the economy, and (b) paid female labor outside the household performs the same work men do for lower pay.

In our discussion, the economic impact of increasing feminization of the labor force works through these two linkages. In relation to the first, *ceteris paribus*, increasing female participation of the labor force has a negative effect on output. For the extent to which the cost of reproducing the labor power is subsidized by unpaid female labor is likely to

diminish as women are drawn in large numbers into paid employment. In relation to the second, *ceteris paribus*, women's increasing labor force participation is likely to have a positive effect on output due to lower wage costs.

The relative weight of these two gender effects are likely to differ among countries that are at different levels of development. It is plausible that in the South the first effect is stronger, especially given the low level of public services; while in the North the second effect is likely to be more important. By contrast, both effects are likely to be operative in an increasing number of newly industrializing countries which are generally, but not exclusively, middle-income.

For our purposes, the stylized distinction between the North and the South can be drawn in connection with the U-shaped, long-term relationship found between the female labor force participation rate and economic development. The evidence for this U-shaped pattern is based on both the historical experiences of developed countries and from several studies that utilized crosscountry data in crosssection. For instance, in the United States, female labor force participation fell during the initial stages of economic growth, thereafter it began to rise, exhibiting a U-shaped pattern (Goldin, 1994). Likewise, crosscountry data show that the poorest and richest countries, identified as such by the manner of the World Bank's classification scheme of high-income (North) and low-income (South) countries, have the highest female labor force participation rates, while middle-income countries have the lowest (Pampel & Tanaka, 1986; Goldin, 1994; Cagatay & Ozler, 1995).

In our discussion, the South refers to the group of countries on the left arm of the U-curve; and the North refers to the countries on the right. The South constitutes countries where a significant share of gross domestic product, say 25% or more, is devoted to agriculture, and where a considerably greater share of the labor force, say 40% or more, is engaged in agriculture. In contrast, the Northern countries are those where the predominant economic activities, as a proportion of gross domestic product, are industrial/technical/professional services. In the North, agriculture constitutes a low share of gross domestic product, typically less than 10%, and the share of the labor force in agriculture is even smaller, typically less than 5%.

Our mode of inquiry utilizes the two differential equations, phase diagram technique, which enables us to explore how cumulative processes unfold over the complete span of time required for them exercise their full effects. The immediate effects of a policy such as trade liberalization may be quite different from its long-term effects as the dynamics of the process of impact unfold over time. Phase diagrams enable us to characterize the ultimate rather the immediate impact.

We also load the dice in favor of trade liberalization with our assumptions about its immediate impact. In other words, our analysis demonstrates grounds for reservations about trade liberalization under conditions most favorable for the consequences of this type of policy reform.

We assume a model which takes the general form:

$$\dot{x} = f(x, y),$$
$$\dot{y} = g(x, y)$$

that can be applied to countries in both the North and the South, where x is per capita income and y is the rate of feminization of employment. [5] The functional relations posited in the two equations refer to slow-changing, long-term variations, while short-term movements in the state variables caused by changes in policy orientation or other exogenous forces are treated as discrete shifts. Treating trade liberalization as one possible example of such a shift, we explore its dynamic implications by means of assessing the likely sign of the four partial derivatives involved in our equation system (i.e., f_x, f_y, g_x, g_y), without, however, specifying any explicit functional form, on the basis of two sets of assumptions.

One set of assumptions draw from the standard claims made on behalf of trade liberalization as an agent of growth. Along with mainstream theory, for the purposes of the theoretical exercise here, we take it for granted that (a) as a first effect, trade liberalization increases the per capita level of output in both the North and the South, (b) countries that have different levels of per capita income tend to converge, (i.e., the so-called convergence thesis), and (c) the possible effects of demand on long-term growth are negligible. These assumptions constitute the package of beliefs imbedded in our analysis that are most favorable towards a policy stance that favors trade liberalization. In our model, the first assump-

tion is treated as a "one-time" shift in per capita output for all levels of feminization of employment, while the second is incorporated into the first equation as a slow-changing, long-term effect.

The second set of assumptions draws from the gender and development literature described above. Again, fast-changing, short-term effects are distinguished from slow-changing, long-term variations in the state variables. For instance, the often observed increase in the female share of employment in developing countries that liberalized their trade is treated as a "one-time" shift in the rate of feminization of labor for all levels of per capita output, while long-term changes in the gender composition of labor—which can be hypothesized on the basis of the U-shaped feminization curve—are incorporated into the second equation as a slow-changing, long-term effect.

We make the following assumptions with respect to the signs of the partial derivatives specified above:

(i) In the first equation, it is assumed that $f_x < 0$ in both the North and the South. This means that the rate of change in per capita level of output is inversely related to its level. The assumption follows from the convergence thesis, and implies that the impact of the level of output on the rate of change of output is negative. [6] It can also be argued that rising per capita income is generally associated with rising real wages and indirect costs of labor which can thwart economic growth to the extent that investment behavior is more sensitive to production costs than to demand (Darity, 1982).

(ii) The impact of the level of feminization of the labor force on the rate of change of output is assumed to be positive in the North ($f_y > 0$) and negative in the South ($f_y < 0$).

In the South, the process of modernization and industrial growth usually takes place in the absence of a developed infrastructure for public services. In these economies, women's unpaid labor within the household plays an invisible role by shouldering the cost of reproducing labor. Thus, women's *en masse* incorporation into paid employment outside the household is likely to put upward pressure on the cost of living, giving rise to increased demands for higher real wages. Rising real wages are, *ceteris paribus*, assumed to check economic growth. [7]

By contrast, in the North, where a more extensive infrastructure and network of public services exist, increased employment of women outside the household need not imply rising labor costs. On the contrary, to the extent that women are the preferred labor supply, either because they do the same work men do for lower pay or because they are more compliant as workers, increased feminization of employment is likely to have a positive effect on the rate of change of output.

(iii) The impact of the level of per capita output on the rate of change of the feminization rate is negative in the South ($g_x < 0$) and positive in the North ($g_x > 0$).

Following the seminal work by Boserup's (1970), the consensus in the 1970s was that industrialization marginalized women, in the sense of curtailing their rate of participation in paid employment (Pearson, 1998). This is also consistent with the empirical regularity represented by the U-shaped feminization curve (Figure 1). On the left side of the U-curve, the feminization rate falls as per capita income rises, and on the right-hand side the feminization rate rises as per capita income goes up.

The historical and crosscountry evidence do not in themselves suffice to conclude that past trends will continue to hold in the future or that the South will follow in the footsteps of the North. Most notably, the increased participation of women in industrial employment in the South in the context of export-led growth in the 1980s might be thought to invalidate the hypothesis of a longitudinal relationship drawn on the basis of the feminization U.

However, given the widespread evidence of defeminization of labor in the many of the first-tier export-industrializing countries in more recent years (Acevedo, 1990; Berik, 1995; Joekes & Weston, 1994) it might be safer to treat the increased feminization of labor associated with export-orientation/trade liberalization as a "shorter term" shift superimposed onto the long-term relationship implied by the feminization U. Increased employment of women in the North due to the changing composition of output toward services, generally agreed to be associated with technological change, can likewise be superimposed as a short-term shift onto the secular trend of increasing feminization of employment.

(iv) We assume that the rate of change of feminization of labor might be inversely related to its level in both regions, ($g_y < 0$).

Evidence from around the world suggests that the share of women's employment in relation to the total labor force varies in the context of three different modalities (Ertürk & Cagatay, 1995). First, women enter the labor force during times of expansion and exit during downturns, acting as a buffer. Second, changes in the composition of output towards sectors where women are concentrated increases their employment in relation to men. Third, women replace men in jobs that are traditionally held by men. While the first two mechanisms by which the rate of feminization rises need not encounter much resistance from men, the third—which is likely to be more prevalent in the long run—might. For instance, it might be plausible that the conservative backlash against various affirmative action programs in the North is in part be a reflection of such resistance.

To recap then, we make the following assumptions about the sign of the partials.

In the South : $f_x < 0$; $f_y < 0$; $g_x < 0$; $g_y < 0$,

In the North : $f_x < 0$; $f_y \geqslant 0$; $g_x > 0$; $g_y < 0$.

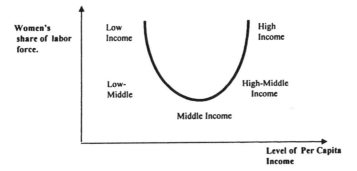

Figure 1. *Feminization U.*

3. EVALUATION OF THE MODEL

It is possible to evaluate the dynamic properties of the equilibrium positions these assumptions yield by means of drawing phase diagrams for both regions. Depending on the relative magnitude of the partial derivatives f_y and g_y, the equilibrium points that emerge for both regions are either stable *nodes* or *saddle points*. Because it is difficult to draw inferences about *saddle point* solutions in the absence of explicit functional forms, save some cursory remarks (see below), we focus on cases that involve stable *nodes* in what is to follow. Thus, we assume that the relative magnitudes of the partial derivatives are such that Case (a) holds in Figures 2 and 3.

The effect of shifts in policy orientation or other exogenous forces which might raise per capita income for all levels of feminization of employment can be depicted by a rightward shift in the $\dot{x} = 0$ locus, while the effect of those that raise the feminization rate for all levels of per capita income can be depicted by an upward shifts in the $\dot{y} = 0$ locus.

In numerous countries in the South, trade liberalization/export orientation have led to increased feminization of employment in the 1980s. Given our earlier assumption that trade liberalization enhances per capita output, we can show this by a simultaneous shift in both demarcation curves. Just as $\dot{x} = 0$ locus shifts to the right, $\dot{y} = 0$ locus shifts up. As depicted in Figure 4, the level of per capita income increases from x_0 to x_1 following the rightward shift in the $\dot{x} = 0$ locus. But, it should be noted that the simultaneous upward shift in the $\dot{y} = 0$ locus at least partially offsets this increase as the level of per capita output is reduced to x_2.

A similar result also holds in the case of the North, where import penetration from poor countries has led to defeminization of labor in low-wage sectors where women are concentrated (see Kucera & Milberg, 2000). In this case, the rightward shift in $\dot{x} = 0$ locus, depicting the beneficial impact of trade liberalization is accompanied by a downward shift in the $\dot{y} = 0$ schedule (see Figure 5). Again, the increase in per capita income from x_0 to x_1 due to trade liberalization is at least partially offset

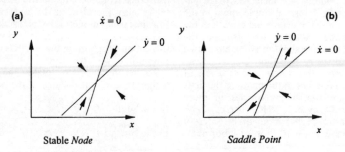

Figure 2. *Possible types of equilibrium in the North.*

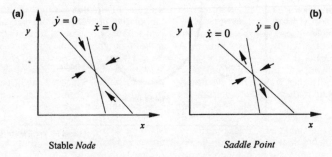

Figure 3. *Possible types of equilibrium in the South.*

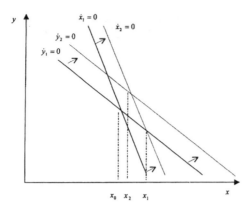

Figure 4. *Impact of trade liberalization in the South.*

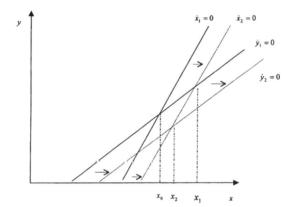

Figure 5. *Impact of trade liberalization in the North.*

by the reduction in the rate of feminization of labor. As depicted in Figure 5, with the downward shift in the $\dot{y} = 0$, the equilibrium level of per capital income is reduced to x_2 from x_1.[8]

Finally, a few comments can be made about the possibility of a saddle point solution. A saddle point means that only a unique set of trajectories converge to the equilibrium position and that all other trajectories eventually become divergent if they are not so from the outset. Given the absence of explicit functional forms in our equation systems, it is possible to specify neither the stable adjustment path nor the exact parameters that yield a saddle point. Two general comments can be made, however. First, a marked contrast exists between the

North and the South in terms of the dynamics implied by the saddle point solution. In the North, depicted in Figure 2(b), the two possible outcomes for divergent time paths are either a cumulative increase in both per capita output and feminization rate or a cumulative decrease in both variables. Thus, any deviation from the unique time path convergent to equilibrium leads to a runaway movement in one or the other direction, which we might call a *win–win* or a *lose–lose* outcome. Thus, trade liberalization possibly can give rise to either outcome.

In contrast, in the South, depicted in Figure 3(b), the two possible divergent time paths are either increasing per capita output along with a falling feminization rate, or a rising feminization rate along with decreasing per capita output. Second, in both regions the likelihood of a saddle point is higher the greater the magnitude of the partial derivative g_y in relation to f_y' in absolute value. In other words, a reduction in men's resistance to women's incorporation to the labor force—which g_y represents—can possibly account for a switch

from a stable *node* to a *saddle point*. Regardless, the long-run impact of trade liberalization in the South does not have salutary implications for growth and female labor force participation simultaneously, even under the most favorable assumptions about the immediate impact of the policy change.

NOTES

1. For the adverse welfare effects of structural adjustment on women, see Standing (1989), Elson (1991, 1993), Moser (1992), Beneria and Roldan (1987), Sen (1991), Beneria and Feldman (1992), Bakker (1994), Sparr (1994), Cagatay and Ozler (1995). For a more extensive bibliography, see Afshar and Dennis (1992).

2. Though, it is admitted that benefits from integration to world markets are not always equitably distributed within national economies, and recognized that pre-existing gender inequalities may also prevent an equitable distribution.

3. See *World Development* (1995) 23(11) special issue on Gender, Adjustment and Macroeconomics.

4. See, for instance Seguino (2000) and Ozler (2000), both in this issue.

5. By the feminization rate of the labor force we mean the ratio of female paid for work performed outside of the household to the total employment of men and women.

6. The controversy around the empirical basis of the *convergence* thesis is beyond the scope of this paper. The

assumption it implies might be especially unsatisfactory in the case of a number of newly and (rapidly) industrializing developing countries. The dynamic properties of *cumulative* growth (where a higher level of output positively affects its rate of change, i.e., $f_x > 0$) in the case of this group of countries is discussed in detail in Erturk and Cagatay (1995).

7. Something along these lines was visible in many newly industrializing countries, where a steady increase in women's paid employment was followed by a general increase in real wages. In part because of higher labor costs, foreign direct investment by multinational corporations has been shifting in recent years away from this group of countries to less developed ones, such as, Bangladesh, China and Vietnam, among others.

8. Some of the gains from trade that are lost due to defeminization in the North can be seen to be recouped if shifts in the composition of output toward services is linked to trade liberalization, causing an upward shift in the $\dot{y} = 0$ locus. But the weight of argument in the literature points to technological change rather than trade as the main cause of the recent increase in the share of services in total output in the North.

REFERENCES

Acevedo, L. (1990). Industrialization and employment: changes in the patterns of women's work in Puerto Rico. *World Development, 18* (2), 231–255.

Afshar, H., & Dennis, C. (1992). *Women and adjustment policies in the Third World*. London: Macmillan.

Bakker, I. (1994). *The strategic silence: gender and economic policy*. London: Zed Press.

Beneria, L., & Feldman, S. (1992). *Unequal burden: economic crisis, persistent poverty and women's work*. Boulder, Co: Westview Press.

Beneria, L., & Roldan, M. (1987). *The crossroads of class and gender: industrial homework, subcontracting and household dynamics in Mexico city*. Chicago: Chicago University Press.

Berik, G. (1995). *Growth with gender inequality: manufacturing employment in Taiwan*. Paper presented at

the Gender, Adjustment and Macroeconomic Models Roundtable Discussion at the Allied Social Science Association Meetings, Washington DC, January.

Black, S., & Brainerd, E. (1999). *Importing equality? The effects of increased competition on the gender wage gap*. Mimeo, Federal Reserve Bank of New York.

Boserup, E. (1970). *Women's role in economic development*. New York: St Martin's Press.

Cagatay, N., & Ozler, S. (1995). Feminization of the labor force: the effects of long-term development and structural adjustment. *World Development, 23* (11), 1883–1894.

Darity, W. (1982). On the long run outcome of the Lewis-Nurkse international growth process. *Journal of Development Economics, 10*, 271–278.

Elson, D. (1991). Male bias in the development process: an overview. In Elson, D., *Male bias in the development process*. Manchester: Manchester University Press.

Elson, D. (1993). Gender-aware analysis and development economics. *Journal of International Development, 5* (2), 237–247.

Ertürk, K., & Cagatay, N. (1995). Macroeconomic consequences of cyclical and secular changes in feminization: an experiment at gendered macromodeling. *World Development, 23* (11), 1969–1977.

Goldin, C. (1994). *The U-shaped female labor force function in economic development and economic history*. NBER Working Papers Series No. 4707, National Bureau of Economic Research, Cambridge, MA, April.

Joekes, S., & Weston, A. (1994). *Women and the new trade agenda*. New York: UNIFEM.

Kucera, D., & Milberg, W. (2000). Gender segregation and gender bias in manufacturing trade expansion: revisiting the wood asymmetry. *World Development, 28* (7), this issue.

Moser, C. (1992). Adjustment from below: low income women, time and the triple role in Guayaquil, Ecuador. In Afshar, H., & Dennis, C., *Women and adjustment policies in the Third World*. London: Macmillan.

Ozler, S. (2000). Exporting and female share of employment: evidence from Turkey. *World Development, 28* (7), 1239–1248.

Pampel, F.C., & Tanaka, K. (1986). Economic development and female labor force participation: a reconsideration. *Social Forces* 64 (3).

Pearson, R. (1998). Nimble fingers revisited: reflections on women and Third World industrialization in the late twentieth century. In Jackson, C., & Pearson, R., *Feminist visions of development: gender analysis and policy*. New York: Routledge.

Segiuno, S. (2000). Gender inequality and economic growth: a cross-country analysis. *World Development* 28 (7), 1211–1230.

Sen, G. (1991). *Macroeconomic policies and the informal sector: a gender sensitive approach*. Working paper No. 13, Vassar College, Department of Economics, Poughkippsee, New York.

Span, P. (1994). *Mortgaging women's lives: feminist critiques of structural adjustment*. London: Zed Books.

Standing, G. (1989). Global feminization through flexible labor. *World Development, 17* (7), 1077–1096.

Standing, G. (1999). Global feminization through flexible labor: a theme revisited. *World Development, 27* (3), 583–602.

[23]

ANNALS, *AAPSS*, **581**, May 2002

Globalization of Production and Women in Asia

By DONG-SOOK S. GILLS

ABSTRACT: Globalization of production represents a new organization of production processes, accompanied by technological advances and neoliberal ideology, which emphasizes the separation of politics from economics. Emanating from these changes, labor relations are being altered, in particular by world trends of the flexibilization and feminization of labor. Women's labor constitutes a foundation of the international competitiveness of most Asian countries. The forces of economic globalization expose women in Asia to diverse mechanisms of exploitation in complex ways. There is no single pattern but rather an array of complex ways in which gender hierarchy, national capital, foreign capital, and the state negotiate and adapt to globalization. Women's social movements have been part of the social actions that have strengthened the counterhegemonic movements against capital-led economic globalization. Women's labor is an important social force that can resist neoliberal global trends and contribute to an alternative globalization based on democratization and greater social inclusion.

Dong-Sook S. Gills is a senior lecturer in sociology at the University of Sunderland in the United Kingdom. She gained her doctorate in sociology from the University of Sheffield. She is a member of the International Advisory Council of the TODA Institute for Global Peace and Policy Research and a faculty affiliate at the Globalization Research Centre, University of Hawaii. Her most recent publications include Women and Triple Exploitation in Korean Development *(1999, Macmillan),* Globalization and Strategic Choice in South Korea: Economic Reform and Labor *(coauthored with Barry Gills) (2000, Cambridge University Press), and* Women and Work in Globalising Asia *(coedited with N. Piper) (2002, Routledge).*

ONE of the most important aspects of contemporary restructuring processes in the global economy is the discord between the
liberal ideology that propels economic globalization and the politics
of labor rights. The present model of
globalization emphasizes the
strength of economic rationalism at
the ideological level and operates
through globalization of production
in practice. This trend of economic
globalization demands a critical assessment of its impact on labor.

GLOBALIZATION: STRUCTURE AND AGENCY

While globalization as a concept is
often overstated by enthusiasts,
notably by neoliberal writers, others
claim that there has been no qualitative change in international economic relations. Even if we accept
that the fundamental structure of
the world economy has not significantly altered, however, there have
certainly been noticeable changes
that affected the ways in which our
contemporary societies are organized. These include the trends
toward increasing market liberalization, greater specialization in production, and higher mobility of capital, goods, and labor around the
globe. Most notably, globalization of
production has been a key element in
the reshaping of the world economy
with visible impact on our daily lives.
Globalization of production represents new organization of production
processes, backed up by new technologies. Emanating from these
changes, labor relations are being
altered, in particular, to world trends

of the flexibilization and feminization of labor.

In general, globalization can be
traced as a set of multidimensional
processes, encompassing many arenas of ideology, economy, politics, and
culture. Perhaps globalization in the
cultural arena is more visible and
immediate to our everyday life, for
example, transborder exchange
through music, fashion, food, films,
and television. Nevertheless, these
are only symptoms of globalization,
not globalization itself. In fact, the
symptoms of globalization are often
(mis)interpreted as being globalization itself, or even as the main
parameters of current globalization.
It is such a (mis)perception that
leads the debate to focus on the globalization of mass-media images and
to the argument that globalization is
a comprehensive transformation of
our lives. This type of interpretation
of globalization tends to ignore structural aspects of globalization while
privileging the symbolic aspects
(Waters 1995).

By contrast, the debate on economic globalization, for example,
concerning international competitiveness, liberalization, and the
global financial markets, focuses on
the economic structure and tends to
ignore agency as an important factor.
To date, much of the debate on economic globalization in the mainstream has been separated from people, for example, as if financial crisis
did not have a direct relevance to the
lives of ordinary people. It is therefore important to find a balance
between emphasis on structure on
one hand and on agents (people) on
the other and to avoid exaggerating

the independence of the symbolic arena. This is not to say that globalization processes in different social arenas are entirely separate from each other. On the contrary, they are tightly interrelated processes. The globalization of Disney culture, for example, might at first appear to be a purely cultural process. However, this happens through material exchange that entails the global expansion of trade in Disney films, *Aladdin* T-shirts, *Lion King* pencil cases, Mickey Mouse story books, and so on. At the same time, global trade of these wares involves globalization of production, which enables the expansion of Disney in the global market. The production (the material) and the symbolic (the ideational) are not at all separated in the process of globalization but tightly integrated.

The globalization of production provides industry with a higher degree of mobility and flexibility not only in its production process but also in industrial relations vis-à-vis labor. In this example of globalization of Disney culture, the *101 Dalmatians* T-shirts are sewn by workers in Haiti for as little as 12 cents an hour (MacAdam 1998), thus providing a cheap global product to the global market. Alternatively, the work could be subcontracted to a sweatshop in Los Angeles that will offer competitive costs (even compared to Haiti) by employing migrant workers (often illegal) at below the legal minimum wage. This globalization of production thus in turn brings forward the question of international labor rights and standards and universal human rights issues, which reside firmly in the political arena. This brief case study of Disney culture illustrates how different, and sometimes seemingly independent, processes of globalization—that is, cultural globalization, financial and economic globalization, and political globalization—are closely tied together in reality. The underlying structure of globalization, even the cultural and symbolic manifestation, is revealed to be largely economic.

Moreover, the logic of globalization cannot be one of globalization itself, of technology alone, or merely of a new ideology, à la Giddens or Castells (Giddens 1990, 1996; Castells 1996). The logic of globalization, as a set of social processes, is mainly derived from the logic of capitalism. The central logic of capitalism is to maintain and expand the process of capital accumulation. The increase in the level of global exchange and flows of materials, people, and ideas can largely be accounted for and explained within the framework of capital accumulation. This is not to put forward a reductionist interpretation of globalization to attribute every aspect of social change to capitalist market expansion. Rather, it is to emphasize the fact that the main driving force of economic globalization is the logic of capitalism and that economic globalization is at the forefront of the globalization processes, as presented above in the example of the globalization of Disney culture. This has important implications in adopting methodological perspectives and constructing analytical frameworks in our overall understanding of globalization. When globalization is understood as multi-dimensional processes led by economic globalization and the logic of capitalism, then we do not need to reinvent the wheel. There is no need to try to imagine a postmodern world as yet, and certainly not a postmodern global world, because the global logic in question is certainly not postcapitalist.

In sum, the historical forces of globalization are mainly derived from the logic of capitalism. Globalization itself is a set of dynamic social practices that bring social change. In this framework, the social relations of globalization are based on the requirements of capital accumulation, while adapting to technological advances. While recognizing the primary tendencies of economic globalization through which labor is "victimized," both economic reductionism and technological determinism should be questioned. The globalization of production hinges on many changes: in the ways financial markets are integrated and regulated, the ever-increasing liberalization of trade, and the relentless expansion of the flexibilization of labor. Clearly, these changes are supported by technological innovations, in particular in the area of information and communication technology, affecting the logistics and viability of these new practices. As the invention of the telegraph, railroads, and steamships supported the expanding nineteenth-century production system, the Internet and satellite communications have a supportive function in the present economic reorganization. However, these new technological advances should not be taken as overwhelming deter-

minants of economic restructuring but only as its adjutants. Technological change is not globalization, only an aspect of it.

Likewise, analysis of women's labor in globalization should not simply be a description of their suffering. There are two axes of analysis involved in women's labor and globalization: one is of women as victims of the economic process; the other is the potential for women as subjects of the process. When women are perceived as an agency in the globalization process, they become a social force capable of acting in their own interest. This, in turn, brings our attention back to our understanding of the relationship between the politics and economics of globalization, or the political economy of globalization.

As the factory system of industrial production increased the rate of exploitation and control of labor in the nineteenth and twentieth centuries, it also brought workers together and stimulated the trade union movement. Similarly, as the current trend of globalization of production brings about an intensification of the exploitation of labor, it also acts as a stimulus to new forms of organization and resistance, in particular global social movements. Today's "global factory" and the new environment of global communications mean that global networking can emerge as a practical tool of resistance and organization. This reveals not only the contradictions of globalization but also the dialectic nature of trend and countertrend in globalization (Gills 2000). In other words, globalization elicits counterglobalization on a global scale, which induces alternative globalization movements in which labor and women play a critical role.

GLOBAL PRODUCTION AND WOMEN IN ASIA

The past experience of many developing countries, including those that adopted the World Bank's structural adjustment programs, has demonstrated that when overriding policy priority is given to gaining international competitiveness and the promotion of exports, less attention is given to the promotion of the welfare of the general population and particularly of labor. Indeed, the emphasis on international competitiveness and export promotion often supplants explicit policy measures against poverty and social inequality. In most cases, it appears that export promotion tends to induce further suppression of labor rights, combined with low wages. In the absence of any substantial increase in domestic consumption via a higher wage structure, the export promotion policies primarily benefit business interests. The labor practices now prevailing in the ever more ubiquitous free export processing zones (EPZs) around the world are a prime example of this tendency. For most countries in the developing world, with a low level of industrial capacity, promotion of exports is gained at the expense of labor, most notably of women.

With the restructuring of the world economy since the 1970s, governments in Asia have been competing for the favors of transnationally mobile capital. There has been an upsurge of free EPZs and free trade zones in which social and environmental standards are lowered while social subsidies to capital are increased, for example, through offering financial and other investment incentives by the host governments (Hoogvelt and Puxty 1997; Thomas 1997). The general historical outcome of this process has been an increase in the rate of exploitation of labor. Therefore, it represents a general redistribution of wealth and resources from labor to capital. That is, through the extension of both international competition and the mobility of capital, the tendency of an increased flow of wealth and resources from labor to capital has been intensified, rather than the trickle down of wealth from capital to labor taking place. As a result, rather than global wealth redistribution, there is further global wealth concentration.

As was the case in the recent history of the industrializing miracle economies, such as the Four Asian Tigers, women's labor continues to play a crucial role in the contemporary liberalization and restructuring of Asia's economies. Women are becoming increasingly active in both the rural and the urban economy, and their labor constitutes the ultimate foundation of international competitiveness of most Asian countries. Women are a direct source of cheap labor, especially in export manufacturing industries, whether as formal, informal, or casual labor. Among the workers of the world, women are all too often the most vulnerable and the most exploited during the so-called adjustment or restructuring processes.

Transnational companies are the main agents that facilitate the globalization of production. These corporations are responsible for 80 percent of foreign direct investment and are the main employers in some 850 EPZs in developing countries, with a workforce that has been estimated at around 27 million (United Nations Conference on Trade and Development 1994; International Labor Organization [ILO] 1998). Women's labor is central to these export factories that produce or assemble commodities for the global market. Female employment in EPZs is significantly higher than national average female employment in many developing economies. In major exporting countries in Asia, for example, in Malaysia, the Philippines, South Korea, and Sri Lanka, the share of women in employment in EPZs is more than 70 percent while women account for only 30 to 40 percent of overall employment in these countries (Kasugo and Tzannatos 1998). According to a study of nine electronics factories in one industrial park in Thailand, among the well-paid managerial-level employment, only 4 percent is female, while 88 percent of shop-floor workers are women (Theobald 2001). In China, women constitute an average 85 percent of the total workforce in state-owned cotton mills in the export sector (Zhao and West 2001). According to data from the Bangladesh Export Processing Zones Authority, in 1996, 70 percent of the employees in the Chittagong EPZ were women. This figure illustrates the point that the pattern of national industrial development, in the context of globalization of production, is being sustained by a predominantly female labor force in many Asian countries.

However, the ways in which women's labor is adopted in global production in Asia is very distinctive from the situation of women workers in core developed countries. Women in these global factories are subjected to a particular set of social relations that are related to the distinctive nature of global factories and the political economies of industrializing Asian countries. To a large extent, the labor experiences of many Asian women can be explained by the particular nature and the role of foreign capital (mostly transnational companies) in Asia. Core capital, in the form of foreign direct investment, as it operates in developing countries, is not strictly comparable to its role within the core states from which this capital originates. Accordingly, the social relations of capital and labor in the developing countries are quite different from those prevailing in the core countries. Therefore, Asian women workers in global production are a special category of labor that is not only different from men in general but also different from women workers in the developed economies.

Conventional wisdom says that foreign direct investment brings jobs and therefore prosperity and progress—for labor and especially for women. However, while the expansion of the export manufacturing sector through foreign capital investment does provide further opportunities to increase employment and exports for many countries in Asia, it also involves excessive competition to attract and maintain foreign direct investment. This in turn creates a tendency toward increase in the level of labor exploitation, via lower wages and longer working hours, with very little job security. In some cases, the minimum wage in the EPZs is lower than the national minimum wage, and many EPZs are excluded altogether from the scope of national labor laws. According to an ILO report, "the classic model of labor regulation is extremely rare in EPZs." In other words, workers in EPZs cannot negotiate binding agreements that regulate their interaction "with a 'floor' or framework of minimum labor standards, and free trade unions and employers (individually or collectively) coming together" (ILO 1998, 21).

Moreover, the footloose nature of globally mobile capital tends to move away from the countries where wages and working conditions have improved, for example, from South Korea, Hong Kong, and Malaysia to less developed economies such as Vietnam, Sri Lanka, Bangladesh, and China. This in turn creates a tendency toward increase in a downward pressure on wages, as expressed in the race-to-the-bottom syndrome. Thus, in global factories, the capital-labor relations for Asian women are becoming more exploitative and oppressive in the process of globalization of production. The flip side of the race to the bottom is the corporations' incessant search for ever-cheaper labor. As a consequence of these two processes, the labor

conditions of many women in contemporary Asia are coming to resemble those of an earlier era of industrialization in the West, characterized by sweatshops, that is, high levels of exploitation.

With increased emphasis on export production in national economic policy and a substantial increase in foreign direct investment in the region, the feminization of the labor force has now been firmly set in motion in many Asian countries. The feminization of labor in Asia is rather unique compared to that type of feminization taking place in the core countries. First of all, in Asia, the feminization of labor is accompanied by a new process of the proletarianization of women's labor. Many of this new pool of Asian women workers who are engaged in industrial production are drawn from the noncapitalist sphere of production, in particular from rural subsistence farming households. As such, many women wageworkers engaged in capitalist production are still a central part of a noncapitalist or nonproletarian household economy located in rural villages. This continued direct link between wage labor in the formal sector and the reproduction of village subsistence economies is a key feature of the political economy of globalization and women's labor in Asia.

Second, while feminization in the West is mainly located in service sector employment, the feminization of labor in Asia is concentrated in the manufacturing and agricultural sectors. While the proletarianization of women's labor in capitalist industries is a visible trend in most Asian countries, nevertheless a large proportion of Asia's women are still engaged in noncapitalist production.[1] Noncapitalist production refers to all activities that do not involve capital-labor relations but are nonetheless both economic and productive. This includes nonwage forms of work in subsistence agriculture, petty trade, community project work, exchange labor, and so on. Many women in Asian countries are engaged in more than one type of work at the same time. For example, they are involved in family farming while simultaneously working in informal and casual economic sectors, such as street vending or subcontracting piecework at home. In this way, they continuously carry out all types of work that fall outside the category of typical wage labor in the Western model of capitalist production. While some jobs in this category generate direct cash income, some do not necessarily remunerate women's labor in money form.

Nevertheless, these kinds of women's work, both paid and unpaid, significantly contribute to maintain the low cost of industrial and capitalist production. Even though women's labor is performed within the noncapitalist sphere of production, it is more often than not still fully integrated into the national economy, which is usually dominated by capitalist relations of production. A unit of economy, say, subsistence farming, may appear to be unrelated to, or separate from, the main capitalist economic system since social relations in the sphere of subsistence family farming are certainly noncapitalist and nonindustrial. Yet farming

production is closely linked to the capitalist production system, especially via market exchange, and by its relation to national industrial policy, which affects the valorization of peasant production, usually to its detriment.

Let us discuss how this linkage works. Subsistence farm households sell their agricultural products in the market while they purchase other industrial goods, including farming materials such as fertilizers, pesticides, seeds, and agricultural tools. The relative exchange values of these two types of production (i.e., subsistence production and capitalist production) are set differently, and thus unequal exchange occurs at the expense of subsistence production.[2] When farm goods produced in a noncapitalist mode of production are exchanged in the capitalist market, the hidden value of noncapitalist labor activities is valorized and realized in disguised forms. The value of the farm products—grain, vegetables, fruits, and so forth—is created from two layers of noncapitalist labor. One is the value directly created by nonwage subsistence farming labor in producing the goods, a larger part of which consists of rural female labor. The other is the hidden value indirectly created within the sphere of reproduction, that is, domestic labor. When both parts of this noncapitalist labor are considered, women's labor accounts for the largest portion. In this way, even when it is not directly exploited via capital-wage relations, women's labor in noncapitalist production is subjected to indirect but more intensive exploitation by industrial

Critical Perspectives on Globalization

capital. Rural women's labor activity in newly industrializing economies thus involves an "articulation of modes of production" in which value created in the noncapitalist sphere actually subsidizes the capitalist sphere (Meillassoux 1975).

Globalization of production affects women not only in terms of the increasing number of women workers but also in terms of the quality of their labor conditions. Contrary to Engels's claim,[3] the proletarianization in both manufacturing and service industries and the feminization of labor in Asia do not in themselves necessarily entail the empowerment of women through labor participation in production. Rather, under the present environment of a male-dominated structure of organized labor, feminization tends to weaken labor power in general. What is more, the feminization of labor occurs as a part of the process of flexibilization of labor, and this increasingly pushes women out of the core workforce and into a marginalized group of workers consisting of part-time, temporary, casual, and subcontracted labor. The direct and more immediate result of this process of economic marginalization, which affects perhaps the majority of women in Asia, is exacerbated by the intensified exploitation of their labor. In noneconomic terms, the predominance of neoliberal ideology may dampen what little exists of the sociopolitical movement of women in Asia and act to prevent radical improvement of their lives. Much empirical evidence indicates that economic globalization, in particular globalization of production, brings with it further exploitation

and impoverishment of women rather than their empowerment and emancipation.

The relative absence of substantive political representation of women and their alienation from political organizations inevitably affects women's position in society, including their legal rights. The political exclusion of women in Asia is directly related to the deepening of their economic marginalization and impoverishment. Therefore, along with further deterioration in the economic position of women, political exclusion of women, if it remains unchallenged, yields very little scope for improvement of women's position. Women will not get more claim on the society as a gender group unless specific women's issues are included in the political and social agenda of globalization.

ALTERNATIVE GLOBALIZATION:
DEMOCRATIC SOCIAL INCLUSION
AND WOMEN'S RIGHTS

Globalization is not just the predetermined triumph of Western consumerism, expressed as "the ultimate victory of VCR" by Francis Fukuyama (1992), for instance. Those who promise such a utopia for consumers while insisting on the separation of politics from economics do not take into account the fact that both the representation of power and the competition among conflicting interests in the sphere of politics are conditioned by economic relations. For example, capital-labor relations are not politically neutral, nor do capital and labor share an equal balance of power to begin with. Capital, by holding property and money and wielding considerable expertise and organizational power, begins in an advantageous position vis-à-vis labor. That is, the unequal distribution of material resources undermines equal access to political decisions and the capacity to influence political outcomes. In this sense, the assumption of fair and open political competition and equal political rights, on which formalistic notions of democracy ultimately depend, does not hold for everyone. In reality, due to underlying social inequalities, the political system operates largely in favor of capital rather than labor (Cohen 1991). Put another way, as Galbraith said, nothing so constrains the freedom of the individual as a complete absence of money.

The depoliticization element in the current economic globalization has a direct bearing on democratization, when democratization is understood as a process of social inclusion rather than merely as formal electoral participation. Democratization is a key process that may counter neoliberal globalization and how it ignores and marginalizes labor rights. In this context, democratization is a form of political and social resistance to capital-led globalization, which can be expressed as "counter-globalization" or "alternative-globalization" (Gills 2001). This claim depends on defining democratization in broad substantive terms rather than narrow formalistic terms. Any definition of democracy must include formal political democracy resting on legitimate civilian government and the rule of law, but a substantive definition of democracy

goes beyond this narrow conventional understanding. Democracy cannot be constituted only by a formal electoral system, and it needs to meet certain types of redistributive socioeconomic criteria.

The concept of democracy as used typically in the liberal tradition emphasizes the economic freedom or liberty of private property and capital, that is, their independence from public (state) control. The function of the state in this conceptual framework is confined to ensure the individual freedom of capital and the optimum conditions of free market competition. Thus, the role of the state in the economy becomes minimal. It is also on this basis, according to liberalism, that the individual liberty of each citizen is best guaranteed. The concept of Western democracy via a minimalist state grants autonomy to those who already occupy an advantageous position, most notably holders of capital. In the absence of political resistance and intervention, jobs, prices, growth, and the standard of living all rest in the hands of businessmen (Sun 1999). According to Charles Lindblom (1977), the privileged position of business gives capital a louder voice than anyone else's on matters not only of economics but also of politics. The "autonomy of the private corporation" thus becomes "the major specific institutional barrier to fuller democracy." The current trend in globalization is driving toward precisely that goal, that is, increasing the autonomy of the private corporation.

Such a process results in the opposite of broadened social inclusion.

The increased autonomy granted to private capital and corporations exacerbates the process of exclusion. The processes of corporate concentration, megamerger, and oligarchization of global capital occurring in the world today mean that more and more workers and ordinary people will be excluded. The idea of the politics of inclusion is that prosperity for the majority can be brought about only by the inclusion of social forces, in particular of labor, into the state and its decision-making procedures. It also means focusing on redistributional economic policies that favor the weak majority rather than the strong minority. The process of inclusion implies decreasing social inequalities, polarization, and marginalization. Democratization, therefore, requires significant changes in the composition of power, allowing the inclusion of a broad spectrum of social forces into the state, or giving them access to influence the state policy decision-making process. This includes labor, not only organized labor but also unorganized labor, such as women's labor, children's labor, and migrants' labor. The problem of the creation and exclusion of the so-called underclass also has to be dealt with within a more inclusive social-political framework.

Above all, in the argument of democratization, what counts most is whether meaningful social change is actually taking place. In recent years, there has been a tendency toward a co-optive strategy. It is characterized by the convergence of opposition programs until there ceases to be any substantive difference between the alternative and the elite conservative position, be it called "the Third Way" or "New Labour" as put forward by Tony Blair. Such an ideology proclaims that capital-labor relations should no longer be characterized by antagonism but rather by a harmony of interests. This implies the class struggle is an irrelevance in globalized politics and social relations. In other words, in the new globalized world, *Left* and *Right* no longer bear any useful meaning in political discourse. In this way, the state both poses as and acts as the instrument conveying the interests of transnational capital onto national society. To borrow Robert Cox's (1987) term, this is the process of the "internationalizing of the state" in which the key state function is primarily to adjust domestic policies and practices to accommodate the functional requirements of the neoliberal global economy.

In contrast, substantive democratization via a politics of inclusion depends on a decisive shift in the balance of forces in favor of the political inclusion of popular social forces and movements. It strives for expanding and enhancing the political centrality of a progressive program, bringing about the empowerment of new social forces. Such democratization requires the prioritizing of social equity over economic growth. It also requires the will of the state to accept public accountability for the role of protection of societal interests from the depredations of private capital and economic interests. The role of the state therefore becomes central in the politics of globalization. In defense of societal interests, the state must be assumed to be neither merely a neutral mediating institution nor powerless vis-à-vis the forces of globalization. The state is a crucial political actor that facilitates social inclusion and overtly resists undesirable aspects of globalization. Rather than assuming that national policy cannot affect global market forces, the state can retain sufficient independence to exert a powerful influence over domestic outcomes, such as unemployment (Ashton and Maguire 1991) or even capital controls, as some governments in east Asia demonstrated during the Asian financial crisis. For the state to behave in this way, it is true that the first minimum condition is electoral competition, which allows the possibility of popular access to state power. Second, it requires that the party(ies) in government represent and defend the interests of the majority and can be held accountable to or be checked by this majority.

The dynamics in the politics of globalization can be detected in the development of global resistance movements in recent years. For example, Sweatshop Watch and the National Labor Committee, two coalitions based in the United States, represent one type of broad popular social movement. They bring together various campaigners for labor rights, human rights, and legal rights as well as community and religious organizations and university students to battle against sweatshop labor throughout the world. Other similar coalitions include the Maquila Solidarity Network, which promotes cooperation between labor and other social movements in NAFTA countries. The International

Center for Trade Union Rights works specifically for the rights of unions and their workers at the international level, while Women Working Worldwide supports women workers through organizing public awareness campaigns and networking efforts. There are many other social organizations active in all parts of the world connected by the Internet. For example, 50 Years is Enough Network organizes a global network of resistance with some twenty-five similar organizations worldwide, including those in Nicaragua, South Africa, the Philippines, India, Senegal, Mauritius, Brazil, Macedonia, Pakistan, and Mexico.

In addition to new types of movements, the traditional union movement is also rejuvenating internationalism, for example, the International Confederation of Free Trade Unions and the International Trade Secretariats (Stevis and Boswell 2000). While these organizations bring together bureaucrats at the top of the organizational structure, others bring the grassroots unionists together for common action, such as the Transnationals Information Exchange (Niemeljer 1996). Labor is organizing worldwide in "the era of globalization," and as new models of solidarity and collective action emerge, they bridge old barriers between North and South (Munck and Waterman 1999).

In the case of women's labor experiences, the complex ways in which gender hierarchy, national capital, foreign capital, and the state negotiate and adapt to the forces of economic globalization expose women to diverse mechanisms of exploitation.

Accordingly, women are responding in a wide range of ways and at different levels. The spectrum of actions by women extends from day-to-day resistance by individuals and informal resistance and support by a group of women to formal organizational actions. The informal organizational resistance includes various social networks based on women's communities, dormitories, workplaces, and even through worldwide Web sites. This type of activity can provide women with moral and material support as well as a foundation on which collective consciousness and actions develop. Such groups as the Union for Civil Liberty and the Friends for Friends Group in Thailand, Women's Shelters, National Network for Solidarity with Migrant Workers, the Working Women's Network in Japan, and various women's support groups and watchdog organizations, including formal organizations in Asian countries, represent different levels and channels of resistance. Trade union movements demanding increased labor rights for women have also gained further momentum in recent years. For example, there has been an unprecedented level of increase in trade union membership during the past few years in Malaysia, while numerous new women's labor unions and organizations were formed after the 1997-1998 financial crisis in spite of the fact that the absolute amount of female employment has been reduced.

It is apparent that there have been various social actions that have strengthened the counterhegemonic movements against capital-led economic globalization. Labor, especially women's labor, is an important social force that can check the power of capital and resist the global trends that encroach on labor rights. Women's movements, however, are now required to be something more than traditional male-oriented labor movements. Cultural norms and values determining women's adverse social position are very much tied to the dominant patriarchal relations within a society. Therefore, any meaningful changes that would raise women's social status will not come about without some form of organized resistance to gender inequality. Rejection of unequal gender relations can only be effectively pursued via organized political-social action. More broadly, social and political responses working for social justice should be based on greater inclusion, including women's rights.

Globalization of production at the expense of women's and workers' rights cannot be maintained without creating volatility that affects both industry and labor. On one hand, such volatility "makes zones less effective as export platforms and limits their potential to attract investment, generate jobs, boost exports and promote broader economic growth" (ILO 1998). On the other hand, further repression of labor as a way of controlling volatility does not offer long-term solutions; rather, it prevents real progress toward democratization. Meaningful democratization can be pushed forward only through a social agenda of redistribution, not only of economic but of political power, between the divided groups within society, which must include gender.

Notes

1. The heavily urbanized and industrialized countries of northeast Asia, such as Japan, South Korea, and Taiwan, and the city-state of Singapore are exceptions. Elsewhere in Asia, from India, through most of southeast Asia, to mainland China, peasant life still predominates.

2. For a detailed discussion of exchange between subsistence and capitalist production, see Gills (1999).

3. Engels presented production relations as the principal factor that conditions the development of society and of social institutions. Along this line of argument, that social production relations determine all power relations, he and subsequent Marxist writers explained women's subordination as the result of their assignment to "unproductive" roles in the domestic sphere.

References

Ashton, D., and M. Maguire. 1991. Patterns and experience of unemployment. In *Poor work: Disadvantage and the division of labor*, edited by P. Brown and R. Scase, 40-55. Milton Keynes, UK: Open University Press.

Castells, M. 1996. *The rise of the network society*. Oxford, UK: Blackwell.

Cohen, J. 1991. Maximising social welfare or institutionalising democratic ideals? Commentary on Adam Prezworski's article. *Politics and Society* 19 (1): 39-58.

Cox, R. 1987. *Production, power and world order: Social forces in the shaping of history*. New York: Columbia University Press.

Fukuyama, F. 1992. *The end of history and the last man*. Harmondsworth, UK: Penguin.

Galbraith, J. 2000. Forward: The social Left and the market system. In *Globalization and politics of resistance*, edited by B. Gills. London: Macmillan.

Giddens, A. 1990. *The consequences of modernity*. Cambridge, UK: Polity.

———. 1996. Globalization: A keynote address. *UNRISD News*:15.

Gills, B. K. 1997. Editorial: Globalization and the politics of resistance. *New Political Economy* 2 (1): 11-15.

Gills, D.-S.S. 1999. *Rural women and triple exploitation in Korean Development*. New York: Macmillan.

———. 2001. Globalization and counter-globalization. In *Women and work in globalizing Asia*, edited by D. S. Gills and N. Piper, 13-29. London: Routledge.

Hoogvelt, A., and A. Puxty. 1997. *Multinational enterprise: An encyclopedic dictionary of concepts and terms*. London: Macmillan.

International Labor Organization (ILO). 1998. *Labor and social issues relating to export processing zones: Report for discussion in the tripartite meeting of export processing zone-operating countries*. Geneva: International Labor Organization.

Kasugo, T., and Z. Tzannatos. 1998. *Export processing zones: A review in need of update*. Discussion paper series 9802. Washington, DC: World Bank.

Lindblom, C. 1977. *Politics and markets*. New York: Basic Books.

MacAdam, M. 1998. Working for the rat. *New Internationalist* 308 (December): 15-17.

Meillassoux, C. 1975. From production to reproduction: A Marxist approach to economic anthropology. *Economy and Society* 1 (1): 93-104.

Munck, R., and P. Waterman, eds. 1999. *Labour worldwide in the era of globalization: Alternative union models in the new world order*. London: Macmillan.

Niemeljer, M. 1996. Grassroots labor internationalism: The transnational information exchange. Unpublished thesis, University of Amsterdam.

Stevis, D., and T. Boswell. 2000. From national resistance to international labor politics. In *Globalization and the politics of resistance*, edited by B. Gills, 150-70. London: Macmillan.

Sun, H. 1999. Democratic consolidation and labor politics. Unpublished paper, University of Newcastle, UK.

Theobald, S. 2001. Working for global factories: Thai women in electronics export companies in the Northern Regional Industrial Estate. In *Women and work in globalizing Asia*, edited by D. S. Gills and N. Piper, 136. London: Routledge.

Thomas, K. 1997. Corporate welfare campaigns in North America. *New Political Economy* 2 (1): 117 26.

United Nations Conference on Trade and Development. 1994. *UNCTAD statistical pocket book*.

Waters, M. 1995. *Globalization*. London: Routledge.

Zhao, M., and J. West. 2001. Adjusting to urban capital: Rural female labor in state cotton mills in China. In *Women and work in globalizing Asia*, edited by D. S. Gills and N. Piper, 169-187. London: Routledge.

[24]

The International Division of Reproductive Labor

The previous chapter established that Filipino men and women usually migrate independently of each other. My query into the lives of migrant Filipina domestic workers now moves to the causes of their independent migration. Significantly, numerous responses of interviewees to the question "Why did you migrate?" concern issues of gender inequality in the Philippines. They include domestic violence, labor market segmentation, and the unequal division of labor in the family. Traditional discussions on the causes of either male or female migration, which usually are based solely on economics, cannot fully explain such responses. However, while these responses do not question the applicability of the political economy of globalization to the causes of migration for Filipina domestic workers, they do suggest that gender distinguishes the structural causes of independent migration for men and women.

To account for the gendered political economy of migration, I extend discussions of the "international division of labor" in globalization from a sole consideration of productive labor to include analyses of reproductive labor. Reproductive labor refers to the labor needed to sustain the productive labor force. Such work includes household chores; the care of elders, adults, and youth; the socialization of children; and the maintenance of social ties in the family (Brenner and Laslett, 1991; Glenn, 1992). By focusing on reproductive labor, I emphasize that gender is a controlling factor of the outflow of labor in globalization and show another dimension by which gender shapes the economic divisions of labor in migration.

Relegated to women more so than men, reproductive labor has long been a commodity purchased by class-privileged women. As Evelyn Nakano Glenn (1992) has observed, white class-privileged women in the United States have historically freed themselves of reproductive labor by purchasing the low-wage services of women of color. In doing so, they maintain a "racial division of reproductive labor" (Glenn 1992), which establishes a two-tier hierarchy among women.

My analysis of reproductive labor extends the important formulation of Glenn to an international terrain so as to consider issues of globalization and the feminization of wage labor. The globalization of the market economy has extended the politics of reproductive labor into an international level. The migration and entrance into domestic work of Filipino women constitute an international division of reproductive labor. This division of labor, which I call the international transfer of caretaking, refers to the three-tier transfer of reproductive labor among women in sending and receiving countries of migration. While class-privileged women purchase the low-wage services of migrant Filipina domestic workers, migrant Filipina domestic workers simultaneously purchase the even lower wage services of poorer women left behind in the Philippines. In light of this transnational transfer of gender constraints that occurs in globalization, the independent migration of Filipina domestic workers could be read as a process of rejecting gender constraints for different groups of women in a transnational economy.

The international transfer of caretaking links two important but separate discourses on the status of women—Glenn's (1992) discussion of the "racial division of reproductive labor" and Sassen's (1984) discussion of the "international division of labor." It demonstrates that these important formulations need to be expanded to take into account transnational issues of reproduction. To develop my argument, I first analyze the situation of migrant Filipina domestic workers in the Philippines and the receiving nations of the United States and Italy. My discussion establishes the subordinate position of women in the labor market and family at both ends of the migration spectrum. I then build on this by adding the migration links that illustrate the international transfer of caretaking. By presenting this division of labor, I establish that global capitalism and patriarchy are macrostructural forces that jointly determine the subject-positions of migrant Filipina domestic workers in globalization.[1]

The Hidden Causes of Migration

Economic and political processes without doubt determine the migration of Filipina domestic workers. In response to one of the first questions that I asked in the interview—"Why did you migrate?"—I expected answers that fit classic theoretical formulations of the causes of migration. Hoping to show that women are also economically motivated migrants and not just passive dependents of male migrants, I anticipated answers that could be explained by economic disparities between developing countries like the Philippines and industrialized countries like the United States and Italy. As expected, all of my respondents had been partially driven by economic motives. For example, Michelle Fonte, a single woman who in 1989 followed her sister to Rome, states:

> My sister was the first one here. The truth is that our family had a lot of debts in the Philippines. Our land was just about to be confiscated by the bank. My sister couldn't afford to pay for the debt on her own. So what she did was she took me over here. When I got here, we helped each other out and we were able to pay for the debt on time.

Many responses mirrored Michelle's. Some respondents even looked at me strangely, seeming to wonder why I would ask such an obvious question before they proceeded to tell me about the economic insecurities of the middle class in the Philippines. In the Philippines, where at least 70 percent of families live in poverty, a middle-class status does not constitute a comfortable and secure lifestyle (Israel-Sobritchea, 1990). The middle class in the Philippines especially took a sharp downturn in the mid-1980s with the further devaluation of the peso by the International Monetary Fund. As Dasch et al. state, "By the 1980s, even a schoolteacher could not afford to buy more than two chickens a month and could only purchase low quality rice" (1994: 232).

Filipino men and women share the economic displacements that spur labor migration in global restructuring. However, the different meanings of "economic" migration for men and women should be elucidated, considering that gender shapes the family and local economy of the Philippines. With this in mind, I now look at the position of women in the family.

In the Philippines, women confront the traditional gender ideology of the patriarchal nuclear family: men are expected to sustain the family and women reproduce family life. Consequently, gender distinguishes the meaning of independent labor migration for men and women. For women, labor migration in itself questions gender prescriptions in society. As ideological constructs of feminine identity are molded from "mothering and caring roles in the domestic arena," the independent migration of women constitutes a direct liberation from traditional duties and roles (Israel-Sobritchea, 1990).

In Rome and Los Angeles, most respondents migrate to help sustain the family, which is an obligation that stems for the most part from the extremely strong bond of family allegiance and filial piety in the Philippines (Chant and McIlwaine, 1995; Paz Cruz and Paganoni, 1989). Yet the meaning of migration as a strategy of family maintenance is very different for men and women. By migrating to sustain the household, women reconstitute the traditional gender division of labor in the family as they take on the role of income provider. Because independent migration frees working women of household constraints, migration is not just a family strategy but a covert strategy to relieve women of burdens in the family. As Filipina feminist scholar Carolyn Israel-Sobritchea observes, "Despite the growth of female labor force participation, there has not been a commensurate decrease in their child care and household responsibilities" (1990: 35). Most Filipino women do not have the means to relieve themselves of the double day, or the "second shift."

If we consider the gender stratification imposed on women in the family, we can then see that migration as a strategy of family maintenance entails a negotiation of how to perform (gendered) family duties. In the traditional Filipino household, daughters—more so than sons—are expected to care for their parents in old age. As the only daughter in her family, Lorna Fernandez of Rome, for instance, felt a great sense of responsibility for her family but simultaneously felt suffocated by the duties she was expected to perform.

> I am the only girl and the oldest in my family. I have all brothers. There were many reasons why I came here. I had a good job. [She finished in the top ten of the national board exam for midwifery.] I was employed in a private office for seven years. I was making decent money. But I wanted to leave because even if you have a decent salary in our country, it does not allow you to save any money. And then, I kept on thinking that my parents are not going to see their situation improve very much. . . . So one of the reasons I came here was for my family. . . . I came here also for the change. I was very tired. I was sick of the routine I was in. Every month, I received my salary and divided it up to my parents, brothers and then hardly any would be left for me. . . . The first thirty-seven years of my life was given to my family, and I feel this is just when I am starting out for myself.

While the family is considered a central site of support and assistance, some single women simultaneously desire to be liberated from the demands and responsibilities of familism.

Examining the position of women in the Philippine labor market also differentiates the meaning of economic migration for men and women. Although the lack of opportunities in the Philippine economy affects both men and women, the sex segmentation in the Philippine labor market further aggravates the already limited opportunities of women. In the Philippines, the ideology of women as caretakers constrains their productive labor activities in many ways, including their segregation in jobs resembling "wife-and-mother roles" such as household work on plantations and professional work in nursing and teaching (Chant and McIlwaine, 1995; Eviota, 1992). Because women are only expected to subsidize the primary income of men, female jobs are often less valued and far less lucrative than comparable men's work.[2] For example, field work on plantations pays more than household work (Eviota, 1992). In addition, women have fewer chances for promotion than do men (Eviota, 1992; Lopez-Rodriguez, 1990).

Despite these constraints, women do participate in the productive labor force. In 1992, the female share of total employment in the Philippines reached 37.7 percent (Chant, 1997). Like migrant women from the Dominican Republic, most migrant Filipina domestic workers have premigration paid work experience (Grasmuck and Pessar, 1991). Since they have greater means than other women to migrate, educated women in the Philippines may turn to employment opportunities outside the Philippines as a method of negotiating their low wages. Many of the research participants in Rome and Los Angeles formerly employed in "female professions" (for example, teachers and administrative assistants) sought the higher wages that they could earn outside the Philippines, even if only as domestic workers.

Examining the positions of Filipino women and men in the family and labor market demonstrates that they are not equally displaced in the overarching structure of the world-system. In the case of the Philippines, women have to contend with a gender-stratified economy, a fact that may have stimulated female outmigration. This assertion possibly contradicts the common assumption that the increased number of manufacturing jobs in free-trade zones in Third World countries, because it creates greater labor market opportunities for women, displaces male workers and, as a result, indirectly causes the emigration of men. It is important to point out that the female labor force in the Philippines is not subsumed under manufacturing. Multinational firms only guarantee a few jobs, significantly less than agriculture, for example. Though only a very small number of women in my study held manufacturing jobs in the Philippines, the constant turnover of the manufacturing workforce may also promote the migration of female manufacturing workers (Eviota, 1992). After factory employment, women face dim prospects in the Philippine labor market and, as a result, may turn to migration.

Corroborating the deduction that independent female migration can hypothetically be seen as a process of escaping gender constraints are the intense responses of women to the simple and seemingly obvious question "Why did you migrate?" In Rome, fourteen of the twenty female respondents who were legally married when they had migrated wanted to leave an abusive or unfaithful husband or had irresponsible partners and could no longer afford to raise dependents as single mothers. For example, some migrated because they could no longer tolerate the infidelity of their husbands.

> You know why I came here? I had to leave the Philippines. If I didn't, I would have ended up killing someone. I had caught my husband with another woman. (Trinidad Borromeo)

> My husband used to beat me up and have affairs. Then he left me for another woman. . . . I went to Kuwait after my husband and I separated. See, I tried to commit suicide two times. The first time I swallowed poison and the second time I slashed my wrists many times. At the hospital, my mother was able to talk to me, and she told me that if I can't take the actions of my husband, I should just go abroad. I was still very young, and I already had my children. (Clarita Sungkay)

In other cases, women had to escape domestic violence.

> I came to Italy in 1983 to look for a job and also a change of environment. . . . You have to understand that my problems were very heavy before I left the Philippines. My husband was abusive. I couldn't even think about my children. The only thing I could think about was the opportunity to escape my situation. If my husband was not going to kill me, I was probably going to kill him. . . . My problems with him were so heavy. He was abusive. He always beat me up, and my parents wanted me to leave him for a long time. My children, I left with my sister. I asked my husband for permission to leave the country, and I told him that I was only going to be gone for two years. . . . I was just telling him that so I could leave the country peacefully. . . . In the plane. . . I felt like a bird whose cage that had been locked for many years had just recently been opened. Nine years he abused me. He was very strict, and he tried to control every situation. Often, I could not leave the house.

> When I was able to escape, I felt free and felt so loose. Deep inside, I felt homesick for my children, but I also felt free for being able to escape the most dire problem that was slowly killing me. (Ruby Mercado)

These disturbing testimonies suggest a pattern of abusive male behavior that pushes women to leave the Philippines. They turn to migration to escape debilitating situations in the household.

According to British sociologists Sylvia Chant and Cathy McIlwaine, institutionalized practices of "male superiority within the Filipino household include the practice of wife-beating. Domestic violence is viewed as 'ordinary' and 'normal' within the context of marriage and stems from the polarized socialization of men as aggressive and assertive and women as passive and submissive" (1995:13). The rampancy of domestic violence in the Philippines truly shows the contradictory process of patriarchy. Patriarchy persists despite the benefits gained by Filipino women from their society's matrilineal and matrilocal culture such as their comparable level of educational attainment and high rate of formal labor market participation (Eviota, 1992).

Women, at least those with resources (such as networks and funds) emigrate instead of facing ostracism in the community against divorce or separation, for which they as women are more often blamed than men (Israel-Sobritchea, 1990).[3] Divorce is not a legal option for couples in the Philippines even though legal separation can now be granted on the basis of physical violence and incest. Moreover, legally separated individuals do not have the option of remarriage. Legal restrictions and the burden of cultural expectations (for example, the tremendous value on family cohesion for the benefit of children and the immense influence of Catholicism) constrain the option of women to leave abusive spouses permanently. Chant and McIlwaine add, "It should also be noted that grounds for separation on the basis of sexual infidelity are strongly weighted in favour of men, in that a wife only has to have sexual intercourse with another man for this to be granted, whereas a charge of adultery against a husband has to involve concubinage" (1995: 14–15). Not surprising then is the fact that some women believe that they can only escape their marriage by taking advantage of the migrant networks and agencies that are well in place in a traditional sending country such as the Philippines.

Other interviewees decided to emigrate after their husbands abandoned them and they were left to raise their children on their own. Jennifer Jeremillo, for example, sought the higher wages of domestic work in Italy because she could no longer support her children with the wages she earned as a public school teacher.

> After three years of marriage, my husband left me for another woman. . . . My husband supported us for just a little over a year. Then, the support was stopped, everything was stopped, the letters stopped. I have not seen him since. . . . I think of my children's future. There I would be the only one working, without a husband and supporting my children on my own. I knew that my salary was not enough for their future, for their schooling and everything. So I decided to come here even though I had to borrow a lot of money. It cost me 200,000 pesos [U.S.$8000] to come here. Just to pay for the agency was 150,000 pesos [U.S.$6000].

While, on the surface, women who are abandoned by their husbands seem to be motivated solely by the economic benefits of migration, their economic motive cannot be situated solely in the overarching world-system of global capitalism. It must also be placed in the context of gender inequalities that have shaped their experiences and positions as single mothers. Since women are more likely to be abandoned by their husbands than vice versa, it is important to emphasize how this is caused by double standards in male and female sexual practices in the Philippines.[4] Thus, it is this gender inequality that places these women in a position of economic need for migration.

The case of married women in Rome is actually not reflected in my Los Angeles sample, which only includes two women who had cited similar reasons for migration. However, the absence of domestic violence or other marital problems as motivating factors for migration to Los Angeles is not caused by social differences between the two groups, because they belong in the same class. Instead of social differences, this discrepancy can likely be attributed to the more difficult process of migration to the United States. More stringent requirements for prospective migrants delay the migration of women wanting to leave the Philippines quickly.

My finding in Rome is actually supported by the observations of the editor of *Tinig Filipino*.

> In my casual talks with lots of my fellow women overseas contract workers especially the married ones, I found out that there seems to be a certain common factor that binds them—that leaving their families for overseas gave them temporary relief from the sacrifices that go with their marriage. Others are blunt enough to share that their main reason for coming abroad is not merely to earn money but to escape from their

bitter relationships with their husbands. Very rightly so. For no mother could ever afford to leave her young children and her home if the situation at home is normal. (Layosa, 1995b: 7)

As my findings in Rome seem to reflect the situation of Filipina domestic workers in some of the other countries of the labor diaspora, theoretical discussions of the causes of migration have to consider the system of gender inequality in the Philippines, which, in the case of these women, manifests itself in the limited options they have for divorce and the double standards in male and female sexual activities. For Filipinos, these inequalities are aggravated by the burden to uphold the traditional norm of nuclear families.

Highlighting the gender relations and divisions in the Philippines complicates discussions of migration. Patriarchy, which operates as a discrete system within the sending country of the Philippines, is a hidden cause of migration for women. Thus, this system must be included in any formulation of the macrostructural determination of female migration, although, not without an equal consideration of the system of gender inequality in receiving countries.

The Racial Division of Reproductive Labor

Migrant Filipina domestic workers depart from a system of gender stratification in the Philippines only to enter another one in the advanced capitalist and industrialized countries of the United States and Italy. In both sending and receiving nations, they confront societies with similar gender ideologies; that is, reproductive labor is relegated primarily to women. Yet racial, class, and citizenship inequalities aggravate their position in receiving nations. This is demonstrated by their labor market incorporation, which is their official entryway into another system of gender inequality. Migration initiates their entrance into the "racial division of reproductive labor" (Glenn, 1992). They are incorporated into the labor market not only to serve the needs of the highly specialized professionals in "global cities" but also to relieve women of their household work.

In the industrialized countries of Asia, the Americas, and Europe, the number of gainfully employed women has climbed dramatically in the last forty years (Licuanan, 1994; O'Connor, 1996; Reskin and Padavic, 1994). In the United States, women represented 46.5 percent of gainfully employed workers in 1992, a considerable increase over 32.1 percent in 1960 (Reskin and Padavic, 1994: 24–25). In Italy, the downward trend in the labor force participation of women from 1959 to 1972 has since taken a reverse direction (Meyer, 1987). In fact, Italy has witnessed an increasing number of married women in the labor force but surprisingly a decline in the number of younger single women engaged in paid work (Goddard, 1996). In the case of Italy, it has been argued that women are turning away from reproducing families and concentrating on their advancement in the labor market (Specter, 1998). Italy, though known to be "the traditional 'bambini' country," has the lowest birth rate in the world at only 9.6 per 1000 inhabitants (Beck and Beck-Gernsheim, 1995: 102).

While the share of female participation in the labor market has risen in industrialized countries, women remain responsible for the reproductive labor in households. According to Hochschild (1989), in these times of a "stalled revolution," at least in the United States, the vast majority of men do less housework than their gainfully employed partners. A significantly larger number of women have to cope with the double day because women still perform a disproportionate amount of housework, childcare, and social relations with kin and community. Similarly in Italy, *doppio lavoro* (literally meaning double work) has been a recurring theme in the Italian feminist movement since the early 1970s (Birnbaum, 1986). While Italian feminists demanded "wages for housework" beginning in 1975 (Birnbaum, 1986: 135), it can be said that Italian women have since taken a new tactic. Refusing to reproduce the family altogether is a unique response to the double day and a means by which many Italian women minimize their reproductive labor directly.

In both Italy and the United States, elderly care should also be included in the long list of women's household responsibilities. Due to advances in medicine and nutrition, the elderly make up a rapidly growing population, but especially so in communities of "middle- and upper-class whites" in the United States (Abel, 1990: 73). In Italy, the elderly likewise make up an increasing proportion of the population, due primarily to the country's zero-population growth (Beck and Beck-Gernsheim, 1995; Specter, 1998).

In her study of the household division of labor in two-income families, Hochschild (1989) found that men who earned less than their wives were those who were less likely to share housework. An economic logic concerning household division of labor is thus too simplistic. It does not consider the backlash caused by what men perceive as the threat of women's labor market participation (Reskin and Padavic, 1994: 21). In the case of men who earn less than their female partners, women's higher gainful earnings destroy the (socialized) identities accorded to them by patriarchy. Avoiding housework is thus the most tangible means by which they can still maintain their place in the patriarchal order. In a patriarchal society such as the United States, the increasing number of working women are left with the choice of purchasing the services of other, meaning less-privileged, women or working a double day.

While a higher joint income does not guarantee a more egalitarian distribution of housework between the sexes, it does give families the flexibility to afford the services of other women. To ease the double day, many overwhelmed working women have turned to day-care centers and family day-care providers, nursing homes, after-school baby-sitters, and also privately hired domestic workers (Glazer, 1993; Glenn, 1986; Hochschild, 1989; Nelson, 1990; Reskin and Padavic, 1994; Rothman, 1989a, 1989b). As Joy Manlapit, a provider of elderly care in Los Angeles, observes:

> Domestics here are able to make a living from the elderly that families abandon. When they are older, the families do not want to take care of them. Some put them in convalescent homes, some put them in retirement homes, and some hire private domestic workers.

The labor market incorporation of migrant Filipina domestic workers fits into Glenn's schema of the racial division of reproduction of labor. In Italy and the United States, they join the ranks of other groups of working-class women who have historically performed the reproductive labor of more privileged women.[5] In doing so, they free their employers to pursue more rewarding gainful employment. Reflecting the observations of Glenn, Jacqueline Andall finds a direct correlation between the entrance of migrant women into Italy and the entrance of native Italian women into the labor force:

> The migration of women into Italy began at the same time as a number of changes were taking place in the role and position of Italian women within society. When, in the 1970s, an increased number of Italian women began to assert themselves outside the domestic sphere, this had repercussions on the Italian family. This change in Italian women's activity became a pull factor in the migration of women from developing countries. (1992: 43)

Not surprisingly, 36.4 percent of illegal workers in Italy are doing domestic work (Calavita, 1994).

Glenn's formulation of the racial division of reproductive labor suggests that the economic demand for the low-wage labor of domestic workers arises not solely from the concentration of highly specialized professional service workers in "global cities" but also from persisting gender inequalities in the families of these professionals. To fully consider the politics of reproductive labor in migration, I now expand and reformulate the concept of the racial division of reproductive labor by placing it in a transnational setting. In doing so, I situate the increasing demand for paid reproductive labor in receiving nations in the context of the globalization of the market economy.

The International Division of Reproductive Labor

Globalization has triggered the formation of a singular market economy. As such, production activities in one area can no longer be understood solely from a unilocal perspective. Likewise, reproduction activities, especially as they have been increasingly commodified, have to be situated in the context of this singular market economy. In this sense, reproduction activities in one area have concrete ties to reproduction activities in another area. With the feminization of wage labor, global capitalism is forging the creation of links among distinct systems of gender inequality. Moreover, the migration of women connects systems of gender inequality in both sending and receiving nations to global capitalism. All of these processes occur in the formation of the international division of reproductive labor.

This division of labor places Glenn's (1992) concept of the racial division of reproductive labor in an international context under the auspices of Sassen's (1984) discussion of the incorporation of women from developing countries in the global economy. It is a transnational division of labor that is shaped simultaneously by global capitalism and systems of gender inequality in both sending and receiving countries of migration. This division of labor determines the migration and entrance into domestic service of women from the Philippines.

The international transfer of caretaking is a distinct form of international division of labor in which Filipina domestic workers perform the reproductive labor of class-privileged women in industrialized countries as they leave their own to other women in the Philippines to perform. This international division of labor refers to a three-tier transfer of reproductive labor among women in two nation-states. These groups of women are (1) middle- and upper-class women in receiving countries, (2) migrant Filipina domestic workers, and (3) Filipina domestic workers in the Philippines who are too poor to migrate.

In the article "Economy Menders," Linda Layosa, the editor of *Tinig Fili-pino*, gives a partial description of the international transfer of caretaking.

> Indeed, our women have partially been liberated from the anguish of their day-to-day existence with their families and from economic problems, only to be enslaved again in the confines of another home, most of the time trampling their rights as human beings . . . . We have to face the reality that many of our women will be compelled to leave the confines of their own tidy bedrooms and their spotless kitchens only to clean another household, to mend others' torn clothes at the same time mend our tattered economy. (1995a: 7)

In her description, she falls short of mentioning who takes up the household work that migrant Filipina domestic workers abandon upon migration. Most likely, they are other female relatives but also, less-privileged Filipina women, women unable to afford the high costs of seeking employment outside of the Philippines. Thus, migrant Filipina domestic workers are in the middle of the three-tier hierarchy of the international transfer of caretaking.

Under the international transfer of caretaking, women's migration from the Philippines is embedded in the process of global capitalism. At the same time, gender is also a central factor of their migration: the process of migration for women involves escaping their gender roles in the Philippines, easing the gender constraints of women who employ them in industrialized countries, and finally relegating their gender roles to women left in the Philippines.

The international transfer of caretaking refers to a social, political, and economic relationship between women in the global labor market. This division of labor is a structural relationship of inequality based on class, race, gender and (nation-based) citizenship. In this division of labor, there is a gradational decline in worth of reproductive labor. As Rothman (1989a: 43) poignantly describes, "When performed by mothers, we call this mothering . . . ; when performed by hired hands, we call it unskilled." Commodified reproductive labor is not only low-paid work but declines in market value as it gets passed down the international transfer of caretaking. As care is made into a commodity, women with greater resources in the global economy can afford the best-quality care for their family. Conversely, the care given to those with fewer resources is usually worth less.

Consequently, the quality of family life progressively declines as care is passed down the international transfer of caretaking. Freed of household constraints, those on top can earn more and consequently afford better-quality care than can the domestic workers whom they hire. With their wages relatively low, these domestic workers cannot afford to provide the same kind of care for their family. They in turn leave them behind in the Philippines to be cared for by even lesser-paid domestic workers. Relegated to the bottom of the three-tier hierarchy of reproductive labor, domestic workers left in the Third World have far fewer material resources to ensure the reproduction of their own family.

In the international transfer of caretaking, Filipina domestic workers do not just ease the entrance of other women into the paid labor force but also assist in the economic growth of receiving countries. Patricia Licuanan, in reference to households in Hong Kong and Singapore, explains:

> Households are said to have benefited greatly by the import of domestic workers. Family income has increased because the wife and other women members of working age are freed from domestic chores and are able to join the labour force. This higher income would normally result in the enlargement of the consumer market and greater demand on production and consequently a growth in the economy. (1994: 109)

By spurring economic development, the international transfer of caretaking retains the inequalities of the global market economy. The low wages of migrant domestic workers increase the production activities of the receiving nation, but the economic growth of the Philippine economy is for the most part limited and dependent on the foreign currency provided by their low wages.

A similar observation can be made of the employing families in the international transfer of caretaking. Freed of reproductive labor, the family employing the migrant domestic worker can increase the productive labor generated in their household. The mobility of the Filipina migrant domestic worker and her family is for the most part dependent on the greater mobility of the employing family. The same relationship goes for domestic workers in the Philippines and the migrant domestics who employ them.

The case of Carmen Ronquillo provides a good illustration of the international transfer of caretaking. Carmen is simultaneously a domestic worker for a professional woman in Rome and an employer of a domestic worker in the Philippines. Carmen describes her relationship to each of these two women:

> When coming here, I mentally surrendered myself and forced my pride away from me to prepare myself. But I lost a lot of weight. I was not used to the work. You see, I had maids in the Philippines. I have a maid

in the Philippines that has worked for me since my daughter was born twenty-four years ago. She is still with me. I paid her three hundred pesos before, and now I pay her 1000 pesos [U.S.$40].

I am a little bit luckier than others because I run the entire household. My employer is a divorced woman who is an architect. She does not have time to run her household so I do all the shopping. I am the one budgeting. I am the one cooking. [Laughs.] And I am the one cleaning too. She has a twenty-four and twenty-six year old. The older one graduated already and is an electrical engineer. The other one is taking up philosophy. They still live with her. . . . She has been my only employer. I stayed with her because I feel at home with her. She never commands. She never orders me to do this and to do that.

The hierarchical and interdependent relationship between Carmen, her employer in Italy, and her domestic worker in the Philippines forms from the unequal development of industrialized and developing countries in transnational capitalism, class differences in the Philippines, and the relegation of reproductive labor to women. The case of Carmen Ronquillo clearly exemplifies how three distinct groups of women participate in the international transfer of caretaking. While Carmen frees her employer (the architect) of domestic responsibilities, a lower-paid domestic worker does the household work for Carmen and her family.

Wage differences of domestic workers illuminate the economic disparity among nations in transnational capitalism. A domestic worker in Italy such as Carmen could receive U.S.$1000 a month for her labor.

I earn 1,500,000 lira [U.S.$1000] and she pays for my benefits [for example, medical coverage]. On Sundays, I have a part-time; I clean her office in the morning and she pays me 300,000 lira [U.S.$200]. I am very fortunate because she always gives me my holiday pay [August] and my thirteenth month pay in December. Plus, she gives me my liquidation pay at the end of the year. Employers here are required to give you a liquidation pay—equivalent to your monthly salary for every year you worked for them, but they usually give it to you when you leave; but she insists on paying me at the end of the year. So, [in] December, I always receive 5,400,000 lira [U.S.$3600].

Carmen's wages easily enable her to hire a domestic worker in the Philippines, who, on average, only earns the below poverty wage of U.S.$40 per month. Moreover, the female domestic worker in the Philippines, in exchange for her labor, does not receive the additional work benefits Carmen receives for the same labor, for example, medical coverage. Not surprisingly, migrant Filipina domestic workers, as shown by their high level of educational attainment, tend to have more resources and belong in a more comfortable class strata than do domestic workers in the Philippines. Such resources often enable Carmen and other migrant Filipina women to afford the option of working outside of the country.

The Overlooked Participants: Children and Women in the Philippines

> The private world remains devalued, as poor people become the wives and moth
> ers of the world, cleaning the toilets and raising the children. The devaluing of cer-
> tain work, of nurturance, of private "domestic" work, remains: rearing children is
> roughly on a par—certainly in terms of salary—with cleaning the toilet (Roth-
> man, 1989a: 252).

While the devaluation of "rearing children" could be lamented as a tragedy for children, the experiences of the different groups of children (and elderly) in the international transfer of caretaking should be distinguished between those who remain cared for and those who are not and those who regularly see their parents/children and those who cannot. The fact that "rearing children is roughly on a par . . . with cleaning the toilet" means that migrant Filipina domestic workers usually cannot afford the higher costs of maintaining a family in industrialized countries due to their meager wages. In the United States, where women of color have traditionally been caregivers and domestic workers for white families, mothering is diverted away from families of people of color. Sau-ling Wong defines "diverted mothering" to be the process in which the "time and energy available for mothering are diverted from those who, by kinship or communal ties, are their more rightful recipients" (1994: 69). Historically, a married black domestic worker in the United States "typically saw her children once every two weeks, leaving them in the care of the husband or older siblings, while remaining on call around the clock for the employer's children" (Wong, 1994: 71). Although now in an international context, the same pattern of "diverted mothering" could be described for Filipina, Latina, and Caribbean domestic workers, as many are forced to leave their children behind in the country of origin (Colen, 1995; Hondagneu-Sotelo and Avila, 1997). The question then is, who cares for these "other" children?

In the Philippines, it is unusual for fathers to nurture and care for their children, but since not all migrant Filipina domestic workers hire domestic workers, some men are forced to give in to the renegotiations of household division of labor led by the migration of their wives. Usually, however, other female relatives take over the household work of migrant Filipinas.[6] In these cases, nonegalitarian relations among family members should be acknowledged, considering that for female family members left in the Philippines, "the mobility they might achieve through migration is severely curtailed" (Basch et al., 1994: 241). However, hired domestic workers—a live-in housekeeper or *labandera* (laundry woman who hand washes clothes)—also free migrant Filipina domestics of their household labor. Almost all of my interviewees hire domestic workers in the Philippines. This should not be surprising considering that the average wage of domestics in the Philippines is considerably less than the average wage of migrant domestics.

In discussions of the international division of (productive) labor, the women who cannot afford to work as domestic workers in other countries are equated with those who do so. For example, migrant Filipina domestic workers and female low-wage workers in the Philippines are considered to be equally displaced in global capitalism. Maya Areza, who dreams of retiring in the Philippines after a few more years in Los Angeles, reminds us of the structural inequalities characterizing relations among women in developing countries when she states:

> When I retire I plan to go home for good. I plan to stay at my parents' house. . . . I would just lounge and smoke. I will get a domestic helper who I can ask to get my cigarettes for me. . . . My children and my cousins all have domestic workers. You can hire one if you have money. It's cheap, only 1000 pesos [U.S.$40]. Here, you earn $1000 doing the same kind of work you would do for one thousand pesos there! I won't have a problem with hiring one.

Because migrant Filipina domestic workers are usually in the middle of the hierarchical chain of caretaking, they maintain unequal relations with less-privileged women in the Philippines. Under the international transfer of caretaking, the unequal economic standing of nation-states and discrepancies in monetary currencies are prominent factors that distinguish the position of female low-wage workers in advanced capitalist and developing countries. They differentiate, for example, the position of domestic workers in the United States and Italy from domestic workers in the Philippines. Migrant Filipina domestic workers surely take advantage of these differences in wages and maintain a direct hierarchical relationship with the domestic workers whom they hire in the Philippines. In the international transfer of caretaking, domestic workers hired by families of domestic workers abroad are the truly subaltern women.

Conclusion

As gender differentiates the causes of migration for men and women, it is very problematic to simply apply women's experiences to traditional male models of migration. To move away from additive approaches in the treatment of women, it is important to consider how gender stratification interlocks with other systems of inequality to determine the causes of women's migration. Migration is a movement from one distinct patriarchal system to another, bound by race and class, in transnational capitalism. Therefore, it should be analyzed from a gendered perspective of the political economy.

The hierarchy of womanhood—involving race, class, and nation, as well as gender—establishes a work transfer system of reproductive labor among women, the international transfer of caretaking. It is a distinct form of transnational division of labor that links women in an interdependent relationship. Filipina domestic workers perform the reproductive labor of more privileged women in industrialized countries as they relegate their reproductive labor to poorer women left in the Philippines. This demonstrates that production is not the only means by which international divisions of labor operate in the global economy. Local economies are not solely linked by the manufacturing production of goods. Under globalization, the transfer of reproductive labor moves beyond territorial borders to connect separate nation-states.

The formulation of the international division of reproductive labor treats gender as a central analytical framework for understanding the migration of Filipina domestic workers. It shows that the movement of Filipina domestic workers is embedded in a gendered system of transnational capitalism. While forces of global capitalism spur the labor migration of Filipina domestic workers, the demand for their labor also results from gender inequalities in receiving nations, for example, the relegation of reproductive labor to women. This transfer of labor strongly suggests that despite their increasing rate of labor market participation, women continue to remain responsible for reproductive labor in both sending and receiving countries. At both ends of the migratory stream, they have not been able to negotiate directly with male counterparts for a fairer division of household work but instead have had to rely on their race and/or class privilege by participating in the transnational transfer of gender constraints to less-privileged women.

A central contradiction in the maintenance of gender inequalities is that they hinder as much as they facilitate the migration of women. In the Philippines, gender stratification spurs the migration of women in resistance to male abuse, the double day, labor market segmentation, and single motherhood. Escaping gender stratification is a hidden cause of migration. For example, migration alleviates the household reproductive labor of married women, while single women escape gender-defined duties in the family. But as they are relegated to domestic work in the labor market, they enter another patriarchal society. Ironically, women in industrialized (Western) countries are often assumed to be more liberated than women are in developing countries. Yet many women are able to pursue careers as their male counterparts do because disadvantaged migrant women and other women of color are stepping into their old shoes and doing their household work for them. As women transfer their reproductive labor to less and less privileged women, the traditional division of labor in the patriarchal nuclear household has not been significantly renegotiated in various countries in the world. This is one of the central reasons why there is a need for Filipina domestic workers in more than a hundred countries today.

Though the underlying theme of dislocations was not the focus of analysis in this chapter, my discussion of the international transfer of caretaking as a division of labor has touched upon some of the dislocations that migrant Filipina domestic workers encounter in migration. First, being in the middle entails the maintenance of a transnational household structure and consequently involves experiencing the pain of family separation. Second, being in the middle also means being part of the middle class of the Philippines. This alludes to the dislocation of contradictory class mobility and the partial citizenship granted to them by receiving nations that fail to acknowledge their educational training prior to migration. Returning to my analysis of dislocations, the next two chapters address the dislocation of the pain of family separation.

References

Abel, Emily K. 1990. "Family Care of the Frail Elderly." Pp. 65–91 in Abel and Nelson, *Circles of Care*.

Basch, Linda, Nina Glick-Schiller, and Christina Szanton Blanc. 1994. *Nations Unbound: Transnational Projects, Postcolonial Predicaments, and Deterritorialized Nation-States*. Langhorne, PA: Gordon and Breach Science.

Beck, Ulrich, and Elisabeth Beck-Gernsheim. 1995. *The Normal Chaos of Love*. Cambridge: Polity Press.

Birnbaum, Lucia Chiavola. 1986. *Liberazione della Donne*. Middletown, CT: Wesleyan University Press.

Brenner, Johanna, and Barbara Laslett. 1991. "Gender, Social Reproduction and Women's Self-Organization: Considering the U.S. Welfare State." *Gender and Society* 5(3): 311–33.

Calavita, Kitty. 1994. "Italy and the New Immigration." Pp. 303–26 in Cornelius, Martin, and Hollifield, *Controlling Immigration*.

Chant, Sylvia, and Cathy McIlwaine. 1995. *Women of a Lesser Cost: Female Labour, Foreign Exchange and Philippine Development*. London and East Haven, CT: Pluto Press.

Colen, Shellee. 1995. "'Like a Mother to Them': Stratified Reproduction and West Indian Childcare Workers and Employers in New York." Pp. 78–102 in Faye D. Ginsburg and Rayna Rapp, editors, *Conceiving the New World Order: The Global Politics of Reproduction*. Berkeley and Los Angeles: University of California Press.

Eviota, Elizabeth Uy. 1992. *The Political Economy of Gender: Women and the Sexual Division of Labour in the Philippines*. London: Zed Books.

Glazer, Nona. 1993. *Women's Paid and Unpaid Labor: The Work Transfer in Health Care and Retailing*. Philadelphia: Temple University Press.

———. 1992. "From Servitude to Service Work: The Historical Continuities of Women's Paid and Unpaid Reproductive Labor." *Signs* 18(1): 1–44.

———. 1986. *Issei, Nisei, Warbride*. Philadelphia: Temple University Press.

Goddard, V. A. 1996. *Gender, Family and Work in Naples*. Oxford and Washington, D.C.: Berg.

Grasmuck, Sherri, and Patricia Pessar. 1991. *Between Two Islands: Dominican International Migration*. Berkeley and Los Angeles: University of California Press.

Hochschild, Arlie. 1989. *The Second Shift*. New York: Avon Books.

———. 1983. *The Managed Heart: Commercialization of Human Feeling*. Berkeley and Los Angeles: University of California Press.

Hondagneu-Sotelo, Pierrette, and Ernistine Avila. 1997. "'I'm Here, but I'm There': The Meanings of Latina Transnational Motherhood." *Gender and Society* 11(5): 548–71.

Israel-Sobritchea, Carolyn. 1990. "The Ideology of Female Domesticity: Its Impact on the Status of Filipino Women." *Review of Women's Studies* 1(1): 26–41.

Layosa, Linda. 1995a. "Economy Menders." *Tinig Filipino* (June): 7.

Licuanan, Patricia. 1994. "The Socio-economic Impact of Domestic Worker Migration: Individual, Family, Community, Country." Pp. 103–16 in Heyzer, Lycklama á Nijeholt, and Weerakoon, *The Trade in Domestic Workers*.

Lopez-Rodriguez, Luz. 1990. "Patriarchy and Women's Subordination in the Philippines." *Review of Women's Studies* 1(1): 15–25.

Meyer, Donald. 1987. *The Rise of Women in America, Russia, Sweden, and Italy*. Middletown, CT: Wesleyan University Press.

Nelson, Margaret K. 1990. "Mothering Other's Children: The Experiences of Family Day Care Providers." Pp. 210–32 in Abel and Nelson, *Circles of Care*.

O'Connor, Julia S. 1996. "From Women in the Welfare State to Gendering Welfare State Regimes." *Current Sociology* 44(2): 1–130.

Paz Cruz, Victoria, and Anthony Paganoni. 1989. *Filipinas in Migration: Big Bills and Small Change*. Quezon City, Philippines: Scalabrini Migration Center.

Reskin, Barbara, and Irene Padavic. 1994. *Women and Men at Work*. Thousand Oaks, CA: Pine Forge Press.

Rothman, Barbara Katz. 1989a. *Recreating Motherhood: Ideology and Technology in a Patriarchal Society*. New York and London: W. W. Norton.

———— 1989b. "Women as Fathers: Motherhood and Child Care under a Modified Patriarchy." *Gender and Society* 3(1): 89–104.

Sassen, Saskia. 1984. "Notes on the Incorporation of Third World Women into Wage Labor through Immigration and Offshore Production." *International Migration Review* 18(4): 1144–67.

Specter, Michael. 1998. "The Baby Bust." *New York Times*, July 10.

Wong, Sau-ling. 1994. "Diverted Mothering: Representations of Caregivers of Color in the Age of 'Multiculturalism.'" Pp. 67–91 in Glenn, Chang, and Forcey, *Mothering*.

[25]

Feminist Economics 10(1), March 2004, 3–35

R Routledge
Taylor & Francis Group

GLOBALIZATION, LABOR STANDARDS, AND WOMEN'S RIGHTS: DILEMMAS OF COLLECTIVE (IN)ACTION IN AN INTERDEPENDENT WORLD

Naila Kabeer

ABSTRACT

This paper challenges the idea that a "social clause" to enforce global labor standards through international trade agreements serves the interests of women export workers in poor countries. Drawing on fieldwork in Bangladesh and empirical studies, the author argues that exploitative as these jobs appear to Western reformers, for many women workers in the South they represent genuine opportunities. Clearly, these women would wish to better their working conditions; yet having no social safety net, and knowing that jobs in the informal economy, their only alternative, offer far worse prospects, women cannot fight for better conditions. Moreover, global efforts to enforce labor standards through trade sanctions may lead to declining employment or to the transfer of jobs to the informal economy. Lacking measures that also address the conditions of workers in this informal economy, demands for "the social clause" will reinforce, and may exacerbate, social inequalities in the labor market.

KEYWORDS

Globalization, women workers, export garments, Bangladesh, labor standards

JEL Codes: J7, J8, I30

INTRODUCTION

For the most part, it is the wretched of the earth who do the world's tailoring. Made in Bangladesh competes with Made in Honduras, Made in the Philippines, Made in Macao, Made in Any Steamy Reservoir of Third World Unemployment: those places where plentiful labor lacks the leverage to command high pay, and the most pitiful thing about the jobs is how hard it is to get them. (Barry Bearak 2001)

My name is Fatema Akhter. I am a garment worker. ... As garment workers, we live and work under difficult conditions but at least we are managing to earn a living. Now we have heard rumors that in the next two to four years, the garment industry may close down. What

Feminist Economics ISSN 1354-5701 print/ISSN 1466-4372 online © 2004 IAFFE
http://www.tandf.co.uk/journals
DOI: 10.1080/1354570042000198227

ARTICLES

will happen to us? You are perhaps all aware of the situation of women in Bangladesh – women have very few opportunities for employment. We are, however, slowly making some progress. Because of jobs in the garment industry, many Fatemas like me are able to work honorably. 'Garments' is the only option for us. We beg you not to take away these jobs and our right to work with dignity. (People's Health Movement 2002: 41–2)

Both these quotations describe the same phenomenon but from very different standpoints. The first, from a US journalist, comments on the apparent contradiction between what he perceives to be the inhuman working conditions prevailing in garment factories in poorer parts of the world and the fact that so many of the "wretched of the earth" in these parts compete fiercely to work in them. Bearak's view represents an influential strand of discourse in the Western media and helps explain growing support for the "social clause," the enforcement of certain minimum labor standards through international trade agreements, with possible sanctions by the WTO against countries that fail to comply.

The second quotation is from a Bangladeshi woman, one of "the wretched of the earth" who works in the kind of factories Bearak describes, but for whom such employment represents one of her few options for "working with dignity." It was part of her testimony to the thousands of activists who attended the International People's Health Assembly, held in Bangladesh in 2000. It echoes sentiments that are voiced by women workers in the "steamy reservoirs of unemployment" elsewhere in the Third World and helps explain why they, and their supporters, strongly resist the idea that global enforcement of labor standards will serve the interests of workers in the Third World.

This paper is written from the latter standpoint and seeks to challenge the former. It recognizes that the debate about global labor standards is both an extremely complex and highly polarized one, in which accusations of protectionism and double standards clash with claims of exploitation and "social dumping." It recognizes, too, that both many who support, and many who oppose, the global enforcement of labor standards are motivated by the spirit of international solidarity with the interests of workers rather than by protectionist or free trade sentiments. While this paper does not support the view that unregulated global competition serves the interests of the working poor of the world, it is equally skeptical of the idea that they would be better off with global enforcement of labor standards. While its skepticism stems from the protectionist practices that continue to characterize international trade, its critique of protectionism derives from an analysis of the workings of an unequal world order rather than from adherence to neoliberal market principles.

4

LABOR STANDARDS AND WOMEN'S RIGHTS

The next section of this paper sketches out the global context in which current debates about standards should be located. I then describe the politics of representation that has shaped the public discourse on, and helped to mobilize public support for, the idea of globally enforced labor standards. Against this background, I go on to explore the experiences of women workers in global garment factories in Bangladesh and elsewhere in order to provide an alternative perspective on the issue of standards. The paper examines their working conditions, explores why they do not protest those aspects they find oppressive, and questions whether campaigning for the global enforcement of standards is the most appropriate response from those concerned with their interests. Finally, it suggests that the spirit of global solidarity would be better served if the international labor movement were to campaign for a universal social floor that would protect the basic needs of all citizens, regardless of their labor market status, instead of a social clause that would only serve the needs of a minority.

THE GLOBALIZATION OF THE ECONOMY AND THE CHANGING DIVISION OF LABOR

The twentieth century began with an international division of labor largely shaped by the practices of colonialism, with the poorer countries exporting primary commodities to the rich while the latter specialized in the production and export of manufactured goods. As the poor countries achieved independence, many embarked on strategies of import-substitution industrialization, building up their manufacturing capacity behind protective barriers. However, since the 1970s, a combination of factors, including rising labor costs in advanced industrialized countries, changes in transport and communications technology, the liberalization of trade, and the deregulation of markets, including financial markets, has effected a radical transformation in the direction and pace of global flows of capital, goods, services, and labor. As a result, many of the protective barriers have fallen. Of the factors cited above, changes in the volume and pattern of trade, and associated changes in the international division of labor, are central to the concerns of this paper.

The volume of trade has increased from around 25 percent of world GNP in 1970 to around 45 percent today (World Bank 1995). Much of this increase is in manufacturing, which accounted for 59 percent of world-merchandise exports in 1984 but reached 74 percent of those exports by the mid-1990s. Developing countries have performed well in this sector: the share of manufactures in their exports tripled between 1970 and 1990 from 20 percent to 60 percent (World Bank 1995). Growth has been most rapid in labor-intensive manufacturing: technological changes allowed for the fragmentation of production processes while international wage differentials encouraged the relocation of labor-intensive production, or stages of

5

ARTICLES

production, from highly paid enclaves of organized labor in the North to a low-paid, less well-organized, and largely female labor force in the South. The decline of the "cut–make–trim" stages of garment manufacturing in the OECD countries in the course of this period and their rise in lower-income regions of the world exemplifies this trend.

Attempts to compete in an increasingly global economy have led many countries to deregulate labor markets with the view to making labor more "flexible" (Guy Standing 1999). Regular, male-dominated, full-time employment, protected by various forms of state regulation, has given way to more diverse and less-protected patterns of work, including outsourcing, contract labor, casual, part-time, and home-based work. The resulting deterioration in employment prospects and working conditions has had the greatest impact on less-skilled members of the labor force in the North, many of whom now find themselves in direct competition for their jobs with workers from the South. These developments have given rise to growing fears of a global race to the welfare bottom.

It is therefore not entirely coincidental that this period has witnessed the rise of a new discourse of "ethics" in international trade. This discourse has helped target public attention to working conditions in precisely those labor-intensive manufacturing industries in which poorer countries have gained what mainstream economists refer to as a "comparative advantage" – and which some have reconstituted as an "unfair advantage." It has also helped to mobilize various constituencies in efforts to address the exploitative conditions under which many of the imports into their countries are produced.

Uniting these constituencies is the view that certain minimum labor standards should be observed in the production of goods and services imported into their countries, regardless of whether the goods were purchased by importing companies or directly produced by them. Most equate this minimum with the International Labor Organization's (ILO) "core" standards – freedom of association, the right to collective bargaining, abolition of child labor, and elimination of discrimination at work – which have received widespread endorsement at the international level and are seen to constitute a shared global morality.[1] A variety of strategies have been adopted to promote these standards, including consumer boycotts, public "naming and shaming" campaigns, the "social labeling" of goods, company codes of conduct, fair trade agreements, and collaborative efforts that bring together companies, trade unions, and NGOs to promote and monitor compliance with agreed-upon standards. In addition, however, there is growing pressure from these groups to link global labor standards to international trade agreements in the form of a "social clause." The distinguishing feature of this clause is its demand that the WTO, with its power to impose sanctions, should oversee the global harmonization of labor standards in place of (or along with) the ILO,

6

LABOR STANDARDS AND WOMEN'S RIGHTS

which is the international body so far entrusted with this responsibility, but one that has traditionally exercised a supportive and supervisory role rather than a compulsion-based one.

In an earlier era, when debates about labor standards were carried out within the context of national economies, divisions were fairly straightforward (Alice Amsden 1994). Employers and right-of-center economists opposed them on the grounds they distorted market forces, inhibiting employment and income, while the labor unions and their left-of-center allies were supporting them, arguing they would improve the motivation and physical capacity of workers and hence their productivity. However, in the closing decades of the twentieth century, when the debate over labor standards moved to the global level, the divisions have become far less clear-cut.

Support for the social clause comes from northern governments as well as from consumer groups, student activists, northern trade unions and their networks, and progressive academics, including feminists, many, but not all, based in the North (Nilufer Cagatay 1996, 2001; Andrew Ross 1997a; Rohini Hensman 2000; Ronaldo Munck 2002). Given the threat to northern jobs by the changing international division of labor, there is inevitably a strong element of self-interest in some of the trade union support for the social clause. However, there are other, disinterested reasons for this support, including moral outrage at the apparent indifference of some of the world's wealthiest corporations to the exploitative conditions under which they employ, directly or indirectly, some of the world's poorest workers. For these groups, the global enforcement of labor standards appears to offer a "win–win" solution for workers around the world: workers in the North stand to benefit from standards that would increase the price of exports from late-industrializing countries and reduce their attractiveness as low-cost production sites for northern investors. Workers in the South would benefit from higher wages and better working conditions which in turn would lead to increases in aggregate demand and employment (Steve Charnowitz 1987; John Cavanagh 1997).

Using an alternative version of the win–win scenario, right-wing economists oppose the idea of the global labor standards. They argue that global free trade allows countries to specialize in those activities in which they have a comparative advantage and to reap mutual gains through exchange. For poorer countries with vast supplies of unskilled labor, their ability to compete in international trade lies in the production of those goods and services that make intensive use of such labor. The imposition of global standards would undermine the basis of their comparative advantage by increasing the cost of labor.

While governments of most developing countries also subscribe to this argument, their opposition to compulsory labor standards is further bolstered by what Eddie Lee has described as the "deep fault line of

7

mistrust" that divides them from the advanced industrial countries (1997: 177). They have expressed their belief that the international trading system is already tilted in favor of rich countries and that attempts to link labor standards to trade agreements are simply a "new form of conditionality" which will further entrench the interests of the North (Nicola Bullard 2001). According to the late Julius Nyerere (1998), the first chairman of the South Centre, a permanent intergovernmental organization of developing countries set up in Geneva in 1996, demands for global labor standards were merely attempts to use the language of workers' rights to disguise the protectionist tendencies of the world's wealthier countries.

These accusations are not entirely groundless. The rich countries of the world have a long history of preaching the virtues of fair trade, but practicing protectionism when it has suited them (Oxfam International 2002). The United States, for instance, has been a leading champion of free trade, using its influence within the international financial institutions to press for the opening up of the world's economies to international capital and taking steps to penalize countries found to be operating barriers to its exports. It has also been at the forefront of moves to link labor standards with trade agreements at bilateral, regional, as well as multilateral level. Yet it initially resisted the idea of an International Trade Organization in 1948 precisely because of the explicit link the ITO made between labor standards and trade (Ajit Singh and Ann Zammit 2000). It has currently ratified only two of the eight conventions that make up the ILO core labor standards, the poorest track record among OECD countries, and among the poorest in the world. And it continues to resort to subsidies and controls when these are considered necessary to protect its own workers from international competition.

The most recent example of this was the decision of the Bush administration, ostensibly dedicated champions of free trade, to support the 2002 Farm Bill, which would provide subsidies of more than $180 billion for US farmers in the coming decade. Although this decision both compromises the ability of the US to challenge the even higher levels of agricultural protection that prevail in Europe and undercuts the ability of farmers in developing countries to compete against cheap American imports, such objections cut little ice with US politicians. According to the *London Times*, Tom Harkin, the Democratic senator who drew up the bill, said, "This isn't a German farm Bill or a Chinese farm Bill or a French farm Bill. It is an American farm Bill for American farmers. Let those other countries worry about their own farmers" (Bronwen Maddox 2002).

It is this long experience with the double standards that rich countries practice in international trade, combined with fears about the implications of attempts to link labor standards to trade agreements for export competitiveness and employment in the South, that explains why resistance to the social clause goes beyond governments of developing countries to

LABOR STANDARDS AND WOMEN'S RIGHTS

many trade unions, nongovernmental organizations, and women's networks, as well as progressive academics, including economists critical of
neoliberal theory as well as feminists (Amsden 1994; Nyerere 1998; Kaushik
Basu 1999; Pranab Bardhan 2000; Naila Kabeer 2000; Jayati Ghosh 2001).
Singh and Zammit (2000: xv) have forcibly argued that

> attempts to enforce labor standards through trade sanctions are likely
> to cause economic harm to most export developing countries, at least
> in the short to medium term, while doing little or nothing to improve
> their labor standards. Indeed, under wholly plausible circumstances,
> this approach could be seriously counterproductive and reduce stan-
> dards overall.

Trade unionists and labor organizations have also raised questions about
the social clause, most consistently in the Indian context but also in other
developing countries (J. John and A. M. Chenoy 1996; Women Working
Worldwide 1996). A number of southern-based NGO networks have
criticized the social clause as well. As Martin Khor of the Third World
Network points out, there is a strong case for improving standards at work
in the North as well as in the South, but "linking labor standards to trade
sanctions is not justified and could well lead to a lowering of workers'
welfare instead of improving it" (Third World Network 1994). He suggests
two conditions that might help dilute the opposition to the social clause
from developing countries; these conditions also summarize the nature of
these countries' concerns. The first – that the introduction of the core labor
standards not be used as the thin end of the wedge to impose a whole range
of other standards that did not command such consensus – reflects
concerns about equal representation. Whatever the limitations of the
"core" labor standards, they are the only ones that command some
agreement within the international community, because they are seen to be
valid, regardless of levels of development. The developing countries fear
that once supporters obtain agreement to a social clause tied to core labor
standards, other "substantive" labor standards, which do not command an
international consensus but are supported by many in the anti-sweatshop
campaign, will be pushed through the back door to further protectionist
interests (see also Bardhan 2000).

The second condition – that the introduction of the social clause not
result in net job losses in developing countries – expresses concerns about
development. Here, countries fear that attempts to implement labor
standards, particularly substantive ones, will raise the costs of labor to levels
where poor countries lose their competitive edge in global markets. Many
have attempted to estimate the likely employment effects associated with
the introduction of labor standards but these efforts have proved
inconclusive. It is difficult to disentangle changes in competitiveness and
employment caused by changes in the costs of labor from the other changes

9

ARTICLES

that occur in an economy (OECD 1996), but ultimately it is likely that the benefits of linking labor standards to trade agreements will vary for different countries. Amsden (1994) suggests that the link will be least effective in larger wage-led economies like India's, which has large domestic markets and relatively insignificant export sectors. On the other hand, in smaller developing countries – like Bangladesh, which increasingly relies on international trade to expand access to markets – higher real wages in the export sector may increase domestic demand, but not to the extent of offsetting the fall in international demand for highly price-elastic goods like clothing. Instead, rising costs in the export sectors would hurt such countries' competitiveness and most certainly reduce their long-term growth.

THE POLITICS OF REPRESENTATION IN INTERNATIONAL TRADE

Unraveling all of the strands of arguments that advocacy groups (themselves internally diverse) use to support or reject efforts to link labor standards to trade agreements is beyond the scope of this paper. Instead, I will confine myself to questioning the view that globally enforced labor standards are in the interests of all workers, particularly those who have been unable to fight for such standards themselves. While such views may be sincere, I believe they are based on an ahistorical and uncontextualized understanding of what is at stake. An important factor in this understanding is the politics of representation that supporters have deployed to make the case for global labor standards. Much of the success of this advocacy with the wider public of student activists and consumer groups has rested on portrayals of Third World factories as "showcases of horrors for the labor abuses sanctioned by the global free trade economy, where child labor, wage slavery, and employer cruelty are legion" (Andrew Ross 1997b: 10).

That many of the export industries in the South produce consumer goods, such as garments, shoes, carpets, footballs, and the like, has worked to the advantage of this form of advocacy because consumer purchasing power can be a powerful weapon. Moreover, that a significant proportion of workers in these factories is women allows such advocacy to both feed on, and feed into, widespread preconceptions about poor, Third World women as helpless victims of the global free-trade economy: "undifferentiated, homogenous, faceless and voiceless" (Diane Wolf 1992). Such portrayals help to both provoke and to justify action by the northern public on behalf of these women workers who are unable to act on their own behalf.

As one of the world's poorest countries, with one of its lowest standards of living, it is not surprising that Bangladesh has featured frequently in these campaigns. A classic example of this politics of representation can be found

10

LABOR STANDARDS AND WOMEN'S RIGHTS

in a contribution by Elinor Spielberg (1997), a member of UNITE, the American garment workers' union, to a collection of essays for the anti-sweatshop movement in the United States. Spielberg begins her account, based on what seems to have been a brief and cursory visit to Bangladesh, with the extraordinary claim that "there's a saying among the girls in the slums of Bangladesh: if you are lucky, you'll be a prostitute – if you're unlucky, you'll be a garment worker" (p. 113). I found no evidence for this saying in my own research on garment workers or in the work of researchers and activists who have been working in the urban slums of Bangladesh for many years. As in many other countries in the world, particularly in sexually conservative societies like Bangladesh, prostitution remains possibly the most socially stigmatized of occupations, despite campaigns by women's organizations, including those of sex workers, to promote their rights and recognition.

However, even more extraordinary than this claim is Spielberg's detailed description of the condition of the *feet* of a young girl she encountered, a description she links, improbably, to working conditions in the girl's garment factory:

> Whatever early malnutrition had started doing to her chances of mar-riage, the garment trade had finished off. The mind cannot register, in the first few seconds, that these appendages are attached to a creature that walks upright on the ground. They have flattened and spread out to such a degree they seem more suited to one that propels itself in the water. Like fins. Like flounders, but curved in toward each other: bot-tom fish that got trapped, and grew, inside a kidney-shaped pan. The mind tries to grasp hold of something more noble, something scienti-fic perhaps, to explain why a child, a child who is now admiring her new plastic bangles and smoothing the hem of her best dress, has been cursed with feet like that on which to toil. Compensation: now that's a scientific word. The bones of her feet were too weak to support the weight of the body, so they accommodated the floor. (p. 114)

The relevance of this horrified description to working conditions in the garment industry is extremely tenuous: the kind of malnutrition she describes is widespread among poorer children, particularly girls, in Bangladesh, but it reflects economic deprivation and gender discrimina-tion from birth in an underdeveloped and patriarchal society rather than the effects of a few years' work in the garment industry. Its inclusion in her account helps to establish her credentials as a caring moral being but it reduces the young girl to the status of "the other," deserving of sympathy, but also a living testimony to the dehumanizing conditions that Spielberg's union claims to be campaigning against.

The tactics used by the National Labor Coalition, another organization extremely active in the anti-sweatshop movement in the US, make for equally disturbing reading (see Kitty Krupat 1997). Its leading activist presents as a virtue the fact that he is "not a professional – not a trained organizer, economist or academic" and that his organization relies instead on "human stories . . . anecdotal examples and accessible language" to win consumer support (cited in Krupat 1997: 74). The NLC considers young workers from Third World factories its best asset and has frequently flown these workers over to testify in their campaigns: "We wanted the most authentic, direct, virtually naïve workers we could find. We had faith that these young kids would simply tell the truth and that would be more damaging than anything an academic could say" (cited in Krupat 1997: 74). Yet, as Krupat's essay goes on to reveal, the NLC does not deal in simple, spontaneous, and unmediated truths but rather on what she describes as an "intensive educational technique" (p. 75) to ensure that their "authentic, direct, virtually naïve" workers make "eloquent witnesses":

> They stay in our apartment. We're together constantly, talking and learning from one another. In my opinion, it's filthy and rude to bring a young worker up from Central America and just say, 'Here's a speech. Go ahead'. She'd say, 'We're oppressed'. What does that mean? No one ever asked her to define it. Why? How? Name it. We do that. We really press them to be specific. 'They yell at us'. 'What do they say'. 'How?'. 'They call us chicken heads, we're born of whores'. 'They hit us'. 'Well how do they hit you?' 'They hit us on the head'. 'How?'. 'With their knuckles'. We make them write it down and practice their delivery till its polished. They're so elevated by the fact that someone has given them their own voice and the chance to speak for all their co-workers, they dig inside themselves and they're unstoppable. (Cited in Krupat 1997: 75)

One could view this "intensive educational technique" as yielding "the truth" as NLC clearly believes it does. Alternatively, of course, it can be viewed as a way of ensuring that the workers in question produce the "correct" story in their testimonies.[2]

The politics of representation can, in other words, slip very easily into a politics of misrepresentation if the activist decides there is little mileage to be gained in presenting nuanced, balanced, and differentiated accounts of ground-level realities in low-income countries – narratives that distinguish between situations in which working conditions are products of poverty and underdevelopment and those that entail the flagrant violation of basic human rights. Yet such distinctions are imperative if poor workers in the South are not to be penalized for their poverty or for the poverty of their country. As Fiona Wilson (1991) points out in her study of women garment workers in Mexico, there is no dearth of literature on the "exploitation and vulnerability of labor in situations of rampant capitalist growth where little

12

LABOR STANDARDS AND WOMEN'S RIGHTS

or no protection is forthcoming from the State, or any other body" (p. 15). However, she goes on to caution:

> when discussing particular instances in the Third World, a more complex view is required if the significance of informalization processes is to be unearthed and distinguished in terms of implications for relations of class and gender. The separate experiences of workers and capitalists and of women and men need to be reviewed in the light of the specific historical conditions *(what was life like before?)* [italics added]. ... The present general tendencies towards informalization and disenfranchisement unleash feelings of concern, at least for those broadly on the "left." Workers' rights are being trampled upon; former victories won by the working class through class struggles have not been permanent. These defeats must be opposed. ...

> But when one moves to the local level and has a view from below, then the same feelings are not necessarily engendered. It is true one can depict the gross exploitation of labor. Nevertheless, new working classes are emerging composed of people who had never been given a chance of joining the old "male" proletariat that had earlier led the confrontation with capital. The new working classes have not been passive but have engaged in struggles of their own.

In the rest of this paper, I will explore this view from below and ask, "what was life like before?" for women workers in a number of developing countries. This question helps shed a somewhat different light on what these jobs might mean to the workers and to provide somewhat different grounds for opposing the idea of compulsory labor standards to those usually expressed in international forums. I draw mainly on research from Bangladesh, partly because it features so frequently in the horror stories of the anti-sweatshop campaign and partly because of my own long-term research on garment workers there that began in 1988 (see Kabeer 2000). However, I will also cite findings from research elsewhere in the world in order to suggest that the arguments made here are not exceptional to Bangladesh but have a wider relevance.

THE SIGNIFICANCE OF EXPORT-ORIENTED GARMENT MANUFACTURING IN BANGLADESH

Bangladesh is officially classified by the UN as among the forty-eight "least-developed countries" of the world. It is a largely agrarian society and agriculture still provides employment for the majority of its workforce. The export of jute and jute products used to be its main source of its foreign exchange earnings but has fallen drastically in the face of declining world prices. However, since the 1980s, the country has seen the

13

ARTICLES

emergence and rapid expansion in export-oriented garment manufacturing in response to a new industrial policy that sought to liberalize the economy in response to pressure from the international financial institutions. The industry was also helped by the imposition of quotas by a number of developed countries on garment exports from the more successful garment-exporting countries in the South under the "anti-surge" provision of the Multi-Fibre Agreement (MFA).[3] The quota regime associated with the MFA has served to regulate world trade in garments, providing favored access to northern markets for some of the poorer developing countries, including Bangladesh.

Bangladesh is also among the world's more patriarchal societies. It belongs to a regional belt stretching across northern Africa, the Middle East, Pakistan, and the northern plains of India which is characterized by patrilineal principles of descent, patriarchal structures of family organization, the practice of female seclusion, and a marked preference for sons over daughters (Naila Kabeer 2003a). Women have not only been discriminated against in access to education and employment, a common pattern in many other parts of the world, but also in access to basic life-preserving resources such as health and food to the extent that this region (unlike other parts of the developed and developing world) has been characterized by higher levels of mortality among women and girls than among men and boys.

Over the past decade, Bangladesh has seen important improvements in its situation. In 1991 it moved from military rule to a fragile and somewhat dysfunctional democracy. Poverty has decreased, particularly in recent decades, and national food security has improved. Nevertheless, around half of its population still continues to live below the poverty line, failing to meet a very minimum definition of its basic needs. And while decades of impoverishment and landlessness drove many women from poorer families to seek work, cultural restrictions on their mobility, as well as the barriers they faced in the marketplace, historically confined them to the hidden, worst paid and most exploitative margins of the informal economy. There they worked as petty traders, domestic servants, sex workers, and casual wage laborers.

Given this history of female invisibility in the public domain, one of the most remarkable aspects of the rise of export-oriented garment manufacturing in the early 1980s was the almost overnight creation of a first generation of female factory workers. Most, but not all, of the women who work in the industry come from poor families and have migrated from the poorer rural districts of Bangladesh in search of work. The reasons this workforce is predominantly female corroborate findings from elsewhere that women's disadvantaged position in the labor market is a "comparative advantage" (Kabeer 2000). Employers in Bangladesh put less emphasis on women's "nimble fingers" – indeed many considered male labor to be

14

LABOR STANDARDS AND WOMEN'S RIGHTS

more productive – and more on the docility that comes with disadvantage. Women workers were aware of why employers preferred them. As one woman put it:

> You see, as women, one of our wings is broken. We don't have the nerve that a man has, because we know we have a broken wing. A man can sleep anywhere, he can just lie down on the street and go to sleep. A woman cannot do that. She has to think about her body, about her security. So the garment factory owner prefers to hire women because men are smarter about their opportunities, you train them and they move on. Even when he compares a small boy and an older girl, he will think, 'She's only a girl, she can't wander too far away'. (Kabeer 2000: 72)

There are now 3,480 export garment factories in Bangladesh, employing around 1.8 million workers, of whom around 1.5 million are women. The industry is made up of a number of different segments (Naila Kabeer and Simeen Mahmud 2003). The largest factories, often employing several thousand workers and dealing directly with international buyers, are to be found in the country's two export processing zones (EPZs), large industrial estates set up by the government as enclaves in which the trade and customs regime of a country do not apply. However, these account for less than 10 percent of the total employment in the industry (personal communication, Ananya Rahman). While the government has prohibited trade unions in the EPZs, both wages and working conditions are far superior to those in the rest of the export industry and indeed in the rest of the economy (Naila Kabeer and Simeen Mahmud, forthcoming).

The rest of the export industry is in factories scattered across the main urban areas of the country. Around 30 percent of these deal directly with buyers (author's interview with employers, 2003). These vary in size, but generally employ between 300 and 500 workers. While unions are legally permitted here, employers strongly resist them using a combination of strong-arm tactics to intimidate organizers or bribes to buy them off. However, working conditions are generally good, reflecting a combination of pressure from international buyers, themselves under pressure from northern consumer groups and labor organizations, as well as rising awareness among employers themselves. The rest of the industry is made up of smaller factories and workshops, operating mainly on orders subcontracted to them by larger factories that would otherwise not meet buyers' deadlines. This segment of the industry merges imperceptibly into the informal economy: it features low pay and poor working conditions, and is generally ignored by the trade union movement which has always preferred to focus on the formal sector employees.

15

PROBLEMATIZING WOMEN'S WORK: THE NEGATIVE ASPECTS OF GARMENT EMPLOYMENT

A number of studies have been carried out into the situation of women workers in the export garment industry. One such study, currently being written up, was carried out by Simeen Mahmud and myself in 2001 and sought to compare wages, working conditions, and attitudes among women working in the export-oriented garment industry and a sample of women from the same low-income neighborhoods, but working in a variety of mainly informal jobs for the domestic market. We will be citing from some of the preliminary analysis coming out of this study (Kabeer and Mahmud 2003; Kabeer and Mahmud, forthcoming).

These studies suggest that the level of wages is not the most significant source of dissatisfaction for workers in the industry. Wages are generally higher in the garment industry than those prevailing in alternative forms of waged labor available to women, both in urban areas and in rural (Kabeer and Mahmud, forthcoming) and gender differentials are generally lower (Debapriya Bhattacharya and Mustafizur Rahman 2001). A more frequent source of dissatisfaction related to irregularity in monthly payments. While employers are not legally obliged to pay monthly wages on the same day each month, there is a legal limit to delays in payment that many employers violate regularly. Wages are often delayed, perhaps by two or three months, sometimes held back deliberately to ensure the worker does not leave, sometimes because employers themselves face delays in payments from buyers. Overtime is also a source of dissatisfaction for some workers, but not always for the same reasons. For married women, the problem is mandatory overtime: given a choice, many prefer to go home to attend to their domestic responsibilities. Unmarried women, on the other hand, often welcome overtime as a means of supplementing their wages. Their problem is that employers seldom show overtime on their time cards, with a resulting lack of clarity regarding the rate of remuneration and the suspicion that they may not be getting their due.

On issues of health and safety, fire hazards in the industry have generated considerable attention in national and international media. However, the workers themselves do not frequently articulate this concern. This may reflect the fact that many employers have started to take more safety precautions; it may reflect that fires are not an everyday occurrence in the factories and hence not a part of workers' everyday consciousness; or it may reflect the fact that such fires are simply one more hazard in contexts where hazards of various kinds are endemic (Geoff Wood and Sarah Salway 2000; Kabeer 2003a). The issue of toilets is a frequent source of complaints, particularly in relation to restrictions imposed on the number of toilet breaks workers are permitted to take. Garment workers view these restrictive practices, together with the long hours of work in confined

16

LABOR STANDARDS AND WOMEN'S RIGHTS

spaces, as taking a toll on their health in the long run. This concern is one of the reasons for high labor turnover in the industry: while exact estimates of turnover are not available, it is worth noting that the average number of years spent in the garment industry by the workers in our survey was five years.

A small percentage of women workers had experienced, while others had heard reports of, incidents of sexual harassment within the factory. However, many more experienced, or heard of such harassment, and in some cases, rape, on the streets on their way to and from work (Protima Paul-Majumder and Anwara Begum 2000; Kabeer and Mahmud 2003). Moreover, studies on child labor in Dhaka's urban slums have found that many parents preferred garment employment for their daughters because they believed the girls would face less sexual harassment there than in other occupations open to them (Emily Delap 1998) and that working mothers saw work in local garment factories as a safer option for their young daughters to leaving them home on their own (Naila Kabeer 2003b). Petra Dannecker (2002) also noted incidents of sexual harassment on the factory floor, but cautioned against the tendency of the local community to perceive women as sexually passive. Some women engaged in romantic liaisons with men they had met on the factory floor, others found husbands there, and still others used their sexuality to promote their own interests within the workplace. Such behavior in a culture that is particularly repressive of female sexuality explains the public perception of garment workers as "loose women" and the unwelcome attention they receive from men on the streets (Kabeer 2000).

Childcare emerged as a central concern for many of the workers. While many women leave the factory at marriage or the birth of a child – another reason for high labor turnover – they often return when children grow older. While a number of studies continue to stereotype women workers in the garment industry as "young unmarried women," the statistical evidence suggests that a high proportion (between 40 and 50 percent) are, or were, married and a significant number of them have children. Most of these women have to make their own arrangements for childcare; some leave young children with their families in the countryside while others rely on older siblings or neighbors.

The other factor that emerges routinely as a source of dissatisfaction in studies is the lack of respect supervisors show for their women workers. As Dannecker (2002: 135) notes in her study: "all the interviewed women articulated their insecurity and their helplessness with regard to the way the supervisors addressed them, talked to them and treated them." Such disrespect has a gendered dimension; managers and supervisors are far more cautious toward male workers, who have the potential to be far more disruptive. It is significant, for instance, that management behavior featured as a reason for job satisfaction or dissatisfaction for women

17

ARTICLES

workers in the industry far more frequently than for men (Salma Chaudhuri Zohir and Pratima Paul-Majumder 1996).

There is thus little doubt that while working conditions are not as dire as anti-sweatshop campaigners claim, they nonetheless leave much room for improvements. Why, then, do women workers endure these conditions with apparently little protest? And why do those who claim to have the workers' interests at heart resist the idea of using internationally enforced sanctions to improve their labor standards? The answer to the first question helps to frame the answer to the second; part of the explanation relates to the more positive aspects of factory employment, aspects to which anti-sweatshop advocates sometimes give short shrift. Yet these positive features must be factored into any attempt to understand the perspectives of women workers on their jobs. A second part of the explanation relates to the weak organizational capacity of women workers and the causes for it. Finally, the last part of the explanation relates to whether alternatives to factory employment exist and the importance of an "exit" option to empower workers to take action on their own behalf. Taken together, these factors indicate that addressing the interests of the working poor requires different strategic priorities than those contained in current versions of the social clause.

EVALUATING WOMEN'S WORK: "WHAT LIFE WAS LIKE BEFORE"

My own research, and that conducted by others in Bangladesh, suggests that along with the many grievances the garment workers expressed, they had also made significant gains. Women valued the satisfaction of a "proper" job in contrast to the casualized forms of employment that had previously been their only options. Their ability to earn on a regular basis gave them a sense of self-reliance, of standing on their own feet. They also valued their access to new social networks on the factory floor, which replaced their previous isolation within the home; the greater voice they exercised in household decision-making because of the value of their economic contribution; their enhanced sense of self-worth; and, in some cases, greater personal freedom and autonomy (Nazli Kibria 1995; Zohir and Paul-Majumder 1996; Sajeda Amin, Ian Diamond, Ruchira T. Naved, and Margaret Newby 1998; Margaret Newby 1998; Kabeer 2000; Paul-Majumder and Begum 2000; Dannecker 2002; Kabeer and Mahmud, forthcoming).

Some women used their newly found earning power to renegotiate their relations within marriage, others to leave abusive marriages, and others to help their parents, a possibility generally denied to women once they were married (Kabeer 2000). Yet others used their earnings to postpone the age of marriage and enjoy a longer period of freedom from the responsibilities

18

LABOR STANDARDS AND WOMEN'S RIGHTS

that came with marriage and children (Amin *et al.* 1998). A UNICEF-supported study on working children in urban slums found that jobs in the garment factories were "coveted" because they were considered "prestigious and well-paid" in comparison to the unsavory alternatives, such as domestic service and prostitution (Najma Chawla 1996). Finally, a national consultation exercise carried out by the NGO Working Group of the World Bank found that garment factories and NGOs were the only formal institutions unanimously considered to have had a positive influence in the lives of the urban poor (Rashed un Nabi, Dipankara Datta, Subrata Chakrabarty, Masuma Begum, and Nasima Jahan Chaudhury 1999).

These findings do not square easily with the one-dimensional portraits of export-oriented factories as "showcases of horror for the labor abuses sanctioned by the global free trade economy" promoted by many in the anti-sweatshop campaign. The complexity of ground-level realities from the perspective of women workers is better captured by Dannecker's conclusion to her study:

> ... women workers do not romanticize their jobs, marriages or other aspects of their lives. They are aware of the exploitation that employment is poorly paid, that they are treated badly inside the factories and unfairly in many different ways. Nevertheless, they are also certain that it has given them material and personal benefits, an aspect often neglected in the literature. (2002: 255)

This paradox of broadly positive subjective evaluations of work within a context of objectively negative conditions working the workplace is by no means unique to Bangladesh. It is evident in the lives of women workers in export manufacturing in a number of other parts of the world. Diane Wolf's ethnographic study of women garment workers in Java documents their awareness of the exploitative conditions under which they work, but it points also to the "material and personal benefits that few would give up" (1992: 256). In Turkey, where, like Bangladesh, there are cultural restrictions on women's work in the public domain, a study of female clothing workers found that many women no longer defined their work purely in terms of their familial roles, to be abandoned when they got married or had children, but as a more permanent way of life (Ayda Eraydin and Asuman Erendil 1999). The overwhelming majority had made their own decision to enter factory work for reasons that varied from wanting to make use of their skills to seeking to escape the control exercised by family and neighbors.

Delia Davin (2001) notes the thousands of young, single women who are migrating from the countryside to live and work in the export-processing zones of southern China. Here, too, wages are low by international standards, the working conditions oppressive, and the assembly-line jobs

ARTICLES

ranked low in the occupational hierarchy for urban women. However, they are fiercely competed for by young rural women, many of whom had previously worked as unpaid laborers on family farms, but now have the opportunity to earn more cash in one month than they, or even the men in their home villages, could make in a year. As Davin points out,

> we cannot dismiss as meaningless the voices of the many young women who affirm a sense of achievement and pride in the lives they make for themselves as factory workers ... And hardship may be a price worth paying if the cash they earn allows them to change something they disliked in their past or that they wish to avoid in their future. (2001: 16)

Virginia Guzman and Rosalba Todaro (2001) arrived at similar conclusions in their research on working women in Latin America. They note that while labor-market deregulation has brought women into the paid workforce in increasing numbers, the jobs are largely casual and insecure. Nevertheless, they observe:

> Even in precarious conditions, unstable labor relations, and with meager social protection, there are many cases where access to insecure work can represent an improvement for women with respect to their previous situation. For instance, women that were expelled from the rural areas because of lack of land or because of agricultural restructuring had no option other than migrating to cities. There again the only alternative available was to work as domestic helpers. Now, women in rural areas have the alternative of working as temporary laborers for export agriculture. The existence of alternatives has even improved the working conditions of domestic helpers. ... Women now have the right to choose their destiny as individuals not only as family members. (2001: 18–19)

And, finally, if we go back in history to the early phase of the industrialization in Europe, we find similar assessments about the experience of industrialization for women workers in the northern context. As Nancy Fraser (1997) points out, feminist scholars who equate the emergence of capitalist employment in Europe with ''wage slavery'' miss the contradictory and gender-specific implications of such employment in the lives of workers:

> To be sure, it was painfully experienced in just that way by some early-nineteenth century proletarianized (male) artisans and yeoman farmers who were losing not only tangible property in tools and in land but also prior control over their work. But their response was contextually specific and gendered. Consider, by way of contrast, the very different

20

LABOR STANDARDS AND WOMEN'S RIGHTS

experience of young single women who left farms – with open-ended work hours, pervasive parental supervision, and little autonomous personal life – for mill towns, where intense supervision in the mill was combined with relative freedom from supervision outside it, as well the increased autonomy of personal life conferred by cash earnings. From their perspective, the employment contract was a liberation. (1997: 230)

Then, as now, factory employment was just one sphere in the totality of women workers' lives. Other spheres included the consumer market, to which their wages bought them entry, but also the domestic sphere, where they were expected to perform the unpaid work of social reproduction. In this arena particularly, itself permeated by power and inequality, women's wages functioned "as a resource and a leverage" (Fraser 1997: 230), helping them to challenge the model of the male breadwinner and transform the nature of the patriarchal contract within the home.

My research with women workers in the Bangladesh garment industry suggests that, in a different time and a different place, another group of newly proletarianized young women have been attempting to effect a similar transformation. These have always been precarious jobs, but now the very future of the industry is uncertain: many factories are likely to close down with the planned phase out of the MFA by the end of 2004 and the accession of China into the WTO and several thousand women are likely to lose their jobs, plunging their families back into poverty. However, the challenge that the women's experience of factory employment has posed for deeply entrenched prejudices regarding their economic capabilities may have a lasting effect on gender relations in Bangladesh.

TRANSLATING NEEDS INTO RIGHTS: VOICE AND ORGANIZATION

Understanding the possibilities that access to waged work has opened up for women in contexts in which they had previously very little choice helps explain why they do not view their jobs in the unequivocally negative light that anti-sweatshop campaigners do. Indeed, studies show that many enter factory employment *against* the wishes of senior family members, including husbands and fathers: Paul-Majumder and Begum (2000) found that 37 percent of 589 workers interviewed in their 1997 survey had taken up jobs in the garment industry despite family opposition, while Kabeer (2000) documents the processes of bargaining, negotiation, and defiance which women resorted to in the face of family opposition. Simply highlighting their problems, and ignoring their gains, erases the possibility that there may have been a calculus of choice involved and that women[4] may consider

21

ARTICLES

these jobs worth defending. At the same time, however, many aspects of their working conditions clearly violate the workers' sense of justice, so, on their own, the positive aspects of their work do not fully explain the absence of protest within the factories. Like most countries, Bangladesh has various commitments to labor standards in place within its national legislation, including the right to form trade unions; while the export processing zones are the exception to this, they account for a very small minority of workers in this sector. It has also ratified seven of the eight ILO conventions pertaining to core labor standards. Although these various commitments are generally not observed in practice, they provide a supportive legal framework for workers' struggles to improve their conditions at work. Garment workers have been known to take their employers to court, usually with the backing of a non-governmental organization, and, more importantly, to win. As a lawyer working with garment workers observed, the courts generally believed the workers over their employers: "the judges are sympathetic to the workers in most of the cases, that is our fortune" (cited in Dannecker 2000: 244). Nearly all the cases she had taken up on behalf of workers had ended positively since the threat of legal notice was often sufficient to persuade employers to settle out of court.

However, such action has generally been on an individualized and sporadic basis rather than as part of a wider collective struggle. This failure to organize collectively can be partly attributed to the active hostility of employers within the industry to trade union activity (Shamsul I. Khan 2002). However, employers' efforts to repress union activity has been made far easier by the failure of the trade unions themselves to take women workers' concerns seriously. Trade unionism is more than a hundred years old in South Asia, and most garment workers are aware of the unions' existence. However, few are members. This is not a purely gender-specific phenomenon. Less than 5 percent of male workers, most of them located in public sector employment in the formal economy, belong to trade unions.

These low membership rates reflect what the unions represent in the context of South Asia generally. Many have strong links with the major political parties and act as the industrial appendage of their political parties rather than as representatives of workers' interests (see Sharit K. Bhowmik 1998 for a description of the Indian context). It is not accidental that trade unions are a largely formal sector phenomenon in a region where the overwhelming majority of workers are in the informal sector. Jan Breman has described the attitudes of Indian trade unions towards such workers as one of "indifference, rising almost to enmity" underpinned by the "fear that pressure from below would lead to gradual erosion of the rights gained during a long struggle by the protected labor" (1996: 247). For women workers, the majority of whom are in the informal sector, such exclusionary behavior takes a markedly gendered form: not only are most male trade unionists largely indifferent to their needs and priorities as workers, but

22

LABOR STANDARDS AND WOMEN'S RIGHTS

they also tend to reproduce the norms and behavior that treat women as a subordinate category and marginalize their needs and priorities as women (Bhowmik 1998; Dannecker 2002).

More responsive to the needs and rights of women workers are various nongovernmental organizations, some of which work directly with them. In Bangladesh, these include Nari Uddug Kendra which provides safe low-cost residential facilities for working women; Uthsao and Phulki which seek to promote childcare facilities for women both within the community as well as located within factories; and Ain-o-Shalish Kendro and the Bangladesh Women's Lawyers' Association which provide legal support to workers. In addition, new kinds of labor organizations are emerging that base themselves within the community and offer a much wider range of support services, including legal literacy, than do the traditional trade unions. The Bangladesh Independent Garment Workers' Union, founded and funded by USAID, is the best-resourced example in Bangladesh, but there are others, such as Kormojibi Nari, affiliated to left-wing parties that have come to realize the significance of gender in their work. Growing cooperation among these different groups is evident in the emergence of coalitions such as the Bangladesh Garment Workers' Protection Alliance that seek to ensure that women workers' voices are heard in national and international forums at a time when the future of the industry is becoming increasingly uncertain.

Such organizations bring with them the recognition that women workers' exercise of agency in the workplace is unlikely to take the form of the heroic mass struggles that make up trade union lore (Sujata Gothoskar 1997). Engaged in unceasing, individual struggles on a daily basis to combine their domestic chores and wage labor, and to negotiate their way in a world hostile to the idea of women working for pay, their agency in the workplace takes a lower key and less confrontational form. Today's garment workers take many more enterprise-based collective actions than they did in the early years of the industry, including sporadic "downing of tools," collective bargaining with management, and a willingness to take their grievances to court (interview with Shireen Akhter of Kormojibi Nari 1999). Yet mass collective action through the trade union movement remains a remote possibility.

Research on women's experiences with trade unions in other parts of the world suggests that the situation in Bangladesh is by no means exceptional (Sheila Rowbotham and Swasti Mitter 1994; Amrita Chhachhi and Renee Pittin 1996). It is part of a problem that exists wherever unions, as champions of the organized sector workers, have acquired male-biased culture and procedures that are out of tune with the lives and priorities of working women (Swasti Mitter 1994). In such contexts, alternative forms of organizations have championed women's needs and priorities through forms of collective action that are not necessarily rooted in trade unionism

23

and do not necessarily adopt the confrontational tactics often associated with traditional trade unionism.

In her account of the Central American Network of Women in Solidarity with Maquila Workers, Jennifer Bickham Mendez (2002) discusses the failure of trade unionism to support the needs and rights of women workers in terms that echo the situation in Bangladesh. Here, too, women's organizations have opted for an incremental accretion of rights at work, what the Network call a strategy of "radical reformism" or "self-contained radicalism," which acknowledges institutional constraints and seeks to work for change within them. Rather than seeking to seize the state or overthrow the capitalist system, radical reformism starts from the current realities of the lives of women workers with a view to a strategy of gradual improvement, given the existing political and economic conditions: as one of its workers said, "We are asking for the minimum. We are not even questioning the exploitation of workers. If the goal of the code of ethics were to dismantle the system of capitalism, we would be fried" (cited in Mendez 2002: 133). Such a negotiating stance clearly has its limitations, but it reflects a perspective, grounded in present reality of women's lives, that distinguishes between what is desirable and what is possible in situations of extreme poverty.

TRANSLATING RIGHTS INTO ACTION: VOICE AND EXIT

The hostility of employers to trade unions, combined with the male-dominated culture of the trade union movement, goes some way towards explaining the low levels of organization among women workers in the export factories in Bangladesh. Upholding the right to organize through trade sanctions may not rectify these deeply entrenched biases within the trade union movement, but it would open the way for alternative forms of organization to flourish. However, it would not necessarily translate into mass activism on the part of women garment workers for reasons that relate to the critical tradeoff that the wage workers, particularly female wage workers, face in an underdeveloped, labor-abundant economy: the tradeoff between access to employment and conditions of employment. The predominantly male workforce in Bangladesh's formal economy, most of whom are employed by the public sector, has not faced this tradeoff in quite the same way. Male workers were able to improve their standards at work *and* retain their jobs because of the protection provided by state employment, by barriers to trade, and by their own ability to exclude less privileged workers, male as well as female. While trade liberalization and the ongoing "de-nationalization" of state-owned industries are changing this situation, the fact that the minimum wage in these sectors is more than double the country's per capita GNP, and several multiples of the wages in the informal economy, is evidence of their success.

24

LABOR STANDARDS AND WOMEN'S RIGHTS

The rest of the workforce, however, has always been denied access to formal employment by various forms of social closure, including the restrictive practices of organized workers themselves. For these nonunionized workers, there is a stark tradeoff between exclusion from work and exploitation at work. Women workers are particularly cautious about taking action because they fear losing jobs in a society that offers women very few economic opportunities (Dannecker 2002; Kabeer and Mahmud 2003). After women's long history of exclusion from paid work in the public domain, the garment industry has provided them with their first large-scale opportunity to enter a relatively formal form of employment. In an era when the male breadwinner model is breaking down under the pressures of poverty, households are increasingly looking to women's economic contributions as an essential component of their livelihoods. And for women themselves, whatever problems they face within the garment industry, the options outside are far bleaker. They are reluctant to jeopardize the concrete gains they have made in the present for the uncertain gains in the future that struggles in the workplace might bring. They know well that for every woman who is prepared to fight, many others are prepared to take her place on acquiescent terms.

This reality suggests a major flaw in how labor standards are being posed in current debates. The focus is almost entirely on the traded sectors of national economies, which are either conflated in the public imagination with the whole economy of the country or else treated in isolation from the rest of the economy. Anti-sweatshop activists constantly compare the wages women earn in these industries with the prices their products sell for in richer countries or, alternatively, with the wages earned by workers in the equivalent sector in richer countries. Yet, while these comparisons may be useful for campaigning purposes, neither of these prices influence the labor-market decisions of women workers in Bangladesh. Instead, it is wages and conditions that prevail in the alternative forms of employment available to them, together with the prospect of having no job at all, that exercise the greatest influence. In other words, it is the conditions that prevail in the wider economy, particularly in the informal economy in which the vast majority of women workers are concentrated, rather than those in the export sector, that help to shape their "exit" options and to determine what they are prepared to risk their jobs for.

Similar considerations operate elsewhere in the world. They explain the cautious approach adopted by the Central Network of Women in Central America discussed earlier. They are also evident in Hart's discussion of the failure of trade unions in South Africa to organize women working in the garment sector to press for higher wages and better working conditions. This failure reflected not only the opposition of the employers, but also "broader processes of labor force formation and the desperate search by

ARTICLES

huge numbers of dispossessed people for a modicum of economic and social security" (Gillian Hart 1995; cited in Shahra Razavi 1999: 678).

As long as there is an untapped pool of female labor available and willing to take up employment in export-oriented manufacturing, or a large informal economy in which wages and conditions are far worse than those that prevailed in the export sector, the ability of workers employed in these sectors to collectively bargain for improvements in their own situation is likely to be limited. Nor will linking global labor standards to trade agreements help them very much. As Jayati Ghosh (2000) puts it,

> One important reason why progressive elements in the South have tended to oppose labor-standards-based trade sanctions, is because typically the worst labor conditions are to be found not in exporting industries but in a range of traditional and service sector activities. Thus, in most developing countries, exporting industries are able to survive and profit from low wages and terrible working conditions simply because the other job alternatives for workers are even worse or are nonexistent ... Quite often, workers themselves see the expansion of employment in export-related activities as a positive enlargement of employment choice, and therefore welcome it, even though it implies conditions, which are in themselves unsatisfactory and certainly much worse than those prevailing in developed countries.

SOCIAL POLICIES FOR THE POOR IN POOR COUNTRIES: GENDER PERSPECTIVES

Perspectives "from below" of the kind discussed in this paper offer a different and a more gendered standpoint from which to view the concerns raised in global debates about labor standards. When those who support the social clause express fears about the "race to the welfare bottom," they serve to remind us that workers in different parts of the world are inserted into this race on very different terms. In the poorer countries of the world, socially protected full-time employment only ever applied to a very small proportion of the total labor force, mainly those who worked in formal, usually public sector, employment, and made up at most 10 percent of the workforce. It applied to an even smaller proportion of working women in these countries, the vast majority of whom were to be found in the informal economy, which provided little or no protection of any kind. These latter are likely to have different livelihood priorities from those who have enjoyed, and are now seeking to defend, relatively high levels of social protection.

Similarly, when those who oppose the social clause express concerns about the possible negative implications for employment, the "view from

26

LABOR STANDARDS AND WOMEN'S RIGHTS

below" reminds us that it is women workers who stand to lose most, should these fears be realized, because they are most likely to be found in industries, or sectors of industries, that are vulnerable to social clause sanctions. And finally, while both sides to the debate refer to the ILO's core labor standards as representing the international consensus, the view from below reminds us that the ILO's tripartite structure of government, business, and organized labor has so far excluded any participation by women workers, particularly those in the informal economy. It may well be that, if they were heard, they would consider the right to organize and to engage in collective bargaining to be meaningless rights in the absence of the right to work or to alternative means of survival.

As noted above, the logic of the analysis in this paper points to the need to move away from the narrow preoccupation with labor standards in the globally traded sector to a consideration of working conditions in the wider economy. These ultimately determine the willingness of workers, all workers, to stand up for their rights. Some of the strategies adopted as part of the anti-sweatshop movement clearly have a role to play in the struggle to improve workers' rights. The development of codes of conduct by companies allows them to be held accountable by their shareholders and the public at large. Initiatives that bring unions, NGOs, and companies together to ensure compliance with agreed codes of conduct help to strengthen the norm and practice of corporate social responsibility. Attempts to enforce the social clause through trade agreements are also likely to improve the labor standards of some workers in some economies.

However, all of these strategies are partial in their focus. As Women Working Worldwide (a UK-based NGO working with labor organizations around the world) points out, most women workers engage in undocumented and often unremunerated work in domestic, agricultural, and industrial sectors, beyond the reach of existing national as well as international regulation. Even within the export industries, women's participation is often carried out within the home or in small workshops at the end of a companies' subcontracting chain so that they are more likely to be employed on a part-time, casual, or temporary basis than men.

The social clause, on the other hand, is targeted to paid work, and moreover, to paid work in the formal economy. It is highly unlikely that the global labor standards it seeks to promote can be enforced beyond the boundaries of the formal economy, given the massive amount of resources, both financial and administrative, that would be required. As a result, the implementation of the social clause could very well lead to even greater differentials in pay and working condition between workers in the formal and informal economy and, by extension, to greater differentials between male and female workers (Women Working Worldwide 1996; see also Angela Hale 1996).

27

ARTICLES

If the struggle for decent conditions at work has become increasingly interdependent at the global level, so that lower labor standards in one country threaten labor standards in all, it is even more interdependent at the local level. As long as an informal economy exists in which workers have no rights at all, it will dampen the willingness of those who have managed to enter the better-paid export sector to fight for improvements in their labor standards. The struggle for labor standards needs to be broadened and made more inclusive by transforming itself into a struggle for a universal "social floor," so that all workers, men as well as women, urban as well as rural, formal as well as informal, in work and without it, are able to organize for their other rights without fear of jeopardizing their means of survival.

For the poor in general, the institution of a social floor that guaranteed access to the basic means of survival could enable them to engage as citizens in wider struggles for social justice in their society. For poor women in particular, it could provide the basis from which they could challenge their dual subordination within the home and at work. It would give them the leverage to challenge the patriarchal contract within the family, a leverage that they have otherwise had to acquire through participation in paid work in highly discriminatory labor markets. And it would promote their leverage vis-à-vis their employers in the workplace by providing them with resources to fall back on should their struggle for rights at work threaten to jeopardize their jobs.

The demand for a "social" floor should consequently be seen as both the object of struggle but also as an important precondition for strengthening the capacity for struggle. An international labor movement that mobilized around the global promotion for workers' rights, rather than the selective enforcement of labor standards, would give strategic and simultaneous importance to a global campaign for a universal social floor. It would also lend legitimacy to local efforts to strengthen the capacity of workers to engage in collective action on their own behalf, regardless of whether they belonged to the formal or the informal economy, or produced for domestic or global markets.

BEYOND LABOR STANDARDS: INTERNATIONAL
SOLIDARITY IN THE CONTEXT OF GLOBAL INEQUALITY

The arguments for a universalist approach to social security at the global level are the contemporary version of the arguments that gave rise to the universalist approaches to social policy at the national level in an earlier era of capitalism and to the "de-commodification" of labor (Gosta Esping-Andersen 1990). European welfare states undertook to make access to a basic real income a matter of right rather than a gift, welfare, or charity, thereby rescuing workers from their status as commodities, to be bought

LABOR STANDARDS AND WOMEN'S RIGHTS

and sold in the marketplace, into citizens with the right to have rights. The New Deal did the same for American workers. Today, as globalization and the threat of capital flight undermines the capacity of the more affluent countries of the world to continue to protect their workers, they, too, face a version of the tradeoff between exploitation and exclusion: "the more [they] do to improve the material situation of the poorest among the workers, the scarcer the jobs become, and the more people there are who are deprived of the privilege of having one" (Philippe Van Paijs 1996: 63).

The idea of a social floor has been taken up in Europe as a campaign for a basic citizenship income (Standing 1999). It argues the principle that every adult citizen within the EU should be automatically and unconditionally entitled to a level of income that allows them a basic modicum of security in their lives. Such an income can be phased in gradually, starting with a partial basic income, and increased to a full basic income, or it can be phased in partially to those whose need is greatest and then spread to achieve universal coverage.

Redistributive cash transfers of this kind are unlikely to be practical in the context of the poorer economies of the world, but the principle of a universal social floor, which covers the minimum basic needs of food, health, and shelter, could be operationalized by building on, and improving, existing systems of social security, including employment guarantee schemes, food-for-work programs, public food distribution systems, micro-finance services, and low-cost health insurance schemes. A commitment to basic universal services, particularly in the fields of health and education, has existed in most developing countries and would have existed in many more if they had not been dismantled under pressure from international financial institutions, which are dominated of course by many of the same richer countries that are now leading the demand for global labor standards (Judith Tendler 2000; Stephen Devereux 2002).

If the rights of labor are to be defended today, social policies will clearly have to defend the principle of universalism at both national and global levels. However, any proposal for inclusive social policies comes up against the barriers posed by the unequal distribution of resources within and across nations. Clearly, some of the costs of instituting a minimum social floor could – and should – be financed through domestic resources. However, as R. Beattie (2000) points out, in countries where large numbers of people cannot afford to contribute to their own social security, these resources have to be provided through the public budget. The extremely low tax to GDP ratio that prevails in a number of countries, including Bangladesh, reflects their failure to take collective responsibility for dealing with consequences of poverty and inequality within their own citizenship.

At the same time, however, the level of per capita GNPs in these countries indicates the limits to redistributive policies within national contexts. The

29

ARTICLES

per capita GNP in Bangladesh, for instance, was $370 in 1999 compared to $32,000 in the United States. The shockingly low ratio of development assistance to GNP in the richer countries is indicative of their failure to seriously address the issue of global inequality. The US, for instance, allocated 0.10 percent of its GNP to development assistance in 1999, of which a minute 0.16 percent went to the least developed countries in the world. The United States is not alone in the meagerness of its contribution to global equity. The wealthier nations of the world in general perform badly in their attempts to address global inequality, with the seven wealthiest countries (the G7) performing proportionately worst (Nancy Birdsall and David Roodman 2003).

In a global economy that is becoming increasingly interdependent and increasingly unequal, a struggle for some degree of redistribution from North to South, from rich to poor, from capital to labor, and from more to less privileged forms of labor can be the only basis on which claims to international solidarity on workers' rights can have any moral force. Such redistribution, moreover, has to be a matter of right rather than gift, welfare, charity, or "aid." It requires measures of the kind proposed by the Brandt Commission at the end of the 1970s, which recommended that countries be taxed on a sliding scale related to national income in order to generate revenue for a global social fund. The Brandt Report was overtaken by the debt crisis in the developing world, the ascendance of neoliberal ideologies within the international community, and the turn to market forces as the solution to social need. By the end of the 1990s, as the failure of unregulated markets to meet social need have become manifestly clear to many in the developed and developing world, proposals for a system of global taxation are once again resurfacing in the global agenda. However, they continue to founder on the rocks of neoliberal resistance. Draft documents for the UN Conference on Financing for Development in Monterey in 2002 called for an international tax organization to develop a system of transfers from richest to poorest countries in an efficient and coherent manner. This resolution was dropped from the final document because a number of the governments, led by the United States, were opposed to considering any type of redistributive measure (Lourdes Benería 2003). They emphasized instead the importance of fostering markets to help poorer countries: in particular, they extolled the virtues of free trade.

In other words, "*plus ça change.* ..." (Benería 2003: 165). Powerful countries continue to preach the value of free trade when faced with demands for global redistribution by poorer countries but practice protectionism to placate powerful political lobbies at home. The late Julius Nyerere, a life-long socialist and one of Africa's most respected elder statesmen, had some blunt words to say on this matter in a speech he delivered shortly before he died. Let me end this article with his

LABOR STANDARDS AND WOMEN'S RIGHTS

observations because they provide a pithy summary of some of my main points:

> Under the relentless pressure of unfettered globalization, the world is becoming one huge free market. That is what the developed countries want. And to avoid trouble from their own workers while facilitating the process of globalization, they now have this idea of demanding universal levels of social standards based on their own capacities to meet them. And this means that by a legally binding treaty, economic sanctions would be applied against any country which fails to enforce such standards internally.
>
> Yet the idea that the rich countries should be legally bound to help the poor ones to meet those social standards is rejected. Proposals for an international tax of any kind, for any purpose, are dismissed as absurd. Indeed, the poor countries come under immense pressure even to cut back on domestic redistributive taxation. Under international conditionalities, it is made increasingly difficult for these countries to tax their own rich in order to improve the social standards of their own poor. (Nyerere 1998: 2)

His conclusion resonates with the conclusion of this paper. The only basis on which global labor standards are likely to be either possible or compatible with the principles of justice, given the present unequal international order, is if they are linked to, and conditional on, a holistic, deliberate, and consistent program to meet the basic needs and promote the human dignity of women and men wherever they are located in the world. In the absence of such a program, the social clause will end up as merely one more weapon with which the powerful countries of the world can continue to dominate the less powerful.

Naila Kabeer, Institute of Development Studies, University of Sussex,
Brighton BN1 9RE, UK
e-mail: N.Kabeer@ids.ac.uk

ACKNOWLEDGMENTS

I would like to thank Lourdes Beneria and Savitri Bisnath for comments on an earlier version of this paper; the two anonymous referees for their insightful and probing comments; and to Nilufer Cagatay for pushing me to think more clearly about my own position. I am grateful also for the editorial support provided by *Feminist Economics*.

ARTICLES

NOTES

[1] It should be noted that not all of the eight conventions have received the same degree of support internationally. Ninety-five countries have ratified all eight conventions and a further thirty-five (including Bangladesh) have ratified seven of the eight. The US, which has ratified only two of these conventions, is on the "less support" end of the spectrum, along with a handful of mainly developing countries.

[2] Some of the facts produced by the NLC were subsequently disputed by journalists writing in the *Los Angeles Times* ("Stitching Together a Crusade") and the *New York Times* ("Hondurans in 'Sweatshops' See Opportunity"), who suggested that many workers in the very factories the NLC had targeted perceived their jobs rather differently than the evaluations provided by the NLC.

[3] The Multi-Fibre Agreement of 1974 was put in place in the interests of "orderly trade" between developed and developing countries in garments and textiles. The anti-surge clause allowed quotas to be imposed when exports from any developing country to a developed country exceeds 6 percent a year.

[4] Such as Fatema Akhter in the opening quote.

REFERENCES

Amin, Sajeda, Ian Diamond, Ruchira T. Naved, and Margaret Newby. 1998. "Transition to Adulthood of Female Garment Factory Workers in Bangladesh." *Studies in Family Planning* 29(22): 185 – 200.

Amsden, Alice H. 1994. "Macro-Sweating Policies and Labor Standards," in Werner Sengenberger and Duncan Campbell (eds.) *International Labor Standards and Economic Interdependence*, pp. 185 – 93. Geneva: International Institute of Labor Studies.

Bardhan, Pranab. 2000. "Social Justice in the Global Economy: Governance and Policy Issues," *ILO Social Policy Lecture*, University of the Western Cape, South Africa. Available http://www.ilo.org/public/english/bureau/inst/papers/sopolecs/bardhan/

Basu, Kaushik. 1999. "International Labor Standards and Child Labor." *Challenge* 42(5): 80 – 93.

Bearak, Barry. 2001. "Lives Held Cheap in Bangladesh Sweatshops." *New York Times*, April 15.

Beattie, R. 2000. "Social Protection for All: But How?" *International Labor Review* 139(2): 129 – 48.

Benería, Lourdes. 2003. *Gender, Development and Globalization. Economics as if All People Mattered*. London: Routledge.

Bhattacharya, Debapriya and Mustafizur Rahman. 2001. "Female Employment Under Export Propelled Industrialization: Prospects for Internalizing Global Opportunities in the Apparel Sector in Bangladesh." Occasional Paper No. 10, United Nations Research Institute for Social Development (UNRISD).

Bhowmik, Sharit K. 1998. "The Labour Movement in India: Present Problems and Future Perspectives." *Indian Journal of Social Work* 59(1): 147 – 66.

Birdsall, Nancy and David Roodman. 2003. *The Commitment-to-Development Index: A Scorecard of Rich-Country Policies*. Washington, DC: Center for Global Development.

Breman, Jan. 1996. *Footloose Labour: Working in India's Informal Economy*. Cambridge, UK: Cambridge University Press.

Bullard, Nicola. 2001. *Social Standards in International Trade*, prepared for the Deutsche Bundestag Commission of Enquiry, "Globalization of the World Economy – Challenges and Answers." Bangkok: Focus on the Global South.

Cagatay, Nilufer. 1996. "Gender and International Labor Standards." *Review of Radical Political Economics* 28(3): 92 – 101.

LABOR STANDARDS AND WOMEN'S RIGHTS

——. 2001. *Trade, Gender, and Poverty.* New York: UNDP.

Cavanagh, John. 1997. "The Global Resistance to Sweatshops," in Andrew Ross (ed.) *No Sweat: Fashion, Free Trade, and the Rights of Garment Workers,* pp. 39–50. London: Verso.

Charnowitz, Steve. 1987. "The Influence of International Labor Standards on the World Trading Regime." *International Labor Review* 126(5): 565–84.

Chawla, Najma. 1996. *In Search of the Best Interests of the Child.* Dhaka: UNICEF.

Chhachhi, Amrita and Renee Pittin (eds.). 1996. *Confronting State, Capital and Patriarchy: Women Organizing in the Process of Industrialization.* Basingstoke, UK: Macmillan.

Dannecker, Petra. 2002. *Between Conformity and Resistance: Women Garment Workers in Bangladesh.* Dhaka: University Press.

Davin, Delia. 2001. "The Impact of Export-Oriented Manufacturing on Chinese Women Workers." Prepared for the UNRISD Project on Globalization, Export-Oriented Employment for Women and Social Policy, UNRISD, Geneva.

Delap, Emily. 1998. "The Determinants and Effects of Children's Income-Generating Work in Urban Bangladesh." Department of Economics and International Development, University of Bath, UK.

Devereux, Stephen. 2002. "Safety Nets in Malawi: The Process of Choice." Presented at IDS Conference on Surviving the Present, Securing the Future: Social Policy for the Poor in Poor Countries, Institute of Development Studies, Brighton, UK.

Eraydin, Ayda and Asuman Erendil. 1999. "The Role of Female Labor in Industrial Restructuring: New Production Processes and Labor Market Relations in the Istanbul Clothing Industry." *Gender, Place and Culture* 6(3): 259–72.

Esping-Andersen, Gosta. 1990. *The Three Worlds of Welfare Capitalism.* Cambridge, UK: Polity Press.

Fraser, Nancy. 1997. *Justice Interruptus: Critical Reflections on the "Post-Socialist" Condition.* London: Routledge.

Ghosh, Jayati. 2000. "Rules of International Economic Integration and Human Rights." Background Paper for the Human Development Report, UNDP, New York.

——. 2001. "Globalization, Export-Oriented Employment for Women and Social Policy: A Case Study for India." Prepared for the UNRISD Project on Globalization, Export-Oriented Employment for Women and Social Policy, UNRISD, Geneva.

Gothoskar, Sujata. 1997. "Introduction," in Sujata Gosthoskar (ed.) *Struggles of Women at Work,* Indian Association for Women's Studies. New Delhi: Vikas Publishing House.

Guzman, Virginia and Rosalba Todaro. 2001. "Apuntes sobres genero en la economia global," in Rosalba Todaro and Regina Rodríguez (eds.) *El Genero en la Economia.* Santiago: Isis Internacional/CEM.

Hale, Angela. 1996. "The Deregulated Global Economy: Women Workers and Strategies of Resistance." *Gender and Development* 6(3): 8–15.

Hensman, Rohini. 2000. "World Trade and Workers' Rights. To Link or Not to Link?" *Economic and Political Weekly,* April 8.

John, J. and A. M. Chenoy (eds.). 1996. *Labor, Environment and Globalization.* New Delhi: New Age International Publications.

Kabeer, Naila. 2000. *The Power to Choose: Bangladeshi Women and Labor Market Decisions in London and Dhaka.* London: Verso.

——. 2003a. *Mainstreaming Gender Equality in Poverty Eradication and the Millennium Development Goals.* London and Ottawa: Commonwealth Secretariat and International Development Research Centre.

——. 2003b. "Past, Present and Future: Child Labor and the Intergenerational Transmission of Poverty in the Urban Slums of India and Bangladesh." Presented at the Chronic Poverty Research Centre Conference: Staying Poor: Chronic Poverty and Development Policy. Available www.idpm.man.ac.uk/cprc/Conference/conferencepapers/Kabeer.pdf.

ARTICLES

—— and Simeen Mahmud. 2003. "Globalization, Gender and the Millennium Development Goals: Women's Employment in the Bangladesh Garment Industry." Presented at OXFAM, Institute of Development Studies, Sussex, UK; and the Bangladesh Institute of Development Studies Workshop: Beyond the Multi-Fibre Arrangements: A Value Chain Perspective on the Bangladesh Garment Industry.

—— 2004. "Globalization, Gender and Poverty: Bangladeshi Women Workers in Global and Domestic Markets." *Journal of International Development* 16(1): 93–109.

Khan, Shamsul I. 2002. "Trade Unions, Gender Issues and the Ready-Made Garment Industry of Bangladesh," in Carol Miller and Jessica Vivian (eds.) *Women's Employment in the Textile Manufacturing Sectors of Bangladesh and Morocco*. Geneva: UNRISD/UNDP.

Kibria, Nazli. 1995. "Culture, Social Class and Income Control in the Lives of Women Garment Workers in Bangladesh." *Gender and Society* 9(3): 289–309.

Krupat, Kitty. 1997. "From War Zone to Free Trade Zone," in Andrew Ross (ed.) *No Sweat: Fashion, Free Trade and the Rights of Garment Workers*, pp. 51–77. London: Verso.

Lee, Eddie. 1997. "Globalization and Labor Standards: A Review of Issues." *International Labor Review* 136(2): 173–89.

Maddox, Bronwen. 2002. "Grotesque Bill Will Set Back Years of Reform." *The Times* (London), May 10.

Mendez, Jennifer Bickham. 2002. "Transnational Organizing for Maquila Workers' Rights," in Nancy A. Naples and Manisha Desai (eds.) *Women's Activism and Globalization: Linking Local Struggles and Transnational Politics*. London: Routledge.

Mitter, Swasti. 1994. "On Organizing Women in Casualised Work: A Global Overview," in Sheila Rowbotham and Swasti Mitter (eds.) *Dignity and Daily Bread: New Forms of Economic Organising among Poor Women in the Third World and the First*, pp. 14–52. London: Routledge.

Munck, Ronaldo. 2002. *Globalization and Labour: The New "Great Transformation."* London: Zed Books.

Nabi, Rashed un, Dipankara Datta, Subrata Chakrabarty, Masuma Begum, and Nasima Jahan Chaudhury. 1999. *Consultation with the Poor: Participatory Poverty Assessment in Bangladesh*. Report of the NGO Working Group on the World Bank, Dhaka.

Newby, M. H. 1998. "Women in Bangladesh: A Study of the Effects of Garment Factory Work on Control over Income and Autonomy." PhD dissertation, University of Southampton, UK.

Nyerere, Julius K. 1998. *Are Universal Social Standards Possible?* Presented to the North/ South Conference for Sustainable Development. Berne: Swiss Coalition for Development.

OECD. 1996. *Trade, Employment and Labor Standards: A Case Study of Core Workers' Rights and International Trade*. Paris: OECD.

Oxfam International. 2002. *Rigged Rules and Double Standards: Trade, Globalization and the Fight Against Poverty*. Oxford, UK: Oxfam.

Paul-Majumder, Pratima and Anwara Begum. 2000. *The Gender Differentiated Effects of the Growth of Export-Oriented Manufacturing: A Case for the Ready-Made Garment Industry in Bangladesh*. Prepared for the Policy Research Report on Gender and Development, World Bank.

People's Health Movement. 2002. *Voices of the Unheard: Testimonies from the People's Health Assembly*. Gonoshasthya Kendra: Savar.

Razavi, Shahra. 1999. "Export-Oriented Employment, Poverty and Gender, Contested Accounts." *Development and Change* 30(3): 653–84.

Ross, Andrew (ed.). 1997a. *No Sweat: Fashion, Free Trade and the Rights of Garment Workers*. London: Verso.

——. 1997b. "Introduction," in Andrew Ross (ed.) *No Sweat: Fashion, Free Trade and the Rights of Garment Workers*. London: Verso.

LABOR STANDARDS AND WOMEN'S RIGHTS

Rowbotham, Sheila and Swasti Mitter (eds.). 1994. *Dignity and Daily Bread: New Forms of Economic Organising Among Poor Women in the Third World and the First.* London: Routledge.

Singh, Ajit and Ann Zammit. 2000. *The Global Labour Standards Controversy: Critical Issues for Developing Countries.* Geneva: South Centre.

Spielberg, Elinor. 1997. "The Myth of Nimble Fingers," in Andrew Ross (ed.) *No Sweat: Fashion, Free Trade and the Rights of Garment Workers,* pp. 113–22. London: Verso.

Standing, Guy. 1999. *Global Labour Flexibility: Seeking Distributive Justice.* Basingstoke, UK: Macmillan.

Tendler, Judith. 2000. "Why Social Policy is Condemned to a Residual Category of Safety Nets and What to Do About It." Prepared for the UNRISD Programme on Social Policy in a Development Context, UNRISD, Geneva.

Third World Network. 1994. *Asian Meet Opposed to Labor Link at WTO.* Available http://www.sunsonline.org/trade/process/towards/09120094.htm.

———. 1996. *Barking Up the Wrong Tree: Trade and Social Clause Links.* Available http://www.twnside.org.sg/south/twn/title/tree-ch.htm.

United Nations. 1999. *1999 World Survey on the Role of Women in Development: Globalization, Gender, and Work.* New York: United Nations.

Van Paijs, Philippe. 1996. "Basic Income and the Two Dilemmas of the Welfare State." *Political Quarterly* 61(1): 63–6.

Wilson, Fiona. 1991. *Sweaters: Gender, Class and Workshop-Based Industry in Mexico.* Basingstoke, UK: Macmillan.

Wolf, Diane Lauren. 1992. *Factory Daughters: Gender, Household Dynamics and Rural Industrialization in Java.* Berkeley, CA: University of California Press.

Women Working Worldwide. 1996. *Trade Liberalization and the Rights of Women Workers: Are Social Clauses the Answer?* Available www.poptel.org.uk/women-ww/trade_liberalisation.htm.

Wood, Geoff and Sarah Salway. 2000. "Securing Livelihoods in Dhaka Slums." *Journal of International Development* 12(5): 669–88.

World Bank. 1995. *World Development Report: Workers in an Integrating World.* London: Oxford University Press.

Zohir, Salma Chaudhuri and Pratima Paul-Majumder. 1996. "Garment Workers in Bangladesh: Economic, Social and Health Conditions." Research Monograph 18, Bangladesh Institute of Development Studies, Dhaka.

Part II
Risks and Threats Associated with Globalization

[26]

Electronic Money and the Casino Economy

Richard Barnet and John Cavanagh

Deregulation of banking and financial markets, combined with the new rules of free trade and the new technologies that offer instantaneous worldwide money transfers, have combined to profoundly transform the modes of financial activity all over the planet. Incomprehensibly large amounts of money are shifting from market to market and then back again in the time it takes to make a keystroke. Governments are left nearly helpless to ensure the stability of markets or currency values in the face of the tremendous acceleration of speculation. The role of the global financial gamblers in creating many of the current money crises has been seriously underreported in the media. In this chapter a condensed history of these enormous changes and their consequences is presented.

Richard J Barnet is a former arms control expert in the Kennedy administration. He has written 14 books, most recently (with Ann Barnet) The Youngest Minds, *and (with John Cavanagh)* Imperial Corporations and the New World Order. *Barnet cofounded the Institute for Policy Studies in 1963 and is currently a Distinguished Fellow at the institute. He has published hundreds of articles on foreign policy, globalization and domestic policy in the* New Yorker, Harpers Magazine, *the* New York Review of Books, *the* Nation *and other publications.*

John Cavanagh is director of the Institute for Policy Studies and vice president of the board of the International Forum on Globalization, where he chairs the Alternatives Working Group. He has coauthored ten books on the global economy, most recently (with Sarah Anderson and Thea Lee) A Field Guide to the Global Economy. *His articles appear in the* Washington Post, *the* New York Times, Foreign Policy *and other publications. Cavanagh has degrees from Dartmouth College and Princeton University and has authored studies on transnational corporations for the United Nations Conference on Trade and Development and the World Health Organization.*

On 30 January 1995, 24 hours before President Bill Clinton orchestrated a US$50 billion bailout of the Mexican economy, the world financial system came perilously close to meltdown. As news spread around global financial markets that Mexico was on the verge of defaulting on government bond payments, capital fled stock markets from Brazil and Argentina and even from countries as far away as Poland and the Czech Republic. On that day, Asian markets were spared only because stock markets were closed in observance of Chinese New Year.

Just two and half years later, in mid 1997, a similar financial panic spread across the world. This time, the crisis began in Thailand but quickly moved to the Philippines, South Korea, Indonesia, Russia and Brazil. As international investors panicked in country after country, their 'hot money' left much faster than it had arrived. Big-time currency speculators such as George Soros deepened the crisis by betting against the currencies of the crisis nations. International Monetary Fund (IMF) policy advice only quickened the exodus. Currencies and stock markets from South Korea to Brazil nosedived, spreading pain, dislocation, death and environmental ruin. This sort of crisis is more than likely to recur in the coming years, and next time it might have even more devastating effects worldwide.

The root causes of these crises are twofold:

1   the total deregulation of the global financial systems that leaves banks and other financial institutions without controls; and
2   the corresponding revolution in communications technology that has brought radical change in the scale, speed and manner of financial activity.

This combination of factors has enabled currency speculators to run wild, moving their immense resources electronically, instantaneously, from country to country, beyond the abilities of any government to control the process. In this cybertech globalized world, money has become free of its place and, as we will see, from most connections to its former sources of value: commodities and services. Money itself is the product that money buys and sells.

Because of the tremendous financial requirements for playing in this global money game, banks and finance houses are quickly diminishing in number but increasing in size; as a result, they are becoming still more difficult to control. The net effect is that the world financial system has become exquisitely vulnerable to technological breakdown, the high-risk consequences of short-term speculation and freelance decision-making. If anything goes wrong in this fragile arrangement, which is increasingly likely in the context of a wired-up economy based on free trade, then the following scenario is likely. When a crisis in one place directly affects financial flows everywhere else, speculators panic, speculative funds will be moved without warning (as happened in Mexico, Asia, Russia and Brazil), and we will be quickly threatened by a rapid domino effect among the world's interdependent stock markets. Global economic collapse is possible.

The following are some elements in this larger story.

The Nature of Electronic Money

Most business and personal financial transactions still involve cash, that is, the exchange of coins and bank notes issued by treasuries and central banks. According to the Federal Reserve, about 85 per cent of dollar transactions are in cash at banks, supermarkets, petrol stations, restaurants and the like. But the trillions sloshing back and forth between countries, within and between corporations, and between large investors and entrepreneurs, are transferred from one account to another through an electronic network. Unlike withdrawals at automated teller machines (ATMs), these large transactions do not take place in public view. The number of electronic transfers amounts to only 2 per cent of the total transfers; yet these transactions involve US$5 out of every US$6 that move in the world economy.

Traders still shout at one another at exchanges around the world, buying and selling money in one form or another, but more and more dollars, yen, or lire move from one account to another hundreds or thousands of kilometres away because someone in a quiet room has hooked into a global electronic network and punched a key. Well over US$2 trillion a day travels across the street or across the world at unimaginable speed as bits of electronic information. A treasury bill, as James Grant, the editor of *Grant's Interest Rate Observer*, puts it, 'no longer exists except as an entry on a computer tape' (Passell, 1992).

Information technology has transformed global banking more than any other economic activity. The software that guides electronic networks now permits 24-hour trading in a wide variety of money products – securities, options, futures and so on – all across the planet, and it has changed the human relations of banking. As Felix Rohatyn of Lazard Freres puts it: 'People buy and sell blips on an electronic screen. They deal with people they never see, they talk to people on the phone in rooms that have no windows. They sit and look at screens. It's almost like modern warfare, where people sit in bunkers and look at screens and push buttons and things happen' (Sampson, 1989).

The sheer size of global financial operations is reducing costs substantially. Any multimillion dollar transfer across the globe can be accomplished for just 18 US cents. By developing the most advanced foreign-exchange software, Bankers Trust was able to achieve a ten-second advantage over other traders – enough time, according to a 1987 Office of Technology Assessment study, to execute four or five trades. The opportunity to react to new information a few seconds ahead of the market can be worth billions (O'Brien, 1992).

The introduction of state-of-the-art information technology has changed what banks are and what banks do. Computers and electronic communications networks have expanded the markets for money products and reduced the costs of making transfers, in large measure by eliminating thousands of jobs for clerks, tellers, messengers and the like. But the installation of the automated systems has required huge capital investments. In 1990, commercial banks in the United

States spent US$15 billion on information technology. The need to amass large investment funds for such purposes has encouraged the consolidation of investment and banking corporations. Firms merge to save costs by sharing expensive data systems. These systems facilitate the speedy settlement of money trading; even a few seconds of exposure before a transfer is settled can spell disaster if millions of dollars are involved.

In other words, global banking has become highly dependent on a few centralized information operations to accomplish and monitor the transfers. CHIPS is the New York Clearing House Interbank Payment System. Inside a reinforced concrete-and-glass office building on a run-down block on Manhattan's West Side, two Unisys A-I5 J mainframe computers about the size of refrigerators dispatch funds across the Earth. Requests for payment stream in through 134 telephone lines, and, after the requests are screened for possible fraud by 22 electronic black boxes, the mainframes move the money, as *New York Times* writer Peter Passell (1992) puts it, in the form of 'weightless photons through the electromagnetic ether'.

As bankers contemplate this electronic money web, the nightmare – which most dismiss – is that a massive fraud, a flash of lightning or a diabolical computer virus could trigger power failure, scrambled money messages, gridlock, and breakdown in the global banking system, and lead to the world's first computer-driven worldwide financial panic. CHIPS takes all this seriously enough to adopt elaborate security arrangements, to put in auxiliary power and water systems, and to replicate the entire Manhattan operation just across the river in New Jersey, down to a maze of white-walled rooms, a network of telephone lines, a Halon fire-protection system and water-resistant ceilings.

According to Peter Passell, a US$20 million theft did occur in 1989, a fraudulent transfer from a Zurich bank to the State Bank of New South Wales via its New York branch. A Malaysian con man secured the cooperation of two employees of the Swiss Bank and conjured up a fictitious bank in Cameroon to work the scheme. The thieves were caught and convicted. The US$20 million had been transferred in a fraction of a second, but recovering it took longer. Three years later, US$12 million of it was still missing. Despite all the technological precautions and hurdles, even more imaginative inside jobs on an even larger scale are possible.

John Lee, president of the New York Clearing House Association, estimates that 99 per cent of CHIPS transactions are legitimate. That may well be true, given the huge volume of daily transactions. Nevertheless, the speed and anonymity of the global money-transfer system presents an opportunity for large-scale criminal operations and tax fraud.

Electronic transfers are secret. Anyone with funds in the bank who prefers to hide them from regulators, creditors, wives or husbands can communicate with the bank by fax or modem and order wire transfers across the globe without ever speaking to a bank officer. Tax havens are nesting grounds for criminal gains or untaxed profits. Indeed, most of the deposits sitting in these out-of-the-way places are there to avoid scrutiny by regulatory and taxing authorities. Typically, tax havens are tiny – Cayman Islands, Bahamas, Bermuda, Cape Verde, Hong Kong, Bahrain – mostly islands featuring warm weather, good flight connections and plenty of faxes. Grand Cayman's financial district is reputed to have the highest concentration of fax machines in the world to serve its 548 banking outposts, which hold assets of about US$400 billion.

The volume and reach afforded by instantaneous banking transactions across the world make global banking highly profitable, but some economists fear that these same characteristics could also be its undoing. On a typical day, well over 100 banks are sending and receiving pay orders via CHIPS at the rate of US$2 billion a minute. Unlike payments in currency, which are final, electronic orders to pay are not settled until the close of the business day, and then the accounts are cleared multilaterally. Passell (1992) likens the process to a poker game: 'Each institution that is in arrears makes payments into the kitty much the way the "bank" settles accounts for a half-dozen players' when the game breaks up. Should a bank lack the funds to settle accounts at the end of its business day, the electronic entries would be reversed – *unwound* in global-banking lingo – and every bank engaged in a transfer to or from the defaulting bank would feel its effects. The gridlock caused by the hundreds of corrections, especially if multiple bank defaults are involved or a stock market crash is also occurring, could trigger a chain reaction of bank failures. The system could be shut down for weeks, during which time corporations would be starved of working capital. Bankers profess great confidence that such scenarios are highly improbable, but they acknowledge that the complexity, speed, and dynamism of global banking arrangements expose the system to hazards we cannot even imagine. That, they say, is always the risk of technological advance. And as with other technological catastrophes – from Chernobyl to Bhopal – a financial markets computer breakdown would ultimately injure innocent workers and civilians just as it has in Mexico, Asia and elsewhere.

GLOBALIZATION AND THE PRESSURE TO DEREGULATE

The technology of money lending and the explosion in money packaging have outpaced banking regulations designed for a simpler and slower age. The pressures of globalization have been used to remove regulations of all sorts from the financial services industry; US banks are subject to more regulations than their German or Japanese competitors and therefore, it is argued, the global playing field is not level. Bigger German and Japanese banks with broader powers are outcompeting global banks that fly the US flag.

Changes in Japanese banking regulations are also putting Tokyo-based banks in a stronger competitive position. On 18 October, two weeks before the 1992 presidential election, Secretary of the Treasury Nicholas Brady gave a speech to the American Bankers Association in which he said that increasing the competitiveness of the US financial services industry was critical to stimulating growth in the US economy. The key, he said, was to eliminate 'the old arbitrary legal framework that governs the banking system, especially outdated restrictions on products and geography'. In other words, banks should be free to leave their original neighbourhoods – where they may have helped local business and the public – and go to Asia or Europe, or wherever the action is, to serve themselves.

The argument that globalization requires deregulation is at least a quarter-century old. Deregulation of the US financial services industry has actually been underway for years, as part of a global shift in the relationship between governments and banks all over the world. To a great extent the US financial services industry deregulated itself. By resorting to creative corporation rearrangements, such as holding companies and mergers, the banking, brokerage and insurance industries slipped out of the legislative restraints intended to limit their geographical reach and their permissible activities long before Congress acted to loosen them. Through its parent corporation, Citicorp, which is not a bank under the law, Citibank could operate as a credit-card banker in all 50 states, rendering irrelevant and unenforceable the New Deal legislation that was supposed to keep banks serving their own communities. To get around legal requirements that banks lend only a certain percentage of their cash reserves, Citibank could sell its loans to Citicorp, which is not subject to these requirements. (In 1998, a giant financial conglomerate, Travelers Group, acquired Citicorp for US$72.6 billion; the new merged firm is called Citigroup.)

Congress had not anticipated that the nation's largest bank would make such effective use of the one-bank holding company to escape regulation, and friends of the banking industry in the US Senate effectively blocked efforts to plug the loophole. By the 1980s, banks were not only operating across state lines but had become sellers of insurance as well. Brokerage houses and automobile manufacturers were now deeply involved in the real estate market. All had, one way or another, jumped over the fences Congress had put up to separate investment banks from commercial banks and to keep brokerage firms, insurance companies and thrifts concentrated on the businesses for which they were chartered. Thanks to information technology and the ingenuity of lawyers, money now travelled faster, farther and in ways never envisioned by banking legislation and regulatory authorities. As Clive Crook in the *Economist* puts it, deregulation 'is often no more than an acknowledgement that the rules are no longer working' (Crook, 1992).

But deregulation, whether by circumvention of official policy or by law, had unanticipated and extremely unpleasant consequences. Like war plans, bank regulations are written with the catastrophes of the previous generation in mind.

After the Great Depression, when the national banking system collapsed because of risky loans, the Federal Reserve was given authority to set interest-rate ceilings on deposits. Regulation Q, as this grant of regulatory authority was known, was designed to stop banks from offering higher interest rates as a way of competing for deposits. The theory was that if banks were paying high interest, they would have to earn more on their loans and would be under pressure to take big risks with depositors' money. Since the deposits were now insured by the Federal Deposit Insurance Corporation (FDIC), the risk would eventually fall on the taxpayers if the economy turned sour. In normal times, the fees all the member banks paid into the FDIC are sufficient to cover the deposits of banks in trouble; but if failures were to reach a certain point, FDIC reserves would be exhausted, and Congress would have to come up with the money to pay off depositors. This is, of course, exactly what happened in the late 1980s in the infamous savings and loan industry debacle. But the roots of the problem were planted decades earlier.

EVOLUTION OF HOMELESS MONEY

All through the Cold War years, US savers were sending more of their money abroad to take advantage of higher returns. In 1966, under pressure from lobbies representing elderly and retired persons, the Federal Reserve Board agreed to let financial institutions such as brokerage houses and insurance companies pay market rates on consumer savings accounts. These new accounts offering higher returns for consumers were known as *money market funds*. As nominal interest rates soared in the 1970s, money market funds accumulated hundreds of billions of dollars. By 1979, savings banks, savings and loan associations (S&Ls) and credit unions, which had their deposits tied up in long-term, low-interest home mortgages arranged before inflation became rampant, tottered on the edge of bankruptcy.

Congress came to the rescue with two pieces of legislation: one known as the Deregulation and Monetary Control Act of 1980 and the other the Garn–St Germain Act of 1982. Essentially, these laws phased out regulatory limits on interest rates for savings institutions, allowed them to offer interest-paying checking accounts, and granted authority to make all sorts of loans. Previously, thrifts had survived by lending most of the home-mortgage money in the nation, but now they were permitted to make consumer loans and commercial real-estate loans. At the same time, companies such as Sears, GM, and Prudential, along with the commercial banks, could expand further into the commercial mortgage market. By tradition and by law, commercial banks were in business to supply working capital and investment funds to industry. But now they rushed into the real estate market. Citibank increased its mortgage portfolio from US$100 million to US$14.8 billion in just ten years. All this competitive zeal to finance unneeded office buildings spelled disaster for the S&Ls. Half of them disappeared. Our children and millions more taxpayers yet unborn will have to come up with something under US$1 trillion to repair the damage.

All through the last three decades, US banks pursued another strategy to escape the regulators. They shifted more and more of their activities beyond US shores, well out of reach of the treasury or the Federal Reserve. Here, too, regulators inadvertently spurred the process. As US corporations, armies, military installations and government aid programmes spread around the world in the 1950s, all spending billions in US currency in other countries, the glut of dollars in the hands of foreigners became a serious world problem. By this time, Germany, Japan, and the other industrial countries were recovering from the shocks of World War II and were producing a flood of goods. It was neither necessary nor advantageous to import so much from the US. Non-Americans had accumulated hundreds of billions of dollars more than they could possibly use to buy goods and services from the US. Except for the fact that the dollar was the world's reserve currency backed by gold, the overvalued offshore dollars were becoming risky holdings. If the holders of offshore dollars were to cash them in, the US would face financial catastrophe, because the treasury promised to redeem dollars with gold at US$35 an ounce. The obvious alternatives for the federal government were either to scale back expensive military commitments or to devalue the dollar. Both were inconsistent with America's self-image in the 1960s as the world's number one superpower.

For the first time, the nation experienced severe balance of payments problems. As foreigners piled up unwanted, overvalued dollars in banks in London, Paris, Geneva and Hong Kong, the doors of the gold depository at Fort Knox kept swinging open to accommodate the heavy traffic in gold bars bound for Europe. To stem the flow of gold, the Kennedy and Johnson administrations tried to limit the amount of dollars US banks could lend to foreigners and taxed foreign bonds issued in the United States. But these measures only succeeded in accelerating the outflow of dollars. US banks, led by Citibank, were now firmly established in Europe and Asia, and offshore lending exploded in reaction to the US government's efforts to keep Wall Street banks from lending to foreigners.

By the 1970s, for every dollar US banks were lending to non-Americans from their domestic bank offices, they were lending six or seven more from vast offshore facilities that collectively came to be called the Euromarket. This pooling of funds, mostly in dollars, started in Europe to accommodate the financial needs of communist China, but it soon became a global money pool that could be used by borrowers anywhere. The distinguishing feature of the Euromarket is that the money is denominated in a currency different from the official currency where the deposits are located. All such money is largely beyond the reach of national regulators in the countries of origin. When US companies in need of capital abroad resorted to the Euromarket, they were complying with the US policy to restrict capital outflow from the United States. But the buildup of this huge pool of offshore dollars created a formidable alternative to the US capital market. IBM was the pioneer among US-based companies to make creative use of the Euromarket, but soon many US companies operating outside the United

States were financing their overseas operations without resorting to banks in their home country. The Euromarket expanded into bond issues and then began offering a menu of increasingly arcane money products. Soon it was serving as a 'connecting rod' for financial markets around the world that once were entirely separate.

EMERGENCE OF CASINO ECONOMICS

Money itself was becoming a truly global product. In 1973, the gross sum in Eurocurrency accounts all over the world was US$315 billion; by 1987, the total was nearly US$4 trillion. This fantastic expansion was hastened by the series of deregulations of international money transactions that began when the Nixon administration forced the end of fixed exchange rates in August 1971, and governments everywhere lost much of their power over money. The value of money was now set in increasingly integrated global marketplaces, as foreign exchange traders all around the world haggled over how many lire or drachmas an ever fluctuating dollar could buy at any instant in time. In the 1970s, the eminent economist Milton Friedman convinced the Chicago Mercantile Exchange, which had established a lively futures market in hog bellies and other agricultural products in order to protect farmers and food companies from the volatility of farm prices, that a futures market for money products would be a smart idea. The more exchange rates fluctuated, the more interested investors would become in hedging their bets with contracts to buy or sell at a set price on a set date. The betting possibilities were limitless. By 1989, 350 varieties of futures contracts, most of which were financial, were traded in Chicago and in the 70-plus new exchanges that had sprouted up across the world.

US officials played the key role in the transformation of world financial markets, most notably on two occasions. The first was in 1971, when Nixon closed the 'gold window'. No longer was it possible to redeem dollars for gold. This meant that non-Americans had to keep their dollars on deposit somewhere in the world or convert them into some other currency. The second event came eight years later when Paul Volcker, then chair of the Federal Reserve Board, tried to fight inflation in the US by cutting the money supply. He used the standard tool – charging substantially higher interest rates to commercial banks to obtain dollars from the Federal Reserve. Since the dollar was the reserve currency for the world, however, the 'Fed' had unwittingly raised interest rates everywhere, and both interest rates and exchange rates began fluctuating wildly. As Michael Lewis puts it in his book *Liar's Poker* (1989), 'Overnight the bond market was transformed from a backwater into a casino. The buying, selling and lending of monetary products worldwide became businesses in themselves. Most of it had little or nothing to do with investment in either production or commerce. (However, as exchange rates became more volatile, hedging became almost a necessity for some transnational businesses.) Foreign direct investment in the developing world fell as the leading commercial banks of the world saw that they could reap quicker profits in commissions, fees and interest by 'recycling' tens of billions of 'petrodollars' from the coffers of Kuwait and Saudi Arabia to the governments and their business associates in poor countries.

As Richard O'Brien, chief economist of American Express Bank, notes (1992), 'Deregulation and liberalization clearly encourage globalization and integration. Liberal markets and systems tend to be open, providing greater ease of access, greater transparency of pricing and information.' The flow of accessible information offers a global environment that is hospitable to homeless money, promoting what O'Brien calls 'the end of geography' in the finance and investment business.

The rise of global financial markets makes it increasingly difficult for national governments to formulate economic policy, much less to enforce it. In the increasingly anarchic world of high-speed money, the dilemma facing national political leaders is clear: impose regulations, then sit back and watch how quickly financial institutions slip away by changing their looks, disappearing into other corporations, or otherwise rearranging their affairs to make life difficult for the regulators. At the same time, bankers argue that to the extent the regulations are observed, they pose a handicap in international competition. Yet, the history of deregulation is littered with scandals and financial foolishness for which a handful of bankers, but mostly millions of taxpayers and depositors, have paid a heavy price.

GLOBAL RACE TO DEREGULATE

On 27 October 1986, the 'Big Bang', as the chair of the London Stock Exchange first called it, went off in the city of London, ending 200 years of comfortable, stately, and expensive trading practices on the London Stock Exchange. Overnight, the market was deregulated and opened to foreign banks and securities firms of all sorts. An electronic marketing system modelled on the new US computer-age stock exchange, NASDAQ, was installed to take the place of old-fashioned floor trading. Traders could now bypass London and deal directly with markets in New York and Tokyo at much less cost. Deregulation was a strategy for trying to get lost business back. As the New York Stock Exchange had done more than ten years earlier, the London Stock Exchange abolished fixed commissions for traders, and it now permitted firms to act as both wholesale dealers and brokers. Suddenly, US commercial banks that were barred from the securities business at home could plunge into this market in London, neatly jumping over the wall of separation between investment and commercial banking provided under the Glass-Steagall Act of 1933, the cornerstone of modern US banking regulation. (With the Great Crash and its consequences still fresh in mind, the act was intended to forbid banks to act as underwriters for corporate securities.)

The global expansion through large corporate mergers and acquisitions gathered steam in the 1970s, and this global restructuring of industry required the amassing of huge amounts of capital. At first, large banks dominated this market because they were the ones with the financial power and connections to syndicate large loans through networks of foreign banks. But in the 1980s, as capital needs mushroomed, corporations in search of funds found that it was much cheaper to raise the capital by issuing bonds and other sorts of commercial paper. Financial institutions of all sorts packaged a bunch of small loans and sold them as securities on world markets.

Borrowers all over the world, including the largest corporations, could now shop around the world for money, and they could borrow it in many different forms on a wide variety of terms. Investors could hedge against risks in one national economy or in one industry by buying foreign stocks. Global markets in securities offered opportunities for diversification. Laws and regulations that had previously put international investments out of bounds came tumbling down. Markets in securities were losing what few geographical ties were left. It was now possible to invest in the New York market by buying New York Stock Exchange index shares on the Chicago Board Options Exchange.

The Big Bang triggered an explosion of deregulation in other financial centres all over the world. Screen-based markets offering instantaneous flows of global information took over an ever larger share of business from traditional floor trading. In addition to the speed and convenience, there were fees and taxes to be saved. Stocks in foreign companies became internationally traded products. London, Amsterdam, Paris, Frankfurt and Zurich competed in offering the most cosmopolitan menu of stocks, options, swaps, and futures in companies around the world. By 1990, the buying and selling of foreign equities on the London Exchange exceeded that of British equities.

THE FINAL BARRIER

With the juggernaut of deregulation having just about completed its sweep across the developed world, there remained one final barrier to ultimate freedom of movement for money and for the ability of the great financial conglomerates to control world markets. That barrier was among the poor countries of the developing world, who still stubbornly refused to open their commercial banking sector to outside domination. The Uruguay Round of the GATT took care of that.

In most of the world's poorest countries, foreign banks were traditionally welcomed for the services they performed, but only up to a certain point. The foreign banks were appreciated as sellers of retail credit and providers of capital under controlled, specific conditions. But foreign banks, with few exceptions, had been prohibited from buying into ownership positions in commercial banking. Developing world governments argued that since finance is central to development, the financial services industry should remain firmly in domestic hands, serve domestic interests, and keep money within the economy.

The US led the challenge against the developing world's control of its own financial markets during the Uruguay Round of GATT negotiations. The US and other Western nations argued that 'efficiency' and 'fairness' required that all foreign banks be accorded national treatment in every country. *National treatment* essentially means that foreign banks must be treated just as if they were local banks, so, for example, US banks must be permitted entry into developing world financial markets even if they gain full control of the local institutions. Local governments would have to give up all attempts to sustain control over local financing activity.

This was one of several important points that kept GATT negotiations stalled for seven years; but eventually the US and the other Western powers forced the poor nations to cave in and, under the WTO, a financial invasion is now underway.

While those negotiations proceeded, the US pushed hard for deregulation of financial services with Mexico and secured an agreement that the US negotiator said would give US banks 'dramatic new opportunities', a situation later solidified by NAFTA. As a result, one treasury official bragged at an off-record briefing, 'They [Mexico] gave us their financial system.' Indeed they had, and in January 1995 the world was given a taste of the consequences. The Mexican economy will not recover for a long while. Ordinary Mexican citizens will ultimately pay the bills for the bailout by the US of hundreds of its own speculators, notably Chase Manhattan and Goldman Sachs.

Clearly, Mexico in 1995 and much of the rest of the world in 1997–1998 were just the first of many such debacles to come. In a globalized economy, wired together by technologies capable of moving unimaginable funds instantaneously around the globe at the behest of speculators and immune to any ability to regulate or control this movement, we are in for more frequent catastrophes. Yet, this is a condition the world will not be able to tolerate for long. It makes banking services even more difficult and distant for local communities, small businesses and ordinary people. Worst of all, it puts the entire international economic apparatus into a most precarious situation. Global finance could tumble down quickly, like the house of cards it has become.

Ultimately, change must come in the form of a financial system not based on speculation, but a system that uses funds with geographic roots and some connection to goods and services that cater, as they once did, to the interests of local and regional economies. The examples of the Grameen Bank in Bangladesh and the South Shore Bank in Chicago, running directly counter to the trend, are informative, optimistic models. Only by such a change in direction can the financial community be remotely in service to ecological and social sustainability.

References

Crook, Clive (1992), 'Fear of Finance', *The Economist* (September 19)

Lewis, Michael (1989), *Liar's Poker: Rising Through the Wreckage on Wall Street*, New York: Norton

O'Brien, Richard (1992), *Global Financial Integration: The End of Geography*, New York: Council on Foreign Relations Press

Passell, Peter (1992), 'Fast Money', *New York Times Magazine* (18 October)

Sampson, Anthony (1989), *The Midas Touch: Money, People and Power from West to East*, London, BBC Books: Hodder and Stoughton

[27]

Journal of Human Development
Vol. 4, No. 2, July 2003

Carfax Publishing
Taylor & Francis Group

The Evolving Infectious Disease Threat: implications for national and global security

DAVID L. HEYMANN

David L. Heymann, M.D., is Executive Director of the Communicable Diseases Cluster at the World Health Organization

Abstract This paper discusses the ways in which the sharply increased danger of bio-terrorism has made infectious diseases a priority in defence and intelligence circles. Against this background, the author sets out a central principle of global public health security: a strengthened capacity to detect and contain naturally caused outbreaks is the only rational way to defend the world against the threat of a bio-terrorist attack. He then discusses the three trends that underscore this point: vulnerability of all nations to epidemics, the capacity of a disease such as AIDS to undermine government and society, and the way in which the determinants of national security have been re-defined in the post-Cold War era.

Key words: Infectious Disease, Epidemics, Microbials, Terrorism, HIV/AIDS, Governance, Human Security

Introduction

The deliberate use of anthrax to incite terror, which quickly followed the events of September 11 2001 in the US, changed the profile of the infectious disease threat in a dramatic and definitive way. Prior to these events, the emergence of new diseases — and, most especially, the devastation caused by AIDS — had sharpened concern about the infectious disease threat as a disruptive and destabilizing force, and given it space in national security debates. The reality of bio-terrorism immediately raised the infectious disease threat to the level of a high-priority security imperative worthy of attention in defence and intelligence circles. In so doing, it also focused attention on several features of the infectious disease situation that make outbreaks — whatever their cause — an especially ominous threat. As smallpox again became a disease of greatest concern, both politicians and the public began to comprehend problems long familiar to public health professionals. These have ranged from silent incubation periods that allow pathogens to cross borders undetected and undeterred, through the finite nature of vaccine manufacturing capacity, to the simple fact that outbreaks have a potential for international spread that transcends the defences of any single country.

ISSN 1464-9888 print/ISSN 1469-9516 online/03/020191-17 © 2003 United Nations Development Programme
DOI: 10.1080/1464988032000087541

The Evolving Infectious Disease Threat

undetected and become endemic. Such theoretical vulnerability has been amply demonstrated in practice.

New diseases, which are poorly understood, difficult to treat, and often highly lethal, are emerging at the unprecedented rate of one per year (Woolhouse and Dye, 2001). Ebola haemorrhagic fever in Africa, hantavirus pulmonary syndrome in the US, and Nipah virus encephalitis in South-East Asia are just a few examples. Older diseases have re-emerged in dramatic ways. Cholera, now in its seventh pandemic, returned to Latin American in 1991 after an absence of almost a century. Within a year, 400 000 cases and 4000 deaths were reported from 11 countries of the Americas (Tauxe *et al.*, 1995). Yellow fever is poised to cause massive urban epidemics in sub-Saharan Africa and Latin America. An urban outbreak in Côte d'Ivoire in 2001 necessitated the emergency immunization of 2.9 million persons in less than 2 weeks, depleting the international reserve of vaccine stocks (World Health Organization, 2003). Urban yellow fever promptly returned in 2002 in outbreaks in Senegal that again caused frantic efforts to secure sufficient emergency vaccine supplies (*Weekly Epidemiology Record*, 2002a). The 1998 epidemics of dengue and dengue haemorrhagic fever were un-precedented in geographical occurrence and numbers of cases, and the epidemics of 2002 have continued this alarming trend (World Health Organization, 2002a, 2003). A new strain of epidemic meningitis, W135, emerged in 2002, defying emergency preparedness in the form of stockpiled vaccines against conventional strains (*Weekly Epidemiology Record*, 2002b; World Health Organization, 2003). New and more severe strains of common food-borne pathogens, including *Escherichia coli* O157:H7, *Campylobacter*, and *Listeria monocytogens*, have made the profile of food-borne diseases distinctly more sinister (Tauxe, 1997; World Health Organization, 2001a, 2002b). The invariably fatal variant Creutzfeldt-Jakob disease, first recognized in 1996 and probably transmitted to humans through beef, has added considerably to this concern (World Health Organization, 2002c). Year by year, the highly unstable influenza virus is a reminder of the ever-present threat of another lethal influenza pandemic (Bonn, 1997).

Disease vectors are equally resilient and adaptable. Some anopheline mosquito species that transmit malaria have developed resistance to virtually all major classes of insecticides. Others, such as the tsetse fly that transmits African sleeping sickness, have returned to areas where they had previously been well controlled. The *Aedes aegypti* mosquito that transmits both yellow fever and dengue, originally confined to tropical jungles, has adapted to breed in urban litter. The diseases carried by vectors have likewise spread to new continents or returned to former homes. Rift Valley fever is now firmly established on the Arabian peninsula. West Nile virus, first introduced on the East coast of the US in 1999, has now been detected in 43 states across the US and in five provinces of Canada as well (Gubler, 2001; Molyneux, 2001; Centers for Disease Control and Prevention, 2002).

The threat posed by drug resistance is particularly ominous and universal. Health care in all countries is now compromised by the shrinking number of effective first-line antimicrobials and the need to resort to more costly, and often more hazardous, alternative drugs, when available. Fuelled by co-infection with HIV, the return of tuberculosis as a global menace has been accompanied by the emergence of multidrug-resistant forms costing up to 100 times more to treat (World Health Organization, 2003). Malaria may soon be resistant worldwide to all currently available first-line drugs (World Health Organization, 2003). Drug resistance to common bacterial infections is now so pervasive that it raises the spectre of a post-antibiotic era in which many life-saving treatments and routine surgical procedures could become too risky to perform (World Health Organization, 2001b).

These developments have eroded past confidence that high standards of living and access to powerful medicines could insulate domestic populations from infectious disease threats abroad. They have also restored the historical significance of infectious diseases as a disruptive force — this time cast in a modern setting characterized by close interdependence of nations and instantaneous communications (Heymann, 2001a). Within affected countries, the disruptive potential of outbreaks and epidemics is expressed in ways ranging from public panic and population displacement to the interruption of routine functions that occurs when containment requires the emergency immunization of populations numbering in the millions. Disruption can also be measured in economic terms. Outbreaks are always expensive to contain. Affected countries can experience heavy additional burdens in the form of lost trade and tourism — estimated at US$2 billion during the 1994 outbreak of plague in India (Cash and Narasimham, 2002). At the global level, some of the most telling efforts to measure economic consequences, in terms of international relations and foreign affairs, have centred on determining what the AIDS epidemic in sub-Saharan Africa means for the economies of wealthy nations. At one extreme, the high mortality caused by this disease and the particular age group it affects have been interpreted as the cost to industrialized countries of lost export markets (Kassalow, 2001). At the other extreme, the economic costs of AIDS to the international community have been expressed in terms of the price of drugs and services needed to rescue a continent (World Health Organization, 2001c). The human suffering caused by this disease defies calculation in any terms.

AIDS: a clear threat to national security

Of all diseases, AIDS provides the most dramatic and disturbing example of the capacity of a previously unknown pathogen to rapidly spread throughout the world, establish endemicity, and cause social and economic upheaval on a scale that threatens to destabilize a large geographical area. Although the disease has a global distribution, its impact is overwhelmingly concentrated in sub-Saharan Africa, where approximately 3.5 million new infections occurred in 2001. This brings the total number of people living with HIV/AIDS in sub-Saharan Africa to 28.5 million, accounting for 71% of the global total. In sub-Saharan Africa, an estimated 9% of all inhabitants between the ages of 15 and 49 carry the virus. In one country, HIV prevalence among pregnant women in urban areas now stands at 44.9%. The region as a whole is home to an estimated 11 million AIDS orphans (UNAIDS, 2002).

Prior to the events of September and October 2001, AIDS already provided a strong case for considering infectious diseases as a security issue. At the most obvious level, any agent with such high rates of mortality — whether infectious or otherwise — that directly threatens to kill a significant proportion of a state's population constitutes a direct threat to state security (Price-Smith, 2002). In this respect, few would argue against the proposition that AIDS is a direct security threat to countries in sub-Saharan Africa. Recent analyses by experts in international security and foreign affairs have defined the nature of this threat in more explicit terms (Eberstadt, 2002; Elbe, 2002; Ostergard, 2002). In Africa, AIDS poses an immediate threat to the organization of many different societies as well as to the security of political institutions, the capacity of military operations, and the performance of the police force (Ostergard, 2002). Evidence from several sources indicates that AIDS has already begun to diminish the operational efficiency of many of Africa's armed forces while also escalating the social costs of ongoing wars to new levels (Elbe, 2002). Other immediate effects on state capacity include the loss of high-level government officials, an overwhelming of the health care system, and an erosion of traditional systems of social support (Ostergard, 2002). Studies of the long-term security impact predict a significant decline in the economic performance of many countries due to absenteeism, the loss of skilled workers, reduced foreign investment, increasing government expenditure on health care, higher insurance costs, and a paucity of teachers to train the next generation of workers (Morrison, 2002; Ostergard, 2002). More, not less, state failure and insecurity is projected, and this is expected to translate into new forms of transnational security threats (Morrison, 2002).

Changing perceptions of security

Efforts to understand the security implications of AIDS have taken place within the context of a reconsideration of what constitutes a security threat in the post-Cold War era.

In its traditional meaning, 'security' has long been a strictly national pursuit aimed at defending territorial integrity and ensuring state survival. It is intrinsically self-centred, focused on shielding state citizens from external danger in an international system ruled by anarchy (Burchill, 1996). Traditional approaches to the defence of national security are military functions: protecting borders, fighting wars, and deterring aggressors (Center for Strategic and International Studies, 2000; Ban, 2001).

Two events have challenged these traditional views. First, the end of the Cold War meant an end to security issues polarized by the ideological conflict and geopolitical interests of the superpowers, and kept on edge by the nuclear arms race. As old threats subsided, more attention focused on threats arising from civil unrest, internal conflicts, mass migration of refugees, and localized wars between neighbouring countries, particularly when these

Critical Perspectives on Globalization

had the capacity to undermine state stability or contribute to state failure (Weiner, 1992; Kelley, 2000; Nichiporuk, 2000; Price-Smith, 2002). The absence of a bipolar power system magnified these threats considerably, as intervention to prop up a failing state of geopolitical strategic interest was no longer assured (Tickner, 1995; Cooper, 1996; Fidler, forthcoming). As a result, security issues became broader and more complex, and attention began to focus on ensuring the internal stability of states by addressing the root causes of unrest, conflict, and mass population movement rather than defending national borders against external aggressors (Holsti, 1996). In the wake of these changes, a number of factors — from environmental conditions to income, education, and health — were put forward as determinants of internal state stability and therefore of potential relevance to the evolving security debate (Ostergard, 2002).

In a second event, the forces of globalization demonstrated the porous nature of national borders and eroded traditional notions of state sovereignty. In a closely interconnected and interdependent world, the repercussions of adverse events abroad easily cross borders to intrude on state affairs in ways that cannot be averted through traditional military defences (Center for Strategic and International Studies, 2000). For example, in the world's tightly inter-related financial system, a crisis in a distant economy can rapidly spread to affect others (Homer-Dixon, 2001). Many other transnational threats — whether arising from environmental pollution or tobacco advertising — were recognized as having an effect on internal affairs that went beyond the control of strictly national actions. Emerging and epidemic-prone diseases qualified as a transnational threat for obvious reasons: they easily cross borders in ways that defy traditional defences and cannot be deterred by any state acting alone (Center for Strategic and International Studies, 2000). In the broadened debate, their disruptive potential gave them added weight as a possible security concern, although this potential differs considerably between industrialized and developing countries (Kelley, 2000; National Intelligence Council, 2000).

In industrialized countries, global pandemics such as influenza, where supplies of vaccines and antivirals are clearly insufficient, have the capacity to destabilize populations, and the panic that they incite could cause great social disruption. In developing countries, where economies are fragile and infrastructures weak, outbreaks and epidemics are far more directly disruptive. In these countries, the destabilizing effect of high-mortality endemic diseases, including malaria and tuberculosis as well as AIDS, is amplified by emerging and epidemic-prone diseases, as they disrupt routine control programmes and health services, often for extended periods, due to the extraordinary resources and logistics required for their control (Heymann and Rodier, 2001). For example, outbreaks of epidemic meningitis, which regularly occur in the African 'meningitis belt', disrupt normal social functions and bring routine health services to the brink of a standstill as containment depends on the emergency vaccination of all populations at risk (World Health Organization, 2003). The resurgence of African sleeping sickness, which is also a disease of livestock, has disrupted productive

The Evolving Infectious Disease Threat

patterns of land use and jeopardized food security in remote rural areas (World Health Organization, 2003). Recent outbreaks of dengue in Latin America required the assistance of military forces, sometimes from neighbouring countries, for their containment. Outbreaks of new or unusual diseases can cause public panic to a degree that calls into question government's capacity to protect its population. In addition, the dramatic interruption of trade, travel, and tourism that can follow news of an outbreak places a further economic burden on impoverished countries with little capacity to absorb such shocks (Heymann and Rodier, 2001).

High priority on the security agenda?

Several recent events suggest that emerging and epidemic-prone diseases are being taken seriously as a threat to national and global security. In an unprecedented step, a US government-supported study concluded in 1995 that emerging and re-emerging infectious diseases, especially AIDS, constituted a national security threat and foreign policy challenge (CISET, 1995). In 1996, the US Department of Defense established the Global Emerging Infections Surveillance and Response System, based on a network of domestic and overseas military laboratories, as an explicit acknowledgement that emerging diseases can threaten military personnel and their families, can reduce medical readiness, and present a risk to US national security (DoD-GEIS, 2003). The threat posed by microbial agents to the security of the US was further acknowledged in 2000 by an equally unprecedented report from the US Central Intelligence Agency's National Intelligence Council (2000). Citing the 'staggering' and 'destabilizing' number of deaths caused by AIDS in sub-Saharan Africa, the report documented specific consequences in the form of diminished gross domestic product, reduced life expectancy, weakened military capacity, social fragmentation, and political destabilization. The report also addressed the growing threat posed by infectious diseases in general, and drew attention to the contributing roles of rapid urban growth, environmental degradation, and cross-border population movements (National Intelligence Agency, 2000). A further acknowledgement that microbial 'foes' could threaten international peace and security came in 2000 when the UN Security Council, in its first consideration of a health issue, concluded that the AIDS pandemic had moved beyond a health crisis to become a threat to global security, the viability of states, and economic development (UN Security Council, 2000).

Although the creation in January 2002 of the Global Fund to Fight AIDS, Tuberculosis and Malaria gives cause for hope, the magnitude of the response falls far short of what is needed to rescue Africa and other areas from a humanitarian crisis of historic proportions (World Health Organization, 2001c; Feachem, 2003). In many ways Africa has become increasingly marginalized as a player in global economics and politics, with the possible exception of South Africa (Eberstadt, 2002). At the same time, the reality of the industrialized country response to Africa's AIDS crisis brings into question the extent to which AIDS and other emerging diseases — even if formally

D. L. Heymann

acknowledged to be a security threat — rank as an absolute priority in national security agendas.

The events of September and October 2001 changed this situation dramatically, as the prospect of bio-terrorism brought infectious disease agents into direct intersection with national security imperatives. It has also brought into sharp focus many of the difficult problems faced by public health on a daily basis. For example, the anthrax incident demonstrated the difficulty of quickly identifying an unfamiliar disease. This difficulty arises with almost all outbreaks, particularly in the developing world, that do not follow a predictable geographical or seasonal pattern. It also arises with the thousands of cases of imported malaria and other tropical diseases that occur each year in temperate countries having large international airports, which are frequently misdiagnosed. It also occurred following the unexpected arrival of West Nile virus in the Western hemisphere, where the disease was initially misdiagnosed as St Louis encephalitis and a full 3 weeks lapsed before the causative agent was correctly identified. The rapid determination of whether a disease might be deliberately caused is likewise notoriously difficult. Plague in India, dengue in Cuba, hantavirus in New Mexico, and West Nile virus in New York are just some examples of diseases initially considered to have a deliberate origin in the recent past.

Also in connection with the anthrax incident, the question of whether a country experiencing a public health emergency has the right to over-ride the patent of a vital drug, such as ciprofloxacin hydrochloride, has been vigorously debated, primarily within the context of the AIDS humanitarian crisis, since shortly after the Agreement on Trade-Related Aspects of International Property Rights was signed in 1994. Concerning the particular problems posed by the sudden demand for smallpox vaccine, the difficulty of quickly building an adequate vaccine reserve as preventive defence is experienced on a daily basis in efforts to contain outbreaks of epidemic meningitis and urban yellow fever, where the finite nature of vaccine manufacturing capacity frequently jeopardizes emergency containment operations (World Health Organization, 2003). In the case of yellow fever, the situation is a particularly disturbing example of the impact of poverty. Because of the expense, few high-risk countries practice routine childhood immunization against yellow fever, although this option is ten times more cost-effective and prevents more cases and deaths than emergency immunization campaigns (World Health Organization, 2003). Vaccine shortages have also, on occasion, threatened the effectiveness of National Immunization Days during the end stage of the drive to eradicate poliomyelitis. Nor is smallpox the only severe infectious disease for which no effective treatment exists. Dengue, yellow fever, Japanese encephalitis, rabies, and the Ebola, Marburg and Crimean-Congo haemorrhagic fevers are just some of the diseases of major public health importance that lack effective treatments. In this sense, some of the terror incited by the prospect of a bio-terrorist attack in industrialized countries is a constant feature of life in the many developing countries prone to outbreaks of these diseases.

As a final example, the question of how the world can best defend itself

---

The Evolving Infectious Disease Threat

---

against the threat of a bio-terrorist attack has also been addressed in a series of practical actions that date back to at least 1997 (World Health Organization, 2002d). On September 5 2001, the US Senate Committee on Foreign Relations, at a hearing on 'The threat of bio-terrorism and the spread of infectious diseases', heard testimony explaining how systems set up to detect and contain naturally caused outbreaks provide global defence against the threat posed by bio-terrorism (Heymann, 2001b).

'Dual use' defence

Efforts to prevent the international spread of infectious diseases have a long history. In the fourteenth century, ships that were potential carriers of plague-infected rats were forcibly quarantined in the harbour of the city-state of Venice to prevent importation of plague (Howard-Jones, 1975). A series of international health agreements between the newly industrialized countries, elaborated during the nineteenth century, culminated in the adoption of the International Health Regulations in 1969 (World Health Organization, 2001d). The regulations are designed to maximize security against the international spread of infectious diseases while ensuring minimum impact on trade and travel. Administered by the World Health Organization (WHO), these are the only international regulations that require reporting of infectious diseases. At the same time, they provide norms and standards for airports and seaports designed to prevent the spread from public conveyances of rodents or insects that may be carrying infectious diseases, and describe best practices to be used to control the spread of these diseases once they have occurred.

The regulations are currently being revised to serve as an up-to-date framework for global surveillance and response in the twenty-first century. To support the revision process, the World Health Assembly has endorsed a series of resolutions aimed at ensuring a global surveillance and response system, operating in real time and under the framework of the International Health Regulations, that facilitates rapid disease detection and rational responses (World Health Organization, 1983, 1995a, 1995b, 1998). The WHO is also now authorized by the Health Assembly to utilize information sources other than official notifications submitted by governments (World Health Organization, 2001d).

The WHO has long argued that the most important defence against the infectious disease threat in all its forms is good intelligence and a rapid response. Intelligence is gleaned through highly sensitive global surveillance systems that keep the world alert to changes in the infectious disease situation. Routine surveillance systems for naturally occurring outbreaks enhance the capacity to detect and investigate those that may be deliberately caused, as the initial epidemiological and laboratory response techniques are the same. Adequate background data on the natural behaviour of known pathogens provide the epidemiological intelligence needed to recognize an unusual event and to determine whether suspicions of a deliberate cause should be investigated (Heymann and Rodier, 2001, World Health Organization, 2001e, 2002d). A global surveillance system, operating in real time, facilitates rapid and rational responses. It ensures that the necessary laboratory and epidemiological skills are kept sharp, since the call-out for natural outbreaks at the global level is almost daily. It provides a mechanism for sharing expertise, facilities, and staff. The performance of routine systems in detecting and containing naturally occurring outbreaks provides an indication of how well they would perform when coping with a deliberately caused outbreak, although the scale of a deliberately caused outbreak would probably be much larger. Strong public health systems are vital, as public health plays the initial and leading role in the response to a deliberately caused outbreak (Knobler *et al.*, 2002).

The mechanisms for global surveillance and response are in place and operational, on a daily basis, in the Global Outbreak Alert and Response Network (Heymann and Rodier, 2001). Under development since 1997, this overarching network interlinks electronically, in real time, 110 existing laboratory and disease reporting networks. Together, these networks possess much of the data, expertise, and skills needed to keep the international community constantly alert and ready to respond.

The network, which was formalized in April 2000, is supported by several new mechanisms and a customized artificial intelligence engine for real-time gathering of disease information. This tool, the Global Public Health Intelligence Network (GPHIN, 2002), maintained by Health Canada, heightens vigilance by continuously and systematically crawling websites, news wires, local online newspapers, public health e-mail services, and electronic discussion groups for rumours of outbreaks. In this way, the network is able to scan the world for informal news that gives cause for suspecting an unusual event. Apart from its comprehensive and systematic search capacity, the GPHIN has brought tremendous gains in time over traditional systems in which an alert is sounded only after case reports at the local level progressively filter to the national level and are then notified to the WHO. The network currently picks up — in real time — more than 40% of the outbreaks subsequently verified by the WHO. However, outbreaks of some diseases, including Ebola haemorrhagic fever, frequently occur in very remote rural areas that fall outside the reach of electronic communications, thus necessitating continued reliance on other sources, including reports from countries.

Additional sources of information linked together in the network include government and university centres, ministries of health, academic institutions, other United Nations agencies, networks of overseas military laboratories, and non-governmental organizations having a strong presence in epidemic-prone countries. Information from all these sources is assessed and verified on a daily basis. 'Suspected accidental or deliberate release' is one of six criteria used to determine whether an outbreak is of international concern, and is routinely considered (Heymann and Rodier, 2001).

Once international assistance is needed, as agreed upon in confidential pro-active consultation with the affected country and with experts in the network, electronic communications are used to coordinate prompt assistance. To this end, global databases of professionals with expertise in specific

The Evolving Infectious Disease Threat

diseases or epidemiological techniques are maintained, together with non-governmental organizations present in countries and in a position to reach remote areas. Such mechanisms, which are further supported by a network of specialized national laboratories and institutes located throughout the world, help make the maximum use of expertise and resources — assets that are traditionally scarce for public health. Surge capacity, insufficient vaccine supplies, and expensive drugs are issues that must be dealt with on a regular basis in order to keep the world ready to respond — issues similar to those needed for preparedness for bio-terrorism. Chronic shortages of vaccines for epidemic meningitis and yellow fever are being addressed through international collaborative mechanisms, also involving manufacturers, that stockpile vaccine supplies and pre-position them in countries at greatest risk of epidemics. The highly unstable influenza virus is kept under close surveillance by a WHO network of 110 institutes and laboratories in 83 countries. The network determines the antigenic composition of each season's influenza vaccine and keeps close watch over conditions conducive to a pandemic.

From July 1998 to August 2001, the network verified 578 outbreaks in 132 countries, indicating the system's broad geographical coverage. The most frequently reported outbreaks were of cholera, meningitis, haemorrhagic fever, anthrax, and viral encephalitis. During this same period, the network launched effective international cooperative containment activities in many developing countries — Afghanistan, Bangladesh, Burkina Faso, Côte d'Ivoire, Egypt, Ethiopia, Kosovo, Sierra Leone, Sudan, Uganda, and Yemen, to name a few (Heymann and Rodier, 2001).

The work of co-ordinating large-scale international assistance, which involves many agencies from many nations, is facilitated by operational protocols that set out standardized procedures for the alert and verification process, communications, co-ordination of the response, emergency evacuation, research, monitoring, ownership of data and samples, and relations with the media. By setting out a chain of command and bringing order to the containment response, such protocols help protect against the very real risk that samples of a lethal pathogen might be collected for later provision to a terrorist group.

A rational response to a shared threat

The source of the evolving infectious disease threat is a microscopic adversary that changes and adapts with great speed and has the advantages of surprise on its side. The possibility that biological agents might be deliberately used to cause harm is yet another divergence of the infectious disease threat. Its capacity to incite terror builds on the fears aroused by the resurgence of naturally caused outbreaks and epidemics. Its significance as a security threat is readily appreciated in light of the well-documented ability of naturally caused infectious diseases to invade, surprise, and disrupt. The issues that require attention and resources — vaccine production, stockpiling of antibiotics, and protective clothing — are vital.

201

D. L. Heymann

The dramatic change in the profile of infectious diseases, which followed the deliberate use of anthrax, has focused high-level attention on features of the infectious disease situation that make all outbreaks especially ominous events, often with international as well as local repercussions. The challenge is to manage this new threat in ways that do not compromise the response to natural outbreaks and epidemics, but rather strengthen the public health infrastructure, locally and globally, for managing both threats. Increasing vaccine manufacturing capacity to counter the bio-terrorism threat should also work in the long term to increase the supply of vaccines needed to control naturally occurring infectious diseases.

In the US, the initial response to the anthrax incident concentrated almost exclusively on the strengthening of domestic public health capacity, with very little attention given to the international dimensions of either the threat itself or the measures needed to ensure protection (Knobler *et al.*, 2002). More recent developments indicate a growing awareness of the inadequacy of a strictly national response. They also indicate a growing willingness to view improved global capacity to detect and contain naturally caused outbreaks as the most rational — and the most reliably protective — way to defend nations, individually and collectively, against the threat of a bio-terrorist attack (Chyba, 2002).

In November 2001, a meeting of G7 + Mexico health ministers culminated in agreement on the *Ottawa Plan for Improving Health Security* (G7 Health Ministers, 2001). The plan acknowledged bio-terrorism as an international issue requiring international collaboration, and launched a series of collective efforts aimed at improving international preparedness and capacity to respond. Additional emergency preparedness and response plans and exercises have moved forward quickly. By the time of its third meeting, held in Mexico in December 2002, the concerns of the group had expanded to include plans for increasing the WHO emergency reserve of smallpox vaccine to manage cases of an outbreak occurring in any country lacking the resources to purchase and stockpile vaccine in advance. The meeting established a working group to address problems surrounding influenza and other epidemic-prone diseases, including insufficient vaccine supplies and preparedness planning for the management of massive numbers of patients. The meeting also launched a global collaborative network of high-security laboratories as a strategy for improving global capacity to rapidly and accurately diagnose diseases "whether naturally or intentionally occurring".

In another significant development, the proposed US *Global Pathogen Surveillance Act 2002* acknowledged the universal nature of the infectious disease threat and frankly admitted that "domestic surveillance and monitoring, while absolutely essential, are not sufficient" to combat bio-terrorism or ensure adequate domestic preparedness. The Act singled out the role played by the Global Outbreak Alert and Response Network, and further noted the inability of developing countries "to devote the necessary resources to build and maintain public health infrastructures", thus underscoring the need for foreign assistance. Finally, the Act treated natural and intentionally caused

The Evolving Infectious Disease Threat

outbreaks as closely related threats and recognized that strengthened capacity to monitor, detect, and respond to infectious disease outbreaks would offer dual dividends in the form of better protection against both threats (US Senate, 2002).

The acceptance of the infectious disease threat as a high-level security imperative has been sudden, ushered in by an equally sudden and previously unthinkable event. Within a year, the repercussions of the anthrax incident have led to an unprecedented appreciation of problems that have long hindered efforts to improve the detection and containment of naturally occurring outbreaks. Although public health has struggled — with little success — for decades to have these problems acknowledged, it can take some satisfaction from the fact that its experiences and advice are now guiding the way forward in a joint public health and security policy endeavour. Recent developments provide encouraging evidence that political leaders have a better understanding of the issues facing public health and — above all — appreciate both the need to strengthen public health infrastructures and the universal benefits of doing so. Equally important is the understanding that strong national and international public health must be considered as elements of national security, and that increased funding for strengthening national and international public health must come from government sectors that go beyond health to include national security, defence, and international development aid. Only then can the world begin to move towards a degree of security that sees the volatile infectious disease threat matched by a stable, alert, and universal system of defence. The lasting benefits for the daily work of outbreak detection and control could be enormous for both industrialized and developing countries.

Infectious diseases and human security

This paper has largely focused on the threat to global health security posed by emerging and epidemic-prone diseases. It is also pointed out that other infectious diseases, such as AIDS, impose a constant and unacceptable burden on individuals and communities, and are a recognized impediment to the achievement of human health security. According to the latest WHO estimates, infectious diseases caused 14.7 million deaths in 2001, accounting for 26% of total global mortality. Most of these deaths could have been prevented through existing drugs and vaccines and simple access to food and drinking water free of faecal contamination (World Health Organization, 2003).

Three diseases — AIDS, tuberculosis, and malaria — continue to account for a large share (39%) of deaths attributed to infectious diseases. Total deaths from these three diseases amounted to 5.6 million in 2001. When deaths from diarrhoeal disease and respiratory infections (5.8 million) are added, these five diseases alone are responsible for approximately 78% of the total infectious disease burden.

Perhaps the most powerful acknowledgement that these diseases compromise human security and impede development is inclusion of the control

203

D. L. Heymann

of HIV/AIDS, malaria, and other diseases as one of the eight time-bound and measurable Millennium Development Goals (United Nations, 2000). These goals, along with the report in December 2001 of the Commission on Macroeconomics and Health, and the establishment in January 2002 of the Global Fund to Fight AIDS, Tuberculosis and Malaria, give health a higher place on the global development agenda and underscore its fundamental importance to human health security (World Health Organization, 2001c; Global Fund to Fight AIDS, Tuberculosis and Malaria, 2003).

Other signs indicate the willingness of the international community to take unprecedented steps to combat infectious diseases, especially those that disproportionately affect poor populations in remote areas of the developing world — the so-called 'neglected diseases'. In just the past few years, partnerships, often involving open-ended donations of high-quality drugs and strongly supported on the ground by non-governmental organizations, have formed to eliminate or control, by a specified date, seven severely disabling diseases of the poor: African sleeping sickness, Chagas disease, guinea worm disease, leprosy, lymphatic filariasis, onchocerciasis, and trachoma. Progress has been strong and results, especially when elimination or eradication targets are met, can be permanent. For lymphatic filariasis, which seriously disables an estimated 40 million people in 80 countries, the annual number of people treated has rapidly risen from 2.9 million (in 12 countries) in 2000, to 26 million (in 22 countries) in 2001, to 65 million (in 34 countries) in 2002.

Growing concern over the issue of global health security, the main focus of this paper, has resulted in heightened vigilance, better disease intelligence, and strengthened capacity to respond when outbreaks occur. Populations in all countries will benefit from this strengthening of basic public health functions. While this trend can be seen as anchored in the enlightened self-interest of nations, the commitment and energy now focused on other diseases that are endemic in the developing world and concentrated among the poor are good evidence that humanitarian concerns are likewise shaping the response to the infectious disease threat in all its dimensions.

References

Ban, J. (2001) *Health, Security, and US Global Leadership*, CBACI Health and Security Series, Special Report 2, Chemical and Biological Arms Control Institute, Washington, DC.

Bonn, D. (1997) 'Spared an Influenza Pandemic for Another Year?', *Lancet*, 349, p. 36.

Burchill, S. (1996) 'Realism and Neo-Realism', in S. Burchill and A. Linklater (Eds), *Theories of international relations*, Macmillan, London.

Cash, R.A. and Narasimham, V. (2002) 'Impediments to Global Surveillance of Infectious Diseases: Consequences of Open Reporting in a Global Economy', *Bulletin of the World Health Organization*, 78, pp. 1353–1367.

Center for Strategic and International Studies (2000) *Contagion and Conflict: Health as a Global Security Challenge*, a report of the Chemical and Biological Arms Control Institute and the CSIS International Security Program, Center for Strategic and International Studies, Washington, DC.

Centers for Disease Control and Prevention (2002) *West Nile Virus Update: Current Case Count* [www.cdc.gov/od/oc/media/wncount.htm].

The Evolving Infectious Disease Threat

Chyba, C.F. (2002) 'Toward Biological Security', *Foreign Affairs*, 81, pp. 122–136.

CISET (1995) *US National Science and Technology Council Committee on International Science, Engineering, and Technology (CISET) Working Group on Emerging and Re-emerging Infectious Diseases: Infectious diseases—A Global Health Threat*, CISET, Washington, DC.

Cooper, R. (1996) *The Post-Modern State and the World Order*, Demos, Los Angeles.

DoD-GEIS (2003) US Department of Defense Global Emerging Infections Surveillance and Response System [http://www.geis.ha.osd.mil/aboutGEIS.asp].

Eberstadt, N. (2002) 'The Future of AIDS: Grim Toll in India, China, and Russia', *Foreign Affairs*, 81, pp. 22–45.

Elbe, S. (2002) 'HIV/AIDS and the Changing Landscape of War in Africa', *International Security*, 27, pp. 1150–1177.

Feachem, R.G.A. (2003) 'AIDS hasn't Peaked Yet—and that's not the worst of it', *Washington Post*, 12 January.

Fidler, D.P. (forthcoming) 'Public Health and National Security in the Global Age: Infectious Diseases, Bioterrorism, and *Realpolitik*', *George Washington International Law Review*, 27 (in press).

G7 Health Ministers (2001) *Ottawa Plan for Improving Health Security*, statement of G7 Health Ministers' Meeting, 7 November, Ottawa [www.g7.utoronto.ca/g7/health/ottawa2001.html].

Global Fund to Fight AIDS, Tuberculosis and Malaria (xxxx) [http://www.globalfundatm.org/].

Gubler, D.J. (2001) 'Human Arbovirus Infections Worldwide', *Annals of the New York Academy of Sciences*, 951, pp. 13–24.

Health Canada (2002) *How Canadian initiatives are changing the face of health care*, Ottawa: Health Canada, 2002. http://www.hc-sc.gc.ca/ohih-bsi/pubs/succ/national_e.html

Heymann, D.L. (2001a) 'The fall and Rise of Infectious Diseases', *Georgetown Journal of International Affairs*, 11, pp. 7–14.

Heymann, D.L. (2001b) 'Strengthening Global Preparedness for Defense Against Infectious Disease Threats', statement for the Committee on Foreign Relations, United States Senate, *Hearing on the Threat of Bioterrorism and the Spread of Infectious Diseases*, 5 September [http://www.who.int/emc/pdfs/Senate—hearing.pdf].

Heymann, D.L. and Rodier, G.R. (2001) 'Hot Spots in a Wired World', *Lancet Infectious Diseases*, 1, pp. 345–353.

Holsti, K.J. (1996) *The State, War, and the State of War*, Cambridge University Press, Cambridge.

Homer-Dixon, T. (2001) 'Now Comes the Real Danger', *Toronto Globe and Mail*, 12 September.

Howard-Jones, N. (1975) *The Scientific background of the International Sanitary Conferences, 1851–1938*, World Health Organization, 2001d.

Kassalow, J.S. (2001) *Why Health is Important to US Foreign Policy*, Council on Foreign Relations and Milbank Memorial Fund, New York.

Kelley, P.W. (2000) 'Transnational Contagion and Global Security', *Military Review*, May–June, pp. 59–64.

Knobler, S.L., Mahmoud, A.A.F. and Pray, L.A. (Eds) (2002) *Biological Threats and Terrorism. Assessing the Science and Response Capabilities*, National Academy Press, Washington, DC.

Lederberg, J., Shope, R.E. and Oaks, S.C., Jr. (Eds) (1992) *Emerging Infections: Microbial Threats to Health in the United States*, National Academy Press, Washington, DC.

Molyneux, D.H. (2001) 'Vector-Borne Infections in the Tropics and Health Policy Issues in the Twenty-First Century', *Transactions of the Royal Society for Tropical Medicines and Hygiene*, 95, pp. 235–238.

Morrison, J.S. (2001) 'The African Pandemic hits Washington', *Washington Quarterly*, 24, pp. 197–209.

National Intelligence Council (2000) *The Global Infectious Disease Threat and its Implications for the United States* [www.cia.gov/cia/publications/nie/report/nie99-17d.html]:

Nichiporuk, B. (2000) *The Security Dynamics of Demographic Factors*, RAND, Santa Monica, CA.

D. L. Heymann

Ostergard, R.L., Jr. (2002) 'Politics in the Hot Zone: AIDS and National Security in Africa', *Third World Quarterly*, 23, pp. 333–350.

Price-Smith, A.T. (2002) *Pretoria's shadow: The HIV/AIDS Pandemic and National Security in South Africa*, CBACI Health and Security Series, Special Report 4, Chemical and Biological Arms Control Institute, Washington, DC.

Rodier, G.R., Ryan, M.J. and Heymann, D.L. (2000) 'Global Epidemiology of Infectious Diseases', in G.T. Strickland (Ed.), *Hunter's Tropical Medicine and Emerging Infectious Diseases*, 8th edition, WB Saunders Company, Philadelphia, PA.

Tauxe, R.V. (1997) 'Emerging Foodborne Diseases: An Evolving Public Health Challenge', *Emerging Infectious Diseases*, 3, pp. 425–434.

Tauxe, R.V., Mintz, E.D. and Quick, R.E. (1995) 'Epidemic Cholera in the New World: Translating Field Epidemiology into New Prevention Strategies', *Emerging Infectious Diseases*, 1, pp. 141–146.

Tickner, J.A. (1995) 'Re-Visioning Security', in K. Booth and S. Smith (Eds), *International Relations Theory Today*, Pennsylvania State University Press, University Park, PA.

UNAIDS (2002) *Report on the Global HIV/AIDS Epidemic*, July, UNAIDS, Geneva.

United Nations (2000) *United Nations Millennium Development Goals*, United Nations, New York [http://www.un.org/millenniumgoals/].

UN Security Council (2000) *Session on HIV/AIDS in Africa*, 10 January.

US Senate (2002) *Global Pathogen Surveillance Act of 2002* [http://thomas.loc.gov/cgi-bin/query/F?c107:5:./temp/~c1076twsgK:e369].

Weekly Epidemiology Record (2002a) 'Yellow Fever, Senegal (Update)', *Weekly Epidemiology Record*, 77, pp. 373–374.

Weekly Epidemiology Record (2002b) 'Urgent Call for Action on Meningitis in Africa—Vaccine Price and Shortage are Major Obstacles', *Weekly Epidemiology Record*, 77, pp. 330–331.

Weiner, M. (1992) 'Security, Stability and International Migration', *International Security*, 17, pp. 91–126.

Woolhouse, M.E.J. and Dye, C. (Eds) (2001) 'Population biology of Emerging and Re-Emerging Pathogens', *Philosophical Transactions of the Royal Society for Biological Sciences*, 356, pp. 981–982.

World Health Organization (1983) *International Health Regulations (1969)*, World Health Organization, Geneva.

World Health Organization (1998) *Revision of the International Health Regulations: Progress Report*, Report by the Director General, World Health Organization, Geneva (World Health Assembly document A51/8).

World Health Organization (1995a) *Revision and Updating of the International Health Regulations*, World Health Organization, Geneva (World Health Assembly resolution WHA48.7).

World Health Organization (1995b) *Communicable Disease Prevention and Control: New, Emerging, and Re-Emerging Infectious Diseases*, World Health Organization, Geneva (World Health Assembly resolution WHA48.13).

World Health Organization (2001a) *The Increasing Incidence of Human Campylobacteriosis*, report and proceedings of a WHO consultation of experts, World Health Organization, Geneva (document number WHO/CDS/CSR/APH 2001.7).

World Health Organization (2001b) *WHO Global Strategy for Containment of Antimicrobial Resistance*, World Health Organization, Geneva (document number WHO/CDS/CSR/DRS/2001.2).

World Health Organization (2001c) *Macroeconomics and Health: Investing in Health for Economic Development*, report of the Commission on Macroeconomics and Health by J.D. Sachs (Chairman), World Health Organization, Geneva.

World Health Organization (2001d) *Global Health Security: Epidemic Alert and Response*, World Health Organization, Geneva (World Health Assembly resolution WHA54.14).

World Health Organization (2001e) *Public Health Response to Biological and Chemical Weapons*, World Health Organization, Geneva [www.who.int/emc/book_2nd_edition.htm].

World Health Organization (2002a) *Dengue Prevention and Control*, report by the Secretariat, World Health Organization, Geneva (World Health Assembly document A55/19).

The Evolving Infectious Disease Threat

World Health Organization (2002b) *Emerging Foodborne Diseases*. WHO Fact Sheet 124. World Health Organization, Geneva.

World Health Organization (2002c) *Understanding the BSE Threat*. World Health Organization, Geneva (document number WHO/CDS/CSR/EPH/2002.6).

World Health Organization (2002d) *Preparedness for the Deliberate Use of Biological Agents: A Rational Approach to the Unthinkable*, World Health Organization. Geneva (document number WHO/CDS/CSR/EPH/2002.16).

World Health Organization (2003) *Global Defence Against the Infectious Disease Threat*. World Health Organization, Geneva.

[28]

Democracy & Nature, Vol. 8, No. 2, 2002

Carfax Publishing
Taylor & Francis Group

The Global 'War' of the Transnational Elite

TAKIS FOTOPOULOS

ABSTRACT The aim of this article is to show that the so-called 'war' against terrorism that was launched by the transnational elite in the aftermath of the events of 11 September, like the previous 'wars' of the transnational elite (Iraq, Yugoslavia), aims at securing the stability of the New World Order (NWO) which is founded on capitalist neoliberal globalisation and representative 'democracy' by crushing any perceived threats against it. However, this is also a new type of war. Unlike the previous 'wars', this is a global and permanent war—a global war, because its targets are not only specific 'rogue' regimes, which are not fully integrated in the NWO or simply do not 'toe the line', but any kind of regime or social group and movement that resists the NWO: from the Palestinian up to the anti-globalisation movements; and permanent war, because it is bound to continue for as long as the NWO and the systemic and state violence associated with it, to protect the present huge asymmetry of power between and within nations (which give rise to counter-violence), are perpetuated.

The first task in an effort to interpret the causes and the significance of the 11 September events is to delineate the meaning of political violence, a form of which is terrorism[1] and to discuss the relationship between terrorism, systemic violence and democracy—the object of the first section. However, the attacks, which functioned as the catalyst for the present so-called 'war' on terrorism (in fact, simply a military suppression of technologically much inferior opponents, as was also the case with the previous 'wars' of the transnational elite) become incomprehensible unless we examine their historical and structural background, something that brings us to an examination of the contours of the New World Order (NWO)—and this is done in the second section. The third section will discuss the events of 11 September and compare and contrast the present war with the previous wars of the transnational elite. The penultimate section examines the aims of this new type of war and its phases up to now, as well as the possible phases of it in the future. Finally, the concluding section discusses the crucial issue of whether there is any way out of the present cycle of violence, which, as one can certainly expect—after the bloody first two phases (Afghanistan, Palestine)—may quite possibly become even bloodier in the future.

---

1. The term terrorism is used here in a technical sense with no moral strings attached to it.

ISSN 1085-5661 print; 1469-3720 online/02/02/0201-40 © 2002 Democracy & Nature
DOI: 10.1080/10855660220148589

Takis Fotopoulos

1. Terrorism, systemic violence and democracy

Systemic violence, counter-violence and terrorism

The attacks of 11 September were presented by the transnational elite-controlled mass media, as well as by the intellectuals who function as the apologists of the NWO, as the act of fanatic fundamentalists who envy the wealth and democratic organisation of the West, if not as pure 'nihilism', that is, as part of the eternal battle of Good and Evil in a dualistic universe fueled by hatred and envy, and by religious/ideological fundamentalism. To my mind, a meaningful discussion of the crucial issues that arose out of these events which, according to the propaganda machine of the transnational elite, were the cause of the 'war against terrorism' that it launched in their aftermath, should involve an examination of the meaning and causes of *political violence* (i.e. the use of violence for political aims) in all its forms: wars, systemic violence, state repression and state terrorism on the one hand and counter-violence and popular terrorism on the other.

As a British analyst pointed out in the aftermath of the September events, 'the tendency in recent years, encouraged by the scale of last month's atrocity in New York, has been to define terrorism increasingly in terms of methods and tactics—particularly the targeting of civilians—rather than the status of those who carry it out'.[2] This is an approach which, as the same analyst stresses, would classify historical liberation movements, like the ANC and the Algerian FLN that attacked civilian targets, as 'terrorist'—an approach which unfortunately has been adopted today by many in the Left, even self-declared libertarians. All this, despite the fact that the concept of modern terrorism derives from the French revolution, where terrorism was only state terrorism.

On the other hand, a useful definition of terrorism that takes into account these crucial considerations is the one given by Johan Galtung, who, starting with Clausewitz's classical definition of war as 'the continuation of politics by other means', defines in a similar way terrorism as 'the continuation of violence by other means'.[3] This definition is particularly helpful because it explicitly takes into account the fact that violence for political aims, which either originates in a socio-economic system and its political expression, the state, or in opposing forces 'from below', is always a cycle and is incomprehensible unless seen as such. Galtung stresses in particular the significance of what he calls *structural violence* (I would better call it *systemic violence* to emphasise its systemic character), i.e. the institutionalisation of highly asymmetric situations, which leads to state repression or even state terrorism on the one hand and its counterparts guerrilla warfare and popular terrorism on the other. The institutionalisation of asymmetric situations, i.e. systemic violence, may refer to:

- the economic level, where the built-in control of economic resources by a minority, which is institutionalised in a market economy system, leads to unemployment, poverty and insecurity for vast parts of the population;

2. Seumas Milne, 'Terror and Tyranny', *The Guardian*, 25 October 2001.
3. Johan Galtung, 'On the Causes of Terrorism and their Removal', *IFDA Dossier 66*, July-August 1988, pp. 29–42

The Global 'War' of the Transnational Elite

- the political level, where the institutionalisation of the control of the political process by a minority in a representative 'democracy' leads the vast majority of the population to political alienation and apathy; or
- the social and cultural levels, where the control of social and cultural institutions by parts of the population leads to various forms of discrimination against the other parts.

All these phenomena, i.e. unemployment, poverty, insecurity, political alienation and apathy, as well as various forms of discrimination against parts of the population on the basis of gender, race, identity, etc., are simply forms of systemic or structural violence, as a result of the institutionalisation of concentration of power in all its forms, that is, the institutionalisation of political, economic and social inequality. It is therefore clear that the ultimate cause of systemic violence is the non-democratic organisation of society, in other words its organisation on the basis of institutions which, instead of aiming to secure the equal distribution of power in all its forms among all citizens, aims at reproducing the pattern of asymmetry of power that has historically been established by privileged social groups.

The privileged social groups in the last two centuries or so, i.e. during the periods of liberal and statist modernity,[4] have established their power mainly through their control of the state machines. However, in the last quarter of a century or so, i.e. during the present era of neoliberal modernity, this is increasingly being achieved through their control of the international institutions established by the transnational elite, as we shall see in the next section. Still, in both cases, it is the concentration of power at the hands of various elites that leads to systemic violence and counter-violence. *Counter-violence* against systemic violence may be undertaken by social groups collectively, or by individuals acting on their own. *Collective counter-violence* may take the form of direct action, violent demonstrations and riots that may culminate in a violent revolution and, in extreme cases, it may assume the form of guerrilla warfare or even popular terrorism. *Individual counter-violence* mainly takes the form of crimes against property (robberies, break-ins, car thefts, etc.), although it may also take the form of physical violence, as in the case of terrorist activities undertaken by individuals or groups (which do not have organic links to popular movements so that they could be classified as forms of popular terrorism) against the elites and their representatives. Collective counter-violence, when it takes mass proportions, could lead to either direct *state repression* (i.e. the violence against civilians, which is undertaken directly by the state apparatus and is bounded by normal legal proceedings, with the aim of fighting collective counter-violence) or, in extreme cases, to state terrorism, whereas individual counter-violence is dealt with stricter legislation on crime and corresponding increases in the prison populations.

It is not accidental that, historically, both state repression and counter-violence have flourished in the last two centuries. This is because representative

4. See for an analysis of the various forms of modernity, Takis Fotopoulos, 'The Myth of Post-modernity', *Democracy & Nature*, Vol. 7, No. 1 (March 2001), pp. 27–76.

Takis Fotopoulos

'democracy' and the market economy, which flourished during this period, not only institutionalised the concentration of political and economic power (i.e. systemic violence) but also made easier the flourishing of counter-violence, some forms of which were legally recognised. No wonder that when counter-violence was suppressed, as for instance in the case of military regimes, extreme forms of counter-violence have developed like guerila warfare or even popular terrorism.

As the above definition of terrorism implies, there are two main types of terrorism: state terrorism 'from above' and popular terrorism 'from below'. Although state terrorism is simply a further elaboration of state repression, it differs from it because state terrorism is unpredictable and not subject to formal legal procedures. We may therefore define *state terrorism* as any kind of violence against civilians, which is undertaken directly or indirectly by the state apparatus, is unbounded by normal legal proceedings and aims at fighting collective counter-violence. Such forms of state terrorism are for instance the US administrations' authorised CIA killings of suspected terrorists (recently extended to include even heads of state of 'rogue' regimes!), the 'targeted killings' by Israel, as well as the collective punishments against the Palestinian population regularly implemented by the Israeli army. It is therefore not surprising that as George Monbiot[5] points out, the US government 'for the past 55 years has been running a terrorist training camp, whose victims massively outnumber the people killed by the attack on New York, the embassy bombings and the other atrocities laid, rightly or wrongly, at al-Qaeda's door. The camp is called the Western Hemisphere Institute for Security Cooperation, or WHISC. It is based in Fort Benning, Georgia, and it is funded by Mr Bush's government'. Another form of state terrorism is *inter-state terrorism*. This is a kind of state terrorism that emerges when the symmetry of power between states leads weak states to clandestinely support terrorist activities against strong states. Inter-state terrorism is proclaimed by the transnational elite as one of the causes of the present war against terrorism.

On the other hand, popular terrorism, which is an extreme form of counter violence, challenges what the state considers its right, i.e. the monopoly of violence. This is the reason why every kind of elite is against popular terrorism—something that could go a long way in explaining the fact that every ruling elite today, from the American up to the Russian and the Chinese ones (each for its own reasons of course), is unanimously in favour of the 'war against terrorism'. Popular terrorism differs from guerrilla warfare because, unlike the latter, it does not presuppose some sort of symmetry in military power. In fact, popular terrorism arises when the asymmetry of power is so great that guerrilla warfare is impossible.

Popular terrorism may be defined as the violence against members of the state apparatus or civilians expressing the interests of the elites, which is planned by organisations that constitute the military wing of a popular movement and is carried out by small groups or even individuals, with the aim to fight systemic violence, state repression and state terrorism (this is the case, for instance, of national liberation organisations, resistance organisations against military regimes, etc.). This definition of popular terrorism rules out forms of terrorism

5. George Monbiot, 'Backyard Terrorism', *The Guardian*, 30 October, 2001.

The Global 'War' of the Transnational Elite

such as the Italian Right's terrorist bombings in the 1970s and the various Latin American death squads. This is not only because these forms of terrorism are usually funded and supported by various parts of the elites that also control the state apparatus, but also because they do not aim at countering the violence of the elites 'from above' but mainly the counter-violence of the oppressed 'from below'. Similarly, the above definition of popular terrorism rules out the activities of the various terrorist organisations of the Left that emerged, mainly in Europe, in the 1970s. Although this type of terrorism aims at fighting systemic violence and state repression, the fact that it is carried out by organisations that are not organically connected to popular movements gives them the character of elitist organisations, which hope that through their actions, will create the objective and subjective conditions that will 'force' the oppressed to rise in an anti-systemic struggle against the oppressors.

Popular terrorism and democracy

It is therefore clear that it is the institutionalisation of the 'asymmetry' (or unequal distribution) of power in all its forms, which is the ultimate cause of popular terrorism. It is equally clear that popular terrorism is a form of political activity, which has the special characteristic that it involves the use of violence against military or civilian targets for political aims. As such, it has to be assessed with political as well as moral criteria. As I will attempt to show next, popular terrorism is not only morally unjustifiable but also incompatible with the democratic project and therefore, on both grounds, should be rejected.

Thus, at the moral level, any political activity which uses as the main means for the achievement of a political aim the destruction of human life, which should be considered as the *absolute good*, has to be rejected. The only cases in which political violence may be justified, as Hannah Arendt[6] also pointed out, are the cases of revolution and collective or individual self-defence against state violence and violence emanating from the elites. Furthermore, it is morally degrading for the oppressed to use the same bestial methods that are employed by the oppressors—something that is bound to accustom them to political violence, through the negative long-term effects on their personalities that the use of violence creates.

Furthermore, popular terrorism should also be rejected at the political level as well, particularly so since physical violence lies outside the field of *logon didonai* (rendering account and reason), which, 'in itself entails the recognition of the value of autonomy in the sphere of thinking'[7] that is synonymous with reason itself. In other words, as Hannah Arendt again stresses, 'violence itself is incapable of speech, and not merely that speech is helpless when confronted with violence ... in so far as violence plays a predominant role in wars and revolutions, both occur outside the political realm'.[8] Democracy, therefore, whose very

6. Hannah Arendt, *On Revolution* (London: Penguin, 1990).
7. C. Castoriadis, 'The Crisis of Marxism and the Crisis of Politics', *Society and Nature*, Vol. 1, No. 2 (1992), p. 209.

Takis Fotopoulos

basis is speech and reason, is incompatible with violence and terrorism—as long, of course, as change by democratic means is possible within a given institutional framework. No wonder that the classical concept of politics, which was developed in the Athenian Democracy, was also incompatible with violence:[9]

> To be political, to live in a *polis*, meant that everything was decided through words and persuasion and not through force and violence. In Greek self-understanding , to force people by violence, to command rather than persuade, were prepolitical ways to deal with people characteristic of life outside the *polis*, of home and family life, where the household head ruled with uncontested , despotic powers, or of life in the barbarian empires of Asia, whose despotism was frequently likened to the organisation of the household

In this problematique, the only political issue is whether political violence can be justified as a means of reaching a genuine democracy, something which brings us to the issue of 'confronting the system', an issue that I have discussed in the past in my dialogue with Ted Trainer.[10] As I stressed in that dialogue, this confrontation can be seen in a broad or a narrow sense. In a broad sense, this confrontation involves any kind of activity, which aims to confront rather than to bypass the system, at any stage of the transition to a new society. Such activities could include direct action and life-style activities, as well as other forms of action aiming at creating alternative institutions at a significant social scale (e.g. the taking over of local authorities through the electoral process). The condition for such activities to be characterised as confronting the system is that they are an integral part of a mass political movement for systemic change. Clearly, this type of confrontation does not involve in principle any physical violence, apart from self-defence in the case, for instance, of direct action, although it should be expected that the elites will extensively use other forms of violence—particularly economic violence—to crush such a movement. On the other hand, in a narrow sense, confrontation means the physical confrontation with the mechanisms of physical violence that the elites may use against an anti-systemic movement and refers exclusively to the final stage of the transition towards an alternative society. For the Inclusive Democracy (ID) project, whether the transition towards an ID will be marked by a physical confrontation with the elites will depend entirely on the attitude of the latter at the final stage of transformation of society, i.e. on whether they will accept peacefully such a transition, or whether they will prefer instead to use physical violence to crush it, as is most likely given that this transition will deprive them of their privileges.

8. Hannah Arendt, *On Revolution*, p. 19.
9. Hannah Arendt, *The Human Condition* (Chicago: University of Chicago Press, 1958), pp. 26–27.
10. See Takis Fotopoulos, 'The Limitations of Life-style Strategies', *Democracy & Nature*, Vol. 6, No. 2 (July 2000), pp. 287–308.

<u>*The Global 'War' of the Transnational Elite*</u>

The violence of the oppressors and the violence of the oppressed

> The experience over the years
> Of nothing getting better
> Only worse
> The humiliation of being able
> To change almost nothing
> The example of those who resist
> Being bombarded to dust
> (John Berger, *The Guardian*, 25 October 2001)

Although popular terrorism and political violence in general are (as a rule) incompatible with the democratic project, and as such rejectable, this does not mean that we can equate all forms of political violence as many, even in the Left, do today, who (consciously or unconsciously adopting the logic of the transnational elite and the NGOs directly or indirectly financed by it) 'put in the same bag' the popular violence of the oppressed (e.g. the Palestinian 'suicide bombers') with the state violence of the oppressors.[11] To my mind, irrespective of the target of violence, the violence of the oppressors should never be equated with that of the oppressed for the following reasons:

First, the violence of the oppressors is normally aggressive and in today's socio-economic system always aims at the reproduction of inequality in all its forms (political, economic, social, military), whereas the violence of the oppressed is normally defensive. Even in the case when the violence of the oppressed is formally aggressive, as when it aims at the overthrow of an oppressive regime (as for instance the Palestinian struggle for liberation), its character is in essence defensive since its aim is the restoration of some form of autonomy (political, economic, national or cultural), which was usurped by the oppressor.

Second, the oppressors, given their superior military power, have always the capacity of selecting targets that do not involve the use of indiscriminate violence against civilians—particularly so today, in the era of laser-guided missiles, etc. If they do not exploit this capacity, this is due to their deliberate decision to terrorise the oppressed to submission. This was the aim of the 'mass wars' that involved indiscriminate killings of civilians, which began with the Nazi bombings in the Spanish civil war and continued with the carpet bombings of Dresden and then of Vietnam, Iraq, Afghanistan and so on, not to mention the nuclear holocaust at Hiroshima and Nagasaki. On the other hand, the oppressed, given the same asymmetry of power, do not have much choice in their targets, particularly when this asymmetry makes even guerrilla warfare non-feasible. This is the case of the suicide-bomber today who resorts to the last resort, i.e. the use of his/her own life as a weapon, in a kind of desperado action against the massive killings of civilians by a vastly superior oppressor (in military terms).

11. As Paul Foot aptly put it: 'anyone who favours the Israeli occupation of the areas, or the settlements, or who denies the right of violent resistance to the Palestinians is siding unequivocally with the oppressor against the oppressed' ("In Defence of Oppression", *The Guardian*, 5 March 2002).

In this problematique, one may easily understand the motives of the Arab suicide[12] bombers in September 2001, or of Palestine suicide bombers in the months that followed, who, unable even to cause any significant military casualties to an enemy that caused thousands of deaths of civilians in Iraq and Palestine, resort to this kind of desperado terrorism. Therefore, the only rational way in which one may understand activities like suicide bombing is as a kind of a desperado irrational response to the present, unprecedented in history, asymmetry of power that is founded on the systemic violence built in within the NWO. This implies that the issue for the radical Left is not simply to ponder on whether it should join the bandwagon of 'anti-terrorism' (as most in the Left have done gaining in the process the approval of the establishment media) or not. The real issue is what alternative ways of response to the systemic violence of the elites are possible today—an issue that we will consider in the last section of this paper.

Finally, whereas the oppressed, being the victims of oppression, are by definition innocent, this does not apply to everybody on the other side, i.e. the side that directly or indirectly takes part in the oppression. Those on the side that carries out the oppression are innocent only when they adopt a stand against the crimes of their elites—if, of course, they are aware of them. However, the crucial problem here is that usually the peoples are not aware of the crimes of their elites or, given the power of the media to distort events, are confused and have a false consciousness about them. Still, to take two obvious topical examples, there are many Americans who are fully aware of the crimes of their elites but nonetheless, tacitly or not, endorse them, with the obvious aim to secure their privileged standard of living—although they have the power to stop such crimes, as they did in the Vietnam war when 'their own boys' began coming back in body bags. Similarly, there are even more Zionists in Israel and all over the world who, being also fully aware of the crimes of the Israeli state against the Palestinians, still, tacitly or not, endorse them. Their motive supposedly is to secure a place of living for the Jews (which, in fact, can be secured in alternative democratic ways rather than through a Zionist state), but in reality their stand is founded on their nationalist/religious ideologies that often verge on racism. In all these cases one would have to agree with Ellen Cantarow, a Jewish writer, who, desperate in the face of the Israeli crimes in Jenin and elsewhere in the April 2002 onslaught, cried: 'those who do not speak out against the abominations of these horrors are complicit by their silence. Those who exonerate or apologize for Israel as it commits them are guilty by association.'[13] Of course, this does not apply to the US Congress whose guilt is much more than that of association. This was made

12. As Robert Fisk, who, together with John Pilger, provide some of the best examples of independent journalism, aptly put it, suicide bombing is 'the new weapon of the Middle East, which neither Americans or any other Westerners could equal: the despair-driven, desperate suicide bomber. All America's power, wealth—and arrogance, the Arabs will be saying—could not defend the greatest power the world has ever known from this destruction (R. Fisk, "The Awesome Cruelty of a Doomed People", *Znet*, 12 September 2001).

13. Ellen Cantarow, 'Speak Out'/'34 years of Israeli Policy have Laid the Groundwork for its Unholy War in the West Bank', *Jerusalem Indymedia*, 6–8 April 2002.

The Global 'War' of the Transnational Elite

evident for instance when, at the very moment the world anger against the Israeli crimes in Zenin and elsewhere was mounting, it passed resolutions of blatant support for the Zionist state, blessing its brutal military campaign as an attempt at 'dismantling the terrorist infrastructure' in Palestinian territory, whereas the House majority leader declared shamelessly that 'I'm content to have Israel grab the entire West Bank!'[14]

2. Systemic violence and counter-violence in the NWO

There is no doubt that counter-violence in all its forms has increased significantly since the rise of neoliberal globalisation. This can only be interpreted in terms of a significant increase in systemic violence (or even state repression) and the associated increase in the concentration of power at the hands of the ruling elites—that is in terms of a growing asymmetry between rulers and ruled. The discussion of the crucial issue of whether there has indeed been a significant increase in systemic violence lately will bring us to an examination of the contours of the NWO. As I have discussed the meaning of the NWO in detail elsewhere,[15] I will only outline here its main dimensions, which are also the dimensions of systemic violence.

At the outset, it should be stressed that the meaning of NWO used in this paper has little relation to the usual meaning given to this term that simply refers to the changes at the political and military level that resulted from the collapse of the Soviet bloc and the end of the Cold War. In this paper, the NWO takes a much broader meaning extending to:

- the economic level, as expressed by the emergence of the present neoliberal economic globalisation in the form of the internationalised market economy, which secures the concentration of economic power in the hands of the transnational economic elite;
- the political–military level, as expressed by the emergence of a new informal political globalisation securing the concentration of political power in the hands of a newly-emerged transnational political elite;
- the ideological level, as expressed by the development of a new transnational ideology of limited sovereignty (supposedly to protect human rights, to fight 'terrorism', etc.)—a kind of ideological globalisation justifying the decrease of national sovereignty, which complements the corresponding decrease of economic sovereignty as a result of economic globalisation.

14. Alison Mitchell, 'Congress Passes Measure of Support for Israel', *New York Times*, 2 May 2002.

15. See for an earlier formulation of the NWO concept in this journal, Takis Fotopoulos, 'The War in the Balkans: The First War of the Internationalised Market Economy', *Democracy & Nature*, Vol. 5, No. 2 (July 1999), pp. 357–382 and for a more recent extended version of it, 'New World Order and NATO's War against Yugoslavia', *New Political Science*, Vol. 24, No. 1 (March 2002), pp. 73–104.

Takis Fotopoulos

The economic dimension of systemic violence

As regards, first, the economic dimension of systemic violence today, the emergence of neoliberal modernity can be traced back to important structural changes and their effects on the parameters of social struggles that brought about the collapse of the statist form of modernity, i.e. the period of the social-democratic consensus lasting from roughly the mid 1930s to the mid 1970s.[16] These structural changes were both technological and economic, although mainly the latter.

The technological changes, which refer mainly to the information revolution, constitute a parallel (though not independent from the economic changes) process that marked the shift of the market economy from the industrial to the post-industrial phase. This resulted in a drastic change in the employment structure and consequently the class structure of advanced market economies (through the decimation of the working class) with significant political and social implications—above all the decline of the labour movement and consequently of the socialist movement.[17]

As far as the economic changes are concerned, they mainly represented the growing internationalisation of the market economy during the 1950s and 1960s, as a result of the expansion of free trade and the corresponding expansion of the newly emerged Transnational Corporations (TNCs). The expanding needs of TNCs led to an informal opening of capital markets, mainly through development of the Euro-dollar market (1970s) which, however, was instrumental for the later lifting of exchange and capital controls.[18] However, growing internationalisation implied that the growth of the market economy was more and more relying on the expansion of the world market rather than the domestic market, making statism (which kept growing throughout the early post-war period under the pressure of the labour movement) incompatible with it, as it encroached on competitiveness. The stagflation crisis of the early 1970s was the result of this incompatibility between growing statism and internationalisation rather than, as is usually argued by orthodox economists, of the oil crisis, or as is argued by Hardt and Negri,[19] of the accumulation of class struggles.

At the same time, the above changes in the 'objective' conditions created the corresponding changes in the 'subjective' conditions, in terms of the rise of the neoliberal movement and the parallel decline of the trade union and socialist movements.

In this problematique, the arrangements adopted by the economic elites to open and liberalise markets, mostly, institutionalised (rather than created) the present form of the internationalised market economy. The opening and liberalising of markets was simply part of the historical trend to minimise social controls over markets, particularly those aiming to protect labour and the environment that

16. See Takis Fotopoulos, *Towards An Inclusive Democracy* (London, Casssell, 1997), ch. 1.
17. See Takis Fotopoulos, 'Class Divisions Today—The Inclusive Democracy Approach', *Democracy & Nature*, Vol. 6, No. 2 (July 2000), pp. 211–252.
18. See Will Hutton, *The State We're In* (London: Jonathan Cape, 1995), ch. 3.
19. See Michael Hardt and Antonio Negri, *Empire, Part 3* (Cambridge, MA: Harvard University Press, 2000).

interfered with economic 'efficiency' and profitability. The combined effects of these changes have been what is called 'neoliberal globalisation', which clearly reflects the structural changes of the market economy and the corresponding changes in business requirements of late modernity. Policies implemented today for the management of neoliberal globalisation are therefore 'systemic' policies, necessitated by and reflecting the dynamics of the market economy, rather than capitalist 'plots' carried out by unscrupulous neoliberal governments and decadent centre-Left parties—as the reformist Left suggests,[20] which has never grasped the significance of the present monumental changes at the economic level and the corresponding consequences at the political, military and ideological levels.

This system already functions as a self-regulating market in which the interests of the elites that control it are satisfied to the full, almost 'automatically', through the mere functioning of the market forces. In fact, both economic theory (radical economic theory and even parts of orthodox theory) as well as empirical evidence can show that the opening and liberalisation of markets, which constitute the essence of neoliberal globalisation, inevitably, leads to the concentration of income, wealth and economic power, given unequal initial conditions. In fact, there is overwhelming evidence today which confirms the huge concentration of income and wealth, as a result of neoliberal globalisation, and also makes obvious the economic dimension of systemic violence: the richest 20% of the world's population receive today 86% of world GDP (vs 1% for the poorest 20%) and control 82% of world export markets and 68% of foreign direct investment.[21]

The political/military dimension of systemic violence

Coming next to the political dimension of the NWO, it is obvious that a transnational economy needs its own transnational elite. In other words, globalisation cannot be seen only in terms of trade, investment and communications but it requires also a political and security dimension, which used to be the domain of nation-states and today is that of the transnational elite. The emergence of such an elite has already been theorised both from the Marxist[22] and the Inclusive Democracy[23] viewpoints and the evidence on it has been increasingly substantiated. The *transnational elite* may be defined as the elite that draws its power (economic, political or generally social power) by operating at the transnational level. It consists of corporate directors, major shareholders, TNC executives, globalising bureaucrats and professional politicians functioning either within major international organisations or in the state machines of the major market economies, as well as important academics and researchers in the various international foundations, members of think tanks and research departments of major international universities, transnational mass media executives, etc. Its members have a dominant position within society, as a result of their economic, political or

---

20. Takis Fotopoulos, 'Globalisation, the Reformist Left and the Anti-Globalisation "Movement" ', *Democracy & Nature*, Vol. 7, No. 2 (July 2001), pp. 233–280.
21. UN, Human Development Report 1999.
22. Leslie Sklair, *The Transnational Capitalist Class* (Oxford: Blackwell, 2001).
23. Takis Fotopoulos, 'Globalisation the Reformist Left and the Anti-Globalisation "Movement" '.

broader social power and, unlike national elites, see that the best way to secure their privileged position in society is not by ensuring the reproduction of any real or imagined nation-state but, instead, by securing the worldwide reproduction of the institutional framework on which the NWO is founded: the system of market economy and representative 'democracy'. In other words, the new transnational elite sees its interests in terms of international markets rather than national markets and is not based on a single nation-state but is a decentred apparatus of rule with no territorial centre of power.

This is clearly an *informal* rather than an institutionalised elite. Thus, in the same way that economic globalisation expresses an informal concentration of economic power at the hands of the members of the economic elite, political globalisation expresses an informal concentration of political power at the hands of the members of the political elite. In other words, the economic elite constitutes that part of the transnational elite that controls the internationalised market economy, whereas the political elite constitutes that part of the transnational elite that controls the distinctly political–military dimension of the NWO. The main institutions securing the concentration of economic and political power at the hands of the transnational elite are the market economy and representative 'democracy' respectively, whereas the main organisations through which the transnational elite exercises its informal control are the EU, NAFTA, the G8, WTO, IMF, World Bank, NATO and the UN.

The three 'wars' launched by the transnational elite so far (i.e. the Gulf war,[24] the war in Kosovo[25] and the on-going 'war on terrorism'), are cases substantiating the existence of an informal system of transnational governance, a political globalisation presided over by a transnational elite. The informal character of globalisation is needed not only in order to keep the façade of a well functioning representative 'democracy' in which local elites are still supposed to take the important decisions but also in order to preserve the nation-state's internal monopoly of violence. The latter is necessary so that local elites are capable of controlling their populations in general and the movement of labour in particular, enhancing the free flow of capital and commodities.

Despite the dominance of the US-based elements within the transnational elite, it is clear that the latter does not consist only of Americans and that therefore it is wrong to talk about an 'American empire'. It is only the uneven distribution of political/military power among the members of the transnational elite that establishes the informal hegemony of the US elite in the present form of political globalisation. This is particularly important if we take into account the fact that the transnational elite, like national elites, is hardly a monolithic body and that there are instead significant divisions within it. Still, these divisions refer not to the common goal of protecting the stability of the universal institutional framework (capitalist neoliberal globalisation and representative 'democracy') but on ways and means of doing so. Such divisions become particularly important today in view of the deteriorating multi-dimensional crisis, mainly with respect to its economic and ecological dimensions, as is shown by the clash of views between

24. See Takis Fotopoulos, *The Gulf War* (Athens: Exantas, 1991)—in Greek.
25. See Takis Fotopoulos, 'The War in the Balkans'.

The Global 'War' of the Transnational Elite

'conservative' elements of the transnational elite (mainly US-based) and 'progressive' elements (mostly Europe-based). An example of this division is the dispute over the Kyoto treaty that has been endorsed by all members of the transnational elite apart from the US elite. A similar division has arisen with respect to the growing concentration of economic power that neoliberal globalisation implies. European elites, having to face stronger reactions against the neoliberal philosophy than their American counterparts (due to the stronger socialist/social-democratic traditions in Europe) propose various measures to reduce absolute (but not relative) poverty, and pursue a policy of fully integrating China, Russia and the 'rogue' states into the internationalised market economy rather than alienating them through aggressive political and military strategies. In other words, the aim of the European parts of the transnational elite is to create a 'capitalist globalisation with a human face' that does not alter the essentials of NWO.[26] Finally, the divisions within the transnational elite concerning the future phases of the war against terrorism is another case illustrating this point.

Still, given the unrivalled power of the US-based parts of the elite, one might expect that a consensus reached between the various trends within it on matters of strategy and tactics will mainly express the US positions. This is particularly so today when the US-based parts of the elite have established a long-term superiority over the other parts of it, not only at the military level, where the events of September 2001 gave them the opportunity to function as the policeman of the NWO, but also at the economic level. The present US economic superiority is based not only on the long-term decline of Japanese elites but also on their unchallenged position in the information revolution placing them well ahead of rivals in the Far East and Europe. A clear indication of the American predominance within the transnational elite is the fact that whereas at the end of the 1980s, eight of the 10 biggest multinationals in the world were Japanese, a decade later all ten were American.[27]

Finally, it should be added here that the New Political Order, a necessary complement of the New Economic Order that is based on neoliberal globalisation, is defined not only by the informal structure of political globalisation which I considered above but also by an important institutional change: the redefinition of NATO's role by the 1999 Washington treaty. As is well known, NATO was founded in 1949 as a collective defence organisation against the communist 'threat' posed by the Soviet bloc. The heart of the North Atlantic Treaty was Article 5, in which the signatory members 'agree that an armed attack against one or more of them in Europe or North America shall be considered an attack against them all'. In fact it was article 5 that was used by the transnational elite in order to involve NATO in the present war against terrorism. However, the 1999

26. See for example an expression of this trend in a recent *Observer leader* under the eloquent title 'The US is Not Fit to Run the World—We must Help Europe Take on the Job', *The Observer*, 1 April 2001. Also, the French paper *Le Monde Diplomatique* plays a significant role with respect to this trend, both in theory and in practice.
27. Madeleine Bunting, 'Smash and Grab Inc.—The US Ruled the Last Century and It will Rule the Next. What will It Do with Its Power?', *The Guardian*, 24 August 1999.

Takis Fotopoulos

Washington summit, which was dedicated to an expanded NATO that included several formerly Soviet block countries, adopted a new 'strategic concept'[28] that radically changed the nature of this crucial military organisation in which all main advanced market economies—apart from Japan—take part.

The new NATO constitution redefined the role of NATO from a mutual defence organisation of a number of nation-states allied against the Soviet bloc into the main military institution of the internationalised market economy. As, the new constitution explicitly states,[29] 'the Alliance therefore not only ensures the defence of its members but contributes to peace and stability in this region'. Then, in a section entitled 'The evolving strategic environment' the document lays out the NATO/UN relationship by stating that 'the United Nations Security Council has the primary responsibility for the maintenance of international peace and security'.[30] It is indicative that at the time of the summit meeting, President Chirac interpreted this clause as implying that NATO could not act without UN authorisation, but this interpretation was immediately contradicted by Solana who stated that a Security Council resolution would not be necessary before making an intervention outside NATO territory.[31] The issue has been resolved in practice by the NATO war against Yugoslavia: if the transnational elite cannot secure the votes of all permanent members of the UN Security Council they will have no hesitation to start military action without prior UN mandate.

Further on, in a section entitled 'Security challenges and risks', the new strategic concept is clearly defined and the transformation of NATO is made explicit: from a defensive alliance that protects specific areas from the communist threat to an aggressive alliance that protects a vaguely defined broad area ('in and around the Euro–Atlantic area and the periphery of the Alliance') against a series of loosely defined 'risks'.[32] In effect, any kind of conflict situation (including 'the disruption of the flow of vital resources' and 'acts of terrorism') within this broadly defined geographical area that might directly or indirectly threaten the stability of the internationalised market economy, may be considered as threatening the Alliance.[33]

The new role of NATO as the defender of the transnational elite and its global interests is therefore obvious from the Washington Treaty. Furthermore, although the above formulations imply that all members of NATO would take part in defining a 'risk situation' and in proposing the appropriate measures to be taken, it is obvious that given the US hegemony, it is basically the US part of the transnational elite that takes the responsibility of defending the New Economic Order. No wonder that the Pentagon explicitly declared that 'a prosperous, largely democratic, market-oriented zone of peace and "prosperity that encompasses more than two-thirds of the world's economy" requires the "stability" that

28. North Atlantic Treaty Organisation, *The Alliance's Strategic Concept*, 24 April 1999.
29. *Ibid.*, article 6.
30. *Ibid.*, article 15.
31. Ben Macintyre, *The Times*, 26 April 1999.
32. NATO, *The Alliance's Strategic Concept*, article 20.
33. *Ibid.*, article 34.

The Global 'War' of the Transnational Elite

only American "leadership can provide" '.[34] Protection of the internationalised market economy and free trade thus 'depend on America's overseas military commitments and power'. An influential New York Times columnist[35] was even more frank on the matter when he stressed that 'For globalisation to work, America can't be afraid to act like the almighty superpower it is ... The hidden hand of the market will never work without a hidden fist ... and the hidden fist that keeps the world safe for Silicon Valley's technologies is called the US Army, Air Force, Navy and Marine Corps.'

Yet, the fact that US military hegemony is recognised by all members of the transnational elite does not mean that there are no parts of it that would like to move toward some degree of independence from the US. The French parts of the transnational elite, in particular, wish to create an independent EU military power with the aim of moderating the American dominance over the other members of the transnational elite. As one could expect in view of the military weakness of the European powers, such wishes can never exceed the stage of pious hopes. As George Robertson, the NATO secretary general, pointed out recently, European countries spend the equivalent of two-thirds of the US defence budget on arms, but have nothing like two-thirds of the US defence capability because of duplication.[36] In fact, all this was before the recent huge rise in US military spending announced by the Bush administration that according to Professor Paul Kennedy at Yale University, will lead to the US spending more each year than the next nine largest national defence budgets combined![37] No wonder that although the Nice Treaty, signed by EU ministers in February 2001, states clearly that common foreign and security policy shall include 'all questions relating to the security of the union', it then goes on to specify in a long annex that 'NATO remains the basis of the collective defence of its members and will continue to play an important role in crisis management. The development of European security and defence policy will contribute to the vitality of a renewed transatlantic link.'[38] It is therefore clear that any European defence force would be fully integrated into NATO, securing the military hegemony of the US elite and, in effect, playing a complementary, rather than a competitive, role to it.

So, the new NATO constitution made it clear that the type of wars envisaged in the future had nothing to do either with the kind of wars between advanced market economies culminating in the two world wars which marked the 20th century, or those that were expected by the original NATO constitution between the two Cold War blocs. In this sense, the new NATO constitution accurately reflects the transnational elite's problematique on wars in the NWO.

34. Christopher Layne and Benjamin Schwarz, 'Making the World Safer for Business: Instability and Aggression are Regarded as a Threat to the Global Stability upon which U.S. Markets Depend', *Los Angeles Times*, 2 April 1999.

35. Thomas Friedman, *New York Times*, 28 March 1999 (quoted in M. Parenti, *To Kill A Nation*, *To Kill A Nation* (Verso, 2000), p. 235.

36. Michael White, *The Guardian*, 10 February 2001.

37. Peter Beaumont and Ed Vulliamy, *The Observer*, 10 February 2002.

38. Richard Norton-Taylor, *The Guardian*, 28 February 2001.

Takis Fotopoulos

Thus, as regards, first, wars among major market economies, the smooth functioning of a self-regulating internationalised market economy, involving free movement of commodities and capital, is incompatible with embargos and military activities. Therefore, the present internationalisation of the market economy makes such armed conflicts between major market economies superfluous, if not impossible. Today, the nation states are essentially the municipalities of the internationalised market economy and their job is to provide, at the cheapest possible cost, the infrastructure and 'public goods' required for the effective functioning of business.[39] It is simply against the general interest of the transnational elite to allow any military conflicts to arise between the major advanced market economies, i.e. the triad (EU, NAFTA and Japan) on which all elements of the transnational elite are based. Furthermore, it is not difficult to see that in the framework of this internationalised economy any attempt by a country or an economic bloc to use military force against another country or bloc within the triad is inconceivable, since it will incur the immediate sanctions of the global financial markets, the first casualty being its own currency. At the same time, a generalised war, like the two previous world wars, will lead to collapse the internationalised market economy, through the collapse of the internationalised stock exchanges and the bankruptcy of the transnational corporations that will have to drastically restrict their activities.

But, if wars among the countries in the triad are ruled out this is not the case as regards wars between them and countries in the periphery and the semi-periphery of the internationalised market economy, nor is this the case with regard to wars (like the present global 'war' on terrorism) to crush any resistance against the NWO, nor, finally, is this the case with regard to wars between peripheral countries (often expressing corresponding divisions within the transnational elite).

Thus, as regards wars between countries in the triad and countries in the periphery and semi-periphery, as well as those against resistance movements, the explosion of inequality in the world distribution of power within the NWO implies that attacks against any 'rogue' regimes or resistance movements challenging it will continue unabated—this is the main aim of the present global 'war'. Such regimes or movements will have to be crushed in the kind of total victory that we have seen in the case of the three 'wars' to date. It is with the purpose of fighting wars of this type that the armies of countries in the Triad are fast being converted into armies of professional killers (a kind of samurai) who are not susceptible, as conscripts are, to ideological influences and feelings of solidarity with the social groups from which they are recruited (usually the poorest groups). Despite the higher cost of professional armies,[40] the NWO elites have no choice but to finance such extra expenses since wars are no longer for the defence of the country but purely for the defence of the NWO and the privileges of those benefiting from it—primarily the transnational elite but also the upper middle classes in the triad countries as well as the elites in the peripheral countries.

39. K. Ohmae, 'The Rise of the Region State', *Foreign Affairs*, Spring 1993.
40. Adrian Hamilton, *The Observer*, 25 February 1996.

The Global 'War' of the Transnational Elite

As for wars among peripheral states, conflicts of a cultural, religious, nationalist or ethnic nature may easily arise between them, often giving outlet to socio-economic frustrations. The reaction of the transnational elite to such wars is not uniform. In some cases, as with ethnic wars in the Balkans, such conflicts may threaten the stability of the NWO and have to be crushed through its military arms, if possible through the UN, alternatively by the new NATO, or as last resort by US military power. If these tensions do not threaten the NWO as such but are useful in financing expansion of the armament industries of the transnational elite then such tensions are left to keep simmering.

In conclusion, the military branch of the transnational elite, i.e. the US Pentagon, with the assistance of the second-in-command, the British Army—with or without the help of NATO—play today the role of managing the security dimension of the NWO. In this framework, the new global 'war' of the transnational elite offers, as we shall see below, the very security apparatus for the process of neoliberal globalisation (a global war for a globalised economy), as well as the protection mechanism with respect to any threat against the NWO in general.

The ideological dimension of systemic violence

Economic and political globalisation are inevitably accompanied by a kind of 'ideological globalisation', i.e. a transnational ideology used to justify the decrease of national sovereignty, which complements the corresponding decrease of economic sovereignty following economic globalisation. The core of this new ideology is the doctrine of 'limited' sovereignty that is used to 'justify' military interventions/attacks against any 'rogue' regimes or political organisations and movements.[41] According to this doctrine, there are certain universal values that should take priority over other values, like that of national sovereignty. The five centuries-old culture of unlimited sovereignty, which nations that participated in the drafting of the UN charter agreed to limit only as regards their right to wage war in case of an attack, in exchange for a promise that the Security Council provide collective security on their behalf (an arrangement blatantly violated by the US 'war' against Afghanistan[42]), is therefore completely abolished in the NWO.

41. Tony Blair's foreign policy guru Robert Cooper expressed clearly the new ideological globalisation when he argued that 'what is needed is a new kind of imperialism, one compatible with human rights and cosmopolitan values: an imperialism which aims to bring order and organisation but which rests today on the voluntary principle', Robert Cooper, *The Observer*, 'Why We Still Need Empires', 7 April 2002.
42. As Monique Chemillier-Gendreau points out 'The end of international law, likely since the Gulf war, is accelerating ... the UN Security Council finally bowed to the US in Resolution 1368 of 12 September 2001. ... By describing the attacks of 11 September as "threats to international peace and security" ... (it) has abandoned any idea of collective action in the name of the UN ... the UN is encouraging a vicious circle where the response to violence and murder is a war of vengeance that may be extended to other lands' ('UN: The End of Collective Action', *Le Monde Diplomatique*, November 2001).

Takis Fotopoulos

In cases where 'universal values' are violated, international organisations expressing the will of the 'international community' (i.e. the UN Security Council, NATO, etc.) should enforce them by any means necessary, irrespective of national sovereignty concerns that should never override the primary significance of these universal values. This new doctrine was formally expressed by the UK Prime Minister in a Chicago speech just before the Washington NATO summit. The upshot of this speech was that democratic states should be allowed to intervene in the internal affairs of other states so long as human rights are at stake—a principle fully endorsed by the 'new' NATO.[43]

There are two obvious conclusions that one may draw from this new doctrine of 'limited sovereignty', which is fast becoming the ideology of the NWO, first with respect to human rights and second with respect to the 'war against terrorism'. The first conclusion is that this doctrine overrides the UN Charter which explicitly states that 'nothing contained in the present Charter shall authorize the United Nations to intervene in matters which are essentially within the domestic jurisdiction of any state' except upon a Security Council finding of a 'threat to the peace, breach of the peace, or act of aggression'.[44] This reversal becomes all too clear when one takes into account that a proposal to ensure the protection of human rights was explicitly rejected at the San Francisco Conference establishing the UN. The second conclusion is that given the huge asymmetry of power in the present world order it is not the sovereignty of the powerful states in the triad countries that is going to suffer because of this new doctrine but only that of the weak ones.

It is therefore clear that this new doctrine is false, asymmetrical and potentially oppressive. It is false, because primacy of 'human rights' or the protection against 'terrorism' over national sovereignty presupposes that we live in a society and a world in which the peoples of this world (and not their elites) can define the meaning of 'human values' and 'terrorism'. It is asymmetrical insofar as it creates a right for the powerful to intervene in the affairs of the weak and not vice versa. This could explain, for instance, why massive violations of Palestinian human rights in the past and the Jenin crimes during the second phase of the 'war' against terrorism in April 2002 at the hands of a brutal Zionist army, with the obvious connivance of the transnational elite, have never warranted any action by the transnational elite (not even a commission of inquiry!), or why the KLA in Kosovo and the Contras in Nicaragua, easily qualifying as 'terrorist' organisations, not only were never pursued by the transnational elite, but instead were armed and financed by it! Finally, it is potentially oppressive, because it can easily be used by the transnational elite to oppress any movement that tries to establish an alternative kind of society in order to abolish the unequal distribution

43. Article 20 of the new strategic concept makes it explicitly clear that only a limited conception of sovereignty is recognised by the new NATO. This is the obvious conclusion from references that article 20 makes to ethnic and religious rivalries, or the abuse of human rights—events that according to the new 'strategic concept', can lead to crises affecting Euro–Atlantic stability and armed conflicts affecting the security of the Alliance by spilling over into neighbouring countries. (NATO, *The Alliance's Strategic Concept*).
44. UN Charter, article 2, No. 7 & article 39.

218

The Global 'War' of the Transnational Elite

of political and economic power. This new doctrine of limited sovereignty, therefore, plays the ideological role of legitimising political and military interventions of the transnational elite in order to guarantee the stability of the NWO.

Finally, it is worth noting the role of the centre-left and the mainstream Greens as the main promoters of the new transnational ideology. Both have played a vital part in justifying the 'wars' of the transnational elite through the doctrine of limited sovereignty. This is not difficult to explain in view of the fact that both the centre-left and the mainstream Greens have already fully adopted the NWO in their economic and political aspects. Thus, all major European centre-left parties (Germany, Britain, France, Italy, etc.) have already adopted the capitalist neoliberal globalisation. Similarly, mainstream Greens have long ago abandoned any ideas about radical economic changes and have adopted instead a kind of 'eco-social-liberalism' that amounts to some version of 'Green capitalism'.

It was therefore hardly surprising that the centre-left endorsed enthusiastically all three 'wars' of the transnational elite, whereas the mainstream Greens, who at the beginning of the 1990s were concerned about the ecological implications of the Gulf war, were dedicated supporters of the war against Yugoslavia by the end of the decade and today have fully endorsed the 'war against terrorism'. The argument used by Greens to justify their stand was that the Green ideology of fighting for human rights and human liberation in general was perfectly compatible with the new role of NATO as protector of human rights! Still, there is an alternative explanation for the Green stand: since ideas about the anti-party party, direct democracy and radical ecology were shelved once the mainstream Green parties became 'normal parties' fighting for government power, it was inevitable that, once in power, they would become 'normal governments', taking part in criminal activities like the NATO war.

However, if the historical role of social democrats on the side of the ruling elites in their various wars can be taken for granted, this does not apply to the left in general or the Greens in particular. As regards the former, it was surprising though not unexpected to see that the 'war' against Yugoslavia was endorsed by most intellectuals of the European 'left': from Anthony Giddens and Alain Tourain to Edgar Morin, Habermas and many others, who, in effect, served as apologists for NATO's attack against the Yugoslavian people when they justified the doctrine of 'limited' sovereignty and talked about a 'new era' in international relations, supposedly marked by the Pinochet affair and the 'war' itself. It is clear that most 'left' intellectuals, having abandoned their critical role are now, as Castoriadis aptly described them, 'enthusiastically adhering to that which is there just because it is there'.[45]

The same applies to the Greens who entered the political arena a quarter a century ago, as a new social movement fighting for the noble goal of liberating Nature and Humanity from the evils of the present society. Their participation in the last two criminal 'wars' of the transnational elite (Yugoslavia, Afghanistan) constitutes a flagrant violation of the *raison d'être* itself of the Green movement. This became particularly obvious in the case of Yugoslavia, when 'realist'

45. Cornelius Castoriadis, 'The Retreat from Autonomy: Postmodernism as Generalised Conformism', *Democracy & Nature*, Vol. 7, No. 1 (March 2001), pp. 17–26.

Takis Fotopoulos

Greens like the ex-leftists and now professional politicians Cohn-Bendit[46] and Joschka Fischer, and 'red-Greens' like Alain Lipietz,[47] as well as the European Green parties, saw no contradiction between the end of this war (liberation of Kosovars from oppression and ethnic cleansing) and the means used for this purpose (the criminal war machine of the transnational elite engaged in the systematic destruction of the country's infrastructure). Mainstream Greens have shown that they no longer have (if they ever did) a vision of an alternative society: they simply endorse the institutional framework of the present internationalised market economy and its political expressions. As socialist critics[48] were quick to point out, mainstream Greens today cannot claim to be any kind of 'anti-systemic force'. Clearly, therefore, from the moment 'realists' won the battle against radical currents within the European Greens, Green parties have become an element of the NWO engaged in environmental 'statecraft' on behalf of the middle classes which they mainly represent, ending any hopes for their anti-systemic potential.

Counter-violence in the NWO

Political violence in all its varieties is not of course a new phenomenon and has always been present in every form of hierarchical (or heteronomous) society. As I attempted to show in the first section, political violence was always associated with the unequal distribution of power at all levels and particularly the political/ military and the economic levels. In other words, the asymmetry of economic and political/military power between and within nations has always been the necessary condition for political violence, both from the point of view of the oppressor as well as that of the oppressed. One may even go further and assume a direct relationship between inequality in the distribution of power and political violence: the higher the inequality in the distribution of power the greater the degree of political violence in all its forms.

As hopefully was made clear in the last section, the NWO has institutionalised an extreme concentration of economic, political/military power, i.e. an extreme form of systemic violence, which is the ultimate cause of the huge rise of counterviolence in the last quarter of the century or so. In contrast to the liberal and statist forms of modernity, when power was concentrated at the national level and therefore terrorism was also nationally focused, in the NWO of neoliberal modernity, power is concentrated at the international level, in the hands of the transnational elite. Not surprisingly, terrorism also takes a globalised form today to hit the centres of the transnational elite and particularly the USA. However, it has been various non-extreme forms of counter-violence rather than terrorism itself that flourished in the NWO, although one may notice some significant variations between the North and the South.

46. Daniel Cohn-Bendit, 'Le recours, c'est la force', *Liberation*, 6 April 1999.
47. Alain Lipietz, 'Ce qu'il faut savoir avant une guerre terrestre', *Liberation*, 13 April 1999.
48. As Paul McGarr stresses: 'Their (Green) politics are a criticism of some aspects of the capitalist system, such as the way it leads to environmental destruction, but not a rejection of the system itself', 'European Greens, Shades of Deep Khaki', *Socialist Worker*, 23 April 1999.

The Global 'War' of the Transnational Elite

In the North, counter-violence in the 1980s and early 1990s used mainly to take the form of individual counter-violence, as expressed through the huge increase in crime. No wonder that today the world prison population is an all-time record, with more than 8.75 million people in prison around the world and about half of them in three countries alone: the US (1.93 million), China (1.43 million) and Russia (0.96 million)[49] where the concentration of power in all its forms is highest. The only North-based terrorist organisations still operating today are either remnants of the 1970s (November 17th Organisation in Greece and the resurrected Red Brigades in Italy) or national liberation movements (ETA in Spain, 'Real IRA' in Northern Ireland). However, with the blooming of neoliberal globalisation in the 1990s, a new form of collective counter-violence has developed recently, as expressed particularly by the activity of the anti-systemic currents within the anti-globalisation movement. No wonder that the new anti-terrorist legislation that was introduced in many countries in the North, even before the 11 September events, but particularly after them, has been designed to be applicable not only with respect to terrorism from the South but also with respect to the anti-systemic currents within the anti-globalisation movement and similar movements outside it. Particularly so, since the systemic violence is at a very high level in the NWO, with inequality, poverty and unemployment having reached record post-war levels, representative 'democracy' not giving any outlet for protest as all main parties agree on the basic principles governing neoliberal globalisation, and the capital-controlled mass media being busy in manufacturing consent around the aims of the transnational elite that manages the NWO. Inevitably, this huge systemic violence can only be sustained through state repression, in case the built-in mechanisms used by the elite to push the oppressed into passivity and individualisation (consumer culture, drug culture, mass media, etc.) are not sufficient for their control.

On the other hand, in the South, the rise of systemic violence represented by the NWO has been met by a corresponding rise of collective counter-violence, including popular terrorism. This is the case of many movements that have emerged in the last decade or so in Latin America—particularly in countries like Brazil where the demands for land redistribution have grown—but also, in Asia, in countries like India and lately China,[50] where demonstrations against the effects of globalisation seem to have flourished lately. Popular terrorism is also rampant in the South. This is on account of two reasons. First, because counter-violence is usually suppressed by the repressive regimes dominating the South (even if they formally adopted the representative 'democracy' paraphernalia), pushing resistant social groups to the use of terrorist methods. In fact, terrorism has almost replaced other forms of collective counter-violence like guerrilla warfare, which used to be the main form of struggle in the periphery. Second, because when counter-violence is directed against the North (or colonizers from the North like the Zionist regime in Israel), the asymmetry of power between

---

49. Alan Travis, 'England Worse than China in Prison Population Rate', *The Guardian*, 13 February 2002.
50. John Gittings, 'Strikes Convulse China's Oil-rich Heartlands', *The Guardian*, 21 March 2002.

oppressors and oppressed is such that the latter have in fact no effective choice but to resort to terrorism.

3. The 11 September events as the catalyst for the new 'war'

The causes of the 11 September events

The common theme of the transnational elite and its ideological commissars in interpreting the September events has been that they constituted an inexplicable attack against democracy and civilisation caused by religious fanatics whereas the more 'sophisticated' of those analysts talked about the 'clash of civilisations'.

Thus, the *New York Times*, the medium *par excellence* of the transnational elite, found the causes of the attack in 'religious fanaticism' and in the anger of those left behind by globalisation.[51] Similarly, several of the ideological commissars of the same elite 'explained' the events as pure 'nihilism'. A Harvard university professor, for instance, writing in the immediate aftermath of the events, gave the following 'interpretation', which obviously aimed at preparing world opinion for the bloody 'war' to come:[52]

> It is important to insist on the apocalyptic content and the nihilistic moral meaning of these events because so many good people persist in believing that the attacks were a cry from the heart of an unjust world, an indictment, wrong in moral form, but right in content, of the injustice of American power. Some even go so far as to claim that America's guilt deprives it of the right to strike back. The mistake is to construe an act of annihilating nihilism as an act of politics. ... Since the politics of reason cannot defeat apocalyptic nihilism, we must fight.

As the above extract makes clear, the aim of the establishment ideologues has been to separate completely the violence of 11 September from systemic violence so that the impression of a nihilistic event could be established. However, neither was the attack inexplicable nor was it directed against democracy and civilisation. In fact, it was clearly an extreme form of popular terrorism directly related to the systemic violence built into the NWO. Thus, the attack becomes far from inexplicable when it is taken into account that the Arabs who carried out it grew up in a world order in which their brothers and sisters in Palestine were murdered on a daily basis in the process of a barbarous ethnic cleansing, the perpetrators of which, far from being bombed as in Yugoslavia for their contempt of numerous UN resolutions, were scandalously supported by the transnational elite—mainly the US-based parts of the elite—for the sake of its control of Middle-East oil, and were rewarded at the rate of over US\$3 billion per year. They also grew up in a world order in which more than a million of their compatriots in Iraq (half of

---

51. Leader, 'The National Defence', *New York Times*, 12 September 2001.
52. Michael Ignatieff, 'It's War—But it Doesn't Have to be Dirty', *The Guardian*, 1 October 2001. A similar position was adopted by 'left philosophers' like Andre Glucksmann (*TO VEMA*, 7 October 2001).

them children) have died out of the mass bombings and the subsequent embargo[53] of the transnational elite.

Also, concerning the allegation that the September events represented an attack against democracy, one may argue that it was the very absence of real democracy in the USA that was the cause of death of innocent victims. Surely, most of these victims were not responsible for the decisions to subjugate the Palestinians, the Iraqis, the Indonesians, or earlier on the Latin Americans and the Vietnamese. It was the political elites, at whose hands political power is concentrated in a representative 'democracy', that have to be blamed for this. Also, most of these victims were probably not even aware of the *avoidable* death (according to UNICEF) of over 10 million children per year, because of the lack of proper living conditions and of the role of Western elites in the development of such conditions. On the other hand, it is the 200 billionaires, who concentrate in their hands an amount of wealth which is eight times higher than the total income of 582 million people in the 'developing' countries,[54] who in a market economy are invested with economic power and, with the support of the privileged social groups, determine the fate of everybody in the planet.

Finally, the allegation that the September events represent a kind of 'clash of civilisations'[55] is obviously an ideological smokescreen to cover the real cycle of systemic violence and counter-violence. Not only has the transnational elite clearly not been motivated by any crusade but there is also no evidence that the Arabs who carried out the attack were motivated by some fervent desire to spread Islamic fundamentalism.[56] This, does not deny of course the possibility that their religious beliefs (which might well have been exploited by their leadership to recruit them in the struggle against the transnational elite) might have helped them in executing (but not in taking) their decision to sacrifice their own lives. As regards the rise of Islamic fundamentalism itself, it was only in the late 1960s that Muslims throughout the Islamic world had begun to develop what we call fundamentalist movements and it was not before 1979, when the ayatollahs took over in Iran, that the Islamic fundamentalist movement flourished—usually enhanced by the West in its struggle to dismantle the Soviet bloc. This was therefore a phenomenon that happened after, and not before, the failure of Arab nationalism/ socialism to stem the continuous decline of Arab societies, despite the political and economic independence that the end of colonialism supposedly brought about. The turn of the Arab populations (including the radical currents within the Palestinian movement) to Islamic fundamentalism is therefore the logical

53. See e.g. John Pilger, 'Inevitable Ring to the Unimaginable', *Znet*, 13 September 2001.
54. UN, *Human Development Report 2000* (New York: Oxford University Press, 2000).
55. See for the theory of the clash of civilisations Samuel Huntington, *The Clash of Civilisations and the Remaking of the World Order* (New York: Simon & Schuster, 1996).
56. As Ric Rouleau pointed out 'Islamic rhetoric became an instrument of mobilisation, serving as a cover for nationalist and anti-imperialist objectives. But it also had a social component, and included denunciations of the injustices, corruption, and tyranny that characterised the reigning oligarchies' (Ric Rouleau, 'Terrorism and Islamism', *Le Monde Diplomatique*, November 2001).

Takis Fotopoulos

outcome of this failure and of the parallel establishment by the transnational elite of semi-dictatorial client regimes that stifle any democratic process.

One may therefore conclude that the ultimate cause of the 11 September attacks should be traced back to the NWO that we considered in the last section, which has established a huge inequality in the distribution of economic and political power *between* and *within* nations. It is this huge asymmetry that inspired the attackers to express themselves in a language of desperation, something that did not represent any clear strategy, with its long-term aims and short-term tactics. From this viewpoint, Saskia Sassen's observation is clearly to the point:[57]

> the attacks are a language of last resort: the oppressed and persecuted have used many languages to reach us so far, but we seem unable to translate the meaning. So a few have taken the personal responsibility to speak in a language that needs no translation.

At the same time, the events of September themselves functioned as catalysts and gave the perfect pretext to the transnational elite, headed by the US-based parts of it, for its present attempt to crush any resistance movement in the South, in the hope that this will eliminate any serious threats to its interests. As the special, correspondent of *Le Monde Diplomatique* put it: 'Having been challenged by a new terrorism, the US is determined to regain control, if only partially, in Afghanistan and Pakistan, Saudi Arabia and Yemen, and even Iraq. It means to eliminate all the political and social forces that pose a violent threat to its interests.'[58] However, despite the fact that *Le Monde Dimplomatique*[59] attempts to differentiate between the US and the European elements of the transnational elite and blames only the former, one may argue that this elite as a whole did not have any other choice and, in spite of the differences on tactics, all its members agree on the long-term tactics of the war, as the European Commission made clear.[60]

It is therefore clear that, despite the differences in tactics that may well exist between the various elements of the transnational elite, it does not make any sense to assume that it will ever take any measures to fight the causes of popular terrorism (i.e. the systemic violence within the NWO) rather than its symptoms, as it does with the global 'war'. Therefore, one could not expect that this elite will ever abandon the client Zionist state, which is the main foundation of the NWO in the area, or that it will stop seeking to overthrow 'rogue' regimes and suppress

---

57. Saskia Sassen, 'A Message from the Global South', *The Guardian*, 12 September 2001.
58. Paul-Marie de la Gorce, 'Uncivil War in Washington', *Le Monde Diplomatique*, November 2001.
59. As Ignatio Ramonet, the editor of *Le Monde Diplomatique*, wrote in a leader in the aftermath of the September events, 'throughout the world, and particularly in the countries of the South, the most common public reaction to the attacks in New York and Washington has been: what happened in New York was sad, but the US deserved it' (*Le Monde Diplomatique*, October 2001).
60. A spokesman for Chris Patten, the EU foreign affairs commissioner, declared on the aftermath of Bush's 'axis of evil' speech that 'although we have the same long-term aims (with the Americans) we have a different policy, a policy of rapprochement, in order to achieve the same aims' (Associated Press/ *Eleftherotypia*, 1 February 2002).

radical movements threatening its vital interests, or finally that it will introduce any effective measures to control neoliberal globalisation for the sake of protecting labour and the environment and against the imperatives of neoliberal globalisation.

The aftermath of 11 September: launching a new type of 'war'

The attacks of 11 September gave the opportunity to the transnational elite, whose military branch is, *de facto*, the US military machine, to start its latest 'war' against terrorism. Despite the fact that the new war has several common characteristics with the previous 'wars', as we shall see below, there are also significant differences between these 'wars'. Thus, the war against terrorism, unlike the previous ones, is a global and permanent war. It is a global war, not in the sense of a generalised war like the two world wars but in the sense that its targets are not only specific 'rogue' regimes (as was the case with the Saddam and Milosevic regimes), which are not fully integrated in the NWO or simply do not 'toe the line', but any kind of regime or social group and movement that resists the NWO: from the Palestinian up to the anti-globalisation movements. As Dan Plesch, senior research fellow at the Royal United Services Institute put it 'the war on terrorism is analogous to civil war on a global scale, in that it is taking place in a world in which globalisation has shrunk and become interconnected'.[61] Furthermore, it is a permanent[62] war, because it is bound to continue for as long as the NWO and the systemic and state violence associated with it are reproduced.

In other words, the 'war against terrorism' is a particularly expedient means of controlling populations that threaten the NWO. The direct targets in its first phases are those populations in the South that are particularly influenced by Islamic fundamentalism. As we have seen above, the selection of these targets does not indicate the kind of 'clash of civilisations' predicted by the ideologues of the NWO but rather the fact that the populations in countries like Afghanistan, Iran and Iraq, as well as Indonesia, Philippines and Malaysia, have been the main victims of the NWO, particularly in its economic dimension, because of their geographical and economic position.

Still, the fundamentalist movements in the South are not the only targets of the 'war against terrorism'. Direct action movements in the North, like the anti-globalisation movement, are also the implicit targets of the transnational elite. The significant curbing of civil liberties introduced at the moment throughout the North (USA, EU, etc.), ostensibly to subdue Islamic terrorists, could easily be used to suppress the more radical elements within the anti-globalisation movement. The tactics used to suppress this movement have already led to violent confrontations (from Seattle to Göteborg and Genoa) which, in the present anti-'terrorist' climate,

---

61. Peter Beaumont, 'America Gears up for a New Kind of War', *The Observer*, 10 March 2002. According to the same report, US forces are now fighting and deploying across the globe—in Afghanistan, the Philippines, Iraq and Colombia and in the former Soviet republics. American arms and money are flooding elsewhere as its military takes up new bases across the globe.

62. According to Dick Cheney, the US Vice President, the new war may last 50 years or more (see John Pilger, *The Mirror*, 29 January 2002, http://www.zmag.org).

could clearly be used by the transnational elite to identify anti-globalisers with 'terrorists'. This is particularly so at a moment when, as Alex Wilks points out[63], a number of official and media commentators have already claimed that the way to fight terrorism is further economic liberalisation, implying that anyone who dares question this is on the side of terrorists.

In this problematique, therefore, the 'war' against terrorism does not aim at 'eradicating' terrorism, as the official propaganda asserts, although, as we shall see in the next section, discouraging counter-violence in general is a basic aim of it. However, counter-violence in all its forms, which under certain conditions may take the extreme form of popular terrorism, will never be eradicated as long as there is systemic violence, state repression and state terrorism. The transnational elite is well aware of this fact, given the historical experience that clearly shows that state repression and state terrorism never managed to eradicate popular terrorism for as long as the asymmetry in power that caused it in the first instance, still continued. This is particularly true today when terrorists are prepared to use even their own lives to resist against a formidable enemy, who is able to use the most deadly technology at a minimum cost (in lives) to itself.

Common characteristics of the transnational elite's wars

Still, despite the novel elements of this war there are also certain common features characterising all the transnational elite's wars so far (i.e. the Gulf war, the NATO war against Yugoslavia and the war against Afghanistan) and in all probability will also characterise the 'wars' to come within the general framework of the 'war against terrorism'. Such characteristics are:

First, the so-called 'wars' are decided by the highest echelons of the transnational elite—the leading role in this decision-taking process being played of course by the American members of this elite that possess the necessary equipment and technology. Despite the fact that the regimes that take part in these 'wars' are called 'democracies', the peoples themselves are never involved directly in these decisions and even the professional politicians in the respective parliaments usually are called to approve these 'wars' after they have already been launched.

Second, the wars are invariably carried out in blatant violation of international law, both when they are formally covered by a capitalist-controlled UN Security Council resolution, as in the case of the Gulf war, and when they are not, as in the cases of Yugoslavia[64] and Afghanistan. As we have seen above, the doctrine of limited sovereignty used to justify these wars is in blatant contradiction to the UN Charter. With regards to the attack against Afghanistan, in particular, it should be noted that Article 51 of the UN Charter, which has been used to justify this 'war', refers to the right of 'self-defense if an armed attack occurs against a Member of the United Nations', not to any 'right' to retaliate against an attack using a civilian airliner, and in no way grants permission to attack a country that offers refuge to the transnational elite's enemies!

63. Alex Wilks, 'Keeping the Pressure On', *The Observer*, 4 November 2001.
64. See Fotopoulos, *The Gulf War* and *The New Order in the Balkans* (Athens: Staxy, 1999).

The Global 'War' of the Transnational Elite

Third, the pattern of military division of labour between the members of the transnational elite, as it emerged from all three 'wars', involves the almost exclusive use of the US military machine, particularly its unrivalled air power, in the first stages of the war effort, with the military machines of the other members mobilised mainly at later stages, for peace-keeping roles, etc. It is this pattern of military division of labour, which has persuaded some analysts to make the untenable assumption of US unilateralism, if not isolationism—at the very moment when US is involved in a global war! However, this pattern has been imposed *de facto* by the US-based members of the elite, exclusively because of military considerations, i.e. as a result of the overwhelming superiority of US military power over the other members of the transnational elite.[65] This has therefore nothing to do with any real divergence between the members of this elite regarding the common long-term aims, although of course the huge asymmetry in military power among the members of the elite gives a much greater weight to the views on tactics adopted by the American members of the elite *vis-à-vis* the views of the other members.

Fourth, any negotiated settlement is ruled out by the transnational elite, which it either sets conditions that no sovereign country could accept (this was the case of Yugoslavia that according to the Rambouillet proposals had to be voluntarily converted into a NATO protectorate to avoid the attack against it[66]) or simply blocks any offers for a negotiated settlement by the country under threat of an attack (this was the case of Iraq in the Gulf war and of Afghanistan in the present 'war').

Fifth, the political–military aim of the 'wars' is the destruction of the infrastructure of the countries concerned and the terrorisation of their peoples (killing thousands of innocent civilians in the process as 'collateral damage') so that they would be 'softened up' to accept alternative elites friendly to the transnational elite.[67] A parallel basic aim is the minimisation of the losses on the side of the transnational elite to undermine the flourishing of any mass anti-war movement, like the one that effectively forced the US elite to stop its war against Vietnam.

Sixth, as I mentioned in the second section, the transnational elite's 'wars' are justified by the doctrine of 'limited' sovereignty, according to which there are certain universal values that should take priority over other values, like that of national sovereignty. However, these universal values change according to the requirements of the 'international community', i.e. the transnational elite. Thus,

65. As a result of the huge US military superiority, according to a well known *New York Times* columnist, 'we are increasingly heading for a military apartheid within NATO: America will be the chef who decides the menu and cooks all the great meals, and the NATO allies will be the bus boys who stay around and clean up the mess and keep the peace—indefinitely', Thomas Friedman, 'America Will be the Chef and its NATO Allies the Bus Boys Who Stay to Clean up the Mess', *The Guardian*, 6 February 2002.

66. See Fotopoulos, 'New World Order and NATO's War against Yugoslavia'.

67. Adm. Sir Michael Boyce, the chief of the British Defence Staff, was explicit about this during the heavy bombing of Afghanistan: 'The squeeze will carry on until the people of the country themselves recognize that this is going to go on until they get the leadership changed'. Michael R. Gordon 'Allies Preparing for Long Fight as Taliban Dig In', *New York Times*, 28 October 2001.

in the war against Iraq it was the protection of the world from a 'new Hitler' that necessitated not only the ousting of his troops from the elite's client state (Kuwait) but also a deadly embargo that cost the lives of hundreds of thousands of innocent people. In the 'war' against Yugoslavia, it was the protection of human rights that was promoted to a universal value justifying any criminal activity by the transnational elite. Still, in the 'war against terrorism' the protection of human rights is bypassed if not suspended in favour of protection from 'terrorism' (as defined by the transnational elite again!), which becomes a new universal value justifying any kind of limitation of civil liberties, if not pure state terrorism and suppression.

Seventh, the mass media, particularly the electronic ones, play a crucial role in the manipulation of popular opinion, either by minimising the significance of the elites' crimes, or by distorting and cutting off the events from their historical context. As Phillip Knightley,[68] the author of *The First Casualty: A History of War Reporting* points out, Western media follow a depressingly familiar formula when it comes to the preparation of the public for conflict. In stage one, an atmosphere of crisis is created that supposedly demands military action to be overcome. In stage two, the enemy's leader is demonised (Sadam is likened to Hitler, the Serbian elite to the Nazis, bin Laden is presented as a maniac Islamist, etc.). In stage three, the demonisation expands to include most of the enemy peoples themselves (the Serbians are presented as Nazi thugs intent on genocide, the Taliban—in fact, most Afghans, even many Muslims—are described as fanatical and cruel, etc.). Finally, in stage four, the demonisation process culminates with the supposed 'atrocities' of the Iraqis, the Serbs, the Afghans (the story of the Kuwaiti babies is a well known scandal of Western mass media fabricating stories against the Iraqis). However, the transnational elite in its new permanent 'war' went much further than this usual process. Thus, following the 11 September attacks, the military branch of this elite, the US Pentagon, opened an Office of Strategic Influence (OSI) with the explicitly Orwellian mandate to spread misinformation aimed at brainwashing the international press and 'influencing public opinion and political leaders in friendly as well as unfriendly countries'.[69]

Eighth, the ideologues of the NWO undertake the theoretical justification of the elite's 'wars' and at the same time try to defame every intellectual that would dare to reveal the criminal character of its actions. In this effort, the most valuable assistance comes from the ideologues of the system, particularly those in the 'left'[70] who, having abandoned any anti-systemic vision after the collapse of the socialist project, have endorsed the NWO in all its aspects. The assimilation process has been gradual: the first war of the transnational elite was adopted only by the centre-left intellectuals and analysts; the second war was endorsed also by

---

68. Phillip Knightley, 'The Disinformation Campaign', *The Guardian*, 4 October 2001.
69. Ignacio Ramonet, *Le Monde Diplomatique*, March 2002.
70. A typical example is ex-Trotskyite Christopher Hitchens, who in a vitriolic attack against the critics of the 'war' against Afghanistan, wrote in the *Spectator* that intellectuals who seek to understand the new enemy are no friends of peace, democracy or human life; see Tariq Ali, 'The New Empire Loyalists', *The Guardian*, 16 March 2002.

most of the Green and broadly 'left' intelligentsia; finally, the present 'war' against terrorism has been adopted by most of the remaining 'left' including several Marxists, ex-communists and others!

4. The aims of the global 'war'

If the eradication of terrorism is mainly a pretext, as I attempted to show above, what are the real aims of this new type of 'war'? To my mind, the transnational elite pursues a series of aims with this 'war'—all within the boundaries set by the general aim of securing the stability of the NWO in its economic and political dimensions through the crushing of any perceived threats against it. Such 'particular' aims are:

* to discourage the flourishing of counter-violence brought about by the growing systemic violence, which is the inevitable by-product of capitalist neoliberal globalisation and its political implications,
* to secure 'stability'[71] in Central Asia and the Middle East, so that the sources of energy (on which the growth of the market economy depends) could be guaranteed; and
* to guarantee the reproduction of the war economy (which went through a '*raison-d'-être*' crisis after the end of the Cold War) that significantly contributes to the growth of the market economy

However, the question still remains why the transnational elite has chosen this particular moment in history to launch this unprecedented new type of war? There are several reasons for this amounting to the fact that this elite has a much better chance to crush any violent reaction against the NWO, which is based on the internationalised market economy and representative 'democracy', than the national elites ever had in the past. Such reasons are, first, the fact that the universalisation of representative 'democracy' has reduced drastically the number of people that would resort to violent action today in order to achieve significant social change when they believe that such change can also be achieved through parliament. This is particularly the case in the periphery and semi-periphery where national elites used to rely in the past on dictatorial or semi-dictatorial regimes that stifled any illusion of change through 'democratic' means, leading to rampant counter-violence in all its forms. Second, the creation of a basically self-regulating internationalised market economy institutionalises systemic violence at the economic level in such a way that few are even aware of the nature and real causes for the huge inequality in the distribution of economic power. Third, the vast improvements in the technology of state repression have created a huge asymmetry of military power that has led to the actual disappearance of the guerrilla strategy in the periphery (apart from a few exceptions in Latin America and the Philippines) and of urban terrorism almost everywhere. Fourth, the collapse of socialist statism, in its forms of 'actually existing socialism' in the East and social democracy in the West, has led to the end of traditional

71. See, for example, Pierre Abramovici, 'The US and the Taliban: A Done Deal', *Le Monde Diplomatique*, January 2002.

Takis Fotopoulos

anti-systemic movements[72] and the collapse of the traditional left in general, given the homogenisation of electoral politics that the internationalisation of the market economy implies.[73]

On the basis of such reasons one could therefore assume that the transnational elite decided to launch this new type of global war in order to secure its unchallenged hegemony for many years to come.

The intermediate targets and means implied by the above aims are the following ones:

- The military crushing of any 'rogue' regime or 'popular terrorism' organisation around the world and the parallel installation of a vast global network of military bases with the aim of encircling any potentially dangerous regime or country that harbours forms of popular terrorism that threaten the elite's interests. Thus, the 'temporary' US bases in Afghanistan, Pakistan and the Caspian states, which were supposedly built for the needs of the war, have already taken a character of permanency, as some US Administration officials made clear.[74] No wonder that, as it was recently reported on the basis of the views of several defence analysts and experts, 'today, almost six months after the attacks on New York and Washington, the US is putting in place a network of forward bases stretching from the Middle East across the entire length of Asia, from the Red Sea to the Pacific. US forces are active in the biggest array of countries since the Second World War.'[75]

- The parallel suppression of the radical currents within the new anti-systemic movements emerging today and particularly the anti-globalisation movement. This is achieved mainly through the introduction of draconian 'anti-terrorist' legislation in the North, supposedly to fight terrorism, but in reality as an effective means to suppress the collective counter-violence against the present intensification of systemic violence. Thus, anti-terrorist legislation 'deepens' everywhere. In the USA, the Patriot Act anti-terror legislation has effectively suspended parts of the US constitution, creating, as a law professor at Columbia University pointed out,[76] 'one of the more dramatic Constitutional crises in United States history' and giving the federal government sweeping new powers to investigate electronic communications, personal and financial records, computer hard drives and other individual documents. Similar legislation in Britain suspended parts of the European convention for Human Rights so that, among other provisions, foreigners could be detained indefinitely without charge or trial, on the basis merely of suspicion, whereas the EU

72. See Takis Fotopoulos, 'The End of Traditional Anti-systemic Movements and the Need for a New Type of Anti-systemic Movement Today', *Democracy & Nature*, Vol. 7, No. 3 (November 2001), pp. 415–456.

73. See Fotopoulos, 'Globalisation, the Reformist Left and the Anti-globalisation Movement'.

74. As Monbiot reports, 'In December, the US assistant secretary of state Elizabeth Jones promised that "when the Afghan conflict is over we will not leave central Asia. We have long-term plans and interests in this region",' *The Guardian*, 12 February 2002.

75. Ewen MacAskill, 'From Suez to the Pacific', *The Guardian*, 8 March 2002.

76. Patricia J. Williams. 'This Dangerous Patriot's Game', *The Observer*, 2 December 2001.

The Global 'War' of the Transnational Elite

embarked on discussions to define terrorism in a way that would allow the arrest as terrorists of students and workers occupying public buildings.[77]

As far as the 'war' itself is concerned, given its global and permanent nature that I mentioned above, we can only describe its phases up to date and make some projections about its possible future phases. The first phase has been the 'war' in Afghanistan. The second phase, though not formally stated as such, involves the suppression of the Palestinian resistance movement. The next stage in all probability would involve an invasion of Iraq to 'finish the job' that began with the Gulf war. From then on several candidates have been mentioned and the list is expanding all the time.

Phase I: The 'war' against Afghanistan

This 'war' was supposedly aimed at the military crushing of the al Quaeda organisation, which is thought to be the perpetrator of the 11 September attacks, but as soon as the massive US air bombardment began, it became obvious that the real target was the infrastructure of Afghanistan and some pitiful military facilities of the Taliban regime, including empty camps and caves where al Quaeda members used to hide in the past. Thus, despite the fact that it is highly unlikely that the Taliban regime itself was involved with the 11 September events and in spite of its desperate efforts to achieve a negotiated solution (even offering to hand Osama bin Laden over to a neutral country for trial), the transnational elite went ahead with its 'war' because obviously it had a very different agenda, i.e. the aims I mentioned above. The brutality of the B-52 carpet bombing and the use of cluster bombs, depleted uranium bombs and other newly developed super bombs[78] against one of the poorest countries on Earth (a country with life expectancy of 46 years (world average: 67 years) and an adult illiteracy rate of 65% (world average: 25%)),[79] which did not have even a remote capability of effecting any signifi- cant damage to the 'brave' attackers, set the pattern for the phases of the war against terrorism to follow and particularly the Israeli massive crimes in Palestine. It is no wonder that experts and informed sources put the total deaths of civilians at between 2000 and 8000 and according to a UN source

77. The draft framework decision on terrorism that the European Commission has presented to the European Council and parliament, as a European civil servant argued, would mean that 'an anti-capitalist action, using dubious but non-violent methods, could be considered as terrorism. As he pointed out "this legislation will target individuals or groups with a perfectly legitimate desire to radically change the political, economic and social organisation of one or more coun- tries. They will not be prosecuted for anything they have actually done, but because they may have done it for ideological reasons." John Brown, "Euro Law Wrongly Defines Terrorism", *Le Monde Diplomatique*, February 2002.

78. Robert James Parsons, 'Depleted Uranium in Bunker Bombs—America's Big Dirty Secret', *Le Monde Diplomatique*, March 2002.

79. World Bank, World Development Report 2000/2001, Tables 2 & 1a.

231

in Kabul 'it is definitely in the four figures'[80]—significantly surpassing those in New York!

The real aims were confirmed as soon as a new protectorate of the transnational elite was established in Kabul.[81] Thus, the conferences, at the end of 2001, in Bonn and in Pakistan (where a parallel economic conference under the auspices of the World Bank took place) sealed the integration of Afghanistan into the NWO, i.e. the internationalised market economy and representative 'democracy'. It is no wonder that on 29 January the IMF's assistant director for monetary and exchange affairs suggested that Afghanistan should abandon its currency and adopt the dollar instead, as a 'temporary' measure![82]

Needless to add the aims of the 'war' against Afghanistan never included the protection of women's rights from the Taliban regime, as the propaganda of the transnational elite, eagerly adopted by the 'left' intelligentsia in the West, had it. As a French feminist pointed out several months after the end of the war—indirectly, also, exonerating the French elite, which however never dissociated itself from the 'war':[83]

> Has the US always fought for women's rights? No. Has it ever? No. On the contrary, it has trampled on them. Afghan women were defended by Marxist governments, and they were the friends of the US' enemy, so the women had to go to the wall. After all, human rights cannot be allowed to interfere with the pursuit of world domination. Women's rights are like Iraqi babies. Their death is the price paid for US power. ... To say that the war may be good for Afghan women is almost to say that it is better for them to die in the bombing, cold or starvation than to live under the Taliban. ... At present the women of Afghanistan are on the road, living in tents or camps, in their millions. There are a million more refugees outside the country than there were before the war and a million displaced persons in the country itself.

Phase II: The suppression of the Palestinian movement

The second phase of the global war involves the suppression of the Palestinian movement at the hands of the transnational elite's proxy in the area, the Zionist state of Israel, which enjoys the full support of the American elements within the transnational elite and the tacit support of the rest. The aim of this informal phase is to terrorise to submission the Palestinian people so that a Palestinian protectorate could be created that will be totally dependent (economically as well as

---

80. Ian Traynor and Julian Borger, 'Storm over Afghan Civilian Victims', *The Guardian*, 12 February 2002.
81. Hamid Karzai (who was appointed by the transnational elite as head of the Afghan interim government agreed at the Bonn meetings) used to be a consultant for the US company, Unocal, during the negotiations over the Afghan oil and gas pipelines from the Caspian Sea to the port of Karachi (Abramovici, 'The US and the Taliban: A Done Deal'). See also George Monbiot, 'America's Pipe Dream', *The Guardian*, 23 October 2001.
82. George Monbiot, 'America's Imperial War', *The Guardian*, 12 February 2002.
83. Christine Delphy, *Le Monde Diplomatique*, March 2002.

The Global 'War' of the Transnational Elite

politically–militarily) on the Zionist regime and through it on the transnational elite. The ultimate aim is to secure the 'stability' of the crucial Middle East area and to guarantee the smooth supply of energy on the transnational elite's terms.

The means employed were the massive use of brutal force, which in the case of Jenin may have reached the level of a massacre that the transnational elite did everything possible to cover up and was carried out by a brutalised army, whose conscripts have grown up in a racist regime that sees Palestinians as 'inferior' to the 'chosen people'. This brutal action against a basically defenceless people enjoyed the massive support of the Israeli public, as indicated by all polls and the lack of any mass anti-war demonstrations. This support could not simply be interpreted in terms of the insecurity that the Israeli public justifiably felt as a result of suicide bombings—as the propaganda of the transnational elite and the Zionists asserts. Suicide bombing is only a very recent phenomenon that can not explain the continuous 'hardening' of Israeli public opinion over the years. Such a hardening becomes obvious by the fact that supporters of the two major parties, who for all these years have carried out the systematic colonisation of the territories through the settlements, constitute the vast majority of the population. The same majority strongly supported the brutal force used to supress the two intifadas and tacitly accepted even the Jenin crimes.

To explain this hardening, we have to refer to the drastic change of the political profile of the Israeli people in the last 50 years since the installation of the new state. This change in the political profile was the result mainly of two demographic factors: the physical withering away of the older generations, who were the real victims of blatant anti-Semitism, and the parallel massive infusion of 'new blood'—often originating from the ultra-conservative parts of the US Jewish community who believe that all of Palestine belongs to them by Biblical right. Similar factors and particularly the massive conversion of Jewish communities abroad into Zionism could explain their fervent support for the colonial and racist regime that has been established in Palestine with the overt protection of the transnational elite. No wonder that the Zionist 'holocaust industry'[84] (i.e. the exploitation of the systematic persecution and liquidation of Jews by the Nazi regime) and the similar 'anti-Semitism industry'[85] (i.e. the defaming of any critic of Zionist ethnic cleansing) was put globally at top gear. The intention was, as always, to impose a kind of severe self-censorship on any well-intended critic of Zionist/transnational elite policies.

A discussion of the real aims of the transnational elite and the Zionists with respect to the present suppression of the Palestinian movement is meaningless unless we examine briefly the establishment of the state of Israel at the end of the Second World War. It was at that time that the Zionists began the ethnic cleansing of Palestine, in the aftermath of the historic UN decision which recognised the establishment of a Jewish state on 55% of British Palestine, despite the fact that the Arabs constituted more than 60% of the total population. Then, under the pretext of Arab hostility against this blatant colonisation, a huge Zionist campaign began to expand this new state further, with the massive support of the

84. See N.G. Finkelstein, *The Holocaust Industry* (London: Verso, 2001).
85. See e.g. P. Beaumont, 'The New Anti-Semitism?', *The Observer*, 17 February 2002.

Takis Fotopoulos

West, at the expense of the Arabs who became refugees in their own lands. The Palestinians, according to the Zionist plans, should never have a sovereign state, i.e. nothing beyond a kind of protectorate dependent on Israel, that could also serve as a permanent source of cheap labour.[86]

Thus, through wars and an overt policy of colonisation of the occupied territories (approved by all major Israeli parties) the Zionists ended up controlling 90% of the Palestinian land in the early 1990s, when, under the threat of another intifada following the first one at the end of the 1980s, they agreed to a process of negotiations at the 1993 Oslo meeting. At that stage the process of creating a Palestinian protectorate began that would allow the Zionists to keep 78% of the land and allow the Arabs to create a Bantustan-type of state, with areas completely encircled by Zionists, in the remaining 28% of the land.[87] The newly emerging Palestinian middle class, facing the establishment of the NWO after the collapse of the Soviet block that supported them, expressed, through the Arafat elite, its willingness to accept this sort of arrangement. However, the lower social groups, as well as the millions of the refugees living under miserable conditions in the neighbouring countries (who were deprived of any right of return under the Oslo accord), were hostile to such plans. Many of those 'rejectionists' joined the Islamic organisations that were engaged in a fierce struggle against the occupation and the continuous expansion, in blatant violation of international law, of the Israeli settlements in the occupied territories. When therefore a final 'settlement' along these lines was offered in 2000 at Camp David,[88] the Palestinian leadership, under severe pressure 'from below' was unable to accept it. This signalled the intensification of repression and the beginning of the second intifada.

In this context, the September events provided the perfect opportunity to crush the Palestinian organisations that could now be declared as 'terrorist' and face a treatment similar to the one given by the transnational elite to the Taliban. Thus, the US elements of the transnational elite, followed by those in the EU, effectively gave the green light to the Zionist regime when they froze the financial resources of the Palestinian organisations, which were classified as terrorist. The 'Afghan treatment' of the Palestinian organisations and people that followed was as inevitable as was the dissociation by most of the left from both the violence of the oppressors and the consequent counter-violence of the oppressed—an attitude implicitly equating the two forms of political violence.

86. George Szamuely, *The Observer*, 12 August 2001; See, also, Noam Chomsky, 'Al-Aqsa Intifada', Alternative Information Centre, 20 October 2000.
87. Dilip Hiro, 'Land is the Issue. Land is Confiscated, Stolen, Kept', *The Guardian*, 22 May 2001.
88. According to an article in the *New York Review of Books* by Robert Malley, a member of the US negotiating team at Camp David, Barak and Clinton used the negotiations to set a trap for the Palestinians. The talks were 'designed to increase the pressure on the Palestinians to reach a quick agreement while heightening the political and symbolic costs if they did not' (George Szamuely, 'Israel Will Always Have a Yankee Friend', *The Observer*, 12 August 2001); see also the article on the same line by David Clark, a special adviser at the Foreign Office until May 2001, 'The Brilliant Offer Israel Never Made', *The Guardian*, 10 April 2002.

The Global 'War' of the Transnational Elite

Still, alternative solutions of democratic co-existence of the peoples of Palestine had been proposed for many years by prominent members of the Jewish Left like Hannah Arendt who, as early as the 1940s, was arguing strongly against Zionism and in favour of a Middle East federation of the peoples in Palestine.[89] In fact, one could argue that even today there is a non-racist solution to the problem in terms of a confederal Inclusive Democracy of the peoples in Palestine. In such a confederal system, all forms of power could be distributed equally between its citizens: Arabs, Jews and those belonging to minorities. Of course, such a solution is anathema to the Zionists and their apologists, as well as to the transnational elite, for, in the case of such a solution being adopted by the peoples involved, they would not be able to control the crucial Middle East area.[90]

Phase III: A new invasion in Iraq?

The next stage of the 'war' seems to involve the elimination of the 'rogue' regime in Iraq, employing the highly successful method used for the removal of the Taliban regime: the massive bombardment of the infrastructure followed by some sort of uprising of the Iraqi opposition, which is funded and armed by the transnational elite. The outrageous excuse used by the elite this time to justify the expected bloodbath is that the Iraqi regime has not implemented all the UN Security Council resolutions and that it has developed dangerous chemical weapons of mass destruction—an excuse which has hardly any connection to the supposed aim of the war, i.e. to punish terrorism. All this, at the very moment when the transnational elite itself is fully aware of the fact that the UN embargo they have imposed on Iraq operates in breach of the UN covenants on human rights, the Geneva and Hague conventions and other international laws and that its client regime, Zionist Israel, has contemptuously ignored all UNSC resolutions passed against it and, on top of this, possesses weapons of mass destruction, including nuclear ones. It is also indicative of the 'democratic' character of the 'international community' (i.e. the transnational elite) that the entire campaign is being organised despite the fact that according to the polls,[91] even strong supporters of such 'wars' in the past, like the British public (as well as the German and French public) are against it, presumably suspecting that the real aim of this new 'war' is to secure absolute control on Iraq's

89. See Moshe Zimmerman, 'Mother of Post-Zionism', *HA'ARETZ*, 20 October 2000.
90. Although it is to Chomsky's credit that he has never been an apologist of Zionism, still, in contradiction to his radical stand on the matter in the past, he declared in a recent NBC chat that 'personally I don't think and have never thought that we should discontinue support of Israel'. He then went on to repeat the strange statement he has made in the past that US is 'a very free, very democratic society' and declare that he agrees with the 'two-states' solution in Palestine which, however, would inevitably involve the backdated vindication of the racist policies of Zionists (see MSNBC.com chat of 2 October 2001, published in *Znet*).
91. A March 2002 poll in Britain showed that a clear majority—51%—would disapprove of British political support for an American-led attack on Iraq, with or without the presence of British troops. As *The Guardian* noted at the time the poll, it shows that the Germans and French are more in tune with British public opinion on this issue than Mr Blair or Mr Duncan Smith (the leader of the opposition) (Alan Travis, 'Say No to Iraq Attack', *The Guardian*, 19 March 2002.

oil reserves. This is not suprising of course if one recalls Henry Kissinger's brutally frank admission that oil to substantiate the propaganda, 'is much too important a commodity to be left in the hands of the Arabs'.[92]

Needless to add, there is no evidence whatsoever of the transnational elite concerning the weapons of mass destruction, supposedly possessed by the Iraqi regime. Scott Ritter, who was a UN weapons inspector in Iraq from 1991 to 1998, declared recently that 'under the most stringent on-site inspection regime in the history of arms control, Iraq's biological weapons programmes were dismantled, destroyed or rendered harmless during the course of hundreds of no-notice inspections'.[93] Even an extensive survey[94] among Western arms inspectors and military and foreign affairs experts drew similar conclusions. Thus, according to this survey, 'most analysts concede that there is considerable doubt about the extent of Saddam's weapons programme, and about how dangerous it could be to the rest of the world'. Furthermore, several experts, including ex-inspectors, agree that the inspectors destroyed 95% of Iraq's weapons of mass destruction and the remaining 5% has been rendered unusable by the fact that Iraq is prevented under sanctions from replacing equipment needed to deploy them. Finally, Rosemary Hollis, head of the Middle East programme at the Royal Institute of International Affairs, reported that from discussions with nuclear scientists it seemed clear that Iraq does not have the capacity to build nuclear weapons, whereas the International Atomic Energy Agency (IAEA), which is responsible for monitoring nuclear weapons and which is still making visits to Iraq, has recently concluded that there is no sign of a surviving programme.

It is not therefore surprising that the transnational elite used every method available to it in order to preclude any independent assessment of the weapons of mass destruction supposedly possessed by Iraq, including an unprecedented coup to oust the director-general of the Organisation for the Prohibition of Chemical Weapons (OPCW) that enforces the chemical weapons convention who has proposed a peaceful solution to 'the problem'. As Monbiot[95] pointed out at the time, 'the coup will also shut down the peaceful options for dealing with the chemical weapons Iraq may possess, helping to ensure that war then becomes the only means of destroying them'.

Phase IV: The 'axis of evil' and beyond

The permanent feature of the new type of 'war' launched by the transnational elite was made clear by its spokesman, Bush, Jr, in his State of the Union address

92. Hans von Sponeck and Denis Halliday, 'The Hostage Nation', *The Guardian*, 29 November 2001. The report by these two ex-UN humanitarian coordinators for Iraq is particularly useful in showing that 'The uncomfortable truth is that the West is holding the Iraqi people hostage, in order to secure Saddam Hussein's compliance to ever-shifting demands'.

93. Scott Ritter, 'Don't Blame Saddam for this One', *The Guardian*, 19 October 2001.

94. Julian Borger, Richard Norton-Taylor, Ewen MacAskill and Brian Whitaker 'Iraq: The Myth and the Reality', *The Guardian*, 15 March 2002.

95. See G Monbiot, 'Chemical coup d'etat', *The Guardian*, 16 April 2002 and 'Diplomacy US Style', *The Guardian*, 23 April 2002.

The Global 'War' of the Transnational Elite

to the Congress in January 2002 in which he extended the war targets to include, after Afghanistan, what he called 'the axis of evil', i.e. Iraq, Iran and North Korea. As Ivo Daalder, a strategic analyst at the Brookings Institution, said 'It was a virtual declaration of war; it enunciated a new doctrine, which says that people we declare bad, with weapons we declare bad, are basically the same as terrorists'.[96] Thus, whereas the original 'Bush doctrine', which was announced in the aftermath of 11 September declared 'war' against the terrorist perpetrators of these attacks and the states harbouring them, the new expanded and improved version of it declared war against anyone the transnational elite, through the US elite, considers as 'bad'.

The rhetoric used by Bush was the usual: 'North Korea is a regime arming with missiles and weapons of mass destruction, while starving its citizens' and Iran aggressively pursues these weapons and exports terror, while an unelected few repress the Iranian people's hope for freedom. These regimes, as well as the usual suspect, Iraq, 'by seeking weapons of mass destruction pose a grave and growing danger' as 'they could attack our allies or attempt to blackmail the United States'.

Of course the truth, as usual, has nothing to do with this rhetoric. There is no evidence that North Korea does have the technology to put credible weapons on its ramshackle missiles. The real problem that North Korea creates for the transnational elite is that it is a major exporter of ballistic missile technology to the Middle East.[97] Also, Iran has committed itself to international inspection of its chemical, biological and nuclear facilities. In fact, the real problem with the fundamentalist regime in Iran is that the Zionist Israeli regime has always seen it as its gravest long-term threat; i.e. the 'rogue state' at its most menacing, combining sponsorship of international terror, nuclear ambition, ideological objection to the existence of the Jewish state and unflagging determination to sabotage the Middle East peace process. As an experienced analyst[98] pointed out, Israel classifies Iran as one of those 'far' threats—Iraq being another—that distinguish it from the 'near' ones: the Palestinians and neighbouring Arab states. It seems therefore that the plan of the transnational elite is that once the Palestinian movement has been crushed and accepts the kind of protectorate status the former designed for it, it will be the turn of Iraq, Iran and possibly North Korea for the 'Afghan treatment'.

As I mentioned above, although all members of the transnational elite share the same long-term goals, still, some members, notably the EU elites, would prefer to 'deal' with Iraq and particularly with Iran through the use of non-military means. However, as I mentioned in previous sections, given the huge asymmetry of power between USA and the other members of the elite, there is little doubt as to which tactical approach will prevail at the end. In fact, the extent of America's power is unprecedented in human history, since, with the latest increases in its military spending announced by Bush Jr, US military spending will account to 40% of the worldwide total, putting the US military predominance miles ahead of any previous military empire—from the Roman to the British—which have never

96. Julian Borger, *The Guardian*, 31 January 2002.
97. Oliver Burkeman, 'North Korea "selling missiles" ', *The Guardian*, 2 February 2002.
98. David Hirst, 'Israel Thrusts Iran in Line of US Fire', *The Guardian*, 2 February 2002.

237

enjoyed anything like this preponderance, let alone America's global reach. The target of this huge military power was made explicit by a report for the US Space Command last year, which, after celebrating about the 'synergy of space superiority with land, sea, and air superiority' that would come with missile defence and other projects to militarise space, drew the conclusion that 'this would "protect US interests and investment" in an era when globalisation was likely to produce a further "widening between haves and have-nots" '.[99]

Finally, the list of states that are candidates for some sort of treatment by the transnational elite if they do not 'behave' is lengthening all the time. At this stage, the transnational elite demands from the local elites to take 'steps', with its help, to crush the indigenous resistance movements and allow the US military to establish its presence there. This applies in particular to the Philippines, where a diplomat was quoted recently in Washington as observing that 'the Americans have been desperate to get back into the Philippines since their armed forces were kicked out of the Clark and Subic Bay bases in 1992'.[100] It also applies to countries like Malaysia, where several terrorist groups are based; Indonesia, where the Islamist tide is rising and mass anti-war demonstrations have taken place; Yemen and Sudan, which are asked to liquidate what remains of the training camps, depots and resources once used by supposedly terrorist groups; and Georgia, where the Pentagon has already outlined plans to take war on terror to it.

Furthermore, Latin American movements resisting the effects of capitalist neoliberal globalisation are already characterised as terrorist. Thus, 'in Brazil, the military has often described the Landless Peasants' Movement (MST) as terrorist, in Mexico, the Zapatistas have been accused, whereas the CIA national intelligence council and the Chilean military research centre have identified "a new challenge to internal security": the indigenous threat, from Mexico to Tierra del Fuego',[101] Very recently, Cuba was added on the list of the targets of the war against terror when in a speech called 'Beyond the Axis of Evil' the under-secretary of state, John Bolton, accused Fidel Castro's regime of developing biological weapons and sharing its expertise with other 'rogue states'[102] No wonder that the Centre for Strategic and International Studies (CSIS) finds a close relationship between the construction of the FTAA (i.e. the process which aims to extend the North American Free Trade Agreement—NAFTA—to the entire hemisphere) and a new 'security architecture in the Americas'.[103]

Naturally, the old big enemies, Russia and China, have not been forgotten, but simply downgraded as 'evil' states, at present, because the ruling elites in these countries are eager to integrate their economies to the internationalised market economy. Still, preparing for the eventuality of a change of regime in these countries, the military part of the transnational elite in the US, as was revealed in

99. Seumas Milne, 'Can the US be Defeated?', *The Guardian*, 14 February 2002.

100. Andrew Murray, 'Challenge in the East', *The Guardian*, 30 January 2002.

101. Janette Habel, 'Latin America Recolonised', *Le Monde Diplomatique*, January 2002.

102. Julian Borger, 'War on Terror May Extend to Cuba', *The Guardian*, 7 May 2002.

103. *Ibid.* Quoted from Patrice M. Franko, 'Toward a New Security Architecture in the Americas'.
     The Strategic Implications of the FTAA', *The CSIS Press*, Vol. 22, No. 3, Washington, 2000.

The Global 'War' of the Transnational Elite

March 2002, has already prepared contingency plans for a nuclear attack on seven countries, which apart from the usual suspects (Iraq, North Korea, Iran, Libya and Syria) includes also Russia and China!

5. Concluding remarks: the way out of the cycle of violence

The obvious conclusion from the above analysis is that systemic violence and therefore state repression (if not state terrorism), as well as counter-violence (including popular terrorism), are built-in elements of any society characterised by an unequal distribution of political and economic power. If the ultimate cause of political violence in all its forms is the asymmetry of power, it is obvious that the only way out of the cycle of violence is the elimination of this asymmetry and particularly the elimination of systemic violence. This involves the establishment of new political and economic institutions that aim at the equal distribution of power in all its forms, between, as well as within, nations and the parallel creation of a culture compatible with it. The cultural factor is particularly important because it would be a serious error to assume that the present socio-economic system relies only on the elites' repression and the media brainwashing and not also on the socialisation by schools, the family and other social institutions which condition people to take the present socio-economic system for granted. The political apathy created by representative democracy and the individualism promoted by the market economy are not only symptoms of the systemic violence that is associated with the concentration of political and economic power institutionalised by these institutions. They form also the constituent elements of a process that leads to a fundamental lack of belief towards an alternative socio-economic organisation—a process that the collapse of the socialist project decisively influenced.

However, if it would be erroneous to minimise the significance of the cultural factor it would be equally erroneous to move to the other extreme, particularly fashionable today among many radical ecologists and feminists, i.e. to minimise the importance of the institutional factor and assume that what is wrong is not the market economy system and representative 'democracy' themselves but the Western culture, as if culture is somehow independent from the institutional framework. These two extremes have led to correspondingly extreme positions as regards the transition to a new society. As I attempted to show elsewhere,[104] the appropriate strategy cannot be in terms of the old Marxist approach, which is based on the building of an anti-systemic movement in the hope that the struggle against the present system and for the establishment of new institutions following a revolution will create the necessary culture. As the Soviet case showed, this strategy failed to create the new culture, even after the lapse of more than 70 years following the revolution. Nor could it be in terms of the anarchist approach of 'prefiguring', i.e. building the new within the old at the small social scale of our commune or neighbourhood, outside of a mass anti-systemic movement and the political arena in general. Such experiments of 'anarchy in action' have been

104. See Takis Fotopoulos, 'Transitional Strategies and the Inclusive Democracy Project', *Democracy & Nature*, Vol. 8, No. 1 (March 2002), pp. 17–62.

tried for more than 30 years, since the late 1960s and early 1970s, and dismally failed to create a new anti-systemic consciousness at a massive scale, remaining always marginalized or even used by social-liberal governments as a kind of alternative system of welfare services at no cost to the budget, in place of the welfare state that is being mercilessly dismantled by the capitalist neoliberal globalisation.

The appropriate strategy may only be a synthesis of these approaches, as well as of the direct action approach used by movements like the anti-globalisation movement. This implies, as I stressed in the last issue,[105] creating a democratic organisation that will fight for the building of a new massive anti-systemic movement with clear long-term and short-term goals and strategy aiming at a new political and economic institutional framework, as a necessary condition (though not a sufficient one) for the elimination of the unequal distribution of political and economic power. Such a movement will combine the fight against the present system with the parallel struggle to create a new system within the old. Building inclusive democracies at the local level, as an integral part of an anti-systemic movement explicitly aiming at the institution of a confederal inclusive democracy, is perhaps the only way leading to the creation of a genuinely alternative society rather than an easily reversible variation of the existing one. It is also the first step towards the creation of a society with no systemic violence, in which the cycle of violence will, for the first time in history, become redundant.

---

105. See Takis Fotopoulos, ' "The Transition to An Alternative Society: The Ecovillage Movement, The Simpler Way and the Inclusive Democracy Project"—Takis Fotopoulos' Reply, *Democracy & Nature*, Vol. 8, No. 1 (March 2002), pp. 150–157.

[29]

Cambridge Review of International Affairs,
Volume 15, Number 3, 2002

Carfax Publishing
Taylor & Francis Group

Reflections on Globalisation, Security and 9/11

Christopher W. Hughes
University of Warwick

Abstract *The study of globalisation carries important conceptual insights into the contemporary security agenda following the events of September 11th 2001 ('9/11'). This article argues that globalisation can be defined in a variety of ways, ranging from liberalisation to Westernisation, and can also be extended into concepts of supra-territorialisation. In combination, these definitions help to explain the generation of 9/11 style-conflict by providing the political-economic motivation for hyper-terrorism, by facilitating the political identities and activities of non-state actors; and by creating an environment for the global reach of terror movements. Additionally, the interconnection between globalisation and security can be seen in the response of the United States to 9/11 and its striving to project military power on a global scale with declining reference to time and geographical distance, and the varied ability of sovereign states to respond to the challenge of trans-sovereign security problems in the future.*

Security has once again reclaimed the centre stage of the international social science and policy agendas. The events of September 11th 2001 and the ensuing conflict in Afghanistan have highlighted many of the unfolding trends and complexities of contemporary security. A variety of social science disciplines, including International Relations (IR) and the traditionally diverse field of Security Studies, have already been brought to bear in order to provide explanatory insights into the aftermath of 9/11. It is also inevitable that another field of enquiry, globalisation studies, should be applied to understanding 9/11. Even if this field might not yet be confident or established enough in its individual status to generally speak of itself in upper case terms, in the discussions amongst both policy and academic circles post-9/11 there was a definite sense in which these events were related to the phenomenon of globalisation, and that those engaged in its study may possess a distinct type of knowledge that could contribute to the debate on security.

The argument of this article is that the study of globalisation does indeed have the capability to make a distinctive and advantageous, if at times supplementary, contribution to the study of security after 9/11. It argues that the processes of globalisation themselves, defined in a variety of ways including liberalisation, convergence and supra-territorialisation, form one conceptual lens and explanation for the perpetration of, and responses to, violent conflict and terrorism. Although, at the same time this article argues that globalisation alone is not responsible for conflict scenarios such as that in Afghanistan, but needs to be understood in combination with other fundamental or 'conjunctural' shifts in the international structure, including decolonisation and bipolarisation.

ISSN 0955-7571 print/ISSN 1474-449X online/02/030421-13 © 2002 Centre of International Studies
DOI: 10.1080/095575702200001095 3

The study of globalisation is inherently a multidisciplinary enterprise, drawing in IR, International Political Economy (IPE), Economics, Sociology, History and a number of other fields of expertise. This type of approach is arguably less constrained by traditional state-centred security debates, and is thus highly suited to getting to grips with the complex and cross-cutting security agenda after 9/11. It offers a means to address its multi-actor nature in terms of the revealed (if not wholly new) proliferation of security actors; its multi-dimensional nature in comprising political-military, economic, societal and environmental security; its multi-regional nature in straddling and connecting the security of a number of regions from the Middle East, to Africa, Europe, East Asia; and its inter-linked nature in seeing all of these actors, dimensions, and regions as potentially conjoined and impacting on the security of each.

Alongside this exhortation to consider the post-9/11 security agenda as one which can be seen in many ways as something akin to a post-globalisation security agenda, this article also throws in three major caveats that limit its scope and ambition. Firstly, there is always the constant danger of overstretching both the concepts of globalisation and security to the point of losing sharpness in their conceptual definition and explanatory power. Susan Strange chided the globalisation studies community by remarking that the phenomenon has been used to analyse everything from the Internet to the hamburger,[1] and this serves as a warning that we should be cautious in applying globalisation to the topic of security, an already well-developed field. There is a risk on various sides of debate of engaging in a 'securitisation' exercise and simply slapping the label of globalisation on 9/11 without delving any deeper in our analysis.[2] Those who perceive themselves as victims of the attacks may argue that terrorism is an anti-globalisation force, but this is a statement, as argued below, that can only penetrate to the truth if globalisation is carefully defined from different perspectives to discover the particular elements of this broad phenomenon that the perpetrators of terror are resisting. Meanwhile, those who perceive themselves as victims of globalisation and its related evils, or in the policy and academic communities that argue the case in favour of such perceived victimisation, may have hit upon globalisation as a genuine force for generating insecurity. However, if this is as far as the examination of the globalisation–security nexus goes, then this runs the risk of caricaturing globalisation and halting in its tracks debate that can unpack the phenomenon and its political and economic dynamics, and in turn the effort to understand in a deeper fashion the interconnection with security. Unfortunately, this deeper understanding of 9/11 has not been overly present in much of the related analysis, with a knee jerk reaction on all sides of locating security with the globalisation process but without actually examining what the term itself means in different contexts.

Secondly, this article should be read with the caveat that it will touch upon events in the Middle East, but that the author is more knowledgeable about

---

[1] Susan Strange, *The Retreat of the State: The Diffusion of Power in the World Economy*, Cambridge, Cambridge University Press, 1996, p. xiii.

[2] For examples of the debate on securitisation, see Barry Buzan, Ole Waever and Jaap de Wilde, *Security: A New Framework for Analysis*, Boulder, Lynne Rienner, 1998, pp. 23–26; and Simon Dalby, 'Contesting an Essential Concept: Reading the Dilemmas in Contemporary Security Discourse', in Keith Krause and Michael C. Williams, eds, *Critical Security Studies: Concepts and Cases*, Minneapolis, University of Minnesota Press, 1997, pp. 3–32.

security studies and globalisation in general and with particular reference to the East Asia region. Thirdly, this article cannot attempt to cover all the events and implications of 9/11 simply due to the massive scope of the agenda and the limited number of words available.

Nonetheless, having outlined these caveats and the risks involved, this article will briefly introduce some areas where the study of globalisation may add explanatory power to the events of 9/11 and the current attempts of Security Studies to grapple with its implications. The problem of conceptual clarity will be overcome by attempting to adopt a two-level definition of globalisation that will highlight how it impacts on security. The problem of how far to stretch the interconnection between globalisation and security will also be addressed by limiting the examination to the ways in which globalisation phenomena have impacted on the generation of, and responses to, violent conflict, rather than in this particular context running the whole gamut of potential security problems opened up by globalisation. The minimal knowledge of the Middle East cannot be readily overcome, but the strategy of the article is on the one hand to hope that some of the lessons about the impact of globalisation on East Asia are transferable to other regions, and, on the other, simply to hope that some of the insights offered resonate with those more expert in this region. Finally, as all events and implications of 9/11 cannot be dealt with, the approach of the article is simply to sample a variety of areas where globalisation has impacted on security and the problems of terrorism and state responses.

Defining Globalisation

Globalisation as Liberalisation and Convergence

Globalisation is a notoriously slippery concept to define. This article suggests a two-step definition and understanding of globalisation as both reflexive and substantive processes which are dialectically related and in many cases nearly indistinguishable. Perhaps the most common understanding of globalisation to date has been that of internationalisation, implying the increasing density and interdependence of interaction amongst nation-states and their markets, or, more accurately, given the lack of congruence in many regions between state entities and their nationalist populations, sovereign states. In turn, these increased flows of capital, personnel and knowledge generally go beyond internationalisation, which implies the state essentially remaining unchanged in this process, and involves the lowering of state borders, which then equates to the process of liberalisation.[3]

The next most common definition of globalisation is derived from the general notion prevalent in the mass media and mass opinion of a general convergence in global affairs in the economic, political and other spheres of social activity. The convergence thesis view of globalisation finds its most extreme form in the hyper-globalisation and 'end of history' literature of the likes of Kenichi Ohmae

---

[3] For this type of understanding of globalisation in government circles as internationalisation and liberalisation, see UK Government, *Eliminating World Poverty: Making Globalisation Work for the Poor, White Paper on International Development*, December 2000, http://www.globalisation.gov.uk/WhitePaper/FullPaper.pdf

424 *Christopher W. Hughes*

and Francis Fukuyama.[4] However, the convergence thesis also feeds through in a variety of extremes into definitions of globalisation that revolve around the idea of the universalisation of standards of social interaction. This is at least the preferred understanding in the discourse of many of the most powerful government and institutional advocates of the benefits of globalisation in the developed world. For even if they may not argue consciously for universalisation and wish to acknowledge heterogeneity, the economic policies and Structural Adjustment Packages (SAPs) which the international financial institutions (IFIs) have championed for the developing world in East Asia, Latin America, Africa and the Middle East imply, at the very least, convergence by default. From the developing world view, such policies which lead to convergence and universalisation can also bring about a definition of globalisation as Westernisation. Even less attractive is the concept of globalisation as a form of Americanisation, as the United States is seen as the principal power pushing for convergence in ways that only serve to reinforce its global political and economic dominance, and that are capable of leading to accusations of neo-imperialism.[5] The implications for security of the perceived congruence between globalisation and Americanisation in the generation of anti-American feeling in the case of 9/11 is addressed in subsequent sections.

Globalisation as Supra-territorialisation

Liberalisation, universalisation, Westernisation and Americanisation are all clearly components of globalisation, and because globalisation is itself a reflexive process (often accentuated by modern telecommunications technology), where perceptions drive forward the process, this means that these definitions and their related discourses are not merely academic matters but have to be dealt with as world views that motivate actual political, economic and security behaviour. However, it is also possible to conceive of globalisation at a second and still higher conceptual level, and which can help to further unlock understanding of its impact upon security. Arguably, the above definitions fail to capture the qualitatively different nature of globalisation from other processes and phenomena associated with the interaction of social forces on a global scale. Globalisation represents a qualitatively different process due to its essential de-territorialisation, or stated in reverse, supra-territorialisation of social interaction. That is to say, globalisation is a process which increasingly reconfigures social space away from and beyond notions of delineated territory, and *transcends* existing physical and human borders imposed upon social interaction.[6] For instance, global financial transactions, facilitated by information technology, can now often operate without reference to physical territorial distance or human-imposed territorial barriers. Hence, globalisation is a process facilitated by economic liberalisation and the growth of new technologies, but it is a

---

[4] Kenichi Ohmae, *The Borderless World*, London, Fontana, 1990; Francis Fukuyama, *The End of History and the Last Man*, Harmondsworth, Penguin, 1992.

[5] For one critical view from the developing world of globalisation as leading to the reinforcement of the power of the North over the South, see Martin Khor, *Globalization and the South: Some Critical Issues*, Penang, Third World Network, 2000, pp. 1–16.

[6] Jan Aart Scholte, 'Global Capitalism and the State', *International Affairs*, vol. 73, no. 3, July 1997, p. 431.

process which may also go beyond these in its functioning and outcomes. Again, it is important to avoid the 'hyper-globalisation' thesis which views the world as moving towards a condition of being totally 'borderless'. For it is apparent that there is considerable territorial 'drag' upon the free flow of globalisation forces; that not all forms of economic interaction such as trade and labour migration are as fully globalised as finance; that there are wide disparities in the degree of globalisation across different regions of the world; and, as pointed out in subsequent sections, that there is both resistance to, and reversibility in, the process itself.[7] Nevertheless, globalisation as a process of supra-territorialisation is increasingly affecting large sections of the world, and must be acknowledged as a different, although certainly related, process from those other definitions of social interaction noted above. Hence, even though liberalisation, internationalisation, universalism, and Westernisation may eventually result in globalisation, the fact that they may not necessarily be entirely detached from territorialisation means that they remain on a qualitatively different level from the inherently supra-territorial phenomena of globalisation.

The phenomena of globalisation as supra-territorialisation and the re-configuration of social space carry significant implications for existing forms of social organisation and, most importantly in the case of security issues, the dominant position of the nation-state within the existing globality. Needless to say, the state with its exclusive jurisdiction—or in other words, *sovereignty*—over a particular social and territorial space, delineated by a combination of physical geography and most especially human construction, has been the basic unit for the division of global space in the modern era. States in the past have attempted in theory and practice to exercise sovereign control over all forms of social interaction in the political, economic and security dimensions, both within and between their territorial borders. Quite clearly, and as elucidated below with reference to the post-colonial states of East Asia and the Middle East, not all states throughout history have been strong enough to be able to exercise the same degree of sovereign control and authority over all forms of social interaction. Nevertheless, sovereign states rooted in territorial notions of social space have been the prime unit for facilitating, impeding and mediating interaction between the societal groups, organisations, and citizens and other categories of collective and individual societal units contained within their borders. Hence, to date, global social space has been primarily international, or inter-sovereign-state, social space.

However, the inherent nature of globalisation as a process which transcends and overrides territoriality as the dominant principle for the organisation of social space now poses a fundamental challenge to the sovereign state as the basic social unit which exemplifies and undergirds this very territorial principle. Sovereign states must contend with the freer flow of social forces on a global scale which move with declining reference to the previous limitations and channels imposed by state borders. This increasing porosity of state borders, relative decline in the *de facto* sovereign authority of states over social interaction, and corresponding increased exposure of 'internal' societal groupings to 'external forces' (or even indeed the removal of the traditional domestic–

---

[7] For a cautiously sceptical view of the extent of globalisation, see Paul Hirst and Grahame Thompson, *Globalisation in Question*, Cambridge, Polity Press, 1999, pp. 1–18.

international divide to create an inter-mestic arena for social interchange) has a number of outcomes for security, as discussed below. For if global social space has been primarily international or inter-sovereign-state space for much of the modern era, then the security order as one aspect of social interaction has been built primarily around the inter-state order. But it is clear that the security order is now pitted against the phenomenon of globalisation which generates security issues diametrically opposed to and often beyond the limits of sovereign-state authority.

Globalisation and Security

The following sections now attempt to examine how globalisation, understood in terms of liberalisation, convergence and supra- or de-territorialisation, can be seen to motivate and facilitate the contemporary security agenda and generation of violence in both general terms and with specific reference to 9/11.

Sovereign-state Units, Decolonisation, Bipolarisation and Globalisation

The influence of globalisation needs to be considered alongside other major processes which have shaped the inter-sovereign-state and related security system. The effects of globalisation should not be disembedded from factors of historical and regional contingency, and, following on this, the particular nature of the state units in each region which underpin (or in many case are increasingly failing to underpin) the global security order. In order to understand these state units it is thus necessary to remember that, prior to the advent of globalisation as the dominant perceived trend in regional politics, the forces of decolonisation and bipolarisation were the most active in shaping sovereign states in the post-war period, and that these forces clearly had differential effects. In the developed world, decolonisation clearly figured less greatly in the reconfiguration of already well-established individual state units, many of which were colonisers themselves, other than to reorder their relative capacities in the inter-sovereign-state system. Bipolarisation served to preserve these sovereign-state units, if to skew the economic development of the states of the communist and non-communist camps. In the developing world, the effects of decolonisation and bipolarisation were more fundamental.[8] Decolonisation in Africa, East Asia and the Middle East brought into existence a number of new sovereign states. In theory these were modelled along the lines of the sovereign and nation-states of their former colonial masters or the developed states, but in practice have not always conformed to these ideals. In many instances, the idea of the sovereign state came before or diverged from that of the nation-state: shown by the fact that the territorial and sovereign space of states in the region was often delineated along former colonial borders which had been drawn arbitrarily and in contradistinction to trans-border ties of ethnicity and religion.

These problems are particularly salient in East Asia and the Middle East, where cross-border minority groups such as the Palestinians, Kurds, Chechens,

---

[8] For an approach which combines the processes of decolonisation and globalisation to explain development across different regions, see Ankie Hoogvelt, *Globalization and the Postcolonial World: The New Political Economy of Development*, Basingstoke, Palgrave, 2001.

Karens and Timorese are often at loggerheads with the state into which they have been principally incorporated. Such contradictions between sovereign space and societal composition clearly weakened from the start the internal political cohesion of states in the region, and laid the ground for the potential divisibility between the security interests of the state and its societal constituents. Hence, these types of states have often been subject to internal political unrest, separatist and insurgency movements. Moreover, the common legacy of distorted development from the colonial period also placed these states in a disadvantageous economic position to maintain their internal stability. For instance, the preoccupation of many states in the East Asia region in the post-colonial period has been to preserve their internal integrity by advancing the process of state building, and particularly in the economic sphere, as a means to reconcile these structural contradictions.[9] In the Middle East, the picture is a similar one of forced economic integration of this region into the international political economy under the influence of the imperial powers, and then the continuing legacy of the structural dependence on raw material and oil exports and limited intra-regional economic integration in the post-colonial period—all obliging the regimes of the region to attempt to secure their legitimacy by state-led development policies.

The problematic position of newly established sovereign states in various regions was also further compounded either during or immediately after the decolonisation phase by the impact of the onset of the Cold War. The division of regions between the competing ideologies and political economies of the socialist and capitalist blocs was to create a legacy of military confrontation and superpower interventionism. Just as important when considering the post-globalisation security agenda is the effect of the Cold War upon the state-building agendas and development of the political economies of many of the states in the East Asia and Middle East regions. The economic dispensations offered by the superpowers to allied, aligned, or even non-aligned states in various regions of the developing world assisted their economic progress but also left them ultimately vulnerable when exposed to the forces of liberal capitalism at the end of the Cold War.

Therefore, the overlapping processes of decolonisation and bipolarisation have had a significant impact upon the development of the sovereign states of the developing world and their ability to respond to the process of globalisation. Firstly, these processes have created states marked by internal contradictions between the delineation of territorial space and societal composition, and a near ineradicable and potential divisibility between the proclaimed security interests of these states and large sections of their citizenry. Secondly, they have created states that are or will be increasingly driven to exploit the benefits of liberal capitalism to paper over the political and security cracks in their own societies, but which have been insulated in the past from the full effects of capitalism's tendency towards periodic crises. The end of the Cold War and the declining incentives on the part of the United States to provide special economic dispensations is also exposing the states of various regions to fully-fledged modes of liberal capitalism and their attendant security costs. In East Asia the end of US

---

[9] Mohammed Ayoob, *The Third World Security Predicament: State Making, Regional Conflict and the International System*, Boulder, Lynne Rienner, 1995, pp. 21–45.

428   *Christopher W. Hughes*

dispensations was highlighted to some degree by its unwillingness to invest significant resources in bailing out the East Asia states from the financial crisis of 1997 onwards. In the Middle East, it seems the end of the Cold War and collapse of oil prices for the oil-producing countries generated major economic shocks, whilst the decline in US and Soviet technical, military and economic aid undermined the economic stability of oil and non-oil-producing Arab states alike.[10]

Motivations for Violent Conflict

The analysis above of the processes of decolonisation and bipolarisation provides an historically contingent backdrop which helps to explain how globalisation processes impact on security across different sovereign states and societies. If the first-stage definition of globalisation as liberalisation is applied, it is immediately apparent how these processes have impacted on the political economies of a variety of states, which in turn has produced the conditions for violent conflict. Economic liberalisation in East Asia has produced mixed effects for economic and political stability. Firstly, globalisation has produced economic exclusion for states and individuals. This may be marked by disparities in welfare, which can feed through into military tension amongst states, or result in internal unrest within states. North Korea is one example of a state which has taken the path of autarchy and found itself lagging behind other states in the region economically.[11] Secondly, globalisation may produce economic rivalry amongst states and their citizens for scarce economic resources, a constant potential problem in East Asia with regard to competition for energy, food and fresh water resources. Thirdly, globalisation may produce economic dislocation within states. In East Asia, this location has been marked by financial crises and the ingraining of poverty in certain sections of society. All these effects of economic liberalisation and globalisation are accentuated by the pre-existing vulnerabilities engendered by the effects of decolonisation and bipolarisation on the political economy of development in such states, and can feed through into social instability. In turn, these problems of instability are compounded by the often declining ability of states under the dominance of neo-liberal IFIs to practise policies which can redistribute these costs away from the most vulnerable in their societies and minimise internal political tensions.

In the Middle East it would appear that globalisation in the form of economic liberalisation has produced similar effects. The oil-producing states of the region are in a sense already globalised owing to their high degree of dependence on the export of one commodity, but have also been able to insulate themselves to a certain degree because of their large market share and the converse dependency of foreign consumers on their products. However, it is also clear that states such as Saudi Arabia that have been able to practise a degree of autarchy

---

[10] Toby Dodge, 'Bringing the Bourgeoisie Back in: Globalization and the Birth of Liberal Authoritarianism in the Middle East', in Toby Dodge and Richard Higgott, eds, *Globalization and the Middle East: Islam, Economy, Society and Politics*, London, Royal Institute of International Affairs, 2002, p. 181.

[11] Christopher W. Hughes, *Japan's Economic Power and Security: Japan and North Korea*, London, Routledge, 1999, pp. 117–60.

in the past, which has also reinforced the autocracy of the ruling regime, are now facing a decline in their economic performance.

Subsequently this presents such states with the need to further liberalise their economies to attract foreign direct investment (FDI), but this presents the dilemma of exacerbating potential internal inequalities in welfare, the exposure to external economic shocks, and the resulting political risks of divergent calls for both greater reform or to reverse reforms. This provides fertile ground for political discontent with the dominant regimes, and the radicalisation of Islam which forms the only outlet for the expression of opposition in states where political parties are banned or subjugated to the state. Recent bomb attacks in Saudi Arabia in early 2002, directed against foreigners, are evidence of the rising dissatisfaction with the Western-oriented but also politically rigid House of Saud. For the non-oil-producing states, these dilemmas are even greater as they are possessed of fewer resources to cushion the economic and political impact of their integration into the global political economy.

Likewise, globalisation perceived as convergence, leading to Westernisation or Americanisation, clearly possesses also the potential to create an environment conducive to political discontent. In East Asia, the confidence that many of the elites possessed in the prowess of their own economic management to simultaneously ride the wave of economic globalisation and to maintain the allegedly common bulwark of 'Asian Values' against the encroachment of 'Western Values' accompanying economic development, has met a serious setback. The perceived dominance of the United States over IFIs and its attempts to roll back the developmental state model in the region resulted in resentment in varying degrees towards the United States and the West amongst both political leaders and on the 'street' amongst the disadvantaged.[12] In the case of Indonesia and Malaysia, the financial crisis also raised fears that moderate or secular governments may not be able to hold the line as anti-globalisation and anti-Western sentiment combined with the radicalisation of Islam.[13] Regarding the situation in the Middle East, there has always been strong to intense strains of anti-Westernism amongst regime elites and the general population. But it would appear that the concerns associated with globalisation can only add to the impetus to the backlash against the West and globalisation, and the United States as their dominant champion.

Meanwhile, technology, and especially information technology, as one of the drivers of globalisation has also served to reinforce these potential anti-globalisation sentiments by enabling the rapid dissemination about its effects to elites and masses alike. It would be too crude an assessment to state that globalisation has provided the only motivations for 9/11 and that its role can be conceived of as laying the ground for the 'clash of the civilisations'. Samuel Huntington's thesis is certainly problematic in seeking to establish distinct

---

[12] Christopher W. Hughes, 'Japanese Policy and the East Asian Currency Crisis: Abject Defeat or Quiet Victory?', *Review of International Political Economy*, vol. 7, no. 2, Summer 2000, pp. 232–33; Richard Higgott, 'The Asian Economic Crisis: A Study in the Politics of Resentment', *New Political Economy*, vol. 3, no. 3, pp. 333–56.

[13] For an analysis of the impact of the East Asian financial crisis on the Indonesia and Malaysian political economies and domestic politics, see Joseph A. Camilleri, *States, Markets and Civil Society in the Asia-Pacific: The Political Economy of the Asia-Pacific Region*, vol. 1, Cheltenham, Edward Elgar, 2000, pp. 262–90.

cultures diametrically opposed to each other and bound to generate conflict.[14] Moreover, it would be simplistic to ascribe 9/11 to being purely a reaction to globalisation. It is clear that opinions on globalisation in the Middle East are divided between those who see their world as already globalised—Islam being the true form of global religion—and those who view globalisation as the inherent threat of convergence, universalisation, Westernisation and Americanisation.[15] Nevertheless, globalisation's role in challenging the existing state dominance of the political economies of Middle Eastern societies, its perception as leading to convergence, and its ability to project these perceptions into the elite and popular 'global consciousness' (to abuse Roland Robertson's terminology which argues for the closure rather than exposure of cultural cleavages) through media organisations such as the satellite broadcasters CNN and al-Jazira, all argue that it has been a contributory factor in the rise of radical Islamic sentiment that found one motivation and expression in the terror of 9/11.[16] In this sense, globalisation's impact on security may be seen to follow the Huntington thesis more than that of Fukuyama, even if the latter's predictions on convergence may be one principal motivating factor for conflict.

Facilitation of Conflict

Globalisation defined as liberalisation, convergence and its higher definition of supra-territorialisation, also offers a perceptual tool for understanding how terrorist acts such as 9/11 have been facilitated. In terms of actors, globalisation's challenge to sovereignty opens up a range of new political identities for non-state actors in the global political economy. As noted above, the attempt to construct states that control social interaction within a delimited territorial space has also often meant an attempt to shoehorn political identities within this state construction. Most typically this construction has been underpinned by the close association between the state and its citizenry in the form of nationalism. However, this association between the apparatus of the state and its population is clearly challenged by globalisation as a process of economic liberalisation which transcends sovereign borders and the capacity of states to deal with trans-sovereign problems. The result of this can be for the citizenry of states to look to alternative political identities distanced from the sovereign-state and inter-sovereign-state systems. These new identities may take the form of nationalism which transcends state borders, leading to problems of separatism of irredentism. It may also take the form of non-state-centred forms of political identity and activity.

The most positive manifestation of this movement is often viewed as the growth of what has been termed 'global civil society' to complement efforts at global governance, manifested in the increasing policy input of non-

---

[14] Samuel P. Huntington, 'The Clash of the Civilizations?', *Foreign Affairs*, vol. 72, no. 3, 1993, pp. 22–49.

[15] Fred Halliday, 'The Middle East and the Politics of Differential Integration', in Dodge and Higgott, *Globalization and the Middle East*, pp. 42–45.

[16] Roland Robertson, *Globalization: Social Theory and Global Culture*, London, Sage, 1992, pp. 8–9.

governmental organisations (NGOs).[17] More worrying from the Western perspective has been the rise of global 'uncivil society', whereby individuals and groups can forge a common cause across sovereign-state boundaries. These groups may consist of trans-sovereign crime groups which enjoy a form of political identity, as in the separatist groups in Burma which fund their campaign from the narcotics campaign.[18] But they may also have a sharper political identity still and have a strong trans-sovereign movement, with implications for security.[19] Arguably, the al-Qaeda network is one such movement, which draws it strength to some degree from traditions of pan-Arabism and a common Islamic identity, and is facilitated by the rise of globalisation which engenders and enables the articulation of such a trans-sovereign political and cultural identity.

In addition, globalisation has manifestly also facilitated the actual terrorist activities of al-Qaeda. Globalisation, again in conjunction with the effects of decolonisation and bipolarisation, has eroded the sovereignty of states, and it is in the areas where the sovereign control of states is weakest—most notably Afghanistan and Somalia—where terrorist networks have accumulated. For such states are where the remit of the central government often fails to run and where groups can practise illicit activities relatively free from interference. Beyond providing a conceptual map to identify sites for the basing of terrorists, globalisation also enhances our understanding of the means by which these networks are able to operate within other societies. Globalisation as economic liberalisation and the transcendence of sovereign control over social interaction, spurred on by improvements in transportation and information technology, has enabled trans-national crime and terrorist organisations to mimic the behaviour of transnational corporations (TNCs), and to move with greater ease across deregulated economic and territorial space.[20] Terrorist organisations are also now able to strike against their targets without even necessarily an attack on their territory *per se*. In the case of the United States, the defence of its homeland now comprises its physical sovereign territory and the extension of its economic presence to the domain of cyberspace engendered by modern telecommunications technology. In this way, al-Qaeda has been able to exploit the open societies of the West to perpetrate terror, and to gain the resources to do so through money laundering and the partial exploitation of globalised financial networks.[21] As President George W. Bush noted in a speech to Congress on 20 September 2001, terrorist organisation such as al-Qaeda have now acquired 'global reach'.[22]

---

[17] Jan Aart Scholte, *Global Civil Society Changing the World?*, Centre for the Study of Globalisation and Regionalisation, University of Warwick, Working Paper no. 31, 1999.

[18] Christopher W. Hughes, 'Conceptualizing the Globalization–Security Nexus in the Asia-Pacific', *Security Dialogue*, vol. 32, no. 4, December 2001, p. 416.

[19] Mary Kaldor, *New and Old Wars: Organized Violence in a Global Era*, Cambridge, Polity Press, 1999, pp. 6–7.

[20] Stephen E. Flynn, 'The Global Drug Trade versus the Nation-state', in Maryann K. Cusimano, ed., *Beyond Sovereignty: Issues for a Global Agenda*, Boston and New York, Bedford/St. Martin's, 2000, p. 52.

[21] For a prescient discussion prior to 9/11 of how terrorist networks such as al-Qaeda could exploit the opportunities of a globalising world, see Steven Simon and Daniel Benjamin, 'America and the New Terrorism', *Survival*, vol. 42, no. 1, Spring 2000, pp. 59–75.

[22] Cited in International Institute for Strategic Studies, *Strategic Survey 2001/2002*, Oxford, Oxford University Press, 2002, p. 231.

432 *Christopher W. Hughes*

Responses to 9/11

The response of the United States and other coalition states to 9/11 also provides interesting insights into the interconnection between understandings of globalisation and the contemporary security agenda. One observation that has emerged from recent events after 9/11 is that the onset of globalisation is neither inevitable nor irreversible, and thus its impact on security can also be channelled and shaped. Contrary to the predictions of the hyper-globalists, the sovereign state retains considerable flexibility not only to take a transformationalist path under conditions of globalisation, but also to firmly re-orient or even reverse the process if necessary. The concerted action by the United States and its allies against international money laundering is one demonstration that the sovereign state, especially in the developed world, lives on and still possesses considerable resources to respond to trans-sovereign terror movements.

At the same time, the response of the United States to 9/11 provokes the observation that globalisation and security are interconnected in terms of the increasing globalisation of military strategy. This occurs not just in the domain of the ability of the United States to coordinate a global coalition stretching from Europe and even to Japan, with more passive support from the likes of China, but also to its ability to project its own military power unilaterally. If globalisation is conceived of as the transcendence of territorial and sovereign barriers, then US military action can be depicted in certain ways as the apogee of this. The United States in the Afghan campaign has certainly demonstrated its progression, again driven by the leveraging of advanced technology, towards being able to exercise power with declining reference to geographical distance and time, and across the four dimensions of land, sea, and especially air and space. For instance, US commanders were able to deploy unmanned aerial vehicles (UAVs) to gather real-time information on enemy activities and to enable real-time responses. In this sense, the United States has moved one step closer to the realisation of the long-envisaged Revolution in Military Affairs (RMA) and the global reach of its power to match that of its terrorist counterpart.[23]

The conflict in Afghanistan, though, has also demonstrated that the United States has still not effected a totally globalised or post-modern military strategy. The United States was not entirely free from territoriality in projecting its power in the Middle East, intent as it was to secure bases for its military forces in Saudi Arabia (unsuccessfully) and in the central Asian republics (with more success) for the assault on Afghanistan. The United States was also forced to fight a ground war for the possession of territory, even if this was limited to the deployment of its own and coalition special forces, as well as the Northern Alliance as a proxy ground army. Above all, the United States may have been able to limit its own engagement on the ground and resulting casualties, but its military campaign in traditional fashion wreaked untold devastation and pain on its enemies and non-combatants in Afghanistan.[24]

---

[23] For US global military strategy and the RMA, see Paul Rogers, *Losing Control: Global Security in the Twenty First Century*, London, Pluto Press, 2000, pp. 58–77; Michael O'Hanlon, *Technological Change and the Future of Warfare*, Washington, DC, Brookings Institution Press, 2000, pp. 7–31.

[24] On the likelihood that globalisation will not necessarily engender a reduced-casualty environment for modern warfare, see Ian Clark, *Globalization and International Relations Theory*, Oxford, Oxford University Press, 1999, p. 115.

Conclusion: Globalisation and Future Responses to Insecurity

This article has argued that globalisation provides a number of conceptual insights to assist understanding of the contemporary security agenda following 9/11. Differing definitions of globalisation, individually or in combination, can shed light on the motivations and facilitation of, as well as the responses to, the activities of al-Qaeda and other extant forms of terrorism. Globalisation as liberalisation engenders tensions in the political economy of societies, which, when synergised with globalisation as the perception of convergence and Westernisation, can lay down the motivations for conflict. In turn, the actualisation of these conflicts is enhanced by globalisation as economic liberalisation and trans-territorialisation which enable terrorist groups to exploit areas of weakening sovereignty and to extend their activities along the same economic networks that are utilised by other agents of globalisation such as TNCs. The response of the United States and other states to 9/11 also provides insights into the globalisation–security nexus. Globalisation, although it can generate security problems, can also be mastered by the developed states and its worst security excesses curbed given sufficient political will and urgency. Lastly, 9/11 is a demonstration of the increasing globalisation of military strategy and power, but simultaneously its continuing limitations.

These observations lead to a final thought about the direction which the post-9/11 and post-globalisation security agendas may take. 9/11 has indeed demonstrated the ability (or at least the effort) of the developed states to channel globalisation in their interests, to tame factors such as international finance, and to reverse the retreat of the state. If these states are intent on reshaping globalisation processes then they may have also hit upon the key to addressing the root causes of the political economy of insecurity that can give rise to the hyper-terrorism of al-Qaeda. However, the concern must be that the developed states have only learned a partial lesson from 9/11. Despite all the talk of state building in Afghanistan, in other areas of international policy the leading powers continue to adhere to policies of globalisation which are, as noted above, more oriented towards state reducing. Therefore, unless there is an effort to harmonise globalisation with the as yet unfinished state-building efforts of other regions, then there will be no solution to trans-sovereign terrorism. Moreover, the meaning of state building here should not be construed as simply Cold War-style Western support for the rigid and autocratic regimes of the Middle East, but an effort to move beyond the *status quo* and nurture the indigenous development of states that will best allow them to filter the benefits of globalisation whilst undergoing the transformation towards modernity. Added to this, 9/11's confirmation of the ability of not only terrorist networks to transcend sovereignty but also major states such as the United States to project power in a globalised fashion does not provide hope for easy solutions to global insecurity. For as long as the US defence community continues to possess the (perhaps mistaken) perception that it can tackle global terrorism with globalised military power, and thus pursue technical rather than genuine political solutions to the threat of terrorism, then insecurity and the threat of terrorism will persist.

[30]

Cambridge Review of International Affairs,
Volume 15, Number 2, 2002

Carfax Publishing
Taylor & Francis Group

A Turning Point for Globalisation? The Implications for the Global Economy of America's Campaign against Terrorism

Lael Brainard
The Brookings Institution

Abstract *Did September 11th herald a turning point for globalisation? Although America's campaign against terrorism could put at risk many of the gains globalisation has brought, the new environment likewise presents opportunities to smooth the rough edges of the globalisation associated with American policies of the past decade. Measures to tighten the security of cross-border flows of goods, people, information and capital may raise entry barriers still higher for poor countries seeking greater integration with the global economy. But September 11th also provided a wake-up call, alerting the wealthier nations and especially Americans to the direct link between their own well-being and ensuring that people around the world have a stake in the international system. Unfortunately, there is little evidence so far these lessons have been taken to heart in policies on trade, financial assistance, and advancing economic reform in the states of the Middle East.*

No sooner had the world comprehended the horror of September 11th than voices on both sides of the debate began making the connection to globalisation. Some observers argued that the attacks were directed at globalisation, while others speculated globalisation would be a direct casualty. Is there indeed any connection between September 11th and the phenomenon of globalisation? Perhaps the unspoken question in this debate is whether September 11th will cast the previous decade in a wholly new light—as a unique period, even an interwar period—belying our earlier assumption that it foreshadowed the shape of the new century.

In some ways, the terrorist attacks in the United States were profoundly about globalisation. For countless Americans, these attacks brought home viscerally the anxious realisation that America's involvement in the world is not a one-way street. Moreover, the terrorists targeted dramatic symbols of America's global projection of military and economic power. America's openness and huge footprint in the international system made it both more vulnerable and more attractive to terrorist attacks. And the technologies touted as handmaidens of globalisation—the Internet, global financial networks, and commercial aviation—proved their moral neutrality by enabling terrorists to wreak havoc on an unimagined scale.

Some observers contend the terrorist attacks were the logical, violent expression of anti-globalisation; they were an act of revenge by people either oppressed or marginalised by the global economy. But this claim makes the

ISSN 0955-7571 print/ISSN 1474-449X online/02/020233-12 © 2002 Centre of International Studies
DOI: 10.1080/0955757022015128 1

common mistake of equating globalisation—the progressive broadening and deepening of international integration—with capitalism, American hegemony, or even modernity more generally.

Even if globalisation was neither target nor victim of the attacks, September 11th could be a pivotal event for the future pace and direction of globalisation if it heralds a sustained redirection of America's national security and economic policy. On one extreme, to the extent that globalisation is driven by technological advances and the logic of the market, globalisation should continue to advance at the same relentless pace. By this logic, globalisation should at most suffer a hiccup as security measures are tightened. But history suggests a very different possibility: globalisation could well be reversed. The policies pursued in the aftermath of the First World War had a profoundly chilling effect on globalisation. It took nearly seventy years to recoup the levels of economic integration seen in the pre-war period—on trade, immigration, and foreign direct investment. Globalisation proved very fragile and heavily dependent for its survival on international rules and institutions and national commitments to maintaining open borders. And it is sobering to recall that globalisation already faced a growing international drumbeat of criticism from both the left and the right in the two years preceding September 11th.

Just as globalisation is not inevitable, neither is its reversal. History suggests the outcome depends not on the terrorists' actions, but on our choices. The international policy response to the Cold War was quite different than to the First World War. The progressive expansion of market rules and institutions has been credited with lifting hundreds of millions out of poverty and helping to provide foundations for democratisation and peace.

Too often, globalisation is either glorified or vilified as an end in itself. Far better to judge it critically on the extent to which it advances our highest aspirations, such as peace, freedom, and broadly shared prosperity. The events of September 11th put at risk many of the gains globalisation has brought, but likewise may present opportunities to smooth some of the rough edges of the globalisation associated with US policies of the previous decade. To skip to the punchline, the future trajectory of globalisation is not preordained; it lies largely in our own hands.

The Terrorism Tax on Cross-Border Flows

With support for globalisation already precarious, many held their breaths following the attacks on the World Trade Center and the Pentagon, fearing a major pendulum swing against cross-border flows. 'The footprints of globalisation have left an obvious and important mark on the economic landscape during the past decade. But the terrorist attacks of September 11th and their aftermath may bring about its demise.'[1] And indeed, there was a major collapse in the volumes of world trade and investment. Trade growth fell from a record 12.5% in 2000 to less than 2% in 2001.[2] Foreign direct investment flows fell by an estimated half in 2001 from the record of US$1.3 trillion reached in 2000—the

---

[1] Stephen Roach, 'Back to Borders', *Financial Times*, 28 September 2001, p. 20.
[2] World Trade Organisation, *International Trade Statistics 2001*, France, WTO Publications, 25 October 2001, pp. 17–18.

sharpest drop in three decades and the first drop since the beginning of the 1990s.[3] Yet most experts agree there is no connection to the campaign against terrorism: these declines were already in the works, reflecting slowing in the world's three biggest economic areas and the collapse of the global tech sector.

There was also considerable concern about the potential for the security response to cause major and lasting disruption to the US economy. And indeed, in the first few weeks, cross-border transactions in the United States were adversely impacted. A large number of international flights were cancelled and air travellers resigned themselves to three-fold increases in wait times. The processing of visas slowed, and 20,000 refugee visas that had already been approved remained on hold months later.[4] With insurance costs soaring, corporations advised their employees to restrict international travel to only the most essential meetings, and took a hard look at the security exposure of their international facilities. And multitudes of US companies were affected when heightened scrutiny at land borders paralysed cross-border truck traffic, idling assembly lines dependent on just-in-time supplies from Mexico and Canada.

There has been considerable debate about the importance of these disruptions to the overall US economy and their contribution to the global recession. Months later, it remains difficult to disentangle the various factors contributing to the recession, most of which, such as the information technology downturn, the inventory cycle, and business investment overhang, pre-dated September 11th. It is even more difficult to estimate the ongoing impact of the so-called 'terrorism tax' because on many fronts it is still unclear what if anything will be enduringly different in the world after September 11th, especially where 'homeland security' legislation or regulatory proposals are pending, and in cases such as maritime trade where emergency measures are still in place. There is no question that the drive to increase the security of national borders runs counter to the very forces that propel globalisation. It is difficult if not impossible to address the demands for greater security and scrutiny of cross-border movements of goods, people, information, financial capital, even snailmail without some setbacks to the drumbeat of *faster, cheaper, less red tape* that drove productivity gains in the 1990s.

Thus far, much of the analysis has focused on the overall cost to the US economy of projected increases in homeland security measures and on the incidence of this tax in the private and public sectors. Observers initially compared the economic impact of the attacks to natural disasters, weighing the one-time loss of physical and human capital against the increased demand for construction services.[5],[6] Subsequent comparisons were made between the increased public and private sector costs of security and the rising incidence of pollution abatement expenditures in the 1970s and 1980s. Important questions

---

[3] Leumi Trade, 'Foreign Direct Investment Fell by Almost Half in 2001', *Global Business Magazine*, 29 January 200, www.bankleumi.co.il

[4] Somini Sengupta, 'Refugees at America's Door Find It Closed after Attacks', *New York Times*, 29 October 2001, p. A1.

[5] Edward Leamer and Christopher Thornberg, 'The Economic Impact of the Terrorist Attack on the World Trade Center Will Be Minor', *UCLA Anderson Forecast*, 13 September 2001, pp. 1–3.

[6] Gary S. Becker, 'Don't Be Surprised if Recovery is Rapid', *Business Week*, 22 October 2001, pp. 26–27.

remain about the extent to which these costs will affect the economy in a one-shot manner, similar to Y2K compliance measures, or on a recurring cost basis.[7]

There is an important related question that has received far less attention: whether the security measures now being implemented or contemplated will disproportionately impact cross-border flows of goods, people, capital, and a services relative to domestic flows. A bias in the incidence of the terrorism tax goes to the underlying plumbing of economic globalisation—and the international cooperation necessary to sustain it. Such a bias seems both logical and likely, since the focus is on the security exposure created by America's extensive involvement with the rest of the world, ranging from immigration to cross-border trade to overseas operations of multinationals to the travel and communications networks that are the lifeblood of international commerce to the dense webs of international financial transactions. To the extent that the costs impact disproportionately on cross-border inflows, there could be important implications for direct transmission to other economies as well as for policies to encourage integration of countries, and particularly poorer countries, into the international trade system.

This kind of bias could derive from a variety of sources. US multinationals facing greater costs of transport among locations and of providing security for overseas operations might reasonably be expected to pull back from those locations where security risks are greatest. Legal immigration flows into the US might slow, with foreign students taking their education dollars to Europe or Canada, deterred by greater scrutiny and wait times, and with skilled workers taking their skills to more hospitable labour markets, alarmed by anecdotes that US employers are increasingly reluctant to take on the security exposure and red tape of foreign hires. US businesses might reasonably be expected to favour domestic suppliers, in an effort to avoid the greater 'just in case' inventory holding and security costs associated with heightened security measures at US ports.

Maritime security experts have pointed out the frightening potential for weapons of mass destruction to be concealed in one of the 11.6 million school-bus-sized metal containers that pass through America's ports and onto America's railways and highways each year with minimal oversight.[8] Addressing this vulnerability will require not only strengthening inspection and scanning capabilities at America's borders, but preventing threatening shipments from ever entering the port system through the adoption of internationally agreed security standards and procedures in all of the world's major ports. It is likewise clear that strengthening immigration surveillance at the borders alone is inadequate when it is clear the terrorists carefully calibrate their visa strategies to exploit differences in scrutiny and oversight.

These examples illustrate a more general phenomenon. The security measures adopted in the wake of September 11th are likely to fall disproportionately on cross-border flows relative to domestic activities, for instance raising the costs

---

[7] David Hale, 'Will Islamic Terrorism Produce a Global Recession?', Zurich Financial Services, 17 September 2001, pp. 1–5.

[8] Thomas Frank, 'Potential for Terrorism at Ports Called Alarming', 15 January 2002, www.Newsday.com; Stephen Flynn, 'America the Vulnerable', *Foreign Affairs*, vol. 81, no. 1, 2002, p. 64.

(or the precautionary inventory holding motive) of imports relative to domestically produced goods. Moreover, the policy response will necessarily put a greater premium on cooperation among enforcement authorities across borders as well as on partnerships with those corporations that have a proven capacity to enforce internal security measures through supply chain management and other practices. The result is likely to be a "slow-lane" bias against transactions involving poorer countries and smaller, less internationalised companies that are unwilling or lack the requisite resources or governance capacity to enforce enhanced security measures. In short, the response to September 11th is likely to create even higher entry barriers to the members club of countries able to take advantage of the upside of globalisation—at a moment when lowering the entry barriers for the poor and disenchanted is more important than ever.

More International Cooperation?

The aftermath of September 11th confronts America with countervailing pressures. When a sense of safety previously taken for granted is profoundly undermined, there is a natural tendency to pull up the drawbridges and pull back from the world. And when jobs and economic security are put at risk, there is a tendency to look towards protectionist solutions. But September 11th also brought a realisation of how much America's well-being depends on the international order and on having friends and allies around the world that share the same basic values. The attacks of September 11th made concrete the certain knowledge that America cannot effectively combat the terrorist threat alone. America cannot alone track and stem the financial lifeblood of international terrorist organisations, combat the roots of terrorism, or win a war against a shadowy enemy. Perhaps for the first time since the end of the Cold War, Americans may see international cooperation in a new light as directly relevant to their well-being.

The progressive globalisation of the past fifty years did not just happen. It was the product of concerted efforts to build an international order. The farsighted statesmen of the day founded the General Agreement on Tariffs and Trade, and eight successive rounds of negotiations have fuelled growth in trade at four times the pace of world income and successively broadened the geographic scope to encompass China and much of the developing world. The International Monetary Fund (IMF), created to help countries facing external imbalances at a time when the gold standard prevailed and capital controls were the norm, has since shifted its focus to financial stabilisation in the face of explosive growth in private capital flows and an unprecedented experiment in floating currencies. The World Bank, created to address reconstruction in war-ravaged developed economies, has since taken on the more complicated challenges of fighting international poverty and complementing rather than replacing private capital investments. The US was both the ringleader and the sugar daddy during the initial decades of these efforts, financing the Marshall Plan, maintaining generous foreign aid, opening its markets, and demonstrating steadfast commitment to the multilateral institutions.

As the Cold War wound down, however, and the US entered a sustained period of strong productivity-driven growth, Americans had the luxury of questioning their international commitment. Entering the first decade of the new century, foreign partners increasingly criticized as unilateral. Critics in Europe and elsewhere increasingly saw America as a double agent—working to extend globalisation to every village, but unwilling to share the authority or spend the resources to shape the international environment in ways that serve America's core interests. For a global power, America appeared remarkably self-absorbed.

And indeed, the first nine months of the Bush administration were characterised by a series of policy announcements that—whether by design or by accident—lent themselves to characterisation as unilateralist and hostile to international treaties, institutions and regimes. In the months immediately following September 11th, however, the pattern was precisely the reverse: at almost every decision point, the Bush administration chose the course of greater international cooperation and involvement. Indeed, some high-ranking officials and advisers are quoted in the *Washington Post* suggesting that the goal of maintaining a broad coalition would help define US military strategy, prompting some commentators to worry out loud about 'paralytic multilateralism'.

However, it is not clear that the new emphasis on coalition building has brought with it an enduring new sensitivity to the concerns and priorities of foreign partners. And there is little evidence that fundamental positions on trade and aid policies have shifted—at a time when they could make a critical difference.

The Root Causes Debate

In searching for the root causes of the terrorists' violent fanaticism, many have pointed to the poverty and inequality associated with globalisation. The reality is far more complicated. First, a sceptic might well point out that if poverty were the driving force, we would expect terrorists to come mostly from the poorest countries in the world, largely concentrated in sub-Saharan Africa, such as Ethiopia, Burundi, Sierra Leone, Guinea Bissau, Malawi, and Niger. Instead, the architects and perpetrators of the September 11th attacks were largely from educated, middle class backgrounds in the relatively more affluent societies of the Middle East. The roots of their anger are more likely to be found in frustration with the blocked routes to political and economic opportunity in their societies than with poverty *per se*.

A careful reading of Bin Laden's *fatwahs* and expert analysis of the perpetrators' worldviews suggest the attacks were motivated by a pan-Islamic radical agenda hostile to US intervention in the Middle East and moderate Middle Eastern governments alike. Research teaches us that conflict is most prevalent in periods of societal transition. The rifts within these societies can be explained without any reference to the global marketplace by the age-old clash between modernity and tradition. Surely, the events of September 11th have far more in common with the Iranian hostage crisis of 1979 than with the Asian financial crisis of 1998. The debates within Saudi Arabia, Egypt, and Iran are only in the most trivial way centred on whether to ban Western television and video games. The real fight is over the relation between political and religious authority and who wields power in these petrified states that have largely failed to modernise.

In contrast, poverty is a critical ingredient in the failed states such as Afghanistan and Somalia that litter the world's landscape, provide the foot soldiers in Al Qaeda's efforts, and play hosts to Al Qaeda's deadly training camps and recruitment efforts. And poverty, poor access to education, and despair clearly help explain why so many in the Islamic world fall prey to the demagoguery of resentment and violence in Bin Laden's message—the impetus that led them to dance in the streets at the news of the September 11th attacks. It is at least plausible that if Pakistan devoted greater resources to public primary education, the *madrassahs*, or religious schools, would have less of a monopoly on the hearts and minds of Pakistan's youth. There is admittedly no simple guarantee that addressing poverty and helping to rescue a state from failure will automatically cause it to lose its appetite for the international opprobrium associated with harbouring or sponsoring terrorism, but it certainly raises the stakes.

But in neither the failed states nor the petrified states of the Middle East and Central and South Asia is the answer less globalisation. The Islamic nations of this region by and large have spurned rather than been split by globalisation. Most have low trade and investment shares of GDP and export bases that are highly concentrated in primary commodities—in several cases, oil—and only a handful are members of the World Trade Organisation (WTO). In many cases, relative insulation from the world economy is combined with heavy state involvement in the domestic economy. With notable exceptions, such as Lebanon, Bahrain and Jordan, the wealthier Middle Eastern states are characterised by striking underperformance, high levels of economic statism, and shallow integration with the international economy. Not surprisingly, many of these countries experienced declining per capita incomes through much of the 1990s— while emerging markets elsewhere made advances. For the Middle East and North Africa region as a whole, unemployment averages 15%.[9] This is a particularly volatile mix in countries with rapidly growing, young populations; population in the Arab countries grew an average of 2.7% between 1975 and 1999—high even compared with the average for all low income countries—and 38% of the population is under 15.[10]

There is an intimate connection between the striking lack of economic and political modernisation in many of these states. Extensive state control over domestic resource allocation is critical in maintaining the legitimacy of existing regimes, giving the ruling elites power over the distribution of plum jobs, state contracts, and social welfare expenditures. In Egypt, for instance, university graduates remain unemployed for years in order to capitalise on the government's guarantee of secure coveted employment.[11] Experience elsewhere suggests that economic liberalisation diminishes the scope for corruption and bureaucratic discretion in allocating jobs and capital (a vital source of power for entrenched interests), introduces ideas from the international arena, and creates sources of power and opportunity independent of the state.

In fact, it appears that more and better globalisation may be an important part of the answer both to help millions escape poverty and to kick-start the

---

[9] World Bank, 'Middle East Northern Africa Region Regional Brief', www.worldbank.org, 27 September 2001, p. 1.

[10] The statistics are for 'Arab countries' as reported in the UNDP 2001 Human Development Report, New York, Oxford University Press, 2001, p. 157.

[11] Paul Blustein, 'Unrest a Chief Product of Arab Economies', *Washington Post*, 26 January 2002, p. A1.

economic reforms that are so sorely needed by the rapidly growing population of the Middle East. Of course, it is up to the governments and citizens of the region to make the choice to embark on a course of international integration and reform in order to reap the benefits of more broadly shared prosperity and opportunity, but the advanced industrial countries can influence the terms of this debate through their trade and financial assistance policies.

A Fair Deal on Trade?

If indeed the attacks herald a sustained shift in the organising principle of US foreign policy, it could lead to a reorganisation of American international economic policy analogous to the Cold War. However, so far there is little evidence of change. Broadly speaking, the 1990s were characterised by profound reconsideration of America's international economic engagement, freed of the customary constraints from the security environment. Critics from both the left and the right converged on a difficult standard for judging US commitments on foreign aid, the international financial institutions, and trade agreements. It came down to the simple question: 'What's in it for us?'

The question now is whether the new security environment will shift the terms of the debate to a broader definition of America's interests. Sensing the opportunity, US Trade Representative Bob Zoellick lost no time in proclaiming trade to be a central element in America's campaign against terror. A month later, President Bush put the case in even stronger terms: 'The terrorists attacked the World Trade Center, and we will defeat them by expanding and encouraging world trade.' Nonetheless, it remains extremely difficult for the most advanced nations to deliver on their promises, given the high domestic salience of the most controversial areas, such as support for the agricultural sector, protection of textiles jobs, the sovereign right to deploy trade remedies to soften the impact of disruptive trade and to set environmental and labour standards, and the distributive issues associated with intellectual property.

Together, the terrorist attacks and the perceptible deepening of recession in the US and around the world upped the ante on both sides of the trade debate. With the US experiencing the first surge of unemployment in years and with the cyclically sensitive manufacturing sector hit particularly hard, domestic concerns moved front and centre. The result has been a mixed record: there have been several achievements of great symbolic significance, but little of a concrete nature so far.

The emphasis on international coalition building in the wake of September 11th created enormous momentum for the successful launch of global trade talks at the WTO ministerial that was scheduled to take place two months after the attacks. Success at Doha became a political imperative. Moreover, although the decision to locate the ministerial in Doha Qatar had been taken months earlier, the determination to follow through was courageous and symbolically important, given Qatar's position as one of a handful of Middle Eastern states that has joined the WTO. Moreover, as evidenced by the term used to describe the outcome, 'the Doha Development Agenda', the tenor of discussions at Doha and the resulting ministerial declaration tipped the balance on the margins towards the developing world. Both the EU and the US made concessions to assure a successful launch. Nonetheless, the developing countries can claim only limited victories, and it is clear that the battles over the most contentious issues will return to be fought another day.

Second, in the US, both Houses of Congress voted to grant the President fast track trade promotion authority, following several years of stalemate. This legislation, which has greater symbolic than practical significance for US trade policy in the immediate term, looks likely to be enacted during 2002, following reconciliation of the House of Senate Versions. However, the House vote was won by a margin of one and was purchased at the expense of a rollback of textile trade concessions already granted to Caribbean Basin nations in earlier legislation.

These agreements to proceed with negotiations, while difficult in themselves, nonetheless are much easier than the follow-on negotiations over concrete trade measures, which will inevitably require concessions in specific sectors where identifiable jobs and livelihoods are directly on the line. So far, domestic considerations have dominated on these more concrete sectoral tradeoffs. Already, several US allies in the fight against terrorism have been disappointed in their efforts to secure greater access to America's markets for particular products. Thus, it is still an open question whether, in the spirit of coalition building, America, the EU and others will be able to bridge the divide with key developing countries by offering greater flexibility in sensitive areas.

Moreover, so far, there has been virtually no discussion of a concerted trade strategy to address the complicated issues discussed above of lagging economic reform and shallow international integration that hamper development in the Middle East. Such a strategy could range from expanded trade preferences for the poorer countries to a systematic effort to increase participation in the WTO to a longer-term plan for regional economic integration within the framework of a free trade arrangement with the US or the EU.

The Foreign Aid Debate

America's commitment to the international financial institutions and bilateral development aid has come under attack since the end of the Cold War. US development aid has declined by over 35% in real terms since its heyday in the early 1960s (to roughly US$11 billion in 2000). US assistance reached a post-1945 low in 1999, both as a share of national income, and as a share of federal budget outlays, where it has fallen from over 3% to under 0.6%.[12] If we compare donor countries, US spending on Official Development Assistance (ODA), which includes aid to the poorest countries, is 0.10% of national income—the lowest among OECD (Organisation for Economic Co-operation and Development) donors and less than half the donor average of 0.22%. And US per capita spending of US$34 per year is far below the average of US$67.[13] Clearly, policy makers had little success in selling the case for foreign aid to the American

---

[12] Isaac Shapiro, *As a Share of the Economy and the Budget. U.S. Development and Humanitarian Aid Would Drop to post-WWII Lows in 2002*, Washington, Center on Budget and Policy Priorities, 18 June 2001, pp. 2, 12.

[13] Jean-Claude Faure, Organisation for Economic Co-operation and Development, Development Assistance Committee, 'Development Co-Operation, 2000 Report', *DAC Journal*, vol. 3, no. 1, 2002, pp. 203, 207.

242 *Lael Brainard*

public during a decade of peace and rising prosperity. But their perceived
salience to America's well-being rises during times of crisis. Already, sanctions
on Pakistan have been lifted, freeing up loans and debt relief. And the US has
joined the international community in pledging hundreds of millions for the
rebuilding of Afghanistan. The Bush Administration has recently proposed
increasing foreign aid by $10 billion over the next three years, representing an
important shift in US aid policy.

In the wake of September 11th, a growing chorus of influential voices has
called for a Marshall Plan for the Middle East. But a close look at the chief
elements of the Marshall Plan raises questions about its relevance to America's
troubled relations with the Islamic countries of the Middle East and Northern
Africa. The stunning 33% increase in European income achieved over the four
years of the Marshall Plan owed far less to the volume of aid than to the fertile
environment to which it flowed. The European recipient nations all had strong
institutional foundations, a wealth of human capital, and a demonstrated commitment to reform. There is little reason to believe that the absorptive capacity
or the commitment to reform of either the failed states or the petrified states of
the Islamic world are comparable to those of post-war Europe.

Nonetheless, a case can be made that the vision and spirit that underlay
conceptualisation of the Marshall Plan are precisely what are needed today. The
post-war visionaries who launched the Marshall Plan and provided the blueprint for the international economic architecture understood the intimate relationship between peace and prosperity in America and in conflict-prone regions
elsewhere. They also displayed an acute understanding of the role of international commerce and financial ties in giving everyone a stake in the international system.

The Marshall Plan debate raises broader questions about the appropriate
role—if any—for financial assistance in the immediate campaign against terrorism as well as in the broader campaign to expand support around the world for
the international trade and financial system. Based on public opinion, the likely
answer would be that few Americans see any connection, and most think the US
already wastes too many dollars on aid. A 2001 University of Maryland poll
found that on average Americans believe 24% of the federal budget is spent on
foreign aid; the actual figure is closer to 0.5%.[14] And it is admittedly difficult to
make the case for assistance—apart from strict humanitarian and reconstruction
aid—in light of the abysmal performance of some of the primary beneficiaries of
largesse in the Middle East. Egypt has received more than US$55 billion in aid
from the international community over the past 25 years—which most experts
agree allowed the government to shrug off genuine economic reform and
maintain a heavily state-directed economic system that stymies private initiative
and generates far too few jobs.

More broadly, critics draw the conclusion that aid is counterproductive by
comparing the stunning economic success of East Asian countries—which received relatively modest shares of aid relative to resources—with the relative
economic failure of more aid-dependent states in sub-Saharan Africa. And
indeed, the raw numbers are compelling. Many countries in sub-Saharan Africa,
where aid flows have exceeded 10% of GNP over the past several decades, have

---

[14] University of Maryland Program on International Policy Attitudes, 'Americans on
Foreign Aid and World Hunger: A Study of U.S. Public Attitudes', 2 February 2001,
www.pipa.org/OnlineReports/BFW/toc.html

yet to see progress. Per capita incomes are declining or stagnant, life expectancy remains well below the world average, and primary school attendance is low. In contrast, in the countries of East and South Asia, which have received aid amounting to less than 2% of GDP on average, there have been stunning growth rates averaging 7.5% and 4.9%, respectively, over the past three decades, life expectancy has risen considerably, and primary school attendance has achieved important gains.[15]

But here, as elsewhere, simple generalities do not do justice to reality. First, research has shown that a prime reason for the poor performance of development aid is that too many resources were allocated on the basis of geostrategic considerations rather than on the basis of the recipient government's commitment to fostering a conducive environment for growth and its accountability and legitimacy. Money is fungible, and too much of the money disbursed during the Cold War was wasted on autocratic and corrupt anti-reform regimes, which used it to beef up military budgets or line their own pockets.

In reality, there have been vastly differing experiences with aid, depending on the intended purpose and the context. A careful reading of the research suggests many valuable lessons have been learned that can help guide the efficient use of aid resources as one component of a sustained poverty reduction effort. A UK government memo cites recent academic research showing that aid's impact on economic growth has increased since the Cold War era. It suggests that every US$1 billion of aid given in 1997 raised 284,000 people permanently out of poverty, and that where a recipient country's policies are sound, aid worth 1% of GDP cuts poverty and infant mortality by 1%.[16]

The green eye shades of the 1990s taught some difficult but valuable lessons about what kind of assistance has the greatest impact on growth and in what conditions. Investments in basic health and education have the best track record. Substantial research has documented the value of primary education for all children as a high yielding long-term investment strategy. Investment in education for girls has important positive spillovers to other areas of human development, encouraging smaller and healthier families. And indeed, there is substantial potential for improvement on primary education among the poorer Islamic countries—and particularly on girls' education. Similarly, scientific advances hold great promise for combating killer infectious diseases and reducing maternal and infant mortality rates through relatively inexpensive prevention strategies. Other areas such as ensuring access to clean drinking water, improving transportation and communications infrastructure especially in rural areas, and facilitating the availability of credit to micro-entrepreneurs have demonstrated value.

The record is also relatively straightforward on the kind of environments where such investments are likely to deliver the greatest bang for the buck. Relative macroeconomic stability, sound overall economic policies, and a well-supervised market-based system of financial intermediation are critical prerequisites. Moreover, the existence of a well-functioning institutional structure with good governance, relative transparency, and democratic accountability are criti-

---

[15] Keith Marsden, 'Trade Helps More than Handouts', *Wall Street Journal Europe*, 4 September 2001, online edition, www.wsje.com.

[16] Editorial, 'Does Aid Help?', *Washington Post*, 9 February 2002, p. A26.

244 *Lael Brainard*

cal to ensure that aid dollars are used for the designated purposes and reflect the needs of the citizenry. In environments where corrupt and illegitimate governments stand in the way of effective anti-poverty programmes, strategies can be devised to work through grassroots organisations and target the private sector directly.

If the foreign assistance spigot is turned back on, driven by the exigencies of coalition building, reconstruction, and addressing the root causes of the current crisis, the big question is whether the US will disburse aid based on sound foundations of reform and good governance rather than the stratetic rationale of whether a country is 'with us or against us'. There are risks that poorly directed spending could do more harm than good in the longer term—helping sustain political regimes that are seen as illegitimate by increasingly radicalised youth. So the prescription for progress must lie not only in the amount of aid but how it is used. It would be a terrible shame if increased flows of assistance discredited the enterprise and reinforced public scepticism by repeating the mistakes of earlier periods—providing pocket money for corrupt autocrats, financing unproductive pet projects, and helping to finance unsustainable currencies and capital flight.

Conclusion

Globalisation was neither the primary target nor necessarily a casualty of September 11th. But September 11th could be a pivotal event for the future course of globalisation. That course is not preordained. It is in the hands of those in the wealthiest countries who have greatest influence on the international system—and especially Americans. Will we have the foresight to respond to the need for greater security without compromising our commitment to open borders and international engagement? Will we have the political will to move forward the trade agenda in a way that demonstrates to the developing nations they have a real stake in it? Will we have the wisdom to address the distributive consequences in our own economy? Will we increase the generosity of our international aid while resisting the pressures to disburse money as a bribe or payback, with the inevitable misuse and backlash that would bring?

[31]

Cambridge Review of International Affairs,
Volume 15, Number 2, 2002

Carfax Publishing
Taylor & Francis Group

Global Intifadah? September 11th and the Struggle within Islam

Arshin Adib-Moghaddam
University of Cambridge

Abstract *Against the background of two dominant world order theories—the 'End of History' and the 'Clash of Civilisations'—this article argues that September 11th epitomised two interrelated patterns in world politics: first, the idiosyncrasies and perils of globalisation and second the struggle between different directions in contemporary 'Muslim' politics. The former challenges the traditional view that links globalisation solely to phenomena such as economic integration or the spread of liberal-democratic values, while the latter refers to intra-regional developments in the 'Muslim' world, questioning the characterisation of 'Islam' as a monolithic entity destined to challenge the security of the 'West'. Taken together, these two patterns defy traditional categories of international relations, touching on issues ranging from the role of the state to national security considerations.*[1]

In the immediate aftermath of the suicide attacks on the Pentagon and the World Trade Center, politicians and intellectuals alike were struggling to evaluate the impact of September 11th, 2001 on the future of world politics. While it seemed, to some, that something, if not everything, had changed, the controversies about the causes and consequences of the attacks in the United States appeared diffuse. Several questions remain unanswered: How does September 11th fit into our traditional understanding of forces opposing and driving globalisation? How does the presence of violent transnational networks challenge traditional categories of the discipline of international relations such as state-centrism or national security? What is the role of political Islam in world politics? What are the prospects of multilateral cooperation in the changed climate of international politics since September 11th?

The facts on the ground created by the attack on the ruling Taliban movement in Afghanistan and blunt suggestions about new paradigms of world politics supersede the debates about the causes and consequences of September 11th, which remain constrained by the initial impediment of eclecticism. In such an environment of guided confusion, persistent myths provide an arsenal of rhetorical abuse, ready to be utilised by radical elements in the governments involved in the current conflict. Scholars writing within the realm of international relations (IR), a discipline that itself is in a state of 'ferment and

---

[1] For his critical reading and helpful comments, the author would like to thank Charles Jones, Centre of International Studies, University of Cambridge.

ISSN 0955-7571 print/ISSN 1474-449X online/02/020203-14 © 2002 Centre of International Studies
DOI: 10.1080/0955757022015126 3

204 *Arshin Adib-Moghaddam*

confusion',[2] implicitly failed to address that normative dilemma of disentangling myths from facts. Driven by the elusive pretext of parsimony dominating the discourse in some academic circles, holistic world order theories oversimplify the inherent complexity of world politics in favour of mono-causal mechanisms based on static, *a priori* defined pseudo-theoretical constructs. The exclusiveness of some of the categories chosen and the chronic lack of empathy translates into the failure of constructing a framework for inclusive dialogue. This paper shares the view that such a reasoned dialogue can only evolve if world politics in general and September 11th in particular are appreciated as global with equally global causes and consequences.[3]

In this article it is argued that September 11th indeed initiated new patterns in world politics that challenge our understanding of the unipolar transition period characterised by the dominance of the US as the triumphant power after the demise of the Soviet Union and confusion about the future world order. The modifications are linked to emerging patterns of engagement on the one side and asymmetrical threats to security on the other. The incentive of diplomatic engagement on the basis of reciprocal dialogue is catalysed by an increased demand for multilateral solutions to existing conflicts and necessitated by a sense of security interdependence on the systemic level of international politics. The argument of interdependence is in sharp contrast to the vitriolic tone of the dominant 'Clash of Civilisations'[4] prophecy and relates to two alternative views on the causes and consequences of September 11th: first, the re-evaluation of the idiosyncrasies and perils of globalisation and second the divergence of different directions in contemporary 'Muslim' politics. The former challenges the persistent view that one can attribute a unidirectional automatism to globalisation. In other words, it is problematic to assume that economic integration or the spread of liberal-democracy are the only, exclusive categories of globalisation and that their triumph on a global scale is inevitable. The implicit claim of the supremacy of supposedly 'Western' values tied to the notion of an unequivocal affirmation of the mechanisms of globalisation is discussed against the background of the 'End of History' thesis espoused by Francis Fukuyama[5] in the first section of this article. It is argued that if we are to accept the convergence among social scientists that globalisation denotes the increasing linkage between human activities across regions and continents as a result both of technological and social change,[6] the forces behind September 11th are as much related to globalisation as MTV Europe is.

Against the background of the second dominant world order theory, namely the 'Clash of Civilisations' paradigm suggested by Samuel P. Huntington,[7] the

[2] Robert O. Keohane, 'International Relations, Old and New', in Robert E. Goodin and Hans-Dieter Klingemann, eds, *A New Handbook of Political Science*, Oxford, Oxford University Press, 1996, p. 462.

[3] Fred Halliday, *Two Hours that Shook the World. September 11, 2001: Causes and Consequences*, London, Saqi Books, 2002, p. 31.

[4] Samuel P. Huntington, 'The Clash of Civilisations?', *Foreign Affairs*, vol. 72, no. 3, 1993, pp. 22–49; Samuel P. Huntington, *The Clash of Civilisations and the Remaking of World Order*, London, Simon & Schuster, 1997. For an 'Islamicist's' critique of Huntington's ideas preceding September 11th, see Roy P. Mottahedeh, 'The Clash of Civilisations: An Islamicist's Critique', *Harvard Middle Eastern and Islamic Review*, vol. 2, no. 1, 1995, pp. 1–26.

[5] Francis Fukuyama, *The End of History and the Last Man*, New York, Free Press, 1992.

[6] David Held, Anthony McGrew, David Goldblatt, and Jonathan Perraton, *Global Transformations*, Stanford, Stanford University Press, 1999, p. 15.

[7] In the aftermath of September 11th both Huntington and Fukuyama reiterated the centrality of their respective thesis for the future world order. See *Washington Post*, 16

second part of this article argues that the attack on the US, rather than being an incidence of inter-civilisational conflict, epitomised the ongoing clash among different constructions within political Islam. What is neglected by the portrayal of civilisations as monolithic blocks is both the scope of constitutional models, ranging from secular systems such as Turkey or Tunisia, to traditionalist monarchies such as Saudi Arabia, to modern syntheses such as Iran, and the range of contemporary discourse in the Middle East and elsewhere in the 'Muslim' world. Rather than being related to inter-civilisational conflict, the 'neo-fundamentalism' espoused by transnational networks such as al-Qaeda is first and foremost designed to destabilise the Arab regimes in the Middle East and derail reform processes in the 'Muslim' world and hence has to be discussed against the background of contemporary 'Muslim' politics. Here, 'neo-fundamentalism' refers to the emergence of a new category within extremist, political Islam, 'ideologically conservative but at times politically radical'.[8] Interrelated with the globalisation of terror, that 'struggle within Islam' influences the future perils of world politics, and thus merits reflection.

Global Political Violence and the End of the 'End of History'

After the demise of Communism as the nemesis of the self-declared 'Free World' and the end of the bipolar world order, two dominant theories dominated normative discourse about the future order of world politics. The first of these was the euphoric thesis of the 'End of History' propounded by Francis Fukuyama; the second, the apocalyptic 'Clash of Civilisations' prophecy suggested by Samuel P. Huntington. With the triumph of liberal-capitalism as the only remaining legitimate ideology, Fukuyama argues, the liberation of humankind has been accomplished and the world will be encompassed by a liberal zone of peace. According to Fukuyama, history as we know it will be terminated by the global inhalation of the core values of 'Western' civilisation. Here, Fukuyama names economic development and the aspiration of individuals to maximise personal freedom as the two mechanisms determining the end of ideological competition, and hence the end of history.

For obvious reasons, the inherent idealism of Fukuyama's thesis is not consistent with the current climate of international politics. Contrary to the view that the triumph of 'Western' modernity ushers in an era of global liberalism as the inevitable path to the salvation of humankind, the forces underlying 11 September question the very legitimacy of the political, economic and cultural supremacy of the supposedly 'Western' values tied to the argument of Fukuyama. While the attack on the US and indeed the assault on the perceived manifestations of capitalism and military hegemony provide another example of the violent eruption of the volcano of anti-Western resentment, there is certainly an intellectual dimension underlying such action which merits attention. The history of terrorism tells us at least two lessons: first, that apart from isolated incidents committed out of revenge or 'psychological disturbance'[9] by indivi-

---

(Footnote continued)

December 2001, *www.washingtonpost.com/wp-dyn/articles/A34207–2001Dec12.html*

[8] Olivier Roy, 'Neo-fundamentalism', *www.ssrc.org/Sept11/essays/roy_text_only.htm*

[9] Fred Halliday, *Islam and the Myth of Confrontation. Religion and Politics in the Middle-East*, London and New York, I. B. Tauris, 1996, p. 36.

206 *Arshin Adib-Moghaddam*

duals or groups, there are real issues beyond the reprehensible use of terror that cannot be ignored and, second, that contrary to its original meaning as a strategy to implement political order during the régime de la terreur of the French Revolution 'terrorism' has become a label attached to declared outsiders of society, either international or domestic, in order to legitimise, in most instances, action against the outside group.[10] In the political climate since September 11th discussion of the issues underlying the attack on the US seems to be politically incorrect and is largely avoided. As a consequence, the current 'war on terrorism' is creating new fronts within states and between them, opening up new potentials for future conflict on a global scale. Without reflecting upon the motivation of terrorist networks, however, both the sources of their criminal behaviour and the strategies they employ remain unclear. While the means of terrorist organisations are reprehensible, discussing issues that motivate these groups might open up alternative modes of explaining the rationale behind their actions.

The underlying assumption of the theory of Fukuyama is a narrow definition of globalisation as unidirectional and driven solely by the twin forces of liberalism and economic integration. This paper has already mentioned the conventional definition of globalisation in social science denoting increasing linkages of human activities across regions and continents as a result of technological and social change.[11] Keohane and Nye define 'globalism' as a 'state of the world involving networks of interdependence at multicontinental distances, linked through flows of capital and goods, information and ideas, people and force, as well as environmentally and biologically relevant substances'.[12] When globalism is understood as multidirectional and occurring on different levels, as in those definitions, the global outreach of contemporary terrorism can itself be regarded as a factor in globalisation.[13] In that vein, 'moving the battle into the heart of America', as proclaimed by Suleiman Abu Gaith,[14] spokesman of bin-Laden, exemplifies the expansion of transnational networks such as al-Qaeda beyond the confines of regional and national boundaries. This is supported by the fact that a large number of al-Qaeda activists have lived, worked and studied in several countries all over the world, adapting to the different environments and taking advantage of modern technologies of communication, transportation and weaponry. Some of the activists linked to al-Qaeda are converts to Islam socialised in London or other major West European cities, and have similar middle-class backgrounds to 'urban' terrorists in other parts of the world.[15] In other words, the globalisation of violence by networks such as al-Qaeda reveals the adverse effects of the supposedly exclusive mechanisms heralded by Fukuyama and others as the catalysts of global liberalism and capitalism.

---

[10] Halliday, *Two Hours that Shook the World*, pp. 81–82.

[11] Held et al., p. 15.

[12] Robert O. Keohane and Joseph S. Nye, *Power and Interdependence*, 3rd edn, New York, Addison Wesley Longman, 2001, p. 229.

[13] Keohane and Nye, *Power and Interdependence*, p. 237.

[14] See the statement of Suleiman Abu Gaith of 9 October 2001, in *Financial Times*, 10 October 2001.

[15] The social background of those al-Qaeda members is hence comparable to leftist movements such as the German Rote Armee Fraktion, the Italian Brigade Rosse, the Angry Brigade in Britain and the range of 'urban guerilla' movements in Central and South America that were especially active during the 1960s and 1970s. The aim of targeting urban centres is shared by the Aum Shinrikyo (Supreme Truth) religious sect in Japan, responsible for the unleashing of nerve gas in the Tokyo underground in March 1995 and the Oklahoma bombing by 'White Supremacists' in the United States in the same year.

September 11th put an abrupt end to such premature prophecies and certainly added a new, disturbing category to the phenomenon of globalisation itself.

To adopt the preceding argument means that September 11th defies the conventional understanding of the effects of globalisation. The global outreach of transnational terrorism adds a new dimension to globalism, while falsifying the unidirectional automatism that constitutes the lifeline of the 'End of History' thesis. The driving agents of globalisation are not simply reducible to the Bill Gateses and George Soroses of this world, but also include criminal groupings travelling around the globe using English and Arabic and sharing a sense of belonging to a common cause with a universal ethos. While that new instance of globalism found its tragic epitome in the death of over 3,000 civilians in New York and at least the same number in Afghanistan, the purpose of the neo-fundamentalism espoused by transnational networks such as al-Qaeda provides a second category of controversy to be focused upon in the following section.

The Myth of the 'Clash of Civilisations'

In direct response to Fukuyama, Samuel P. Huntington cautioned against the euphoria underlying the 'End of History' thesis. Instead, Huntington painted the picture of a potential new world disorder in which competing civilisations struggle for the dominance of international politics. His main hypothesis is 'that the fundamental source of conflict in this new world will not be primarily ideological or primarily economic. The great divisions among humankind and the dominating source of conflict will be cultural [...] The clash of civilisation will dominate global politics.'[16] According to that view, conflict along the cultural fault lines of 'Islam' and the 'West' epitomises the emerging 'West against the Rest'[17] dichotomy, positing the worse case scenario for the equilibrium of future world politics. By externalising the significant 'other' as representation of an imagined enemy, the West against the rest dichotomy is not very different from the mental disposition behind the *dar al-Islam* (house of Islam, forces of good) *dar al-harb* (forces of evil) distinction espoused by both Arab nationalists and 'Islamic' fundamentalist movements. Both positions, Islam vs. infidels and West vs. the rest, are intended to enforce categories and draw strict boundaries between supposedly incompatible worldviews. In Edward Said's words,

> primitive passions and sophisticated know-how converge in ways that give the lie to a fortified boundary not only between 'West' and 'Islam' but also between past and present, us and them ... A unilateral decision made to draw lines in the sand, to undertake crusades, to oppose their evil with our good, to extirpate terrorism and, in Paul Wolfowitz's nihilistic vocabulary, to end nations entirely, doesn't make the supposed entities any easier to see; rather, it speaks to how much simpler it is to make bellicose statements for the purpose of mobilising collective passions than to reflect, examine, sort out what it is we are dealing with in reality, the interconnectedness of innumerable lives, 'ours' as well as 'theirs'.[18]

In the current climate of cataclysmic transformations, the inherent essentialism of dichotomous world categories provides a ready-made affirmation of the

---

[16] Huntington, *The Clash of Civilisations*, p. 22.

[17] Huntington, *The Clash of Civilisations*, p. 41.

[18] Edward W. Said, 'The Clash of Ignorance', *The Nation*, 22 October 2001, *www.thenation.com/docPrint.mhtml?i = 20011022&s = said*

lowest common denominator in the domestic and international context, namely the sense of an inescapable standoff between 'Western' and 'Islamic' world-views. From the arrest of 'Muslim' activists in the US and Europe to the international war on terrorism, the issues concerned mostly relate to the people and states of the 'Western' and the ('Muslim') eastern hemispheres. Except for the most purblind, it seems, it should be evident that the theory of a West against the rest dichotomy, narrowed down to a conflict between the challenger civilisation 'Islam' and the 'West', found its manifestation in the attacks on the most prominent symbols of 'Western' capitalism and military power.[19]

The theory of Huntington, constructed as a meta-narrative for a new world order in the aftermath of the demise of the Soviet Union, continues to have a serious impact on the psychology of international politics. Among the few international relations theories that gained prominence both in academic and in decision-making circles, its provocative conclusions even inspired the emergence of a symbolic counter-approach in the form of the 'Dialogue among Civilisa-tions' initiative, suggested by Iranian President Mohammad Khatami and adopted by the United Nations as the political motto of 2001. In his speech to the United Nations on 21 September 1998, Khatami countered the idea of civilisa-tional conflict by stressing the importance of dialogue on the basis of universal norms:

> Among the worthiest achievements of this century is the acceptance of the necessity and significance of dialogue and rejection of force, promotion of under-standing ... and strengthening of the foundations of liberty, justice, and human rights ... If humanity at the threshold of the new century and millennium devotes all efforts to institutionalise dialogue, replacing hostility and confrontation with discourse and understanding, it would leave an invaluable legacy for the benefit of the future generations.[20]

Apart from such rare occurrences of constructive engagement, the pervasive myth of an 'Islamic' threat continues to provide enough potential for polemical misuse, both among those in the 'West' who would like to castigate a religion stretching from North Africa to Southeast Asia into one supposedly homoge-neous entity, and among 'Muslim' extremists who propagate the utopia of a single Muslim *umma* (community) destined to challenge the tenets of 'Western' civilisation. After September 11th, the Huntington thesis regained its promi-nence among politicians, including Italian Prime Minister Silvio Berlusconi, who pontificated about the 'supremacy of western values',[21] or former British Prime Minister Margaret Thatcher, who in an article published in *The Guardian* equated Islamism with Bolshevism.[22] In the spirit of the prophecy of Huntington, September 11th has been turned into proof that it is the 'Islamic menace' that undermines the security of 'Western' democracies and the very foundations of the capitalist world system.

---

[19] By using the headline 'Why They Hate Us: The Roots of Islamic Rage and What We Can Do about It', the 15 October 2001 edition of *Newsweek* captured this mood accurately.

[20] President Mohammad Khatami's address at the UN General Assembly on 21 September 1998, *Iranian Journal of International Affairs*, vol. 10, nos 1–2, 1998, p. 132.

[21] The statement of Berlusconi during a state visit to Germany on 26 September 2001 triggered widespread criticism by both the European Union and 'Islamic' states, prompting him to make a half-hearted apology for his ignorance about the various contributions of 'Islam' to human affairs.

[22] Margaret Thatcher, 'Islamism Is the New Bolshevism', *The Guardian*, 12 February 2002, *www.guardian.co.uk/bush/story/0,7369,648935,00.html*

What is neglected by the portrayal of civilisations as supposedly homogeneous units is the complexity of intra-regional developments, which begets far more insights into the causes and consequences of September 11th than either Huntington or Fukuyama appreciates. Discussed against the context of forces pulling and pushing the direction of political Islam from within, the transnational terrorism employed by the members of al-Qaeda can be seen as an attempt to escalate the ongoing struggle between progressive Islam and extremist Islam on a global scale. The most violent exemplification of the propaganda by deed policy followed by anarchists from the end of the 19th century onwards, the strategy behind September 11th is aimed at radicalising public opinion in the various domestic contexts of the 'Muslim' world in order to attain political power. The outcome of this clash within civilisation—not only after September 11th—relates to the contemporary perils of international politics and thus requires further discussion.

The Context of September 11th: The Politics of 'Islam'

More than two decades after the success of the Iranian revolution brought political Islam to the forefront of international politics, the direction of fundamentalism in the Arab world and the non-Arab states of Iran, Afghanistan, Pakistan and Turkey is changing. Two interrelated issues merit analysis: first, the emergence of a new form of transnational and fundamentalist movements and second the modified challenges to the legitimacy of the nation-state and established 'Islamist' agendas evolving from these movements. In conjunction with the impact of a long-term crisis such as the conflict over Palestine and the colonial and Cold War legacies that have been discussed elsewhere,[23] those two developments add to the instability of the regions involved and provide the breeding ground for the emergence of terrorist organisations such as al-Qaeda.

'Islamism' denotes the politicisation of Islam by movements, operating mainly within the Middle East, aiming to implement religious principles in the realm of society, state and culture.[24] As opposed to 'fundamentalism', which urges passive adherence to literal reading of the Qu'ran, 'Islamism can embrace both "progressive" *ulema* and those urban intellectuals who believe Islamic tenets are compatible with such modern values as freedom and democracy.'[25]

While the renaissance of 'Islam' as an all-encompassing political ideology can be traced back to the early 1920s, it was the triumph of the Iranian revolution of 1979 that for the first time created a modern Islamic state.[26] The causes of the resurgence of 'Islam' and the various forms and shapes it takes in the different national contexts are diverse and exceed the limits of this article. Suffice it to

---

[23] See among others John L. Esposito, *The Islamic Threat: Myth or Reality?*, New York, Oxford University Press, 1992; Halliday, *Islam and the Myth of Confrontation*, pp. 36–41.

[24] Halliday, *Two Hours that Shook the World*, p. 43.

[25] Ali R. Abootalebi, 'Islam, Islamists and Democracy', *Middle East Review of International Affairs*, vol. 3, no. 1, 1999, *www.biu.ac.il/SOC/besa/meria/journal/1999/issue1/jv3n1a2.html* . The same distinction was used earlier by Robin Wright, 'Islam, Democracy and the West', *Foreign Affairs*, vol. 71, no. 3, 1992, pp. 131–45.

[26] See among others Roger Owen, *State, Power and Politics in the Making of the Modern Middle-East*, 2nd edn, London and New York, Routledge, 2000, p. 173; Halliday, *Two Hours that Shook the World*, p. 43.

keep in mind that the success of Islamism is closely linked to disillusionment with secular nationalism and may be traced back to the challenges of 'Western' modernity that confronted the societies of the Middle East from the beginning of the 20th century onwards. In domestic contexts, the authoritarian governments in 'Muslim' countries failed to secure public legitimacy and heavily relied upon repressive security apparatus to enforce their political power. In terms of international politics, the defeat of the Arab forces by Israel in 1967 discredited Arab nationalism and opened up the vacuum for Islamist agendas. Against this background and the widespread popular dissent with corruption, mismanagement and the inability of the ruling elite to resist perceived 'Western' political and cultural imperialism, Islamist movements successfully generated popular support for their respective socioeconomic and political programmes.

While Islamist movements differ with regard to their motives, they have in common the quest to synthesise modernity with the main tenets of the *shari'a* (Islamic law). In Turkey, where Islamism rose as a protest movement against the secularisation of the Turkish state espoused by Mustafa Kemal 'Atatürk' during the 1920s and 1930s and later in Iran as a reaction against the repressive policies of Reza Khan and his son Mohammad Reza Shah Pahlavi during the reign of the Pahlavi dynasty between 1925 and 1979, the main mass support for Islamic movements came from urban, well-educated youth with a secular background.

While 'Islamism' describes a broad narrative currently dominant in the Middle East and elsewhere, there is no such thing as a coherent 'Islamic' movement. The success of the Iranian revolution had very distinct features—from the charismatic leadership of Ayatollah Ruhollah Khomeini to the history of opposition in Shia religious thought[27]—and thus did not spread to other countries. While the Islamic Republic in its first decade of existence endeavoured to export its revolution (*sudur-e enquilab*) to other states with significant Shia populations, such as Bahrain, Iraq, Afghanistan and Lebanon, it failed to generate a mass movement that would seriously threaten the regimes in power.[28]

Rather than representing a coherent political movement, Islamism is a product of specific national circumstances. As opposed to al-Qaeda, Hamas is not calling for a jihad against the 'West' and is limiting its activities to the

---

[27] The main tenet of Iranian Shi'ism is that the last in the line of the Twelve Imams, who the Shi'ites believe are the legitimate heirs of the Prophet Mohammad, went into hiding, and will return to establish the just rule of God on earth. The inherent mysticism of this belief in the occultation (*gheibat*) of the twelfth Imam is accompanied by a moral stress on the sufferings of Shi'ites at the hands of perceived unjust rulers, and upon the cult of the Shi'ite martyrs, Imam Ali and his sons, Imam Hassan and Imam Hossein. In particular, the powerful imagery of the martyrdom (*shahadat*) of Imam Hossein against superior forces has served the cause of popular mobilisation in modern Iran, both in the domestic context against foreign interference and authoritarianism and in perceived injustice in world politics. In this regard, Ayatollah Khomeini employed the *mostazafan—mostakbaran* dichotomy to refer to the fight of the 'oppressed' against the 'oppressors' both in the domestic context in order to mobilise the masses against the repressive regime of the Shah and in the international realm in order to confront perceived imperialism and political injustice ranging from Apartheid to the occupation of Palestine. For a discussion of the oppositional role of the 'Muslim' clergy in Iran, see among others Hamid Algar, 'The Oppositional Role of the Ulema in Twentieth Century Iran', in Nikki Keddie, ed., *Scholars, Saints and Sufis*, Berkeley, University of California Press, 1972, or Shahrough Akhavi, *Religion and Politics in Contemporary Iran*, Albany, State University of New York, 1980.

[28] See also Olivier Roy, *The Failure of Political Islam*, London, I. B. Tauris, 1994, pp. 183–193.

occupied territories and Israel. The Refah party (now Fazilet) of Necmettin Erbakan is inspired by Ottoman legacies and intends to address the effects of Kemalism on the constitution of Turkey, rather than to create an Islamic state. The Shia opposition inside and outside of Iraq works closely together with nationalist movements in the country. The Front Islamique du Salut (FIS) in Algeria portrays itself as the heir of the anti-colonialist fight against colonial occupation, and has had only marginal success in Morocco and Tunisia.[29] While these organisations act within the limits and constraints of established nation-state institutions and under the banner of a well-known political and social agenda, loose networks such as al-Qaeda are divorced from any regulatory context. Consequently, they rely on increasing violence in order to advance their political aspirations. This violence is not at all restricted to US institutions. Employing a radical interpretation of the Wahhabi school of Islamic thought, the ascendancy of the Taliban–al-Qaeda coalition in Afghanistan led also to an increasing anti-Shia bias in the region. As a result, sectarian violence led to the murder of dozens of Shi'ites in Pakistan, damaging relations between Sunni Pakistan and Shia Iran. In Afghanistan, the Taliban assassinated Iranian diplomats after capturing the northern town of Mazar-i Sharif in August 1998, further escalating anti-Shia sentiments and worsening the situation of the Hazara minority in the country.[30]

A quick look at the arrested and killed members of the Taliban–al-Qaeda coalition show that the militants are recruited mainly among radicalised Sunnis in Pakistan, Afghanistan, the Arab world and Chechnya and among uprooted and disillusioned youths with secular backgrounds in 'Western', mainly Western European circles. The composition of the coalition is thus fundamentally different from Islamist organisations, which are mostly rooted within the confines of the nation-state and act within a specific political context. Even radical groups such as Hamas or Islamic Jihad adapt to the regulations of the nation-state and regional politics. For the Taliban–al-Qaeda coalition, however, Afghanistan had been reduced to the status of an emirate, rather than a state, without an official capital and without a definition of Afghan nationhood.[31] Mollah Omar, a village preacher with no religious credentials among the *ulema* (Muslim clergy), did not take up a position as head of state but declared himself *Amir al-Mu'minin* (commander of the faithful), staying in Kandahar rather than caring to travel to the Afghan capital Kabul.

As a transnational force, the presence of networks such as al-Qaeda threatens the very legitimacy of the nation-state. The repeated call of the al-Qaeda leadership to 'rise and defend the holy lands' and to 'remove evil from

---

[29] Olivier Roy, 'Neo-fundamentalism', *www.ssrc.org/Sept11/essays/roy_text_only.htm*. Both the Refah Party in Tukey and the FIS in Algeria managed to gain power by winning elections but have been ousted by political—military opponents, while Hamas, at least officially, has not yet dictated *mainstream* Palestinian politics.

[30] Fred Halliday, 'Nervous Tehran Has a Wider Role to Play', *The Guardian*, 21 October 2001, www.observer.co.uk/islam/story/0,1442,577958,00.html

[31] Olivier Roy, 'Neo-fundamentalism', www.ssrc.org/Sept11/essays/roy_text_only.htm

212 *Arshin Adib-Moghaddam*

the Peninsula of Mohammad'[32] during the US American military offensive against the Taliban in Afghanistan, for instance, was implicitly designed to question the sovereignty of the Saudi state. Osama bin Laden did expect that the US would retaliate in full force. His rationale for taking that chance was that he anticipated a mass movement among Muslims, mainly in the Arab world, Afghanistan and Pakistan, a calculation that was as wrong as Saddam Hussein's speculation about 'Muslim' support against the Allied forces during the second Persian Gulf War.

The most apparent factor distinguishing movements such as al-Qaeda or the Taliban from Islamist movements is the lack of a social, political, economic, let alone intellectual agenda. In the Iranian/Shia context Ayatollah Ruhollah Khomeini, along with other pioneers of Shia political thought such as Ayatollah Hassan Shariatmadari, Ayatollah Baqer al-Sadr and Ali Shariati, addressed a wide range of social interaction, from the individual to the nation-state, and elaborated their respective agendas in relation to acknowledged facts of modernity, while endeavouring to embed their constructs in an 'Islamic' discourse. The same applies to other 'Islamic' thinkers such as Hassan Al-Ban'na and Abul A'la Mawdudi, to name but two.[33] The political and social movements that were enhanced by the propagated 'Islamic' resurgence and refer to the manifestos of these thinkers had and have legitimate concerns with regard to domestic and international issues. The reason why even the most radical of these movements have not endorsed bin-Laden's struggle against the 'West,' is that both the Taliban and al-Qaeda lack any kind of economic, social and intellectual agenda and that unresolved concerns, ranging from domestic reform to the occupation of Palestine, would be delegitimised by any association with September 11th.

The Implications of September 11th for World Politics

The causes and consequences of September 11th are much more diverse than the theories of Huntington and Fukuyama can comprehend. The preceding discussion about the struggle for Islam as the dominant narrative of contemporary 'Muslim' politics defies a portrayal of civilisations as monolithic polities. In this regard, the rationale behind the terrorist attacks against the US has been mainly to radicalise public opinion in 'Muslim' countries. Certainly, one might contend that bin-Laden had calculated that the US would retaliate and expected that the demagogy of a jihad against the West would unite significant segments of the Arab, Pakistani and Afghan populations behind the Taliban–al-Qaeda coalition, silencing moderate voices and threatening the stability of collaborating states such as Saudi Arabia or Pakistan. September 11th hence may be regarded as a new incident of globalisation bringing the 'clash within Islam' to the global stage. Neither a narrow vision of the universal triumph of capitalism and liberalism nor the myth of an Islamic colossus aimed at destroying the tenets of 'Western' civilisation explains the implications of September 11th for global politics.

---

[32] As requested by Osama bin Laden during his speech broadcasted on al-Jazira television on 7 October 2001, and published on 8 October 2001 in the *International Herald Tribune*.

[33] Roy, *The Failure of Political Islam*, pp. 35–39.

What then are the likely effects of September 11th on world politics? Certainly, it is too early to answer that question, and what follows is certainly not to be understood as some kind of deterministic prediction. Instead, the lines below will characterise patterns, building upon the preceding analysis about the globalisation of violence and the struggle for Islam. Two dominant factors merit further attention. First, the globalisation of violence typified by the events on September 11th altered the traditional view of security and geographical barriers. The success of 'bringing the battle into the heart of America', as proclaimed by bin-Laden, carried out by the network of a non-state actor, motivated by a common universal cause, without established battle lines and territorial boundaries, blurs the traditional security calculus with regard to physical invulnerability due to geographic barriers. That new dimension of globalisation means that states such as the US which were traditionally geographically separated from the devastation in other parts of the world suddenly find themselves in a situation where the meaning of geographical barriers and the security assumption tied to it have become obsolete. While the threat from thermonuclear war, which equally blurred the barriers of geographical space, was calculable during the Cold War, the transnational terrorism of the kind of September 11th is not.

The second factor is related to the first and is linked to the argument about the global outreach of the struggle for 'Islam'. The sense of security interdependence that has been generated by the attacks on the United States and the underlying issues relating to 'Muslim' politics suddenly pushed the isolationist policies of the Bush administration towards military and diplomatic engagements in regions it had previously intended to abandon. Initially, the ability of the United States to orchestrate an international response has been greatly enhanced by the powerful 'international coalition against terrorism' narrative. Even states that have been known to challenge US foreign policy, such as Syria, Libya and Iran, were quick to condemn the events of September 11th and used their diplomatic influence to stabilise the situation in Afghanistan. Iran, together with Russia the main contributor to the Northern Alliance for the past seven years, even offered search and rescue missions for downed US pilots on Iranian territory, and actively contributed to the establishment of the Afghan interim government of Hamid Karzai.[34]

From the repeated announcement of decision makers in Europe and the United States that the war on terrorism is not a war against 'Islam' to the deepened engagement of the European Union with states such as Iran that until recently had represented the archetypal 'Muslim' polity in 'Western' imagery, the various challenges of political Islam appear to dominate the agenda of world politics. Here, there is no contradiction to the argument about the struggle within Islam and the inherent diversity of the 'Muslim' world. It is simply inaccurate to argue that there exists some kind of 'Islamic' menace, first because there is no 'Muslim' consensus on how to deal with the 'West' (and vice versa) and second because 'Islamic' states are much more concerned with domestic crisis than international confrontation. In the context of 'Muslim' politics, the use and misuse of 'Islam' as a political instrument, however, constitutes an ideological

---

[34] Daniel Brumberg, 'End of a Brief Affair? The United States and Iran', *Carnegie Endowment for International Peace*, Policy Brief, 14 March 2002.

determination, both in domestic and in systemic settings, and reached global dimensions after September 11th. That politicisation of 'Islam' has proven to provide enough potentiality to generate mass movements, providing a powerful instrument ready to be utilised by states, transnational networks or individuals. The struggle to dominate 'Muslim' politics, thus, will remain a dominant factor in international politics and its outcome will certainly have an impact on the order of future world politics.

As opposed to Huntington's prescription that the US should refrain from meddling in the affairs of 'alien civilisations', the current foreign policy restructuring of the Bush administration hints towards more engagement on the international level than one would have anticipated before September 11th. The inherent morality of the struggle against terrorism, enhanced by the emotionally charged atmosphere in the aftermath of September 11th, has given the United States the mandate to forge a fragile alliance that allowed a military attack on Afghanistan without systematic opposition by other states. The legitimising instrumentality of this war on terrorism will remain a powerful force, not only on the systemic level of international politics but also in the various domestic contexts.[35]

Conclusions: Foreign Policy Lessons and Theoretical Ramifications

Against the background of the world order theories of Fukuyama and Huntington this article has argued that the causes and consequences of September 11th can be explained in terms neither of the end of history nor of a clash among civilisations. Two interrelated arguments have been discussed: first, September 11th can be characterised as one incident of globalisation, questioning the assumption that we can attribute a unidirectional automatism to global affairs, and, second, that the attack on the United States can be related to the ongoing struggle between different constructs of political Islam. In order to appreciate the perils and idiosyncrasies of that changed climate of interaction, drawing lines between supposedly different entities might provide policy guidelines and legitimise unilateral military campaigns, it does not, however, appreciate the complex interconnectedness of contemporary world politics. These issues are, of course, by no means exclusive. Adopting them as alternative causes and consequences for September 11th, however, yields practical and theoretical implications that were previously ignored.

In regard to practical ramifications, the globalisation of political violence has altered the traditional understanding of security threats. After September 11th, globalisation means that the barriers of geographical space and the security associated with them are further blurred. While the likelihood of thermonuclear confrontation during the Cold War and the symmetry of a bipolar world order provided a calculable threat, transnational networks such as al-Qaeda strike out of nowhere, and do not react towards deterrence or any form of missile defence system for that matter. The global reach of that political violence links the security of the United States to the ongoing struggle within 'Islam', and hence requires international and indeed multilateral resolve to be managed.

---

[35] The label 'war on terrorism' hence provides enough potentiality to be employed in various contexts, from the continuing dispute between India and Pakistan over Kashmir to

After September 11th the Bush administration for a short period abandoned the unilateralist policies that had previously led the US to opt out of international treaties such as the Kyoto protocol against global warming.[36] By forging an international alliance via the UN Security Council[37] and implementing careful diplomacy with regard to the war against Afghanistan, the US successfully managed to minimise the opposition to the use of military force. Now that the Taliban movement in Afghanistan appears to be defeated, however, the rhetoric of the Bush administration regarding the future of the war on terrorism has turned back to the tenor of unilateralism, to the detriment of both the diplomatic initiatives of the European Union and future stability in Afghanistan and the Middle East.

The issues underlying what Halliday calls the 'Greater West Asian Crisis',[38] ranging from the legacies of colonialism and the Cold War to the quest for Palestinian statehood, Kashmir and Afghanistan, require multilateral resolve on the basis of international norms and against the background of genuine dialogue and engagement. This is certainly not some remote utopia. The historical fact that the United Nations evolved out of the mayhem of the Second World War proves that international crisis can generate international cooperation. My discussion of the politics pulling and pushing the 'Islamic' world from within should have conveyed the message that the forces behind September 11th are a threat to universal values transcending both the 'Muslim' world and the 'West'. An appreciation of that interconnectedness provides the common denominator that could generate stronger multilateral cooperation on a global scale. If boundaries, in terms of national, civilisational or other imagined constructs, are enforced, however, the vast majority of people might get alienated from essentially universal principles, enforcing the dangerous disposition that the future world order is somehow determined by irrefutable self-fulfilling prophecies.[39]

In theoretical terms the globalisation of political violence and security interdependence challenge traditional realist views of the roles of states in international relations. In an essay published in the aftermath of September 11th, Keohane argues that

> Most problematic are the assumptions in international relations theory about the roles played by states. There has been too much 'international relations,' and too little 'world politics,' not only in work on security but also in much work on

---

(Footnote continued)
the escalating violence between Israelis and Palestinians and the continued military campaigns of Russia against Chechnya, and Turkey against Islamist and Kurdish leftist opposition forces. Taking this together with the fact that since September 11th the US has embarked upon a major military operation in Afghanistan and minor, not necessarily related, operations in various regions of the world (Georgia, Colombia, Philippines), one might well conclude that the war on terrorism is indeed a dominant current in international politics since September 11th.

[36] Robert O. Keohane, 'The Globalization of Violence, Theories of World Politics and "The Liberalism of Fear"', *www.ssrc.org/sept11/essays/keohane.htm*

[37] Security Council Resolution 1373 passed on 28 September 2001 used the mandatory provisions of Chapter VII of the United Nations Charter to require all states to deny safe haven 'both to terrorists' and to those who 'provide safe haven' to terrorists. Resolution 1373 also required states to prevent potential terrorists from using their territories, and to 'prevent and suppress the financing of terrorist acts'.

[38] Halliday, *Two Hours that Shook the World*, p. 38.

[39] The 'Enhanced Border Security and Visa Entry Reform Act' which passed unanimously (97.0) in the US American Senate on 18 April 2002, further constraining the entry of citizens of so called 'state sponsors of terrorism' into the US is certainly to be considered a step into the wrong direction.

216 *Arshin Adib-Moghaddam*

international institutions. States no longer have a monopoly on the means of mass destruction: more people died in the attacks on the World Trade Center and the Pentagon than in the Japanese attack on Pearl Harbor in 1941. Indeed, it would be salutary for us to change the name of our field, from 'international relations' to 'world politics.' The language of 'international' relations enables us to slip back into state-centric assumptions too easily.[40]

If one were to take the argument of Keohane one step further and delve deeper into international relations theory, the 'states systemic project', originally pioneered by Kenneth Waltz,[41] requires modification in the direction of what constructivists refer to as the appreciation of agency in world politics.[42] While the war on terrorism reinforced the centrality of states to the current conflict, the presence of non-state actors, either violent, as in the case of al-Qaeda, or non-violent, as in the case of non-governmental organisations (NGOs), multinational companies, inter-governmental organisations (IGOs) and so forth, modifies the role of states in world politics. Like states, all of these group actors have their specific interests, defined in terms of their constructed identities. In the case of many NGOs, interest is defined in terms of the enhancement of environmental standards, health services, third world debt relief and so forth. At the other, darker end of the spectrum, terrorist organisations define interest in terms of political power, chaos, violence, media coverage and so on. As much as globalisation cannot be solely referred to in terms of economic integration, the modified challenges to the state in world politics cannot be merely defined in terms of orthodox concepts. Without the inclusion of new categories in the repertoire of international relations theory, these new nuances of world politics remain unaccounted for, and will certainly further question the practical utility of some of the contemporary debates occurring within the discipline.

[40] Robert O. Keohane, 'The Globalization of Violence, Theories of World Politics and "The Liberalism of Fear"', *www.ssrc.org/sept11/essays/keohane.htm*

[41] Waltz argues, 'So long as the major states are the major actors, the structure of international politics is defined in terms of them. That theoretical statement is of course borne out in practice. States set the scene in which they, along with non-state actors, stage their dramas or carry on their humdrum affairs ... When the crunch comes, states remake the rules by which other actors operate'; Kenneth N. Waltz, 'Political Structures', in Robert O. Keohane, ed., *Neorealism and Its Critics*, New York, Columbia University Press, 1986, p. 89. See also Kenneth N. Waltz, *Man, the State, and War*, New York, Columbia University Press, 1959; Kenneth N. Waltz, *Theory of International Politics*, New York, McGraw-Hill, 1979.

[42] For a constructivist version of the state-systemic project see Alexander Wendt, *Social Theory of International Politics*, Cambridge, Cambridge University Press, 1999.

[32]

GLOBALISED CULTURE:
THE TRIUMPH OF THE WEST?

John Tomlinson

GLOBAL AND GLOBALISED CULTURE

The idea of a single, unified culture encompassing the whole world has a long and, so far as I know, relatively undocumented history. An inventory of the various historical dreams, visions and speculations about a global culture would, I suppose, have to include at least those of: the imperial projects of the ancient 'world empires' such as China or Rome; the great proselytising 'world religions' and the communities of faith established around them – Christendom, the Ummah Islam etc.; the utopian global visions of early socialists such as Saint-Simon; the various movements dedicated to establishing world peace; the ideas, beginning in the nineteenth century, of enthusiasts for artificial 'international' languages such as Esperanto; and many more.[1] These ideas clearly differ from each other in all sorts of ways. For example, some (probably most) were simply naïve, unproblematised, often dogmatic, projections of a particular cultural outlook onto a 'universal' screen, while others were driven by the desire to reconcile cultural differences and to usher in a new, pacified ideal home for humankind. But two things unite all these visions. First, that they all approached the idea of a single global culture with enthusiasm, and second that none of them came anywhere near to seeing it achieved.

The ideas of a global culture in the air today – in the intellectual and critical discourses of the 1990s – are different. They are not, in the main, visionary or utopian ideas.[2] Rather they are speculations that arise in response to processes that we can actually see occurring around us. These processes, which are generally referred to collectively as 'globalisation', seem, whether we like it or not, to be tying us all – nations, communities, individuals – closer together. It is in the context of globalisation, then, that current discussions of an emergent global culture assume a different significance from earlier speculations. It is not only that the current social, economic and technological context makes a global culture in some senses more plausibly attainable – a concrete possibility rather than a mere dream. It is also that this very sense of imminence brings with it anxieties, uncertainties and suspicions.

Talk of a global culture today is just as likely, probably more likely, to focus on its dystopian aspect, to construct it as a threat rather than a promise. This, at any rate, is the sort of talk I want to consider here. To grasp its close relation to the processes of globalisation and to distinguish it from earlier traditions of thought, I shall refer in what follows to the idea of a *globalised* rather than global culture. A globalised culture refers here specifically to the way in which people, integrating the general signs of an increasing interdependence that characterises the globalisation process with other critical positions and assumptions, have constructed a pessimistic 'master scenario' (Hannerz 1991) of cultural domination. This is the speculative discourse that I want to criticise.

In order to develop this discussion in a relatively short piece, I shall have to leave on one side some pretty big and thorny related and contextual issues. Most of these relate to the way in which the notion of globalisation has been theorised. Though I shall offer later a brief description of what globalisation broadly means, it must be recognised that there are all sorts of unresolved controversies in globalisation theory which this discussion will necessarily rub up against from time to time without explicitly recognising. If readers recognise these, and develop the argument themselves, so much the better!

GLOBALISED CULTURE AS WESTERNISED CULTURE

The argument I want to focus on can be set out quite briefly in outline, though we shall see that it contains some crucial assumptions that will require unpacking presently. It goes like this. The globalised culture that is currently emerging is not a global culture in any utopian sense. It is not a culture that has arisen out of the mutual experiences and needs of all of humanity. It does not draw equally on the world's diverse cultural traditions. It is neither inclusive, balanced, nor, in the best sense, synthesising. Rather, globalised culture is the installation, world-wide, of one particular culture born out of one particular, privileged historical experience. It is, in short, simply the global extension of *Western* culture. The broad implications – and the causes of critical concern – are that: (a) this process is homogenising, that it threatens the obliteration of the world's rich cultural diversity; (b) that it visits the various cultural ills of the West on other cultures; (c) that this is a particular threat to the fragile and vulnerable cultures of peripheral, 'Third World' nations; and (d) that it is part and parcel of wider forms of domination – those involved in the ever-widening grip of transnational capitalism and those involved in the maintenance of post-colonial relations of (economic and cultural) dependency.

This is, of course, to view the globalisation process through a now familiar critical prism – that of the critique of Western 'cultural imperialism' (Friedman 1994; Hannerz 1991; and McQuail 1994). As I and others have argued elsewhere (Boyd-Barrett 1982; Schlesinger 1991; Sinclair 1992; Tomlinson 1991, 1995, 1997), this is a peculiarly vexed and often confused critical discourse which rolls a number of complex questions up together. In the space available here I shall have to take for granted most of this criticism. But before I come to my central argument it will be useful just to mention a couple of the most common objections to the general idea of Westernisation, so as to distinguish them from the specific, rather different line of criticism I want to follow later.

What do people mean when they talk about 'Westernisation'? A whole range of things: the consumer culture of Western capitalism with its now all-too-familiar icons (McDonald's, Coca-Cola, Levi Jeans), the spread of European languages (particularly English), styles of dress, eating habits, architecture and music, the adoption of an urban lifestyle based around industrial production, a pattern of cultural experience dominated by the mass media, a range of cultural values and attitudes – about personal liberty, gender and sexuality, human rights, the political process, religion, scientific and technological rationality and so on. Now, although all of these aspects of 'the West' can be found throughout the world today, they clearly do not exist as an indivisible package. To take but one example, an acceptance of the technological culture of the West and of aspects of its consumerism may well co-exist with a vigorous rejection of its sexual permissiveness and its generally secular outlook – as is common in many Islamic societies. A prime instance of this contradiction is the current attempt to regulate or even ban the use of satellite television receivers in countries like Iran, since they are seen by the authorities to be the source of various images of Western decadence. This sort of cultural-protectionist legislation is almost impossible to implement, partly because of the huge numbers of dishes involved (estimated at more than 500,000 in Tehran alone) but also because use of this technology is vital for education and scientific research. Restriction of access is thus resisted by these constituencies within the intelligentsia who might otherwise hold quite 'conventional' Muslim attitudes towards, for example, images of sexuality or nudity in Western television programmes (Haeri 1994).

So there is obviously a need to *discriminate* between various aspects of what is totalised as 'Westernisation', and such discrimination will reveal a much more complex picture: some cultural goods will be broader in their appeal than others, some values and attitudes easily adopted while others are actively resisted or found simply odd or irrelevant. All this will vary from society to society and between different groupings and divisions – class, age, gender, urban/rural, etc. – within societies. The first objection to the idea of Westernisation, then, is that it is too broad a generalisation. Its rhetorical force is bought at the price of glossing over a multitude of complexities, exceptional cases and contradictions. This criticism also connects with another one: that the Westernisation/homogenisation/cultural imperialism thesis itself, ironically, displays a sort of Western ethnocentrism (Hannerz 1991; Tomlinson 1991, 1995). Ulf Hannerz puts this point nicely:

> The global homogenisation scenario focuses on things that we, as observers and commentators from the centre, are very familiar with: our fast foods, our soft drinks, our sitcoms. The idea that they are or will be everywhere, and enduringly powerful everywhere, makes our culture even more important and worth arguing about, and relieves us of the real strains of having to engage with other living, complicated, puzzling cultures.
>
> (Hannerz 1991: 109)

A second set of objections concerns the way in which Westernisation suggests a rather crude model of the one-way flow of cultural influence. This criticism has – rightly – been the one most consistently applied to the whole cultural imperialism idea. Culture, it is argued, simply does not transfer in this way. Movement between cultural/geographical areas always involves translation, mutation and adaptation as the 'receiving culture' brings its own cultural resources to bear, in dialectical fashion, upon 'cultural imports' (Appadurai

1990; Garcia Canclini 1995; Lull 1995; Robins 1991; Tomlinson 1991). So, as Jesus Martin-Barbero describes the process of cultural influence in Latin America: 'The steady, predictable tempo of homogenising development [is] upset by the counter-tempo of profound differences and cultural discontinuities' (1993: 149). What follows from this argument is not simply the point that the Westernisation thesis underestimates the cultural resilience and dynamism of non-Western cultures, their capacity to 'indigenise' Western imports. It is also draws attention to the *counter-flow* of cultural influence – for instance in 'world music' (Abu-Lughod 1991) – from the periphery to the centre. Indeed this dialectical conception of culture can be further developed so as to undermine the sense of the West as a stable homogeneous cultural entity. As Pieterse puts it: 'It ... implies an argument with Westernisation: the West itself may be viewed as a mixture and Western culture as Creole culture' (1995: 54). Of course, the ultimate implication is that whatever globalised culture is emerging, it will not bear the stamp of any particular cultural-geographical or national identity, but will be *essentially* a hybrid, *mestizaje*, 'cut-and-mix' culture (Pieterse 1995; Garcia Canclini 1995).

These sorts of criticism quickly take some of the wind out of the sails of the Westernisation argument, at least in its most dramatic, polemical formulations. However, they do not entirely resolve the issue of the contemporary cultural power of the West. For it could very reasonably be argued that, when all is said and done and all these criticisms met, Western cultural practices and institutions still remain firmly in the driving seat of global cultural development. No amount of attention to the processes of cultural reception and translation, no anthropological scruples about the complexities of particular local contexts, no dialectical theorising, can argue away the massive and everywhere manifest power of Western capitalism, both as a general cultural configuration (the commodification of everyday experience, consumer culture) and as a specific set of global cultural industries (CNN, Times-Warner, News International). What, it might be asked, is this, if not evidence of some sort of Western cultural hegemony? What ensues from this is a sort of critical stand-off. Both positions are convincing within their own terms, but seem somehow not precisely to engage.

To try to take the argument a little further I want, in what follows, to focus on one particular, largely implicit assumption that seems to be embedded in the idea of globalised culture as Westernised culture. This is the assumption that the process of globalisation is *continuous* with the long, steady, historical rise of Western cultural dominance. By this I mean that the sort of cultural power generally attributed to the West today is seen as of the same *order* of power that was manifest in, say, the great imperial expansion of European powers from the seventeenth century onwards. So, for example, this implicit understanding of globalised culture would see the massive and undeniable spread of Western cultural goods – 'Coca-colonisation' – as, at least broadly, part of the same process of domination as that which characterised the *actual* colonisation of much of the rest of the world by the West. I do not mean that no distinction is made between the obviously coercive and often bloody history of Western colonial expansion and the 'soft' cultural imperialism of McDonald's hamburgers, Michael Jackson videos or Hollywood movies. But I think it is often the case that these and many other instances of Western cultural power get lumped together – 'totalised' – by the term 'Westernisation' and that the result is an impression of the inexorable advance – even the 'triumph' of the West.

It is this particular totalising assumption that I think could benefit from being unpacked and critically examined. This is for two reasons: first because it mistakes the nature of the globalisation process and secondly because by conflating a number of different issues it overstates the general cultural power of the West. I do not want to deny that the West is in a certain sense 'culturally powerful', but I do want to suggest that this power, which is closely aligned with its technological, industrial and economic power, is not the whole story. It does not amount to the implicit claim that 'the way of life' of the West is now becoming installed, via globalisation, as the unchallengeable cultural model for all of humanity.

Indeed, as I shall now go on to argue, there are ways in which the globalisation process, properly conceived, can be shown to be actively problematic for the continuation of Western cultural dominance: to signal not the triumph of the West, but its imminent decline.

GLOBALISATION AS THE 'DECLINE OF THE WEST'

In this section I want to examine some observations by two important and influential British social theorists, Anthony Giddens and Zygmunt Bauman, which connect globalisation with the decline, rather than the triumph of the West. Giddens in particular has been highly influential in theorising the globalisation process and in relating this to the wider debate about the nature of social modernity. Neither of these particular arguments, however, is developed at any great length and there will not be space here to develop them much further. I present them simply as suggestive ways of thinking against the grain of the arguments we have so far reviewed. First, however, it will be useful to say a little more about the nature of the globalisation process itself.

Probably the most important thing to be clear about is that globalisation is not *itself* the emergence of a globalised culture. Rather, it refers to the complex pattern of interconnections and interdependencies that have arisen in the late-modern world. Globalisation is heavy with implications for all spheres of social existence – the economic, the political, the environmental, as well as the cultural. In all these spheres it has the effect of tying 'local' life to 'global' structures, processes and events. So, for example, the economic fate of local communities – levels of economic activity, employment prospects, standard of living – is increasingly tied to a capitalist production system and market that is global in scope and operation – to global 'market forces'. Similarly, our local environment (and consequently our health and physical quality of life) is subject to risks arising at a global level – global warming, ozone depletion, eco-disasters with global 'fall-out' such as Chernobyl.

What these aspects of globalisation represent, then, is a rapidly growing context of global interdependence which already 'unites' us all, if only in the sense of making us all subject to certain common global influences, processes, opportunities and risks. But clearly this sort of 'structural unity' does not of itself imply the emergence either of a common 'global culture' (in the utopian sense) or of the globalised (Westernised) culture we have been discussing. Neither, it should be added, does this interdependence imply a levelling out of advantages and disadvantages globally. Globalisation is generally agreed to be an *uneven* process in which neither the opportunities nor the risks are evenly distributed (McGrew 1992; Massey 1994). But, again, this does not mean that it necessarily reproduces – or will reproduce – the precise historical patterns of inequality supposed in the dualism of the 'West versus the Rest'. More complex, contradictory patterns of winners and losers in the globalisation process may be emerging.

Another important aspect of globalisation is, of course, the increasing level of social-cultural *awareness* of global interdependence. As Robertson puts it, globalisation 'refers both to the compression of the world and the intensification of consciousness of the world as a whole' (1992: 8). Our sense of the rest of the world and of our connections with it are 'brought home to us' routinely via globalising media and communications technology. Now, of course, it can be argued that the *contents* of these images of a wider world are often highly selective and restricted ones. For instance, it has long been observed that the picture of developing countries portrayed on Western televisions tends to be restricted to 'the narrow agenda of conflicts and catastrophes' (Cleasby 1995: iii). Thus as Peter Adamson of UNICEF has argued, with 'no equivalent sense of the norms in poor countries to set against this constant reporting of the exceptional ... the cumulative effect of the way in which the developing world is portrayed by the media is grossly misleading' (quoted, Cleasby 1995: iii).

However, the point I want to stress is the routine *availability* of distanciated imagery (however accurate) that globalising media technology provides. In the affluent Western world we take the experience provided by such technology pretty much for granted. We *expect* to have instant images of events happening in every remote corner of the world on our television screens. It is with no sense of wonder that we pick up the phone and speak to people on other continents. We just as quickly – some of us – become used to communicating globally on the Internet and the 'World Wide Web'. So globalisation seems also to involve, as Giddens puts it (1990: 187), the extension of our 'phenomenal worlds' from the local to the global. Of course, access to this technology is obviously not evenly distributed and so we must avoid the mistake of extrapolating from the Western experience. But, on the other hand, it would be equally misleading to treat such communications technology, and the experience it affords as, somehow, the exclusive property of the West. Again, we have to recognise the possibility that globalisation may be producing shifting global and local patterns in what has been called the 'information rich and the information poor'.

Perhaps the most widely recognised property of globalisation amongst those who have theorised it is its *ambiguous* nature – its mixture of risk and opportunity, its 'dialectical' counterposing of generalising and particularising tendencies, its confusing capacity both to enable and to disempower.

It is within this broad conceptualisation of globalisation that Anthony Giddens writes of '[t]he gradual decline in European or Western global hegemony, the other side of which is the increasing expansion of modern influences world-wide', of 'the declining grip of the West over the rest of the world' or of 'the evaporating of the privileged position of the West' (1990: 51–3). What can he mean by this?

Well, Giddens has written a good deal about the globalisation process and at a fairly high level of abstraction and really these comments need to be read in the context of his overall theorisation of the globalising nature of modernity (Giddens 1990, 1991, 1994a, 1994b). But to put it at its simplest, his argument is that, though the process of 'globalising modernity' may have *begun* in the extension of Western institutions, the very fact of the current global ubiquity of these institutions (capitalism, industrialism, the nation-state system and so on) – in a sense the West's 'success' in disseminating its institutional forms – also represents a decline in the differentials between it and the rest of the world, thus a loss of the West's (once unique) social/cultural 'edge'. As he puts the point in a more recent discussion:

> The first phase of globalisation was plainly governed, primarily, by the expansion of the West, and institutions which originated in the West. No other civilisation made anything like as pervasive an impact on the world, or shaped it so much in its own image ... Although still dominated by Western power, globalisation today can no longer be spoken of only as a matter of one-way imperialism ... increasingly there is no obvious 'direction' to globalisation at all and its ramifications are more or less ever present. The current phase of globalisation, then, should not be confused with the preceding one, whose structures it acts increasingly to subvert.
>
> (Giddens 1994b: 96)

There are various ways in which this 'loss of privilege' and even the 'subversion' of Western power may be understood. For example, it might be pointed out that certain parts of what we were used to calling the 'Third World' are now actually more advanced – technologically, industrially, economically – than some parts of the West. The comparison here might be, for example, between the so-called 'Asian Tiger' economies and some of the economically depressed heavy-industrial regions of Europe or the US. And there might be a complex causal relationship between the rise and decline of such regions connected by a globalised capitalist market (Giddens 1990: 65, 1994a: 65). Or, to put this slightly differently, it might be argued that capitalism has no 'loyalty' to its birthplace, and so provides no guarantees that the geographical patterns of dominance established in early modernity – the elective affinity between the interests of capitalism and of the West – will continue (Tomlinson 1997). There are signs of this, for example, in the increasingly uneasy relation between the capitalist money markets and the governments of Western nation-states – the periodic currency crises besetting the Western industrial nations. A rather spectacular instance of the capitalist system deserting the West could be seen in the débâcle of Britain's

oldest merchant bank, Baring Brothers, in February 1995 as a result of its high risk globalising speculations carried out, appropriately enough, on the Singapore market.

On a more directly cultural level, the loss of privilege of the West can be seen in the shifting orientation and self-understanding of the discipline of anthropology, the academic discipline which, perhaps more than any other, displays the cultural assumptions on which the West has presumed to organise a discourse about other cultures. As Giddens points out (1994b: 97), anthropology in its formative stage was a prime example of the West's self-assured assumption of cultural superiority. Because of its 'evolutionary' assumptions, early taxonomising anthropology established itself as a practice to which the West had exclusive rights – the 'interrogation' of all other cultures. Other cultures were there, like the flora and fauna of the natural world, to be catalogued and observed, but there was no thought that they could ever *themselves* engage in the practice – they were categorised as 'if not inert, no more than a "subject" of enquiry' (1994b: 97).

Early anthropology was part of the cultural armoury of an imperialist West during 'early globalisation' precisely because it had not developed its inner logic. As this emerges, with the recognition of the integrity of traditions, the knowledgeability of all cultural agents and the growing sense of 'cultural relativism', so anthropology becomes simultaneously both a more modest and humble undertaking and, significantly, a globalised practice. Present-day anthropologists have to approach their study in the role of the *ingenu* – the innocent abroad – rather than as the confident explorer and taxonomist. Without the assurance of a taken-for-granted superior cultural 'home-base', anthropological study becomes a matter of 'learning how to go on' rather than of detached, *de haut en bas* interrogation. Not only this, it becomes clear that in this later phase of globalisation, *all* cultures have a thoroughly reflexive anthropological sensibility: 'In British Columbia the present day Kwakiutl are busy reconstructing their traditional culture using [Franz] Boas' monographs as their guide, while Australian Aboriginals and other groups across the world are contesting

land-rights on the basis of parallel anthropological studies' (Giddens 1994b: 100).

So, the trajectory of the development of
anthropology, as Giddens puts it, 'leads to its
effective dissolution today' (1994b: 97). This
could also stand, more broadly, for the way in
which current globalisation subverts and undermines the cultural power of the West from
which it first emerged.

To conclude this section I want to comment
briefly on an interesting distinction that Zygmunt Bauman makes between the 'global' and
the 'universal':

> Modernity once deemed itself *universal*.
> Now it thinks of itself instead as *global*.
> Behind the change of term hides a watershed
> in the history of modern self-awareness and
> self-confidence. Universal was to be the rule
> of reason – the order of things that would
> replace the slavery to passions with the
> autonomy of rational beings, superstition
> and ignorance with truth, tribulations of the
> drifting plankton with self-made and thor-
> oughly   monitored   history-by-design.
> 'Globality', in contrast, means merely that
> everyone   everywhere   may   feed   on
> McDonald's hamburgers and watch the latest
> made-for-TV docudrama. Universality was a
> proud project, a Herculean mission to
> perform. Globality in contrast, is a meek
> acquiescence to what is happening 'out there'
> ...
>
> (Bauman 1995: 24)

Mapping this onto Giddens' distinction
between early and late globalisation, the key
difference becomes that between a Western
culture with pretensions to universalism and
one without.[3] The globalisation of the West's
cultural practices is simply occurring without
any real sense either that this is part of its
collective project or 'mission', or that these
practices are, indeed, the tokens of an ideal
human civilisation. Early globalisation involves
the self-conscious cultural project of univer-
sality, whilst late globalisation – globality – is
mere ubiquity.

Now, whilst it may be argued that Bauman
erects a rather contrived dualism here between
the 'high cultural' project of enlightenment
rationalism and some rather specific 'popular
cultural' practices, I do think his stress on the
cultural self-image and self-confidence of the
West is an important one. The specific doubts

he detects that now 'sap the ethical confidence
and self-righteousness of the West' tend to be
those of the intellectual. These are doubts
about the capacity of the Enlightenment
project ever to deliver full emancipation for all
human beings, about 'whether the wedlock
between the growth of rational control and
the growth of social and personal autonomy,
that crux of modern strategy, was not ill-
conceived from the start ... ' (1995: 29)

However we can read the idea of the loss of
Western self-confidence in more mundane
ways. Bauman's description of globality as a
meek acquiescence to what is happening 'out
there' may be a little overstated, but it does
grasp something of the spirit in which ordinary people in the West probably experience
the global spread of their 'own' cultural practices. Indeed a lot probably hangs on the
extent to which Westerners actually feel
'ownership' of the sorts of cultural practices
that, typically, get globalised. Although this is
an immensely complicated issue, my guess is
that there is only a very low level of correspondence between people's routine interaction with
the contemporary 'culture industry' and their
sense of having a distinctive *Western* cultural
identity, let alone feeling proud of it. It seems
more likely to me that things like McDonald's
restaurants are experienced as simply 'there' in
our cultural environments: things we use and
have become familiar and perhaps comfortable with, but which we do not – either
literally or culturally – 'own'. In this sense the
decline of Western cultural self-confidence
may align with the structural properties of
globalising modernity – the 'disembedding' (to
use Giddens' term) of institutions from
contexts of local to global control. In a world
in which increasingly our mundane 'local'
experience is governed by events and processes
at a distance, it may become difficult to maintain a sharp sense of (at least 'mass') culture as
distinctively 'the way we do things' in the
West – to understand these practices as having
any particular connection with our specific
histories and traditions. Thus, far from
grasping globalised culture in the complacent,
proprietorial way that may have been associated with, say, the *Pax Britannica*, late-modern
Westerners may experience it as a largely
undifferentiated, 'placeless' modernity to which

they relate effortlessly, but without much sense of either personal involvement or of control.

CONCLUSION

The arguments reviewed above are obviously not conclusive and leave many issues unresolved. In particular the complex phenomenology of cultural identity in a globalised world requires far more extensive and nuanced treatment than has been possible here. What I have tried to offer is simply a glimpse of alternative ways of thinking about the complex cultural issues forced upon us by the globalisation process. Nothing in this is meant to deny the continuing *economic* power of the West, nor even that particular, limited, sense of 'cultural' power that proceeds from this – the power of Western transnational capitalism to distribute its goods around the world. Nor, to be clear, do these arguments entail the idea of a simple 'turning of the tables'; the 'decline of the West' does not mean the inevitable 'rise' of any other particular hegemonic power (no matter how tempting it is to speculate about the 'Asian Tigers' and so forth). In the short term at least, much of the 'Third World' will probably continue to be marginalised by globalising technologies (Massey 1994). But, to look beyond this, these reflections do suggest that what is happening in globalisation is not a process firmly in the

cultural grip of the West and that, therefore, the global future is much more radically open than the discourses of homogenisation and cultural imperialism suggest. We surely need to find new critical models to engage with the emerging 'power geometry' of globalisation, but we will not find these by rummaging through the theoretical box of tricks labelled 'Westernisation'.

NOTES

1 On some of the historical – particularly nineteenth-century – utopian visions of global unity see Armytage (1968). More generally, see Robertson (1992) on the broad history of ideas about globalisation.

2 Although some are. The stance of some of the writing on 'cyberspace' – for example *Wired* magazine – might be described as awe-struck techno-utopianist, making extravagant claims for the power of globalising communications technology. This applies even more so to some of the material actually transmitted on the Internet and the World Wide Web. I shall not deal with this very specific discourse here. For a critical discussion, see Stallabrass (1995).

3 In the interests of brevity I ignore here the ideological issues surrounding the discourse of universalism. Bauman is, of course, aware of the discursive position of power – including the power of patriarchy – from which the Enlightenment notion of universalism arose and his comparison is not meant to be celebratory of this earlier cultural self-confidence. But this is not to deny, of course, that globalisation might *eventually* issue in some 'universally' shared cosmopolitan human values recognising commonality of interests and a respect for cultural difference (see Giddens 1994a: 253). These would, of course, have to draw on non-Western as well as Western traditions and perspectives (Therborn 1995: 137).

References

Abu-Lughod, J. (1991), 'Going beyond global babble', in A.D. King (ed.) *Culture, Globalization and the World System*, London: Macmillan.

Appadurai, A. (1990), 'Disjuncture and difference in the global cultural economy', in M. Featherstone (ed.) *Global Culture*, London: Sage.

Bauman, Z. (1973), *Culture as Praxis*, London: Routledge & Kegan Paul.

—— (1995), *Life in Fragments*, Oxford: Blackwell.

Boyd-Barrett, O. (1982), 'Cultural dependency and the mass media', in M. Gurevitch *et al.* (eds) *Culture, Society and the Media*, London: Methuen.

Cleasby, A. (1995), *What in the World is Going On?: British Television and Global Affairs*, London: Third World and Environment Broadcasting Project.

Friedman, J. (1994), *Cultural Identity and Global Process*, London: Sage.

Garcia Canclini, N. (1995), *Hybrid Cultures*, Minneapolis, MN: University of Minnesota Press.

Giddens, A. (1990) *The Consequences of Modernity*, Cambridge: Polity.

—— (1991) *Modernity and Self-Identity: Self and Society in the Late Modern Age*, Cambridge: Polity.

—— (1994a) *Beyond Left and Right*, Cambridge: Polity.

—— (1994b) 'Living in a post-traditional society', in U. Beck, A. Giddens and S. Lash (eds) *Reflexive Modernization*, Cambridge: Polity.

—— (1997) *Sociology*, Cambridge: Polity.

Haeri, S. (1994), 'A fate worse than Saudi,' *Index on Censorship* 23, 4–5: 49–51.

Lull, J. (1995), *Media, Communication, Culture: A Global Approach*, Cambridge: Polity.

McGrew, T. (1992), 'A global society?', in S. Hall, D. Held and T. McGrew (eds) *Modernity and its Futures*, Cambridge: Polity.

McQuail, D. (1994), *Mass Communication Theory*, London: Sage.

Martin-Barbero, J. (1993), *Communication, Culture and Hegemony*, London: Sage.

Massey, D. (1994), *Space, Place and Gender*, Cambridge: Polity.

Pieterse, J.N (1995), 'Globalization as hybridization', in M. Featherstone, S. Lash and R. Robertson (eds) *Global Modernities*, London: Sage.

Robertson, R. (1992), *Globalization: Social Theory and Global Culture*, London: Sage.

Robins, K. (1991), 'Tradition and translation: National culture in its global context', in J. Corner and S. Harvey (eds) *Enterprise and Heritage*, London: Routledge.

Schlesinger, P. (1991), *Media, State and Nation*, London: Sage.

Sinclair, J. (1992), 'The decentring of globalization: Television and globalization', in E. Jacka (ed.) *Continental Shift: Globalisation and Culture*, Double Bay, NSW: Local Consumption Publications.

Tomlinson, J. (1991), *Cultural Imperialism: A Critical Introduction*, London: Pinter.

—— (1995), 'Homogenisation and globalisation', *History of European Ideas* 20, 4–6: 891–7.

—— (1997), 'Internationalism, globalization and cultural imperialism', in K. Thompson (ed.) *Cultural Change and Regulation: Policies and Controversies* (Block Six of D318: *Media, Culture and Identities*), London: Sage and Open University.

[33]

The New Risk Regulators? International Organisations and Globalisation

DESMOND KING AND AMRITA NARLIKAR

THE present reach of international organisations into domestic areas is a far cry from their initial mandates. The World Trade Organisation (WTO) legislates and adjudicates in areas that go well beyond the border measures that occupied its predecessor institution, the General Agreement on Tariffs and Trade (GATT). The conditionalities set by the International Monetary Fund (IMF) and the World Bank are far wider in scope than their initial macroeconomic ones and now involve the functioning of local government and judicial systems. New organisations focused on issues of environment and crime with greater intrusive capacities are in the offing. Faced with the imperatives of globalisation, international organisations have today acquired the role of global risk regulators. The prism of risk is crucial because it provides insights into the expanding reach of international organisations and also explains how global governance is changing.

Identifying risk in the context of globalisation

Scholars in several disciplines have argued that modern techno-economic developments are accompanied, even overshadowed, by the production of risks. Ulrich Beck writes:

unlike the factory-related or occupational hazards of the nineteenth century and the first half of the twentieth century, these can no longer be limited to certain localities or groups, but rather exhibit a tendency to

globalisation which spans production *and* reproduction as much as national borders, and in this sense brings into being '*supra*-national and *non*-class-specific *global hazards*' with a new type of social and political dynamism.[1]

In domestic politics and public policy, risk has been defined as 'a probability, not necessarily calculable in practice, of adverse consequences'.[2] Developing this definition further, we conceptualise 'global risk' as risk that is not attributable to a single actor, but is a result of globalisation. The term includes risks in several issue areas: health risks (e.g. caused by the import of hazardous materials or foods); environmental risks (e.g. caused by the relocation of polluting industries from developed to developing countries); the risk of contagion present in localised financial crises; or the risk of socio-economic destabilisation caused by restructuring in response to globalisation (for example, mass migration or local impoverishment because of the enforcement of strict economic criteria). Further, global risk may have global geographical impact, such as global warming caused by the use of chlorofluorocarbons (CFCs). Examples of global risk (that is, caused by globalisation) with local impact are the adverse side-effects of financial instability and subsequent IMF conditionality on even small communities within developing countries. Global risk may have local effects. Risk may be defined as global as long as it is a by-product of globalisation and irrespective of its geographical or temporal scope.

The emergence of this new set of problems affects the policy autonomy of

© The Political Quarterly Publishing Co. Ltd. 2003
Published by Blackwell Publishing Ltd, 9600 Garsington Road, Oxford OX4 2DQ, UK and 350 Main Street, Malden, MA 02148, USA 337

states. But the impact is just as significant for international organisations. They face problems of regulation for which their traditional mandates provide no obvious tools. Some international organisations have responded by going deep into the regulatory regimes of states, which raises concerns about their accountability and may presage their institutional restructuring. Other international organisations find themselves incapacitated to deal with some of the major problems of globalisation.

Whether domestic or global, risk belongs to the category of market failures. Global risk may be seen more specifically as an externality of globalisation. It is a special type of externality with two distinguishing features.

First, unlike traditional international market failures which could be corrected at the border level, global risk management requires coordinated changes in domestic regulation. As such, it differs from the 'crisis of interdependence' of the 1970s that was captured by the interdependence literature. The oil crisis, for instance, still related to the price of a commodity; today, most trade crises involve a (relatively) stronger WTO intervening in domestic regulatory regimes such as a state's taxation policies or national safety standards. Having a Non-Proliferation Treaty on nuclear weapons offers little protection today against the risk of nuclear piracy, made easier by the greater movement of people. Proliferating terrorist networks (bolstered by globalisation through easier flow of ideas via the internet and movement of people) have necessitated not only stronger border defences but also controversial encroachments of states on civil liberties, expanded powers to freeze certain financial assets and so forth. While the need for international coordination is not new, the need for international coordination at the *domestic* level is a phenomenon unique to risks associated with globalisation.

The second distinguishing feature of

global risk as a special type of externality (which it shares with its domestic variant) is its technical content. The risk itself and its effects can be understood only through scientific investigation rather than by direct lay observation. As such, risk is associated with the application of 'recondite language—by scientists and government at least—to ordinary activities like eating and drinking, instead of qualitative and dichotomous judgements, like safe/unsafe, wholesome/unhealthy'.[3] Risk and its regulation necessitates technical pools of knowledge rather than informal observation or even lay monitoring. Examples include scientific assessments that are necessary to estimate the impact of environmental degradation on climate change or the safety of genetically modified organisms for consumption.

The domestic response to the problems of risk assessment and management has been the rise of regulation, often dubbed the rise of the 'regulatory state'.[4] It is possible to trace a similar development in the rise of regulatory international organisations dealing with the challenges of global risk. For example, international financial institutions (IFIs) have seen, since the 1970s, a dramatic change in their functions from controlling capital movements and maintaining stable exchange rates to ensuring financial liberalisation and preventing any crises resulting therefrom. The leap from border measures and goods to non-tariff barriers and the 'new issues' brought the GATT into a qualitatively new regulatory role with ever-expanding possibilities. Through risk regulation, the GATT/WTO and the IFIs entered into areas of not only domestic sovereignty but also legal and technical expertise. Trade negotiations today, for instance, are no longer a matter just for trade negotiators or ministers but involve scientists, lawyers and technocrats.

The appearance of global risk as a factor in global governance fundamentally alters the calculations that international organisations make (see Table 1). First, while international organisations continue to overcome certain market failures (e.g. competitive protectionism), many of these initial aims are either obsolete (e.g. the Bretton Woods institutions and coordination of capital controls) or achieved (e.g. the binding of tariff levels in a very large proportion of traded goods in the case of the WTO). Increasingly, the work of international organisations today is to manage global risk. Second, global risk management is often both more intrusive and more technical than the correction of market failures at the cross-border level. Echoing domestic developments, the international regulation of risk is progressively becoming a highly technical task involving specialised international bodies or sub-committees and national experts. Third, the new regulatory role of international organisations is a product of globalisation. The IMF's preoccupation with preventing the occurrence and spread of financial crises today (and the conditionalities that accompany these attempts) result directly from the freeing up of financial flows. New technologies associated with globalisation have created new demands for international environmental legislation, while the increased movement of peoples and information has necessitated a greater regulatory

role to address international crime and terrorism. Hence the rise of the regulatory state in domestic politics is accompanied by the decline of the market-failure-correcting international organisation and the rise of the risk-regulating international organisation, thereby revising conventional expectations about the division between domestic and international governance.

Managing risk in the international political economy: trade and finance

Much international economic legislation extends beyond administering traditional border measures, a change observable in the expanding agenda of the WTO, IMF and World Bank. In 2001, of the twenty-seven disputes that were brought for consultation within the dispute settlement mechanism of the WTO, only one related to traditional border measures (on the Generalised System of Preferences, brought by Thailand against the European Communities). The two IFIs initiated similar regulatory intrusions into domestic economies, in the 1980s, through the tool of conditionality. Since then, the number and scope of conditionalities has expanded. In a study of twenty-five sample countries conducted

Table 1: Evolving role of international organisations in context of globalisation

	Before globalisation	*In globalisation*
Principal function	Correction of market failure to reach Pareto-optimal solutions	Management of global risk
Method	Positive coordination	Negative coordination/ regulation
Scope	Border measures: improved transparency; issue-linkages; institutionalization; shallow integration	Domestic: intrusions to facilitate harmonisation of standards; deep integration
Nature	Direct, interstate, accessible	Specialised and technical
Directly affected parties	Member governments	National populations affected by international legislation and regulation

by Devesh Kapur and Richard Webb, IFI loans were conditional upon six 'performance criteria' in the 1970s, ten in the 1980s and twenty-six in the 1980s, even with conditionality narrowly defined. IFI conditionality, loosely defined, yielded an average of 114 conditionalities for sub-Saharan Africa, of which eighty-two were governance related (57.4 of these were institutional and 24.6 were financial).[5] Never before has international regulation been this expansive or intrusive in scope.

The rise of international regulation of trade can be traced to the late 1970s/early 1980s, in parallel with the rise of globalisation and its attendant risks. Beginning cautiously with the Kennedy Round and then in a much bigger way through the Tokyo Round, non-tariff measures (NTMs) were included within the GATT purview through voluntary codes of conduct on almost all non-tariff issues.[6]

The second significant jump in the mandate of the GATT came about with the Uruguay Round, when the 'new issues' of trade in services, investment and intellectual property were added to the multilateral trade regime. The inclusion was an almost natural consequence of the process of globalisation, since enterprises needed access to efficient service inputs. All but one (cross-border supply or mode 1) of the four modes of supply already brought the GATT into areas of domestic regulation. The General Agreement on Trade in Services (GATS) addresses transparency, domestic regulation, recognition of licences and service suppliers, exceptions, employment law, consumer protection, policies regarding payments and transfers for services, and the behaviour of public monopolies. Intellectual property rights, traditionally defined as country-specific and within the purview of national legislation, came under GATT auspices with the signing of the Trade Related Intellectual Property Rights Agreement. The Trade Related Investment Measures Agreement reaffirmed

that GATT principles apply in the area of investment measures. By doing so, the agreement formally brings international regulation even further within the domain of the domestic.

The third and biggest jump in the regulatory scope of the GATT occurred with the creation of the WTO, whose mandate exceeded that of the GATT in two ways. The single undertaking was to be managed by a much stronger dispute settlement mechanism (DSM), where the rulings of the panel can be rejected only by consensus. By allowing cross-sectoral retaliation in case of violation of an agreement, the WTO can penalise members where it hurts most. Additionally, the WTO has expanded rules on non-tariff measures and their regulation to an extent that the change is a qualitative one. The intrusiveness of WTO regulation and its impact on domestic regulatory regimes, ethics, consumer choice and cultural habits is illustrated by the beef hormones dispute. The US case against the EU's prohibition of the import of meat produced using hormones was based on the provisions of the Agreement on the Application of Sanitary and Phytosanitary measures (SPS). The aim of this agreement is 'to maintain the sovereign right of any government to provide the level of health protection it deems appropriate, but to ensure that these sovereign rights are not misused for protectionist purposes and do not result in unnecessary barriers to international trade'. The WTO dispute panel ruled that the EU ban was inconsistent with the SPS agreement; the appellate body upheld the ruling albeit on narrower grounds. This decision meant that the EU prohibition violated the requirements of the SPS agreement regarding the scientific justification of national norms and the use of risk assessment procedures that take into account techniques developed by the relevant international organisations.[7] The announcement by the EU of its inability to comply with the ruling led a WTO arbitration panel to authorise retaliation by the US and later Canada. The incident illustrates how the WTO can impose international regulatory standards that violate domestic regulatory regimes and affect such basic cultural characteristics as people's food habits.

The rise in the regulatory content of international trade legislation is a direct response by the GATT/WTO to the challenges of globalisation. Increasing trade, a vehicle and consequence of globalisation, created this new regulatory mandate by introducing two sets of risks. The first was simply a danger that countries would now resort to non-tariff measures as a form of protectionism. The second was that as trade increased and products (goods or services) crossed borders, countries might use national standards as an excuse to discriminate against imported products. To prevent this happening but also to guard against the risk that hazardous products might enter importing nations in the name of free trade, the WTO entered the domestic regulatory domain.

Standards would be set with respect to goods that might pose risks of health or safety and undermine consumer protection, but also touch upon products that violate national cultural preferences. Examples of the former include products infected with foot-and-mouth disease; of the latter, products manufactured using child labour, or goods whose production causes deforestation or endangers certain animal species. Many products, however, lie at the intersection of the two categories: that is, their consumption is seen as hazardous by certain cultures but this assessment is not easily verifiable objectively or agreed upon universally.

In an attempt to deal with such risks, the WTO has become increasingly involved in setting standards of regulation. This agenda of 'deep integration' ranges from the coordinated application of national policies to the harmonisation of regulatory regimes. Both strategies involve the penetration of the WTO behind borders into 'trade and' issues (see Table 2).

Table 2: Global risk and the rise of regulation by the GATT/ WTO

	Phase I: GATT, Kennedy and Tokyo Rounds	Phase II: GATT, Uruguay Round	Phase III: WTO, Singapore, Geneva, Seattle, Doha ministerials
Type of risk	Resort to NTMs for protectionism and unfair domestic practices for trade advantage		Risk to consumer health and choice, expanding into issues such as environment
Means of global risk regulation	Codes on NTMs	Expansion of agenda to 'new' issues (services, TRIPs and TRIMs) and old issues (agriculture, textiles)	(a) Single undertaking that includes SPS, TBT and other standards; (b) Strengthened DSM; (c) Possible inclusion of environment, labour standards as well as 'new-new' issues of competition policy, government procurement, trade facilitation and investment policy

Moving on to consider finance, we see that the changing agenda of the IFIs has arguably surpassed the expansion of the WTO into regulatory issues. The entry point of IFI regulation has been conditionality. Originally, the rationale of conditionality was to protect the financial integrity of the Bretton Woods institutions. The IMF's conditionalities had a narrow focus on macroeconomic issues, while the World Bank focused on micro-level, sector-specific, financial issues. For the IMF, the importance of conditionality began to grow significantly from the 1970s. One reason for this change was the new risk of financial crises and contagion, which in turn was partly a result of the abandonment of the fixed exchange rate system and the increase in speculative capital flows. Conditionality became central to IMF operations in 1979, when the introduction of new guidelines made it a lender of first instead of last resort. Growth became an increasingly prominent objective in these conditionalities, particularly as IMF programmes were criticised for focusing on austerity to the neglect of growth.

Through the 1980s, the scope of conditionalities of both organisations widened sufficiently to signify a new phase in the capacity of the IFIs to intrude in domestic regulation. In the case of the IMF, the average number of criteria associated with upper-tranche arrangements rose from about six in the 1970s to ten in the 1980s. The average number of World Bank conditions increased from thirty-two in 1980–3 to fifty-six by the end of the decade.[8] Their prescriptions were much more detailed. The logic of this expansion was simple: it was necessary to achieve macroeconomic stabilisation in borrowing economies if they were eventually to repay their debts to the IFIs or the private sector, and an expanding list of conditions was the way of ensuring that borrowers would follow 'sound' policies.

The third, and possibly the most significant, expansion in the reach of IMF and World Bank conditionality occurred in the 1990s. This decade demonstrated that even initially localised financial crises could threaten the world economy through contagion. The Mexican crisis of 1994 generated fears of a 'Tequila effect' of contagion. The East Asian financial crisis beginning in 1997 and the crisis of the Russian rouble in 1998 reinforced these fears. The record of conditionality was, at best, controversial, and even countries with sound macroeconomic credentials became vulnerable to crises. Economic adjustment provided inadequate safeguards against the risk of financial crises and contagion if the institutional underpinnings of a market economy were flawed. The result was the expansion of conditionality into second-generation reforms.

The World Bank devised the 'Comprehensive Development Framework', which was designed to replace both the old approach of an exclusive focus on growth and the 'trickle-down approach'. While the Bank had previously recognised the importance of governance, its prescriptions in the 1980s were confined to bureaucratic downsizing, for example through imposition of hard budget constraints on wage expenditures. After a brief change in which governments were given salary supplements to equip them to do more, the Bank introduced a new class of measures: institutional reforms such as regulatory reform within the public sector, and external checks and balances to improve the transparency, efficiency and accountability of governments. Having begun as principal upholders of the Bretton Woods system of fixed exchange rates and limited capital mobility, the IFIs have found a way into the domestic regulatory systems of their borrowing members (Table 3).

Table 3: Rise of risk and increasing regulation by the IFIs

	Phase I: old Bretton Woods system	Phase II: 1970s–1980s	Phase III: 1990s
Type of risk	Volatile financial flows	Problems of growth: loss of state control of major instruments of state policy, necessitating expansion of IMF lending and attention to issues of growth. Risk of default	Increased volatility of financial flows; risk of localised financial crises and systemic contagion
Nature of regulation	Fixed exchange rates and limitations on capital account convertibility	Structural adjustment conditionalities to ensure 'sound' macroeconomic policies and repayment of loans	Second-generation conditionality: institution-building, corporate restructuring, governance, poverty reduction and ownership of reforms to guard against capital flight and sustain growth

Inadequacy of risk management: migration

Differences in international regulation are seldom a function of the differential threats posed by different risks. In fact, risks of similar proportion all deriving from globalisation can generate quite distinct international regulatory regimes, suggesting that risk assessment and regulation are neither as technocratic nor as politically neutral as they sometimes appear. Take the case of migration, which generates two sorts of risks affecting both asylum seekers and economic migrants: first, that some states will be overwhelmed with migrants and second, the harsh circumstances facing migrants in a globalised economy. The former risk is heavily regulated by states and international regimes; the latter risk is little regulated.

Globalisation is a phenomenon that comprises the flow of not only concrete goods and capital, and images and ideas, but also people. As Arthur Helton notes, 'the movement of people is frequently neglected as an important aspect of globalisation.'[9] Increased communications and cheaper transportation costs have stimulated more people to move; images of developed economies have acted as a powerful pull for migration, while traditional push factors endure. Although not extending freedom of movement to labour, trade agreements such as the North American Free Trade Agreement (NAFTA) have a logic propelling greater migration, as rates of illegal immigration to the US and Canada confirm. NAFTA's effects are not confined to the three participants: it has contagion effects, as a pull factor, upon Latin American countries south of Mexico. For illegal migrants the risks of movement can be life-threatening; but even for legal migrants, mistreatment is a real risk. The tragedies of this international movement of peoples graphically set an agenda for international organisations involved in globalisation and its risks.

Even while globalisation has increased migratory (refugee and otherwise) movements, regimes to protect such movements have weakened in the 1990s. During the Cold War, Western states recognised a duty to assist refugees fleeing totalitarian communism; since 1989 this openness has been replaced with a view that the lifting of communism should enable former communist states to construct internal solutions to problems of nationality and membership. States have been reluctant to acknowledge as refugees persons fleeing general conditions of violence and, as Loescher writes, have interpreted the rule of *non-refoulement* narrowly: 'in the current restrictionist climate, many national policymakers claim that *non-refoulement* does not apply to persons seeking asylum if they are encountered before they actually enter a state's territory.'[10] The upshot is that states engage in ad hoc definition of who is a refugee and dilute the UNHCR's authority to provide full protection to refugees. This retention of power by states makes the application of uniform standards immensely difficult. States' efforts to patrol more rigorously their borders and points of entry (often at considerable cost) have intensified the global risks for refugees by increasing the demand for organised criminal trafficking organisations—in turn a development which, by importing criminality, also poses dangers for developed states' internal politics.

While migration is fuelled by globalisation, decisions about migration still remain fundamentally state-controlled. No international organisation has the power to affect how an individual state sets targets for immigrants, even though international organisations have displayed the capacity and political will to promulgate statements about the acceptable treatment of migrants and asylum see-

kers. For instance, the UN Convention Relating to the Status of Refugees (1951) defined a refugee as an individual with a well-founded anxiety of being persecuted in their home country for reasons of race, religion, nationality or membership of a social group. This definition has provided an international benchmark, and the right of refugees not to be forcibly returned has been established in international law. But this definition overlooks internal exiles within a country and those forced abroad because of a general condition of violence in their home country rather than following an identifiable individual threat to them personally. And the right to asylum remains one decided by the receiving state, though the UN Convention on Refugees does impose an obligation on receiving states to process the asylum seeker's application. Political concerns shape the exercise of this discretion. The state retains a decisive role in setting immigration policy: for instance, many states differentiate between potential immigrants by favouring those with particular skills,[11] applying rigorous 'economic needs' tests; furthermore, states are careful to distinguish between immigrants and temporarily visiting personnel with valuable skills.

To address the risks that unregulated movements can generate, two sorts of expansion in international regulation have developed. First, certain international organisations, including the EU, NAFTA and the WTO, have engaged in policy-making about the movement of people. The EU does not allow asylum seekers to move between member states; instead, their case must be assessed in the EU country which they first reach. Saskia Sassen points out that within both NAFTA and GATT/WTO the transnationalisation of immigration has made the creation of a 'special regime for the circulation of service workers' necessary. She argues that 'this regime . . . is a regime for labor mobility which is in good part under the oversight of entities that are quite autonomous from the government.'[12] But the GATS specifies that its rules are applicable only to the temporary movement of labour and not to migration. Under NAFTA, the regulation of people working in countries of which they are not citizens has been formalised across the three member states. Second, there are international human rights codes, including the UN's statement on refugees, designed to protect migrants, refugees and asylum seekers. Increasingly, these are employed by judges making decisions in national courts. An example is the UN's 1990 Resolution (No. 45/158), adopted by the General Assembly, committing member states to the protection of migrant workers and their families. This adds to the law used by judges in reaching decisions about the status of migrant workers or their rights to family reunion.

Whose risk regulation?

The international regulation of the risks flowing from migration and refugees thus contrasts with the regulation of economic risks. Both types of risk arise from an increasingly globalised world economy. But the capacity of international organisations to address them differs. The divergent reach of international organisations across areas that are equally risk-prone begs the question: whose risk is it that international organisations seek to regulate? And what are the implications of their expansion into the regulatory domain?

Areas that have proved most resistant to international regulation are ones that developed countries are reluctant to open up to such regulation, or even to international assessment. Hence migration policy is couched in terms of core issues of sovereignty while environmental policy and corporate structures are not, as international regulation in the latter set of areas is beneficial to developed countries. The WTO has a Committee on Trade and

Environment and the IFIs' conditionalities have included corporate restructuring. In contrast, the WTO takes special care to ensure that its rules on the temporary movement of labour are not interpreted as international regulation of migration. Debates about regulating labour have focused largely on labour standards as opposed to economic migration. On migration itself, while refugees have rights to assessment established by the UN Convention on Refugees, the right to remain and naturalise lies in the gift of receiving states. And while developing countries bring their domestic regulations in line with WTO requirements and IFI conditionalities, foreign direct investment and short-term capital flows are subject to no comparable international regulations by the major international organisations. The UN Code on Transnational Corporations (UNCTC), a proposal backed by developing countries, proved to be for all practical purposes a non-starter and was finally scuttled in 1991. But codes on state behaviour towards TNCs were established in the GATT with the introduction of trade-related investment measures (TRIMs). Hence both the existence of international regulation and its direction are determined crucially by the balance of interests expressed in power politics. Risks that threaten the weak and have only marginal effects on the powerful often fail to reach the agenda of international regulation. And international regulation can have some serious repercussions that undermine protectionism for developed countries and influential lobbies within them.[13]

For international organisations already entrenched in the agenda of risk regulation, certain inevitabilities follow. First, risk regulation involves greater intrusion of international organisations into the domestic domain, often creating a fundamental contradiction between the very foundational principle of all international organisations (as articulated, for example, in Article 2(7) of the UN Charter) and their effective reach today. Besides the examples discussed above, several others may be cited. The establishment of the International Criminal Court (April 2002) and international conventions that allow crimes against humanity to be tried in countries where they were not committed is representative of this shift. Initiatives to build international protocols that control domestic emissions of pollution or guarantee minimum human rights, and even assist in democratisation, are further examples of international regulation behind borders.

Second, whether domestic or international, risk regulation is characterised by highly technical knowledge, often inaccessible to popular understanding. When international organisations regulate global risk through information collection, standard-setting and behaviour modification, they rely on the technical inputs of their members (in the case of member-driven organisations like the WTO) or the expertise of their staff (in the case of staff-driven organisations like the IFIs or the UNHCR). Scientific investigation is crucial in the assessment of risk and for the negotiation of international standards. Often, delegates from poorer countries find that they are unable to keep abreast of the multi-sector, technical discussions on rules and standards in the WTO and on conditionality in the IFIs. For instance, in the WTO, developed countries are able to fly in technical experts when issues such as telecoms come up for negotiation. In contrast, in 2001, twenty-four developing countries had no diplomatic presence in Geneva, let alone technical expertise specific to the issues under negotiation. As the reach of international organisations expands, developing countries find themselves pushed into a corner from both sides. Simply in terms of selection of risk, it is the powerful countries that exercise effective veto power across organisations. And in the risks that do come up for regulation by an

international organisation, developing countries are unable to participate effectively in regulation-building. Risk regulation, very seldom a democratic or easily accountable process, becomes even more undemocratic by curbing the participation of developing countries.

Were risk regulation even mainly a technocratic process based on an epistemic consensus, limited participation by some members of international organisations might not matter to the members themselves or the organisation concerned. But all international organisations are first and foremost political organisations. Not only is the structure of the international regulatory organisations political, so is the content of their regulation. Risk, by definition, is characterised by unpredictability, and there are no absolutes in terms of the health risks posed by genetically modified organisms or the financial contagion risks of certain domestic practices of corporate governance. The regulation that results is often pseudo-technocratic and reflects the concerns of the most powerful members of international organisations. This is true of the WTO, where risks of socio-economic destabilisation as a result of implementation of agreements in poorer countries— e.g. health risks resulting from price increases in pharmaceuticals due to trade-related intellectual property rights—are often conveniently ignored. But the 'risk' of large-scale movement of labour for services provision is carefully monitored. The pseudo-technocratic language of international regulation is just as evident in the IFIs, where borrowing countries are given loans on conditions of radical restructuring of their governance systems, and the interpretation of what policies actually characterise 'good governance' is left to the discretion of the IFIs. Political manipulation significantly affects both risk selection and regulation.

As a result of the rise of regulatory international organisations, the weak in the international system face several new challenges. First, the domestic autonomy of developing countries declines in the face of international regulations with which they must comply on pain of adverse consequences, such as cross-sectoral retaliation under the WTO and the IFIs' refusal to grant desperately needed loans. Second, although these regulations are negotiated and administered by interstate organisations, weak states find it difficult to set the agenda and influence rule-making on proliferating technical issues. Third, most measures prescribed by the IFIs or the WTO usually involve a replication of standards of the developed countries in the developing countries. The WTO agreements on trade-related intellectual property rights, customs valuation, and sanitary and phytosanitary measures present examples of 'advanced countries saying to the others, "Do it my way!"'[14] The new function of international organisations is to act as global risk regulators. But whose risk they regulate and how is still determined by the old game of power politics.

Conclusion

A return to their original mandates by international organisations as a corrective to some of the problems described in the previous paragraphs would not remedy the complexities of their roles in risk regulation. Global risks require international regulation, and the role of international organisations in that task is essential. If international organisations are becoming risk-regulating organisations and if examples of domestic risk regulation are germane, it is almost inevitable that an increasing proportion of their work will become more intrusive and more inaccessible to scrutiny. To ensure that it does not result in further marginalisation of the weak and a deepening democratic deficit on the part of the international organisation, new enabling and constraining mechanisms will have to be formulated to match the evolving

functions of these organisations. One thing is certain: as the current backlash against globalisation indicates, a serious rethinking of the mandates and methods of international organisations is necessary. Recognising international organisations for what they actually do today, namely regulate global risk, will provide the first significant step in this rethinking.

Acknowledgements

We are very grateful to Christopher Hood, Matthew Gibney, John Odell and David Stasavage for their comments on an earlier version of this article.

Notes

1 Ulrich Beck, *Risk Society*, London, Sage 1992, p. 13.
2 Christopher Hood, Henry Rothstein and Robert Baldwin, *The Government of Risk*, Oxford, Oxford University Press, 2001, p. 3.
3 Ibid., p. 4.
4 Giandomenico Majone, 'From the Positive to the Regulatory State: Causes and Consequences of Changes in the Mode of Governance', *Journal of Public Policy*, vol. 17, 1997, pp. 139–67; Kanishka Jayasuriya, 'Globalisation and the Changing Architecture of the State: The Regulatory State and the Politics of Negative Co-ordination', *Journal of European Public Policy*, vol. 8, 2001, pp. 101–23.
5 Devesh Kapur and Richard Webb, *Governance-related Conditionalities of the International Financial Institutions*, G-24 Discussion Paper Series, no. 6, New York, United Nations, August 2000, p. 21.
6 Bernard M. Hoekman and Michel M. Kostecki, *The Political Economy of the World Trading System: The WTO and Beyond*, Oxford, Oxford University Press, 2001.
7 N. Woods and A. Narlikar, 'Governance and the Limits of Accountability: The WTO, IMF and World Bank', *International Social Science Journal*, vol. 53, no. 170, 2001, pp. 569–83.
8 Kapur and Webb, *Governance-related Conditionalities of the International Financial Institutions*.

9 Arthur C. Helton, *The Price of Indifference: Refugees and Humanitarian Action in the New Century*, New York, Oxford University Press, 2002, pp. 7–8; Astri Suhrke, 'Uncertain Globalisation: Refugee Movement in the Second Half of the Twentieth Century', in Wang Gungwu, ed., *Global History and Migrations*, Boulder, CO, Westview, 1997.

10 Gil Loescher, *The UNHCR and World Politics*, Oxford, Oxford University Press, 2001, p. 352.

11 Jeanette Money, 'No Vacancy: The Political Geography of Immigration Control in Advanced Industrial Countries', *International Organisation*, vol. 51, 1997, pp. 685–720; also Gary P. Freeman, 'The Decline of Sovereignty? Politics and Immigration Restriction in Liberal States', in Christian Joppke, ed., *Challenge to the Nation-State*, Oxford, Oxford University Press, 1998.

12 Saskia Sassen, 'The de facto Transnationalizing of Immigration Policy', in Christian Joppke, ed., *Challenge to the Nation-State*, Oxford, Oxford University Press, 1998, pp. 63–4; 'Annex on Movement of Natural Persons Supplying Services under the Agreement', GATS para. 2: www.wto.org.

13 Jim Rollo and L. Alan Winters, 'Subsidiarity and Governance Challenges for the WTO: Environmental and Labour Standards', *World Economy*, vol. 23, no. 4, 2001, pp. 561–76.

14 J. M. Finger and P. Schuler, *Implementation of Uruguay Round Commitments: The Development Challenge*, Policy Research Working Paper no. 2215, Washington DC, World Bank, 1999.

Name Index